400 wor

THE CONTINUING DEBATE
Essays on Education

Leslie A. Fiedler & Jacob Vinocur

The Continuing Debate

Essays on Education

ST MARTIN'S PRESS   NEW YORK

For
LILLIAN FIEDLER
and
PAUL VINOCUR

Preface

THERE IS ONE SUBJECT ABOUT WHICH THE COLLEGE STUDENT IS deeply concerned, and about which he knows a good deal. He has lived through four years of high school which he must have paused to consider· at one point or another, and he must have speculated a little, too, about college education or he would not be in the college classroom. The essays collected here give him the opportunity to write on the one subject about which he has a certain expertness.

These essays deal not only with what the student knows best, but also say well what their authors know and feel about it. Some of these authors assert firm opinions; some are heated and polemical; but all open rather than close issues. And this seems to us precisely to the point. For our intention is not to indoctrinate but to stimulate students by providing them with models of how to comment meaningfully on their experience.

They will find here much that is new to them and perhaps much with which they disagree. This should not dismay them, for disagreement with others' assessments may lead them to see their own backgrounds in a new light. They will also find it profitable to compare the series of statements about the goals of liberal or scientific education found here with their own experience in school.

If some of the essays included in this collection are less than flattering to the kind of institution the student attends he should be neither surprised nor chagrined. The sooner he becomes aware that *all* colleges and universities are imperfect institutions sharing the strengths and weaknesses of the people who create them, the sooner he will be able to make a wise and efficient use of those institutions. In the course of developing such an awareness he will at any rate have learned to think more clearly and to write better.

Although these essays represent a variety of opinions on many educational issues, there are three main themes which run through most of them. These are libertarianism as opposed to authoritarianism in the schools, the conflicting claims of science and the humanities for the student's attention, and the relationship of education to the larger issues of society. This book, therefore, can easily be used for what has come to be known "controlled research." That is, the student may find here evidence for a reasoned estimate of the means and ends of his own education. The questions provided for each of these essays aim to enhance this process.

Table of Contents

THE CONTINUING DEBATE
Essays on Education

Introduction

THE ESSAY DEALING WITH EDUCATION IS AS OLD AS EDUCATION ITSELF, older in fact than any surviving institution of learning. Plato, for instance, though he wrote in a world which had not yet invented higher education, imagined a world that could not survive without it. The school system which he describes in *The Republic*, however, is primarily designed to sustain and support his ideal state, that is, to inhibit social change. And whatever disagreements he may have had with Plato about the nature of a desirable society, no writer on education up to the eighteenth century contested the view that its end was to inculcate currently accepted values in a ruling class, and myths reinforcing those values in the rest of society.

This view still persists, of course, though almost universally now it is "the people" in general rather than a governing elite who are thought of as the intended beneficiaries of indoctrination. And we are likely to call such indoctrination "brain-washing" when it serves values and ideals obviously different from our own. Not until the time of Jean-Jacques Rousseau, however, was the Platonic or conservative theory of education successfully challenged by a libertarian or revolutionary one; until that time, modern educational theory cannot be said properly to have begun.

This book, therefore, opens with an excerpt from Rousseau's *Émile*, in which a peculiarly modern series of questions is posed: Shall man be educated to challenge rather than accept, dissent rather than pledge allegiance, seek change rather than oppose it? Shall he be educated not to suit the needs of a church or state, but rather to satisfy the demands of his own nature? Shall he, in short, be educated not to submit, but to be free? Once sounded, Rousseau's key words—"freedom" and "nature"—never cease ringing in the heads of the participants in the continuing great debate to which many of the essays collected here contribute.

Some of Rousseau's questions were anticipated, to be sure, as early as the fifteenth century, in the section of Rabelais' *Gargantua and Pantagruel* to which Leslie Fiedler refers in his essay, "The Crumbling Ivory Tower." But Rabelais still envisaged the education of a tiny minority who, even when they learned to do what they willed rather than what they were told, would have willed the maintenance of an existing aristocratic society based on courtesy and honor and privilege. He therefore seems remote from our world of unceremonious candor, self-interest and equality. Rousseau, however, in whom the modes of thought which produced the French Revolution are already operative, does not seem remote. Treating the most pressing current problems of, say, integration in the grade schools or the opening of college classrooms to larger and larger numbers of inadequately prepared students, we are likely to find ourselves thinking in terms of "natural rights," and, doing so, we realize that *Émile,* despite its envisioning an ideal relationship of a single teacher to a single pupil, speaks a language still viable in a society pledged to mass education. It speaks *our* language, as Plato or Rabelais do not.

Even in Rousseau's style, in his tone and vocabulary, we can sense an impatience with formal restraints and conventions which strikes us as familiar. We may not subscribe to, but we cannot help recognizing as congenial, his desire to speak from personal feeling rather than some objective set of principles, and to settle educational problems in terms of libertarian impulse rather than cold rational consideration. Certainly we can see how a similar commitment to feeling and impulse determines analagous styles in certain of the extreme present-day libertarians anthologized here, in Paul Goodman, for example, and A. S. Neill and C. Wright Mills.

In such writers, as in Rousseau, the libertarian attitude toward education is associated not only with a free-swinging, unbuttoned style, but also with radical politics, socialist or anarchist, and a radical approach to marriage and the family. In other modern instances, we find similar attitudes toward schools and learning more moderately expressed and, perhaps by the same token, more moderately grounded in liberal rather than revolutionary politics. John Dewey, David Riesman, and Edgar Z. Friedenberg, perhaps also Herbert Gold and Alfred Kazin, provide examples of the latter; though the politics as well as the educational program of Gold and Kazin, who are literary men—as compared with a philosopher like Dewey, or social scientists like Riesman and Friedenberg—are presented by implication in personal narratives, and are qualified by an irony and distance more appropriate to works of art than to the manifestoes of reformers.

Not all the essayists represented in this collection speak for the libertarian point of view, however, for Rousseau's thesis has by no means been universally accepted. Nonetheless, conservatives and authoritarians in the field of education have been on the defensive since the eighteenth century, feeling no doubt that it is history they fight as well as individual theorists, the French and American and Russian revolutions as well as Rousseau and those who follow him. Cardinal Newman, for instance, speaks not with the self-assurance of, say, an Augustine still close to the beginnings of Christianity, but from the embattled position of a Catholic convert in non-Catholic England, addressing an entire culture, many of whose intellectuals had already decided that Newman's God was dead, and a good thing, too. Certainly there is already something a little nostalgic about his version of the Christian gentleman, and we cannot help suspecting from his tone that he was aware of it.

By the same token, Irving Babbitt writing in the twentieth century in America betrays an even greater uncertainty, more revealed than masked by his pontifical tone. He spent much of his polemical energy in combating at long distance and two hundred years later the pernicious influence of Rousseau; and yet he must have felt, even inside the citadel of a Harvard still nominally committed to tradition and classicism, how much his own position went against the American grain, which was and remains—in the theory at least—Rousseauistic, romantic, progressive, and unredeemably hopeful. Moreover, his theory that man's nature needed curbing rather than expression was no longer based on inherited Christian doctrines about original sin, but was only theoretically sustained by reference to the great literature of the past, which other minds disconcertingly insisted on reading in quite other ways.

Similarly, Robert Hutchins, whose program of General Education at the University of Chicago depended on a similar attempt to synthesize secular scriptures, the famous One Hundred Great Books, found his chief supporters among a few neo-Aristotelian, Roman Catholic conservatives; yet most of his faculty was liberal in politics and sceptical in religion, and they fought and finally destroyed his program. Certainly we sense in Hutchins' writing the voice of one convinced that his cause is just, but also suspicious that it has been lost before he begins. And the less learned, less theoretically well-grounded opponents of "modernism" in education who have succeeded him, the newest advocates of a return to the standards of some bygone, and presumably golden, age of education—Arthur Bestor, for instance—grow shriller and shriller, more and more exaggerated in their claims. Finally, their pleas are vulgarized and distorted by certain extremists on the radical right, who manage to combine a belief in reading-writing-and-arithmetic in the schools plus the classics and Christianity in the colleges, with opposition to Jews, Negroes, Democrats, the federal income tax and the United Nations.

The conservatives' despair at the apparent defeat of their cause, and the dismay of their more intelligent theorists at how the mass mind has debased when it has not ignored that cause, is, however, matched by the despair and dismay of the libertarians over their apparent victory. For, despite the triumph of Progressive Education at the grade and high school levels and the displacement of rigid curricula by the "free elective" system in colleges, intelligent libertarians find little to applaud in our educational system.

Freed from the weight of the past, our schools have almost foundered under the pressures of the present. Alumni groups and parents' organizations, associations of war veterans and self-styled patriots, timid school boards and testy administrators have conspired to ban "controversial" books and intimidate teachers who question the *status quo* by suggesting that our present social order does not provide all the freedom we can stand. Even when teachers espoused doctrines already accepted by all but the least enlightened elements of the community, there have been reprisals from officials more committed to bureaucracy than democracy, more concerned with public relations than the pursuit of knowledge. Worst of all, teachers themselves have precensored their own texts and classroom lectures on the basis of an odd conviction that they are able to remain "free" so long as they advocate nothing which disturbs those who fear freedom.

Meanwhile, even in schools where the teachers are relatively free and the students are exposed to books which teach them to prize liberty, those students are likely to find themselves living under a totalitarian regime. This is particularly true in the case of girls, who are considered, if not less worthy of freedom than their male compeers, at least less able to enjoy it without moral disaster. At any rate, in all educational institutions where students live away from their families, and to a lesser degree in day-schools as well, students are subjected to regulations concerning smoking, drinking, relations with the opposite sex—even hours of going to bed—much more illiberal and restrictive than those invoked by their families. The rather irrational taboos which curtail liberty are based, apparently, on two totally contradictory beliefs: one, that in high school and even in college, students are still children, and therefore are not yet qualified to be free; and two, that female students are only too likely to prove their adulthood by becoming pregnant. Consequently, the legitimate aims of education, such as the encouragement of responsibility, the fostering of self-reliance and the development of independence of spirit, are lost.

Where grades and examinations, class attendance and the withdrawal of books from the library are concerned, even the university student finds it easy to believe himself in a police state, where everything that is not forbidden is required, and his teachers are cast in the role of spies and cops. It is Deans of Men and Women and the student's own organizations which enforce morality upon him; but it is his professors who, losing faith in their own ability to compel his attention and in the power of the books they teach, finally attempt to enforce learning itself. In the end, our colleges are characterized by liberality in their catalogues and authoritarianism in the dorms. The student, that is to say, is permitted with the help of an advisor to choose his own courses and thus determine the basic pattern of his education; but he is refused the right even with the aid of a counselor to lead his own social and romantic life. Yet he is likely to be infinitely more experienced and competent in the latter area than in the former. This is one aspect of a prevailing ambivalence toward the adolescent in our society which is examined by Paul Goodman, and more profoundly, though more ponderously, by Edgar Friedenberg.

Often, oddly enough, the harshest classroom taskmasters and the staunchest advocates of repressive student social regulations are teachers who ask for themselves the broadest kinds of academic freedom; indeed, they consider themselves enlightened Rousseau-ists because they despise traditional classical curricula. Such teachers are more likely than not to be scientists, or at least technologists who dignify themselves with the more honorific title; and who, in any case, think of science as the heart of modern, progressive, rational education, as compared to the older kind of humanistic studies, associated in their mind with a worship of the past and a fear of the future.

The attempt on the part of such scientists to arrogate the liberal movement in education to themselves is as old as their quarrel with the humanities. That quarrel assumed its current form during the reign of Queen Victoria in the debate between Thomas Henry Huxley and Matthew Arnold, whose key documents appear in this book. It has been vigorously espoused recently by C. P. Snow, whose much overrated and much too often reprinted essay, "The Two Cultures," is referred to by R. Buckminster Fuller. Snow confuses science and technology, and arrogantly contends that only the scientist has in our time dedicated himself to progress and the cause of freedom. Snow is unaware of the sense in which the Huxley-Arnold quarrel is only a special subcase in the much more ancient debate begun by Rousseau.

Other more eminent scientists and technologists (Snow's chief fame, after all, comes from his novels), J. Robert Oppenheimer, for example, have been less sanguine about the prospects of science taking the lead in guiding us toward a more desirable future. Better grounded in the humanities, perhaps, and cer-

tainly more disturbed by the way in which science flourishes in
totalitarian regimes like the Russian one (to whose defects Snow
remains stubbornly blind), as well as more oppressed by the
guilt the scientist bears for having brought us to the verge of
atomic destruction, Oppenheimer recognizes that neither technology nor the "scientific method" can, unaided, redefine and
unify our sundered culture. In his search for a new total
humanism, one more aware of the possibilities of technology but
not less tragic or complex than the old, Oppenheimer is joined
by such fellow-scientists as Jerome Bruner and R. Buckminster
Fuller, as well as by philosophers like Whitehead and Dewey
and a literary man like I. A. Richards, who were, in fact, there
first.

Like Snow, however, most scientists and humanists alike have
imagined a future which is merely an extension of the present,
for they have been limited by a theoretical vocabulary incapable
of expressing an imaginative leap out of our own time. The one
writer included in this collection who speaks the language of the
future, and seems thereby to have escaped from the limits imposed on our thinking by the Huxley-Arnold debate, is Buckminster Fuller. His vision of "comprehensive anticipatory design
science" may seem to some more nightmare than sanguine dream,
but it cannot help leaving with all who read him the exhilarating
sense of having been transported into the utopian world of
science-fiction.

In the universities, however, not only is there a resistance to
such passionate extrapolations as Buckminster Fuller's, but
also even to the more moderate kind of hope expressed by Oppenheimer. Most academicians regard any demand that they learn
each other's language, or some common human tongue, as a
challenge to the ideal of specialization, as an infringement on
their privacy in the laboratory and the library. Meanwhile, in
the world of mass-culture beyond the campus, the world out of
which all students come and into which most subside with a sigh
after graduation, "science" means the man in the white coat on
TV who advises Bufferin rather than aspirin; "humanities" is
associated vaguely with literature, literature with poetry—and
poetry with things learned in school and forgotten in life, except

for, perhaps, "Thirty days hath September, April, June and November. . . ."

Finally, our schools are neither scientific in the Huxleyan sense nor humanistic in the Arnoldian, any more than they are libertarian as Rousseau would have understood the term, or authoritarian as Newman would have conceived it. They neither indoctrinate the young in a tested tradition, nor free their minds for the creation of traditions still unconceived; they only teach them to submit to the tyranny of mediocrity, the lowest common denominator of value in the world of mass-production, mass-consumption, and the degradation of standards. Or worse, the young are taught that to seem to submit to such a tyranny, to maintain the appearance of what society agrees to call virtue, though not to live by it, is all that is required of them.

Indeed, the fact rather than the semblance of virtue would give the game away. So, too, the fact rather than the semblance of intellectual curiosity could prove disturbing in institutions geared to providing larger and larger numbers of well-trained professionals guaranteed to disturb nothing in the society which foots the bills for their training—including future teachers destined to provide other well-trained professionals guaranteed to disturb nothing in the society (still unchanged) which will be footing the bills for *their* training, etc., etc.

Recent studies (most of them too successfully couched in sociological jargon to be included in a collection of essays for writing classes) have proved conclusively, at any rate, that colleges, whether Ivy League schools like the Princeton memorialized by Edmund Wilson and John Peale Bishop, or the Harvard three times commented on in this book, or the large coeducational state universities described by David Boroff—these colleges neither forge the minds of students in a traditional mold nor free them for courageous speculation, but only re-enforce the values learned by those students from their families and friends. These values are likely to be less adventurous, less progressive, less committed and less generous even than those of the teachers in whose classes the students have sat for four years or more.

The ironies implicit in this situation are reflected upon with some bitterness by sociologists David Riesman and C. Wright Mills, literate enough to have been included in the present anthology. But the silent protest of more and more well-qualified students who leave college after a year or two of bafflement and disillusion is even more eloquent. Such students sense that the university which is neither rationally conservative nor boldly libertarian, which is modeled neither on the vision of Plato nor on the dream of Rousseau, is not properly a university at all— but a vocational school with pretensions, combined with a baby-sitting establishment for those already capable of producing babies of their own. Rousseau prophesied two hundred years ago that: "Yet things would be worse without this traditional education. . . . Prejudice, authority, necessity, example, all the social conditions into which we are plunged, would stifle nature and put nothing in her place." That "worse" we now endure.

It is, however, not quite "nothing" which the modern university offers its superior students, but a minimum sort of "something" which they find even more appalling. Asking to be prepared for a rapidly changing, increasingly confused world, and for a future less perilous and chaotic, they are taught instead how to adjust and succeed in a world which they distrust. And they register their disappointment by choosing failure; they walk out. To many of their fellow-students the withdrawal seems an act of heroism. At any rate, when one of the refugees from college turns author and creates a hero (like those of Salinger or Kerouac) who sees through academic fraud and gets the hell out, he becomes a favorite among undergraduates, who seem to have dreamed all along the escape they did not dare attempt.

Meanwhile, of course, the schools are succeeding only too well with career-oriented, success-oriented students (see, for instance, the essay by C. Wright Mills), good boys and girls who, whatever their IQ's, question nothing—at least in public; and quarrel with the world only because it does not open for them quite fast enough. Norman Mailer in a little poem caricatures one of them at the moment he is getting ready for college:

Heroes

I applied
to
Harvard

                                but I've
                                picked
                                Yale
                                Columbia
                                and
                                Brown
                                as my
                                            fall-back
                                            said the
                                            child of
                                            the new
                                            frontier.

Only literature—an occasional poem, novel or story—catches
the real comedy and pathos of the current crisis in education, the
felt truth of actual academic experience. It seems only fair, therefore, that the students asked to read certain essays in this book,
also find here (we have placed it at the end, but not as an after-
thought) a list of works of fiction which can give them real
pleasure as well as terrifying insights into the world in which
they now live. They may indeed respond more deeply to the
direct rendering of experience in these stories than to the generalizations derived from experience in the essays.

Such generalizations are, however, important too. For we all
must, if we are not to fall into cynicism and despair about the
future of education, attempt to understand what we are not yet
able to control. Understanding is not a guarantee of eventual
control, but it is a necessary precondition, a first step. Yet even
that is hard to come by at this point, since, despite years of impassioned discussion, we have only begun to identify the basic
problems: the libertarian versus the authoritarian approach, the
relative importance of science and the humanities, the relationship between learning and social regulations, the role of the
teacher and the responsibility of the student, the function of the
small private college and the large state-supported institution,
the impact of the new mass media on the traditional curriculum,
the training of the gifted versus the education of everybody.

The subject of mass higher education in particular is new, the
way ahead is long, and success far from assured, even if, for

the first time, all the participants involved, students as well as faculty and administration, try to know what they are doing as they do it. But the pressures on us all are great, because understanding education has come to seem as little a luxury as education itself. Any expense of spirit (and in this area spirit, not money, is required) seems justified, for when we talk now about college we are talking about the ordinary pattern of life, about, certainly, the kind of life we all expect for all of our children. But this changes the very way in which the topic must be discussed. What was once a privilege and a distinction, to be speculated on at leisure among the few, is now a common possession, a common fate, to be discussed urgently and among the many, however reluctant the many may be to join in. It is in the interest of such urgency, and out of faith in such discussion, that this collection has been assembled.

I. THE TRADITION

Émile

From Book I

JEAN JACQUES ROUSSEAU

(1712–1778)

Julie, or the New Héloïse, 1761
Émile, 1762
The Social Contract, 1762
Confessions, 1784

JEAN JACQUES ROUSSEAU, social philosopher, educational theorist, autobiographer, pioneer novelist and first modern bohemian, is a figure who has stirred controversy and misunderstanding. To some he seems an apostle of freedom, one of the voices prophesying the French Revolution and the world of expanding liberties which succeeded it; to others he seems a vain, half-mad vagabond, who formulated notions of man's natural goodness which have led only to confusion and disillusion. For our purposes, he is important as the author, in *Émile*, of the first attempt to define a kind of education aimed not at preparing a man to take his place in an already established society, but rather at releasing in him his full human potentiality.

GOD MAKES ALL THINGS GOOD; MAN MEDDLES WITH THEM AND THEY become evil. He forces one soil to yield the products of another, one tree to bear another's fruit. He confuses and confounds time, place, and natural conditions. He mutilates his dog, his horse, and his slave. He destroys and defaces all things; he loves all that is deformed and monstrous; he will have nothing as nature made it, not even man himself, who must learn his paces like a saddle-horse, and be shaped to his master's taste like the trees in his garden.

Yet things would be worse without this education, and mankind cannot be made by halves. Under existing conditions a man

From *Émile* by Jean Jacques Rousseau, transl. Barbara Foxley. Everyman's Library. Reprinted by permission of E. P. Dutton & Co., Inc.

left to himself from birth would be more of a monster than the
rest. Prejudice, authority, necessity, example, all the social conditions into which we are plunged, would stifle nature in him
and put nothing in her place. She would be like a sapling chance
sown in the midst of the highway, bent hither and thither and
soon crushed by the passers-by.

Tender, anxious mother,[1] I appeal to you. You can remove this
young tree from the highway and shield it from the crushing
force of social conventions. Tend and water it ere it dies. One
day its fruit will reward your care. From the outset raise a wall
round your child's soul; another may sketch the plan, you alone
should carry it into execution.

Plants are fashioned by cultivation, man by education. If a man
were born tall and strong, his size and strength would be of no
good to him till he had learnt to use them; they would even harm
him by preventing others from coming to his aid;[2] left to him-

---

1. The earliest education is most important and it undoubtedly is
woman's work. If the author of nature had meant to assign it to men
he would have given them milk to feed the child. Address your treatises
on education to the women, for not only are they able to watch over
it more closely than men, not only is their influence always predominant
in education, its success concerns them more nearly, for most widows
are at the mercy of their children, who show them very plainly whether
their education was good or bad. The laws, always more concerned
about property than about people, since their object is not virtue but
peace, the laws give too little authority to the mother. Yet her position is
more certain than that of the father, her duties are less trying; the right
ordering of the family depends more upon her, and she is usually
fonder of her children. There are occasions when a son may be excused
for lack of respect for his father, but if a child could be so unnatural as
to fail in respect of the mother who bore him and nursed him at her
breast, who for so many years devoted herself to his care, such a monstrous wretch should be smothered at once as unworthy to live. You say
mothers spoil their children, and no doubt that is wrong, but it is worse
to deprave them as you do. The mother wants her child to be happy
now. She is right, and if her method is wrong, she must be taught a
better. Ambition, avarice, tyranny, the mistaken foresight of fathers,
their neglect, their harshness, are a hundredfold more harmful to the
child than the blind affection of the mother. Moreover, I must explain
what I mean by a mother and that explanation follows.

2. Like them in externals, but without speech and without the ideas
which are expressed by speech, he would be unable to make his wants

self he would die of want before he knew his needs. We lament the helplessness of infancy; we fail to perceive that the race would have perished had not man begun by being a child.

We are born weak, we need strength; helpless, we need aid; foolish, we need reason. All that we lack at birth, all that we need when we come to man's estate, is the gift of education.

This education comes to us from nature, from men, or from things. The inner growth of our organs and faculties is the education of nature, the use we learn to make of this growth is the education of men, what we gain by our experience of our surroundings is the education of things.

Thus we are each taught by three masters. If their teaching conflicts, the scholar is ill-educated and will never be at peace with himself; if their teaching agrees, he goes straight to his goal, he lives at peace with himself, he is well-educated.

Now of these three factors in education nature is wholly beyond our control, things are only partly in our power; the education of men is the only one controlled by us; and even here our power is largely illusory, for who can hope to direct every word and deed of all with whom the child has to do.

Viewed as an art, the success of education is almost impossible, since the essential conditions of success are beyond our control. Our efforts may bring us within sight of the goal, but fortune must favour us if we are to reach it.

What is this goal? As we have just shown, it is the goal of nature. Since all three modes of education must work together, the two that we can control must follow the lead of that which is beyond our control. Perhaps this word Nature has too vague a meaning. Let us try to define it.

Nature, we are told, is merely habit. What does that mean? Are there not habits formed under compulsion, habits which never stifle nature? Such, for example, are the habits of plants trained horizontally. The plant keeps its artificial shape, but the sap has not changed its course, and any new growth the plant may make will be vertical. It is the same with a man's disposition; while the conditions remain the same, habits, even the least

known, while there would be nothing in his appearance to suggest that he needed their help.

natural of them, hold good; but change the conditions, habits vanish, nature reasserts herself. Education itself is but habit, for are there not people who forget or lose their education and others who keep it? Whence comes this difference? If the term nature is to be restricted to habits conformable to nature we need say no more.

We are born sensitive and from our birth onwards we are affected in various ways by our environment. As soon as we become conscious of our sensations we tend to seek or shun the things that cause them, at first because they are pleasant or unpleasant, then because they suit us or not, and at last because of judgments formed by means of the ideas of happiness and goodness which reason gives us. These tendencies gain strength and permanence with the growth of reason, but hindered by our habits they are more or less warped by our prejudices. Before this change they are what I call Nature within us.

Everything should therefore be brought into harmony with these natural tendencies, and that might well be if our three modes of education merely differed from one another; but what can be done when they conflict, when instead of training man for himself you try to train him for others? Harmony becomes impossible. Forced to combat either nature or society, you must make your choice between the man and the citizen, you cannot train both.

The smaller social group, firmly united in itself and dwelling apart from others, tends to withdraw itself from the larger society. Every patriot hates foreigners; they are only men, and nothing to him.[3] This defect is inevitable, but of little importance. The great thing is to be kind to our neighbors. Among strangers the Spartan was selfish, grasping, and unjust, but unselfishness, justice, and harmony ruled his home life. Distrust those cosmopolitans who search out remote duties in their books and neglect those that lie nearest. Such philosophers will love the Tartars to avoid loving their neighbour.

The natural man lives for himself; he is the unit, the whole,

---

3. Thus the wars of republics are more cruel than those of monarchies. But if the wars of kings are less cruel, their peace is terrible; better be their foe than their subject.

dependent only on himself and on his like. The citizen is but the numerator of a fraction, whose value depends on its denominator; his value depends upon the whole, that is, on the community. Good social institutions are those best fitted to make a man unnatural, to exchange his independence for dependence, to merge the unit in the group, so that he no longer regards himself as one, but as a part of the whole, and is only conscious of the common life. . . .

Two conflicting types of educational systems spring from these conflicting aims. One is public and common to many, the other private and domestic.

If you wish to know what is meant by public education, read Plato's *Republic*. Those who merely judge books by their titles take this for a treatise on politics, but it is the finest treatise on education ever written.

In popular estimation the Platonic Institute stands for all that is fanciful and unreal. For my own part I should have thought the system of Lycurgus far more impracticable had he merely committed it to writing. Plato only sought to purge man's heart; Lycurgus turned it from its natural course.

The public institute does not and cannot exist, for there is neither country nor patriot. The very words should be struck out of our language. The reason does not concern us at present, so that though I know it I refrain from stating it.

I do not consider our ridiculous colleges[4] as public institutes, nor do I include under this head a fashionable education, for this education facing two ways at once achieves nothing. It is only fit to turn out hypocrites, always professing to live for others, while thinking of themselves alone. These professions, however, deceive no one, for every one has his share in them; they are so much labour wasted.

---

4. There are teachers dear to me in many schools and especially in the University of Paris, men for whom I have a great respect, men whom I believe to be quite capable of instructing young people, if they were not compelled to follow the established custom. I exhort one of them to publish the scheme of reform which he has thought out. Perhaps people would at length seek to cure the evil if they realised that there was a remedy.

Our inner conflicts are caused by these contradictions. Drawn
this way by nature and that way by man, compelled to yield to
both forces, we make a compromise and reach neither goal. We
go through life, struggling and hesitating, and die before we
have found peace, useless alike to ourselves and to others.

There remains the education of the home or of nature; but how
will a man live with others if he is educated for himself alone?
If the twofold aims could be resolved into one by removing the
man's self-contradictions, one great obstacle to his happiness
would be gone. To judge of this you must see the man full-
grown; you must have noted his inclinations, watched his progress,
followed his steps; in a word you must really know a natural man.
When you have read this work, I think you will have made some
progress in this inquiry.

What must be done to train this exceptional man! We can do
much, but the chief thing is to prevent anything being done. To
sail against the wind we merely follow one tack and another; to
keep our position in a stormy sea we must cast anchor. Beware,
young pilot, lest your boat slip its cable or drag its anchor before
you know it.

In the social order where each has his own place a man must
be educated for it. If such a one leave his own station he is fit
for nothing else. His education is only useful when fate agrees
with his parents' choice; if not, education harms the scholar, if
only by the prejudices it has created. In Egypt, where the son was
compelled to adopt his father's calling, education had at least
a settled aim; where social grades remain fixed, but the men who
form them are constantly changing, no one knows whether he is
not harming his son by educating him for his own class.

In the natural order men are all equal and their common calling is that of manhood, so that a well-educated man cannot fail
to do well in that calling and those related to it. It matters little
to me whether my pupil is intended for the army, the church, or
the law. Before his parents chose a calling for him nature called
him to be a man. Life is the trade I would teach him. When he
leaves me, I grant you, he will be neither a magistrate, a soldier,
nor a priest; he will be a man. All that becomes a man he will
learn as quickly as another. In vain will fate change his station,

he will always be in his right place. *"Occupavi te, fortuna, atque cepi; omnes-que aditus tuos interclusi, ut ad me aspirare non posses."* The real object of our study is man and his environment. To my mind those of us who can best endure the good and evil of life are the best educated; hence it follows that true education consists less in precept than in practice. We begin to learn when we begin to live; our education begins with ourselves, our first teacher is our nurse. The ancients used the word "Education" in a different sense, it meant "Nurture." *"Educit obstetrix,"* says Varro. *"Educat nutrix, instituit paedagogus, docet magister."* Thus, education, discipline, and instruction are three things as different in their purpose as the dame, the usher, and the teacher. But these distinctions are undesirable and the child should only follow one guide.

We must therefore look at the general rather than the particular, and consider our scholar as man in the abstract, man exposed to all the changes and chances of mortal life. If men were born attached to the soil of our country, if one season lasted all the year round, if every man's fortune were so firmly grasped that he could never lose it, then the established method of education would have certain advantages; the child brought up to his own calling would never leave it, he could never have to face the difficulties of any other condition. But when we consider the fleeting nature of human affairs, the restless and uneasy spirit of our times, when every generation overturns the work of its predecessor, can we conceive a more senseless plan than to educate a child as if he would never leave his room, as if he would always have his servants about him? If the wretched creature takes a single step up or down he is lost. This is not teaching him to bear pain; it is training him to feel it.

People think only of preserving their child's life; this is not enough, he must be taught to preserve his own life when he is a man, to bear the buffets of fortune, to brave wealth and poverty, to live at need among the snows of Iceland or on the scorching rocks of Malta. In vain you guard against death; he must needs die; and even if you do not kill him with your precautions, they are mistaken. Teach him to live rather than to avoid death: life is not breath, but action, the use of our senses, our mind, our faculties, every part of ourselves which makes us conscious of our being. Life consists less in length of day than in the keen sense of living. A man may be buried at a hundred and may never have lived at all. He would have fared better had he died young.

Our wisdom is slavish prejudice, our customs consist in control, constraint, compulsion. Civilised man is born and dies a slave. The infant is bound up in swaddling clothes, the corpse is nailed down in his coffin. All his life long man is imprisoned by our institutions.

I am told that many midwives profess to improve the shape of the infant's head by rubbing, and they are allowed to do it. Our heads are not good enough as God made them, they must be moulded outside by the nurse and inside by the philosopher. The Caribs are better off than we are. "The child has hardly left the mother's womb, it has hardly begun to move and stretch its limbs, when it is deprived of its freedom. It is wrapped in swaddling bands, laid down with its head fixed, its legs stretched out, and its arms by its sides; it is wound round with linen and bandages of all sorts so that it cannot move. It is fortunate if it has room to breathe, and it is laid on its side so that water which should flow from its mouth can escape, for it is not free to turn its head on one side for this purpose."

The new-born child requires to stir and stretch his limbs to free them from the stiffness resulting from being curled up so long. His limbs are stretched indeed, but he is not allowed to move them. Even the head is confined by a cap. One would think they were afraid the child should look as if it were alive.

Thus the internal impulses which should lead to growth find an insurmountable obstacle in the way of the necessary movements. The child exhausts his strength in vain struggles, or he gains strength very slowly. He was freer and less constrained in the womb; he has gained nothing by birth. . . .

Fix your eyes on nature, follow the path traced by her. She keeps children at work, she hardens them by all kinds of difficulties, she soon teaches them the meaning of pain and grief. They cut their teeth and are feverish, sharp colics bring on convulsions, they are choked by fits of coughing and tormented by worms, evil humours corrupt the blood, germs of various kinds ferment in it, causing dangerous eruptions. Sickness and danger play the chief part in infancy. One half of the children who are born die before their eighth year. The child who has overcome hardships has gained strength, and as soon as he can use his life he holds it more securely.

This is nature's law; why contradict it? Do you not see that in your efforts to improve upon her handiwork you are destroying it; her cares are wasted? To do from without what she does within is according to you to increase the danger two-fold. On the contrary, it is the way to avert it; experience shows that children delicately nurtured are more likely to die. Provided we do not overdo it, there is less risk in using their strength than in sparing it. Accustom them therefore to the hardships they will have to face; train them to endure extremes of temperature, climate, and condition, hunger, thirst, and weariness. Dip them in the waters of Styx. Before bodily habits become fixed you may teach what habits you will without any risk, but once habits are established any change is fraught with peril. A child will bear changes which a man cannot bear, the muscles of the one are soft and flexible, they take whatever direction you give them without any effort; the muscles of the grown man are harder and they only change their accustomed mode of action when subjected to violence. So we can make a child strong without risking his life or health, and even if there were some risk, it should not be taken into consideration. Since human life is full of dangers, can we do better than face them at a time when they can do the least harm?

A child's worth increases with his years. To his personal value must be added the cost of the care bestowed upon him. For himself there is not only loss of life, but the consciousness of death. We must therefore think most of his future in our efforts for his preservation. He must be protected against the ills of youth before he reaches them: for if the value of life increases until the child reaches an age when he can be useful, what madness to spare some suffering in infancy only to multiply his pain when he reaches the age of reason. Is that what our master teaches us?

Man is born to suffer; pain is the means of his preservation.

His childhood is happy, knowing only pain of body. These bodily sufferings are much less cruel, much less painful, than other forms of suffering, and they rarely lead to self-destruction. It is not the twinges of gout which make a man kill himself, it is mental suffering that leads to despair. We pity the sufferings of childhood; we should pity ourselves; our worst sorrows are of our own making.

The new-born infant cries, his early days are spent in crying. He is alternately petted and shaken by way of soothing him; sometimes he is threatened, sometimes beaten, to keep him quiet. We do what he wants or we make him do what we want, we submit to his whims or subject him to our own. There is no middle course; he must rule or obey. Thus his earliest ideas are those of the tyrant or the slave. He commands before he can speak, he obeys before he can act, and sometimes he is punished for faults before he is aware of them, or rather before they are committed. Thus early are the seeds of evil passions sown in his young heart. At a later day these are attributed to nature, and when we have taken pains to make him bad we lament his badness.

In this way the child passes six or seven years in the hands of women, the victim of his own caprices or theirs, and after they have taught him all sorts of things, when they have burdened his memory with words he cannot understand, or things which are of no use to him, when nature has been stifled by the passions they have implanted in him, this sham article is sent to a tutor. The tutor completes the development of the germs of artificiality which he finds already well grown, he teaches him everything except self-knowledge and self-control, the arts of life and happiness. When at length this infant slave and tyrant, crammed with knowledge but empty of sense, feeble alike in mind and body, is flung upon the world, and his helplessness, his pride, and his other vices are displayed, we begin to lament the wretchedness and perversity of mankind. We are wrong; this is the creature of our fantasy; the natural man is cast in another mould.

Would you keep him as nature made him? Watch over him from his birth. Take possession of him as soon as he comes into the world and keep him till he is a man; you will never succeed otherwise. The real nurse is the mother and the real teacher is the father. Let them agree in the ordering of their duties as well as in their method, let the child pass from one to the other. He will be better educated by a sensible though ignorant father than by the cleverest master in the world. For zeal will atone for lack of knowledge, rather than knowledge for lack of zeal. But the duties of public and private business! Duty indeed! Does a father's duty come last.[5] It is not surprising that the man whose wife despises the duty of suckling her child should despise its education. There is no more charming picture than that of family life; but when one feature is wanting the whole is marred. If the mother is too delicate to nurse her child, the father will be too busy to teach him. Their children, scattered about in schools, convents, and colleges, will find the home of their affections elsewhere, or rather they will form the habit of caring for nothing. Brothers and sisters will scarcely known each other; when they are together in company they will behave as strangers. When there is no confidence between relations, when the family society ceases to give savour to life, its place is soon usurped by vice. Is there any man so stupid that he cannot see how all this hangs together?

A father has done but a third of his task when he begets children and provides a living for them. He owes men to humanity, citizens to the state. A man who can pay this threefold debt and neglects to do so is guilty, more guilty, perhaps, if he pays it in part than when he neglects it entirely. He has no right to be a father if he cannot fulfil a father's duties. Poverty, pressure of business, mistaken social prejudices, none of these can

---

5. When we read in Plutarch that Cato the Censor, who ruled Rome with such glory, brought up his own sons from the cradle, and so carefully that he left everything to be present when their nurse, that is to say their mother, bathed them; when we read in Suetonius that Augustus, the master of the world which he had conquered and which he himself governed, himself taught his grandsons to write, to swim, to understand the beginnings of science, and that he always had them with him, we cannot help smiling at the little people of those days who amused themselves with such follies, and who were too ignorant, no doubt, to attend to the great affairs of the great people of our own time.

excuse a man from his duty, which is to support and educate his own children. If a man of any natural feeling neglects these sacred duties he will repent it with bitter tears and will never be comforted.

But what does this rich man do, this father of a family, compelled, so he says, to neglect his children? He pays another man to perform those duties which are his alone. Mercenary man! Do you expect to purchase a second father for your child? Do not deceive yourself; it is not even a master you have hired for him, it is a flunkey, who will soon train such another as himself.

There is much discussion as to the characteristics of a good tutor. My first requirement, and it implies a good many more, is that he should not take up his task for reward. There are callings so great that they cannot be undertaken for money without showing our unfitness for them; such callings are those of the soldier and the teacher.

"But who must train my child?" "I have just told you, you should do it yourself." "I cannot." "You cannot! Then find a friend. I see no other course."

A tutor! What a noble soul! Indeed for the training of a man one must either be a father or more than man. It is this duty you would calmly hand over to a hireling!

The more you think of it the harder you will find it. The tutor must have been trained for his pupil, his servants must have been trained for their master, so that all who come near him may have received the impression which is to be transmitted to him. We must pass from education to education, I know not how far. How can a child be well educated by one who has not been well educated himself?

Can such a one be found? I know not. In this age of degradation who knows the height of virtue to which man's soul may attain? But let us assume that this prodigy has been discovered. We shall learn what he should be from the consideration of his duties. . . .

Contrary to the received opinion, a child's tutor should be young, as young indeed as a man may well be who is also wise. Were it possible, he should become a child himself, that he may be the companion of his pupil and win his confidence by sharing his games. Childhood and age have too little in common for the formation of a really firm affection. Children sometimes flatter old men; they never love them.

People seek a tutor who has already educated one pupil. This is too much; one man can only educate one pupil; if two were essential to success, what right would he have to undertake the first? With more experience you may know better what to do, but you are less capable of doing it; once this task has been well done, you will know too much of its difficulties to attempt it a second time—if ill done, the first attempt augurs badly for the second.

It is one thing to follow a young man about for four years, another to be his guide for five-and-twenty. You find a tutor for your son when he is already formed; I want one for him before he is born. Your man may change his pupil every five years; mine will never have but one pupil. You distinguish between the teacher and the tutor. Another piece of folly! Do you make any distinction between the pupil and the scholar? There is only one science for children to learn—the duties of man. This science is one, and, whatever Xenophon may say of the education of the Persians, it is indivisible. Besides, I prefer to call the man who has this knowledge master rather than teacher, since it is a question of guidance rather than instruction. He must not give precepts, he must let the scholar find them out for himself.

If the master is to be so carefully chosen, he may well choose his pupil, above all when he proposes to set a pattern for others. This choice cannot depend on the child's genius or character, as I adopt him before he is born, and they are only known when my task is finished. If I had my choice I would take a child of ordinary mind, such as I assume in my pupil. It is ordinary people who have to be educated, and their education alone can serve as a pattern for the education of their fellows. The others find their way alone. . . .

I must add that there is just one other point arising out of this; we must never be separated except by mutual consent. This clause is essential, and I would have tutor and scholar so inseparable that they should regard their fate as one. If once they perceive the time of their separation drawing near, the time which must make them strangers to one another, they become strangers then and there; each makes his own little world, and both of them being busy in thought with the time when they will no longer be together, they remain together against their will. The disciple regards his master as the badge and scourge of childhood, the master regards his scholar as a heavy burden which he longs to be rid of. Both are looking forward to the time when they will part, and as there is never any real affection between them, there will be scant vigilance on the one hand, and on the other scant obedience.

But when they consider they must always live together, they must needs love one another, and in this way they really learn to love one another. The pupil is not ashamed to follow as a child the friend who will be with him in manhood; the tutor takes an interest in the efforts whose fruits he will enjoy, and the virtues he is cultivating in his pupil form a store laid up for his old age. . . .

Liberal Knowledge Its Own End

JOHN HENRY CARDINAL NEWMAN
(1801–1890)

The Idea of a University, 1852
Apologia pro Vita Sua, 1864
An Essay in Aid of a Grammar of Assent, 1870

JOHN HENRY CARDINAL NEWMAN belonged to the Church of England until he became a convert to the Roman Catholic Church. In 1852 he was named Rector of the new Irish Catholic University in Dublin where, in preparation for his position, he delivered a series of lectures later published as *On the Scope and Nature of a University Education*. He struggled with a problem then crucial, and even more pressing in our own times, that of the formation of student minds which are both thoroughly educated and thoroughly religious.

A UNIVERSITY MAY BE CONSIDERED WITH REFERENCE EITHER TO ITS students or to its Studies; and the principle, that all Knowledge is a whole and the separate Sciences parts of one, which I have hitherto been using in behalf of its studies, is equally important when we direct our attention to its students. Now then I turn to the students, and shall consider the education which, by virtue of this principle, a University will give them; and thus I shall be introduced, gentlemen, to the second question, which I proposed to discuss, viz., whether and in what sense its teaching, viewed relatively to the taught, carries the attribute of Utility along with it.

I have said that all branches of knowledge are connected together, because the subject-matter of knowledge is intimately united in itself, as being the great Creator and His work. Hence it is that the Sciences, into which our knowledge may be said to be

On the Scope and Nature of a University Education, London: J. M. Dent, 1915.

cast, have multiplied bearings one on another, and an internal
sympathy, and admit or rather demand, comparison and adjustment. They complete, correct, balance each other. This consideration, if well-founded, must be taken into account, not only as
regards the attainment of truth, which is their common end, but
as regards the influence which they exercise upon those whose education consists in the study of them. I have said already, that to
give undue prominence to one is to be unjust to another; to
neglect or supersede these is to divert those from their proper
object. It is to unsettle the boundary lines between science and
science, to disturb their action, to destroy the harmony which
binds them together. Such a proceeding will have a corresponding
effect when introduced into a place of education. There is no
science but tells a different tale, when viewed as a portion of a
whole, from what it is likely to suggest when taken by itself, without the safeguard, as I may call it, of others.

Let me make use of an illustration. In the combination of
colours, very different effects are produced by a difference in their
selection and juxtaposition; red, green, and white change their
shades, according to the contrast to which they are submitted.
And, in like manner, the drift and meaning of a branch of
knowledge varies with the company in which it is introduced to
the student. If his reading is confined simply to one subject,
however such division of labour may favour the advancement
of a particular pursuit, a point into which I do not here enter,
certainly it has a tendency to contract his mind. If it is incorporated with others, it depends on those others as to the kind
of influence which it exerts upon him. Thus the Classics, which
in England are the means of refining the taste, have in France
subserved the spread of revolutionary and deistical doctrines. In
Metaphysics, again, Butler's "Analogy of Religion," which has
had so much to do with the conversion of members of the University of Oxford, appeared to Pitt and others, who had received
a different training, to operate only in the direction of infidelity.
And so again, Watson, Bishop of Llandaff, as I think he tells us
in the narrative of his life, felt the science of Mathematics to
indispose the mind to religious belief, while others see in its
investigations the best defence of the Christian Mysteries. In

like manner, I suppose, Arcesilas would not have handled logic as Aristotle, nor Aristotle have criticized poets as Plato; yet reasoning and poetry are subject to scientific rules.

It is a great point then to enlarge the range of studies which a University professes, even for the sake of the students; and, though they cannot pursue every subject which is open to them, they will be the gainers by living among those and under those who represent the whole circle. This I conceive to be the advantage of a seat of universal learning, considered as a place of education. An assemblage of learned men, zealous for their own sciences, and rivals of each other, are brought, by familiar intercourse and for the sake of intellectual peace, to adjust together the claims and relations of their respective subjects of investigation. They learn to respect, to consult, to aid each other. Thus is created a pure and clear atmosphere of thought, which the student also breathes, though in his own case he only pursues a few sciences out of the multitude. He profits by an intellectual tradition, which is independent of particular teachers, which guides him in his choice of subjects, and duly interprets for him those which he chooses. He apprehends the great outlines of knowledge, the principles on which it rests, the scale of its parts, its lights and its shades, its great points and its little, as he otherwise cannot apprehend them. Hence it is that his education is called "Liberal." A habit of mind is formed which lasts through life, of which the attributes are, freedom, equitableness, calmness, moderation, and wisdom; or what in a former Discourse I have ventured to call a philosophical habit. This then I would assign as the special fruit of the education furnished at a University, as contrasted with other places of teaching or modes of teaching. This is the main purpose of a University in its treatment of its students.

And now the question is asked me, What is the *use* of it? and my answer will constitute the main subject of the Discourses which are to follow.

Cautious and practical thinkers, I say, will ask of me, what, after all, is the gain of this Philosophy, of which I make such account, and from which I promise so much. Even supposing it to enable us to give the degree of confidence exactly due to every science respectively, and to estimate precisely the value of every truth which is anywhere to be found, how are we better for this master view of things which I have been extolling? Does it not reverse the principle of the division of labour? will practical objects be obtained better or worse by its cultivation? to what then does it lead? where does it end? what does it do? how does it profit? what does it promise? Particular sciences are respectively the basis of definite arts, which carry on to results tangible and beneficial the truths which are the subjects of the knowledge attained; what is the Art of this science of sciences? what is the fruit of such a Philosophy? what are we proposing to effect, what inducements do we hold to the Catholic community, when we set about the enterprise of founding a University?

I am asked what is the end of University Education, and of the Liberal or Philosophical Knowledge which I conceive it to impart: I answer, that what I have already said has been sufficient to show that it has a very tangible, real, and sufficient end, though the end cannot be divided from that knowledge itself. Knowledge is capable of being its own end. Such is the constitution of the human mind, that any kind of knowledge, if it be really such, is its own reward. And if this is true of all knowledge, it is true also of that special Philosophy, which I have made to consist in a comprehensive view of truth in all its branches, of the relations of science to science, of their mutual bearings, and their respective vlaues. What the worth of such an acquirement is, compared with other objects which we seek—wealth or power or honour or the conveniences and comforts of life, I do not profess here to discuss; but I would maintain, and mean to show, that it is an object, in its own nature so really and undeniably good, as to be the compensation of a great deal of thought in the compassing, and a great deal of trouble in the attaining.

Now, when I say that Knowledge is, not merely a means to something beyond it, or the preliminary of certain arts into which it naturally resolves, but an end sufficient to rest in and to pursue for its own sake, surely I am uttering no paradox, for I am stating what is both intelligible in itself, and has ever been the common judgment of philosophers and the ordinary feeling of mankind. I am saying what at least the public opinion of this day ought to be slow to deny, considering how much we have heard of late years, in opposition to Religion, of entertaining, curious, and various knowledge. I am but saying what whole volumes have been written to illustrate, by a "selection from the records of Philosophy, Literature, and Art, in all ages and countries, of a body of examples, to show how the most unpropitious circumstances have been unable to conquer an ardent desire for the acquisition of knowledge."[1] That further advantages accrue to us and redound to others by its possession, over and above what it is in itself, I am very far indeed from denying; but, independent of these, we are satisfying a direct need of our nature in its very acquisition; and, whereas our nature, unlike that of the inferior creation, does not at once reach its perfection, but depends, in order to it, on a number of external aids and appliances, Knowledge, as one of the principal gifts or accessories by which it is completed, is valuable for what its very presence in us does for us by a sort of *opus operatum,* even though it be turned to no further account, nor subserve any direct end.

Hence it is that Cicero, in enumerating the various heads of mental excellence, lays down the pursuit of Knowledge for its own sake, as the first of them. "This pertains most of all to human nature," he says, "for we are all of us drawn to the pursuit of Knowledge; in which to excel we consider excellent, whereas to mistake, to err, to be ignorant, to be deceived, is both evil and a disgrace."[2] And he considers Knowledge the very first object to which we are attracted, after the supply of our physical wants. After the calls and duties of our animal existence, as they may be termed, as regards ourselves, our family, and our neighbours, follows, he tells us, "the search after truth. Accordingly, as soon as we escape from the pressure of necessary cares, forthwith we desire to see, to hear, to learn; and consider the knowledge of what is hidden or is wonderful as a condition of our happiness."

This passage, though it is but one of many similar passages in a multitude of authors, I take for the very reason that it is so

---

1. "Pursuit of Knowledge under Difficulties." Introd.
2. Cicer. Offic. init.

familiarly known to us; and I wish you to observe, gentlemen, how distinctly it separates the pursuit of Knowledge from those ulterior objects to which certainly it can be made to conduce, and which are, I supose, solely contemplated by the persons who would ask of me the use of a University or Liberal Education. So far from dreaming of the cultivation of Knowledge directly and mainly in order to our physical comfort and enjoyment, for the sake of life and person, of health, of the conjugal and family union, of the social tie and civil security, the great Orator implies, that it is only after our physical and political needs are supplied, and when we are "free from necessary duties and cares," that we are in a condition for "desiring to see, to hear, and to learn." Nor does he contemplate in the least degree the reflex or subsequent action of Knowledge, when acquired, upon those material goods which we set out by securing before we seek it; on the contrary, he expressly denies its bearing upon social life altogether, strange as such a procedure is to those who live after the rise of the Baconian philosophy, and he cautions us against such a cultivation of it as will interfere with our duties to our fellow-creatures. "All these methods," he says, "are engaged in the investigation of truth; by the pursuit of which to be carried off from public occupations is a transgression of duty. For the praise of virtue lies altogether in action; yet intermissions often occur, and then we recur to such pursuits; not to say that the incessant activity of the mind is vigorous enough to carry us on in the pursuit of knowledge, even without any exertion of our own." The idea of benefiting society by means of "the pursuit of science and knowledge" did not enter at all into the motives which he would assign for their cultivation.

This was the ground of the opposition which the elder Cato made to the introduction of Greek Philosophy among his countrymen, when Carneades and his companions, on occasion of their embassy, were charming the Roman youth with their eloquent expositions of it. The fit representative of a practical people, Cato estimated everything by what it produced; whereas the Pursuit of Knowledge promised nothing beyond Knowledge itself. He despised that refinement or enlargement of mind of which he had no experience.

Things, which can bear to be cut off from everything else and yet persist in living, must have life in themselves; pursuits, which issue in nothing, and still maintain their ground for ages, which are regarded as admirable, though they have not as yet proved themselves to be useful, must have their sufficient end in themselves, whatever it turn out to be. And we are brought to the same conclusion by considering the force of the epithet, by which the knowledge under consideration is popularly designated. It is common to speak of *"liberal* knowledge," of the *"liberal* arts and studies," and of a *"liberal* education," as the especial characteristic or property of a University and of a gentleman; what is really meant by the word? Now, first, in its grammatical sense it is opposed to *servile;* and by "servile work" is understood, as our catechisms inform us, bodily labour, mechanical employment, and the like, in which the mind has little or no part. Parallel to such works are those arts, if they deserve the name, of which the poet speaks,[3] which owe their origin and their method to hazard, not to skill; as, for instance, the practice and operations of an empiric. As far as this contrast may be considered as a guide into the meaning of the word, liberal knowledge and liberal pursuits are such as belong to the mind, not to the body.

But we want something more for its explanation, for there are bodily exercises which are liberal, and mental exercises which are not so. For instance, in ancient times the practitioners in medicine were commonly slaves; yet it was an art as intellectual in its nature, in spite of the pretence, fraud, and quackery with which it might then, as now, be debased, as it was heavenly in its aim. And so in like manner, we contrast a liberal education with a commercial education or a professional; yet no one can deny that commerce and the professions afford scope for the highest and most diversified powers of mind. There is then a great variety of intellectual exercises, which are not technically called "liberal"; on the other hand, I say, there are exercises of the body which do receive that appellation. Such, for instance, was the palaestra, in ancient times; such the Olympic games, in which strength and dexterity of body as well as of mind gained

---

3. Vid. Arist. Nic. Ethic. vi.

the prize. In Xenophon we read of the young Persian nobility being taught to ride on horseback and to speak the truth; both being among the accomplishments of a gentleman. War, too, however rough a profession, has ever been accounted liberal, unless in cases when it becomes heroic, which would introduce us to another subject.

Now comparing these instances together, we shall have no difficulty in determining the principle of this apparent variation in the application of the term which I am examining. Manly games, or games of skill, or military prowess, though bodily, are, it seems, accounted liberal; on the other hand, what is merely professional, though highly intellectual, nay, though liberal in comparison of trade and manual labour, is not simply called liberal, and mercantile occupations are not liberal at all. Why this distinction? because that alone is liberal knowledge, which stands on its own pretensions, which is independent of sequel, expects no complement, refuses to be *informed* (as it is called) by any end, or absorbed into any art, in order duly to present itself to our contemplation. The most ordinary pursuits have this specific character, if they are self-sufficient and complete; the highest lose it, when they minister to something beyond them. It is absurd to balance, in point of worth and importance, a treatise on reducing fractures with a game of cricket or a fox-chase; yet of the two the bodily exercise has that quality which we call "liberal," and the intellectual has it not. And so of the learned professions altogether, considered merely as professions; although one of them be the most popularly beneficial, and another the most politically important, and the third the most intimately divine of all human pursuits, yet the very greatness of their end, the health of the body, or of the commonwealth, or of the soul, diminishes, not increases, their claim to the appellation in question, and that still more, if they are cut down to the strict exigencies of that end. If, for instance, Theology, instead of being cultivated as a contemplation, be limited to the purposes of the pulpit or be represented by the catechism, it loses—not its usefulness, not its divine character, not its meritoriousness (rather it increases these qualities by such charitable condescension)—but it does lose the particular attribute which I am illustrating; just as a face worn by tears and fasting loses its beauty, or a labourer's hand loses its delicateness; for Theology thus exercised is not simple knowledge, but rather is an art or a business making use of Theology. And thus it appears that even what is supernatural need not be liberal, nor need a hero be a gentleman, for the plain reason that one idea is not another idea. And in like manner the Baconian Philosophy, by using its physical sciences for the purpose of fruit, does thereby transfer them from the order of Liberal Pursuits to, I do not say the inferior, but the distinct class of the Useful. And, to take a different instance, hence again, as is evident, whenever personal gain is the motive, still more distinctive an effect has it upon the character of a given pursuit; thus racing, which was a liberal excrcise in Greece, forfeits its rank in times like these, so far as it is made the occasion of gambling.

All that I have been now saying is summed up in a few characteristic words of the great Philosopher. "Of possessions," he says, "those rather are useful, which bear fruit; those *liberal, which tend to enjoyment*. By fruitful, I mean, which yield revenue; by enjoyable, where *nothing accrues of consequence beyond the use*."[4]

Do not suppose, gentlemen, that in thus appealing to the ancients, I am throwing back the world two thousand years, and fettering Philosophy with the reasonings of paganism. While the world lasts, will Aristotle's doctrine on these matters last, for he is the oracle of nature and of truth. While we are men, we cannot help, to a great extent, being Aristotelians, for the great Master does but analyse the thoughts, feelings, views, and opinions of human kind. He has told us the meaning of our own words and ideas, before we were born. In many subject-matters, to think correctly, is to think like Aristotle; and we are his disciples whether we will or no, though we may not know it. Now, as to the particular instance before us, the word "liberal" as applied to Knowledge and Education, expresses a specific idea, which ever has been, and ever will be, while the nature of man is the same, just as the idea of the Beautiful is specific, or of the Sublime,

----

4. Aristot. Rhet. i. 5.

or of the Ridiculous, or of the Sordid. It is in the world now, it was in the world then; and, as in the case of the dogmas of faith, it is illustrated by a continuous historical tradition, and never was out of the world, from the time it came into it. There have indeed been differences of opinion from time to time, as to what pursuits and what arts came under that idea, but such differences are but an additional evidence of its reality. That idea must have a substance in it, which has maintained its ground amid these conflicts and changes, which has ever served as a standard to measure things withal, which has passed from mind to mind unchanged, when there was so much to colour, so much to influence any notion or thought whatever, which was not founded in our very nature. Were it a mere generalisation, it would have varied with the subjects from which it was generalised; but though its subjects vary with the age, it varies not itself. The palaestra may seem a liberal exercise to Lycurgus, and illiberal to Seneca; coach-driving and prize-fighting may be recognised in Elis, and be condemned in England; music may be despicable in the eyes of certain moderns, and be in the highest place with Aristotle and Plato—(and the case is the same in the particular application of the idea of Beauty, or of Goodness, or of Moral Virtue, there is a difference of tastes, a difference of judgments)—still these variations imply, instead of discrediting, the archetypal idea, which is but a previous hypothesis or condition, by means of which issue is joined between contending opinions, and without which there would be nothing to dispute about.

I consider, then, that I am chargeable with no paradox, when I speak of a Knowledge which is its own end, when I call it liberal knowledge, or a gentleman's knowledge, when I educate for it, and make it the scope of a University. And still less am I incurring such a charge, when I make this acquisition consist, not in Knowledge in a vague and ordinary sense, but in that Knowledge which I have especially called Philosophy or, in an extended sense of the word, Science; for whatever claims Knowledge has to be considered as a good, these it has in a higher degree when it is viewed not vaguely, not popularly, but precisely and transcendently as Philosophy. Knowledge, I say, is then especially liberal, or sufficient for itself, apart from every external and ulterior object, when and so far as it is philosophical, and this I proceed to show.

Now bear with me, gentlemen, if what I am about to say, has at first sight a fanciful appearance. Philosophy, then, or Science, is related to Knowledge in this way:—Knowledge is called by the name of Science or Philosophy, when it is acted upon, informed, or if I may use a strong figure, impregnated by Reason. Reason is the principle of that intrinsic fecundity of Knowledge, which, to those who possess it, is its especial value, and which dispenses with the necessity of their looking abroad for any end to rest upon external to itself. Knowledge, indeed, when thus exalted into a scientific form, is also power; not only is it excellent in itself, but whatever such excellence may be, it is something more, it has a result beyond itself. Doubtless; but that is a further consideration, with which I am not concerned. I only say that, prior to its being a power, it is a good; that it is, not only an instrument, but an end. I know well it may resolve itself into an art, and terminate in a mechanical process, and in tangible fruit; but it also may fall back upon Reason, and resolve itself into Philosophy. In one case it is called Useful Knowledge, in the other Liberal. The same person may cultivate it in both ways at once; but this again is a matter foreign to my subject; here I do but say that there are two ways of using Knowledge, and in matter of fact those who use it in one way are not likely to use it in the other, or at least in a very limited measure. You see then, gentlemen, here are two methods of Education; the one aspires to be philosophical, the other to be mechanical; the one rises towards ideas, the other is exhausted upon what is particular and external. Let me not be thought to deny the necessity, or to decry the benefit, of such attention to what is particular and practical, the useful or mechanical arts; life could not go on without them; we owe our daily welfare to them; their exercise is the duty of the many, and we owe to the many a debt of gratitude for fulfilling it. I only say that Knowledge, in proportion as it tends more and more to be particular, ceases to be Knowledge. It is a question whether Knowledge can in any proper sense be predicated of the brute creation; without pretending to metaphysical exactness of phraseology, which would be unsuitable to an occasion

like this, I say, it seems to me improper to call that passive sensation, or perception of things, which brutes seem to possess, by the
name of Knowledge. When I speak of Knowledge, I mean something intellectual, something which grasps what it perceives
through the senses; something which takes a view of things; which
sees more than the senses convey; which reasons upon what it
sees, and while it sees; which invests it with an idea. It expresses
itself, not in a mere enunciation, but by an enthymeme: it is of the
nature of science from the first, and in this consists its dignity.
The principle of real dignity in Knowledge, its worth, its desirableness, considered irrespectively of its results, is this germ
within it of a scientific or a philosophical process. This is how it
comes to be an end in itself; this is why it admits of being called
Liberal. Not to know the relative disposition of things is the state
of slaves or children; to have mapped out the Universe is the
boast of Philosophy.

Moreover, such knowledge is not a mere extrinsic or accidental
advantage, which is ours to-day and another's to-morrow, which
may be got up from a book, and easily forgotten again, which we
can command or communicate at our pleasure, which we can
borrow for the occasion, carry about in our hand, and take into
the market; it is an acquired illumination, it is a habit, a
personal possession, and an inward endowment. And this is the
reason, why it is more correct, as well as more usual, to speak of
a University as a place of education, than of instruction, though,
when knowledge is concerned, instruction would at first sight
have seemed the more appropriate word. We are instructed, for
instance, in manual exercises, in the fine and useful arts, in
trades, and in ways of business; for these are methods, which
have little or no effect upon the mind itself, are contained in rules
committed to memory, to tradition, or to use, and bear upon an
end external to themselves. But education is a higher word; it
implies an action upon our mental nature, and the formation of a
character; it is something individual and permanent, and is
commonly spoken of in connection with religion and virtue.
When, then, we speak of the communication of Knowledge as
being Education, we thereby really imply that that Knowledge
is a state or condition of mind; and since cultivation of mind is

surely worth seeking for its own sake, we are thus brought once more to the conclusion, which the word "Liberal" and the word "Philosophy" have already suggested, that there is a Knowledge, which is desirable, though nothing come of it, as being of itself a treasure, and a sufficient remuneration of years of labour.

This, then, is the answer which I am prepared to give to the question with which I opened this Discourse. Before going on to speak of the object of the Church in taking up Philosophy, and the uses to which she puts it, I am prepared to maintain that Philosophy is its own end, and, as I conceive, I have now begun proving it. I am prepared to maintain that there is a knowledge worth possessing for what it is, and not merely for what it does; and what minutes remain to me to-day I shall devote to the removal of some portion of the indistinctness and confusion with which the subject may in some minds be surrounded.

It may be objected then, that, when we profess to seek Knowledge for some end or other beyond itself, whatever it be, we speak intelligibly; but that, whatever men may have said, however obstinately the idea may have kept its ground from age to age, still it is simply unmeaning to say that we seek Knowledge for its own sake, and for nothing else; for that it ever leads to something beyond itself, which therefore is its end, and the cause why it is desirable;—moreover, that this end is twofold, either of this world or of the next; that all knowledge is cultivated either for secular objects or for eternal; that if it is directed to secular objects, it is called Useful Knowledge, if to eternal, Religious or Christian Knowledge;—in consequence, that if, as I have allowed, this Liberal Knowledge does not benefit the body or estate, it ought to benefit the soul; but if the fact be really so, that it is neither a physical or a secular good on the one hand, nor a moral good on the other, it cannot be a good at all, and is not worth the trouble which is necessary for its acquisition.

And then I may be reminded that the professors of this Liberal or Philosophical Knowledge have themselves, in every age, recognised this exposition of the matter, and have submitted to the issue in which it terminates; for they have ever been attempting to make men virtuous; or, if not, at least have assumed that refinement of mind was virtue, and that they themselves were

the virtuous portion of mankind. This they have professed on
the one hand; and on the other, they have utterly failed in
their professions, so as ever to make themselves a proverb
among men, and a laughing-stock both to the grave and the dissipated portion of mankind, in consequence of them. Thus they
have furnished against themselves both the ground and the
means of their own exposure, without any trouble at all to any
one else. In a word, from the time that Athens was the University of the world, what has Philosophy taught men, but to
promise without practising, and to aspire without attaining?
What has the deep and lofty thought of its disciples ended in but
eloquent words? Nay, what has its teaching ever meditated, when
it was boldest in its remedies for human ill, beyond charming
us to sleep by its lessons, that we might feel nothing at all? like
some melodious air, or rather like those strong and transporting
perfumes, which at first spread their sweetness over everything
they touch, but in a little while do but offend in proportion as
they once pleased us. Did Philosophy support Cicero under the
disfavour of the fickle populace, or nerve Seneca to oppose an
imperial tyrant? It abandoned Brutus, as he sorrowfully confessed, in his greatest need, and it forced Cato, as his panegyrist
strangely boasts, into the false position of defying heaven. How
few can be counted among its professors, who, like Polemo,
were thereby converted from a profligate course, or like Anaxa-
goras, thought the world well lost in exchange for its possession?
The philosopher in Rasselas taught a superhuman doctrine, and
then succumbed without an effort to a trial of human affection.
"He discoursed," we are told, "with great energy on the government of the passions. His look was venerable, his action
graceful, his pronunciation clear, and his diction elegant. He
showed, with great strength of sentiment and variety of illustration, that human nature is degraded and debased, when the lower
faculties predominate over the higher. He communicated the
various precepts given, from time to time, for the conquest of
passion, and displayed the happiness of those who had obtained
the important victory, after which man is no longer the slave
of fear, nor the fool of hope. . . . He enumerated many examples
of heroes immovable by pain or pleasure, who looked with in-

difference on those modes or accidents to which the vulgar give the names of good and evil."

Rasselas in a few days found the philosopher in a room half darkened, with his eyes misty, and his face pale. "Sir," said he, "you have come at a time when all human friendship is useless; what I suffer cannot be remedied, what I have lost cannot be supplied. My daughter, my only daughter, from whose tenderness I expected all the comforts of my age, died last night of a fever." "Sir," said the prince, "mortality is an event by which a wise man can never be surprised; we know that death is always near, and it should therefore always be expected." "Young man," answered the philosopher, "you speak like one who has never felt the pangs of separation." "Have you, then, forgot the precept," said Rasselas, "which you so powerfully enforced? . . . consider that external things are naturally variable, but truth and reason are always the same." "What comfort," said the mourner, "can truth and reason afford me? Of what effect are they now, but to tell me that my daughter will not be restored?"

Better, far better, to make no professions, you will say, than to cheat others with what we are not, and to scandalise them with what we are. The sensualist, or the man of the word, at any rate is not the victim of fine words, but pursues a reality and gains it. The Philosophy of Utility, you will say, gentlemen, has at least done its work; it aimed low, but it has fulfilled its aim. If that man of great intellect who has been its Prophet in the conduct of life played false to his own professions, he was not bound by his philosophy to be true to his friend or faithful in his trust. Moral virtue was not the line in which he undertook to instruct men; and though, as the poet calls him, he were the "meanest" of mankind, he was so in what may be called his private capacity, and without any prejudice to the theory of induction. He had a right to be so, if he chose, for anything that the Idols of the den or the theatre had to say to the contrary. His mission was the increase of physical enjoyment and social comfort;[5] and most wonderfully, most awfully has he ful-

---

5. It will be seen that on the whole I agree with Lord Macaulay in his Essay on Bacon's Philosophy. I do not know whether he would agree with me.

filled his conception and his design. Almost day by day have we fresh and fresh shoots, and buds, and blossoms, which are to ripen into fruit, on that magical tree of Knowledge which he planted, and to which none of us perhaps, except the very poor, but owes, if not his present life, at least his daily food, his health, and general well-being. He was the divinely provided minister of temporal benefits to all of us so great, that, whatever I am forced to think of him as a man, I have not the heart, from mere gratitude, to speak of him severely. And, in spite of the tendencies of his philosophy, which are, as we see at this day, to depreciate, or to trample on Theology, he has himself, in his writings, gone out of his way, as if with a prophetic misgiving of those tendencies, to insist on it as the instrument of that beneficent Father,[6] who, when He came on earth in visible form, took on Him first and most prominently the office of assuaging the bodily wounds of human nature. And truly, like the old mediciner in the tale, "he sat diligently at his work, and hummed, with cheerful countenance, a pious song"; and then in turn "went out singing into the meadows so gaily, that those who had seen him from afar might well have thought it was a youth gathering flowers for his beloved, instead of an old physician gathering healing herbs in the morning dew."[7]

Alas, that men, in the action of life or in their heart of hearts, are not what they seem to be in their moments of excitement, or in their trances or intoxications of genius—so good, so noble, so serene! Alas, that Bacon too[8] in his own way should after all be but the fellow of those heathen philosophers who in their disadvantages had some excuse for their inconsistency, and who sur-

6. De Augment. iv. 2, vid. Macaulay's Essay; vid. also "In principio operis ad Deum Patrem, Deum Verbum, Deum Spiritum, preces fundimus humillimas et ardentissimas, ut humani generis aerumnarum memores, et peregrinationis istius vitae, in qua dies paucos et malos terimus, *novis suis eleemosynis, per manus nostras,* familiam humanam dotare dignentur. Atque illud insuper supplices rogamus, ne *humana divinis officiant*; neve *ex reseratione viarum sensus,* et accensione majore luminis naturalis, *aliquid incredulitatis* et noctis, animis nostris erga divina mysteria oboriatur," &c. *Praef. Instaur. Magn.*

7. Fouqué's "Unknown Patient."

8. Te maris et terrae, &c. Hor. Od. i.28.

prise us rather in what they did say than in what they did not do! Alas, that he too, like Socrates or Seneca, must be stripped of his holy-day coat, which looks so fair, and should be but a mockery amid his most majestic gravity of phrase; and, for all his vast abilities, should, in the littleness of his own moral being, but typify the intellectual narrowness of his school! However, granting all this, heroism after all was not his philosophy: I cannot deny he has abundantly achieved what he proposed. His is simply a Method whereby bodily discomforts and temporal wants are to be most effectually removed from the greatest number; and already, before it has shown any signs of exhaustion, the gifts of nature, in their most artificial shapes and luxurious profusion and diversity, from all quarters of the earth, are, it is undeniable, by its means brought even to our doors, and we rejoice in them.

Useful Knowledge then certainly has done its work; and Liberal Knowledge as certainly has not done its work—supposing, that is, as the objectors assume, its direct end, like Religious Knowledge, is to make men better; but this I will not for an instant allow. For all its friends, or its enemies, may say, I insist upon it, that it is as real a mistake to burden it with virtue or religion as with the mechanical arts. Its direct business is not to steel the soul against temptation or to console it in affliction, any more than to set the loom in motion, or to direct the steam carriage; be it ever so much the means or the condition of both material and moral advancement; still, taken by and in itself, it as little mends our hearts as it improves our temporal circumstances. And if its eulogists claim for it such a power, they commit the very same kind of encroachment on a province not their own as the political economist who should maintain that his science educated him for casuistry or diplomacy. Knowledge is one thing, virtue is another; good sense is not conscience, refinement is not humility, nor is largeness and justness of view faith. Philosophy, however enlightened, however profound, gives no command over the passions, no influential motives, no vivifying principles. Liberal Education makes not the Christian, not the Catholic, but the gentleman. It is well to be a gentleman, it is well to have a cultivated intellect, a delicate taste, a candid, equitable, dispassionate mind, a noble and courteous bearing in the conduct of life;—these are the con-natural qualities of a large knowledge; they are the objects of a University; I am advocating, I shall illustrate and insist upon them; but still, I repeat, they are no guarantee for sanctity or even for conscientiousness, they may attach to the man of the world, to the profligate, to the heartless—pleasant, alas, and attractive as he shows when decked out in them. Taken by themselves, they do but seem to be what they are not; they look like virtue at a distance, but they are detected by close observers, and on the long run; and hence it is that they are popularly accused of pretence and hypocrisy, not, I repeat, from their own fault, but because their professors and their admirers persist in taking them for what they are not, and are officious in arrogating for them a praise to which they have no claim. Quarry the granite rock with razors, or moor the vessel with a thread of silk; then may you hope with such keen and delicate instruments as human knowledge and human reason to contend against these giants, the passion and the pride of man.

Surely we are not driven to theories of this kind in order to vindicate the value and dignity of Liberal Knowledge. Surely the real grounds on which its pretensions rest are not so very subtle or abstruse, so very strange or improbable. Surely it is very intelligible to say, and that is what I say here, that Liberal Education, viewed in itself, is simply the cultivation of the intellect as such, and its object is nothing more or less than intellectual excellence. Every thing has its own perfection, be it higher or lower in the scale of things; and the perfection of one is not the perfection of another. Things animate, inanimate, visible, invisible, all are good in their kind, and have a *best* of themselves, which is an object of pursuit. Why do you take such pains with your garden or your park? You see to your walks and turf and shrubberies; to your trees and drives; not as if you meant to make an orchard of the one, or corn or pasture land of the other, but because there is a special beauty in all that is goodly in wood, water, plain, and slope, brought all together by art into one shape, and grouped into one whole. Your cities are beautiful, your palaces, your public buildings, your territorial mansions, your churches; and their beauty leads to nothing beyond itself. There is a physical beauty and a moral: there is a beauty of person, there is a beauty of our moral being, which is natural virtue; and in like manner there is a beauty, there is a perfection, of the intellect. There is an ideal perfection in these various subject-matters, towards which individual instances are seen to rise, and which are the standards for all instances whatever. The Greek divinities and demigods, as the statuary has moulded them, with their symmetry of figure, and their high forehead and their regular features, are the perfection of physical beauty. The heroes, of whom history tells, Alexander, or Caesar, or Scipio, or Saladin, are the representatives of that magnanimity or self-mastery which is the greatness of human nature. Christianity too has its heroes, and in the supernatural order, and we call them Saints. The artist puts before him beauty of feature and form; the poet, beauty of mind; the preacher, the beauty of grace; then intellect too, I repeat, has its beauty, and it has those who aim at it. To open the mind, to correct it, to refine it, to enable it to know, and to digest, master, rule, and use its knowledge, to give it power over its own faculties, application, flexibility, method, critical exactness, sagacity, resource, address, eloquent expression, is an object as intelligible (for here we are inquiring, not what the object of a Liberal Education is worth, nor what use the Church makes of it, but what it is in itself). I say, an object as intelligible as the cultivation of virtue, while, at the same time, it is absolutely distinct from it.

This indeed is but a temporal object, and a transitory possession: but so are other things in themselves which we make much of and pursue. The moralist will tell us that man, in all his functions, is but a flower which blossoms and fades, except so far as a higher principle breathes upon him, and makes him and what he is immortal. Body and mind are carried on into an eternal state of being by the gifts of Divine Munificence; but at first they do but fail in a failing world; and if the powers of intellect decay, the powers of the body have decayed before them, and, as an Hospital or an Almshouse, though its end be ephemeral, may be sanctified to the service of religion, so surely may a University, even were it nothing more than I have as yet described it. We attain to heaven by using this world well, though it is to pass away; we perfect our nature, not by undoing it, but by adding to it what is more than nature, and directing it towards aims higher than its own.

Science and Culture

THOMAS HENRY HUXLEY
(1825–1895)

Evidence as to Man's Place in Nature, 1870
Lay Sermons, Addresses, and Reviews, 1877
American Addresses, 1877
Science and Culture and Other Essays, 1881
Evolution and Ethics, 1894

THOMAS HENRY HUXLEY did not regard himself as a literary man but as the proponent of scientific truth. Largely self-educated as a child, as an adult he was trained as a physician. But his real passions were scientific research and popular education. He became an exponent of Darwin's theories of biological evolution, at the same time urging the place of science in general education. He wrote mainly for the express purpose of expounding his ideas on science and defending Darwin against attack. His was a highly refined literary talent, coupled with a real genius for the lucid exposition of the most complex subjects. A scientist with a philosophic mind, Huxley recognized that "Science and literature are not two things, but two sides of one thing."

. . . FROM THE TIME THAT THE FIRST SUGGESTION TO INTRODUCE physical science into ordinary education was timidly whispered, until now, the advocates of scientific education have met with opposition of two kinds. On the one hand, they have been pooh-poohed by the men of business who pride themselves on being the representatives of practicality; while, on the other hand, they have been excommunicated by the classical scholars, in their capacity of Levites in charge of the ark of culture and monopolists of liberal education.

The practical men believed that the idol whom they worship —rule of thumb—has been the source of the past prosperity, and

Science and Culture and Other Essays, London: Macmillan & Co., Ltd., 1881.

will suffice for the future welfare of the arts and manufactures. They are of opinion that science is speculative rubbish; that theory and practice have nothing to do with one another; and that the scientific habit of mind is an impediment, rather than an aid, in the conduct of ordinary affairs.

I have used the past tense in speaking of the practical men— for although they were very formidable thirty years ago, I am not sure that the pure species has not been extirpated. In fact, so far as mere argument goes, they have been subjected to such a *feu d'enfer* that it is a miracle if any have escaped. But I have remarked that your typical practical man has an unexpected resemblance to one of Milton's angels. His spiritual wounds, such as are inflicted by logical weapons, may be as deep as a well and as wide as a church door, but beyond shedding a few drops of ichor, celestial or otherwise, he is no whit the worse. So, if any of these opponents be left, I will not waste time in vain repetition of the demonstrative evidence of the practical value of science; but knowing that a parable will sometimes penetrate where syllogisms fail to effect an entrance, I will offer a story for their consideration.

Once upon a time, a boy, with nothing to depend upon but his own vigorous nature, was thrown into the thick of the struggle for existence in the midst of a great manufacturing population. He seems to have had a hard fight, inasmuch as, by the time he was thirty years of age, his total disposable funds amounted to twenty pounds. Nevertheless, middle life found him giving proof of his comprehension of the practical problems he had been roughly called upon to solve, by a career of remarkable prosperity.

Finally, having reached old age with its well-earned surroundings of "honour, troops of friends," the hero of my story bethought himself of those who were making a like start in life, and how he could stretch out a helping hand to them.

After long and anxious reflection this successful practical man of business could devise nothing better than to provide them with the means of obtaining "sound, extensive, and practical scientific knowledge." And he devoted a large part of his wealth and five years of incessant work to this end.

I need not point the moral of a tale which, as the solid and spacious fabric of the Scientific College assures us, is no fable, nor can anything which I could say intensify the force of this practical answer to practical objections.

We may take it for granted then, that, in the opinion of those best qualified to judge, the diffusion of thorough scientific education is an absolutely essential condition of industrial progress; and that the College which has been opened today will confer an inestimable boon upon those whose livelihood is to be gained by the practise of the arts and manufactures of the district.

The only question worth discussion is, whether the conditions, under which the work of the College is to be carried out, are such as to give it the best possible chance of achieving permanent success.

Sir Josiah Mason, without doubt most wisely, has left very large freedom of action to the trustees, to whom he proposes ultimately to commit the administration of the College, so that they may be able to adjust its arrangements in accordance with the changing conditions of the future. But, with respect to three points, he has laid most explicit injunctions upon both administrators and teachers.

Party politics are forbidden to enter into the minds of either, so far as the work of the College is concerned; theology is as sternly banished from its precincts; and finally, it is especially declared that the College shall make no provision for "mere literary instruction and education."

It does not concern me at present to dwell upon the first two injunctions any longer than may be needful to express my full conviction of their wisdom. But the third prohibition brings us face to face with those other opponents of scientific education, who are by no means in the moribund condition of the practical man, but alive, alert, and formidable.

It is not impossible that we shall hear this express exclusion of "literary instruction and education" from a College which, nevertheless, professes to give a high and efficient education, sharply criticised. Certainly the time was that the Levites of culture would have sounded their trumpets against its walls as against an educational Jericho.

How often have we not been told that the study of physical science is incompetent to confer culture; that it touches none of the higher problems of life; and, what is worse, that the continual devotion to scientific studies tends to generate a narrow and bigoted belief in the applicability of scientific methods to the search after truth of all kinds? How frequently one has reason to observe that no reply to a troublesome argument tells so well as calling its author a "mere scientific specialist." And, as I am afraid it is not permissible to speak of this form of opposition to scientific education in the past tense; may we not expect to be told that this, not only omission, but prohibition, of "mere literary instruction and education" is a patent example of scientific narrow-mindedness?

I am not acquainted with Sir Josiah Mason's reasons for the action which he has taken; but if, as I apprehend is the case, he refers to the ordinary classical course of our schools and universities by the name of "mere literary instruction and education," I venture to offer sundry reasons of my own in support of that action.

For I hold very strongly by two convictions: The first is, that neither the discipline nor the subject-matter of classical education is of such direct value to the student of physical science as to justify the expenditure of valuable time upon either; and the second is, that for the purpose of attaining real culture, an exclusively scientific education is at least as effectual as an exclusively literary education.

I need hardly point out to you that these opinions, especially the latter, are diametrically opposed to those of the great majority of educated Englishmen, influenced as they are by school and university traditions. In their belief, culture is obtainable only by a liberal education; and a liberal education and instruction in literature, but in one particular form of literature, namely, that of Greek and Roman antiquity. They hold that the man who has learned Latin and Greek, however little, is educated; while he who is versed in other branches of knowledge, however deeply, is a more or less respectable specialist, not admissible into the cultured caste. The stamp of the educated man, the University degree, is not for him.

I am too well acquainted with the generous catholicity of spirit, the true sympathy with scientific thought, which pervades the writings of our chief apostle of culture to identify him with these opinions; and yet one may cull from one and another of those epistles to the Philistines, which so much delight all who do not answer to that name, sentences which lend them some support.

Mr. Arnold tells us that the meaning of culture is "to know the best that has been thought and said in the world." It is the criticism of life contained in literature. That criticism regards "Europe as being, for intellectual and spiritual purposes, one great confederation, bound to a joint action and working to a common result; and whose members have, for their common outfit, a knowledge of Greek, Roman, and Eastern antiquity, and of one another. Special, local, and temporary advantages being put out of account, that modern nation will in the intellectual and spiritual sphere make most progress, which most thoroughly carries out this program. And what is that but saying that we too, all of us, as individuals, the more thoroughly we carry it out, shall make the more progress?"

We have here to deal with two distinct propositions. The first, that a criticism of life is the essence of culture; the second, that literature contains the materials which suffice for the construction of such criticism.

I think that we must all assent to the first proposition. For culture certainly means something quite different from learning or technical skill. It implies the possession of an ideal, and the habit of critically estimating the value of things by comparison with a theoretic standard. Perfect culture should supply a complete theory of life, based upon a clear knowledge alike of its possibilities and of its limitations.

But we may agree to all this, and yet strongly dissent from the assumption that literature alone is competent to supply this knowledge. After having learnt all that Greek, Roman, and Eastern antiquity have thought and said, and all that modern literature have to tell us, it is not self-evident that we have laid a sufficiently broad and deep foundation for that criticism of life, which constitutes culture.

Indeed, to any one acquainted with the scope of physical

science, it is not at all evident. Considering progress only in the "intellectual and spiritual sphere," I find myself wholly unable to admit that either nations or individuals will really advance, if their common outfit draws nothing from the stores of physical science. I should say that an army, without weapons of precision and with no particular base of operations, might more hopefully enter upon a campaign on the Rhine, than a man, devoid of knowledge of what physical science has done in the last century, upon a criticism of life.

When a biologist meets with an anomaly, he instinctively turns to the study of development to clear it up. The rationale of contradictory opinions may with equal confidence be sought in history.

It is, happily, no new thing that Englishmen should employ their wealth in building and endowing institutions for educational purposes. But, five or six hundred years ago, deeds of foundation expressed or implied conditions as nearly as possible contrary to those which have been thought expedient by Sir Josiah Mason. That is to say, physical science was practically ignored, while a certain literary training was enjoined as a means to the acquirement of knowledge which was essentially theological.

The reason of this singular contradiction between the actions of men alike animated by a strong and disinterested desire to promote the welfare of their fellows, is easily discovered.

At that time, in fact, if any one desired knowledge beyond such as could be obtained by his own observation, or by common conversation, his first necessity was to learn the Latin language, inasmuch as all the higher knowledge of the western world was contained in works written in that language. Hence, Latin grammar, with logic and rhetoric, studied through Latin, were the fundamentals of education. With respect to the substance of the knowledge imparted through this channel the Jewish and Christian Scriptures, as interpreted and supplemented by the Romish Church, were held to contain a complete and infallibly true body of information.

Theological dicta were, to the thinkers of those days, that which the axioms and definitions of Euclid are to the geometers of these. The business of the philosophers of the middle ages was to deduce from the data furnished by the theologians, conclusions in accordance with ecclesiastical decrees. They were allowed the high privilege of showing, by logical process, how and why that which the Church said was true, must be true. And if their demonstrations fell short of or exceeded this limit the Church was materially ready to check their aberrations; if need were, by the help of the secular arm.

Between the two, our ancestors were furnished with a compact and complete criticism of life. They were told how the world began and how it would end; they learned that all material existence was but a base and insignificant blot upon the fair face of the spiritual world, and that nature was, to all intents and purposes, the play-ground of the devil; they learned that the earth is the center of the visible universe, and that man is the cynosure of things terrestrial, and more especially was it inculcated that the course of nature had no fixed order, but that it could be, and constantly was, altered by the agency of innumerable spiritual beings, good and bad, according as they were moved by the deeds and prayers of men. The sum and substance of the whole doctrine was to produce the conviction that the only thing really worth knowing in this world was how to secure that place in a better which, under certain conditions, the Church promised.

Our ancestors had a living belief in this theory of life, and acted upon it in their dealings with education, as in all other matters. Culture meant saintliness—after the fashion of the saints of those days; the education that led to it was, of necessity, theological, and the way to theology lay through Latin.

That the study of nature—further than was requisite for the satisfaction of everyday wants—should have any bearing on human life was far from the thoughts of men thus trained. Indeed, as nature had been cursed for man's sake, it was an obvious conclusion that those who meddled with nature were likely to come into pretty close contact with Satan. And, if any born scientific investigator followed his instincts, he might safely reckon upon earning the reputation, and probably upon suffering the fate, of a sorcerer.

Had the western world been left to itself in Chinese isolation, there is no saying how long this state of things might have endured. But, happily, it was not left to itself. Even earlier than the thirteenth century, the development of Moorish civilisation in Spain and the great movement of the Crusades had introduced the leaven which, from that day to this, has never ceased to work. At first, through the intermediation of Arabic translations, afterwards by the study of the originals, the western nations of Europe became acquainted with the writings of the ancient philosophers and poets, and, in time, with the whole of the vast literature of antiquity.

Whatever there was of high intellectual aspiration or dominant capacity in Italy, France, Germany, and England, spent itself for centuries in taking possession of the rich inheritance left by the dead civilisations of Greece and Rome. Marvellously aided by the invention of printing, classical learning spread and flourished. Those who possessed it prided themselves on having attained the highest culture then within the reach of mankind.

And justly. For, saving Dante on his solitary pinnacle, there was no figure in modern literature at the time of the Renascence to compare with the men of antiquity; there was no physical science but that which Greece had created. Above all, there was no other example of perfect intellectual freedom—of the unhesitating acceptance of reason as the sole guide to truth and the supreme arbiter of conduct.

The new learning necessarily soon exerted a profound influence upon education. The language of the monks and schoolmen seemed little better than gibberish to scholars fresh from Virgil and Cicero, and the study of Latin was placed upon a new foundation. Moreover, Latin itself ceased to afford the sole key to knowledge. The student who sought the highest thought of antiquity, found only a second-hand reflection of it in Roman literature, and turned his face to the full light of the Greeks. And after a battle, not altogether dissimilar to that which is at present being fought over the teaching of physical science, the study of Greek was recognized as an essential element of all higher education.

Thus the Humanists, as they were called, won the day; and the great reform which they effected was of incalculable service to mankind. But the Nemesis of all reformers is finality; and the reformers of education, like those of religion, fell into the profound, however common, error of mistaking the beginning for the end of the work of reformation.

The representatives of the Humanists, in the nineteenth century, take their stand upon classical education as the sole avenue to culture, as firmly as if we were still in the age of Renascence. Yet, surely, the present intellectual relations of the modern and the ancient worlds are profoundly different from those which obtained three centuries ago. Leaving aside the existence of a great and characteristically modern literature, of modern painting, and, especially, of modern music, there is one feature of the present state of the civilized world which separates it more widely from the Renascence, than the Renascence was separated from the middle ages.

This distinctive character of our own times lies in the vast and constantly increasing part which is played by natural knowledge. Not only is our daily life shaped by it; not only does the prosperity of millions of men depend upon it, but our whole theory of life has long been influenced, consciously or unconsciously, by the general conceptions of the universe, which have been forced upon us by physical science.

In fact, the most elementary acquaintance with the results of scientific investigation shows us that they offer a broad and striking contradiction to the opinion so implicitly credited and taught in the middle ages.

The notions of the beginning and the end of the world entertained by our forefathers are no longer credible. It is very certain that the earth is not the chief body in the material universe, and that the world is not subordinated to man's use. It is even more certain that nature is the expression of a definite order with which nothing interferes, and that the chief business of mankind is to learn that order and govern themselves accordingly. Moreover this scientific "criticism of life" presents itself to us with different credentials from any other. It appeals not to authority, nor to what anybody may have thought or said, but to nature. It admits that all our interpretations of natural fact are more or less imperfect and symbolic, and bids the learner seek for truth not among words but among things. It warns us that the assertion which outstrips evidence is not only a blunder but a crime.

The purely classical education advocated by the representatives
of the Humanists in our day, gives no inkling of all this. A man
may be a better scholar than Erasmus, and know no more of the
chief causes of the present intellectual fermentation than Erasmus
did. Scholarly and pious persons, worthy of all respect, favour us
with allocutions upon the sadness of the antagonism of science
to their medieval way of thinking, which betray an ignorance of
the first principles of scientific investigation, an incapacity for
understanding what a man of science means by veracity, and an
unconsciousness of the weight of established scientific truths,
which is almost comical.

There is no great force in the *tu quoque* argument, or else the
advocates of scientifice education might fairly enough retort upon
the modern Humanists that they may be learned specialists, but
that they possess no such sound foundation for a criticism of
life as deserves the name of culture. And, indeed, if we were disposed to be cruel, we might urge that the Humanists have brought
this reproach upon themselves, not because they are too full of
the spirit of the ancient Greek, but because they lack it.

The period of the Rennaisance is commonly called that of the
"Revival of Letters," as if the influences then brought to bear
upon the mind of Western Europe had been wholly exhausted
in the field of literature. I think it is very commonly forgotten
that the revival of science, effected by the same agency, although
less conspicuous, was not less momentous.

In fact, the few and scattered students of nature of that day
picked up the clue to her secrets exactly as it fell from the hands
of the Greeks a thousand years before. The foundations of mathematics were so well laid by them, that our children learn their
geometry from a book written for the schools of Alexandria two
thousand years ago. Modern astronomy is the natural continuation
and development of the work of Hipparchus and of Ptolemy;
modern physics of that of Democritus and of Archimedes; it was
long before modern biological science outgrew the knowledge
bequeathed to us by Aristotle, by Theophrastus, and by Galen.

We cannot know all the best thoughts and saying of the Greeks
unless we know what they thought about natural phenomena. We
cannot fully apprehend their criticism of life unless we under-

stand the extent to which that criticism was affected by scientific conceptions. We falsely pretend to be the inheritors of their culture, unless we are penetrated, as the best minds among them were, with an unhesitating faith that the free employment of reason, in accordance with scientific method, is the sole method of reaching truth.

Thus I venture to think that the pretensions of our modern Humanists to the possession of the monopoly of culture and to the exclusive inheritance of the spirit of antiquity must be abated, if not abandoned. But I should be very sorry that anything I have said should be taken to imply a desire on my part to depreciate the value of classical education, as it might be and as it sometimes is. The native capacities of mankind vary no less than their opportunities; and while culture is one, the road by which one man may best reach it is widely different from that which is most advantageous to another. Again, while scientific education is yet inchoate and tentative, classical education is thoroughly well organised upon the practical experience of generations of teachers. So that, given ample time for learning and estimation for ordinary life, or for a literary career, I do not think that a young Englishman in search of culture can do better than follow the course usually marked out for him, supplementing its deficiencies by his own efforts.

But for those who mean to make science their serious occupation; or who intend to follow the profession of medicine; or who have to enter early upon the business of life; for all these, in my opinion, classical education is a mistake; and it is for this reason that I am glad to see "mere literary education and instruction" shut out from the curriculum of Sir Josiah Mason's College, seeing that its inclusion would probably lead to the introduction of the ordinary smattering of Latin and Greek.

Nevertheless, I am the last person to question the importance of genuine literary education, or to suppose that intellectual culture can be complete without it. An exclusively scientific training will bring about a mental twist as surely as an exclusively literary training. The value of the cargo does not compensate for a ship's being out of trim; and I should be very sorry to think that the Scientific College would turn out none but lopsided men.

There is no need, however, that such a catastrophe should happen. Instruction in English, French, and German is provided, and thus the three greatest literatures of the modern world are made accessible to the student.

French and German, and especially the latter language, are absolutely indispensable to those who desire full knowledge in any department of science. But even supposing that the knowledge of these languages acquired is not more than sufficient for purely scientific purposes, every Englishman has, in his native tongue, an almost perfect instrument of literary expression; and, in his own literature, models of every kind of literary excellence. If an Englishman cannot get literary culture out of his Bible, his Shakespeare, his Milton, neither, in my belief, will the profoundest study of Homer and Sophocles, Virgil and Horace, give it to him.

Thus, since the constitution of the College makes sufficient provision for literary as well as for scientific education, and since artistic instruction is also contemplated, it seems to me that a fairly complete culture is offered to all who are willing to take advantage of it.

But I am not sure that at this point the "practical" man, scotched but not slain, may ask what all this talk about culture has to do with an Institution, the object of which is defined to be "to promote the prosperity of the manufactures and the industry of the country." He may suggest that what is wanted for this end is not culture, nor even a purely scientific discipline, but simply a knowledge of applied science.

I often wish that this phrase, "applied science," had never been invented. For it suggests that there is a sort of scientific knowledge of direct practical use, which can be studied apart from another sort of scientific knowledge, which is of no practical utility, and which is termed "pure science." But there is no more complete fallacy than this. What people call applied science is nothing but the application of pure science to particular classes of problems. It consists of deductions from those general principles, established by reasoning and observation, which constitute pure science. No one can safely make these deductions until he has a firm grasp of the principles; and he can obtain that grasp only by personal experience of the operations of observation and of reasoning on which they are founded.

Almost all the processes employed in the arts and manufactures fall within the range either of physics or of chemistry. In order to improve them, one must thoroughly understand them; and no one has a chance of really understanding them, unless he has obtained that mastery of principles and that habit of dealing with facts, which is given by long-continued and well-directed purely scientific training in the physical and the chemical laboratory. So that there really is no question as to the necessity of purely scientific discipline, even if the work of the College were limited by the narrowest interpretation of its stated aims.

And, as to the desirableness of a wider culture than that yielded by science alone, it is to be recollected that the improvement of manufacturing processes is only one of the conditions which contribute to the prosperity of industry. Industry is a means and not an end; and mankind work only to get something which they want. What that something is depends partly on their innate, and partly on their acquired, desires.

If the wealth resulting from prosperous industry is to be spent upon the gratification of unworthy desires, if the increasing perfection of manufacturing processes is to be accompanied by an increasing debasement of those who carry them on, I do not see the good of industry and prosperity.

Now it is perfectly true that men's views of what is desirable depend upon their characters; and that the innate proclivities to which we give that name are not touched by any amount of instruction. But it does not follow that even mere intellectual education may not, to an indefinite extent, modify the practical manifestation of the characters of men in their actions, by supplying them with motives unknown to the ignorant. A pleasure-loving character will have pleasure of some sort; but, if you give him the choice, he may prefer pleasures which do not degrade him to those which do. And this choice is offered to every man, who possesses in literary or artistic culture a never-failing source of pleasures, which are neither withered by age, nor staled by custom, nor embittered in the recollection by the pangs of self-reproach.

If the Institution opened today fulfils the intention of its founder, the picked intelligences among all classes of the population of this district will pass through it. No child born in Birmingham, henceforward, if he have the capacity to profit by the opportunities offered to him, first in the primary and other schools, and afterwards in the Scientific College, need fail to obtain, not merely the instruction, but the culture most appropriate to the conditions of his life.

Within these walls, the future employer and the future artisan may sojourn together for a while, and carry, through all their lives, the stamp of the influences then brought to bear upon them. Hence, it is not beside the mark to remind you, that the prosperity of industry depends not merely upon the improvement of manufacturing processes, not merely upon the ennobling of the individual character, but upon a third condition, namely, a clear understanding of the conditions of social life, on the part of both the capitalist and the operative, and their agreement upon common principles of social action. They must learn that social phenomena are as much the expression of natural laws as any others; that no social arrangements can be permanent unless they harmonise with the requirements of social statics and dynamics; and that, in the nature of things, there is an arbiter whose decisions execute themselves.

But this knowledge is only to be obtained by the application of the methods of investigation adopted in physical researches to the investigation of the phenomena of society. Hence, I confess, I should like to see one addition made to the excellent scheme of education propounded for the College, in the shape of provision for the teaching of Sociology. For though we are all agreed that party politics are to have no place in the instruction of the College; yet in this country, practically governed as it is now by universal suffrage, every man who does his duty must exercise political functions. And, if the evils which are inseparable from the good of political liberty are to be checked, if the perpetual oscillation of nations between anarchy and despotism is to be replaced by the steady march of self-restraining freedom; it will be because men will gradually bring themselves to deal with political, as they now deal with scientific questions; to be as ashamed of undue haste and partisan prejudice in the one case as in the other; and to believe that the machinery of society is at least as delicate as that of a spinning-jenny, and as little likely to be improved by the meddling of those who have not taken the trouble to master the principles of its action.

In conclusion, I am sure that I make myself the mouthpiece of all present in offering to the venerable founder of the Institution, which now commences its beneficent career, our congratulations on the completion of his work; and in expressing the conviction, that the remotest posterity will point to it as a crucial instance of the wisdom which natural piety leads all men to ascribe to their ancestors.

Literature and Science

MATTHEW ARNOLD
(1822–1888).

Essays in Criticism, 1865
Culture and Anarchy, 1869
Literature and Dogma, 1873
Discourses in America, 1885

MATTHEW ARNOLD had a long connection with British education. His father, a historian and liberal churchman, was headmaster of Rugby School, from which the young Arnold proceeded to Oxford, first to Balliol College and then to Oriel. He began his career as a poet; appointed an Inspector of Schools in 1851, a position he was to hold for thirty-five years, Arnold continued as a poet and later also as Professor of Poetry at Oxford. In addition he became one of the foremost literary critics of his age, and somewhat later, one of its most effective social critics. During 1883-84 he first visited the United States where he delivered a series of lectures. In the essay which follows he joins Thomas Henry Huxley in discussing what is now known as the issue of "The Two Cultures."

PRACTICAL PEOPLE TALK WITH A SMILE OF PLATO AND OF HIS absolute ideas; and it is impossible to deny that Plato's ideas do often seem unpractical and unpracticable, and especially when one views them in connexion with the life of a great work-a-day world like the United States. The necessary staple of the life of such a world Plato regards with disdain; handicraft and trade and the working professions he regards with disdain; but what becomes of the life of an industrial modern community if you take handicraft and trade and the working professions out of it? The base mechanic arts and handicrafts, says Plato, bring about a natural weakness in the principle of excellence in a man, so that he can-

Discourses in America, London: Macmillan & Co., Ltd., 1885.

not govern the ignoble growths in him, but nurses them, and cannot understand fostering any other. Those who exercise such arts and trades, as they have their bodies, he says, marred by their vulgar businesses, so they have their souls, too, bowed and broken by them. And if one of these uncomely people has a mind to seek self-culture and philosophy, Plato compares him to a bald little tinker, who has scraped together money, and has got his release from service, and has had a bath, and bought a new coat, and is rigged out like a bridegroom about to marry the daughter of his master who has fallen into poor and helpless estate.

Nor do the working professions fare any better than trade at the hands of Plato. He draws for us an inimitable picture of the working lawyer, and of his life of bondage; he shows how this bondage from his youth up has stunted and warped him, and made him small and crooked of soul, encompassing him with difficulties which he is not man enough to rely on justice and truth as means to encounter, but has recourse, for help out of them, to falsehood and wrong. And so, says Plato, this poor creature is bent and broken, and grows up from boy to man without a particle of soundness in him, although exceedingly smart and clever in his own esteem.

One cannot refuse to admire the artist who draws these pictures. But we say to ourselves that his ideas show the influence of a primitive and obsolete order of things, when the warrior caste and the priestly caste were alone in honour, and the humble work of the world was done by slaves. We have now changed all that; the modern majority consists in work, as Emerson declares; and in work, we may add, principally of such plain and dusty kind as the work of cultivators of the ground, handicraftsmen, men of trade and business, men of the working professions. Above all is this true in a great industrious community such as that of the United States.

Now education, many people go on to say, is still mainly governed by the ideas of men like Plato, who lived when the warrior caste and the priestly or philosophical class were alone in honour, and the really useful part of the community were slaves. It is an education fitted for persons of leisure in such a community. This education passed from Greece and Rome to the

feudal communities of Europe, where also the warrior caste and
the priestly caste were alone held in honour, and where the
really useful and working part of the community, though not
nominally slaves as in the pagan world, were practically not
much better off than slaves, and not more seriously regarded.
And how absurd it is, people end by saying, to inflict this education upon an industrious modern community, where very
few indeed are persons of leisure, and the mass to be considered
has not leisure, but is bound, for its own great good, and for
the great good of the world at large, to plain labour and to
industrial pursuits, and the education in question tends necessarily to make men dissatisfied with these pursuits and unfitted
for them!

That is what is said. So far I must defend Plato, as to plead
that his view of education and studies is in the general, as it
seems to me, sound enough, and fitted for all sorts and conditions
of men, whatever their pursuits may be. "An intelligent man,"
says Plato, "will prize those studies which result in his soul
getting soberness, righteousness, and widom, and will less value
the others." I cannot consider *that* a bad description of the aim
of education, and of the motives which should govern us in the
choice of studies, whether we are preparing ourselves for a
hereditary seat in the English House of Lords or for the pork
trade in Chicago.

Still I admit that Plato's world was not ours, that his scorn of
trade and handicraft is fantastic, that he had no conception of
a great industrial community such as that of the United States,
and that such a community must and will shape its education
to suit its own needs. If the usual education handed down to it
from the past does not suit it, it will certainly before long drop
this and try another. The usual education in the past has been
mainly literary. The question is whether the studies which were
long supposed to be the best for all of us are practically the best
now; whether others are not better. The tyranny of the past,
many think, weighs on us injuriously in the predominance given
to letters in education. The question is raised whether, to meet
the needs of our modern life, the predominance ought not now
to pass from letters to science; and naturally the question is

nowhere raised with more energy than here in the United States. The design of abasing what is called "mere literary instruction and education," and of exalting what is called "sound, extensive, and practical scientific knowledge," is, in this intensely modern world of the United States, even more perhaps than in Europe, a very popular design, and makes great and rapid progress.

I am going to ask whether the present movement for ousting letters from their old predominance in education, and for transferring the predominance in education to the natural sciences, whether this brisk and flourishing movement ought to prevail, and whether it is likely that in the end it really will prevail. An objection may be raised which I will anticipate. My own studies have been almost wholly in letters, and my visits to the field of the natural sciences have been very slight and in-adequate, although those sciences have always strongly moved my curiosity. A man of letters, it will perhaps be said, is not com-petent to discuss the comparative merits of letters and natural science as means of education. To this objection I reply, first of all, that his incompetence, if he attempts the discussion but is really incompetent for it, will be abundantly visible; nobody will be taken in; he will have plenty of sharp observers and critics to save mankind from that danger. But the line I am going to follow is, as you will soon discover, so extremely simple, that perhaps it may be followed without failure even by one who for a more ambitious line of discussion would be quite incom-petent.

Some of you may possibly remember a phrase of mine which has been the object of a good deal of comment; an observation to the effect that in our culture, the aim being *to know ourselves and the world*, we have as the means to this end, *to know the best which has been thought and said in the world*. A man of science, who is also an excellent writer and the very prince of debaters, Professor Huxley, in a discourse at the opening of Sir Josiah Mason's college at Birmingham, laying hold of this phrase, expanded it by quoting some more words of mine, which are these: "The civilised world is to be regarded as now being, for intellectual and spiritual purposes, one great confederation, bound to a joint action and working to a common result; and

whose members have for their proper outfit a knowledge of
Greek, Roman, and Eastern antiquity, and of one another. Special local and temporary advantages being put out of account,
that modern nation will in the intellectual and spiritual sphere
make most progress, which most thoroughy carries out this
programme."

Now on my phrase, thus enlarged, Professor Huxley remarks
that when I speak of the above-mentioned knowledge as enabl-
ing us to know ourselves and the world, I assert *literature* to
contain the materials which suffice for thus making us know
ourselves and the world. But it is not by any means clear, says
he, that after having learnt all which ancient and modern literatures have to tell us, we have laid a sufficiently broad and deep
foundation for that criticism of life, that knowledge of ourselves
and the world, which constitutes culture. On the contrary,
Professor Huxley declares that he finds himself "wholly unable
to admit that either nations or individuals will really advance,
if their outfit draws nothing from the stores of physical science.
An army without weapons of precision, and with no particular
base of operations, might more hopefully enter upon a campaign on the Rhine, than a man, devoid of a knowledge of what
physical science has done in the last century, upon a criticism of
life."

This shows how needful it is for those who are to discuss any
matter together, to have a common understanding as to the
sense of the terms they employ,—how needful, and how difficult.
What Professor Huxley says, implies just the reproach which is
so often brought against the study of *belles lettres,* as they are
called: that the study is an elegant one, but slight and ineffec-
tual; a smattering of Greek and Latin and other ornamental
things, of little use for any one whose object is to get at truth,
and to be a practical man. So, too, M. Renan talks of the "superficial humanism" of a school-course which treats us as if we
were all going to be poets, writers, preachers, orators, and he op-
poses this humanism to positive science, or the critical search
after truth. And there is always a tendency in those who are
remonstrating against the predominance of letters in education,
to understand by letters *belles lettres,* and by *belles lettres* a

superficial humanism, the opposite of science or true knowledge.

But when we talk of knowing Greek and Roman antiquity, for instance, which is the knowledge people have called the humanities, I for my part mean a knowledge which is something more than a superficial humanism, mainly decorative. "I call all teaching *scientific*," says Wolf, the critic of Homer, "which is sytematically laid out and followed up to its original sources. For example: a knowledge of classical antiquity is scientific when the remains of classical antiquity are correctly studied in the original languages." There can be no doubt that Wolf is perfectly right; that all learning is scientific which is systematically laid out and followed up to its original sources, and that a genuine humanism is scientific.

When I speak of knowing Greek and Roman antiquity, therefore, as a help to knowing ourselves and the world, I mean more than a knowledge of so much vocabulary, so much grammar, so many portions of authors in the Greek and Latin languages. I mean knowing the Greeks and Romans, and their life and genius, and what they were and did in the world; what we get from them, and what is its value. That, at least, is the ideal; and when we talk of endeavouring to know Greek and Roman antiquity, as a help to knowing ourselves and the world, we mean endeavouring so to know them as to satisfy this ideal, however much we may still fall short of it.

The same also as to knowing our own and other modern nations, with the like aim of getting to understand ourselves and the world. To know the best that has been thought and said by the modern nations, is to know, says Professor Huxley, "only what modern *literatures* have to tell us; it is the criticism of life contained in modern literature." And yet "the distinctive character of our times," he urges, "lies in the vast and constantly increasing part which is played by natural knowledge." And how, therefore, can a man, devoid of knowledge of what physical science has done in the last century, enter hopefully upon a criticism of modern life?

Let us, I say, be agreed about the meaning of the terms we are using. I talk of knowing the best which has been thought and uttered in the world; Professor Huxley says this means

knowing *literature*. Literature is a large word; it may mean
everything written with letters or printed in a book. Euclid's
Elements and Newton's *Principia* are thus literature. All knowledge that reaches us through books is literature. But by literature Professor Huxley means *belles lettres*. He means to make
me say, that knowing the best which has been thought and said
by the modern nations is knowing their *belles lettres* and no
more. And this is no sufficient equipment, he argues, for a criticism of modern life. But as I do not mean, by knowing ancient
Rome, knowing merely more or less of Latin *belles lettres,* and
taking no account of Rome's military, and political, and legal,
and administrative work in the world; and as, by knowing ancient
Greece, I understand knowing her as the giver of Greek art, and
the guide to a free and right use of reason and to scientific
method, and the founder of our mathematics and physics and
astronomy and biology,—I understand knowing her as all this,
and not merely knowing certain Greek poems, and histories, and
treatises, and speeches,—so as to the knowledge of modern nations also. By knowing modern nations, I mean not merely
knowing their *belles letters,* but knowing also what has been
done by such men as Copernicus, Galileo, Newton, Darwin.
"Our ancestors learned," says Professor Huxley, "that the earth
is the centre of the visible universe, and that man is the cynosure
of things terrestrial and more especially was it inculcated that
the course of nature had no fixed order, but that it could be,
and constantly was, altered." "But for us now," continues Professor Huxley, "the notions of the beginning and the end of
the world entertained by our forefathers are no longer credible.
It is very certain that the earth is not the chief body in the
material universe, and that the world is not subordinated to
man's use. It is even more certain that nature is the expression
of a definite order, with which nothing interferes." "And yet,"
he cries, "the purely classical education advocated by the representatives of the humanists in our day gives no inkling of all
this!"

In due place and time I will just touch upon that vexed
question of classical education; but at present the question is as
to what is meant by knowing the best which modern nations

have thought and said. It is not knowing their *belles lettres* merely which is meant. To know Italian *belles lettres* is not to know Italy, and to know English *belles lettres* is not to know England. Into knowing Italy and England there comes a great deal more, Galileo and Newton amongst it. The reproach of being a superficial humanism, a tincture of *belles lettres,* may attach rightly enough to some other disciplines; but to the particular discipline recommended when I proposed knowing the best that has been thought and said in the world, it does not apply. In that best I certainly include what in modern times has been thought and said by the great observers and knowers of nature.

There is, therefore, really no question between Professor Huxley and me as to whether knowing the great results of the modern scientific study of nature is not required as a part of our culture, as well as knowing the products of literature and art. But to follow the processes by which those results are reached, ought, say the friends of physical science, to be made the staple of education for the bulk of mankind. And here there does arise a question between those whom Professor Huxley calls with playful sarcasm "the Levites of culture," and those whom the poor humanist is sometimes apt to regard as its Nebuchadnezzars.

The great results of the scientific investigation of nature we are agreed upon knowing, but how much of our study are we bound to give to the processes by which those results are reached? The results have their visible bearing on human life. But all the processes, too, all the items of fact, by which those results are reached and established, are interesting. All knowledge is interesting to a wise man, and the knowledge of nature is interesting to all men. It is very interesting to know, that, from the albuminous white of the egg, the chick in the egg gets the materials for its flesh, bones, blood, and feathers, while, from the fatty yolk of the egg, it gets the heat and energy which enable it at length to break its shell and begin the world. It is less interesting, perhaps, but still it is interesting, to know that when a taper burns, the wax is converted into carbonic acid and water. Moreover, it is quite true that the habit of dealing with facts, which is given by the study of nature, is, as the friends of

physical science praise it for being, an excellent discipline. The
appeal, in the study of nature, is constantly to observation and
experiment; not only is it said that the thing is so, but we can
be made to see that it is so. Not only does a man tell us that
when a taper burns the wax is converted into carbonic acid and
water, as a man may tell us, if he likes, that Charon is punting
his ferryboat on the river Styx, or that Victor Hugo is a sublime poet, or Mr. Gladstone the most admirable of statesmen;
but we are made to see that the conversion into carbonic acid
and water does actually happen. This reality of natural knowledge it is, which makes the friends of physical science contrast it, as
a knowledge of things, with the humanist's knowledge, which
is, say they, a knowledge of words. And hence Professor Huxley
is moved to lay it down that, "for the purpose of attaining real
culture, an exclusively scientific education is at least as effectual
as an exclusively literary education." And a certain President of
the Section for Mechanical Science in the British Association is,
in Scripture phrase, "very bold," and declares that if a man, in
his mental training, "has substituted literature and history for
natural science, he has chosen the less useful alternative." But
whether we go these lengths or not, we must all admit that in
natural science the habit gained of dealing with facts is a most
valuable discipline, and that every one should have some experience of it.

More than this, however, is demanded by the reformers. It
is proposed to make the training in natural science the main
part of education, for the great majority of mankind at any rate.
And here, I confess, I part company with the friends of physical
science, with whom up to this point I have been agreeing. In
differing from them, however, I wish to proceed with the utmost
caution and diffidence. The smallness of my own acquaintance
with the disciplines of natural science is ever before my mind,
and I am fearful of doing these disciplines an injustice. The
ability and pugnacity of the partisans of natural science make
them formidable persons to contradict. The tone of tentative
inquiry, which befits a being of dim faculties and bounded knowledge, is the tone I would wish to take and not to depart from. At
present it seems to me, that those who are for giving to natural

knowledge as they call it, the chief place in the education of the majority of mankind, leave one important thing out of their account: the constitution of human nature. But I put this forward on the strength of some facts not at all recondite, very far from it; facts capable of being stated in the simplest possible fashion, and to which, if I so state them, the man of science will, I am sure, be willing to allow their due weight.

Deny the facts altogether, I think, he hardly can. He can hardly deny, that when we set ourselves to enumerate the powers which go to the building up of human life, and say that they are the power of conduct, the power of intellect and knowledge, the power of beauty, and the power of social life and manners—he can hardly deny that this scheme, though drawn in rough and plain lines enough, and not pretending to scientific exactness, does yet give a fairly true representation of the matter. Human nature is built up by these powers; we have the need for them all. When we have rightly met and adjusted the claims of them all, we shall then be in a fair way for getting soberness and righteousness, with wisdom. This is evident enough, and the friends of physical science would admit it.

But perhaps they may not have sufficiently observed another thing: namely, that the several powers just mentioned are not isolated, but there is, in the generality of mankind, a perpetual tendency to relate them one to another in diverse ways. With one such way of relating them I am partciularly concerned now. Following our instinct for intellect and knowledge, we acquire pieces of knowledge; and presently, in the generality of men, there arises the desire to relate these pieces of knowledge to our sense for conduct, to our sense for beauty,—and there is weariness and dissatisfaction if the desire is baulked. Now in this desire lies, I think, the strength of that hold which letters have upon us.

All knowledge is, as I said just now, interesting; and even items of knowledge which from the nature of the case cannot well be related, but must stand isolated in our thoughts, have their interest. Even lists of exceptions have their interest. If we are studying Greek accents, it is interesting to know that *pais* and *pas*, and some other monosyllables of the same form of de-

clension, do not take the circumflex upon the last syllable of the
genitive plural, but vary, in this respect, from the common rule.
If we are studying physiology, it is interesting to know that the
pulmonary artery carries dark blood and the pulmonary vein
carries bright blood, departing in this respect from the common
rule for the division of labour between the veins and the arteries.
But every one knows how we seek naturally to combine the
pieces of our knowledge together, to bring them under general
rules, to relate them to principles; and how unsatisfactory
and tiresome it would be to go on for ever learning lists of exceptions, or accumulating items of fact which must stand isolated.

Well, that same need of relating our knowledge, which operates here within the sphere of our knowledge itself, we shall find
operating, also, outside that sphere. We experience, as we go on
learning and knowing—the vast majority of us experience—
the need of relating what we have learnt and known to the sense
which we have in us for conduct, to the sense which we have
in us for beauty.

A certain Greek prophetess of Mantineia in Arcadia, Diotima
by name, once explained to the philosopher Socrates that love,
and impulse, and bent of all kinds, is, in fact, nothing else but
the desire in men that good should for ever be present to them.
This desire for good, Diotima assured Socrates, is our fundamental desire, of which fundamental desire every impulse in us
is only some one particular form. And therefore this fundamental desire it is, I suppose,—this desire in men that good
should be for ever present to them,—which acts in us when we
feel the impulse for relating our knowledge to our sense for
conduct and to our sense for beauty. At any rate, with men in
general the instinct exists. Such is human nature. And the instinct, it will be admitted, is innocent, and human nature is
preserved by our following the lead of its innocent instincts.
Therefore, in seeking to gratify this instinct in question, we are
following the instinct of self-preservation in humanity.

But, no doubt, some kinds of knowledge cannot be made to
directly serve the instinct in question, cannot be directly related to the sense for beauty, to the sense for conduct. These
are instrument-knowledges; they lead on to other knowledges,

which can. A man who passes his life in instrument-knowledges is a specialist. They may be invaluable as instruments to something beyond, for those who have the gift thus to employ them; and they may be disciplines in themselves wherein it is useful for every one to have some schooling. But it is inconceivable that the generality of men should pass all their mental life with Greek accents or with formal logic. My friend Professor Sylvester, who is one of the first mathematicians in the world, holds transcendental doctrines as to the virtue of mathematics, but those doctrines are not for common men. In the very Senate House and heart of our English Cambridge I once ventured, though not without an apology for my profaneness, to hazard the opinion that for the majority of mankind a little mathematics, even, goes a long way. Of course this is quite consistent with their being of immense importance as an instrument to something else; but it is the few who have the aptitude for thus using them, not the bulk of mankind.

The natural sciences do not, however, stand on the same footing with these instrument-knowledges. Experience shows us that the generality of men will find more interest in learning that, when a taper burns, the wax is converted into carbonic acid and water, or in learning the explanation of the phenomenon of dew, or in learning how the circulation of blood is carried on, than find in learning that the genitive plural of *pais* and *pas* does not take the circumflex on the termination. And one piece of natural knowledge is added to another, and others are added to that, and at last we come to propositions so interesting as Mr. Darwin's famous proposition that "our ancestor was a hairy quadruped furnished with a tail and pointed ears, probably arboreal in his habits." Or we come to propositions of such reach and magnitude as those which Professor Huxley delivers, when he says that the notions of our forefathers about the beginning and the end of the world were all wrong, and that nature is the expression of a definite order with which nothing interferes.

Interesting, indeed, these results of science are, important they are, and we should all of us be acquainted with them. But what I now wish you to mark is, that we are still, when they are

propounded to us and we receive them, we are still in the sphere
of intellect and knowledge. And for the generality of men there
will be found, I say, to arise, when they have duly taken in the
proposition that their ancestor was "a hairy quadruped furnished
with a tail and pointed ears, probably arboreal in his habits,"
there will be found to arise an invincible desire to relate this
proposition to the sense in us for conduct, and to the sense in us
for beauty. But this the men of science will not do for us, and
will hardly even profess to do. They will give us other pieces of
knowledge, other facts, about other animals and their ancestors,
or about plants, or about stones, or about stars; and they may
finally bring us to those great "general conceptions of the universe, which are forced upon us all," says Professor Huxley, "by
the progress of physical science." But still it will be *knowledge*
only which they give us; knowledge not put for us into relation
with our sense for conduct, our sense for beauty, and touched
with emotion by being so put; not thus put for us, and therefore,
to the majority of mankind, after a certain while, unsatisfying,
wearying.

Not to be the born naturalist, I admit. But what do we mean
by a born naturalist? We mean a man in whom the zeal for ob-
serving nature is so uncommonly strong and eminent, that it
marks him off from the bulk of mankind. Such a man will pass
his life happily in collecting natural knowledge and reasoning
upon it, and will ask for nothing, or hardly anything, more. I
have heard it said that the sagacious and admirable naturalist
whom we lost not very long ago, Mr. Darwin, once owned to a
friend that for his part he did not experience the necessity for
two things which most men find so necessary to them,—religion
and poetry; science and the domestic affections, he thought,
were enough. To a born naturalist, I can well understand that
this should seem so. So absorbing is his occupation with nature,
so strong his love for his occupation, that he goes on acquiring
natural knowledge and reasoning upon it, and has little time
or inclination for thinking about getting it related to the desire
in man for conduct, the desire in man for beauty. He relates it
to them for himself as he goes along, so far as he feels the need;
and he draws from the domestic affections all the additional

solace necessary. But then Darwins are extremely rare. Another great and admirable master of natural knowledge, Faraday, was a Sandemanian. That is to say, he related his knowledge to his instinct for conduct and to his instinct for beauty, by the aid of that respectable Scottish sectary, Robert Sandeman. And so strong, in general, is the demand of religion and poetry to have their share in a man, to associate themselves with his knowing, and to relieve and rejoice it, that probably, for one man amongst us with the disposition to do as Darwin did in this respect, there are at least fifty with the disposition to do as Faraday.

Education lays hold upon us, in fact, by satisfying this demand. Professor Huxley holds up to scorn mediaeval education, with its neglect of the knowledge of nature, its poverty even of literary studies, its formal logic devoted to "showing how and why that which the Church said was true and must be true." But the great mediaeval Universities were not brought into being, we may be sure, by the zeal for giving a jejune and contemptible education. Kings have been their nursing fathers, and queens have been their nursing mothers, but not for this. The mediaeval Universities came into being, because the supposed knowledge, delivered by Scripture and the Church, so deeply engaged men's hearts, by so simply, easily, and powerfully relating itself to their desire for conduct, their desire for beauty. All other knowledge was dominated by this supposed knowledge and was subordinated to it, because of the surpassing strength of the hold which it gained upon the affections of men, by allying itself profoundly with their sense for conduct, their sense for beauty.

But now, says Professor Huxley, conceptions of the universe fatal to the notions held by our forefathers have been forced upon us by physical science. Grant to him that they are thus fatal, that the new conceptions must and will soon become current everywhere, and that every one will finally perceive them to be fatal to the beliefs of our forefathers. The need of humane letters, as they are truly called, because they serve the paramount desire in men that good should be for ever present to them,— the need of humane letters, to establish a relation between the new conceptions, and our instinct for beauty, our instinct for

conduct, is only the more visible. The Middle Age could do
without humane letters, as it could do without the study of
nature, because its supposed knowledge was made to engage its
emotions so powerfully. Grant that the supposed knowledge disappears, its power of being made to engage the emotions will of
course disappear along with it—but the emotions themselves,
and their claim to be engaged and satisfied, will remain. Now if
we find by experience that humane letters have an undeniable
power of engaging the emotions, the importance of humane
letters in a man's training becomes not less, but greater, in proportion to the success of modern science in extirpating what it
calls "mediaeval thinking."

Have humane letters, then, have poetry and eloquence, the
power here attributed to them of engaging the emotions, and do
they exercise it? And if they have it and exercise it, *how* do they
exercise it, so as to exert an influence upon man's sense for conduct, his sense for beauty? Finally, even if they both can and do
exert an influence upon the senses in question, how are they to
relate to them the results—the modern results—of natural science? All these questions may be asked. First, have poetry and
eloquence the power of calling out the emotions? The appeal is
to experience. Experience shows that for the vast majority of
men, for mankind in general, they have the power. Next, do they
exercise it? They do. But then *how* do they exercise it so as to
affect man's sense for conduct, his sense for beauty? And this is
perhaps a case for applying the Preacher's words: "Though a
man labour to seek it out, yet he shall not find it; yea, farther,
though a wise man think to know it, yet shall he not be able to
find it." Why should it be one thing, in its effect upon the emotions, to say, "Patience is a virtue," and quite another thing, in
its effect upon the emotions, to say with Homer, "for an enduring heart have the destinies appointed to the children of men"?
Why should it be one thing, in its effect upon the emotions, to
say with the philosopher Spinoza, *"Felicitas in eo consistit quod
homo suum esse conservare potest*—Man's happiness consists in
his being able to preserve his own essence," and quite another
thing, in its effect upon the emotions, to say with the Gospel,
"What is a man advantaged, if he gain the whole world, and

lose himself, forfeit himself?" How does this difference of effect arise? I cannot tell, and I am not much concerned to know; the important thing is that it does arise, and that we can profit by it. But how, finally, are poetry and eloquence to exercise the power of relating the modern results of natural science to man's instinct for conduct, his instinct for beauty? And here again I answer that I do not know *how* they will exercise it, but that they can and will exercise it I am sure. I do not mean that modern philosophical poets and modern philosophical moralists are to come and relate for us, in express terms, the results of modern scientific research to our instinct for conduct, our instinct for beauty. But I mean that we shall find, as a matter of experience, if we know the best that has been thought and uttered in the world, we shall find that the art and poetry and eloquence of men who lived, perhaps, long ago, who had the most limited natural knowledge, who had the most erroneous conceptions about many important matters, we shall find that this art, and poetry, and eloquence, have in fact not only the power of refreshing and delighting us they have also the power,—such is the strength and worth, in essentials, of their author's criticism of life—they have a fortifying, and elevating, and quickening, and suggestive power, capable of wonderfully helping us to relate the results of modern science to our need for conduct, our need for beauty. Homer's conceptions of the physical universe were, I imagine, grotesque; but really, under the shock of hearing from modern science that "the world is not subordinated to man's use, and that man is not the cynosure of things terrestrial," I could, for my own part, desire no better comfort than Homer's line which I quoted just now, "for an enduring heart have the destinies appointed to the children of men"!

And the more that men's minds are cleared, the more that the results of science are frankly accepted, the more that poetry and eloquence come to be received and studied as what in truth they really are,—the criticism of life by gifted men, alive and active with extraordinary power at an unusual number of points;—so much the more will the value of humane letters, and of art also, which is an utterance having a like kind of power with theirs, be felt and acknowledged, and their place in education be secured.

Let us therefore, all of us, avoid indeed as much as possible any invidious comparison between the merits of humane letters, as means of education, and the merits of the natural sciences. But when some President of a Section for Mechanical Science insists on making the comparison, and tells us that "he who in his training has substituted literature and history for natural science has chosen the less useful alternative," let us make answer to him that the student of humane letters only, will, at least, know also the great general conceptions brought in by modern physical science; for science, as Professor Huxley says, forces them upon us all. But the student of the natural sciences only, will, by our very hypothesis, know nothing of humane letters; not to mention that in setting himself to be perpetually accumulating natural knowledge, he sets himself to do what only specialists have in general the gift for doing genially. And so he will probably be unsatisfied, or at any rate incomplete, and even more incomplete than the student of humane letters only.

I once mentioned in a school-report, how a young man in one of our English training colleges having to paraphrase the passage in *Macbeth* beginning,

> Can'st thou not minister to a mind diseased?

turned this line into, "Can you not wait upon the lunatic?" And I remarked what a curious state of things it would be, if every pupil of our national schools knew, let us say, that the moon is two thousand one hundred and sixty miles in diameter, and thought at the same time that a good paraphrase for

> Can'st thou not minister to a mind diseased?

was, "Can you not wait upon the lunatic?" If one is driven to choose, I think I would rather have a young person ignorant about the moon's diameter, but aware that "Can you not wait upon the lunatic?" is bad, than a young person whose education had been such as to manage things the other way.

Or to go higher than the pupils of our national schools. I have in my mind's eye a member of our British Parliament who comes to travel here in America, who afterwards relates his travels, and who shows a really masterly knowledge of the geology of this great country and of its mining capabilities, but who ends by gravely suggesting that the United States should borrow a prince from our Royal Family, and should make him their king, and should create a House of Lords of great landed proprietors after the pattern of ours; and then America, he thinks, would have her future happily and perfectly secured. Surely, in this case, the President of the Section for Mechanical Science would himself hardly say that our member of Parliament, by concentrating himself upon geology and mineralogy, and so on, and not attending to literature and history, had "chosen the more useful alternative."

If then there is to be separation and option between humane letters on the one hand, and the natural sciences on the other, the great majority of mankind, all who have not exceptional and overpowering aptitudes for the study of nature, would do well, I cannot but think, to choose to be educated in humane letters rather than in the natural sciences. Letters will call out their being at more points, will make them live more.

I said that before I ended I would just touch on the question of classical education and I will keep my word. Even if literature is to retain a large place in our education, yet Latin and Greek, say the friends of progress, will certainly have to go. Greek is the grand offender in the eyes of these gentlemen. The attackers of the established course of study think that against Greek, at any rate, they have irresistible arguments. Literature may perhaps be needed in education, they say; but why on earth should it be Greek literature? Why not French or German? Nay, "has not an Englishman models in his own literature of every kind of excellence?" As before, it is not on any weak pleadings of my own that I rely for convincing the gainsayers; it is on the constitution of human nature itself, and on the instinct of self-preservation in humanity. The instinct for beauty is set in human nature, as surely as the instinct for knowledge is set there, or the instinct for conduct. If the instinct for beauty is served by Greek literature and art as it is served by no other literature and art, we may trust to the instinct of self-preservation in humanity for keeping

Greek as part of our culture. We may trust to it for even making the study of Greek more prevalent than it is now. Greek will come, I hope, some day to be studied more rationally than at present; but it will be increasingly studied as men increasingly feel the need in them for beauty, and how powerfully Greek art and Greek literature can serve this need. Women will again study Greek, as Lady Jane Grey did; I believe that in that chain of forts, with which the fair host of the Amazons are now engirdling our English universities, I find that here in America, in colleges like Smith College in Massachusetts, and Vassar College in the State of New York, and in the happy families of the mixed universities out West, they are studying it already.

Defuit una mihi symmetria prisca,—"The antique symmetry was the one thing wanting to me," said Leonardo da Vinci; and he was an Italian. I will not presume to speak for the Americans, but I am sure that, in the Englishman, the want of this admirable symmetry of the Greeks is a thousand times more great and crying than in any Italian. The results of the want show themselves most glaringly, perhaps, in our architecture, but they show themselves, also, in all our art. *Fit details strictly combined, in view of a large general result nobly conceived;* that is just the beautiful *symmetria prisca* of the Greeks, and it is just where we English fail, where all our art fails. Striking ideas we have, and well-executed details we have; but that high symmetry which, with satisfying and delightful effect, combines them, we seldom or never have. The glorious beauty of the Acropolis at Athens did not come from single fine things stuck about on that hill, a statue here, a gateway there;—no, it arose from all things being perfectly combined for a supreme total effect. What must not an Englishman feel about our deficiencies in this respect, as the sense for beauty, whereof this symmetry is an essential element, awakens and strengthens within him! What will not one day be his respect and desire for Greece and its *symmetria prisca,* when the scales drop from his eyes as he walks the London streets, and he sees such a lesson in meanness as the Strand, for instance, in it true deformity! But here we are coming to our friend Mr. Ruskin's province, and I will not intrude upon it, for he is its very sufficient guardian.

And so we at last find, it seems, we find flowing in favour of the humanities the natural and necessary stream of things, which seemed against them when we started. The "hairy quadruped furnished with a tail and pointed ears, probably arboreal in his habits," this good fellow carried hidden in his nature, apparently, something destined to develop into a necessity for humane letters. Nay, more; we seem finally to be even led to the further conclusion that our hairy ancestor carried in his nature also a necessity for Greek.

And therefore, to say the truth, I cannot really think that humane letters are in much actual danger of being thrust out from their leading place in education, in spite of the array of authorities against them at this moment. So long as human nature is what it is, their attractions will remain irresistible. As with Greek, so with letters generally; they will some day come, we may hope, to be studied more rationally, but they will not lose their place. What will happen will rather be that there will be crowded into education other matters besides, far too many; there will be, perhaps, a period of unsettlement and confusion and false tendency; but letters will not in the end lose their leading place. If they lose it for a time, they will get it back again. We shall be brought back to them by our wants and aspirations. And a poor humanist may possess his soul in patience, neither strive nor cry, admit the energy and brilliancy of the partisans of physical science, and their present favour with the public, to be far greater than his own, and still have a happy faith that the nature of things works silently on behalf of the studies which he loves, and that, while we shall all have to acquaint ourselves with the great results reached by modern science, and to give ourselves as much training in its disciplines as we can conveniently carry, yet the majority of men will always require humane letters; and so much the more, as they have the more and the greater results of science to relate to the need in man for conduct, and to the need in him for beauty.

II. THE CLARIFICATION OF EXPERIENCE

Jobs

PAUL GOODMAN
(1911–   )

The Structure of Literature, 1954
The Empire City, 1959
Communitas (with Percival Goodman), 1960
Growing Up Absurd, 1960
The Community of Scholars, 1962

PAUL GOODMAN has written novels, short stories and poems, as well as articles and books that speculate about city planning, politics, depth psychology and the nature of literature. He has been a teacher and a lay analyst, but is primarily a social reformer with a commitment to anarchism and a belief in non-violent resistance. Recently he has concerned himself more and more exclusively with the role, status and psychological health of the young in an industrial society.

IT'S HARD TO GROW UP WHEN THERE ISN'T ENOUGH MAN'S WORK. There is "nearly full employment" (with highly significant exceptions), but there get to be fewer jobs that are necessary or unquestionably useful; that require energy and draw on some of one's best capacities; and that can be done keeping one's honor and dignity. In explaining the widespread troubles of adolescents and young men, this simple objective factor is not much mentioned. Let us here insist on it.

By "man's work" I mean a very simple idea, so simple that it is clearer to ingenuous boys than to most adults. To produce necessary food and shelter is man's work. During most of economic history most men have done this drudging work, secure that it was justified and worthy of a man to do it, though often feeling that the social conditions under which they did it were *not* worthy of a man, thinking, "It's better to die than to live so hard"—but they worked on. When the environment is forbidding, as in the Swiss Alps or the Aran Islands, we regard such work with poetic awe. In emergencies it is heroic, as when the bakers of Paris maintained the supply of bread during the French Revolution, or the milkman did not miss a day's delivery when the bombs recently tore up London.

At present there is little such substance work. In *Communitas* my brother and I guess that one-tenth of our economy is devoted to it; it is more likely one-twentieth. Production of food is actively discouraged. Farmers are not wanted and the young men go elsewhere. (The farm population is now less than 15 per cent of the total population.) Building, on the contrary, is immensely needed. New York City needs 65,000 new units a year, and is getting, net, 16,000. One would think that ambitious boys would flock to this work. But here we find that building, too, is discouraged. In a great city, for the last twenty years hundreds of thousands have been ill housed, yet we do not see science, industry, and labor enthusiastically enlisted in finding the quick solution to a definite problem. The promoters are interested in long-term investments, the real estate men in speculation, the city planners in votes and graft. The building craftsmen cannily see to it that their own numbers remain few, their methods antiquated, and their rewards high. None of these people is much interested in providing shelter, and nobody is at all interested in providing new manly jobs.

Once we turn away from the absolutely necessary subsistence jobs, however, we find that an enormous proportion of our production is not even unquestionably useful. Everybody knows and also feel this, and there has recently been a flood of books about our surfeit of honey, our insolent chariots, the follies of exurban ranch houses, our hucksters and our synthetic demand. Many acute things are said about this useless production and advertising, but not much about the workmen producing it and their frame of mind; and nothing at all, so far as I have noticed, about the plight of a young fellow looking for a manly occupation. The eloquent critics of the American way of life have themselves been

so seduced by it that they think only in terms of selling commod-
ities and point out that the goods are valueless; but they fail to
see that people are being wasted and their skills insulted. (To
give an analogy, in the many gleeful onslaughts on the Popular
Culture that have appeared in recent years, there has been little
thought of the plight of the honest artist cut off from his audience
and sometimes, in public arts such as theater and architecture,
from his medium.)

What is strange about it? American society has tried so hard
and so ably to defend the practice and theory of production for
profit and not primarily for use that now it has succeeded in
making its jobs and products profitable and useless.

2.

Consider a likely useful job. A youth who is alert and willing
but not "verbally intelligent"—perhaps he has quit high school
at the eleventh grade (the median), as soon as he legally could—
chooses for auto mechanic. That's a good job, familiar to him, he
often watched them as a kid. It's careful and dirty at the same
time. In a small garage it's sociable; one can talk to the customers
(girls). You please people in trouble by fixing their cars, and a
man is proud to see rolling out on its own the car that limped
in behind the tow truck. The pay is as good as the next fellow's,
who is respected.

So our young man takes this first-rate job. But what when he
then learns that the cars have a built-in obsolescence, that the
manufacturers do not want them to be repaired or repairable?
They have lobbied a law that requires them to provide spare
parts for only five years (it used to be ten). Repairing the new cars
is often a matter of cosmetics, not mechanics; and the repairs are
pointlessly expensive—a tail fin might cost $150. The insurance
rates therefore double and treble on old and new cars both. Gone
are the days of keeping the jalopies in good shape, the artist-work
of a proud mechanic. But everybody is paying for foolishness, for
in fact the new models are only trivially superior; the whole thing
is a sell.

It is hard for the young man now to maintain his feelings of justification, sociability, serviceability. It is not surprising if he quickly becomes cynical and time-serving, interested in a fast buck. And so, on the notorious *Reader's Digest* test, the investigators (coming in with a disconnected coil wire) found that 63 per cent of mechanics charged for repairs they didn't make, and lucky if they didn't also take out the new fuel pump and replace it with a used one (65 per cent of radio repair shops, but *only* 49 per cent of watch repairmen "lied, overcharged, or gave false diagnoses").

There is an hypothesis that an important predisposition to juvenile delinquency is the combination of low verbal intelligence with high manual intelligence, delinquency giving a way of self-expression where other avenues are blocked by lack of schooling. A lad so endowed might well apply himself to the useful trade of mechanic.

3.

Most manual jobs do not lend themselves so readily to knowing the facts and fraudulently taking advantage oneself. In factory jobs the workman is likely to be ignorant of what goes on, since he performs a small operation on a big machine that he does not understand. Even so, there is evidence that he has the same disbelief in the enterprise as a whole, with a resulting attitude of profound indifference.

Semiskilled factory operatives are the largest category of workmen. (I am leafing through the U. S. Department of Labor's *Occupational Outlook Handbook*, 1957.) Big companies have tried the devices of applied anthropology to enhance the loyalty of these men to the firm, but apparently the effort is hopeless, for it is found that a thumping majority of the men don't care about the job or the firm; they couldn't care less and you can't make them care more. But this is *not* because of wages, hours, or working conditions, or management. On the contrary, tests that show the men's indifference to the company show also their (unaware) admiration for the way the company has designed and manages the plant; it is their very model of style, efficiency, and correct behavior. (Robert Dubin, for the U. S. Public Health Service.)

Maybe if the men understood more, they would admire less. The union and the grievance committee take care of wages, hours, and conditions; these are the things the workmen themselves fought for and won. (Something was missing in that victory, and we have inherited the failure as well as the success.) The conclusion must be that workmen are indifferent to the job because of its intrinsic nature: it does not enlist worth-while capacities, it is not "interesting"; it is not his, he is not "in" on it; the product is not really useful. And indeed, research directly on the subject, by Frederick Herzberg on Motivation to Work, shows that it is defects in the intrinsic aspects of the job that make workmen "unhappy." A survey of the literature (in Herzberg's *Job Attitudes*) shows that Interest is second in importance only to Security, whereas Wages, Conditions, Socializing, Hours, Ease, and Benefits are far less important. But foremen, significantly enough, think that the most important thing to the workman is his wages. (The investigators do not seem to inquire about the usefulness of the job—as if a primary purpose of *working* at a job were not that it is good *for* something! My guess is that a large factor in "Security" is the resigned reaction to not being able to take into account whether the work of one's hand is useful for anything; for in a normal life situation, if what we do is useful, we feel secure about being needed. The other largest factor in "Security" is, I think, the sense of being needed for one's unique contribution, and this is measured in these tests by the primary importance the workers assign to being "in" on things and to "work done being appreciated." (Table prepared by Labor Relations Institute of New York.)

Limited as they are, what a remarkable insight such studies give us, that men want to do valuable work and work that is somehow theirs! But they are thwarted.

Is not this the "waste of our human resources"?

The case is that by the "sole-prerogative" clause in union contracts the employer has the sole right to determine what is to be produced, how it is to be produced, what plants are to be built and where, what kinds of machinery are to be installed, when workers are to be hired and laid off, and how production operations are to be rationalized. (Frank Marquart.) There is *none* of this that is inevitable in running a machine economy; but *if* these are the circumstances, it is not surprising that the factory operatives' actual code has absolutely nothing to do with useful service or increasing production, but is notoriously devoted to "interpersonal relations"; (1) don't turn out too much work; (2) don't turn out too little work; (3) don't squeal on a fellow worker; (4) don't act like a big-shot. This is how to belong.

4.

Let us go on to the Occupational Outlook of those who are verbally bright. Among this group, simply because they cannot help asking more general questions—e.g., about utility—the problem of finding man's work is harder, and their disillusion is more poignant.

> He explained to her why it was hard to find a satisfactory job of work to do. He had liked working with the power drill, testing the rocky envelope of the shore, but then the employers asked him to take a great oath of loyalty.
>
> "What!" cried Rosalind. "Do you have scruples about telling a convenient fib?"
>
> "No, I don't. But I felt uneasy about the sanity of the director asking me to swear to opinions on such complicated questions when my job was digging with a power drill. I can't work with a man who might suddenly have a wild fit."
>
> . . . "Why don't you get a job driving one of the big trucks along here?"
>
> "I don't like what's in the boxes," said Horatio sadly. "It could just as well drop in the river—and I'd make mistakes and drop it there."
>
> "Is it bad stuff?"
>
> "No, just useless. It takes the heart out of me to work at something useless and I begin to make mistakes. I don't mind putting profits in somebody's pocket—but the job also has to be useful for something."
>
> . . . "Why don't you go to the woods and be a lumberjack?"
>
> "No! they chop down the trees just to print off the *New York Times*"
>
>   (*The Empire City*, III, i, 3, Bobbs-Merrill Co.)

The more intelligent worker's "indifference" is likely to appear more nakedly as profound resignation, and his cynicism may sharpen to outright racketeering.

"Teaching," says the *Handbook,* "is the largest of the professions." So suppose our now verbally bright young man chooses for teacher, in the high school system or, by exception, in the elementary schools if he understands that the elementary grades are the vitally important ones and require the most ability to teach well (and of course they have less prestige). Teaching is necessary and useful work; it is real and creative, for it directly confronts an important subject matter, the children themselves; it is obviously self-justifying; and it is ennobled by the arts and sciences. Those who practice teaching do not for the most part succumb to cynicism or indifference—the children are too immediate and real for the teachers to become callous—but, most of the school systems being what they are, can teachers fail to come to suffer first despair and then deep resignation? Resignation occurs psychologically as follows: frustrated in essential action, they nevertheless cannot quit in anger, because the task is necessary; so the anger turns inward and is felt as resignation. (Naturally, the resigned teacher may then put on a happy face and keep very busy.)

For the job is carried on under impossible conditions of overcrowding and saving public money. *Not* that there is not enough social wealth, but first things are not put first. Also, the school system has spurious aims. It soon becomes clear that the underlying aims are to relieve the home and keep the kids quiet; or, suddenly, the aim is to produce physicists. Timid supervisors, bigoted clerics, and ignorant school boards forbid real teaching. The emotional release and sexual expression of the children are taboo. A commercially debauched popular culture makes learning disesteemed. The academic curriculum is mangled by the demands of reactionaries, liberals, and demented warriors. Progressive methods are emasculated. Attention to each case is out of the question, and all the children—the bright, the average, and the dull—are systematically retarded one way or another, while the teacher's hands are tied. Naturally the pay is low—for the work is hard, useful, and of public concern, all three of which qualities tend to bring lower pay. It is alleged that the low pay is why there is a shortage of teachers and why the best do not choose the profession. My guess is that the best avoid it because of the certainty of miseducating. Nor are the best *wanted* by the system, for they are not safe. Bertrand Russell was rejected by New York's City College and would not have been accepted in a New York grade school.

5.

Next, what happens to the verbally bright who have no zeal for a serviceable profession and who have no particular scientific or artistic bent? For the most part they make up the tribes of salesmanship, entertainment, business management, promotion, and advertising. Here of course there is no question of utility or honor to begin with, so an ingenuous boy will not look here for a manly career. Nevertheless, though we can pass by the sufferings of these well-paid callings, much publicized by their own writers, they are important to our theme because of the model they present to the growing boy.

Consider the men and women in TV advertisements, demonstrating the product and singing the jingle. They are clowns and mannequins, in grimace, speech, and action. And again, what I want to call attention to in this advertising is not the economic problem of synthetic demand, and not the cultural problem of Popular Culture, but the human problem that these are human beings working as clowns; that the writers and designers of it are human beings thinking like idiots; and the broadcasters and underwriters know and abet what goes on—

> Juicily glubbily
> *Blubber* is dubbily
> delicious and nutritious
> —eat it, Kitty, it's good.

Alternately, they are liars, confidence men, smooth talkers, obsequious, insolent, etc., etc.

The popular-cultural content of the advertisements is somewhat neutralized by *Mad* magazine, the bible of the twelve-year-olds who can read. But far more influential and hard to counteract is the *fact* that the workmen and the patrons of this enterprise are human beings. (Highly approved, too.) They are not good models for a boy looking for a manly job that is useful and necessary, requiring human energy and capacity, and that can be done with honor and dignity. They are a good sign that not many such jobs will be available.

The popular estimation is rather different. Consider the following: "As one possible aid, I suggested to the Senate subcommittee that they alert celebrities and leaders in the fields of sports, movies, theater and television to the help they can offer by getting close to these [delinquent] kids. By giving them positive 'heroes' they know and can talk to, instead of the misguided image of trouble-making buddies, they could aid greatly in guiding these normal aspirations for fame and status into wholesome progressive channels." (Jackie Robinson, who was formerly on the Connecticut Parole Board.) Or again: when a mass cross-section of Oklahoma high school juniors and seniors was asked which living person they would like to be, the boys named Pat Boone, Ricky Nelson, and President Eisenhower; the girls chose Debbie Reynolds, Elizabeth Taylor, and Natalie Wood.

The rigged Quiz shows, which created a scandal in 1959, were a remarkably pure distillate of our American cookery. We start with the brute facts that (a) in our abundant expanding economy it is necessary to give money away to increase spending, production, and profits; and (b) that this money must not be used for useful public goods in taxes, but must be plowed back as "business expenses," even though there is a shameful shortage of schools, housing, etc. Yet when the TV people at first tried simply to give the money away for nothing (for having heard of George Washington), there was a great Calvinistic outcry that this was demoralizing (we may gamble on the horses only to improve the breed). So they hit on the notion of a real contest with prizes. But then, of course, they could not resist making the show itself profitable, and competitive in the (also rigged) ratings with other shows, so the experts in the entertainment-commodity manufactured phony contests. And to cap the climax of fraudulence, the hero of the phony contests proceeded to persuade himself, so he says, that his behavior was educational!

The behavior of the networks was correspondingly typical. These business organizations claim the loyalty of their employees, but at the first breath of trouble they were ruthless and disloyal to their employees. (Even McCarthy was loyal to his gang.) They want to maximize profits and yet be absolutely safe from any risk. Consider their claim that they knew nothing about the fraud. But if they watched the shows that they were broadcasting, they could not *possibly,* as professionals, not have known the facts, for there were obvious type-casting, acting, plot, etc. If they are not professionals, they are incompetent. But if they don't watch what they broadcast, then they are utterly irresponsible and on what grounds do they have the franchises to the channels? We may offer them the choice: that they are liars or incompetent or irresponsible.

The later direction of the investigation seems to me more important, the inquiry into the bribed disk-jockeying; for this deals directly with our crucial economic problem of synthesized demand, made taste, debauching the public and preventing the emergence and formation of natural taste. In such circumstances there cannot possibly be an American culture; we are doomed to nausea and barbarism. And *then* these baboons have the effrontery to declare that they give the people what the people demand and that they are not responsible for the level of the movies, the music, the plays, the books!

Finally, in leafing through the *Occupational Outlook Handbook,* we notice that the armed forces employ a large number. Here our young man can become involved in a world-wide demented enterprise, with personnel and activities corresponding.

6.

Thus, on the simple criteria of unquestioned utility, employing human capacities, and honor, there are not enough worthy jobs in our economy for average boys and adolescents to grow up toward. There are of course thousands of jobs that are worthy and self-justifying, and thousands that can be made so by stubborn integrity, especially if one can work as an independent.

Extraordinary intelligence or special talent, also, can often carve out a place for itself—conversely, their usual corruption and waste are all the more sickening. But by and large our economic society is *not* geared for the cultivation of its young or the attainment of important goals that they can work toward.

This is evident from the usual kind of vocational guidance, which consists of measuring the boy and finding some place in the economy where he can be fitted; chopping him down to make him fit; or neglecting him if they can't find his slot. Personnel directors do not much try to scrutinize the economy in order to find some activity that is a real opportunity for the boy, and then to create an opportunity if they can't find one. To do this would be an horrendous task; I am not sure it could be done if we wanted to do it. But the question is whether anything less makes sense if we mean to speak seriously about the troubles of the young man.

Surely by now, however, many readers are objecting that this entire argument is pointless because people in *fact* don't think of their jobs in this way at all. *Nobody* asks if a job is useful or honorable (within the limits of business ethics). A man gets a job that pays well, or well enough, that has prestige, and good conditions, or at least tolerable conditions. I agree with these objections as to the fact. (I hope we are wrong.) But *the question is what it means to grow up into such a fact as: "During my productive years I will spend eight hours a day doing what is no good."*

7.

Yet, economically and vocationally, a very large population of the young people are in a plight more drastic than anything so far mentioned. In our society as it is, there are not enough worthy jobs. But if our society, being as it is, were run more efficiently and soberly, for a majority there would soon not be any jobs at all. There is at present nearly full employment and there may be for some years, yet a vast number of young people are rationally unemployable, useless. This paradox is essential to explain their present temper.

Our society, which is not geared to the cultivation of its young, *is* geared to a profitable expanding production, a so-called high standard of living of mediocre value, and the maintenance of nearly full employment. Politically, the chief of these is full employment. In a crisis, when profitable production is temporarily curtailed government spending increases and jobs are manufactured. In "normalcy"—a condition of slow boom—the easy credit, installment buying, and artificially induced demand for useless goods create jobs for all and good profits for some.

Now, back in the Thirties, when the New Deal attempted by hook or crook to put people back to work and give them money to revive the shattered economy, there was an outcry of moral indignation from the conservatives that many of the jobs were "boondoggling," useless made-work. It was insisted, and rightly, that such work was demoralizing to the workers themselves. It is a question of a word, but a candid critic might certainly say that many of the jobs in our present "normal" production are useless made-work. The tail fins and built-in obsolescence might be called boondoggling. The $64,000 Question and the busy hum of Madison Avenue might certainly be called boondoggling. Certain tax-dodge Foundations are boondoggling. What of business lunches and expense accounts? fringe benefits? the comic catergories of occupation in the building trades? the extra stagehands and musicians of the theater crafts? These jolly devices to put money back to work no doubt have a demoralizing effect on somebody or other (certainly on me, they make me green with envy), but where is the moral indignation from Top Management?

Suppose we would cut out the boondoggling and gear our society to a more sensible abundance, with efficient production of quality goods, distribution in a natural market, counterinflation and sober credit. At once the work week would be cut to, say, twenty hours instead of forty. (Important People have already mentioned the figure thirty.) Or alternately, half the labor force would be unemployed. Suppose too—and how can we not suppose it?—that the automatic machines are used generally, rather than just to get rid of badly organized unskilled labor. The unemployment will be still more drastic.

(To give the most striking example: in steel, the annual increase in productivity is 4 per cent, the plants work at 50 per cent

of capacity, and the companies can break even and stop producing at *less than 30 per cent* of capacity. These are the conditions
that forced the steel strike, as desperate self-protection. (Estes
Kefauver, quoting Gardiner Means and Fred Gardner.)

Everybody knows this, nobody wants to talk about it much, for
we don't know how to cope with it. The effect is that we are
living a kind of lie. Long ago, labor leaders used to fight for the
shorter work week, but now, they don't, because they're pretty
sure they don't want it. Indeed, when hours are reduced, the
tendency is to get a second, part-time, job and raise the standard
of living, *because* the job is meaningless and one must have
something; but the standard of living is pretty meaningless, too.
Nor is this strange atmosphere a new thing. For at least a
generation the maximum sensible use of our productivity could
have thrown a vast population out of work, or relieved everybody of a lot of useless work, depending on how you take it.
(Consider with how little cutback of useful civilian production
the economy produced the war goods and maintained an Army,
economically unemployed.) The plain truth is that at present
very many of us are useless, not needed, rationally unemployable. It is in this paradoxical atmosphere that young persons
grow up. It looks busy and expansive, but it is rationally at a
stalemate.

8.

These considerations apply to all ages and classes; but it is of
course among poor youth (and the aged) that they show up first
and worst. They are the most unemployable. For a long time our
society has not been geared to the cultivation of the young. In
our country 42 per cent have graduated from high school (pre-
dicted census, 1960); less than 8 per cent have graduated from
college. The high school trend for at least the near future is not
much different: there will be a high proportion of drop-outs
before the twelfth grade; but *markedly more* of the rest will go
on to college; that is, the stratification will harden. Now the
schooling in neither the high schools nor the colleges is much
good—if it were better more kids would stick to it; yet at present,

if we made a list we should find that a large proportion of the dwindling number of unquestionably useful or self-justifying jobs, in the humane professions and the arts and sciences, require education; and in the future, there is no doubt that the more educated will have the jobs, in running an efficient, highly technical economy and administrative society placing a premium on verbal skills.

(Between 1947 and 1957, professional and technical workers increased 61 per cent, clerical workers 23 per cent, but factory operatives only 4½ percent and laborers 4 per cent.—Census.)

For the uneducated there will be no jobs at all. This is humanly most unfortunate, for presumably those who have learned something in schools, and have the knack of surviving the boredom of those schools, could also make something of idleness; whereas the uneducated are useless at leisure too. It takes application, a fine sense of value, and a powerful community-spirit for a people to have serious leisure, and this has not been the genius of the Americans.

From this point of view we can sympathetically understand the pathos of our American school policy, which otherwise seems so inexplicable; at great expense compelling kids to go to school who do not want to and who will not profit by it. There are of course unpedagogic motives, like relieving the home, controlling delinquency, and keeping kids from competing for jobs. But there is also this desperately earnest pedagogic motive, of preparing the kids to take *some* part in a democratic society that does not need them. Otherwise, what will become of them, if they don't know anything?

Compulsory public education spread universally during the nineteenth century to provide the reading, writing, and arithmetic necessary to build a modern industrial economy. With the overmaturity of the economy, the teachers are struggling to preserve the elementary system when the economy no longer requires it and is stingy about paying for it. The demand is for scientists and technicians, the 15 per cent of the "academically talented." "For a vast majority [in the high schools]," says Dr. Conant in *The Child, the Parent, and the State,* "the vocational courses are the vital core of the program. They represent something related directly to the ambitions of the boys and girls." But somehow, far more than half of these quit. How is that?

9.

Let us sum up again. The majority of young people are faced with the following alternative: Either society is a benevolently frivolous racket in which they'll manage to boondoggle, though less profitably than the more privileged; or society is serious (and they hope still benevolent enough to support them), but they are useless and hopelessly out. Such thoughts do not encourage productive life. Naturally young people are more sanguine and look for man's work, but few find it. Some settle for a "good job"; most settle for a lousy job; a few, but an increasing number, don't settle.

I often ask, "What do you want to work at? If you have the chance. When you get out of school, college, the service, etc."

Some answer right off and tell their definite plans and projects, highly approved by Papa. I'm pleased for them, but it's a bit boring, because they are such squares.

Quite a few will, with prompting, come out with astounding stereotyped, conceited fantasies, such as becoming a movie actor when they are "discovered"—"like Marlon Brando, but in my own way."

Very rarely somebody will, maybe defiantly and defensively, maybe diffidently but proudly, make you know that he knows very well what he is going to do; it is something great; and he is indeed already doing it, which is the real test.

The usual answer, perhaps the normal answer, is "I don't know," meaning, "I'm looking; I haven't found the right thing; it's discouraging but not hopeless."

But the terrible answer is, "Nothing." The young man doesn't want to do anything.

I remember talking to half a dozen young fellows at Van Wagner's Beach outside of Hamilton, Ontario; and all of them had this one thing to say: "Nothing." They didn't believe that what to work at was the kind of thing one *wanted*. They rather expected that two or three of them would work for the electric company in town, but they couldn't care less. I turned away from the conversation abruptly because of the uncontrollable burning tears in my eyes and constriction in my chest. Not feeling sorry for them, but tears of frank dismay for the waste of our humanity (they were nice kids). And it is out of that incident that many years later I am writing this book.

The White Cool Record Book

ALFRED KAZIN
(1915–   )

On Native Ground, 1942
A Walker in the City, 1951
The Inmost Leaf, 1955

ALFRED KAZIN'S first critical book, On Native Ground, appeared when he was a young man just out of college. His criticism has since gained in sensitivity and depth, but in some quarters he tends still to be thought of in terms of his early, socially-oriented approach. The selection that follows comes from A Walker in the City, itself a part of a longer work with which Mr. Kazin is still involved, an autobiography intended to be as well a record of the times. For most of his life a freelance writer, Mr. Kazin is at present a teacher at The New School for Social Research in New York City.

ALL MY EARLY LIFE LIES OPEN TO MY EYE WITHIN FIVE CITY BLOCKS. When I passed the school, I went sick with all my old fear of it. With its standard New York public-school brown brick courtyard shut in on three sides of the square and the pretentious battlements overlooking that cockpit in which I can still smell the fiery sheen of the rubber ball, it looks like a factory over which has been imposed the façade of a castle. It gave me the shivers to stand up in that courtyard again; I felt as if I had been mustered back into the service of those Friday morning "tests" that were the terror of my childhood.

It was never learning I associated with that school: only the necessity to succeed, to get ahead of the others in the daily struggle to "make a good impression" on our teachers, who grimly, wearily, and often with ill-concealed distaste watched against our relapsing into the natural savagery they expected of Brownsville boys. The white, cool, thinly ruled record book sat over us from their desks all day long, and had remorselessly entered into it each day—in blue ink if we had passed, in red ink if we had not—our attendance, our conduct, our "effort," our merits and demerits; and to the last possible decimal point in calculation, our standing in an unending series of "tests"—surprise tests, daily tests, weekly tests, formal midterm tests, final tests. They never stopped trying to dig out of us whatever small morsel of fact we had managed to get down the night before. We had to prove that we were really alert, ready for anything, always in the race. That white thinly ruled record book figured in my mind as the judgment seat; the very thinness and remote blue lightness of its lines instantly showed its cold authority over me; so much space had been left on each page, columns and columns in which to note down everything about us, implacably and forever. As it lay there on a teacher's desk, I stared at it all day long with such fear and anxious propriety that I had no trouble believing that God, too, did nothing but keep such record books, and that on the final day He would face me with an account in Hebrew letters whose phonetic dots and dashes looked strangely like decimal points counting up my every sinful thought on earth.

All teachers were to be respected like gods, and God Himself was the greatest of all school superintendents. Long after I had ceased to believe that our teachers could see with the back of their heads, it was still understood, by me, that they knew everything. They were the delegates of all visible and invisible power on earth —of the mothers who waited on the stoops every day after three for us to bring home tales of our daily triumphs; of the glacially remote Anglo-Saxon principal, whose very name was King; of the incalculably important Superintendent of Schools who would someday rubberstamp his name to the bottom of our diplomas in grim acknowledgment that we had, at last, given satisfaction to him, to the Board of Superintendents, and to our benefactor the City of New York—and so up and up, to the government of the United States and to the great Lord Jehovah Himself. My belief in teachers' unlimited wisdom and power rested not so much on what I saw in them—how impatient most of them looked, how wary—but on our abysmal humility, at least in those of us who were "good" boys, who proved by our ready compliance and "manners" that we wanted to get on. The road to a professional future would be shown us only as we pleased *them*. *Make a good impression the first day of the term, and they'll help you out. Make a bad impression, and you might as well cut your throat.* This was the first article of school folklore, whispered around the classroom the opening day of each term. You made the "good impression" by sitting firmly at your wooden desk, hands clasped; by silence for the greatest part of the live-long day; by standing up obsequiously when it was so expected of you; by sitting down noiselessly when you had answered a question; by "speaking nicely," which meant reproducing their painfully exact enunciation; by "showing manners," or an ecstatic submissiveness in all things; by outrageous flattery; by bringing little gifts at Christmas, on their birthdays, and at the end of the term—the well-known significance of these gifts being that they came not from us, but from our parents, whose eagerness in this matter showed a high level of social consideration, and thus raised our standing in turn.

It was not just our quickness and memory that were always being tested. Above all, in that word I could never hear without automatically seeing it raised before me in gold-plated letters, it was our *character*. I always felt anxious when I heard the word pronounced. Satisfactory as my "character" was, on the whole, except when I stayed too long in the playground reading; outrageously satisfactory, as I can see now, the very sound of the word as our teachers coldly gave it out from the end of their teeth, with a solemn weight on each dark syllable, immediately struck my heart cold with fear—they could not believe I really had it. Character was never something you had; it had to be trained in you, like a technique. I was never very clear about it. On our side *character* meant demonstrative obedience; but teachers already had it—how else could they have become teachers? They had it; the aloof Anglo-Saxon principal whom we remotely saw only on ceremonial occasions in the assembly was positively encased in it; it glittered off his bald head in spokes of triumphant light; the President of the United States had the greatest conceivable amount of it. Character belonged to great adults. Yet we were constantly being driven onto it; it was the great threshold we had to cross. *Alfred Kazin, having shown proficiency in his course of studies and having displayed satisfactory marks of character . . .* Thus someday the hallowed diploma, passport to my further advancement in high school. But there—I could already feel it in my bones—they would put me through even more doubting tests of character; and after that, if I should be good enough and bright enough, there would be still more. *Character* was a bitter thing, racked with my endless striving to please. The school— from every last stone in the courtyard to the battlements frowning down at me from the walls—was only the stage for a trial. I felt that the very atmosphere of learning that surrounded us was fake—that every lesson, every book, every approving smile was only a pretext for the constant probing and watching of me, that there was not a secret in me that would not be decimally measured into that white record book. All week long I lived for the blessed sound of the dismissal gong at three o'clock on Friday afternoon.

I was awed by this system, I believed in it, I respected its force. The alternative was "going bad." The school was notoriously the toughest in our tough neighborhood, and the dangers of "going bad" were constantly impressed upon me at home and in school in dark whispers of the "reform school" and in examples of boys who had been picked up for petty thievery, rape, or flinging a heavy inkwell straight into a teacher's face. Behind any failure in school yawned the great abyss of a criminal career. Every refractory attitude doomed you with the sound "Sing Sing." Anything less than absolute perfection in school always suggested to my mind that I might fall out of the daily race, be kept back in the working class forever, or—dared I think of it?—fall into the criminal class itself.

I worked on a hairline between triumph and catastrophe. Why the odds should always have felt so narrow I understood only when I realized how little my parents thought of their own lives. It was not for myself alone that I was expected to shine, but for them— to redeem the constant anxiety of their existence. I was the first American child, their offering to the strange new God; I was to be the monument of their liberation from the shame of being—what they were. And that there was shame in this was a fact that everyone seemed to believe as a matter of course. It was in the gleeful discounting of themselves—what do we know?—with which our parents greeted every fresh victory in our savage competition for "high averages," for prizes, for a few condescending words of official praise from the principal at assembly. It was in the sickening invocation of "Americanism"—the word itself accusing us of everything we apparently were not. Our families and teachers seemed tacitly agreed that we were somehow to be a little ashamed of what we were. Yet it was always hard to say why this should be so. It was certainly not—in Brownsville!—because we were Jews, or simply because we spoke another language at home, or were absent on our holy days. It was rather that a "refined," "correct," "nice" English was required of us at school that we did not naturally speak, and that our teachers could never be quite sure we would keep. This English was peculiarly the ladder of advancement. Every future young lawyer was known by it. Even the Communists and Socialists on Pitkin Avenue spoke it. It was bright and clean and polished. We were expected to show it off like a new pair of shoes. When the teacher sharply called a question out, then your name, you were expected to leap up, face the class, and eject those new words fluently off the tongue.

There was my secret ordeal: I could never say anything except in the most roundabout way; I was a stammerer. Although I knew all those new words from my private reading—I read walking in the street, to and from the Children's Library on Stone Avenue; on the fire escape and the roof; at every meal when they would let me; read even when I dressed in the morning, propping my book up against the drawers of the bureau as I pulled on my long black stockings—I could never seem to get the easiest words out with the right dispatch, and would often miserably signal from my desk that I did not know the answer rather than get up to stumble and fall and crash on every word. If, angry at always being put down as lazy or stupid, I did get up to speak, the black wooden floor would roll away under my feet, the teacher would frown at me in amazement, and in unbearable loneliness I would hear behind me the groans and laughter: *tuh-tuh-tuh-tuh.*

The word was my agony. The word that for others was so effortless and so neutral, so unburdened, so simple, so exact, I had first to meditate in advance, to see if I could make it, like a plumber fitting together odd lengths and shapes of pipe. I was always preparing words I could speak, storing them away, choosing between them. And often, when the word did come from my mouth in its great and terrible birth, quailing and bleeding as if forced through a thornbush, I would not be able to look the others in the face, and would walk out in the silence, the infinitely echoing silence behind my back, to say it all cleanly back to myself as I walked in the streets. Only when I was alone in the open air, pacing the roof with pebbles in my mouth, as I had read Demosthenes had done to cure himself of stammering; or in the street, where all words seemed to flow from the length of my stride and the color of the houses as I remembered the perfect tranquility of a phrase in Beethoven's *Romance in F* I could sing back to myself as I walked—only then was it possible for me to speak without the infinite premeditations and strangled silences I toiled through whenever I got up at school to respond with the expected, the exact answer.

It troubled me that I could speak in the fullness of my own voice only when I was alone on the streets, walking about. There was something unnatural about it; unbearably isolated. I was not like the others! I was not like the others! At midday, every freshly shocking Monday noon, they sent me away to a speech clinic in a school in East New York, where I sat in a circle of lispers and cleft palates and foreign accents holding a mirror before my lips and rolling difficult sounds over and over. To be sent there in the full light of the opening week, when everyone else was at school or going about his business, made me feel as if I had been expelled from the great normal body of humanity. I would gobble down my lunch on my way to the speech clinic and rush back to the school in time to make up for the classes I had lost. One day, one unforgettable dread day, I stopped to catch my breath on a corner of Sutter Avenue, near the wholesale fruit markets, where an old drugstore rose up over a great flight of steps. In the window were dusty urns of colored water floating off iron chains; cardboard placards advertising hairnets,

Ex-Lax; a great illustrated medical chart headed THE HUMAN FACTORY, which showed the exact course a mouthful of food follows as it falls from chamber to chamber of the body. I hadn't meant to stop there at all, only to catch my breath; but I so hated the speech clinic that I thought I would delay my arrival for a few minutes by eating my lunch on the steps. When I took the sandwich out of my bag, two bitterly hard pieces of hard salami slipped out of my hand and fell through a grate onto a hill of dust below the steps. I remember how sickeningly vivid an odd thread of hair looked on the salami, as if my lunch were turning stiff with death. The factory whistles called their short, sharp blasts stark through the middle of noon, beating at me where I sat outside the city's magnetic circle. I had never known, I knew instantly I would never in my heart again submit to, such wild passive despair as I felt at that moment, sitting on the steps before THE HUMAN FACTORY, where little robots gathered and shoveled the food from chamber to chamber of the body. They had put me out into the streets, I thought to myself; with their mirrors and their everlasting pulling at me to imitate their effortless bright speech and their stupefaction that a boy could stammer and stumble on every other English word he carried in his head, they had put me out into the streets, had left me high and dry on the steps of that drugstore staring at the remains of my lunch turning black and grimy in the dust.

In the great cool assembly hall, dominated by the gold sign above the stage KNOWLEDGE IS POWER, the windowsills were lined with Dutch bulbs, each wedged into a mound of pebbles massed in a stone dish. Above them hung a giant photograph of Theodore Roosevelt. Whenever I walked in to see the empty assembly hall for myself, the shiny waxed floor of the stage dangled in the middle of the air like a crescent. On one side was a great silk American flag, the staff crowned by a gilt eagle. Across the dry rattling of varnish-smelling empty seats bowing to the American flag, I saw in the play of the sun on those pebbles wildly sudden images of peace. *There* was the other land, crowned by the severe and questioning face of Theodore Roosevelt, his eyes above the curiously endearing straw-dry mustache, behind the pince-nez glittering with light, staring and staring me through as if he were uncertain whether he fully approved of me.

The light pouring through window after window in that great empty varnished assembly hall seemed to me the most wonderful thing I had ever seen. It was that thorough varnished cleanness that was of the new land, that light dancing off the glasses of Theodore Roosevelt, those green and white roots of the still raw onion-brown bulbs delicately flaring up from the hill of pebbles into which they were wedged. The pebbles moved me in themselves, there were so many of them. They rose up around the bulbs in delicately strong masses of colored stone, and as the sun fell between them, each pebble shone in its own light. Looking across the great rows of empty seats to those pebbles lining the windowsills, I could still smell summer from some long veranda surrounded by trees. On that veranda sat the family and friends of Theodore Roosevelt. I knew the name: Oyster Bay. Because of that picture, I had read *The Boy's Life of Theodore Roosevelt;* knew he had walked New York streets night after night as Police Commissioner, unafraid of the Tenderloin gangsters; had looked into *Theodore Roosevelt's Letters to His Children,* pretending that those hilarious drawings on almost every page were for me. *There* was America, I thought, the real America, *his* America, where from behind the glass on the wall of our assembly hall he watched over us to make sure we did right, thought right, lived right.

"Up, boys! Up San Juan Hill!" I still hear our roguish old civics teacher, a little white-haired Irishman who was supposed to have been with Teddy in Cuba, driving us through our Friday morning tests with these shouts and cries. He called them "Army Navy" tests, to make us feel big, and dividing the class between Army and Navy, got us to compete with each other for a coveted blue star. Civics was city government, state government, federal government; each government had functions; you had to get them out fast in order to win for the Army or the Navy. Sometimes this required filling in three or four words, line by line, down one side of the grimly official yellow foolscap that was brought out for tests. (In the tense silence just before the test began, he looked at us sharply, the watch in his hand ticking as violently as the sound of my heart, and on command, fifty boys simultaneously folded their yellow test paper and evened the fold with their thumbnails in a single dry sigh down the middle of the paper.) At other times it meant true-or-false tests; then he stood behind us to make sure we did not signal the right answers to each other in the usual way—for true, nodding your head; for false, holding your nose. You could hear his voice barking from the rear. *"Come on now, you Army boys! On your toes like West Point cadets! All ready now? Get set! Go! Three powers of the legislative branch? The judiciary? The executive? The subject of the fifteenth amendment? The capital of Wyoming? Come on, Navy! Shoot those landlubbers down! Give 'em a blast from your big guns right through the middle! The third article of the Bill of Rights? The thirteenth amendment? The sixteenth? True or false, Philadelphia is the capital of Pennsylvania. Up and at 'em, Navy! Mow them down! COME ON!!!"* Our "average" was calculated each week, and the boys who scored 90 per cent or over were rewarded by seeing *their own names* lettered on the great blue chart over the blackboard. Each time I entered that room for a test, I looked for my name on the blue chart as if the sight of it would decide my happiness for all time.

Down we go, down the school corridors of the past smelling of chalk, lysol out of the open toilets, and girl sweat. The staircases were a gray stone I saw nowhere else in the school, and they were shut in on both sides by some thick unreflecting glass on which were pasted travel posters inviting us to spend the summer in the Black Forest. Those staircases created a spell in me that I had found my way to some distant, cool, neutral passageway deep in the body of the school. There, enclosed within the thick, green boughs of a classic summer in Germany, I could still smell the tense probing chalk smells from every classroom, the tickling high surgical odor of lysol from the open toilets, could still hear that continuous babble, babble of water dripping into the bowls. Sex was instantly connected in my mind with the cruel openness of those toilets, and in the never-ending sound of the bowls being flushed I could detect, as I did in the maddeningly elusive fragrance of cologne brought into the classroom by Mrs. B., the imminence of something severe, frightening, obscene. Sex, as they said in the "Coney Island" dives outside the school, was like going to the toilet; there was a great contempt in this that made me think of the wet rings left by our sneakers as we ran down the gray stone steps after school.

Outside the women teachers' washroom on the third floor, the tough guys would wait for the possible appearance of Mrs. B., whose large goiterous eyes seemed to bulge wearily with mischief, who always looked tired and cynical, and who wore thin chiffon dresses that affected us much more than she seemed to realize. Mrs. B. often went about the corridors in the company of a trim little teacher of mathematics who was a head shorter than she and had a mustache. Her chiffon dresses billowed around him like a sail; she seemed to have him in tow. It was understood by us as a matter of course that she wore those dresses to inflame us; that she *was* tired and cynical, from much practice in obscene love-making; that she was a "bad one" like the young Polish blondes from East New York I occasionally saw in the "Coney Island" dives sitting on someone's lap and smoking a cigarette. How wonderful and unbelievable it was to find this in a teacher; to realize that the two of them, after we had left the school, probably met to rub up against each other in the faculty toilet. Sex was a grim test where sooner or later you would have to prove yourself doing things to women. In the smell of chalk and sweat and the unending smirky babble of the water as it came to me on the staircase through my summer's dream of old Germany, I could feel myself being called to still another duty—to conquer Mrs. B., to rise to the challenge she had whispered to us in her slyness. I had seen pictures of it on the block—they were always passing them around between handball games—the man's face furious, ecstatic with lewdness as he proudly looked down at himself; the woman sniggering as she teased him with droplets from the contraceptive someone had just shown me in the gutter—its crushed, filmy slyness the very sign of the forbidden.

They had never said anything about this at home, and I thought I knew why. Sex was the opposite of books, of pictures, of music, of the open air, even of kindness. They would not let you have both. Something always lingered to the sound of those toilets to test you. In and out of the classroom they were always testing you. *Come on, Army! Come on, Navy!* As I stood up in that school courtyard and smelled again the familiar sweat, heard again the unending babble from the open toilets, I suddenly remembered how sure I had always been that even my failures in there would be entered in a white, thinly ruled, official record book.

The Senior-High-School Years

MARTIN MAYER
(1928–   )

Madison Avenue, U.S.A. 1958
The Schools, 1961

MARTIN MAYER is a perceptive and articulate journalist. His analysis of the advertising industry and its effect on our lives in *Madison Avenue, U.S.A.* has been spectacularly successful. Having heard much about the problems of the schools, he went to the best possible source of information, the school itself. He observed schools and students, and reported factually and objecively what he saw. The essay which follows is an example of his findings.

1.

From the classroom. At Regis High School in the heart of the prime residential district of East Side Manhattan—"a Jesuit school of the New York province," says its principal, Father McCoska, "subject to the legislation of this province. We follow the curriculum prescribed for this area, but we are allowed to enrich it." Like so many men in positions of authority in Jesuit education, McCoska is young, handsome and deft, with a well-developed sense of humor. The school he runs, though it has fewer than six hundred students in a four-year program, wins first or second place every year in the great New York race for number of winners of National Merit Scholarships.

The Regis student body is the most highly selected group in American secondary education. In 1960, Regis had 4,300 applicants for the 175 places in ninth grade, and the schools which were sending the applicants had to be restricted to a maximum of 10 per cent of their graduating class, because only 1,800 could be seated in the gymnasium to take the entrance examination. The 175 eventually selected came from 100 different feeder schools, scattered all over the New York metropolitan area. McCoska estimates that about 5 per cent of his boys are from rich families, about 15 per cent from poor families, and about 50 per cent from middle-class families who can afford to buy their sons a private-school secondary education, but would feel the strain. No strain is felt at Regis, where the endowment is large enough to permit the school to operate without any tuition charge whatever. Virtually all Regis graduates (60 to 80 per cent of the entrants) go to college, almost always to the Honors Program of a Jesuit college, and more than nine out of ten get scholarship aid. Because it supplies top students in considerable numbers, Regis stands in a unique position in its relations with the colleges. Much of the recent turmoil in the Fordham engineering school, for example, was caused by a threat from Regis that it would no longer send potential science majors to Fordham unless the university established a more rigorous program for them.

The class is in English, at the sophomore level, and the teacher, Mr. Gallen, is a young "scholar," doing the three years of teaching which are part of the training of all Jesuit priests. He may or may not serve as a teacher after he become a priest: his superiors will decide. The fact that he is an excellent teacher may influence their decision, and may not. Unlike most Regis teachers, Gallen calls his students by their first names. The class opens, as all Regis classes do, with a paternoster (spoken in the foreign language when the class is a language class), and Gallen gets right to work.

"There are a number of Hopkins poems I'd like you to hear today, but before doing that I'd like you to look at this Thurber essay." The boys open their book—a paperback Cardinal edition of *Great Essays*—and look at the Thurber essay. "By the way," Gallen says, "be sure you see *The Battle of the Sexes,* and over the summer *The Thurber Carnival.* They're very, very good." Printed with the essay in the book are several of the greatest Thurber cartoons, including the seal in the bedroom, the first wife atop the bookcase, and the psychiatrist with rabbit ears. Gallen asks for some analysis of the cartoons, and proposes that the psychiatrist really *has* rabbit ears, which does not go down well with the class. "Sir," says one boy, "aren't you misinterpreting it?"—and the class roars. A hint that the Thurber cartoons are related to sicknesses in modern society provokes considerable somber analysis, which Gallen finally breaks up. "I don't mean," he says, "that you should flush all the humor out of this stuff, and go looking for meanings on a second level. No, no, no. But you want to see the impact, too."

Gallen then reads Hopkins' "Spring"—

> . . . What is all this juice and all this joy?
>   A strain of the earth's sweet being in the beginning
> In Eden garden.—Have, get, before it cloy,
>   Before it cloud, Christ, lord, and sour with sinning.

—and reads it beautifully, too. He calls the class to attention with the admonition that "You're used to wrenching all the meaning out of things and throwing words around without any respect for what you're trying to convey." He points out that "Hopkins draws on Anglo-Saxon words, rather than those Latin words we're more used to—because they're strong and hard, more masculine. Did anyone see that about a noun becoming a verb? What does that mean? Jerry?"

Jerry says, "It has life in it."

"Right," says Gallen.

Regis is lucky in the fact that one of the greatest of recent English poets was also a Catholic monk: though only a handful of them will ever be priests, these boys will take Hopkins all the more seriously because of what he was. But Regis takes all literature seriously. Over the summer, for example, in preparation for their third-year course, these fifteen-year-old boys will read Shakespeare's *Henry IV* (both parts) and *V*, *Midsummer Night's Dream* and *Romeo and Juliet*, plus Cervantes' *Don Quixote*. During the year, the program will be broken into a unit on the drama before Shakespeare (*Everyman*, *Gammer Gurton's Needle*, Kyd's *Spanish Tragedy*, and Marlowe's *Faustus*, *Tamburlaine* and *The Jew of Malta*) a unit on Shakespeare (*Richard II* and *III*, *Love's Labour Lost*, *The Tempest* and some sonnets); a unit on the modern theater (*Hedda Gabler, The Cherry Orchard, Emperor Jones, Riders to the Sea, Juno and the Paycock, The Plough and the Stars, Murder in the Cathedral, The Glass Menagerie, Our Town* and *J. B.,* with Shaw "ad lib."); a unit on nineteenth-century and modern poetry; and a unit on the American novel (*The Scarlet Letter, Huckleberry Finn, The Red Badge of Courage, Moby Dick, The Great Gatsby* and *The Old Man and the Sea*). Few if any college literature courses—or European secondary courses —ask as much work in one year.

The habit of picking up whatever book anybody mentions does not always lead Regis in the desired straight line. A few years back, a visiting lecturer from Canisius delivered a talk at Regis contrasting Hopkins' view of the Jesuit order with the view in James Joyce's *A Portrait of the Artist.* "The next week," McCoska recalls, "all the kids were wandering around carrying *Portrait.* I was a little concerned. . . ."

At the Wandsworth Comprehensive School, a former grammar school converted to handle the entire range of boys in an upper-working-class district south of the Thames in London. The class is made up of fifteen-year-old boys who would not have won entrance to a grammar school, but whose measured intelligence is above average, hovering about 110 IQ. At Wandsworth, they follow a program permitting them to try for GCE status. Significantly, the teacher thinks they are the second-best group in the school. They are studying English, and today's unit is on the movies. The teacher opens the class with a question:

"How many of you went to the cinema over the holiday?"

Nearly all hands are raised.

"Well, what's the latest thriller?"

The unit is most recognizable to an American, and the textbook, though more literate, urges the same "values." The book comments, "Someone once said that when people go to the cinema they leave their critical senses at the box office. If we do that we are missing half the fun and most of the point of the film." Later in the section, the book deals with propaganda: "Every theme is propaganda for something . . . for the British Navy, for gangsterism, for wine, women and song, for American prosperity, for

Soviet courage, or for the abolition of unnecessary poverty. What matters is the worth-whileness of the propaganda."

From the cinema we move to grammar, and the teacher draws on the board a tabular form with four headings—"Clause, Kind, Function, Relation." Each sentence is broken into its clauses, and their nature written neatly in the boxes.

The boys have also been writing papers on personal experiences. The papers show the unspeakable benefits of a mastery of the tabular organization of clauses. One of them begins, "One morning while I was on the way to school. It began to snow." Another sets a scene, and then describes the personae: "There was sixteen of us consisting of two adults and fourteen teenages. . . ."

At the Wamogo Regional High School in the northwestern section of Connecticut, a new building on a hilltop, drawing from the elementary schools of three towns. The teacher is Miss Barker, a trim, stocky, lively Bostonian lady who handles Latin as well as English. The class is the top of sophomore year, and it has been reading *Macbeth* and *The Tale of Two Cities*. This day is given to a more or less standard grammar lesson, but Miss Barker handles the subject with unusual intelligence, prying from the students their own ideas about why a given sentence was wrong, never insisting on the book verbiage.

These kids, too, have been writing papers. One was on the character of Lady Macbeth, by no means an easy subject for fifteen-year-olds. "I think," one girl writes, "Lady Macbeth was more to be pitied than condemned, for her thoughts and actions seemed to me to be the workings of a twisted mind." There is also a set of papers on "My Goal in Life," fascinating documents, one and all. This bright class, for example, contained (among others):

1 astronomer
1 "Physical Therapist"
1 doctor ("In helping people who need it I would feel good inside and probably proud of myself.")
1 nurse

1 "teacher in foreign places"
1 "minor post in State Department"
1 "grammar-school teacher"
1 musician ("Those who play good music not only stimulate themselves, but gladden the lives of the people around them.")
1 "professional water skier"

Grading the paper of the professional water skier, Miss Barker added to her comment on its quality, which was rather high for sophomore work, a quote from Browning: "Always a man's reach should exceed his grasp. . . ."

2.

The most convincing proof that the American high school has its heart in the right place is its leaders' continuing advocacy of a free press. No other American institution in the last generation has received the lambasting in print that has been absorbed by the high school. Newspapers stories, magazine articles and books have implied that the high schools are breeding grounds for crime and vice, that their teachers are ill-educated weaklings unable to cope with the students, that the kids spend their time playing skip-to-my-lou and taking driving lessons when they are not pulling switch-blade knives on the teachers or taking dope in the bathrooms.

And most of the individual stories, of course, are true. There are nearly nine million adolescents and 450,000 teachers in American high schools. It is by no means remarkable that hundreds of thousands of the children and tens of thousands of the teachers are, to coin a phrase, no good.

The reasons the newspapers devote so much space to this fraction are interesting in themselves, but not germane here. One cannot resist pointing out, however, the extent to which the focus of the press has been determined by the increasing segregation of adult from adolescent in the modern community. A high proportion of the world's famous gangsters—including most of the gunmen of the Old West—were adolescents, and nobody paid much attention to the fact. Today, offenses by high-school kids are "juvenile delinquency" rather than crime, which seems to put the matter in an entirely different light.

But the shocking stories are only part of it; the press has also given its headlines to strong statements by experts about the low quality of the work in the high schools. The outstanding "expert" on education, inevitably, is the college president, though his actual knowledge of secondary education may not qualify him to give advice to his own admissions officer.

Now, it is characteristic of all educational systems everywhere that teachers at higher levels sneer at the teachers through whose hands the child has already passed. A teacher who gets a first-class student admires the boy; but when he gets a poor student he declares that they've ruined the poor lad down below. "In the history of the human race," says Arthur Adams, until recently head of the American Council on Education, "the scapegoat occupies an heroic place." Russian university professors feel about Russian secondary education precisely as American university professors feel about American high schools. In France, the universities recently refused to recognize the *Baccalauréat*, which is administered by the secondary department, as a matriculation examination, forcing French kids to spend yet another year in school preparing for yet another set of examinations.

Some high schools, some high-school teachers, some superintendents of schools and some professors of education undoubtedly deserve the contempt poured upon them from the universities and reported in the press. Most of them, however, are honestly doing the best they can. Their best is very far from perfect. The American high school is a monstrously inefficient operation. As B. F. Skinner puts the matter, "It is utterly ridiculous to believe that it requires from eight-thirty to four, plus homework, for the high-school student to learn what he actually learns in a day." Teaching methods and the technology of education are astonishingly ill-developed. Nevertheless, the problem is more wasted effort than lack of effort. The high-school student in America, especially on the academic track, works harder than he has worked at any time since he left the primary grades.

3.

Though an assortment of programs is offered, and the variations from school to school are great, it is possible to speak of *the* academic secondary course covered in Britain, France and Scandinavia. In these countries, each child who is "graduated" from an academic secondary school must pass an external examination, and school programs must be drawn up to prepare children for it. The only equivalents to this situation in the United States are the Advanced Placement courses of the College Board and the mathematics and science program in New York State, resting upon the so-called "Regents course" and leading to an examination administered by the state Board of Regents. There are Regents examinations in other subjects, too, but except in math and science the Board has tried to find common denominators in existing school programs rather than to write an "agreed syllabus" leading to the exam. The extent and variety of the choice offered in the Regents examinations in English and history indicate how very different programs in such subjects are from school to school.

There is no such thing as *the* high-school program in the United States. Even where surface appearances are similar, differences from school to school may be very great. In *The American High School Today*, James Bryant Conant offers "academic inventories" of twenty-two comprehensive high schools located in small cities, and judges the schools on the basis of how many "academically talented" children were taking four "years" of mathematics or three "years" of language or seven "years" of English and social studies. In America, however, the term "years" is meaningless by itself, and Conant offers no evidence except in math and science (and not much there) to support the hypothesis that there is a close correspondence between "years" of a subject studied in different schools. Early in their second year of studying French, students at Regis High School are given the "Third-Year Regents" examination, and are expected to get a grade better than 90 on it. How many "years" of French have they had? Even where the same textbooks are employed, the abilities and attitudes of teachers, parents and school supervisors determine the depth to which a child will be asked to explore what he is studying.

Most American comprehensive high schools require sixteen "Carnegie units"—i.e., classes that meet five periods a week for an entire term—before a child can be graduated. Work done in the ninth grade, in junior high, counts in the Carnegie unit tally; though the 6-3-3 form of organization has spread widely, state administrators are still more at home with an 8-4 analysis. Typically, three or four of these units must be in English, two or three in social studies, (including one in American history) one in mathematics (satisfied by "General Mathematics," a dragged-out course in remedial arithmetic which Edward Begle of the School Mathematics Study Group describes as "the most horrible thing that exists"), one or two in science and one or two in physical education. Beyond these requirements, the child makes up his own program, with pressures in one direction or another from guidance counselors and parents. Where the state university must accept all applicants with high-school diplomas—a condition that prevails in nearly half the states—even the college-bound child need take only seven to ten units of *academic* work during his "four years" of high school. It must be pointed out, however, that only a very stupid child would think he could get along in college with so little secondary preparation. Those who see themselves going to college (about half of all high-school entrants have this vision, and three-fifths of these will actually go) ordinarily take a minimum of four academic courses a year, adding "electives" to fill in the six-period or seven-period day, and finishing with twenty or more Carnegie units on their record card.

For reasons of organizational convenience, high schools regard their entrants as following various "tracks"—academic, business, general or vocational, most often in that order of prestige within the school. This track system may be formal and pervasive (a child may take all his courses with his fellows in the same track) or it may be purely for record-card purposes (students from all tracks take their required courses together, and separate for electives). American educational theoreticians have strongly advocated "heterogeneous" classes, with no grouping by ability or track, for the social studies and even the English program, on the grounds that democratic values are thereby promoted. Conant is still urging a "heterogeneous" compulsory "Problems of Democracy" course in senior year. Efforts to run social studies and English programs on this basis, however, have been disastrous, because it is impossible to maintain a level of discussion which satisfies more than a fraction of the students in the classroom. The majority of comprehensive high schools therefore "group" their children for required subjects as well as track subjects (which are to some extent self-grouping).

Not every high school in the United States is "comprehensive" in the special sense that it offers many varieties of education. Small high schools cannot afford to offer many courses, and therefore gear their programs, more or less adequately, to run on what would be the academic track in a larger institution. In most larger cities there are one or more strictly vocational schools providing terminal education and, hopefully, "salable skills." A very few cities have managed to combine the vocational and academic curricula in an open-ended "technical school" which can lead either to a job or to college; usually, however, such schools (like New York's Brooklyn Tech or Chicago's Lane Technical) have rapidly become college-preparatory for nearly all the students. Large Eastern cities may also have selective high schools which take bright kids from all over town for an exclusively college-preparatory program—indeed, a parent whose child is admitted to Boston Latin must sign a declaration of intent to send the child to college. West of Cincinnati, the competitive-entrance, selective high school is frowned upon, and everybody not in a vocational school goes to the comprehensive high school which serves his district. The districts themselves, however, are selective by social class, and every city has its neighborhoods—or at least suburbs—where two-thirds or more of the kids are college-bound. (City headquarters in Phoenix, Arizona, refers to Central and Camelback High Schools as Harvard and Yale.) All larger cities also run district high schools in wretched slums, where no more than a handful of the kids have even considered the possibility of a college education, and the academic options are severely restricted.

Part of the educational program of the high school is carried on outside classrooms, in "extracurricular" activities—stamp, chess, art, French, math, Future Farmers, Future Teachers and similar clubs; student government activities and student publications; the school orchestra and band and glee club and Little Players, which give public performances; athletic teams and so forth. The supervision of such activities takes anywhere from one-tenth to one-third of the time of the staff of the school, and most cities do not pay teachers for their work in this area. With a few exceptions, fraternity-sorority groups and the like, these activities contribute substantially to the child's education, extending his knowledge of himself and of something else. The spark of interest falls, for once, on inflammable material, with no official course of study to smother the fire. Though the club programs are quintessentially middle-class, and though they unquestionably do reinforce within the school some of the more distasteful aspects of the community culture, proposals that they be curbed to make time for more homework show a profound misunderstanding of what does and what does not educate a child. Indeed, the clubs could probably carry more of the weight of the secondary program, especially in music and art, where the schools must offer some preconservatory or art-school training for those who wish it, and should arrange exposure to real music and real art for virtually everybody. But the course structure—the endless *talking* and reading and writing about art which Virgil Thomson labeled "the appreciation racket"—is usually a hindrance to the creation or reception of artistic communication.

4.

The worst crisis through which the American high school passed during the last decade was the threatened collapse of the vocational wing. A steadily decreasing absolute number of blue-collar jobs, combined with a steadily rising average income which permitted more parents to think of college for their children, drove down to rock bottom the quality of the children on the vocational track. Nobody anywhere in the world knows how to give a secondary education to the bottom third of the intelligence distribution, and in many vocational programs in the early 1950's every single child was drawn from that bottom third. The program was highly repetitive, and the standard of work in the shops was far below what would be acceptable in an apprentice. In New York in the late 1950's the *average* IQ in the vocational schools was under 85, and the trade unions were informing the schools that they could no longer support the vocational programs, if *that* was the kind of child the schools thought ought to go into their trade. Elsewhere, businessmen were complaining bitterly about the ham-handedness and general stupidity of the kids coming out of the vocational program. In Louisville an unofficial committee from the Chamber of Commerce waited on an assistant superintendent to tell him that from now on they were going to give preference to kids who had been through the academic or even the general high-school program, on the grounds that they could train an adequate child on the job but could do nothing with allegedly trained inadequacy. As late as 1958, New York's publication *Guidance News* quoted a State Employment Service official as saying that "these young people [vocational school graduates] will probably have to start on unskilled jobs."

Most cities have weathered the crisis by quietly instituting competitive examinations for entrance to the vocational schools. Agreeing with the businessmen and labor union leaders that there was a minimum level of intelligence below which people could not be trained to do skilled jobs, the schools began to screen students through both aptitude and achievement tests. Children in the vocational programs, suddenly, were no longer rejects from the other branches, but successful candidates to this branch. Guidance counselors in the junior highs were urged at least to permit children of average intelligence to elect vocational programs. To demonstrate good will, many vocational divisions launched potentially college-preparatory math-and-science courses for their best entrants, giving the entering child a direct path to engineering school, provided he could climb the hills. This part of the reform movement has been strongest in New York, where the vocational schools had virtually disintegrated before entrance exams were established—two-thirds of the entrants were failing to complete the course, and the third that got its diploma was failing to find jobs. Starting with an experiment at the most successful and intelligent of its vocational schools—Aviation Trades —New York began a project which may lead vocational education to the quality (and thus the status) of technical education.

There is a dark side to this shield, blazoned with the arms of the children who are rejected by the vocational schools. Usually they get shunted to what is known as a "general" program, which can be described fairly accurately as a course of study in which nothing in particular is learned. Such courses are given in "comprehensive" or academic high schools which used to be able to push their most hopeless fraction over to the vocationalists, and neither teachers nor principals are happy about the return of such sheep to the fold. "I have five classes," said an English teacher in New York, "one bright, two average and two dull. And when we say dull, we mean *dull*—these kids can barely read." In Louisville, the principal of the largely college-preparatory Atherton High School, a district school in a good district, commented bitterly that most of his kids were pretty bright, but he also had "a few mentally retarded which Ahrens the vocational school rejects." A very few cities—among them Columbus—maintain "occupational" schools below the vocational program to take the rejects, but the heavy incidence of truly feeble-minded children in these schools makes them less than wholly suitable for the group that is just very dumb. It is easy to argue that because these kids are dumb they are insensitive or incapable of feeling bored, but the look of resentment on their faces indicates that they know what is happening to them and do not like it. They are caught in a pattern of failure and rejection that is likely to last all their lives—the Army certainly won't have them—and they have the right to ask the schools for something more than purely custodial treatment. A few able and compassionate men (high among them Kansas City's Clyde Baer) are working to see if there isn't some way these kids can be got interested in their own education, but they are still far from a solution.

Public agitation has been at the opposite pole of the intelligence spectrum, stirring up the question of what the high schools should do for their brightest fraction, known in editorialese as "the academically talented." Like bird dogs the critics have pointed to the high-school elective system—but the bird they see is a decoy. The accusation is that the free choice of electives operates to lure bright kids to take fly-casting or ballroom-dancing rather than French, because French involves homework. Undoubtedly, a few such cases do come up, but the high-IQ child who opts for a low-IQ program has shown remarkable strength of spirit in resisting the alternating blandishments and scorn of his teachers and his guidance counselor, and can probably be trusted to make his way in the world without French. Long before Conant returned from Germany, the high schools were pressuring the high-IQ kids into the academic program, where most of them wanted to go, anyway.

Yet the elective system *does* hurt bright kids—because it is not elective enough. Serious specialization of any sort is denied the child who might wish to probe more deeply into some aspect of an intellectual discipline. Typically, the high school offers one course in world history (9 sections, 34 children per section), one in American history (15 sections), one in problems of democracy (4 sections unless compulsory) and one in economics (2 sections). For each year in school, there is a math course. There is a year of biology, a year of chemistry, a year of physics. The English Department may offer a year of speech, a year of journalism, and a year of drama in addition to English 1, 2, 3, 4—but the first of these is usually remedial and the other two are essentially activities rather than academic specialization. The child who works up a strong interest in organic chemistry must leave his subject after part of a year's contact with it. The child who becomes fascinated with the Civil War has no chance to study this event intesively and get credit for his work. The child who would like to go on a Russian literature jag must steal the time from schoolwork to do so.

"Mankind is naturally specialist," Whitehead wrote in *The Aims of Education*. "It seems contradictory to allow for specialism in a curriculum especially designed for a broad culture. Without contradictions the world would be simpler and perhaps duller. But I am certain that in education wherever you exclude specialism you destroy life."

Here is the greatest difference between American and European education for bright children. The European child, by electing programs rather than courses, loads his schedule with the sort of work that interests him, and receives an opportunity to go much more deeply into the area that attracts him. He studies physics for three or four years, not one. Specialization can easily be overdone, as it often is in England, where many grammar schools so arrange their program that the child who opts for math and science never studies history again after the age of fourteen. And it can be achieved rather cruelly, as it is in France, where the *lycée* student has so much work thrown at him in every class that he must concentrate on what he does best, and hope to pull up his inevitably poor grades in the less appealing subjects with excellent grades in the subjects that attract him. Only in the United States is it believed that an "A" student is "A" in everything, or that "academically talented" children should spread themselves thin through secondary education (and even through the first two years of college, under the new "general education" programs) by swallowing an equal bite of every intellectual goody displayed in the school showcase. The twentieth-century school which takes the Renaissance Man as its ideal, and expects to educate adolescents to the point where there are no "gaps" in their knowledge of the world, can produce only that combination of glibness and shallowness which is so glowingly rewarded on the College Board examinations—and then so bitterly condemned the next year by the college freshman, who complains that his high school never taught him "how to study" or "how to think."

Logically, it would seem that the American high school, freed of the need to construct false fronts for external examinations, would be studded with courses for beginning specialists. The psychology of teaching would seem to demand such courses, too. Any world history teacher would respect himself and his career the more if he were given an opportunity to teach the Renaissance, say, as well as the section after section of hasty "survey." And adolescents are entitled to occasional escape from the parade of half-truths that constitutes formal knowledge on the survey-course level.

One of the great handicaps of secondary education is the

school's inability to discover methods suitable for teaching what
has been discovered in the last fifty years. The poem does not
mean what the teacher says it means, Bismarck's policies were
not what the textbooks say they were, the "laws" of physics are
special cases of larger laws and not significant in themselves, the
"rules" of algebra can be and have been changed to fit specific
problems. Most of what the child learns in high school he will
have to unlearn if he wishes to understand the subject he is
studying. As Bagehot put it in 1885, "the academies are asylums
of the ideas and the tastes of the last age." the only known approach to the teaching of what is now regarded as True in advanced circles passes through the teaching of what is now regarded
as not-True. In the absence of superior methods, the only way
to avoid the child's total immersion in antiquated information
is to provide specialized courses.

The introduction of specialized courses will become easier
(indeed, harder to avoid) once the junior high school is freed
of the content of seventh- and eighth-grade elementary education and permitted to embark on a genuinely secondary program.
Nevertheless, it would be helpful if administrators could bring
themselves to consign the Carnegie unit form of organization to
whichever circle of Hell will receive it. As Paul Woodring wrote
in *A Fourth of a Nation,* elimination of the Carnegie unit would
involve a lot of work for school principals—but only the sort of
work for which educational administrators are paid. Educationally, there is no conceivable justification for a scheme that assigns
equal time and equal weight to all subjects of study at all stages
of mastery. Even the people who complain most bitterly about
courses in driver education, ballroom dancing and vocational
guidance might be willing to suffer in silence if the school allotted to such useful or ornamental trivia no more than one or
two hours of classroom time a week—which is, after all, what
they warrant.

Even now, however, all high schools could offer the sort of
"seminar" program given in Tucson's Pueblo to the very top of
the class. "Seminar" as Pueblo uses the word does not imply sitting around every day and talking. It means working on one's own
pet project—in literature or history or science—with a teacher

available to answer questions as they come up, and with a meeting of the class as a unit once a week so that children who have found something particularly interesting can talk about it with children who are working along different lines—as the Junior Fellows at Harvard meet at lunch to see what they can learn from each other.

Actually, all reasonably intelligent children—not just the "academically talented"—would find school more interesting and rewarding if they were not forever pulled away from what they would like to study. Ignorance of most of the universe is an inescapable aspect of the human condition, most gracefully borne by those who are not equally ignorant in all directions. Indeed, it is probably true that "average" children would benefit more than their betters by the chance to specialize, because the bright child may see intuitively how much there is to be learned, while the average child must be shown how to find the problems to be solved.

At present, the approved procedure for relieving the boredom of the bright child in high school is the Advanced Placement course, which offers college-level survey work and leads to a chance of earlier specialization at college for those who pass it with high grades. But surely it would be preferable, for both high-school students and high-school teachers, to give a foretaste of specialization on the secondary level. The child who comes to his college survey course with a specialist's knowledge of one element in the course has a center around which he can organize what he learns, and give it meaning.

5.

From the Classroom. At Collegiate, a kindergarten-to-age-18 college-preparatory boys' school on the West Side of New York, now much in the educational news because it is the center of a large pilot project on the use of teaching machines. The six boys in this class, however, are seniors, too old to have enjoyed any of the advantages of programmed instruction. They are off to good colleges next year, and in preparation for one aspect or another of what they will find in college they are taking a course in philosophy. The course is not a survey. The boys are expected to familiarize themselves with some of the essential points in Plato, Aristotle, Descartes, Hume, Kant and Hegel, but in class most of the work is given to modern philosophers. At present, the class is talking over Paul Tillich, having read his book *The Courage to Be.*

The kids are fascinated by Tillich, especially by the concept of ontology, the examination of the meaning of the verb "to be." As one of them says, wonderingly, "In terms of Tillich, if one does not act ontologically, one doesn't exist." All the jargon comes from the boys; their teacher, Mr. Johnson, places the problems to be analyzed in a common-sense frame, and lets the boys use their new vocabulary in discussing them. The question for today is, "Is it possible to have anxiety without being scared to death?" The example chosen is Dostoevsky before the firing squad as a young man in Czarist Russia. "Analyze if you can," Johnson says, "the nature of his experience."

A boy mutters, "One of the men with him went nuts."

Another boy proposes to a classmate, *ad hominem,* a situation in which one enters a tunnel, with light coming in through the other side, knowing that as one crosses the halfway mark in the tunnel one must die. It is too good a situation for classroom discussion—it wants one of those evenings in college, when half a dozen freshmen are standing around a mantelpiece with nothing much to do, spinning a half-dollar, relishing the knowledge that there is nobody who can tell them to go to bed. Johnson tries to bring it down by referring to a specific paragraph in Tillich: "To use Tillich's terminology, and I think we must so long as we're discussing his book . . ." Eventually, however, he has to assert authority, and he claps his hands loudly and says, "Cut it off now." Which they do, and return to Dostoevsky.

At Highland High School in Salt Lake City the senior class has for its teacher Miss Eardley, a pretty girl with a round face and hair carefully disarranged. They are discussing together a test which is going to be given the next day, and a boy asks, "On these parallel adjectives before a noun, are you going to count off very much for those we can't distinguish?"

"It depends on the situation," says Miss Eardley brightly. "Now, remember, this is a one-shot test, kids. You do it or you don't do it. I would suggest that for tomorrow you look up and know the following words—voluble, sarcasm, profound. Obviously, I'm not going to count them very high because they weren't on the lists, but I think it best you know them. It took me about four and a half hours to make up this test. It's a hard test. . . ."

A few days after the test, there is to be a book report written in class. The kids have chosen their own book, but they will have to comment on only one aspect of it—the author's use of "sensory impressions." A boy asks, "About how many quotations should it have?"

"Depends on what you want to say and how it looks to you. But I want you to group your quotes—visual, hearing, smelling. If he uses sensory impressions well and he's a well-rounded sensory impression writer, say so. If you find his description of sensory impression is weak, say so. Ask him what he *means,* even though he isn't here to defend himself. Incidentally, though you're going to write it here, this paper is to be *organized* before you come to class. Think about it. You can say, 'This use of sensory impression made the scene *more vivid,* the story *more convincing.*' But you'd better not; I want something more specific. Or you can say, 'I have been short all my life, and I know what it means to have people look down on me. . . .' "

As part of this general unit, the students have written their own sensory-impression papers. The papers are handed in, and the class forms six groups of five or six each. Miss Eardley goes around the room, handing out to each group several papers written by members of other groups, and tells the class, which is used to this procedure, how she wants the papers graded. "I would like to have you evaluate these papers by these criteria—how well does the person use sensory impressions, and how well do the sensory impressions fit into the paper?"

As the kids begin reading, she adds, "Remember. We have declared death ultimata on certain things. One is spelling, the other is apostrophe mistakes. If you find one of these, take it to the person who wrote it and say, 'Hmmmm . . . how much is it worth to you?' Finally, Mother's little tip on how to succeed in college:

always have someone read your papers before you hand them in."

While the kids read each other's papers and discuss grades, Miss Eardley comes back to find out what her visitor is doing in her classroom. She teaches 130 seniors and 40 juniors every day and she has her students read each other's papers because she wants a lot of writing and knows she can't do a thorough job on everything herself. She does not pay too much attention to the grades which the kids give each other, except that when she feels a grade is way out of line she calls over the group which has given it and seeks an explanation. "I find," she says, "they learn more from judging each other's work than they learn from doing their own." Her seniors read a minimum of two full-length books every six weeks, and she likes to have them read fiction, "though if they want to read *The Organization Man,* that's all right. This is my second year of teaching, and the assignments I give this year are not the ones I gave last year." Miss Eardley stops for a minute and looks down at her seated visitor. "I work very hard at my job," she says slowly. "Too hard . . ."

Some of the papers are handed back to the visitor for his perusal, and Miss Eardley glances at one or two of them as they pass by. "I can see," she says to the class, "that we're going to have to go over our intransitive verbs, aren't we?" The visitor reads the papers, which are several cuts above what one finds even in top classes in cities much more sophisticated than Salt Lake. The prose is too Latinate, as high-school seniors' prose always is; but there is in the writing an unusual effort to convey excitement, rather than simply to fulfill an assignment. Most of the boys have written about sports, and most of the girls about dances, though automobiles and horses are also present. What they have to say is almost uniformly silly, but they feel it as part of themselves; and because Miss Eardley wants correct grammar and spelling, they give her correct grammar and spelling.

The visitor is impressed, and says as much a few minutes later to the principal of the school, who nods glumly. "Yes," he says, "but we're going to lose her. Some boy will come around one of these days and take her away. Whoever he is, he won't let her work those hours. . . ."

6.

In Junior high school, the child accepts guidance from a guidance counselor or orders from his parents, or suggestions from the gang. In senior high school he comes up against the reality of occupational choice. The outside world draws near; work done in school suddenly relates to a real future; gleefully or anxiously, the older adolescent, no longer quite so concerned about who he is, begins to worry about the role he will play when all this nonsense of high school is history.

Even those who will go on to further education—nearly half the group of high-school seniors—must begin to make decisions which look (and often are) irreversible. On the Eastern Seaboard, among ambitious children and the children of ambitious parents, the worry about occupational choice is sublimated in a prior but related worry about college admissions. The children who are and always have been destined for the state university, and will enter it automatically, begin to think more or less seriously about the sort of career for which they plan to use their college education. By and large, college freshmen think they know what they want to be, and though they may change their minds during the course of their college work they feel a need to "make a decision" before finishing high school—a need only slightly less strong than that felt by the boy who is going right out to a job, and will have far less opportunity to change his mind.

Surprisingly little is know about this question of occupational choice and about the forces that influence adolescents to head for one job rather than another. The first attempt to pull together all the forces and form a "general theory" of the choice process was made only a decade ago, by a team consisting of economist Eli Ginzberg, psychiatrist Sol Ginsburg, sociologist Sidney Axelrad and psychologist John Herma, under the auspices of the "Conservation of Human Resources Project" at Columbia University. In their book *Occupational Choice* they divided the process into three phases—the childish period of fantasy choice (the fireman-baseball-player-Indian-chief phase), the early adolescent period of tentative choice based on the child's interests and sense of his own capacities, and the later adolescent period of realistic choice, based on a complicated interplay of self-image, interests, an estimate of the available opportunity, and an understanding of what it means to work for a living.

While making his choice, the adolescent relies upon

a group of external supports. The most important of these is the educational system, with its specified curriculum embracing certain areas of choice, its techniques of grading the work of students, the formal prerequisites which it lays down for promotion and graduation, the prizes which it awards. All-pervasive is the pressure of time. There is a time to enter high school and a time to graduate; a time to enter college and a time to graduate. The struggling adolescent probably finds that these pressures and compulsions help him to order what might otherwise be diffuse and undirected action on his part.

It is, however, from people, from key persons in the environment, that adolescents receive most support. . . . Children during the period of fantasy choices . . . express their occupational goals with reference to particular adults with whom they identify—the father, the policeman in the neighborhood, a baseball idol. They are unable to think about the complexities of an adult world except in terms of specific individuals whom they know. . . .

Other key persons act as intermediaries or counsellors. They help the adolescent to gain a somewhat sharper view of the complex reality which he should include in his purview before reaching a decision. . . . Key persons may be influential even when they are not directly approached. . . . Probably one of the most serious handicaps of the lower income group is the absence of informed and sympathetic adults.

The high-school boy, then, functions with the future somewhere in his head. But the school is entirely an affair of the present. Aside from the abstract "educational qualifications" required for certain careers, the school operates in this context as a formal set of restrictions—curriculum, grades, prerequisites, prizes, time of entrance, time of graduation. The attempt to break out of this formality and enter the boy's inner nature has been at the root of much "educational reform" in this century: if the school could only relate itself more closely to life, the school could do more for its students. Ginzberg and his colleagues still follow this line of argument when they claim that at the high-school ages "the most important incentive to learn is provided when the individual sees a relation between his present activity and his future goals."

Yet there is reason, both empirical and theoretical, to doubt that the schools can succeed in this effort. Where semiskilled trades are involved, all the school can promise is a year's delay before starting the same job. Such inducements exert little pull on a boy who wants to make his own money and who does not know that factory work on an assembly line is not just dull (like school) but positively unpleasant. In skilled trades, when the employment market is tight, the boy knows he can get his job and learn more about it during his first year on it than he could hope to learn in school; when the employment market is loose, he feels he gains an advantage by scrounging for something now rather than later. He smells the dishonesty of the stay-in-school propaganda, with its averaged-out statistics. For many children, what the high school offers that relates to their future is simply that piece of paper, the diploma, lack of which, they understand, can cause trouble later on.

School is only a small part of the context in which the occupational choice is made, and it can serve adequately only one of the elements that go into the choice—the element of interest. The boy who wants to become an auto mechanic because he loves to fool with machinery will do well in the vocational program; the boy will do poorly who seeks such a career because his father is a day laborer and the auto mechanic stands a step up on the status scale. It is simply dishonest to claim that "the whole child comes to school" but only "the salable skill" leaves it. The whole man comes to work, too. The "life adjustment" which is needed is the art of relishing the satisfactions and bearing the discontents of work. Such an art can be developed only by the discovery, enlargement and cultivation of fields of interest, preferably fields which contain the work to be done but spread out far beyond it. "A good teacher," Paul Woodring writes, "can lead a child to be interested in almost anything within his range of comprehension." This is the task of the schools; this is the meaning of "secondary education for all." Nobody should pretend the task is easy.

The Impact of the School:
The Clarification of Experience

EDGAR Z. FRIEDENBERG

(1921–   )

Self-perception in the University, 1954
The Vanishing Adolescent, 1959

Though EDGAR Z. FRIEDENBERG was himself not educated in a public school, he has been an adviser to students in high school and college, has observed education at work day by day, and has thought deeply about his experience. The essay below is taken from *The Vanishing Adolescent,* a book which explores educational problems in the light of present American attitudes toward teen-agers; it represents one of the most original recent contributions to an understanding of such problems.

IN WHAT WAYS DOES THE SCHOOL INFLUENCE THE GROWTH OF adolescents? It is society's formal provision for them. It is charged with their intellectual and moral development. In a culture like ours, in which tragedy is regarded as a problem and problems are assumed to have solutions, the school is held responsible for observable deficiencies in the adolescent much as a department store is held responsible for defects in the quality of its merchandise.

For the most part the school accepts this responsibility. It tries to meet it professionally; that is, by means of a program planned to meet stated objectives through techniques derived from empirical research. The statements of objectives are often so naïve philosophically, and derived from so vulgar a conception of what life will demand of its students, as to be indefensible; the research is often so stupidly planned and executed as to be irrelevant to the conclusions drawn from it. But the school is seldom frivolous or irresponsible in its attitude toward youngsters; it tries to understand its job and do it as conscientiously as the quality of its staff permits.

Indeed, in discussing the role of the school in the social order, professional educationists are frequently unrealistic through being *overly* responsible and conscientious in their point of view. They see the school as a much more active influence on society than it is. They may regard the school as primarily the agent of society, but they still perceive it as an *agent*. They assume that it can and does *act* rather independently, on behalf either of society or of its own educational ends, and that its policies, if properly executed, ought decisively to influence the outcome of events.

In this conception of the function of the school there is some truth; but the school overstates its agency. It takes too much on itself, and speaks as if it were responsible for the outcomes of social processes that it has scarcely influenced. For in much that transpires within the school—and that is undoubtedly highly educational—the school is not an agent. It is the arena in which social forces interact, employing students, teachers, and administrative officials in roles with which they have become familiar but into which they have not developed much insight. The committee reports and public statements by which the school attests its professional orientation and benevolent concern are as sincerely meant as Polonius' advice to Laertes. But the school's intentions are seldom independent influences on educational events. The drama of Prince Hamlet did not work out quite as Polonius intended; and Polonius was not its hero. Too many other people were trying to do too many other things; and even the adolescent Hamlet, who came closest, did not quite grasp all that was going on.

What is going on? If we were to attempt to analyze the complex web of activity of a typical American high school with the affectionate but detached interest of an observer from another planet, what social functions would be discernible? They will obviously vary from one school to another and, more significantly perhaps, according to the categories of thought of the observer. But I think we might expect to find something like the following social processes occurring simultaneously and in interaction. I indicate them here in order of the importance I would attribute to their actual impact on the adolescent and on his subsequent life as an adult in society.

First: The school is where you learn to be an American. Americanization is a process, not a result; it is carried on chiefly by the youngsters themselves. The teachers play a fairly important role as manipulators of the *mise en scène*; but they do not much influence the process by direct instruction. There is plenty of nationalist propaganda in our textbooks and courses, but there is not much evidence that it influences the students. The informal processes of Americanization produce, in fact, so stubborn a resistance to direct indoctrination with any ideology that we have had to evolve other means of propagating our own. They are effective, and the school is one of the principal loci of their application; but they are informal and fit cleverly into our image of ourselves as an independent people given to irreverence.

Second: The school serves as a hydraulic mechanism designed to provide a measure of fluidity and stability of equilibrium for a society which is far more stratified than its members care to admit. How a youngster reacts to the school largely determines his chance to get on in the world; whether he wants to get on the world largely determines what his attitude toward the school will be. What the school contributes in the process is complex, and formal instruction is probably not a very important part of it. Those who set themselves professional goals receive some elementary instruction in the relevant sciences and techniques; it is not usually very good. For the rest, the vast majority, the school serves as what C. Wright Mills has called "a seed-bed of . . . white-collar skills."[1] For all, it is the source of the certification prerequisite to getting a decent job in a society grown much too impersonal to depend on face-to-face assessment of competence.

Third: The school transmits some of the knowledge and some of the intellectual skills and attitudes on which the tradition of

1. In an unpublished address before the New Orleans Conference of the Center for the Study of Liberal Education for Adults, 3 April, 1954.

Western civility depends—depends more precariously than ever. The quality of general education in the American high school is not high, particularly in comparison with a European secondary school of university or preparatory grade. But it is probably underestimated by most observers. It has contributed substantially to the development of a middle class which is interested in the arts, capable of quite fine discrimination in consumption, intellectually alert and anxious to maintain a broad and just interest in its involvement in world affairs. This class continues, however, to lack sufficient depth of education and confidence in the authority of the mind to use its intellectual capacities fully.

Fourth: The school functions as an administrative and records center for various activities with reference to the young. The high school adds substantially to the dossier which has now become standard equipment for Americans. It records a youth's intelligence, interests, medical history, and emotional stability. It notes, should it occur, the rare complication produced by the development of political interests. It observes—and often sets down on microfilm, for permanence and economy—its appraisal of his personality and of his over-all promise for the future, and it transmits this appraisal, and sometimes the raw data on which the appraisal is based, in response to what it regards as legitimate inquiry, forever afterward.

It is probably idle to question at this point whether these processes are conducive to the good of society; they are in any event part of its workings. Processes having a similar function have always occurred in schools. One can hardly imagine a school system which did not somehow provide an ambience congenial to the values and attitudes of the culture which supported it. In every society complex enough to provide formal schooling for postpubescent youngsters, the schools strongly influence the social mobility of individuals. In every culture education aims to develop individuals whose sensitivities and whose anxieties will be useful and reassuring to the kind of people who already wield power. (Indeed, the distinction between liberal and professional education seems to be peculiar to an age of self-made men. Harvard College was founded as a vocational school for clergymen; it was hardly necessary to stipulate that it should also turn out

Harvard men.) And schools have doubtless always managed to provide interested authorities with estimates of their students' character and potential for various kinds of action; in this, as today, their judgments were colored by the ideologies then prevailing.

These functions are traditional, but their impact upon the adolescent is new. They become something different in a society in which school attendance is universal and compulsory, the educational establishment correspondingly enormous, the teaching staff correspondingly specialized, bureaucratic, and lacking in prestige and self-esteem.

Regardless of the uses to which any society may put its schools, education has an obligation that transcends its own social function and society's purposes. That obligation is to clarify for its students the meaning of their experinece of life in their society. The school exists fundamentally to provide the young people of a community—a nation may be a community; it had better be—with a fairly tough and firmly fixed philosophical apparatus for making a certain kind of sense out of their lives, and communicating with other people who may be assumed to have a basically similar apparatus.

This does *not* mean propagating similar views, or social attitudes and beliefs as such. A great deal of this sort of propagandizing does go on concomitantly and perhaps inevitably, but it is not helpful in accomplishing the purpose of clarification. Neither does it mean teaching the truth—though it certainly does mean not teaching the false—for the truth usually cannot be taught; it is too subtle and iridescent, and can only be recognized by persons who expect that it will look entirely different when viewed from different angles. The first and fundamental step is certainly to get the relevant facts right, if facts are involved, and deal with them honestly and consistently; facts can be taught. But they are not the truth.

What it does mean is teaching people to mean the same thing by the truth; to establish in their minds similar categories of thought; to approach understanding with roughly the same unconscious predispositions; to admit the same considerations as relevant; to share a common intellectual—though it sometimes is scarcely that—methodology. In any generation, a few souls will use this apparatus to formulate the truth about themselves and the world they live in; and they do not necessarily go mad or get themselves hanged. We simply remember more vividly those who do. But the social purpose of education is not to create a nation of actively insatiable truth-seekers; truth-seeking is a highly specialized function. It is to create a nation which can see clearly, and agree on what it sees, when it looks in certain directions.

The American school seems to do this. We do indeed share a common culture. There is as yet no other nation in which individual regional differences have been so swamped. Whether the man from the car rental agency meets you at New York, Miami, New Orleans, or San Francisco International Airport hardly matters. And the commonness goes further: American mass gratifications, from soft drinks to comic books and movies, have turned out to be the common coin of mass culture the world over; so that it hardly matters either whether he meets you in Ankara, Tokyo, or Rome. This is not conquest, but genuine cultural diffusion. All over the world, man in the mass has turned out to be exactly our type of fellow.

It is nearly as deep as it is wide, too. As we view ourselves being ourselves, the differences between the patterns of lives of city folk and country folk, rich people and poor ones, those with a Ph.D. and those who never finished grade school are minimal. There are, of course, superficial differences in *how* and *where* people of different social groups spend their leisure, but not fundamental differences in what they *do* with it and what it does to them.

Our schools are a precise expression of our culture; they do prevent it flying apart; they do polarize our vision in certain directions; they do certainly establish in young Americans common categories of thought and unconscious predispositions. But they do not clarify the meaning of experience.

Our schools act as if America were still a melting pot. This is a strong tradition that developed through the decades when the nation was being built up through immigration. Free public secondary education was created in the United States in order to supply its expanding economy with a labor force and a technical staff equal to its growing demands. In order to do so, it had to take youngsters from the most diverse ethnic backgrounds and turn them into an article sufficiently standardized to fit efficiently into a productive system that had very little interest in their personal characteristics and no wish to be troubled by them. In return, the youngsters could count on a rising standard of living. The high school was intended to produce not an industrial proletariat, but a group of individuals who could be trusted with complex technical and administrative machinery and trusted not to raise awkward questions about the place of that machinery in the universe of values. The youngsters by and large agreed with the high school that they were being given an unprecedented opportunity.

Still, adolescents need clarity. If adolescence is the process of defining oneself through conflict with society, it is helpful if the educational institutions with which the adolescent must deal remain loyal thorughout the struggle to the task of clarifying the meaning of experience. For him this amounts, after all, to the same thing: one defines oneself by clarifying the meaning of one's experience. As an individual, he is responsible for achieving more clarity than the school can give him; for the school's cultural biases will in any case camouflage many vitally important phenomena and relationships. Each youngster must correct as best he can for the astigmatism induced by social institutions. But if the school is consistent, honest, and sufficiently sophisticated to be aware of important things and coherent about the relations between them, it will be of great assistance in giving the adolescent something on which to build himself.

Adolescents are ill-served by schools which act as melting pots. When they get into a stew, it is best if the stew is like a properly prepared Japanese soup: crystal clear, with the individual qualities of all the odd ingredients preserved; the soft things soft, the tough things tough, the green things green, and the yellow things yellow. From this kind of heterogeneity it is possible to learn something.

In this respect, the high school has been getting worse for years, for society has. It has always devoted itself to the interests of uniformity more than to individuality; but the uniformities used to be more *external* than they are now. I shall not labor this point, which has already been dealt with so thoroughly by Riesman, W. L. Whyte, and many others; but will simply point out that the school today is less a stew pot than a blender. What comes out, when it is functioning effectively, is not merely uniform but bland and creamy; by its very nature inimical to clarity, yet retaining in a form difficult to detect all the hostile or toxic ingredients present in the original mixture.

This is really serious. It is one thing for the schools of a culture to impart to adolescents a distorted picture of reality, seen from a limited point of view, but *clearly.* So long as the school is not simply an agent of propaganda, or psychotic—so long, that is, as what it talks about is really there, even if what it says is much different from the whole truth—it may still contribute effectively to adolescent growth. Adolescents are alive, and the school is not the whole of life; given a consistent, honest, and coherent picture of the world, they can correct for themselves its biases and omissions. But it is quite another thing for the school to limit perception and responsiveness in every direction to what the society can tolerate without discord. Society thereby establishes within its members a cut-off point; no matter what happens, they do not see too much, get too involved, or try to overthrow the system.

This is happening increasingly in our schools; though nobody intends that it should—in principle, that is; the school staff do intend that it should in particular instances. When a specific conflict arises, the school almost automatically seeks to *mediate* rather than to clarify. It assesses the power of the conflicting interests, works out a compromise among them, and keeps its name out of the papers. The loyalty oath is accepted with gentle chidings about singling out teachers for undue suspicion; *The Merchant of Venice* is omitted from the reading list in favor of something just as good in which all the Jewish characters are pleasant; the aggressive candidate for student council member is quietly barred from office on grounds of emotional immaturity.

We do not know that universal education can retain a commitment to clarity; being in the business, I am sometimes skeptical of it myself. The problem is one of dignity. We have had in all history no experience of any society in which a large proportion of the members could take a good, hard look at life without breaking and running. The examined life has always been pretty well confined to a privileged class. Liberal thought has held that this confinement was deliberate: the members of the privileged class knew that knowledge was power, and excluded those subordinate to them so as to maintain the existing inequities. Liberal thought was here based on sound observation. But it was inclined to overlook certain converse processes.

The most important privilege of a privileged class is freedom from some of the vicissitudes of fortune. Its members are running the show and can divert much that is disagreeable elsewhere. It is often easier, therefore, for them to be honest with themselves about what they see and about what it portends. They can afford to be; they have to be if they are not to lose control, and control is important to them. Ruling classes differ, of course, in the degree to which they understand this and can bear to go on understanding it. De Tocqueville, standing at the point of no return in history, noticed that the *ancien régime français* had forgotten it, and that we had not learned it. Most elites do forget it, and become convinced that destiny, rather than equestrian skill, is keeping them in the saddle. Their members can be distinguished in historical engravings by the hoofprints in the small of their backs.

With respect to this issue, our expectations of education are mixed and conflicting. Our public-school system was not designed to nurture an elite—just the contrary; it was designed to train the boys who would work uncomplainingly in its mills and vote unquestioningly for its measures. The school, by and large, is still devoted to the twin ideals of success and contentment, though it pursues them with greater technical sophistication. But our cultural tradition is a lot broader than our school system, and is less purely pragmatic. It is slightly Hellenistic, a good deal more British, and in any case humanistic and Western. Whether we want to or not, when we think of education—rather than of what school was really like—we think of a process which is expected to prepare the young to accede as well as to succeed. Educators like Robert Hutchins have maintained that democracy demands just this view of public education because in it every man must behave as a ruler of men.

This seems to me rather fanciful, because what actually happens in a modern democratic state seems to be abdication of popular sovereignty in favor of an equally undistinguished and ephemeral ruling clique. But this does not erase the connection, established in our minds by a hardy tradition of our culture, between education and a large measure of responsibility, detachment, and discipline.

In this tradition the common man, exposed as he is to economic, social, and personal pressures, has never fully shared. That, given the opportunity, he would consent to do so is merely an educated guess. He has not yet received the protections of status and property on which the tradition was based; these, or their equivalent, are only now being devised in the form of a less completely material conception of the welfare state in which new social forms guarantee leisure and continued high-level economic security rather than bare survival.

And more widely applicable sources of security and status also lead to a clearer sense of self. *Lucky Jim* is just as trustworthy and really just as brave as Archdeacon Grantly, as well as a great deal more human. But he is far less sure of himself; he cannot count on his nerves and judgment as well in a threatening situation, and situations have much more power to threaten him. He is more vulnerable; he has a much shorter lease on life.

The modern school, then, serves people who lack the protections enjoyed by those who taught us what to expect of an educated class. It is also staffed by people who are, in fact, vulnerable to public opinion and dependent on the approval and support of their colleagues, even in matters of detail, in order to be effective. We cannot be sure that they will ever feel free themselves, or accept any large measure of responsibility to teach youngsters to examine what they are learning against the criteria of their own values, traditions, and experience of life. It may be that we cannot expect them to analyze experience sharply, and tell the truth about what the analysis reveals.

It is difficult to put what we feel to be wrong into words, and we very often use the wrong ones. We complain that standards are too low; yet research report after research report confirms that students, by and large, are learning more rather than less

of the kind of fact and simple skill on which schools convention-
ally base their claim. We feel that the students are getting lazier;
but they seem to work hard, and the worst of all often work the
hardest of all; they voluntarily assail the teacher with volumes of
mediocrity because, they say, they want to raise their grade. Students who do badly in a course frequently argue that they should
have a higher mark because what they did took them so long.
We feel the students are duller, and it is true that the public
school reaches students of lower ability than it was formerly able
to enroll. But it is not they who are the focus of public concern;
in fact it is precisely with them that the school often does its most
clearly professional and original work. We feel that the students
are less disciplined, and are here a little closer to the mark. But it
is an inner discipline that is lacking; the school fails to provide a
basis for it. The undisciplined behavior which sometimes results
is often a sign of the anguish which results from having no core of
one's own.

Standards are unsatisfactory, not because they are low, but because they are fragmentary and incoherent. They exist, and to
the extent that they exist, they add to the general confusion. The
academic curriculum consists of shards of a predemocratic academic culture; relics of a way of life in which many of the people
who had gone through school read poetry for fun, spelled properly
and wrote cogently because they sometimes worked on public
documents, spoke French correctly and fluently because they occasionally had to communicate as equals with civilized Frenchmen.
Their schools were technically far worse than ours; the teachers
untrained in the special concerns of education, usually unimagina-
tive and occasionally brutal. But in that culture, as in ours, the
students were quick to learn what made sense in relation to
their view of themselves and their social role, either with the
school's help or despite it.

The problem today is to determine what does make sense in
terms of one's view of oneself and one's social role. Our schools
are socially heterogeneous, and deeply riven by discontinuities of
experience between the staff, the students, and those earlier individuals who wrote the major works and participated in the
events with which the curriculum must deal. Between the high-

school staff and the street corner boy there is no common ground. Between the high-school staff and Shakespeare there is not likely to be much common ground either. If Sir John Falstaff can only reach the corner boy—who would find him very meaningful—by passing through the high school, he is pretty sure to get lost on the way.

This social heterogeneity is not simply a matter of incongruous courses of study and students with very diverse cultural backgrounds. These would be, as they are commonly thought to be, unique strengths of our system, if only the school had a philosophical structure by which to order them—not into a hierarchy, but according to the existing and potential relationships among them and a coherent set of values. A school having white and Negro students ought to be able, for example—if it is sustained by a conception of democracy that is both profound and sophisticated —to make use of the problems attending desegregation as a living exercise in American social democracy as it actually is. This would require intense historical scholarship and keen and detached sociological analysis. But neither the teachers nor the students are usually capable of either; faced with so controversial an issue they would more likely panic when they found that they lacked the necessary scholarly skills and discipline, and each would run to his particular pressure group to try to get his story in first.

The social changes of the past century have been diastrophic in magnitude; they have produced faulting in several different planes. Growth and education, which depend on continuity of meaning, are likely to be suddenly arrested by running into social groups or institutions—within the school as well as outside it—which are *intrusive* in every sense of the word and which, developmentally speaking, ought not to be there at all. Parents intercede directly with the principal or even the school board to get their children grades high enough to admit them to an Ivy League college. The janitor becomes a channel for gossip that originates among the he-men of the vocational departments as they play poker in the boiler room.[2] Neighbors, peeping through the

2. Wilbur B. Brookover, *A Sociology of Education* (New York: American Book Co., 1955), pp. 196-202.

lace curtains of their parlors, complain that students are walking to school in Bermuda shorts just as if they came from rich homes. Student publications are scanned by committees of self-styled mothers, and textbooks and syllabi by committees of self-appointed patriots, for signs of heterodoxy. Teachers who pride themselves on their toughness indignantly whisper that young Mr. So-and-so who cannot keep order in class ought not to be given tenure; and that the principal, if he ever fails to support them after they have mishandled a problem of discipline, does not know how to run a school. Nobody is ever told not to interfere in matters he does not understand.

This lack of philosophical structure I should judge to be the chief obstacle to the development of high-school curricula which would use our best cultural resources to help students make sense out of the lives they actually lead. The resources are there. One really has to be a cultural snob or a professional alarmist to feel that American arts are barren today. Our poetry is good; our ballet may well be the best in the world; we have excellent literary critics, and they have excellent critics of their own; the *Partisan Review* snaps at the *New Yorker* with the colorful fury of a moray eel attacking a parrotfish. The novel is said to be dying, and it is perhaps a clumsy form in which to attack the existential problems of contemporary life; but it is also extremely broad in scope. Every social level, every sort of human and administrative relationship now receives serious treatment in respectable literary work. The social sciences are not so flourishing; work expressing the seminal ideas of a reflective and experienced specialist has yielded prominence to the teamwork of well-financed committees. But this is comprehensive and disciplined enough to yield insights useful to adolescents, even if not very original or individualized. The natural sciences seem to have abdicated the responsibility for commenting on the meaning of human existence, which they discharged enthusiastically through Einstein's lifetime, and this is a real loss, for only science can hope to keep technology in some sort of moral order. Still, there is quite a lot to work with.

American artists and intellectuals are addressing themselves competently to a very wide range of issues deeply relevant to modern life. But the schools no longer accept intellectual and humanistic authority. The prestige of the intellectual and artist in America is not as low as intellectuals and artists feel; in fact, it is quite high. Nevertheless, they are merely one of the heterogeneous components of American social life. Most school personnel would probably agree; if the statement were made to them, that the function of the humanities is to illuminate life. But they have not grown up with any personal experience of using the humanities for this purpose; and they enthusiastically or apathetically mishandle them. They fear that students will find passages too difficult, and assume that it is the artist's job to say no more than can be easily understood. They fear that the American Legion or a Catholic action group will object to the implications of other passages, and they also fear that they themselves will be called censors; so rather than suppress a work, they set up committees to *edit* it and forestall any possible objections. They note details which they regard as errors from the viewpoint of their own special interests and pounce upon them; if the administration clears Ibsen's *Ghosts* with the PTA by warning it that *Ghosts* is a classic and can therefore be allowed to deal with venereal disease, the chairman of the biology department will be noisily unhappy because it deals with venereal disease inaccurately.

The staff and the students may approve of the use of materials which, if properly handled, would clarify the meaning of modern experience. They approve of most advances. But their total experience of life has not fitted them to use the best of these materials with respect for their properties. They are like a housewife who enjoys hearing about what the science of nutrition can do for her family, but who has no interest in learning what vitamins are destroyed by heat and which minerals are washed out by boiling. It is up to God and Birdseye to put these things in so they will survive any short cuts she may take.

Unlike the housewife, the school is apt to accept considerable responsibility for the solution of technical and methodological problems. But it cannot apply this sense of technical responsibility to the problem of maintaining meanings in its curriculum. It has no sense of texture or structure with reference to meanings, and is likely to be antagonized by any difficulties it encounters, recognizing in them a residual implication of social inferiority. The school may get as far as translating the problem of meaning into the problem of communication; that is, the problem of determining what may be said or done in the school that can be understood by a maximum number of very different students with a minimum of effort. It is not likely to get much further, or to have a sympathetic understanding of how its quest for simplicity rather than meaning reduces its power to clarify the lives of students.

It is easy to mistake the urgent technical difficulties of teaching a heterogeneous student group for the moral and development problems, less urgent and far more serious, which it creates; it is easy to solve the former expediently and evade the latter. Some of the youngsters, for example, are juvenile delinquents or are growing up in slums; they may have become a threat to the manners and morals of more decorous middle-class boys and girls. Some of them have begun thinking and reading in the classroom, and are making the others feel inferior. A teacher, threatened with a switchblade knife, fears at the very least a certain loss of face. Undoubtedly, something must be done about it.

But just what must be done ought to be determined by the school's perception of its function. The problem of preventing a boy from slashing up a teacher is not so simple morally. A juvenile delinquent and a middle-class teacher are incompatible; yet the school is supposed to be able to guide itself by its own purposes, and the human relationship between boy and teacher is its most powerful instrument for achieving its purposes. If the main purpose of the school is to clarify the meaning of experience, its response must do a good deal more than protect the teacher. It must convey to the boy the school's determination to maintain order in its own house; its respect for boys as human beings; its anger at him for having abused that respect in this instance; and its sense of the provocation to which slum boys are sometimes subjected by middle-class behavior. It must convey to the teacher confidence that he will be supported in his role and an awareness that he has probably been playing it badly. It must get the boy and the teacher working together again on the development of the boy as a human being.

The school may do it, too; it will certainly try, and this is greatly to its credit. The American school system has come to conceive itself, in principle and on a very wide scale, as something more than a law-enforcement agency when confronted with student behavior that it cannot accept. The school is now likely to see youngsters who break its regulations as the victims of a maladjustment in the relationship between it and themselves, rather than as miscreants to be punished. It very often applies this point of view sentimentally and has been subjected to a great deal of derision for adopting it. It frequently fails to live up to this view in practice, because in practice the school usually assumes that it is the *youngster,* rather than the relationship or the school itself, that needs to be readjusted. But the viewpoint must, in my judgment, be accepted as one of the few major advances in decency that the twentieth century can justly claim.

The difficulty is that the school seldom goes about applying it with enough dignity and self-confidence to help the student in defining himself. Its motives are weighted toward administrative expedience rather than toward awareness of what is going on in the youngster and respect for what he is and what he may become, even though these more humane motives are now stronger than in the past. Where a full human response to him would previously have been blocked by arrogance, rigidity, and punitiveness, it is now blocked by status anxiety, manipulativeness, and the absence of a firm habit of respect for individuality of any kind. The school has lost confidence in its authority to maintain order, and has specially trained experts to crawl inside the miscreant, exorcise him from himself, and engineer his consent to its guidance. But even a boy who pulls a knife on a teacher—the action is actually rather rare—is entitled to respect for his privacy and some security against invasion. He may need counseling; he may need a formal and effective paddling; he may need a little money and a decent job; he may need glasses and a longer knife. But he does not need to be treated as a problem in social integration. Nobody does.

Yet the school attacks the problems of self-definition in a heterogeneous student group as if they were problems in social integration. Integration is the only attack a school that works like a blender can take; no matter how hard it tries, the problem of preserving the integrity of individual experience is beyond it. This is the approach to morality that grows out of our cultural situation. The most important social process taking place in the high school is learning to be an American. But so much of learning to be an American is learning not to let your individuality become a nuisance. We conceive our country as having achieved a position of leadership and dominance by carefully subordinating personal and ethnic disparity to the interests of teamwork in a colossal technical and administrative enterprise. For us, conformity is a moral mandate. When we insist on taking a personal stand and bucking the system, we feel not only anxious, but guilty as well.

Much as the American tendency to conformity has been emphasized recently, this point, it seems to me, has been understressed. We do conform, but not primarily (as is supposed) because of fear and alienation. There is a strong positive element in our conformity; we do not merely huddle together in little smug or frightened clusters. One has only to watch a committee at work to see that consensus is regarded as a good thing in itself, and intransigence a bad one. The members are eager to accept one another's point of view; awkward data are dismissed, not cynically, but as an act of public spirit. The old joke about a statesman needing the ability to rise above principle turns out to be no joke; an individual who cannot is made to feel as willfully self-indulgent as a timid courtesan in an old, established house.

We are an obsessively moral people, but our morality is a team morality. What is good for the team is good for the player; fair play means playing according to the rules and asking for[3] no special advantage. It is important to win, but the passions of victory must not lead to personal pride, the passions of defeat to personal anger or permanent resentment.

On the team, individual differences must be minimized. "Who cares about his race, religion, or national origin—he can pitch!" baseball players constantly exhort one another; so, at least,

3. Cf. Chapter 8, "Reflections on the American Identity," of Erik Homburger Erikson's *Childhood and Society* (New York: Norton, 1950) for a most insightful exposition of this point.

the posters of the Mayor's Council Against Discrimination proclaim. Yet, discrimination seems an odd thing to be against. One would like to suppose that Jews and Negroes are now admitted to the local chapters of an increasing number of college fraternities because these have finally adopted a policy of *greater* discrimination rather than less, and are basing their discrimination on factors of greater immediate relevance to what a boy could contribute to fraternity life—possibly through the very differences in character and personality that stem from his unusual race, religion, or national origin. This, in fact, is probably what *is* happening, but we dislike putting it so, even though confidence that differences enrich is a basic article of liberal faith. It is no article of American faith. We know what "discrimination" means in our language, and it does not mean sensitivity to significant differences.

Or perhaps it does, and this is what we are against. Our melting pot really works, and even the most stupid and vicious of us is beginning to believe that race no longer refers to any meaningful heritage, that Jews share nothing significant in Judaism. This is integration with a vengeance, and a victory for democracy to delight the heart of the bitterest anti-Semite. The exotic toxins have been almost all absorbed, denatured, removed from the robust bloodstream of American life. America's rugged institutions have been too much for them altogether. They are lost, assimilated; and no organ of society has done so much to assimilate them as the school system.

The process of becoming an American, as it goes on in high school, tends to be a process of renunciation of differences. This conflicts directly, of course, with the adolescent need for self-definition; but the conflict is so masked in institutionalized gaiety that the adolescent himself usually does not become aware of it. He must still deal with the alienation it engenders. He may do this by marginal differentiation, like Riesman's glad-handing boy with the special greeting style.[4] He may do it by erupting into bouts of occasionally violent silliness, which does not make

---

4. David Riesman, in collaboration with Reuel Denney and Nathan Glazer, *The Lonely Crowd* (New Haven: Yale University Press, 1950), p. 82.

him seem queer to other people because it is unconsciously recognized as a form of self-abnegation rather than self-assertion, and is not, therefore, threatening. He may, if he has sufficient ego-strength, become the adolescent equivalent of a genuine revolutionary—rather than a rebel—that is, he may actually succeed in rejecting the folkways of the school without identifying with them and becoming guilty and raucous; he can then replace them with constructive patterns of behavior based on his own homemade values. This is a position which may lead to the growth of a splendid human being, but one which imposes a considerable strain on the boy.

In any case, he is unlikely to get much help from the school's routines. The constant attention to his adjustment; the ratings on cooperativeness and citizenship; the informal but virtually universal policy of limiting the number of failing grades in each class, which undercuts the meaning of competence in the classroom; the mock democratic institutions for student government and student discipline with their committees, juries, and rather studied use of informality to weaken any possible effort he might make to stand on his rights—all these work against him. On his side he has a variable number of factors: possibly a residual academic tradition in certain teachers that leads them to respect his competence; possibly a real evolving political competence of his own that makes him something of an adolescent statesman; possibly a family which is not sympathetic to "groupsy" values; possibly himself. Some youngsters resist standardization very well.

So much for Americanization. The other three social functions of the school also play very important parts in the clarification of experience. The next I mentioned, in order of importance, was the school's role in the distribution of status: in teaching students that they ought to want to get ahead in the world, how to go about doing it, what the terms are on which it can be done. Obviously, the process involves many value-assumptions and conscious and unconscious responses to subtle social cues; it therefore bears on the meaning of experience very fundamentally. However, this process is directly relevant to another aspect of adolescent growth—the establishment of a basis for self-esteem—which I shall treat in the next chapter. We shall look at this function more closely then.

I have already briefly considered certain relationships of the next of these social processes to the clarification of experience. This is the function we commonly mean by education: formal instruction in the natural and social sciences and the humanities —the impact of the school's course of study itself. I have said that this works rather better than it usually gets credit for, and that the most difficult obstruction to the school's use of major cultural resources for the clarification of experience is that the school is now so socially heterogeneous. A large proportion of the students and staff come from social groups in which the authority of the mind and its work is simply not accepted. From the arts they expect diversion and decoration; from the sciences the solution to technical problems; they demand these quickly and under all conditions without back talk. They have had no experience of the arts and sciences as elucidators of life, and mishandle and emasculate them in such a way that their power to serve is impaired or destroyed. Even though the arts now address themselves with profound respect and reduced sentimentality to the experiences of the common life, and the sciences consider its dynamics in detail, the school still regards them in practice as essentially external devices and adornments.

We are, of course, a sufficiently barbarous people to delight in both devices and adornments, so the curriculum includes an enormous lot of good things and handles them with a commendable if superficial sophistication. I suspect it will be a long time before an American high-school drama club performs *Aaron Slick of Punkin Crick* again. *No Exit* is in every way superior; it takes only four actors and one set, and Sartre has *cachet*. The youngsters and the school, in fact, enjoy the complex moral message of the play. It teaches us that in death as in life people who want to get along must cooperate; it teaches us that Hell is like a bad hotel; heaven, by contrast, is probably very much like the Caribe Hilton, with lots of charming, well-to-do people around the pool. Sartre shows keen insight into the moral problems of our day; and the school by producing him shows its courageous determination to grapple with them.

There are listening rooms and good record collections from which a high-school student can learn to appreciate music and consume it intelligently. There is the band, which doubles in brass as a social organization, lends color to athletic spectacles, keeps in time to the drum majorettes, and teaches everybody the value of teamwork. It appears in public, and it sounds good. There are classes in painting and sculpture with excellent Kodachrome slides of classical and contemporary masterpieces; in their own work, the school encourages the students to be creative, which means at least undisciplined but sometimes something more.

Students participate in seminars on all kinds of current social and scientific problems, sometimes carried on the local TV. These ought surely to lead to clarity and understanding, for rigorous precautions are taken. Books on the subject are discussed in class prior to the seminar; not usually the books with most to say, but those most suited to the student's level of reading comprehension. The organizers of the seminar are careful to see that everyone participates, and that all possible points of view are given equal time. There is a mediator, whose function is to continually focus the discussion, which means to demonstrate that the participants are not in fundamental disagreement; and to summarize the main points that have emerged, thus demonstrating that progress has been made toward more agreement. There is usually even a resource person who has been selected because he knows something about the topic and cautioned to keep his comments neutral and factual so that no biases will be introduced. There is no actual rehearsal, which would not be fair; but none is needed since the procedure is similar in practice and identical in its underlying assumptions to the daily procedures of the classroom.

In this way, the very concept of intellectual authority derived from competence and insight is prevented from ever becoming established. No educated person, recalling those steps in his education of which he was conscious, would hit on anything remotely like this. Schools may never have done much to further clarity of mind, though they have seldom in the past systematically sought to derive authority by pooling the viewpoints of persons incompetent to testify on the questions at issue. But the schools cannot forestall clarity altogether. All education is ultimately self-education, and it occurs even under quite adverse circumstances. Clear-minded adolescents do emerge, not unwillingly, from the American high school.

The last social function I attributed to the school—and, to an even greater degree, the college—was that of serving as an administrative center in which a dossier is compiled on each student's health, character, personality, and predilection for social action. This, since it is done as inconspicuously as possible and often by utter stealth, might seem to have little influence on the school's contribution to the clarification of the adolescent's experience. Actually it has an enormous—often a decisive—effect.

The school uses its student records as a basis for dealing with individuals and agencies outside the school. What goes into them determines, of course, the school's recommendations to prospective employers and the answers it gives to security agents. The information that it gives about what it regards as maturity or emotional stability, or about the student's political attitudes if he dared to develop any, can set his career back for a decade. Students—perhaps fortunately—are well aware of this and correspondingly cautious and skeptical about making use of the school's services. I have seldom heard, except at a performance of *Faust*, laughter as sardonic as that with which a student assembly greeted a recent statement by an apologist for their school's guidance service that "Security agents are *not* permitted access to our files—only to a summary of the relevant material in them." The statement, incidentally, was quite true, though not quite reassuring.

Schools, too, are aware that this is a problem, and "Confidentiality of student records" is frequently on the agenda of personnel groups.[5] But their discussions tend to center on externals: on whether the school can maintain viable public relations if it

---

5. "Students Wary of Psychiatrists," a special report by Emma M. Harrison to *The New York Times* of October 24, 1956, of an address by Dr. Orville Rogers, former director of the Yale University Department of University Health to the annual Mental Health Forum of New York State.

gets a reputation for not cooperating with the FBI or its local equivalent; whether students are being frightened away altogether and reducing the case load on which budgets ultimately depend; or, more piously, on just where the moral responsibility of the school lies in a conflict of interest between student and society.

I am much more worried about the effect on the student's inner life and emotional dynamics. By permitting agencies outside the student-counselor relationship to use its records, the school strikes at the very roots of clarity and growth. It invades the unconscious and disrupts the processes by which meanings are organized there by throwing up barriers of anxiety against self-understanding. That it has made it dangerous for the student to deal honestly with it is shameful, but not frightening; that it has made it dangerous for the student to deal honestly with himself is alarming; for to make unconscious processes dangerous is to forestall them. For example, a courageous boy who has come to feel that he has been drinking too much—and needs help badly—may be able by conscious effort to force himself to go to the therapist, even though he knows that this may stain his record; he is a person, and he makes a choice. But if one major factor in his excessive drinking is repressed homosexual longing —as in our culture, among young men, it often is—he probably will not be able to get the help he needs, because his perfectly realistic anxiety about revealing this to the school will keep him from becoming conscious of it himself and making it accessible to therapy.

This is tragic. Many schools have interrupted the development of one of their most valuable and rapidly developing areas of service to students in order to set themselves up as Little Brother and Junior G-Man. The incidence of serious emotional disturbance in American life is high, and it is high among adolescents. The old name for schizophrenia, after all, was *dementia praecox,* which referred to the frequency with which gross symptoms of alienation tended to appear precociously—in adolescence rather than at a later age. This is evidence not that adolescents are emotionally unstable, but that in adolescence a human being is crucially devoted to building a stable and consistent self, and that any latent difficulties are likely to show themselves dramatically.

The anxieties of modern life have certainly not made adolescence any easier and a large proportion of individual boys and girls do need professional help with problems of emotional development. The school is the logical place to give such help, if it can be arranged; it involves least disruption of the youngster's routine of life and least dramatization of his plight, which not only saves him pain and embarrassment but keeps the therapeutic process more effectively tied, as it should be, to the daily realities of living.

There has not been very much the school could do until recently, because there were no psychotherapeutic procedures that could safely be undertaken by nonmedical personnel, or that in any case were not so protracted, costly, and completely individualized as to be unfeasible for more than a handful of students. But this is no longer true. Individual psychoanalysis is still the therapy most clinicians would recommend for a very sick youngster, and it is still unavailable to most. But there have been two developments which have proved most helpful in the school situation, which require neither medically trained personnel nor a protracted series of individual sessions. These are the client-centered psychotherapy, developed by Carl Rogers and his associates over the past decade, which is designed to give considerable help in relatively few sessions; and various techniques of group psychotherapy, client-centered and other, which permit a skilled clinician to help a reasonable number of quite disturbed individuals—say, ten—at the same time, and to help them to help one another.

Client-centered and group psychotherapists must be carefully trained professional people; but they need not be physicians, and it is customary for them to accept appointments to the staffs of schools, school systems, or educational clinics. But their services to students are as fully dependent as those of a psychoanalyst on mutual trust between therapist and client and on unconcious processes. The unconscious processes in therapy are themselves dependent on this trust. There is no question of will involved; if the client fears or distrusts the therapist—quite a different matter from disliking him—fruitful associations and insights simply do not occur. Whatever we may, as good Freudians, think of our Censor, we must agree that it tries to protect us when it can; that is what it is for.

It is therefore usually impossible for a disturbed adolescent to accept any help, even if he is willing to risk it, from a therapist who may be building up a dossier against him. The session must be confidential; the student must be certain that his material will be used by others, at most, purely for research and in disguised form. School principals and deans who permit their personnel records to be used for administrative or security purposes find that they are no longer really offering a therapeutic service of which students can effectively avail themselves, even though they wish to regard this as still their major function.

Then, those students to whom the clarification of experience has become a mortal necessity are beyond the help of the school, cut off by the school's choice to add yet one more to its diverse group of public functions. To argue that the school is obligated to provide the agencies of legitimate government with personal information about its students because it is itself a public agency seems to me vicious nonsense. The school has indeed an obligation to society: to provide all the resources it can in support of the necessary intellectual and moral growth of future citizens. The record of the American school in this respect has been most seriously marred by the frequency with which it has willingly set its responsibility aside in order to perform a minor chore for the community or for influential private groups, from the maintenance of athletic spectacles to blood drives. But it might at least have drawn the line at serving as a police spy.

Perhaps the political realities seldom permit the school to maintain the privacy of its students against local vigilance or governmental agents of inquiry. But one cannot have much familiarity with American public education and retain the belief that this is the fundamental reason why the school so often does not maintain it. There is seldom much desire to, much conviction that it ought to be maintained. What is most seriously lacking is not merely courage but dignity. There is no sense of one's own business and the propriety of minding it; no professional pride in the legitimate restriction of the school's function to its own professional responsibilities such as any physician must have if he is to walk through a patient's home without reading the mail on his desk.

All schools appraise their students; if the appraisal deals with competence and character, which are the school's legitimate responsibility, it is obligated to do so. The high school must obviously inform the college candidly of its judgment of an applicant's chances for a successful college career, whether or not this blasts his hopes of admission; otherwise the college cannot accurately select students who can profitably use its services. It must give prospective employers a candid judgment as to whether a student can be trusted to do a job well. It is true that personality is now demonstrably a more important influence on subsequent success than competence, and that we must now live in an ideologically divided world. It may be argued, then, that the school is merely being realistic in including personality, social, and political attitudes in its appraisal. Have not these greater bearing on the decisions that must be made about the student than his mathematical aptitude, grade-point average, or his ability to perform work undertaken consistently and responsibly?

No doubt. But it is precisely the need to live in a world in which one is judged more by personality than by character, more by flexibility than competence, that fragments adolescent experience and injures the growing boy or girl. The dossier-building school contributes to their difficulties and betrays its primary responsibility to the growth of students as human beings free to feel and think as deeply as their experience of life permits, with no more anxiety or constraint than can be avoided.

The record of the school as a contributor to the clarification of the meaning of the adolescent life is, in the balance, poor. Its specific consequences seem to me usually negative. Good is done, too; but almost because things are not working quite right. The system falters: and scholarly teachers, warmly understanding and professionally oriented counselors, appear and sustain themselves on the satisfactions of their work till their colleagues catch them at it. Pockets of privacy develop, in informal groups and minor clubs and organizations, and deeply felt relations between persons develop in them. High standards of competence are set in certain areas like sports or stagecraft, or in courses dealing with deep concerns of adolescents, because the youngsters will settle for nothing less.

Perhaps the best that can be said for the school in this respect is that it is passively lavish. It provides much good equipment and efficient administrative organization; it brings all the youngsters together and provides them a social role as students that is neutral and acceptable. If they are gifted, spontaneous, emotionally responsive, and genuinely interested in their relationship to what goes on around them, the school will like them none the better. But it nevertheless gives them a great deal to work with.

III. THE HIGHER LEARNING

THE HIGHER LEARNING Promise

My Pedagogic Creed

JOHN DEWEY
(1859–1952)

The School and Society, 1900
The Child and the Curriculum, 1902
Experience and Nature, 1926
Art as Experience, 1932

JOHN DEWEY is universally ranked among the two or three most significant American philosophers. He may indeed be the most original philosopher we have produced; certainly, his speculations have influenced people on every level of our society. Extended, expanded and applied, his insights about "doing and learning" have been the theoretical basis for what is called "Progressive Education." In debates about the state of our schools, he is still cited both as hero and villain.

Article I—*What Education Is*

I BELIEVE THAT

—ALL EDUCATION PROCEEDS BY THE PARTICIPATION OF THE individual in the social consciousness of the race. This process begins unconsciously almost at birth, and is continually shaping the individual's powers, saturating his consciousness, forming his habits, training his ideas, and arousing his feelings and emotions. Through this unconscious education the individual gradually comes to share in the intellectual and moral resources which humanity has succeeded in getting together. He becomes an inheritor of the funded capital of civilization. The most formal and technical education in the world cannot safely depart from this general process. It can only organize it or differentiate it in some particular direction.

My Pedagogic Creed, Washington, D. C.: The Progressive Education Association. First published in 1897.

—the only true education comes through the stimulation of the child's powers by the demands of the social situations in which he finds himself. Through these demands he is stimulated to act as a member of a unity, to emerge from his original narrowness of action and feeling, and to conceive of himself from the standpoint of the welfare of the group to which he belongs. Through the responses which others make to his own activities he comes to know what these mean in social terms. The value which they have is reflected back into them. For instance, through the response which is made to the child's instinctive babblings the child comes to know what those babblings mean; they are transformed into articulate language, and thus the child is introduced into the consolidated wealth of ideas and emotions which are now summed up in language.

—this educational process has two sides—one psychological and one sociological—and that neither can be subordinated to the other, or neglected, without evil results following. Of these two sides, the psychological is the basis. The child's own instincts and powers furnish the material and give the starting-point for all education. Save as the efforts of the educator connect with some activity which the child is carrying on of his own initiative independent of the educator, education becomes reduced to a pressure from without. It may, indeed, give certain external results, but cannot truly be called educative. Without insight into the psychological structure and activities of the individual, the educative process will, therefore, be haphazard and arbitrary. If it chances to coincide with the child's activity it will get a leverage; if it does not, it will result in friction, or disintegration, or arrest of the child nature.

—knowledge of social conditions, of the present state of civilization, is necessary in order properly to interpret the child's powers. The child has his own instincts and tendencies, but we do not know what these mean until we can translate them into their social equivalents. We must be able to carry them back into a social past and see them as the inheritance of previous race activities. We must also be able to project them into the future to see what their outcome and end will be. In the illustration just used, it is the ability to see in the child's babblings the promise and potency of a future social intercourse and conversation which enables one to deal in the proper way with that instinct.

—the psychological and social sides are organically related, and that education cannot be regarded as a compromise between the two, or a superimposition of one upon the other. We are told that the psychological definition of education is barren and formal—that it gives us only the idea of a development of all the mental powers without giving us any idea of the use to which these powers are put. On the other hand, it is urged that the social definition of education, as getting adjusted to civilization, makes of it a forced and external process, and results in subordinating the freedom of the individual to a preconceived social and political status.

—each of these objections is true when urged against one side isolated from the other. In order to know what a power really is we must know what its end, use, or function is, and this we cannot know save as we conceive of the individual as active in social relationships. But, on the other hand, the only possible adjustment which we can give to the child under existing conditions is that which arises through putting him in complete possession of all his powers. With the advent of democracy and modern industrial conditions, it is impossible to foretell definitely just what civilization will be twenty years from now. Hence it is impossible to prepare the child for any precise set of conditions. To prepare him for the future life means to give him command of himself; it means so to train him that he will have the full and ready use of all his capacities; that his eye and ear and hand may be tools ready to command, that his judgment may be capable of grasping the conditions under which it has to work, and the executive forces be trained to act economically and efficiently. It is impossible to reach this sort of adjustment save as constant regard is had to the individual's own powers, tastes, and interests —that is, as education is continually converted into psychological terms.

In sum, I believe that the individual who is to be educated is a social individual, and that society is an organic union of individuals. If we eliminate the social factor from the child we are left only with an abstraction; if we eliminate the individual factor from society, we are left only with an inert and lifeless mass. Education, therefore, must begin with a psychological insight into the child's capacities, interests, and habits. It must be controlled at every point by reference to these same considerations. These powers, interests, and habits must be continually interpreted—we must know what they mean. They must be translated into terms of their social equivalents—into terms of what they are capable of in the way of social service.

Article II—*What the School Is*

I BELIEVE THAT

—the school is primarily a social institution. Education being a social process, the school is simply that form of community life in which all those agencies are concentrated that will be most effective in bringing the child to share in the inherited resources of the race, and to use his own powers for social ends.

—education, therefore, is a process of living and not a preparation for future living.

—the school must represent present life—life as real and vital to the child as that which he carries on in the home, in the neighborhood, or on the playground.

—that education which does not occur through forms of life, forms that are worth living for their own sake, is always a poor substitute for the genuine reality, and tends to cramp and to deaden.

—the school, as an institution, should simplify existing social life; should reduce it, as it were, to an embryonic form. Existing life is so complex that the child cannot be brought into contact with it without either confusion or distraction; he is either overwhelmed by the multiplicity of activities which are going on, so that he loses his own power of orderly reaction, or he is so stimulated by these various activities that his powers are prematurely called into play and he becomes either unduly specialized or else disintegrated.

—as such simplified social life, the school life should grow gradually out of the home life; that it should take up and continue the activities with which the child is already familiar in the home.

—it should exhibit these activities to the child, and reproduce them in such ways that the child will gradually learn the meaning of them, and be capable of playing his own part in relation to them.

—this is a psychological necessity, because it is the only way of securing continuity in the child's growth, the only way of giving a background of past experience to the new ideas given in school.

—it is also a social necessity because the home is the form of social life in which the child has been nurtured and in connection with which he has had his moral training. It is the business of the school to deepen and extend his sense of the values bound up in his home life.

—much of present education fails because it neglects this fundamental principle of the school as a form of community life. It conceives the school as a place where certain information is to be given, where certain lessons are to be learned, or where certain habits are to be formed. The value of these is conceived as lying largely in the remote future; the child must do these things for the sake of something else he is to do; they are mere preparations. As a result they do not become a part of the life experience of the child and so are not truly educative.

—the moral education centers upon this conception of the school as a mode of social life, that the best and deepest moral training is precisely that which one gets through having to enter into proper relations with others in a unity of work and thought. The present educational systems, so far as they destroy or neglect this unity, render it difficult or impossible to get any genuine, regular moral training.

—the child should be stimulated and controlled in his work through the life of the community.

—under existing conditions far too much of the stimulus and control proceeds from the teacher, because of neglect of the idea of the school as a form of social life.

—the teacher's place and work in the school is to be interpreted from this same basis. The teacher is not in the school to impose certain ideas or to form certain habits in the child, but is there as a member of the community to select the influences which shall affect the child and to assist him in properly responding to these influences.

—the discipline of the school should proceed from the life of the school as a whole and not directly from the teacher.

—the teacher's business is simply to determine, on the basis of larger experience and riper wisdom, how the discipline of life shall come to the child.

—all questions of the grading of the child and his promotion should be determined by reference to the same standard. Examinations are of use only so far as they test the child's fitness for social life and reveal the place in which he can be of the most service and where he can receive the most help.

Article III—*The Subject-Matter of Education*

I BELIEVE THAT

—the social life of the child is the basis of concentration, or correlation, in all his training or growth. The social life gives the unconscious unity and the background of all his efforts and of all his attainments.

—the subject-matter of the school curriculum should mark a gradual differentiation out of the primitive unconscious unity of social life.

—we violate the child's nature and render difficult the best ethical results by introducing the child too abruptly to a number of special studies, of reading, writing, geography, etc., out of relation to this social life.

—the true center of correlation on the school subjects is not science, nor literature, nor history, nor geography, but the child's own social activities.

—education cannot be unified in the study of science, or so-called nature study, because apart from human activity, nature itself is not a unity; nature in itself is a number of diverse objects in space and time, and to attempt to make it the center of work by itself is to introduce a principle of radiation rather than one of concentration.

—literature is the reflex expression and interpretation of social experience; that hence it must follow upon and not precede such experience. It, therefore, cannot be made the basis, although it may be made the summary of unification.

—once more that history is of educative value in so far as it presents phases of social life and growth. It must be controlled by reference to social life. When taken simply as history it is thrown into the distant past and becomes dead and inert. Taken as the record of man's social life and progress it becomes full of meaning. I believe, however, that it cannot be so taken excepting as the child is also introduced directly into social life.

—the primary basis of education is in the child's powers at work along the same general constructive lines as those which have brought civilization into being.

—the only way to make the child conscious of his social heritage is to enable him to perform those fundamental types of activity which make civilization what it is.

—in the so-called expressive or constructive activities as the center of correlation.

—this gives the standard for the place of cooking, sewing, manual training, etc., in the school.

—they are not special studies which are to be introduced over and above a lot of others in the way of relaxation or relief, or as additional accomplishments. I believe rather that they represent, as types, fundamental forms of social activity; and that it is possible and desirable that the child's introduction into the more formal subjects of the curriculum be through the medium of these activities.

—the study of science is educational in so far as it brings out the materials and processes which make social life what it is.

—one of the greatest difficulties in the present teaching of science is that the material is presented in purely objective form, or is treated as a new peculiar kind of experience which the child can add to that which he has already had. In reality, science is of value because it gives the ability to interpret and control the experience already had. It should be introduced, not as so much new subject-matter, but as showing the factors already involved in previous experience and as furnishing tools by which that experience can be more easily and effectively regulated.

—at present we lose much of the value of literature and language studies because of our elimination of the social element. Language is almost always treated in the books of pedagogy simply as the expression of thought. It is true that language is a logical instrument, but it is fundamentally and primarily a social instrument. Language is the device for communication; it is the tool through which one individual comes to share the ideas and feelings of others. When treated simply as a way of getting individual information, or as a means of showing off what one has learned, it loses its social motive and end.

—there is, therefore, no succession of studies in the ideal school curriculum. If education is life, all life has, from the outset, a scientific aspect, an aspect of art and culture, and an aspect of communication. It cannot, therefore, be true that the proper studies for one grade are mere reading and writing, and that at a later grade, reading, or literature, or science, may be introduced. The progress is not in the succession of studies, but in the development of new attitudes towards, and new interests in, experience.

—education must be conceived as a continuing reconstruction of experience; that the process and the goal of education are one and the same thing.

—to set up any end outside of education, as furnishing its goal and standard, is to deprive the educational process of much of its meaning, and tends to make us rely upon false and external stimuli in dealing with the child.

ARTICLE IV—*The Nature of Method*

I BELIEVE THAT

—the question of method is ultimately reducible to the question of the order of development of the child's powers and interests. The law for presenting and treating material is the law implicit within the child's own nature. Because this is so I believe the following statements are of supreme importance as determining the spirit in which education is carried on:

—the active side precedes the passive in the development of the child-nature; that expression comes before conscious impression; that the muscular development precedes the sensory; that movements come before conscious sensations; I believe that consciousness is essentially motor or impulsive; that conscious states tend to project themselves in action.

—the neglect of this principle is the cause of a large part of the waste of time and strength in school work. The child is thrown into a passive, receptive, or absorbing attitude. The conditions are such that he is not permitted to follow the law of his nature; the result is friction and waste.

—ideas (intellectual and rational processes) also result from action and devolve for the sake of the better control of action. What we term reason is primarily the law of orderly or effective action. To attempt to develop the reasoning powers, the powers of judgment, without reference to the selection and arrangement of means in action, is the fundamental fallacy in our present methods of dealing with this matter. As a result we present the child with arbitrary symbols. Symbols are a necessity in mental development, but they have their place as tools for economizing effort; presented by themselves they are a mass of meaningless and arbitrary ideas imposed from without.

—the image is the great instrument of instruction. What a child gets out of any subject presented to him is simply the images which he himself forms with regard to it.

—if nine-tenths of the energy at present directed towards making the child learn certain things were spent in seeing to it that the child was forming proper images, the work of instruction would be indefinitely facilitated.

—much of the time and attention now given to the preparation and presentation of lessons might be more wisely and profitably expended in training the child's power of imagery and in seeing to it that he was continually forming definite, vivid, and growing images of the various subjects with which he comes in contact in his experience.

—interests are the signs and symptoms of growing power. I believe that they represent dawning capacities. Accordingly the constant and careful observation of interests is of the utmost importance for the educator.

—these interests are to be observed as showing the state of development which the child has reached.

—they prophesy the stage upon which he is about to enter.

—only through the continual and sympathetic observation of childhood's interests can the adult enter into the child's life and see what it is ready for, and upon what material it could work most readily and fruitfully.

—these interests are neither to be humored nor repressed. To repress interest is to substitute the adult for the child, and so to weaken intellectual curiosity and alertness, to suppress initiative, and to deaden interest. To humor the interests is to substitute the transient for the permanent. The interest is always the sign of some power below; the important thing is to discover this power. To humor the interest is to fail to penetrate below the surface, and its sure result is to substitute caprice and whim for genuine interest.

—the emotions are the reflex of actions.

—to endeavor to stimulate or arouse the emotions apart from their corresponding activities is to introduce an unhealthy and morbid state of mind.

—if we can only secure right habits of action and thought, with reference to the good, the true, and the beautiful, the emotions will for the most part take care of themselves.

—next to deadness and dullness, formalism and routine, our education is threatened with no greater evil than sentimentalism.

—this sentimentalism is the necessary result of the attempt to divorce feeling from action.

ARTICLE V—*The School and Social Progress*

I BELIEVE THAT

—education is the fundamental method of social progress and reform.

—all reforms which rest simply upon the enactment of law, or the threatening of certain penalities, or upon changes in mechanical or outward arrangements, are transitory and futile.

—education is a regulation of the process of coming to share in the social consciousness; and that the adjustment of individual activity on the basis of this social consciousness is the only sure method of social reconstruction.

—this conception has due regard for both the individualistic and socialistic ideals. It is duly individual because it recognizes the formation of a certain character as the only genuine basis of right living. It is socialistic because it recognizes that this right character is not to be formed by merely individual precept, example, or exhortation, but rather by the influence of a certain form of institutional or community life upon the individual, and that the social organism through the school, as its organ, may determine ethical results.

—in the ideal school we have the reconciliation of the individualistic and the institutional ideals.

—the community's duty to education is, therefore, its paramount moral duty. By law and punishment, by social agitation and discussion, society can regulate and form itself in a more or less haphazard and chance way. But through education society can formulate its own purposes, can organize its own means and resources, and thus shape itself with definiteness and economy in the direction in which it wishes to move.

—when society once recognizes the possibilities in this direction, and the obligations which these possibilities impose, it is impossible to conceive of the resources of time, attention, and money which will be put at the disposal of the educator.

—it is the business of every one interested in education to insist upon the school as the primary and most effective interest of social progress and reform in order that society may be awakened to realize what the school stands for, and aroused to the necessity of endowing the educator with sufficient equipment properly to perform his task.

—education thus conceived marks the most perfect and intimate union of science and art conceivable in human experience.

—the art of thus giving shape to human powers and adapting them to social service is the supreme art; one calling into its service the best of artists; that no insight, sympathy, tact, executive power, is too great for such service.

—with the growth of psychological service, giving added insight into individual structure and laws of growth; and with growth of social science, adding to our knowledge of the right organization of individuals, all scientific resources can be utilized for the purposes of education.

—when science and art thus join hands the most commanding motive for human action will be reached, the most genuine springs of human conduct aroused, and the best service that human nature is capable of guaranteed.

—the teacher is engaged, not simply in the training of individuals, but in the formation of the proper social life.

—every teacher should realize the dignity of his calling; that he is a social servant set apart for the maintenance of proper social order and the securing of the right social growth.

—in this way the teacher always is the prophet of the true God and the usherer in of the true kingdom of God.

After John Dewey, What?

JEROME S. BRUNER
(1915–   )

A Study of Thinking, 1956
The Process of Education, 1960
On Knowing, 1962

JEROME BRUNER, a professor of psychology, has long been interested in how people learn. Now at the Center for Cognitive Studies at Harvard, he is studying memory, perception, thinking and attitude formation, in short, all of the factors involved in learning. The book from which the following essay is taken, *On Knowing,* is subtitled *Essays for the Left hand.* It is the product of an informed and wide-ranging mind which eschews the cant of many professional psychologists. It makes delightful reading.

IN 1897, AT THE AGE OF THIRTY-EIGHT, JOHN DEWEY PUBLISHED a stirring and prophetic work entitled *My Pedagogic Creed.* Much of his later writing on education is foreshadowed in this brief document. Five articles of faith are set forth. The first defines the educational process: "All education proceeds by the participation of the individual in the social consciousness of the race. This process begins unconsciously almost at birth, and is continually shaping the individual's powers, saturating his consciousness, forming his habits, training his ideas, and arousing his feelings and emotions."

The second article of faith embodies Dewey's concept of the school: "Education being a social process, the school is simply that form of community life in which all those agencies are concentrated that will be most effective in bringing the child to share in the inherited resources of the race, and to use his own powers for social ends. Education, therefore, is a process of living and not a preparation for future living." In the third thesis Dewey speaks to the subject matter of education: "The social life of the child is the basis of concentration or correlation in all his training or growth. The social life gives the unconscious unity and the background of all his efforts and all his attainments. . . . The true center . . . is not science, nor literature, nor history, nor geography, but the child's own social activities." A view of educational method gives form to Dewey's fourth article: "The law for presenting and treating material is the law implicit in the child's own nature." For Dewey, the law was that of action: "the active side precedes the passive in the development of the child-nature. I believe that consciousness is essentially motor or impulsive; that conscious states tend to project themselves in action." And, finally, Dewey's fifth thesis: "Education is the fundamental method of social progress and reform."

One reads the document today with mixed feelings. Its optimism is classically American in its rejection of the tragic view of life. It defines truth in the pragmatic spirit: truth is the fruit of inquiry into the consequences of action. It expresses a firm faith not only in the individual's capacity to grow but in society's capacity to shape man in its own best image. The final lines of the creed are these: "Every teacher should realize the dignity of his calling; that he is a social servant set apart for the maintenance of proper social order and the securing of the right social growth. In this way the teacher always is the prophet of the true God and the usherer in of the true kingdom of heaven."

Yet the very wholesomeness—the optimism, the pragmatism, the acceptance of man's harmonious continuity with society— leaves one uneasy. For in the two thirds of a century between 1897 and today, there has been a profound change not only in our conception of nature but also of society and the world of social institutions. Perhaps more important, we have lived through a revolution in our understanding of the nature of man, his intelligence, his capabilities, his passions, and the forms of his growth.

Dewey's thinking reflected the changes, though he was limited by the premises of his philosophical position. But between

Dewey's first premises and our day, there bristles a series of revolutionary doctrines and cataclysmic events that change the very character of the inquiry. Two world wars, the dark episode of Hitler and genocide, the Russian revolution, the relativistic revolution in physics and psychology, the Age of Energy with its new technology, the sardonic reign of skeptical philosophy— all of these have forced a reappraisal of the underlying terms by which we construct a philosophy of education.

Let us then re-examine the terms, guided by what we know today of the world and of human nature. There is matter here, however, that is liable to some misinterpretation and we do well to clear it up at the outset. One writes against the background of one's day. Dewey was writing with an eye to the sterility and rigidity of school instruction in the 1890s—particularly its failure to appreciate the nature of the child. His emphasis upon the importance of direct experience and social action was an implied critique of the empty formalism that did little to relate learning to the child's world of experience. Dewey did mighty service in inspiring a correction. But an excess of virtue is vice. We, in our day, are reconsidering education against the background of such an excess.

Then, too, misunderstanding often converted Dewey's ideas into the sentimental practices he so deplored: "Next to deadness and dullness, formalism and routine," he wrote in his creed, "our education is threatened by no greater evil than sentimentalism." The sentimental cult of "the class project," of "life adjustment" courses, the reluctance to expose the child to the startling sweep of man and nature for fear it might violate the comfortable domain of his direct experience, the cloying concept of "readiness"—these are conceptions about children, often with no experimental support, that are justified in the name of Dewey. His was a noble yet tender view in his time. But what of our times? In what form shall we speak our beliefs?

What education is. Education seeks to develop the power and sensibility of mind. On the one hand, the educational process transmits to the individual some part of the accumulation of knowledge, style, and values that constitutes the culture of a people. In doing so, it shapes the impulses, the consciousness, and the way of life of the individual. But education must also seek to develop the processes of intelligence so that the individual is capable of going beyond the cultural ways of his social world, able to innovate in however modest a way so that he can create an interior culture of his own. For whatever the art, the science, the literature, the history, and the geography of a culture, each man must be his own artist, his own scientist, his own historian, his own navigator. No person is master of the whole culture; indeed, this is almost a defining characteristic of that form of social memory that we speak of as culture. Each man lives a fragment of it. To be whole, he must create his own version of the world, using that part of his cultural heritage he has made his own through education.

In our time, the requirements of technology constrain the freedom of the individual to create images of the world that are satisfying in the deepest sense. Our era has also witnessed the rise of ideologies that subordinate the individual to the defined aims of a society, a form of subordination that is without compassion for idiosyncracy and respects only the instrumental contribution of a man to the progress of the society. At the same time, and in spite of ideologies, man's understanding of himself and of his world—both the natural and social world—has deepened to a degree that warrants calling our age an intellectually golden one. The need is now to employ our deeper understanding not only for the enrichment of society but also for the enrichment of the individual.

It is true, as Dewey said, that all education proceeds by the participation of the individual in the social consciousness of the race, but it is a truth with a double edge. For all education, good and bad alike, is of this order. We know now to what degree this is so. To take but one example, the very language one speaks conditions the style and structure of thought and experience. Indeed, as we have seen, there is reason to believe that thought processes themselves are internalizations of social intercourse, an inner colloquy patterned by early external dialogues. It is this that makes education possible. But education, by giving shape and expression to our experience, can also be the principal instrument for setting limits on the enterprise of mind. The guarantee against limits is the sense of alternatives. Education must, then, be not only a process that transmits culture but also one that provides alternative views of the world and strengthens the will to explore them.

After a half century of startling progress in the psychological sciences, we know that mental health is only a minimum condition for the growth of mind. The tragedy of mental illness is that it so preoccupies the person with the need to fend off realities with which he cannot cope that it leaves him without either the nerve or the zest to learn. But mental health is only a state from which to start: the powers of mind grow with their exercise. Adjustment is too modest an ideal, if it is an ideal at all. Competence in the use of one's powers for the development of individually defined and socially relevant excellence is much more to the point. After a half century of Freud, we know that the freeing of instinct and inclination is not an end in itself but a way station along the road to competence. What is most prophetic for us about Freud in this second half of the century is not his battle against the fetters of rigid moralism, but his formula: "Where there was id, let there be ego."

Education must begin, as Dewey concluded his first article of belief, "with a psychological insight into the child's capacities, interests, habits," but a point of departure is not an itinerary. It is just as mistaken to sacrifice the adult to the child as to sacrifice the child to the adult. It is sentimentalism to assume that the teaching of life can be fitted always to the child's interests just as it is empty formalism to force the child to parrot the formulas of adult society. Interests can be created and stimulated. In this sphere it is not far from the truth to say that supply creates demand, that the provocation of what is available creates response. One seeks to equip the child with deeper, more gripping, and subtler ways of knowing the world and himself.

What the school is. The school is an entry into the life of the mind. It is, to be sure, life itself and not merely a preparation for living. But it is a special form of living, one carefully devised for making the most of those plastic years that characterize the development of *homo sapiens* and distinguish our species from all others. School should provide more than a continuity with the broader community or with everyday experience. It is primarily the special community where one experiences discovery by the use of intelligence, where one leaps into new and unimagined realms of experience, experience that is discontinuous with what went before. A child recognizes this when he first understands what a poem is, or what beauty and simplicity inhere in the idea of the conservation theorems, or that measure is universally applicable. If there is one continuity to be singled out, it is the slow converting of the child's artistic sense of the omnipotence of thought into the realistic confidence in the use of thought that characterizes the effective man.

In insisting upon the continuity of the school with the community on the one side and the family on the other, John Dewey overlooked the special function of education as an opener of new perspectives. If the school were merely a transition zone from the intimacy of the family to the life of the community, it would be a way of life easily enough arranged. In the educational systems of primitive societies, there almost always comes a point, usually at puberty, where there is a sharp change in the life of the boy, marked by a *rite de passage* that establishes a boundary between childhood ways and the ways of the adolescent.

It would be romantic nonsense to pattern our practices upon those found in preliterate societies. I would only ask that we attend to one parallel: education must not confuse the child with the adult and must recognize that the transition to adulthood involves an introduction to new realms of experience, the discovery and exploration of new mysteries, the gaining of new powers.

In the *shtetl* of Eastern Europe, the traditional Jewish ghetto, the scholar was a particularly important figure—the *talmid khokhem*. In his mien, his mode of conversation so rich in allusion, his form of poise, the wise man was the image not of a competent but, rather, of a beautiful person. Traditional Chinese society also had its image of the beautiful person, one who blended knowledge and sentiment and action in a beautiful way of life. The ideal of the gentleman served much the same function in the Europe of the seventeenth and eighteenth centuries. It is perhaps in this spirit that Alfred North Whitehead declared that education must involve an exposure to greatness if it is to leave its mark. For men the yeast of education is the idea of excellence, and that comprises as many forms as there are individuals to develop a personal image of excellence. The school must have as one its principal functions the nurturing of images of excellence.

A detached conception of idealized excellence is not enough. A doctrine of excellence, to be effective, must be translatable into the individual lives of those who come in contact with it. What is compelling about the *talmid khokhem*, the Chinese scholar-administrator, and the eighteenth-century gentleman is that they embody ways of life to which any man can aspire in his own way and from which he can draw in his own style. I believe, then, that the school must also contain men and women who, in their own way, seek and embody excellence. This does not mean that we shall have to staff our schools with men and women of great genius but that the teacher must embody in his own approach to learning a pursuit of excellence. And, indeed, with the technical resources opened by television and its adjuncts, one can present the student and also his teacher with the working version of excellence in its highest sense. In the years ahead, we shall find that the great scholar, scientist, or artist can speak as easily and honestly to the beginner as to the graduate student.

The subject matter of education. The issue of subject matter in education can be resolved only by reference to one's view of the nature of knowledge. Knowledge is a model we construct to give meaning and structure to regularities in experience. The organizing ideas of any body of knowledge are inventions for rendering experience economical and connected. We invent concepts such as force in physics, the bond in chemistry, motives in psychology, style in literature as means to the end of comprehension.

The history of culture is the history of the development of great organizing ideas, ideas that inevitably stem from deeper values and points of view about man and nature. The power of great organizing concepts is in large part that they permit us to understand and sometimes to predict or change the world in which we live. But their power lies also in the fact that ideas provide instruments for experience. Having grown up in a culture dominated by the ideas of Newton, and so with a conception of time flowing equably, we experience time moving inexorably and steadily, marked by a one-way arrow. Indeed, we know now, after a quarter of a century of research on perception, that experience is not to be had directly and neatly, but filtered through the programmed readiness of our senses. The program is constructed with our expectations and these are derived from our models or ideas about what exists and what follows what.

From this, two convictions follow. The first is that the structure of knowledge—its connectedness and the derivations that make one idea follow from another—is the proper emphasis in education. For it is structure, the great conceptual inventions that bring order to the congeries of disconnected observations, that gives meaning to what we may learn and makes possible the opening up of new realms of experience. The second conviction is that the unity of knowledge is to be found within knowledge itself, if the knowledge is worth mastering.

To attempt a justification of subject matter, as Dewey did, in terms of its relation to the child's social activities is to misunderstand what knowledge is and how it may be mastered. The significance of the concept of commutativity in mathematics does not derive from the social insight that two houses with fourteen people in each is not the same as fourteen houses with two people in each. Rather, it inheres in the power of the idea to create a way of thinking about number that is lithe and beautiful and immensely generative—an idea at least as powerful as, say, the future conditional tense in formal grammar. Without the idea of commutativity, algebra would be impossible. If set theory—now often the introductory section in newer curriculums in mathematics—had to be justified in terms of its relation to immediate experience and social life, it would not be worth teaching. Yet set theory lays a foundation for the understanding of order and number that could never be achieved with the social arithmetic of interest rates and bales of hay at so much per bale. Mathematics, like any other subject, must begin with experience, but progress toward abstraction and understanding requires precisely that there be a weaning away from the obviousness of superficial experience.

There is one consideration of cognitive economy, discussed in an earlier chapter, that is paramount. One cannot "cover" any subject in full, not even in a lifetime, if coverage means visiting all the facts and events and morsels. Subject matter presented so as to emphasize its structure will perforce be of that generative kind that permits reconstruction of the details or, at very least, prepares a place into which the details, when encountered, can be put.

What then of subject matter in the conventional sense? The answer to the question, "What shall be taught?" turns out to be the answer to the question, "What is nontrivial?" If one can first answer the question, "What is worth knowing about?" then it is not difficult to distinguish between the aspects of it that are worth teaching and learning and those that are not. Surely, knowledge of the natural world, knowledge of the human condition, knowledge of the nature and dynamics of society, knowledge of the past so that it may be used in experiencing the present and aspiring to the future—all of these, it would seem reasonable to suppose, are essential to an educated man. To these must be added another: knowledge of the products of our artistic heritage that mark the history of our aesthetic wonder and delight.

A problem immediately arises concerning the symbolism in terms of which knowledge is understood and talked about. There is language in its natural sense and language in its mathematical sense. I cannot imagine an educated man a century from now who will not be largely bilingual in this special sense—concise and adept in both a natural language and mathematics. For these two are the tools essential to the unlocking of new experience and the gaining of new powers. As such, they must have a central place in any curriculum.

Finally, it is as true today as it was when Dewey wrote that one cannot foresee the world in which the child we educate will live. Informed powers of mind and a sense of potency in action are the only instruments we can give the child that will be invariable across the transformations of time and circumstance. The succession of studies that we give the child in the ideal school need be fixed in only one way: whatever is introduced, let it be pursued continuously enough to give the student a sense of the power of mind that comes from a deepening of understanding. It is this, rather than any form of extensive coverage, that matters most.

The nature of method. The process and the goal of education are one and the same thing. The goal of education is disciplined understanding; that is the process as well.

Let us recognize that the opposite of understanding is not ignorance or simply "not knowing." To understand something is, first, to give up some other way of conceiving of it. Confusion all too often lies between one way of conceiving and another, better way. It is one of our biological inheritances that confusion produces emergency anxiety, and with anxiety there come the defensive measures—flight, fright, or freezing—that are antithetical to the free and zestful use of mind. The binding fact of mental life in child and adult alike is that there is a limited capacity for processing information—our span, as it is called, can comprise six or seven unrelated items simultaneously. Go beyond that and there is overload, confusion, forgetting. As George Miller has put it, the principle of economy is to fill our seven mental-input slots with gold rather than dross. The degree to which material to be learned is put into structures by the learner will determine whether he is working with gold or dross.

For this reason, as well as for reasons already stated, it is essential that, before being exposed to a wide range of material on a topic, the child first have a general idea of how and where things fit. It is often the case that the development of the general idea comes from a first round of experience with concrete embodiments of ideas that are close to a child's life. The cycle of learning begins, then, with particulars and immediately moves toward abstraction. It comes to a temporary goal when the abstraction can then be used in grasping new particulars in the deeper way that abstraction permits.

Insofar as possible, a method of instruction should have the objective of leading the child to discover for himself. Telling children and then testing them on what they have been told inevitably has the effect of producing bench-bound learners whose motivation for learning is likely to be extrinsic to the task—pleasing the teacher, getting into college, artificially maintaining self-esteem. The virtues of encouraging discovery are of two kinds. In the first place, the child will make what he learns his own, will fit his discovery into the interior world of culture that he creates for himself. Equally important, discovery and the sense of confidence it provides is the proper reward for learning. It is a reward that, moreover, strengthens the very process that is at the heart of education—disciplined inquiry.

The child must be encouraged to get the full benefit from what he learns. This is not to say that he should be required to put it to immediate use in his daily life, though so much the better if he has the happy opportunity to do so. Rather, it is a way of honoring the connectedness of knowledge. Two facts and a relation joining them is and should be an invitation to generalize, to extrapolate, to make a tentative intuitive leap, even to build a tentative theory. The leap from mere learning to using what one has learned in thinking is an essential step in the use of the mind. Indeed, plausible guessing, the use of the heuristic hunch, the best employment of necessarily insufficient evidence—these are activities in which the child needs practice and guidance. They are among the great antidotes to passivity.

Most important of all, the educational process must be free of intellectual dishonesty and those forms of cheating that explain without providing understanding. I have expressed the conviction elsewhere that any subject can be taught to anybody at any age in some form that is honest. It is not honest to present a fifth-grade social-studies class with an image of town government as if it were a den of cub scouts presided over by a parent figure interpreting the charter—even if the image set forth does happen to mesh with the child's immediate social experience. A lie is still a lie—even if it sounds like familiar truth. Nor is it honest to present a sixth-grade science class with a garbled but concrete picture of the atom that is, in its way, as sweeteningly false as the suburban image of town government given them the year before. A dishonest image can only discourage the self-generating intellectual inquiry out of which real understanding grows.

The school and social progress. I believe that education is the fundamental method of social change. Revolutions themselves are no better and are often less good than the ideas they embody and the means invented for their application. Change is swifter in our times than ever before in human history and news of it is almost instantaneous. If we are to be serious in the belief that school must be life itself and not merely preparation for life, then school must reflect the changes through which we are living.

The first implication of this belief is that means must be found to feed back into our schools the ever deepening insights that are developed on the frontiers of knowledge. This is an obvious point in science and mathematics, and continuing efforts are now being instituted to assure that new, more powerful, and often simpler ways of understanding find their way back into the classrooms of our primary and secondary schools. But it is equally important to have this constant refreshment from fields other than the sciences—where the frontiers of knowledge are not always the universities and research laboratories but political and social life, the arts, literary endeavor, and the rapidly changing business and industrial community. Everywhere there is change, and with change we are learning.

I see the need for a new type of institution, a new conception in curriculum. What we have not had and what we are beginning to recognize as needed is something that is perhaps best called an "institute for curriculum studies"—not one of them, but many. Let it be the place where scholars, scientists, men of affairs, and artists come together with talented teachers continually to revise and refresh our curriculums. It is an activity that transcends the limits of any of our particular university faculties—be they faculties of education, arts and science, medicine, or engineering. We have been negligent in coming to a sense of quickening change of life in our time and its implications for the educational process. We have not shared with our teachers the benefits of new discovery, new insight, new artistic triumph. Not only have we operated with the notion of the self-contained classroom but also with the idea of the self-contained school—and even the self-contained educational system.

The Nobel poet or the ambassador to the United Nations, the brilliant cellist or the perceptive playwright, the historian making use of the past or the sociologist seeking a pattern in the present—these men, like the student, are seeking understanding and mastery over new problems. They represent excellence at the frontiers of endeavor. If a sense of progress and change toward greater excellence is to illuminate our schools, there must be a constant return of their wisdom and effort to enliven and inform teacher and student alike. There is no difference in kind between the man at the frontier and the young student at his own frontier, each attempting to understand. Let the educational process be life itself as fully as we can make it.

The Social Value of the College-Bred

WILLIAM JAMES
(1842–1910)

The Principles of Psychology, 1890
The Varieties of Religious Experience, 1902
Pragmatism, 1907

The first American school of philosophy, Pragmatism, was founded by William James. Unlike some of his followers (John Dewey, for instance), he was not only a first-rate thinker, but also an eminent stylist; indeed, part of his authority stems from the lucidity with which he expressed his ideas. He was the brother of Henry James, the American novelist. His work on psychology remains still a major contribution to the field.

OF WHAT USE IS A COLLEGE TRAINING? WE WHO HAVE HAD IT SELDOM hear the question raised; we might be a little nonplussed to answer it offhand. A certain amount of meditation has brought me to this as the pithiest reply which I myself can give: The best claim that a college education can possibly make on your respect, the best thing it can aspire to accomplish for you, is this: that it should *help you to know a good man when you see him.* This is as true of women's as of men's colleges; but that it is neither a joke nor a one-sided abstraction I shall now endeavor to show.

What talk do we commonly hear about the contrast between college education and the education which business or technical

From *Memoirs and Studies,* New York: Longmans, Green and Co., reprinted by permission of Paul R. Reynolds & Son, New York. Copyright 1911 by William James.

or professional schools confer? The college education is called
higher because it is supposed to be so general and so disinterested. At the "schools" you get a relatively narrow practical
skill, you are told, whereas the "colleges" give you the more
liberal culture, the broader outlook, the historical perspective,
the philosophic atmosphere, or something which phrases of that
sort try to express. You are made into an efficient instrument for
doing a definite thing, you hear, at the schools; but, apart from
that, you may remain a crude and smoky kind of petroleum, incapable of spreading light. The universities and colleges, on the
other hand, although they may leave you less efficient for this or
that practical task, suffuse your whole mentality with something
more important than skill. They redeem you, make you well-bred;
they make "good company" of you mentally. If they find you
with a naturally boorish or caddish mind, they cannot leave you
so, as a technical school may leave you. This, at least, is pre-
tended; this is what we hear among college-trained people when
they compare their education with every other sort. Now, exactly
how much does this signify?

It is certain, to begin with, that the narrowest trade or professional training does something more for a man than to make
a skillful practical tool of him—it makes him also a judge of
other men's skill. Whether his trade be pleading at the bar or
surgery or plastering or plumbing, it develops a critical sense
in him for that sort of occupation. He understands the difference
between second-rate and first-rate work in his whole branch of
industry; he gets to know a good job in his own line as soon as
he sees it; and getting to know this in his own line, he gets a faint
sense of what good work may mean anyhow, that may, if circumstances favor, spread into his judgments elsewhere. Sound
work, clean work, finished work: feeble work, slack work, sham
work—these words express an identical contrast in many different departments of activity. In so far forth, then, even the
humblest manual trade may beget in one a certain small degree
of power to judge of good work generally.

Now, what is supposed to be the line of us who have the higher
college training? Is there any broader line—since our education
claims primarily not to be "narrow"—in which we also are made

good judges between what is first-rate and what is second-rate only? What is especially taught in the colleges has long been known by the name of the "humanities," and these are often identified with Greek and Latin. But it is only as literature, not as languages, that Greek and Latin have any general humanity-value; so that in a broad sense the humanities mean literature primarily, and in a still broader sense the study of masterpieces in almost any field of human endeavor. Literature keeps the primacy; for it not only *consists* of masterpieces, but is largely *about* masterpieces, being little more than an appreciative chronicle of human master-strokes, so far as it takes the form of criticism and history. You can give humanistic value to almost anything by teaching it historically. Geology, economics, mechanics, arc humanities when taught with reference to the successive achievements of the geniuses to which these sciences owe their being. Not taught thus literature remains grammar, art a catalogue, history a list of dates, and natural science a sheet of formulas and weights and measures.

The sifting of human creations!—nothing less than this is what we ought to mean by the humanities. Essentially this means biography; what our colleges should teach is, therefore, biographical history, that not of politics merely, but of anything and everything so far as human efforts and conquests are factors that have played their part. Studying in this way, we learn what types of activity have stood the test of time; we acquire standards of the excellent and durable. All our arts and sciences and institutions are but so many quests of perfection on the part of men; and when we see how diverse the types of excellence may be, how various the tests, how flexible the adaptations, we gain a richer sense of what the terms "better" and "worse" may signify in general. Our critical sensibilities grow both more acute and less fanatical. We sympathize with men's mistakes even in the act of penetrating them; we feel the pathos of lost causes and misguided epochs even while we applaud what overcame them.

Such words are vague and such ideas are inadequate, but their meaning is unmistakable. What the colleges—teaching humanities by examples which may be special, but which must be typical and pregnant—should at least try to give us, is a general sense of what, under various disguises, *superiority* has always signified and may still signify. The feeling for a good human job anywhere, the admiration of the really admirable, the disesteem of what is cheap and trashy and impermanent—this is what we call the critical sense, the sense for ideal values. It is the better part of what men know as wisdom. Some of us are wise in this way naturally and by genius; some of us never become so. But to have spent one's youth at college, in contact with the choice and rare and precious, and yet still to be a blind prig or vulgarian, unable to scent out human excellence or to divine it amid its accidents, to know it only when ticketed and labelled and forced on us by others, this indeed should be accounted the very calamity and shipwreck of a higher education.

The sense for human superiority ought, then, to be considered our line, as boring subways is the engineer's line and the surgeon's is appendicitis. Our colleges ought to have lit up in us a lasting relish for the better kind of man, a loss of appetite for mediocrities, and a disgust for cheapjacks. We ought to smell, as it were, the difference of quality in men and their proposals when we enter the world of affairs about us. Expertness in this might well atone for some of our awkwardness at accounts, for some of our ignorance of dynamos. The best claim we can make for the higher education, the best single phrase in which we can tell what it ought to do for us, is, then, exactly what I said: it should enable us to *know a good man when we see him.*

That the phrase is anything but an empty epigram follows from the fact that if you ask in what line it is most important that a democracy like ours should have its sons and daughters skillful, you see that it is this line more than any other. "The people in their wisdom"—this is the kind of wisdom most needed by the people. Democracy is on its trial, and no one knows how it will stand the ordeal. Abounding about us are pessimistic prophets. Fickleness and violence used to be, but are no longer, the vices which they charge to democracy. What its critics now affirm is that its preferences are inveterately for the inferior. So it was in the beginning, they say, and so it will be world without end. Vulgarity enthroned and institutionalized, elbowing everything superior from the highway, this, they tell us, is our irremediable destiny; and the picture-papers of the European continent are already drawing Uncle Sam with the hog instead of the eagle for his heraldic emblem. The privileged aristocracies of the foretime, with all their iniquities, did at least preserve some taste for higher human quality, and honor certain forms of refinement by their enduring traditions. But when democracy is sovereign its doubters say, nobility will form a sort of invisible church, and sincerity and refinement, stripped of honor, precedence, and favor, will have to vegetate on sufferance in private corners. They will have no general influence. They will be harmless eccentricities.

Now, who can be absolutely certain that this may not be the career of democracy? Nothing future is quite secure; states enough have inwardly rotted; and democracy as a whole may undergo self-poisoning. But, on the other hand, democracy is a kind of religion, and we are bound not to admit its failure. Faiths and utopias are the noblest exercise of human reason, and no one with a spark of reason in him will sit down fatalistically before the croaker's picture. The best of us are filled with the contrary vision of a democracy stumbling through every error till its institutions glow with justice and its customs shine with beauty. Our better men *shall* show the way and we *shall* follow them; so we are brought round again to the mission of the higher education in helping us to know the better kind of man whenever we see him.

The notion that a people can run itself and its affairs anonymously is now well known to be the silliest of absurdities. Mankind does nothing save through initiatives on the part of inventors, great or small, and imitation by the rest of us—these are the sole factors active in human progress. Individuals of genius show the way, and set the patterns, which common people then adopt and follow. *The rivalry of the patterns is the history of the world.* Our democratic problem thus is statable in ultrasimple terms: Who are the kind of men from whom our majorities shall take their cue? Whom shall they treat as rightful leaders? We and our leaders are the x and the y of the equation here; all other historic circumstances, be they economical, political, or intellectual, are only the background of occasion on which the living drama works itself out between us.

In this very simple way does the value of our educated class define itself: we more than others should be able to divine the worthier and better leaders. The terms here are monstrously simplified, of course, but such a bird's-eye view lets us immediately take our bearings. In our democracy, where everything else is so shifting, we alumni and alumnae of the colleges are the only permanent presence that corresponds to the aristocracy in older countries. We have continuous traditions, as they have; our motto, too, is *noblesse oblige;* and, unlike them, we stand for ideal interests solely, for we have no corporate selfishness and wield no powers of corruption. We ought to have our own class-consciousness. *"Les Intellectuels!"* What prouder club-name could there be than this one, used ironically by the party of "redblood," the party of every stupid prejudice and passion, during the anti-Dreyfus craze, to satirize the men in France who still retained some critical sense and judgment! Critical sense, it has to be confessed, is not an exciting term, hardly a banner to carry in processions. Affections for old habit, currents of self-interest, and gales of passion are the forces that keep the human ship moving: and the pressure of the judicious pilot's hand upon the tiller is a relatively insignificant energy. But the affections, passions, and interests are shifting, successive, and distraught; they blow in alternation while the pilot's hand is steadfast. He knows the compass, and, with all the leeways he is obliged to tack toward, he always makes some headway. A small force, if it never lets up, will accumulate effects more considerable than those of much greater forces if these work inconsistently. The ceaseless whisper of the more permanent ideals, the steady tug of truth and justice, give them but time, *must* warp the world in their direction.

This bird's-eye view of the general steering function of the college-bred amid the driftings of democracy ought to help us to a wider vision of what our colleges themselves should aim at. If we are to be the yeast-cake for democracy's dough, if we are to make it rise with culture's preferences, we must see to it that culture spreads broad sails. We must shake the old double reefs out of the canvas into the wind and sunshine, and let in every modern subject, sure that any subject will prove humanistic, if its setting be kept only wide enough.

Stevenson says somewhere to his reader: "You think you are just making this bargain, but you are really laying down a link in the policy of mankind." Well, your technical school should enable you to make your bargain splendidly; but your college should show you just the place of that kind of bargain—a pretty poor place, possibly—in the whole policy of mankind. That is the kind of liberal outlook, of perspective, of atmosphere, which should surround every subject as a college deals with it.

We of the colleges must eradicate a curious notion which numbers of good people have about such ancient seats of learning as Harvard. To many ignorant outsiders, that name suggests little more than a kind of sterilized conceit and incapacity for being pleased. In Edith Wyatt's exquisite book of Chicago sketches called *Every One his Own Way* there is a couple who stand for culture in the sense of exclusiveness, Richard Elliot and his feminine counterpart—feeble caricatures of mankind, unable to know any good thing when they see it, incapable of enjoyment unless a printed label gives them leave. Possibly this type of culture may exist near Cambridge and Boston. There may be specimens there, for priggishness is just like painter's colic or any other trade-disease. But every good college makes its students immune against this malady, of which the microbe haunts the neighborhood of printed pages. It does so by its general tone being too hearty for the microbe's life. Real culture lives by sympathies and admirations, not by dislikes and disdains; under all misleading wrappings it pounces unerringly upon the human core. If a college, through the inferior human influences that have grown pregnant there, fails to catch the robuster tone, its failure is colossal, for its social function stops; democracy gives it a wide berth, turns toward it a deaf ear.

"Tone," to be sure, is a terribly vague word to use, but there is no other, and this whole meditation is over questions of tone. By their tone are all things human either lost or saved. If democracy is to be saved it must catch the higher, healthier tone. If we are to impress it with our preferences, we ourselves must use the proper tone, which we, in turn, must have caught from our own teachers. It all reverts in the end to the action of innumerable imitative individuals upon each other and to the question of whose tone has the highest spreading power. As a class, we college graduates should look to it that *ours* has spreading power. It ought to have the highest spreading power.

In our essential function of indicating the better men, we now have formidable competitors outside. *McClure's Magazine,* the *American Magazine, Collier's Weekly,* and in its fashion, the *World's Work,* constitute together a real popular university along this very line. It would be a pity if any future historian were to have to write words like these: "By the middle of the twentieth century the higher institutions of learning had lost all influence over public opinion in the United States. But the mission of raising the tone of democracy, which they had proved themselves so lamentably unfitted to exert, was assumed with rare enthusiasm and prosecuted with extraordinary skill and success by a new educational power; and for the clarification of their human sympathies and elevation of their human preferences, the people at large acquired the habit of resorting exclusively to the guidance of certain private literary adventures, commonly designated in the market by the affectionate name of ten cent magazines."

Must not we of the colleges see to it that no historian shall ever say anything like this? Vague as the phrase of knowing a good man when you see him may be, diffuse and indefinite as one must leave its application, is there any other formula that describes so well the result at which our institutions *ought* to aim? If they do that, they do the best thing conceivable. If they fail to do it, they fail in very deed. It surely is a fine synthetic formula. If our faculties and graduates could once collectively come to realize it as the great underlying purpose toward which they have always been more or less obscurely groping, a great clearness would be shed over many of their problems; and, as for their influence in the midst of our social system, it would embark upon a new career of strength.

Literature and the College

IRVING BABBITT
(1865–1933)

Literature and the American College, 1908
The New Laokoön, 1910
Rousseau and Romanticism, 1919

IRVING BABBITT, a professor of French literature at Harvard, exerted a profound influence on his students. He was no Mr. Chips; many students resented him, but most admitted that he had helped shape their minds and lives. His books border on polemic. In *Literature and the American College* he asserted his central thesis that art and literature stand in vital relationship to the whole of human nature. He was the central figure in the development of a way of thought secular yet moral; now called the "New Humanism," it has been much execrated, chiefly by liberal thinkers, and much praised, chiefly by conservatives.

IT WAS WITH SOMETHING OF THE SPIRIT OF TRUE PROPHECY THAT Herbert Spencer proclaimed, in his work on Education, the approaching triumph of science over art and literature. Science, he said, was to reign supreme, and was no longer to be the "household drudge" who had "been kept in the background that her haughty sisters might flaunt their fripperies in the eyes of the world." The tables indeed have been turned so completely that art and literature have not only ceased to be "haughty", but have often been content to become the humble handmaids of science. It is to this eagerness of the artistic imagination to don the livery of science that we already owe the "experimental" novel. A Harvard Commencement speaker promised, not long ago, that we are soon to have poetry that shall be less "human" and more "biological." While awaiting these biological bards of the future,

Reprinted by permission from *Literature and the American College*, Boston: Houghton Mifflin Company, 1908.

we may at least deal scientifically with the poets of the past, if
we are to trust the title of a recently published Laboratory
Method for the study of poetry. Another writer, after heaping
contempt on the traditional views of poetry, produces his own
formula, and informs us that

$$Poem = x + HI + VF.$$

Many of us nowadays would seem to be convinced, with the
French naturalist, that if happiness exists anywhere it will be
found at the bottom of a crucible. Renan regretted in his old
age that he had spent his life on so unprofitable a subject as
the history of Christianity instead of the physical sciences. For
the proper study of mankind is not man, but chemistry; or,
perhaps, our modern attitude might be more correctly defined as
an attempt to study man by the methods of physics and chemistry.
We have invented laboratory sociology, and live in a nightmare
of statistics. Language interests us, not for the absolute human
values it expresses, but only in so far as it is a collection of facts
and relates itself to nature. With the invasion of this hard literal-
ness, the humanities themselves have ceased to be humane. I was
once told as convincing proof of the merit of a certain classical
scholar that he had twenty thousand references in his card catalogue.

The humanism of the Renaissance was a protest against the
excesses of the ascetic. Now that science aspires to be all in all,
somewhat after the fashion of theology in the Middle Ages, the
man who would maintain the humane balance of his faculties
must utter a similar protest against the excesses of the analyst,
in whom a "literal obedience to facts has extinguished every
spark of that light by which man is truly man." It is really about
as reasonable to use a dialogue of Plato merely as a peg on which
to hang philological disquisitions as it was in the Middle Ages
to turn Ovid's "Art of Love" into an allegory of the Christian life.
In its mediaeval extreme, the human spirit strove to isolate itself entirely from outer nature in a dream of the supernatural;
it now tends to the other extreme, and strives to identify itself
entirely with the world of phenomena. The spread of this scientific positivism, with its assimilation of man to nature, has had
especially striking results in education. Some of our higher in-

stitutions of learning are in a fair way to become what a certain eminent scholar thought universities should be—"great scientific workshops." The rare survivors of the older generation of humanists must have a curious feeling of loneliness and isolation.

The time has perhaps come, not so much to react against this nineteenth-century naturalism, as to define and complete it, and especially to insist on its keeping within proper bounds. The nature cult is in danger of being pushed too far, not only in its scientific but in its sentimental form. The benefits and blessings that Herbert Spencer promises us from the scientific analysis of nature are only to be matched by those that Wordsworth promises from sentimental communion with nature.

> One impulse from a vernal wood
> May teach you more of man,
> Of moral evil and of good,
> Than all the sages can.

The sentimental and scientific worship of nature, however far apart they may be at some points, have much in common when viewed in relation to our present subject—their effect on college education. The former, working up into the college from the kindergarten, and the latter, working downward from the graduate school, seem likely between them to leave very little of humanistic standards. The results are sometimes curious when the two tendencies actually meet. I once overheard a group of undergraduates, in search of "soft" courses, discussing whether they should elect a certain course in Old Egyptian. The exaggerations of Wordsworth and Herbert Spencer may have served a purpose in overcoming a counter-excess of tradition and conventionalism. But now the nature cult itself is degenerating into a kind of cant. The lover of clear thinking cannot allow to pass unchallenged many of the phrases that the votaries of the Goddess Natura have come to utter so glibly,—such phrases, for instance, as "obedience to nature" and "natural methods." The word nature—covering as it does both the human world and the world of phenomena —has been a source of intellectual confusion almost from the dawn of Greek philosophy to the present day. To borrow an example from French literature, it is equally in the name of "nature" that La Fontaine humanizes his animals and that Zola bestializes his men. By juggling with the twofold meaning of the word, Renan arrived only a few years ago at his famous dictum that "nature does not care for chastity."

It is a disquieting fact that Rousseau, the man whose influence is everywhere in the new education, was remarkable for nothing so much as his inability to distinguish between nature and human nature. He counts among his disciples all those who, like him, trust to the goodness of "nature," and so tend to identify the ideal needs of the individual with his temperamental leaning; who exalt instinct and idiosyncrasy; who, in their endeavor to satisfy the variety of temperaments, would push the principle of election almost down to the nursery, and devise, if possible, a separate system of education for every individual. For we are living in a privileged age, when not only every man, as Dr. Donne sang, but every child

> thinks he hath got
> To be a Phoenix, and that there can be
> None of that kind, of which he is, but he.

Our educators, in their anxiety not to thwart native aptitudes, encourage the individual in an in-breeding of his own temperament, which, beginning in the kindergarten, is carried upward through the college by the elective system, and receives its final consecration in his specialty. We are all invited to abound in our own sense, and to fall in the direction in which we lean. Have we escaped from the pedantry of authority and prescription, which was the bane of the old education, only to lapse into the pedantry of individualism? One is sometimes tempted to acquiesce in Luther's comparison of mankind to a drunken peasant on horseback, who, if propped up on one side, slips over on the other. What would seem desirable at present is not so much a Tory reaction toward the old ideal as a sense of measure to save us from an opposite excess—from being entirely "disconnected," as Burke has expressed it, "into the dust and powder of individuality." The need of discipline and community of ideal enters into human nature no less than the craving for a free play of one's individual faculties. This need the old curriculum, with all its faults, did something to satisfy. According to Dean Briggs of Harvard, discipline is often left in the new education to athletics; and athletics also meet in part the need for fellowship and communion. However much members of the same college may be split up in their intellectual interests by different electives, they can at least commune in an intercollegiate football game. Yet there should likewise be a place for some less elemental form of communion; so many of the very forces in the modern world that make for material union would seem at the same time to tend toward spiritual isolation. In this as in other respects we are at the furthest remove from mediaeval Europe, when men were separated by almost insuperable obstacles in time and space, but were knit together by common standards. When it comes to the deeper things of life, the members of a modern college faculty sometimes strike one, in Emersonian phrase, as a collection of "infinitely repellent particles." The mere fact that men once read the same book at college was no slight bond of fellowship. Two men who have taken the same course in Horace have at least a fund of common memories and allusions; whereas if one of them elect a course in Ibsen instead of Horace, they will not only have different memories, but, so far as they are touched by the spirit of their authors, different ideals. Only a pure radical can imagine that it is an unmixed gain for education to be so centrifugal, or that the outward and mechanical devices that are being multiplied to bring men together can take the place of this deeper understanding.

The sentimental naturalist would claim the right to elect Ibsen instead of Horace simply because he finds Ibsen more "interesting;" he thus obscures the idea of liberal culture by denying that some subjects are more humane than others in virtue of their intrinsic quality, and quite apart from individual tastes and preferences. The scientific naturalist arrives at the same result by his tendency to apply only quantitative tests and to translate everything into terms of power. President Eliot remarks significantly that the old distinction between the degrees of Bachelor of Arts and Bachelor of Science "is fading away, and may soon disappear altogether; for the reason that the object in view with candidates for both degrees is fundamentally the same, namely, training for power." Our colleges are very much taken up at present with the three years' scheme; but what a small matter this is, after all, compared with the change in the degree itself from a qualitative basis to a quantitative and dynamic one! If some of our educational radicals have their way, the A. B. degree will mean merely that a man has expended a certain number of units of intellectual energy on a list of elective studies that may range from boiler-making to Bulgarian; the degree will simply serve to measure the amount and intensity of one's intellectual current and the resistance overcome; it will become, in short, a question of intellectual volts and amperes and ohms. Here again what is wanted is not a hard and fast hierarchy of studies, but a sense of measure that will save us from the opposite extreme, from the democratic absurdity of asserting that all studies are, and by right should be, free and equal. The rank of studies will finally be determined, not by the number of intellectual foot pounds they involve, but by the nearness or remoteness of these studies to man, the boundaries of whose being by no means coincide with those of physical nature:—

> man hath all which Nature hath, but more,
> And in that *more* lie all his hopes of good.

The future will perhaps arrive at a classification of studies as more or less humane. However, desirable this humane revival may be, we should not hope to bring it about mechanically by proposing some brand-new educational reform. For this would be to fall into the great error of the age, and attempt to create the spirit by means and appliances instead of taking as our very point of departure the doctrine that man is greater than machinery. The hope for the humane spirit is not in the munificence of millionaires, but in a deeper and more earnest reflection on the part of the individual. Emerson's address on the American Scholar is a plea for a humanism that shall rest on pure intuition; the only drawback to Emerson's programme is that he assumes genius in his scholar, and genius of a rare kind at that. On the other hand, a humanism so purely traditional as that of Oxford and the English universities has, along with elements of great strength, certain obvious weaknesses. Perhaps the chief of these is that it seems, to the superficial observer at least, to have forgotten real for conventional values—the making of a man for the making of a gentleman. Herbert Spencer writes of this English education: "As the Orinoco Indian puts on his paint before leaving his hut, . . . so, a boy's drilling in Latin and Greek is insisted on, not because of their intrinsic value, but that he may have the 'education of a gentleman.' " All that may be affirmed with certainty is that if the humane ideal appear at all in the future, it must be in the very nature of things more a matter of individual insight and less a matter of tradition than heretofore. The weakening of traditional authority that our age has seen has some analogy with what took place in the Greece of Pericles. One may perhaps say, without pushing the analogy too far, that we are confronted with the same alternative,—either to attain to the true individualism of Socrates, the first of the humanists as he has been called, or else to fall away into the intellectual and moral impressionism of the sophists. Unpleasant signs of this impressionism have already appeared in our national theatre and newspaper press, in our literary criticism, our philosophy, and our popular novel. Our greatest danger, however, is educational impressionism.

Changes may very well be made in the mere form of the A.B. degree, provided we are careful to retain its humane aspiration. But through lack of clear thinking, we seem likely to forget the true function of the college as opposed to the graduate school on the one hand, and the preparatory school on the other. This slighting of the college is also due in part to German influences. Some of our educational theorists would be willing to unite the upper part of the college course with the graduate school and surrender the first year or two of it to the preparatory school, thus arriving at a division similar to the German gymnasium and university. This division is logical if we believe with Professor Münsterberg that there are but two kinds of scholars, "productive" and "receptive" scholars—those who discover knowledge and those who "distribute" it; and if we also agree with him in thinking that we need give "the boy of nineteen nothing different in principle from what the boy of nine receives."[1] But the youth

---

1. *American Traits*, p. 89.

of nineteen does differ from the boy of nine in one important particular,—he has become more capable of reflection. This change from the receptive to the reflective and assimilative attitude of mind is everything from the humane point of view, and contains in fact the justification of the college. Professor Münsterberg stigmatizes our college scholarship not only as "receptive," but as "passive" and "feminine" (though, to be sure, this bad state of affairs has been somewhat mended of late by the happy influence of Germany). But this is simply to overlook that humane endeavor which it is the special purpose of the college to foster— that effort of reflection, virile above all others, to coordinate the scattered elements of knowledge, and relate them not only to the intellect but to the will and character; that subtle alchemy by which mere learning is transmuted into culture. The task of assimilating what is best in the past and present, and adapting it to one's own use and the use of others, so far from lacking in originality, calls for something akin to creation. Professor Münsterberg regards the relation between the productive scholar and the college teacher as about that between an artist like Sargent and a photographer. He goes on to say that "the purely imitative thinker may make a most excellent teacher. Any one who has a personality, a forcible way of presentation, and an average intellect, will be able to be a fine teacher of any subject at six weeks' notice."[2] This German notion of knowledge as something that is dumped down on one mind and then "distributed" in the same mechanical fashion to other minds, is precisely what we need to guard against. The ambition of the true college teacher is not to "distribute" knowledge to his students, not "to lodge it with them," as Montaigne says, "but to marry it to them and make it a part of their very minds and souls." We shall have paid a heavy price for all the *strengwissenschaftliche Methode* we have acquired from Germany if it makes us incapable of distinguishing between mere erudition and true scholarship.

Granting, then, that the receptive attitude of mind must largely prevail in the lower schools, and that the productive scholar should have full scope in the graduate school, the college, if it is

2. *Ibid.*, p. 95.

to have any reason at all for existing separately, must stand, not for the advancement, but for the assimilation of learning, and for the perpetuation of culture. This distinction is fairly obvious, and one would almost be ashamed to recall it, did it not seem to be overlooked by some of the men who are doing the most to mould the American education. The late President Harper, for example, in his address on the future of the small college, proposed that some of these colleges be reduced to the rank of high schools, that others be made into "junior colleges" (in due subordination to the larger institutions, and taking the student only to the end of the sophomore year), and that others justify their existence by cultivating specialties. The great universities, for their part, are to be brought into closer relations with one another so as to form a sort of educational trust. Now President Harper was evidently right in thinking that small colleges are too numerous, and that no one would be the loser if some of them were reduced to the rank of high schools. Yet he scarcely makes mention in all his scheme of what should be the real aim of the small college that survives, namely, to teach a limited number of standard subjects vivified and informed by the spirit of liberal culture. From whatever side we approach them, these new theories are a menace to the small college. Thus the assumption that a student is ready for unlimited election immediately on completing his preparatory course puts at a manifest disadvantage all save a very few institutions; for only a few institutions have the material resources that will permit them to convert themselves into educational Abbeys of Theleme and write over their portals the inviting legend: Study what you like. The best of the small colleges will render a service to American education if they decide to make a sturdy defense of the humane tradition instead of trying to rival the great universities in displaying a full line of educational novelties. In the latter case, they may become third-rate and badly equipped scientific schools, and so reënact the fable of the frog that tried to swell itself to the size of the ox.

The small colleges will be fortunate if they appreciate their own advantages; if they do not fall into the naturalistic fallacy of confusing growth in the human sense with mere expansion;

if they do not allow themselves to be overawed by size and quantity, or hypnotized by numbers. Even though the whole world seem bent on living the quantitative life, the college should remember that its business is to make of its graduates men of quality in the real and not the conventional meaning of the term. In this way it will do its share toward creating that aristocracy of character and intelligence that is needed in a community like ours to take the place of an aristocracy of birth and to counteract the tendency toward an aristocracy of money. A great deal is said nowadays about the democratic spirit that should pervade our colleges. This is true if it means that the college should be in profound sympathy with what is best in democracy. It is false if it means, as it often does, that the college should level down and suit itself to the point of view of the average individual. Some of the arguments advanced in favor of a three years' course imply that we can afford to lower the standard of the degree, provided we thereby put it within reach of a larger number of students. But from the standpoint of the college one thoroughly cultivated person should be more to the purpose than a hundred persons who are only partially cultivated. The final test of democracy, as Tocqueville has said, will be its power to produce and encourage the superior individual. Because the claims of the average man have been slighted in times past, does it therefore follow that we must now slight the claims of the superior man? We cannot help thinking once more of Luther's comparison. The college can only gain by close and sympathetic contact with the graduate school on the one hand, and the lower schools on the other, provided it does not forget that its function is different from either. The lower schools should make abundant provision for the education of the average citizen, and the graduate school should offer ample opportunity for specialization and advanced study; the prevailing spirit of the college, however, should be neither humanitarian nor scientific—though these elements may be largely represented —but humane, and, in the right sense of the word, aristocratic.

In thus sketching out an ideal it costs nothing, as a French writer remarks, to make it complete and pretentious. One reason why we are likely to fall so far short of our ideal in practice is the difficulty, as things now are, of finding the right kind of college teacher. Professor Münsterberg praises his German teachers because they never aspired to be more than enthusiastic specialists, and he adds that "no one ought to teach in a college who has not taken his doctor's degree." This opinion is also held by many Americans, and hence the fetish worship of the doctor's degree on the part of certain college presidents. But one may shine as a productive scholar, and yet have little or nothing of that humane insight and reflection that can alone give meaning to all subjects and is especially appropriate in a college teacher. The work that leads to a doctor's degree is a constant temptation to sacrifice one's growth as a man to one's growth as a specialist. We must be men before being entomologists. The old humanism was keenly alive to the loss of mental balance that may come from knowing any one subject too well. It was perhaps with some sense of the dangers of specialization that the ancient flute-player replied to King Philip, who wished to argue a point of music with him: "God forbid that your majesty should know as much about these things as I do." England is perhaps the only country in which something of this ideal of the elegant amateur—"l'honnête homme qui ne se pique de rien"—has survived to our own day. Compared with the Germans the English still are, as some one recently called them, a nation of amateurs. However, a revulsion of feeling is taking place, and one might imagine from the tone of some recent English articles that the writers would like to see Oxford converted into a polytechnic school. The whole problem is a most difficult one: the very conditions of modern life require us nearly all to be experts and specialists, and this makes it the more necessary that we should be on our guard against that maiming and mutilation of the mind that come from over-absorption in one subject. Every one remembers the passage in which Darwin confesses with much frankness that his humane appreciation of art and poetry had been impaired by a one-sided devotion to science.

We should at least insist that the college teacher of ancient or modern literature be something more than a mere specialist. To regard a man as qualified for a college position in these subjects simply because he has investigated some minute point of linguistics or literary history—this, to speak plainly, is preposterous.

If we are told that this is a necessary test of his originality and mastery of method, we should reply that as much originality is needed for assimilation as for production—far more, indeed, than enters into the mechanical compilations so often accepted for doctors' theses in this country and Germany. This outcry about originality is simply the scientific form of that pedantry of individualism, so rampant at the present hour, which, in its sentimental form, leads, as we have seen, to an exaggerated respect for temperament and idiosyncrasy. One of the surest ways of being original nowadays, since that is what we are all straining so anxiously after, would be simply to become a well-read man (in the old-fashioned sense of the term), to have a thorough knowledge and imaginative appreciation of what is really worthwhile in the literature of the past. The candidate for the doctor's degree thinks he can afford to neglect this general reading and reflection in the interests of his own private bit of research. This pedantic effort to be original is especially flagrant in subjects like the classics, where, more than elsewhere, research should be subordinated to humane assimilation. What are we to think of the classical student who sets out to write his thesis before he has read widely, much less assimilated, the masterpieces of Greece and Rome? Unfortunately, this depreciation of assimilative and reflective scholarship falls in with what is most superficial in our national temperament—our disregard for age and experience in the race or the individual, our small esteem for the "ancient and permanent sense of mankind" as embodied in tradition, our prejudice in favor of young men and new ideas. In our attitude toward age and tradition, some of us seem bent on going as far in one direction as the Chinese have gone in the other. Youth has already come to be one of the virtues chiefly appreciated in a minister of the gospel! Tocqueville remarks that the contempt for antiquity is one of the chief dangers of a democracy, and adds with true insight that the study of the classics, therefore, has special value for a democratic community. In point of fact, the classical teacher could attempt no higher task than this imaginative interpretation of the past to the present. It is to be accounted one of the chief disasters to our higher culture that our classical teachers as a body have fallen so far short of this task, that they have come instead so entirely under the influence of the narrowest school of German philology, the school of Lachmann and Gottfried Hermann. The throng of scholiasts and commentators whom Voltaire saw pressing about the outer gates of the Temple of Taste now occupy the sanctuary. The only hope for the future of classical studies is in a quite radical change of direction, and, first of all, in an escape from their present isolation. For instance, a better test than a doctor's degree of a man's fitness to teach classics in the average college would be an examination designed to show the extent and thoroughness of his reading in the classical languages and his power to relate this knowledge to modern life and literature. This foundation once laid, the research instinct might develop naturally in those who had a turn for research, instead of being developed, as it is now, in all alike under artificial pressure. But it is hardly probable that our classical teachers will welcome any such suggestion. For, unlike the old humanists as they may be in most other respects, they still retain something of their pride and exclusiveness; they are still careful to remind us by their attitude that Latin and Greek are *litterae humaniores*, however little they do to make good the claim of this proud distinction. They may be compared to a man who inherits a great name and estate, the possession of which he does not sufficiently justify by his personal achievement.

The teaching of the classics will gain fresh interest and vitality by being brought into close contact with mediaeval and modern literature; we should hasten to add that the teaching of modern languages will gain immensely in depth and seriousness by being brought into close contact with the classics. Neither condition is fulfilled at present. The lack of classical teachers with an adequate foreground and of modern language teachers with an adequate background is one of the chief obstacles to a revival of humane methods. Yet nothing could be more unprofitable under existing conditions than the continuance in any form of the old quarrel of the Ancients and Moderns. "I prefer the philosophy of Montaigne," says Charles Francis Adams in his address on the College Fetish, "to what seem to me the platitudes of Cicero." As though it were possible to have a full understanding of Montaigne without knowledge of the "platitudes" of Cicero, and the whole of

Latin literature into the bargain! The teacher of French especially, if he would avoid superficiality, needs to be steadied and
ballasted by a thorough classical training. It is so much easier to
interest a class in Rostand than in Racine that he is in constant
danger of falling into cheap contemporaneousness. A French instructor in an Eastern college told me that as a result of long
teaching of his subject he had come to know the "Trois Mousquetaires" better than any other work in all literature; and the "Trois
Mousquetaires" is a masterpiece compared to other texts that have
appeared, texts whose literary insignificance is often equaled only
by the badness of the editing.[3] The commercialism of the large
publishers works hand in hand here with the impressionism of
modern language teachers, so that the undergraduate of to-day
sometimes has the privilege of reading a novel of Georges Ohnet
where a generation ago he would have read Plato.

Those who have faith in either ancient or modern languages
as instruments of culture should lose no time in healing their
minor differences if they hope to make head against their common enemies,—the pure utilitarians and scientific radicals.
Herbert Spencer, who may be taken as the type of these latter,
holds that scientific analysis is a prime necessity of life, whereas
art and literature are only forms of "play," the mere entertainment at most of our idle moments. And he concludes in regard
to these subjects: "As they occupy the leisure part of life, so
should they occupy the leisure part of education." That this
doctrine which reduces art and literature to a sort of dilettante-
ism should find favor with pure naturalists is not surprising. The
case is more serious when it is also accepted, often unconsciously
perhaps, by those who are working in what should be the field of
literature. Many of the students of linguistics who have in-
trenched themselves in our college faculties are ready to grant a
place to literature as an occasional relaxation from the more serious and strenuous labors of philological analysis. Only a man must
not be too interested in literature under penalty of being thought
a dilettante. A young philologist once said to me of one of his

_____

3. There has been improvement in this respect during the past few
years.

colleagues: "He is almost a dilettante—he reads Dante and Shakespeare." It is perhaps the Spencerian view of art that accounts also for a curious predilection I have often noticed in philologists for vaudeville performances and light summer fiction. Certain teachers of literature, it must be confessed,—especially teachers of English,—seem to have a similar conception of their role, and aspire to be nothing more than graceful purveyors of aesthetic solace, and arbiters of the rhetorical niceties of speech. The philologist and the dilettante are equally far from feeling and making others feel that true art and literature stand in vital relation to human nature as a whole, that they are not, as Spencer's theory implies, mere refined modes of enjoyment, mere titillations of the aesthetic sensibility. Some tradition of this deep import of humane letters for the higher uses of man was maintained, along with other knowledge of value, in the old college curriculum. Now that this humane tradition is weakening, the individual left to his own resources, must seek a substitute for it in humane reflection.

In other words,—and this brings us once more to the central point of our discussion,—even if we sacrifice the letter of the old Bachelor of Arts degree, we should strive to preserve its spirit. This spirit is threatened at present in manifold ways,—by the upward push of utilitarianism and kindergarten methods, by the downward push of professionalism and specialization, by the almost irresistible pressure of commercial and industrial influences. If we sacrifice both the letter and the spirit of the degree, we should at least do so deliberately, and not be betrayed through mere carelessness into some educational scheme that does not distinguish sufficiently between man and an electric dynamo. The time is above all one for careful thinking and accurate definition. Money and enthusiasm, excellent as these things are, will not take the place of vigorous personal reflection. This, it is to be feared, will prove unwelcome doctrine to the ears of an age that hopes to accomplish its main ends by the appointment of committees, and has developed, in lieu of real communion among men, nearly every form of gregariousness. Professor Münsterberg thinks that our highest ambition should be to rival Germany in productive scholarship. To this end he would have us establish a number of twenty-five-thousand dollar professorships, and appoint to them our most meritorious investigators and masters of scientific method; in addition he would have us heap on these chosen heroes of research every manner of honor and distinction. But he will seriously mislead us if he persuades us that productive scholarship is our chief educational problem. We must insist that a far more important problem just now is to determine the real meaning and value of the A.B. degree. However, we should be grateful to Professor Münsterberg for one thing: in dealing with these fundamentals of education, he is comparatively free from that indolent and impressionistic habit of mind that so often marks our own manner of treating them. He does us a service in forcing us to search more carefully into our own ideas if only in order to oppose him. Almost any opinion that has been thoroughly thought out is better than a mush of impressionism. For, as Bacon has said, truth is more likely to be helped forward by error than by confusion.

The Aims of Education

ALFRED NORTH WHITEHEAD
(1861–1947)

Principia Mathematica (with Bertrand Russell), 1910
Science and the Modern World, 1925
Process and Reality, 1929
The Aims of Education and Other Essays, 1929

ALFRED NORTH WHITEHEAD, philosopher and mathematician, sought to bridge the gap between the sciences and the humanities. His *Principia Mathematica,* written with Bertrand Russell, is one of the key works of our time, a primer of a new logic. He taught at the Imperial College of Science in London before coming to Harvard University, where he exerted great influence, becoming after his retirement one of the Senior Fellows of that institution. The *Aims of Education* is the result of his own experience as well as his philosophical speculation, and deals with what has become a central problem in our own time.

CULTURE IS ACTIVITY OF THOUGHT, AND RECEPTIVENESS TO BEAUTY and humane feeling. Scraps of information have nothing to do with it. A merely well-informed man is the most useless bore on God's earth. What we should aim at producing is men who possess both culture and expert knowledge in some special direction. Their expert knowledge will give them the ground to start from, and their culture will lead them as deep as philosophy and as high as art. We have to remember that the valuable intellectual development is self-development, and that it mostly takes place between the ages of sixteen and thirty. As to training, the most important part is given by mothers before the age of twelve. A saying due to Archbishop Temple illustrates my meaning. Surprise was expressed at the success in after-life of a man, who as a boy at Rugby had been somewhat undistinguished. He answered, "It is not what they are at eighteen, it is what they become afterwards that matters."

In training a child to activity of thought, above all things we must beware of what I will call "inert ideas"—that is to say, ideas that are merely received into the mind without being utilised, or tested, or thrown into fresh combinations.

In the history of education, the most striking phenomenon is that schools of learning, which at one epoch are alive with a ferment of genius, in a succeeding generation exhibit merely pedantry and routine. The reason is, that they are overladen with inert ideas. Education with inert ideas is not only useless: it is, above all things, harmful—*Corruptio optimi, pessima*. Except at rare intervals of intellectual ferment, education in the past has been radically infected with inert ideas. That is the reason why uneducated clever women, who have seen much of the world, are in middle life so much the most cultured part of the community. They have been saved from this horrible burden of inert ideas. Every intellectual revolution which has ever stirred humanity into greatness has been a passionate protest against inert ideas. Then, alas, with pathetic ignorance of human psychology, it has proceeded by some educational scheme to bind humanity afresh with inert ideas of its own fashioning.

Let us now ask how in our system of education we are to guard against this mental dryrot. We enunciate two educational commandments, "Do not teach too many subjects," and again, "What you teach, teach thoroughly."

The result of teaching small parts of a large number of subjects is the passive reception of disconnected ideas, not illumined with any spark of vitality. Let the main ideas which are introduced into a child's education be few and important, and let them be thrown into every combination possible. The child should make them his own, and should understand their application here and now in the circumstances of his actual life. From the very beginning of his education, the child should experience the joy of discovery. The discovery which he has to make, is that general ideas give an understanding of that stream of events which pours through his life, which is his life. By understanding I mean more than a mere logical analysis, though that is included. I mean "understanding" in the sense in which it is used in the French proverb, "To understand all, is to forgive all." Pedants sneer at an education which is useful. But if education is not useful, what is it? Is it a talent, to be hidden away in a napkin? Of course, education should be useful, whatever your aim in life. It was useful to Saint Augustine and it was useful to Napoleon. It is useful, because understanding is useful.

I pass lightly over that understanding which should be given by the literary side of education. Nor do I wish to be supposed to pronounce on the relative merits of a classical or a modern curriculum. I would only remark that the understanding which we want is an understanding of an insistent present. The only use of a knowledge of the past is to equip us for the present. No more deadly harm can be done to young minds than by depreciation of the present. The present contains all that there is. It is holy ground; for it is the past, and it is the future. At the same time it must be observed that an age is no less past if it existed two hundred years ago than if it existed two thousand years ago. Do not be deceived by the pedantry of dates. The ages of Shakespeare and of Moliere are no less past than are the ages of Sophocles and of Virgil. The communion of saints is a great and inspiring assemblage, but it has only one possible hall of meeting, and that is, the present; and the mere lapse of time through which any particular group of saints must travel to reach that meeting-place, makes very little difference.

Passing now to the scientific and logical side of education, we remember that here also ideas which are not utilised are positively harmful. By utilising an idea, I mean relating it to that stream, compounded of sense perceptions, feelings, hopes, desires, and of mental activities adjusting thought to thought, which forms our life. I can imagine a set of beings which might fortify their souls by passively reviewing disconnected ideas. Humanity is not built that way—except perhaps some editors of newspapers.

In scientific training, the first thing to do with an idea is to prove it. But allow me for one moment to extend the meaning of "prove"; I mean—to prove its worth. Now an idea is not worth much unless the propositions in which it is embodied are true. Accordingly, an essential part of the proof of an idea is the proof, either by experiment or by logic, of the truth of the propositions. But it is not essential that this proof of the truth should constitute the first introduction to the idea. After all, its assertion by the authority of respectable teachers is sufficient evidence to begin with. In our first contact with a set of propositions, we commence by appreciating their importance. That is what we all do in after-life. We do not attempt, in the strict sense, to prove or to disprove anything, unless its importance makes it worthy of that honour. These two processes of proof, in the narrow sense, and of appreciation, do not require a rigid separation in time. Both can be proceeded with nearly concurrently. But in so far as either process must have the priority, it should be that of appreciation by use.

Furthermore, we should not endeavour to use propositions in isolation. Emphatically I do not mean, a neat little set of experiments to illustrate Proposition I and then the proof of Proposition I, a neat little set of experiments to illustrate Proposition II and then the proof of Propostion II, and so on to the end of the book. Nothing could be more boring. Interrelated truths are utilised *en bloc,* and the various propositions are employed in any order, and with any reiteration. Choose some important applications of your theoretical subject; and study them concurrently with the systematic theoretical exposition. Keep the theoretical exposition short and simple, but let it be strict and rigid so far as it goes. It should not be too long for it to be easily known with thoroughness and accuracy. The consequences of a plethora of half-digested theoretical knowledge are deplorable. Also the theory should not be muddled up with the practice. The child should have no doubt when it is proving and when it is utilising. My point is that what is proved should be utilised, and that what is utilised should—so far as is practicable —be proved. I am far from asserting that proof and utilisation are the same thing.

At this point of my discourse, I can most directly carry forward my argument in the outward form of a digression. We are only just realising that the art and science of education require a genius and a study of their own; and that this genius and this science are more than a bare knowledge of some branch of science or of literature. This truth was partially perceived in the past generation; and headmasters, somewhat crudely, were apt to supersede learning in their colleagues by requiring left-hand bowling and a taste for football. But culture is more than cricket, and more than football, and more than extent of knowledge.

Education is the acquisition of the art of the utilisation of knowledge. This is an art very difficult to impart. Whenever a text-book is written of real educational worth, you may be quite certain that some reviewer will say that it will be difficult to teach from it. Of course it will be difficult to teach from it. If it were easy, the book ought to be burned; for it cannot be educational. In education, as elsewhere, the broad primrose path leads to a nasty place. This evil path is represented by a book or a set of lectures which will practically enable the student to learn by heart all the questions likely to be asked at the next external examination. And I may say in passing that no educational system is possible unless every question directly asked of a pupil at any examination is either framed or modified by the actual teacher of that pupil in that subject. The external assessor may report on the curriculum or on the performance of the pupils, but never should be allowed to ask the pupil a question which has not been strictly supervised by the actual teacher, or at least inspired by a long conference with him. There are a few exceptions to this rule, but they are exceptions, and could easily be allowed for under the general rule.

We now return to my previous point, that theoretical ideas should always find important applications within the pupil's curriculum. This is not an easy doctrine to apply, but a very hard one. It contains within itself the problem of keeping knowledge alive, of preventing it from becoming inert, which is the central problem of all education.

The best procedure will depend on several factors, none of which can be neglected, namely, the genius of the teacher, the intellectual type of the pupils, their prospects in life, the opportunities offered by the immediate surroundings of the school, and allied factors of this sort. It is for this reason that the uniform external examination is so deadly. We do not denounce it because we are cranks, and like denouncing established things. We are not so childish. Also, of course, such examinations have their use in testing slackness. Our reason of dislike is very definite and very practical. It kills the best part of culture. When you analyse in the light of experience the central task of education, you find that its successful accomplishment depends on a delicate adjustment of many variable factors. The reason is that we are dealing with human minds, and not with dead matter. The evocation of curiosity, of judgment, of the power of mastering a complicated tangle of circumstances, the use of theory in giving foresight in special cases—all these powers are not to be imparted by a set rule embodied in one schedule of examination subjects.

I appeal to you, as practical teachers. With good discipline, it is always possible to pump into the minds of a class a certain quantity of inert knowledge. You take a text-book and make them learn it. So far, so good. The child then knows how to solve a quadratic equation. But what is the point of teaching a child to solve a quadratic equation? There is a traditional answer to this question. It runs thus: The mind is an instrument, you first sharpen it, and then use it; the acquisition of the power of solving a quadratic equation is part of the process of sharpening the mind. Now there is just enough truth in this answer to have made it live through the ages. But for all its half-truth, it embodies a radical error which bids fair to stifle the genius of the modern world. I do not know who was first responsible for this analogy of the mind to a dead instrument. For aught I know, it may have been one of the seven wise men of Greece, or a committee of the whole lot of them. Whoever was the originator, there can be no doubt of the authority which it has acquired by the continuous approval bestowed upon it by eminent persons. But whatever its weight of authority, whatever the high approval which it can quote, I have no hesitation in denouncing it as one of the most fatal, erroneous, and dangerous conceptions ever introduced into the theory of education. The mind is never passive; it is a perpetual activity, delicate, receptive, responsive to stimulus. You cannot postpone its life until you have sharpened it. Whatever interest attaches to your subject-matter must be evoked here and now; whatever powers you are strengthening in the pupil, must be exercised here and now; whatever possibilities of mental life your teaching should impart, must be exhibited here and now. That is the golden rule of education, and a very difficult rule to follow.

The difficulty is just this: the apprehension of general ideas, intellectual habits of mind, and pleasurable interest in mental achievement can be evoked by no form of words, however accurately adjusted. All practical teachers know that education is a patient process of the mastery of details, minute by minute, hour by hour, day by day. There is no royal road to learning through an airy path of brillant generalisations. There is a proverb about the difficulty of seeing the wood because of the trees. That difficulty is exactly the point which I am enforcing. The problem of education is to make the pupil see the wood by means of the trees.

The solution which I am urging, is to eradicate the fatal disconnection of subjects which kills the vitality of our modern curriculum. There is only one subject-matter for education, and that is Life in all its manifestations. Instead of this single unity, we offer children—Algebra, from which nothing follows; Geometry, from which nothing follows; Science, from which nothing follows; History, from which nothing follows; a Couple of Languages, never mastered; and lastly, most dreary of all, Literature, represented by plays of Shakespeare, with philological notes and short analyses of plot and character to be in substance committed to memory. Can such a list be said to represent Life, as it is known in the midst of the living of it? The best that can be said of it is, that it is a rapid table of contents which a deity might run over in his mind while he was thinking of creating a world, and had not yet determined how to put it together.

Let us now return to quadratic equations. We still have on hand the unanswered question. Why should children be taught their solution? Unless quadratic equations fit into a connected curriculum, of course there is no reason to teach anything about them. Furthermore, extensive as should be the place of mathematics in a complete culture, I am a little doubtful whether for many types of boys algebraic solutions of quadratic equations do not lie on the specialist side of mathematics. I may here remind you that as yet I have not said anything of the psychology or the content of the specialism, which is so necessary a part of an ideal education. But all that is an evasion of our real question, and I merely state it in order to avoid being misunderstood in my answer.

Quadratic equations are part of algebra, and algebra is the intellectual instrument which has been created for rendering clear the quantitative aspects of the world. There is no getting out of it. Through and through the world is infected with quantity. To talk sense, is to talk in quantities. It is no use saying that the nation is large,—How large? It is no use saying that radium is scarce,—How scarce? You cannot evade quantity. You may fly to poetry and to music, and quantity and number will face you in your rhythms and your octaves. Elegant intellects which despise the theory of quantity, are but half developed. They are more to be pitied than blamed. The scraps of gibberish, which in their school-days were taught to them in the name of algebra, deserve some contempt.

This question of the degeneration of algebra into gibberish, both in word and in fact, affords a pathetic instance of the uselessness of reforming educational schedules without a clear conception of the attributes which you wish to evoke in the living minds of the children. A few years ago there was an outcry that school algebra was in need of reform, but there was general agreement that graphs would put everything right. So all sorts of things were extruded, and graphs were introduced. So far as I can see, with no sort of idea behind them, but just graphs. Now every examination paper has one or two questions on graphs. Personally, I am an enthusiastic adherent of graphs. But I wonder whether as yet we have gained very much. You cannot put life into any schedule of general education unless you succeed in exhibiting its relation to some essential characteristic of all intelligent or emotional perception. It is a hard saying, but it is true; and I do not see how to make it any easier. In making these little formal alterations you are beaten by the very nature of things. You are pitted against too skilful an adversary, who will see to it that the pea is always under the other thimble. Reformation must begin at the other end. First, you must make up your mind as to those quantitative aspects of the world which are simple enough to be introduced into general education; then a schedule of algebra should be framed which will about find its exemplification in these applications. We need not fear for our pet graphs, they will be there in plenty when we once begin to treat algebra as a serious means of studying the world. Some of the simplest applications will be found in the quantities which occur in the simplest study of society. The curves of history are more vivid and more informing than the dry catalogues of names and dates which comprise the greater part of that arid school study. What purpose is effected by a catalogue of undistinguished kings and queens? Tom, Dick, or Harry, they are all dead. General resurrections are failures, and are better postponed. The quantitative flux of the forces of modern society is capable of very simple exhibition. Meanwhile, the idea of the variable, of the function, of rate of change of equations and their solution, of elimination, are being studied as an abstract science for their own sake. Not, of course, in the pompous phrases with which I am alluding to them here, but with that iteration of simple special cases proper to teaching.

If this course be followed, the route from Chaucer to the Black Death, from the Black Death to modern Labour troubles, will connect the tales of the mediaeval pilgrims with the abstract science of algebra, both yielding diverse aspects of that single theme, Life. I know what most of you are thinking at this point. It is that the exact course which I have sketched out is not the particular one which you would have chosen, or even see how to work. I quite agree. I am not claiming that I could do it myself. But your objection is the precise reason why a common external examination system is fatal to education. The process of exhibiting the applications of knowledge must, for its success, essentially depend on the character of the pupils and the genius of the teacher. Of course I have felt out the easiest applications with

which most of us are more at home. I mean the quantitative sides
of sciences, such as mechanics and physics.

Again, in the same connection we plot the statistics of social
phenomena against the time. We then eliminate the time between suitable pairs. We can speculate how far we have exhibited a real causal connection, or how far a mere temporal coincidence. We notice that we might have plotted against the
time one set of statistics for one country and another set for another country, and thus, with suitable choice of subjects, have
obtained graphs which certainly exhibited mere coincidence.
Also other graphs exhibit obvious causal connections. We wonder
how to discriminate. And so are drawn on as far as we will.

But in considering this description, I must beg you to remember what I have been insisting on above. In the first place,
one train of thought will not suit all groups of children. For example, I should expect that artisan children will want something more concrete and, in a sense, swifter than I have set down
here. Perhaps I am wrong, but that is what I should guess. In
the second place, I am not contemplating one beautiful lecture
stimulating, once and for all, an admiring class. That is not the
way in which education proceeds. No; all the time the pupils
are hard at work solving examples, drawing graphs, and making
experiments, until they have a thorough hold on the whole subject. I am describing the interspersed explanations, the directions
which should be given to their thoughts. The pupils have got
to be made to feel that they are studying something, and are not
merely executing intellectual minuets.

Finally, if you are teaching pupils for some general examination, the problem of sound teaching is greatly complicated. Have
you ever noticed the zig-zag moulding round a Norman arch?
The ancient work is beautiful, the modern work is hideous. The
reason is, that the modern work is done to exact measure, the
ancient work is varied according to the idiosyncrasy of the workman. Here it is crowded, and there it is expanded. Now the essence of getting pupils through examinations is to give equal
weight to all parts of the schedule. But mankind is naturally
specialist. One man sees a whole subject, where another can find
only a few detached examples. I know that it seems contradictory

to allow for specialism in a curriculum especially designed for a broad culture. Without contradictions the world would be simpler, and perhaps duller. But I am certain that in education wherever you exclude specialism you destroy life.

We now come to the other great branch of a general mathematical education, namely Geometry. The same principles apply. The theoretical part should be clearcut, rigid, short, and important. Every proposition not absolutely necessary to exhibit the main connection of ideas should be cut out, but the great fundamental ideas should be all there. No omission of concepts, such as those of Similarity and Proportion. We must remember that, owing to the aid rendered by the visual presence of a figure, Geometry is a field of unequalled excellence for the exercise of the deductive faculties of reasoning. Then, of course, there follows Geometrical Drawing, with its training for the hand and eye.

But, like Algebra, Geometry and Geometrical Drawing must be extended beyond the mere circle of geometrical ideas. In an industrial neighbourhood, machinery and workshop practice form the appropriate extension. For example, in the London Polytechnics this has been achieved with conspicuous success. For many secondary schools I suggest that surveying and maps are the natural applications. In particular, plane-table surveying should lead pupils to a vivid apprehension of the immediate application of geometric truths. Simple drawing apparatus, a surveyor's compass, should enable the pupils to rise from the survey and mensuration of a field to the construction of the map of a small district. The best education is to be found in gaining the utmost information from the simplest apparatus. The provision of elaborate instruments is greatly to be deprecated. To have constructed the map of a small district, to have considered its roads, its contours, its geology, its climate, its relation to other districts, the effects on the status of its inhabitants, will teach more history and geography than any knowledge of Perkin Warbeck or of Behren's Straits. I mean not a nebulous lecture on the subject, but a serious investigation in which the real facts are definitely ascertained by the aid of accurate theoretical knowledge. A typical mathematical problem should be: Survey such and such a field, draw a plan of it to such and such a scale, and find the area. It would be quite a good procedure to impart the necessary geometrical propositions without their proofs. Then, concurrently in the same term, the proofs of the propositions would be learnt while the survey was being made.

Fortunately, the specialist side of education presents an easier problem than does the provision of a general culture. For this there are many reasons. One is that many of the principles of procedure to be observed are the same in both cases, and it is unnecessary to recapitulate. Another reason is that specialist training takes place—or should take place—at a more advanced stage of the pupil's course, and thus there is easier material to work upon. But undoubtedly the chief reason is that the specialist study is normally a study of peculiar interest to the student. He is studying it because, for some reason, he wants to know it. This makes all the difference. The general culture is designed to foster an activity of mind; the specialist course utilises this activity. But it does not do to lay too much stress on these neat antitheses. As we have already seen, in the general course foci of special interest will arise; and similarly in the special study, the external connections of the subject drag thought outwards.

Again, there is not one course of study which merely gives general culture, and another which gives special knowledge. The subjects pursued for the sake of a general education are special subjects specially studied; and, on the other hand, one of the ways of encouraging general mental activity is to foster a special devotion. You may not divide the seamless coat of learning. What education has to impart is an intimate sense for the power of ideas, for the beauty of ideas, and for the structure of ideas, together with a particular body of knowledge which has peculiar reference to the life of the being possessing it.

The appreciation of the structure of ideas is that side of a cultured mind which can only grow under the influence of a special study. I mean that eye for the whole chessboard, for the bearing of one set of ideas on another. Nothing but a special study can give any appreciation for the exact formulation of general ideas, for their relations when formulated, for their service in the comprehension of life. A mind so disciplined should be both more abstract and more concrete. It has been trained in the comprehension of abstract thought and in the analysis of facts.

Finally, there should grow the most austere of all mental qualities; I mean the sense for style. It is an aesthetic sense, based on admiration for the direct attainment of a foreseen end, simply and without waste. Style in art, style in literature, style in science, style in logic, style in practical execution have fundamentally the same aesthetic qualities, namely, attainment and restraint. The love of a subject in itself and for itself, where it is not the sleepy pleasure of pacing a mental quarter-deck, is the love of style as manifested in that study.

Here we are brought back to the position from which we started, the utility of education. Style, in its finest sense, is the last acquirement of the educated mind; it is also the most useful. It pervades the whole being. The administrator with a sense for style hates waste; the engineer with a sense for style economises his material; the artisan with a sense for style prefers good work. Style is the ultimate morality of mind.

But above style, and above knowledge, there is something, a vague shape like fate above the Greek gods. That somthing is Power. Style is the fashioning of power, the restraining of power. But, after all, the power of attainment of the desired end is fundamental. The first thing is to get there. Do not bother about your style, but solve your problem, justify the ways of God to man, administer your province, or do whatever else is set before you.

Where, then, does style help? In this, with style the end is attained without side issues, without raising undesirable inflammations. With style you attain your end and nothing but your end. With style the effect of your activity is calculable, and foresight is the last gift of gods to men. With style your power is increased, for your mind is not distracted with irrelevancies, and you are more likely to attain your object. Now style is the exclusive privilege of the expert. Whoever heard of the style of an amateur painter, of the style of an amateur poet? Style is always the product of specialist study, the peculiar contribution of specialism to culture.

English education in its present phase suffers from a lack of definite aim, and from an external machinery which kills its vitality. Hitherto in this address I have been considering the aims which should govern education. In this respect England halts between two opinions. It has not decided whether to produce amateurs or experts. The profound change in the world which the nineteenth century has produced is that the growth of knowledge has given foresight. The amateur is essentially a man with appreciation and with immense versatility in mastering a given routine. But he lacks the foresight which comes from special knowledge. The object of this address is to suggest how to produce the expert without loss of the essential virtues of the amateur. The machinery of our secondary education is rigid where it should be yielding, and lax where it should be rigid. Every school is bound on pain of extinction to train its boys for a small set of definite examinations. No headmaster has a free hand to develop his general education or his specialist studies in accordance with the opportunities of his school, which are created by its staff, its environment, its class of boys, and its endowments. I suggest that no system of external tests which aims primarily at examining individual scholars can result in anything but educational waste.

Primarily it is the schools and not the scholars which should be inspected. Each school should grant its own leaving certificates, based on its own curriculum. The standards of these schools should be sampled and corrected. But the first requisite for educational reform is the school as a unit, with its approved curriculum based on its own needs, and evolved by its own staff. If we fail to secure that, we simply fall from one formalism into another, from one dung-hill of inert ideas into another.

In stating that the school is the true educational unit in any national system for the safeguarding of efficiency, I have conceived the alternative system as being the external examination of the individual scholar. But every Scylla is faced by its Charybdis—or, in more homely language, there is a ditch on both sides of the road. It will be equally fatal to education if we fall into the hands of a supervising department which is under the impression that it can divide all schools into two or three rigid categories, each type being forced to adopt a rigid curriculum. When I say that the school is the educational unit, I mean exactly what I say, no larger unit, no smaller unit. Each school must have the claim to be considered in relation to its special circumstances. The classifying of schools for some purposes is necessary. But no absolutely rigid curriculum, not modified by its own staff, should be permissible. Exactly the same principles apply, with the proper modifications, to universities and to technical colleges.

When one considers in its length and in its breadth the importance of this question of the education of a nation's young, the broken lives, the defeated hopes, the national failures, which result from the frivolous inertia with which it is treated, it is difficult to restrain within oneself a savage rage. In the conditions of modern life the rule is absolute, the race which does not value trained intelligence is doomed. Not all your heroism, not all your social charm, not all your wit, not all your victories on land or at sea, can move back the finger of fate. To-day we maintain ourselves. To-morrow science will have moved forward yet one more step, and there will be no appeal from the judgment which will then be pronounced on the uneducated.

We can be content with no less than the old summary of educational ideal which has been current at any time from the dawn of our civilisation. The essence of education is that it be religious.

Pray, what is religious education?

A religious education is an education which inculcates duty and reverence. Duty arises from our potential control over the course of events. Where attainable knowledge could have changed the issue, ignorance has the guilt of vice. And the foundation of reverence is this perception, that the present holds within itself the complete sum of existence, backwards and forwards, that whole amplitude of time, which is eternity.

The Higher Learning

ROBERT MAYNARD HUTCHINS
(1899–   )

The Higher Learning in America, 1936
No Friendly Voice, 1937
Education for Freedom, 1943
The Conflict in Education in a Democratic Society, 1953

ROBERT MAYNARD HUTCHINS became at 32 the President of the New York Stock Exchange, where he remained until he was made Chancellor of the University of Chicago. With Mortimer Alder, Stringfellow Barr and others, he created an experimental college based on one of the most radical curricula ever designed in this country. Able students were permitted to enter college early and to move through at their own rate. The "Great Books Program" was a by-product of his original educational reform. A system of nondirected learning, rooted in the study and discussion of one hundred classics, it still flourishes throughout the country—a monument to the mind that created it.

THE MOST CHARACTERISTIC FEATURE OF THE MODERN WORLD IS bewilderment. It has become the fashion to be bewildered. Anybody who says he knows anything or understands anything is at once suspected of affectation of falsehood. Consistency has become a vice and opportunism a virtue. We do not know where we are going, or why; and we have almost given up the attempt to find out.

This is an extraordinary situation. Certainly we have more facts about the world, about ourselves, and the relations among ourselves than were available to any of our ancestors. We console ourselves with the delusion that the world is much more complicated than the one our ancestors inhabited. It does not seem possible that its complexity has increased at anywhere near the same rate as our knowledge of facts about it. If, as Descartes led us to believe, the soul's good is the domination of the physical universe, our souls have achieved a very high degree of good indeed. If, as we have been convinced since the Renaissance, the advance of the race is in direct proportion to the volume of information it possesses, we should by now have reached every imaginable human goal. We have more information, more means of getting more information, and more means of distributing information than at any time in history. Every citizen is equipped with information, useful and useless, sufficient to deck out a Cartesian paradise. And yet we are bewildered.

For three hundred years we have cherished a faith in the beneficent influences of facts. As Hilaire Belloc's doggerel puts it:

> The path of life, men said, is hard and rough
> Only because we do not know enough.
> When science has discovered something more,
> We shall be happier than we were before.

Our faith in facts grew with every succeeding century, until it became the dominant force in our society. It excluded every other interest and determined every procedure. Let us get the facts, we said, serene in the confidence that, if we did, all our problems would be solved. We got them. Our problems are insoluble still.

Since we have confused science with information, ideas with facts, and knowledge with miscellaneous data, and since information, facts, and data have not lived up to our high hopes of them, we are witnessing today a revulsion against science, ideas, and knowledge. The anti-intellectualism of the nineteenth century was bad enough. A new and worse brand is now arising. We are in despair because the keys which were to open the gates of heaven have let us into a larger but more oppressive prison-house. We thought those keys were science and the free intelligence of man. They have failed us. To what can we now appeal? One answer comes in the undiluted animalism of the last works of D. H. Lawrence, in the emotionalism of demagogues, in Hitler's scream: "We think with our blood." Man, satisfied that he has weighed reason and found it wanting, turns now to passion. He attempts to cease to be a rational animal, and endeavors to become merely animal. In this attempt he is destined to be unsuccessful. It is his reason which tells him he is bewildered.

My thesis is that in modern times we have seldom tried reason at all, but something we mistook for it; that our bewilderment results in large part from this mistake; and that our salvation lies not in the rejection of the intellect but in a return to it. Let me say at once that in urging a return to the intellect I do not urge a return to that vicious intellectualism whose leading exponent is Descartes. He turned his back to the world and its past, and there by his German stove in a heavy woolen bathrobe thought himself into a mathematical universe which was to be understood by measurement alone. His thinking produced a reaction in succeeding generations which led at the last to a denial of the intellectual powers of mankind.

Let me say, too, that in advocating a return to reason I do not advocate abandonment of our interest in facts. I proclaim the value of observation and experiment. I would proclaim, also, the value of rational thought and would suggest that without it facts may prove worthless, trivial, and irrelevant. In the words of a great contemporary, "The flame remains feeble on which piles of green wood are flung." During the nineteenth century and since, we have been flinging piles of green wood on the fire and have almost succeeded in putting it out. Now we can hardly see through the smoke.

Our program has amounted to a denial of the nature of man. Tested a priori, such denial results in self-contradiction; tested by its consequences, it has been found unsuccessful. It has led us to devote ourselves to measuring and counting the phenomena which passed before our eyes. It has diverted us from the task of understanding them. Modern empirical science which in origin was the application of mathematics to experience by means of measurement and experiment, has come in recent exposition to be considered exclusively an affair of experiment and measurement. Contemporary physical and biological research inherited the analytical procedures which, combined with observation, constitute a science; and to a great extent the heritage has been fruitful. But contemporary physical and biological scientists have also inherited the nineteenth century's anti-intellectual account of empirical science, which placed primary emphasis upon the accumulation of observed facts. The practice of contemporary scientists is thus paradoxically better than what they preach about the nature and ideals of science. In this paradox we have a source of our bewilderment. And, unfortunately, other disciplines, the social studies and the humanities, have been more influenced by the precepts of the natural scientists than by their practices. They, too, even in the fine arts, have decided they must be scientific and have thought they could achieve this aim merely by accumulating facts. So we have lots of "gadgets" in the natural sciences and lots of information in the other fields of knowledge. The gadgeteers and the data-collectors, masquerading as scientists, have threatened to become the supreme chieftains of the scholarly world.

Now, a university should be a center of rational thought. Certainly it is more than a storehouse of rapidly aging facts. It should be the stronghold of those who insist on the exercise of reason, who will not be moved by passion or buried by blizzards of data. The gaze of a university should be turned toward ideas. By the light of ideas it may promote understanding of the nature of the world and of man. Its object is always understanding. In the faith that the intellect of men may yet preserve him, it seeks to emphasize, develop, and protect his intellectual powers. Facts and data it will obtain to assist in formulating and to illustrate the principles it establishes, as Galileo used experiments to assist and exemplify his analysis, not as a substitute for it. Rational thought is the only basis of education and research. Whether we know it or not, it has been responsible for our scientific successes; its absence has been responsible for our bewilderment. A university is the place of all places to grapple with those fundamental principles which rational thought seeks to establish.

A university so organized and so conducted might stand unmoved by public clamor; it might be an island in a sea of turmoil; it might be a rallying-point of all honest and upright men. It might show us the social order we should desire, and help us keep it when it was achieved. A university may make these contributions not by having its professors politicians on the one hand or hermits on the other. Both extremes are equally disastrous. The university must find better and better means of communicating the ideas which it is its duty to foster and develop. A university without these means of communication will die, or at least will not be fruitful. Its ideas are not intellectual playthings, but forces which will drive the world. A university must be intelligible as well as intelligent.

If we look at the modern American university, we have some difficulty in seeing that it is uniformly either one. It sometimes seems to approximate a kindergarten at one end and a clutter of specialists at the other. The specialists are frequently bent on collecting more and more information rather than grappling with fundamentals. So much is already known, so much is being discovered, so many new fields are opening up, that this approach requires more courses, more hours, more laboratories, and more departments. And the process has carried with it surprising losses in general intelligibility. Since the subject matter is intelligible only in terms of the volume of known facts which must be familiar to the scholar, universities have broken down into smaller and smaller compartments. And yet Whitehead may have been right when he said, not long ago, that "the increasing departmentalization of universities has trivialized the intellect of professors."

Nor do we seem always to grapple with fundamentals when we come to education as distinguished from research. The system has been to pour facts into the student with splendid disregard of the certainty that he will forget them, that they may not be facts by the time he graduates, and that he won't know what to do with them if they are. It is a system based on the false notion that education is a substitute for experience, and that therefore little imitation experiences should be handed out day by day until the student is able to stand the shock of a real experience when he meets one. Yet we know that it is impossible to imitate experience in the classroom and that the kind of experience we might reconstruct there would not be the kind the student will meet when he leaves us.

To tell a law student that the law is what the courts will do, and have him reach his conclusions on this point by counting up what they have done, is to forego rational analysis, to deny the necessity of principles, and to prevent the exercise of the intellect. To remit a business student to cases representing what business used to do, not only provides little intellectual experience but also little practical experience, for the cases of the past might be a positive disservice in solving the problems of the present. To turn the divinity student away from the great intellectual tradition of the church and teach him how to organize a party in the parish house is neither to prepare him for the ministry nor to contribute to its improvement. To instruct a medical student in the mechanics of his trade and to fill him full of the recollection of particular instances may result in a competent craftsman, but hardly in a product of which a university may be proud. If professional schools are to rise above the level of vocational training, they must restore ideas to their place in the educational scheme.

The three worst words in education are "character," "personality," and "facts." Facts are the core of an anti-intellectual curriculum. Personality is the qualification we look for in an anti-intellectual teacher. Character is what we expect to produce in the student by the combination of a teacher or personality and a curriculum of facts. How this result can emerge from the mixture of these elements is a mystery to me. Apparently we insist on personality in the teacher because we cannot insist on intellect; we are anti-intellectual. We talk of character as the end of education because an anti-intellectual world will not accept intelligence as its proper aim. Certainly since the *Meno* of Plato, we have had little reason to suppose that we could teach character directly. Courses in elementary, intermediate, and advanced character will fail of their object. The moral virtues are formed by lifelong habit; a university education contributes to them, but it is not its primary purpose to supply them. A university education must chiefly be directed to inculcating the intellectual virtues, and these are the product of rigorous intellectual effort. Such effort is the indispensable constituent of a university course of study.

We see, then, that an anti-intellectual university involves a contradiction in terms. Unless we are to deny forever the essential nature of man, unless we are to remain content with our bewilderment, we must strive somehow to make the university once again the home of the intellect. I repeat: a university is the place of all places to grapple with those fundamental principles which may be established by rational thought. A university course of study, therefore, will be concerned first of all not with current events, for they do not remain current, but with the recognition, application, and discussion of ideas. These ideas may chiefly be discovered in the books of those who clarified and developed them. These books are, I suggest, at once more interesting and more important than the textbooks which, consumed at the rate of ten pages a day, now constitute our almost exclusive diet from the grades to the Ph. D. To aid in his understanding of ideas the student should be trained in those intellectual techniques which have been developed for the purpose of stating and comprehending fundamental principles. Armed with these, he may at length be able to effect transformations and combinations in any subject matter.

Such a course of study would involve in the fine arts, for example, more aesthetics and far less biographical and factual material. In the physical sciences and in experimental biology it would require more attention to the nature of measurement and its relation to the formulation of a science, and far fewer of the countless isolated measurements and exercises now performed in the laboratory. Here I am referring, of course, to the laboratory as an educational institution, not to the laboratory method as a method of research. In so far as biology deals with evolution, a university course of study would diminish the emphasis now given to innumerable details about innumerable organisms and place it on the comprehension of the general scheme of evolution as a theory of history. And in all that study which appears in every department and which is called "history," a university would endeavor to transmit to the student, not a confused list of places, dates, and names, but some understanding of the nature and schemes of history, through which alone its multitudinous facts become intelligible. By some such course of study the university might pass on the tremendous intellectual heritage of the race.

The scholars in a university which is trying to grapple with fundamentals will, I suggest, devote themselves first of all to the rational analysis of the principles of each subject matter. They will seek to establish general propositions under which the facts they gather may be subsumed. I repeat: they would not cease to gather facts, but would know what facts to look for, what they wanted them for, and what to do with them after they got them. They would not confine themselves to rational analysis and ignore the latest bulletin of the Department of Commerce. But they would understand that without analysis current data remain a meaningless tangle of minute facts. They would realize that without some means of ordering and comprehending their material they would sink deeper and deeper beneath the weight of the information they possessed, as the legal scholar has long since sunk beneath the countless decisions and statutes rained down upon him every year.

Since the multiplicity and overlapping of specialties are caused by the superficiality of our analysis, and since grappling with fundamentals should show us what our subject matters are, the ordering of our concrete material by rational means should show us, too, the absurdity of many intellectual barriers that now divide us. We might see again the connections of ideas, and thus of subject matters. We might recapture the grand scheme of the intellect and the unity of thought. Once the three "departments" of the European university, and the only ones, were medicine, theology, and law. These three fields were so studied as to deal with the same propositions and facts, but with different ultimate references. Each one thus penetrated the whole of contemporary thought and was penetrated by the other two. The scholar and student laboring in one of these fields never lost consciousness of the rest. Thus, wherever he was working he remained aware of the individual, living in society, and under God. To this formal organization of a university we cannot and should not return. But it may suggest to us some consequences of believing that the result of general education should be clear and distinct ideas; the end of university training, some notion of humanity and its destiny; and the aim of scholarship, the revelation of the possibilities of the highest powers of mankind.

THE HIGHER LEARNING *Fulfillment*

Harvard College (1854-1858)

HENRY ADAMS
(1838–1918)

Mont-Saint-Michel and Chartres, 1904
The Education of Henry Adams, 1906 (privately printed), 1918
History of the United States of America, 1909-1911

HENRY BROOKS ADAMS, great grandson of one president of the United States and grandson of another, son of the United States ambassador to England during the Civil War, was educated at Harvard and later taught there. He saw his whole life as a process of education and was concerned not only with the university curriculum, but also with the educational effects of milieu and experience. He ranks high among the men who have dealt with the relationship between American life and the European tradition, and with the related subject of the conflict between modern technology and older religious points of view. The chapter on "The Virgin and the Dynamo" in his *Education* represents a classic treatment of these themes.

ONE DAY IN JUNE, 1854, YOUNG ADAMS WALKED FOR THE LAST TIME down the steps of Mr. Dixwell's school in Boylston Place, and felt no sensation but one of unqualified joy that this experience was ended. Never before or afterwards in his life did he close a period so long as four years without some sensation of loss— some sentiment of habit—but school was what in after life he commonly heard his friends denounce as an intolerable bore. He was born too old for it. The same thing could be said of most New England boys. Mentally they never were boys. Their education as men should have begun at ten years old. They were fully five years more mature than the English or European boy for

Reprinted by permission from *The Education of Henry Adams, An Autobiography,* Boston: Houghton Mifflin Company, 1927.

whom schools were made. For the purposes of future advancement, as afterwards appeared, these first six years of a possible education were wasted in doing imperfectly what might have been done perfectly in one, and in any case would have had small value. The next regular step was Harvard College. He was more than glad to go. For generation after generation, Adamses and Brookses and Boylstons and Gorhams had gone to Harvard College, and although none of them, as far as known, had ever done any good there, or thought himself the better for it, custom, social ties, convenience, and, above all, economy, kept each generation in the track. Any other education would have required a serious effort, but no one took Harvard College seriously. All went there because their friends went there, and the College was their ideal of social self-respect.

Harvard College, as far as it educated at all, was a mild and liberal school, which sent young men into the world with all they needed to make respectable citizens, and something of what they wanted to make useful ones. Leaders of men it never tried to make. Its ideals were altogether different. The Unitarian clergy had given to the College a character of moderation, balance, judgment, restraint, what the French called *mesure;* excellent traits, which the College attained with singular success, so that its graduates could commonly be recognized by the stamp, but such a type of character rarely lent itself to autobiography. In effect, the school created a type but not a will. Four years of Harvard College, if successful, resulted in an autobiographical blank, a mind on which only a watermark had been stamped.

The stamp, as such things went, was a good one. The chief wonder of education is that it does not ruin everybody concerned in it, teachers and taught. Sometimes in after life, Adams debated whether in fact it had not ruined him and most of his companions, but, disappointment apart, Harvard College was probably less hurtful than any other university then in existence. It taught little, and that little ill, but it left the mind open, free from bias, ignorant of facts, but docile. The graduate had few strong prejudices. He knew little, but his mind remained supple, ready to receive knowledge.

What caused the boy most disappointment was the little he

got from his mates. Speaking exactly, he got less than nothing, a result common enough in education. Yet the College Catalogue for the years 1854 to 1861 shows a list of names rather distinguished in their time. Alexander Agassiz and Phillips Brooks led it; H. H. Richardson and O. W. Holmes helped to close it. As a rule the most promising of all die early, and never get their names into a Dictionary of Contemporaries, which seems to be the only popular standard of success. Many died in the war. Adams knew them all, more or less; he felt as much regard, and quite as much respect for them then, as he did after they won great names and were objects of a vastly wider respect; but, as help towards education, he got nothing whatever from them or they from him until long after they had left college. Possibly the fault was his, but one would like to know how many others shared it. Accident counts for much in companionship as in marriage. Life offers perhaps only a score of possible companions, and it is mere chance whether they meet as early as school or college, but it is more than a chance that boys brought up together under like conditions have nothing to give each other. The Class of 1858, to which Henry Adams belonged, was a typical collection of young New Englanders, quietly penetrating and aggressively commonplace; free from meannesses, jealousies, intrigues, enthusiasms, and passions; not exceptionally quick; not consciously sceptical; singularly indifferent to display, artifice, florid expression, but not hostile to it when it amused them; distrustful of themselves, but little disposed to trust any one else; with not much humor of their own, but full of readiness to enjoy the humor of others; negative to a degree that in the long run became positive and triumphant. Not harsh in manners or judgment, rather liberal and open-minded, they were still as a body the most formidable critics one would care to meet, in a long life exposed to criticism. They never flattered, seldom praised; free from vanity, they were not intolerant of it; but they were objectiveness itself; their attitude was a law of nature; their judgment beyond appeal, not an act either of intellect or emotion or of will, but a sort of gravitation.

This was Harvard College incarnate, but even for Harvard College, the Class of 1858 was somewhat extreme. Of unity this band of nearly one hundred young men had no keen sense, but they had equally little energy of repulsion. They were pleasant to live with, and above the average of students—German, French, English, or what not—but chiefly because each individual appeared satisfied to stand alone. It semed a sign of force; yet to stand alone is quite natural when one has no passions; still easier when one has no pains.

Into this unusually dissolvent medium, chance insisted on enlarging Henry Adams's education by tossing a trio of Virginians as little fitted for it as Sioux Indians to a treadmill. By some further affinity, these three outsiders fell into relation with the Bostonians among whom Adams as a schoolboy belonged, and in the end with Adams himself, although they and he knew well how thin an edge of friendship separated them in 1856 from mortal enmity. One of the Virginians was the son of Colonel Robert E. Lee, of the Second United States Cavalry; the two others who seemed instinctively to form a staff for Lee, were town-Virginians from Petersburg. A fourth outsider came from Cincinnati and was half Kentuckian, N. L. Anderson, Longworth on the mother's side. For the first time Adams's education brought him in contact with new types and taught him their values. He saw the New England type measure itself with another, and he was part of the process.

Lee, known through life as "Roony," was a Virginian of the eighteenth century, much as Henry Adams was a Bostonian of the same age. Roony Lee had changed little from the type of his grandfather, Light Horse Harry. Tall, largely built, handsome, genial, with liberal Virginian openness towards all he liked, he had also the Virginian habit of command and took leadership as his natural habit. No one cared to contest it. None of the New Englanders wanted command. For a year, at least, Lee was the most popular and prominent young man in his class, but then seemed slowly to drop into the background. The habit of command was not enough, and the Virginian had little else. He was simple beyond analysis; so simple that even the simple New England student could not realize him. No one knew enough to know how ignorant he was; how childlike; how helpless before the relative complexity of a school. As an animal, the Southerner seemed to have every advantage, but even as an animal he steadily lost ground.

The lesson in education was vital to these young men, who, within ten years, killed each other by scores in the act of testing their college conclusions. Strictly, the Southerner had no mind; he had temperament. He was not a scholar; he had no intellectual training; he could not analyze an idea, and he could not even conceive of admitting two; but in life one could get along very well without ideas, if one had only the social instinct. Dozens of eminent statesmen were men of Lee's type, and maintained themselves well enough in the legislature, but college was a sharper test. The Virginian was weak in vice itself, though the Bostonian was hardly a master of crime. The habits of neither were good; both were apt to drink hard and to live low lives; but the Bostonian suffered less than the Virginian. Commonly the Bostonian would take some care of himself even in his worst stages, while the Virginian became quarrelsome and dangerous. When a Virginian had brooded a few days over an imaginary grief and substantial whiskey, none of his Northern friends could be sure that he might not be waiting, round the corner, with a knife or pistol, to revenge insult by the dry light of *delirium tremens*; and when things reached this condition, Lee had to exhaust his authority over his own staff. Lee was a gentleman of the old school, and, as every one knows, gentlemen of the old school drank almost as much as gentlemen of the new school; but this was not his trouble. He was sober even in the excessive violence of political feeling in those years; he kept his temper and his friends under control.

Adams liked the Virginians. No one was more obnoxious to them, by name and prejudice; yet their friendship was unbroken and even warm. At a moment when the immediate future posed no problem in education so vital as the relative energy and endurance of North and South, this momentary contact with Southern character was a sort of education for its own sake; but this was not all. No doubt the self-esteem of the Yankee, which tended naturally to self-distrust, was flattered by gaining the slow conviction that the Southerner, with his slave-owning limitations, was as little fit to succeed in the struggle of modern life as though he

were still a maker of stone axes, living in caves, and hunting the
bos primigenius, and that every quality in which he was strong,
made him weaker; but Adams had begun to fear that even in
this respect one eighteenth-century type might not differ deeply
from another. Roony Lee had changed little from the Virginian
of a century before; but Adams was himself a good deal nearer
the type of his great-grandfather than to that of a railway superintendent. He was little more fit than the Virginians to deal with
a future America which showed no fancy for the past. Already
Northern society betrayed a preference for economists over diplo-
mats or soldiers—one might even call it a jealousy—against which
two eighteenth-century types had little chance to live, and which
they had in common to fear.

Nothing short of this curious sympathy could have brought
into close relations two young men so hostile as Roony Lee and
Henry Adams, but the chief difference between them as col-
legians consisted only in their difference of scholarship: Lee was
a total failure more sensibly, so that he gladly seized the chance
of escape by accepting a commission offered him by General Win-
field Scott in the force then being organized against the Mormons.
He asked Adams to write his letter of acceptance, which flattered
Adams's vanity more than any Northern compliment could do,
because, in days of violent political bitterness, it showed a certain
amount of good temper. The diplomat felt his profession.

If the student got little from his mates, he got little more from
his masters. The four years passed at college were, for his purposes, wasted. Harvard College was a good school, but at bottom
what the boy disliked most was any school at all. He did not
want to be one in a hundred—one per cent of an education. He
regarded himself as the only person for whom his education had
value, and he wanted the whole of it. He got barely half of an
average. Long afterwards, when the devious path of life led him
back to teach in his turn what no student naturally cared or
needed to know, he diverted some dreary hours of faculty-meet-
ings by looking up his record in the class-lists, and found himself graded precisely in the middle. In the one branch he most
needed—mathematics—barring the few first scholars, failure was
so nearly universal that no attempt at grading could have had

value, and whether he stood fortieth or ninetieth must have
been an accident or the personal favor of the professor. Here his
education failed lamentably. At best he could never have been
a mathematician; at worst he would never have cared to be one;
but he needed to read mathematics, like any other universal language, and he never reached the alphabet.

Beyond two or three Greek plays, the student got nothing from
the ancient languages. Beyond some incoherent theories of free-
trade and protection, he got little from Political Economy. He
could not afterwards remember to have heard the name of Karl
Marx mentioned, or the title of "Capital." He was equally ignorant of Auguste Comte. These were the two writers of his time
who most influenced its thought. The bit of practical teaching he
afterwards reviewed with most curiosity was the course in Chemistry, which taught him a number of theories that befogged his
mind for a lifetime. The only teaching that appealed to his
imagination was a course of lectures by Louis Agassiz on the
Glacial Period and Palaeontology, which had more influence on
his curiosity than the rest of the college instruction altogether.
The entire work of the four years could have been easily put
into the work of any four months in after life.

Harvard College was a negative force, and negative forces have
value. Slowly it weakened the violent political bias of childhood,
not by putting interests in its place, but by mental habits which
had no bias at all. It would also have weakened the literary bias,
if Adams had been capable of finding other amusement, but the
climate kept him steady to desultory and useless reading, till he
had run through libraries of volumes which he forgot even to
their title-pages. Rather by instinct than by guidance, he turned
to writing, and his professors or tutors occasionally gave his English composition a hesitating approval; but in that branch, as
in all the rest, even when he made a long struggle for recognition, he never convinced his teachers that his abilities, at their
best, warranted placing him on the rank-list, among the first
third of his class. Instructors generally reach a fairly accurate
gauge of their scholars' powers. Henry Adams himself held the
opinion that his instructors were very nearly right, and when he
became a professor in his turn, and made mortifying mistakes

in ranking his scholars, he still obstinately insisted that on the
whole, he was not far wrong. Student or professor, he accepted
the negative standard because it was the standard of the school.

He never knew what other students thought of it, or what
they thought they gained from it; nor would their opinion have
much affected his. From the first, he wanted to be done with it,
and stood watching vaguely for a path and a direction. The world
outside seemed large, but the paths that led into it were not many
and lay mostly through Boston, where he did not want to go. As
it happened, by pure chance, the first door of escape that seemed
to offer a hope led into Germany, and James Russell Lowell
opened it.

Lowell, on succeeding Longfellow as Professor of Belles-Lettres,
had duly gone to Germany, and had brought back whatever he
found to bring. The literary world then agreed that truth survived in Germany alone, and Carlyle, Matthew Arnold, Renan,
Emerson, with scores of popular followers, taught the German
faith. The literary world had revolted against the yoke of coming
capitalism—its money-lenders, its bank directors, and its railway magnates. Thackeray and Dickens followed Balzac in scratching and biting the unfortunate middle class savage ill-temper,
much as the middle class had scratched and bitten the Church and
Court for a hundred years before. The middle-class had the
power, and held its coal and iron well in hand, but the satirists
and idealists seized the press, and as they were agreed that the
Second Empire was a disgrace to France and a danger to England, they turned to Germany because at that moment Germany
was neither economical nor military, and a hundred years behind
western Europe in the simplicity of its standard. German thought,
method, honesty, and even taste, became the standards of scholarship. Goethe was raised to the rank of Shakespeare—Kant
ranked as a law-giver above Plato. All serious scholars were
obliged to become German, for German thought was revolu-
tionizing criticism. Lowell had followed the rest, not very enthusiastically, but with sufficient conviction, and invited his
scholars to join him. Adams was glad to accept the invitation,
rather for the sake of cultivating Lowell than Germany, but still
in perfect good faith. It was the first serious attempt he had made

to direct his own education, and he was sure of getting some education out of it; not perhaps anything that he expected, but at least a path.

Singularly circuitous and excessively wasteful of energy the path proved to be, but the student could never see what other was open to him. He could have done no better had he foreseen every stage of his coming life, and he would probably have done worse. The preliminary step was pure gain. James Russell Lowell had brought back from Germany the only new and valuable part of its universities, the habit of allowing students to read with him privately in his study. Adams asked the privilege, and used it to read a little, and to talk a great deal, for the personal contact pleased and flattered him, as that of older men ought to flatter and please the young even when they altogether exaggerate its value. Lowell was a new element in the boy's life. As practical a New Englander as any, he leaned towards the Concord faith rather than towards Boston where he properly belonged; for Concord, in the dark days of 1856, glowed with pure light. Adams approached it in much the same spirit as he would have entered a Gothic Cathedral, for he well knew that the priests regarded him as only a worm. To the Concord Church all Adamses were minds of dust and emptiness, devoid of feeling, poetry or imagination; little higher than the common scourings of State Street; politicians of doubtful honesty; natures of narrow scope; and already, at eighteen years old, Henry had begun to feel uncertainty about so many matters more important than Adamses that his mind rebelled against no discipline merely personal, and he was ready to admit his unworthiness if only he might penetrate the shrine. The influence of Harvard College was beginning to have its effect. He was slipping away from fixed principles; from Mount Vernon Street; from Quincy; from the eighteenth century; and his first steps led toward Concord.

He never reached Concord, and to Concord Church he, like the rest of mankind who accepted a material universe, remained always an insect, or something much lower—a man. It was surely no fault of his that the universe seemed to him real; perhaps—as Mr. Emerson justly said—it was so; in spite of the long-continued effort of a lifetime, he perpetually fell back into the heresy that if anything universal was unreal, it was himself and not the appearances; it was the poet and not the banker; it was his own thought, not the thing that moved it. He did not lack the wish to be transcendental. Concord seemed to him, at one time, more real than Quincy; yet in truth Russell Lowell was as little transcendental as Beacon Street. From him the boy got no revolutionary thought whatever—objective or subjective as they used to call it—but he got good-humored encouragement to do what amused him, which consisted in passing two years in Europe after finishing the four years of Cambridge.

The result seemed small in proportion to the effort, but it was the only positive result he could ever trace to the influence of Harvard College, and he had grave doubts whether Harvard College influenced even that. Negative results in plenty he could trace, but he tended towards negation on his own account, as one side of the New England mind had always done, and even there he could never feel sure that Harvard College had more than reflected a weakness. In his opinion the education was not serious, but in truth hardly any Boston student took it seriously, and none of them seemed sure that President Walker himself, or President Felton after him, took it more seriously than the students. For them all, the college offered chiefly advantages vulgarly called social, rather than mental.

Unluckily for this particular boy, social advantages were his only capital in life. Of money he had not much, of mind not more, but he could be quite certain that, barring his own faults, his social position would never be questioned. What he needed was a career in which social position had value. Never in his life would he have to explain who he was; never would he have need of acquaintance to strenghten his social standing; but he needed greatly some one to show him how to use the acquaintance he cared to make. He made no acquaintance in college which proved to have the smallest use in after life. All his Boston friends he knew before, or would have known in any case, and contact of Bostonian with Bostonian was the last education these young men needed. Cordial and intimate as their college relations were, they all flew off in different directions the moment they took their degrees. Harvard College remained a tie, indeed, but a tie little stronger than Beacon Street and not so strong as State Street. Strangers might perhaps gain something from the college if they were hard pressed for social connections. A student like H. H. Richardson, who came from far away New Orleans, and had his career before him to chase rather than to guide, might make valuable friendships at college. Certainly Adams made no acquaintance there that he valued in after life so much as Richardson, but still more certainly the college relation had little to do with the later friendship. Life is a narrow valley, and the roads run close together. Adams would have attached himself to Richardson in any case, as he attached himself to John LaFarge or Augustus St. Gaudens or Clarence King or John Hay, none of whom were at Harvard College. The valley of life grew more and more narrow with years, and certain men with common tastes were bound to come together. Adams knew only that he would have felt himself on a more equal footing with them had he been less ignorant, and had he not thrown away ten years of early life in acquiring what he might have acquired in one.

Socially or intellectually, the college was for him negative and in some ways mischievous. The most tolerant man of the world could not see good in the lower habits of the students, but the vices were less harmful than the virtues. The habit of drinking —though the mere recollection of it made him doubt his own veracity, so fantastic it seemed in later life—may have done no great or permanent harm; but the habit of looking at life as a social relation—an affair of society—did no good. It cultivated a weakness which needed no cultivation. If it had helped to make men of the world, or give the manners and instincts of any profession—such as temper, patience, courtesy, or a faculty of profiting by the social defects of opponents—it would have been education better worth having than mathematics or languages; but so far as it helped to make anything, it helped only to make the college standard permanent through life. The Bostonian educated at Harvard College remained a collegian, if he stuck only to what the college gave him. If parents went on, generation after generation, sending their children to Harvard College for the sake of its social advantages, they perpetuated an inferior social type, quite as ill-fitted as the Oxford type for success in the next generation.

Luckily the old social standard of the college, as President Walker or James Russell Lowell still showed it, was admirable, and if it had little practical value or personal influence on the mass of students, at least it preserved the tradition for those who liked it. The Harvard graduate was neither American nor European, nor even wholly Yankee; his admirers were few, and his critics many; perhaps his worst weakness was his self-criticism and self-consciousness; but his ambitions, social or intellectual, were not necessarily cheap even though they might be negative. Afraid of serious risks, and still more afraid of personal ridicule, he seldom made a great failure of life, and nearly always led a life more or less worth living. So Henry Adams, well aware that he could not succeed as a scholar, and finding his social position beyond improvement or need of effort, betook himself to the single ambition which otherwise would scarcely have seemed a true outcome of the college, though it was the last remnant of the old Unitarian supremacy. He took to the pen. He wrote.

The College Magazine printed his work, and the College Societies listened to his addresses. Lavish of praise the readers were not; the audiences, too, listened in silence; but this was all the encouragement any Harvard collegian had a reasonable hope to receive; grave silence was a form of patience that meant possible future acceptance; and Henry Adams went on writing. No one cared enough to criticize, except himself, who soon began to suffer from reaching his own limits. He found that he could not be this—or that—or the other; always precisely the things he wanted to be. He had not wit or scope or force. Judges always ranked him beneath a rival, if he had any; and he believed the judges were right. His work seemed to him thin, commonplace, feeble. At times he felt his own weakness so fatally that he could not go on; when he had nothing to say, he could not say it, and he found that he had very little to say at best. Much that he then wrote must be still in existence in print or manuscript, though he never cared to see it again, for he felt no doubt that it was in reality just what he thought it. At best it showed only a feeling for form; an instinct of exclusion. Nothing shocked—not even its weakness.

Inevitably an effort leads to an ambition—creates it—and at that time the ambition of the literary student, which almost took place of the regular prizes of scholarship, was that of being chosen as the representative of his class—the Class Orator—at the close of their course. This was political as well as literary success, and precisely the sort of eighteenth-century combination that fascinated an eighteenth-century boy. The idea lurked in his mind, at first as a dream, in no way serious or even possible, for he stood outside the number of what were known as popular men. Year by year, his position seemed to improve, or perhaps his rivals disappeared, until at last, to his own great astonishment, he found himself a candidate. The habits of the college permitted no active candidacy; he and his rivals had not a word to say for or against themselves, and he was never even consulted on the subject; he was not present at any of the proceedings, and how it happened he never could quite divine, but it did happen, that one evening, on returning from Boston, he received notice of his election, after a very close contest, as Class Orator over the head of the first scholar, who was undoubtedly a better orator and a more popular man. In politics the success of the poorer candidate is common enough, and Henry Adams was a fairly trained politician, but he never understood how he managed to defeat not only a more capable but a more popular rival.

To him the election seemed a miracle. This was no mock-modesty; his head was as clear as ever it was in an indifferent canvass, and he knew his rivals and their following as well as he knew himself. What he did not know, even after four years of education, was Harvard College. What he could never measure was the bewildering impersonality of the men, who, at twenty years old, seemed to set no value either on official or personal standards. Here were nearly a hundred young men who had lived together intimately during four of the most impressionable years of life, and who, not only once but again and again, in different ways, deliberately, seriously, dispassionately, chose as their representatives precisely those of their companions who seemed least to represent them. As far as these Orators and

Marshals had any position at all in a collegiate sense, it was that
of indifference to the college. Henry Adams never professed the
smallest faith in universities of any kind, either as boy or man,
nor had he the faintest admiration for the university graduate,
either in Europe or America; as a collegian he was only known
apart from his fellows by his habit of standing outside the college; and yet the singular fact remained that this commonplace
body of young men chose him repeatedly to express his and their
commonplaces. Secretly, of course, the successful candidate flattered himself—and them—with the hope that they might perhaps not be so commonplace as they thought themselves; but
this was only another proof that all were identical. They saw in
him a representative—the kind of representative they wanted—
and he saw in them the most formidable array of judges he
could ever meet, like so many mirrors of himself, an infinite
reflection of his own shortcomings.

All the same, the choice was flattering; so flattering that it
actually shocked his vanity; and would have shocked it more, if
possible, had he known that it was to be the only flattery of the
sort he was ever to receive. The function of Class Day was, in
the eyes of nine-tenths of the students, altogether the most important of the college, and the figure of the Orator was the most
conspicuous in the function. Unlike the Orators at regular Com-
mencements, the Class Day Orator stood alone, or had only the
Poet for rival. Crowded into the large church, the students, their
families, friends, aunts, uncles and chaperones, attended all the
girls of sixteen or twenty who wanted to show their summer
dresses or fresh complexions, and there, for an hour or two, in a
heat that might have melted bronze, they listened to an Orator
and a Poet in cleryman's gowns, reciting such platitudes as their
own experience and their mild censors permitted them to utter.
What Henry Adams said in his Class Oration of 1858 he soon
forgot to the last word, nor had it the least value for education;
but he naturally remembered what was said of it. He remembered
especially one of his eminent uncles or relations remarking that,
as the work of so young a man, the oration was singularly wanting in enthusiasm. The young man—always in search of education
—asked himself whether, setting rhetoric aside, this absence of

enthusiasm was a defect or a merit, since, in either case, it was all that Harvard College taught, and all that the hundred young men, whom he was trying to represent, expressed. Another comment threw more light on the effect of the college education. One of the elderly gentlemen noticed the orator's "perfect self-possession." Self-possession indeed! If Harvard College gave nothing else, it gave calm. For four years each student had been obliged to figure daily before dozens of young men who knew each other to the last fibre. One had done little but read papers to Societies, or act comedy in the Hasty Pudding, not to speak of all sorts of regular exercises, and no audience in future life would ever be so intimately and terribly intelligent as these. Three-fourths of the graduates would rather have addressed the Council of Trent or the British Parliament than have acted Sir Anthony Absolute or Dr. Ollapod before a gala audience of the Hasty Pudding. Self-possession was the strongest part of Harvard College, which certainly taught men to stand alone, so that nothing seemed stranger to its graduates than the paroxysms of terror before the public which often overcame the graduates of European universities. Whether this was, or was not, education, Henry Adams never knew. He was ready to stand up before any audience in America or Europe, with nerves rather steadier for the excitement, but whether he should ever have anything to say, remained to be proved. As yet he knew nothing. Education had not begun.

American College, 1916

MALCOLM COWLEY
(1898–   )

Exiles' Return, 1935; rev. 1956
The Literary Situation, 1954

MALCOLM COWLEY is an editor, freelance writer and critic, best known for his contributions to such liberal magazines as *The New Republic.* Recently he has concerned himself with literary matters, producing useful studies of Whitman and William Faulkner. His primary interest for a long time, however, was the sociology of the American writer. In *Exiles' Return* (from which the essay below is taken) he wrote the classical account of the American "expatriates": an analysis of why they left America for Europe in the twenties and returned in the thirties. *Exiles' Return* is an autobiography as well as the story of a man's education and of his growing to maturity.

IT OFTEN SEEMS TO ME THAT OUR YEARS IN SCHOOL AND AFTER school, in college and later in the army, might be regarded as a long process of deracination. Looking backward, I feel that our whole training was involuntarily directed toward destroying whatever roots we had in the soil, toward eradicating our local and regional peculiarities, toward making us homeless citizens of the world.

In school, unless we happened to be Southerners, we were divested of any local pride. We studied Ancient History and American History, but not, in my own case, the history of western Pennsylvania. We learned by name the rivers of Siberia—Obi, Yenisei, Lena, Amur—but not the Ohio with its navigable tributaries, or why most of them had ceased to be navigated, or why Pittsburgh was built at its forks. We had high-school courses in

Latin, German, Chemistry, good courses all of them, and a class
in Civics where we learned to list the amendments to the Constitution and name the members of the Supreme Court; but we
never learned how Presidents were really chosen or how a law was
put through Congress. If one of us had later come into contact
with the practical side of government—that is, if he wished to
get a street paved, an assessment reduced, a friend out of trouble
with the police or a relative appointed to office—well, fortunately
the ward boss wouldn't take much time to set him straight.

Of the English texts we studied, I can remember only one, "The
Legend of Sleepy Hollow," that gave us any idea that an American valley could be be as effectively clothed in romance as Ivan-
hoe's castle or the London of Henry Esmond. It seemed to us
that America was beneath the level of great fiction; it seemed
that literature in general, and art and learning, were things
existing at an infinite distance from our daily lives. For those of
us who read independently, this impression became even stronger:
the only authors to admire were foreign authors. We came to
feel that wisdom was an attribute of Greece and art of the Renaissance, that glamour belonged only to Paris or Vienna and
that glory was confined to the dim past. If we tried, notwithstanding, to write about more immediate subjects, we were forced
to use a language not properly our own. A definite effort was
being made to destroy all trace of local idiom or pronunciation
and have us speak "correctly"—that is, in a standardized Amer-
english as colorless as Esperanto. Some of our instructors had
themselves acquired this public-school dialect only by dint of
practice, and now set forth its rules with an iron pedantry, as if
they were teaching a dead language.

In college the process of deracination went on remorselessly.
We were not being prepared for citizenship in a town, a state
or a nation; we were not being trained for an industry or profession essential to the common life; instead we were being ex-
horted to enter that international republic of learning whose
traditions are those of Athens, Florence, Paris, Berlin and Oxford. The immigrant into that high disembodied realm is supposed to come with empty hands and naked mind, like a recruit

into the army. He is clothed and fed by his preceptors, who furnish him only with the best of intellectual supplies. Nothing must enter that world in its raw state; everything must be refined by time and distance, by theory and research, until it loses its own special qualities, its life, and is transformed into the dead material of culture. The ideal university is regarded as having no regional or economic ties. With its faculty, students, classrooms and stadium, it exists in a town as if by accident, its real existence being in the immaterial world of scholarship—or such, at any rate, was the idea to be gained in those years by any impressionable student.

Take my own experience at Harvard. Here was a university that had grown immediately out of a local situation, out of the colonists' need for trained ministers of the Gospel. It had transformed itself from generation to generation with the transformations of New England culture. Farming money, fishing money, trading money, privateering money, wool, cotton, shoe and banking money, had all contributed to its vast endowment. It had grown with Boston, a city whose records were written on the face of its buildings. Sometimes on Sundays I used to wander through the old sections of Beacon Hill and the North End and admire the magnificent doorways, built in the chastest Puritan style with profits from the trade in China tea. Behind some of them Armenians now lived, or Jews; the Old North Church was in an Italian quarter, near the house of Paul Revere, a silversmith. Back Bay had been reclaimed from marshland and covered with mansions during the prosperous years after the Civil War (shoes, uniforms, railroads, speculation in government bonds). On Brattle Street, in Cambridge, Longfellow's house was open to the public, and I might have visited Brook Farm. All these things, Emerson, doorways, factory hands and fortunes, the Elective System, the Porcellian Club, were bound together into one civilization, but of this I received no hint. I was studying Goethe's *Dichtung und Wahrheit* and the Elizabethan drama, and perhaps, on my way to classes in the morning, passing a Catholic church outside of which two Irish boys stood and looked at me with unfriendly eyes. Why was Cambridge an Irish provincial city, almost like Cork or Limerick? What was the reason, in all the territory round Boston, for the hostility between "nice people" and "muckers"? When a development of houses for nice Cambridge people came out on the main street of Sommerville (as one of them did), why did it turn its back on the street, build a brick wall against the sidewalk, and face on an interior lawn where nurses could watch nice children playing? I didn't know; I was hurrying off to a section meeting in European History and wondering whether I could give the dates of the German peasant wars.

I am not suggesting that we should have been encouraged to take more "practical" courses—Bookkeeping or Restaurant Management or Sewage Disposal or any of the hundreds that clutter the curriculum of a big university. These specialized techniques could wait till later, after we had chosen our life work. What we were seeking, as sophomores and juniors, was something vastly more general, a key to unlock the world, a picture to guide us in fitting its jigsaw parts together. It happened that our professors were eager to furnish us with such a key or guide; they were highly trained, earnest, devoted to their calling. Essentially the trouble was that the world they pictured for our benefit was the special world of scholarship timeless, placeless, elaborate, incomplete and bearing only the vaguest relationship to that other world in which fortunes were made, universities endowed and city governments run by muckers.

It lay at a distance, even, from the college world in which we were doing our best to get ahead. The rigorous methods and high doctrines taught by our professors applied only to parts of our lives. We had to fill in the gaps as best we could, usually by accepting the unspoken doctrines of those about us. In practice the college standards were set, not by the faculty, but by the leaders among the students, and particularly by the rich boys from half-English preparatory schools, for whose benefit the system seemed to be run. The rest of us, boys from public high schools, ran the risk of losing our own culture, such as it was, in our bedazzlement with this new puzzling world, and of receiving nothing real in exchange.

Young writers were especially tempted to regard their own experience as something negligible, not worth the trouble of recording in the sort of verse or prose they were taught to imitate from the English masters. A Jewish boy from Brooklyn might win a scholarship by virtue of his literary talent. Behind him there would lie whole generations of rabbis versed in the Torah and the Talmud, representatives of the oldest Western culture now surviving. Behind him, too, lay the memories of an exciting childhood: street gangs in Brownsville, chants in a Chassidic synagogue, the struggle of his parents against poverty, his cousin's struggle, perhaps, to build a labor union and his uncle's fight against it—all the emotions, smells, and noises of the ghetto. Before him lay contact with another great culture, and four years of leisure in which to study, write and form a picture of himself. But what he would write in those four years were Keatsian sonnets about English abbeys, which he had never seen, and nightingales he had never heard.

I remember a boy from my own city, in this case a gentile and a graduate of Central High School, which then occupied a group of antiquated buildings on the edge of the business section. Southeast of it was a Jewish quarter; to the north, across the railroad, was the Strip, home of steelworkers, saloons and small-time politicians; to the east lay the Hill, already inhabited by Negroes, with a small red-light district along the lower slopes of it, through which the boys occasionally wandered at lunch-time. The students themselves were drawn partly from these various slums, but chiefly from residential districts in East Liberty and on Squirrel Hill. They followed an out-of-date curriculum under the direction of teachers renowned for thoroughness and severity; they had every chance to combine four years of sound classical discipline with a personal observation of city morals and sociology and politics in action.

This particular student was brilliant in his classes, editor of the school paper, captain of the debating team; he had the sort of reputation that spreads to other high schools; everybody said he was sure to be famous some day. He entered Harvard two or three years before my time and became a fairly important figure. When I went out for the *Harvard Crimson* (incidentally, without making it) I was sent to get some news about an activity for which he was the spokesman. Maybe he would take an interest in a boy from the same city, who had debated and written for the school paper and won a scholarship like himself. I hurried to his room on Mt. Auburn Street. He was wearing—this was my first impression —a suit of clothes cut by a very good tailor, so well cut, indeed, that it made the features above it seem undistinguished. He eyed me carelessly—my own suit was bought in a department store— and began talking from a distance in a rich Oxford accent put on like his clothes. I went away without my news, feeling ashamed. The story wasn't printed.

Years later I saw him again when I was writing book reviews for a New York newspaper. He came into the office looking very English, like the boss's son. A friendly reporter told me that he was a second-string dramatic critic who would never become first-string. "He ought to get wise to himself," the reporter said. "He's got too much culture for this game."

In college we never grasped the idea that culture was the outgrowth of a situation—that an artisan knowing his tools and having the feel of his materials might be a cultured man; that a farmer among his animals and his fields, stopping his plow at the fence corner to meditate over death and life and next year's crop, might have culture without even reading a newspaper. Essentially we were taught to regard culture as a veneer, a badge of class distinction—as something assumed like an Oxford accent or a suit of English clothes.

Those salesrooms and fitting rooms of culture where we would spend four years were not ground-floor shops, open to the life of the street. They existed, as it were, at the top of very high buildings, looking down at a far panorama of boulevards and Georgian houses and Greek temples of banking—with people outside them the size of gnats—and, vague in the distance, the fields, mines, factories that labored unobtrusively to support us. We never glanced out at them. On the heights, while tailors transformed us into the semblance of cultured men, we exercised happily, studied in moderation, slept soundly and grumbled at our food. There was nothing else to do except pay the bills rendered semi-annually, and our parents attended to that.

College students, especially in the big Eastern universities, in-

habit an easy world of their own. Except for very rich people and
certain types of childless wives, they have been the only American class that could take leisure for granted. There have always
been many among them who earned their board and tuition by
tending furnaces, waiting on table or running back kickoffs for
a touchdown; what I am about to say does not apply to them.
The others—at most times the ruling clique of a big university,
the students who set the tone for the rest—are supported practically without efforts of their own. They write a few begging
letters; perhaps they study a little harder in order to win a scholarship; but usually they don't stop to think where the money comes
from. Above them, the president knows the source of the hard
cash that runs this great educational factory; he knows that the
stream of donations can be stopped by a crash in the stock market or reduced in volume by newspaper reports of a professor gone
bolshevik; he knows what he has to tell his trustees or the state
legislators when he goes to them begging for funds. The scrub-
women in the library, the chambermaids and janitors, know how
they earn their food; but the students themselves, and many of
their professors, are blind to economic forces and they never think
of society in concrete terms, as the source of food and football
fields and professors' salaries.

The university itself forms a temporary society with standards
of its own. In my time at Harvard the virtues instilled into students were good taste, good manners, cleanliness, chastity, gentle-
manliness (or niceness), reticence and the spirit of competition
in sports; they are virtues often prized by a leisure class. When a
student failed to meet the leisure-class standards someone would
say, "He talks too much," or more conclusively, "He needs a
bath." Even boys from very good Back Bay families would fail
to make a club if they paid too much attention to chorus girls.
Years later, during the controversy over the New Humanism, I
read several books by Professor Irving Babbitt, the founder of
the school, and found myself carried back into the atmosphere of
the classroom. Babbitt and his disciples liked to talk about
poise, proportionateness, the imitation of great models, decorum
and the Inner Check. Those too were leisure-class ideals and I
decided that they were simply the student virtues rephrased in

loftier language. The truth was that the New Humanism grew out of Eastern university life, where it flourished as in a penthouse garden.

Nor was it the only growth that adorned these high mansions of culture. There was also, for example, the college liberalism that always drew back from action. There was the missionary attitude of Phillips Brooks House and the college Y.M.C.A.'s, that of reaching down and helping others to climb not quite up to our level. There was later the life-is-a-circus type of cynicism rendered popular by the *American Mercury:* everything is rotten, people are fools; let's all get quietly drunk and laugh at them. Then, too, there was a type of aestheticism very popular during my own college years. The Harvard Aesthetes of 1916 were trying to create in Cambridge, Massachusetts, an after-image of Oxford in the 1890s. They read the *Yellow Book*, they read Casanova's memoirs and *Les Liaisons Dangereuses*, both in French, and Petronius in Latin; they gathered at tea-time in one another's rooms, or at punches in the office of the *Harvard Monthly*; they drank, instead of weak punch, seidels of straight gin topped with a maraschino cherry; they discussed the harmonies of Pater, the rhythms of Aubrey Beardsley and, growing louder, the volup-tuousness of the Church, the essential virtue of prostitution. They had crucifixes in their bedrooms, and ticket stubs from last Saturday's burlesque show at the Old Howard. They wrote, too; dozens of them were prematurely decayed poets, each with his invocation to Antinoüs, his mournful descriptions of Venetian lagoons, his sonnets to a chorus girl in which he addressed her as "little painted poem of God." In spite of these beginnings, a few of them became good writers.

They were apparently very different from the Humanists, who never wrote poems at all, and yet, in respect to their opinions, they were simply Humanists turned upside down. For each of the Humanist virtues they had an antithesis. Thus, for poise they substituted *ecstasy*; for proportionateness, the Golden Mean, a worship of *immoderation*; for imitating great models, the oppo-site virtue of following each impulse, of *living in the moment*. Instead of decorum, they mildly preached a *revolt* from middle-class standards, which led them toward a sentimental reverence for sordid things; instead of the Inner Check, they believed in the duty of *self-expression*. Yet the Humanist and the Aesthete were both products of the same milieu, one in which the productive forces of society were regarded as something alien to poetry and learning. And both of them, though they found different solutions, were obsessed by the same problem, that of their individual salvation or damnation, success or failure, in a world in which neither was at home.

Whatever the doctrines we adopted during our college years, whatever the illusions we had of growing toward culture and self-sufficiency, the same process of deracination was continuing for all of us. We were like so many tumbleweeds sprouting in the rich summer soil, our leaves spreading while our roots slowly dried and became brittle. Normally the deracination would have ended when we left college; outside in the practical world we should have been forced to acquire new roots in order to survive. But we weren't destined to have the fate of the usual college generation and, instead of ceasing, the process would be intensified. Soon the war would be upon us; soon the winds would tear us up and send us rolling and drifting over the wide land.

Harvard

MARCUS CUNLIFFE
(1922–   )

The Nation Takes Shape, 1789-1837, 1959
The Literature of the United States, rev. ed. 1961

MARCUS CUNLIFFE is an Englishman interested in America, and an historian concerned with literature. This double interest has let him see things in our books and life not readily apparent to others. The essay below appeared in *Encounter,* a magazine dedicated, like Mr. Cunliffe himself, to making clear the connections between Great Britain and the United States, as well as between the social sciences and the arts.

HARVARD IS A NUMBER OF DIFFERENT PLACES. TO THE UNINFORMED foreigner—say myself fifteen years ago, before I ever visited the United States—it stands with Yale and Princeton as an American version of Oxford-and-Cambridge. The foreigner may have heard something about Columbia or Chicago or Berkeley, or vaguely envisage vast education-factories that are given over to football and fraternity life. But in such a view only Harvard, followed by Yale and Princeton, has much standing. These are *known* to exist among the general European public: the other colleges are a blurred comedy-world in which the students are all athletes or crooners and the severe lady-professors become beautiful and impulsive simply by removing their spectacles.

To the ordinary American without first-hand knowledge Harvard is also a little special. It is newsworthy. All the American papers, even those three thousand miles from Massachusetts, found space for a paragraph on Harvard's recent success in raising through one sustained drive the unprecedented sum of $82½ million. Harvard was in the news, more than other colleges that took the same line, when it declared its opposition to

From *Encounter,* XVII (July 1961).

the loyalty-oath clause in the National Defence Education Act.
Most newspapers in reporting the death of Bernard Berenson
reported too that he had bequeathed to Harvard his Florentine
house and library at I Tatti. Every political journalist has dwelt
on the fact that Senator John F. Kennedy, the victorious candidate for the presidency, is a Harvard man (like the other senator
from Massachusetts, Leverett Saltonstall, who campaigned for
re-election under the slogan "*Salty for Sixty!*"); and that Henry
Cabot Lodge, the defeated Republican nominee for the vice-
presidency, likewise went to Harvard as did his father before him.
More than that: the commentators have been struck by Harvard's
part in planning political strategy. Harvard professors such as
the historian Arthur Schlesinger Jr. and the economist Seymour
Harris enlivened the campaigns of Adlai Stevenson. They, and
Harvard's John Kenneth Galbraith, have been equally prominent
as supporters of Kennedy. Two professors in the Harvard Law
School, Archibald Cox and Abram Chayes, attracted attention
in the same cause. Another Harvard professor of some celebrity,
William Yandell Elliot, was listed as a Republican strategist.
Politics aside, the non-academic American is likely to be familiar
with the faces and names of plenty of other Harvard figures—
Henry Kissinger of the Centre for International Affairs, David
Riesman the sociologist, Archibald MacLeish the poet-play-
wright, and possibly President Nathan B. Pusey.

To the American tourist, Harvard is part of what the brochures
call "Historic Massachusetts." Almost the whole schoolbook lore
of early American patriotism is to be found in the vicinity. In
Boston are Faneuil Hall, the obelisk of Bunker Hill, the gun-
decks of the *U. S. Constitution*. A few miles away, where Paul
Revere took his midnight ride, are Lexington and Concord and
all their legends of embattled farmers. Near Concord is Thoreau's
Walden Pond. And in Cambridge, Harvard itself, embedded in
associations. The tourist on the trail of "Historic Massachusetts,"
doing his best to excuse the bedragglement of post-historic Boston, is quite likely to approach Harvard along the Storrow
Drive—the highway that hugs the right bank of the Charles
River. His impressions? First the brick cliffs of Beacon Street:
white-coated dentists at the windows, turning their backs to the

panorama like the houses they work in. Sailing-boats on the
water. Then a bridge, leading to the bulky acres of M.I.T.
(Massachusetts Institute of Technology). On the near side, more
institutional sprawl—that of Boston University. The road winds
along the narrowing river for a couple of miles until Harvard
appears along the skyline of the *rive gauche*. Again on the right
bank are the Harvard stadium, at Soldiers' Field, and the neo-
Georgian barracks of the Business School. But it is the scene opposite that takes the eye: crews sculling on the river, hectored
through megaphones; couples lolling on the bright green banks,
solitary people squatting over books; and beyond, the spires and
cupolas of Harvard, in terra-cotta, blue, white, and gold, immacu-
late and slightly improbable as in a coloured photograph—except
for two square new towers that are as incongruous as black teeth
in an otherwise ideal smile.

Turning across the river into Cambridge, the tourist will probably find that the place answers his expectations, though if he is
honest he will admit to himself that parts of it are a little scruffy,
a little too much like Anytown, U.S.A. Still, he can sit under the
striped umbrellas of the *Window Shop,* an establishment of almost intimidating good taste, and discover that Longfellow's
smithy and chestnut-tree once occupied the very same spot. He
can walk along Brattle Street, past a sumptuous new undergraduate theatre (the Loeb *Drama Centre*), past the alley known as
Appian Way in whose little wooden houses the women's college,
Radcliffe, began obscurely eighty years ago; past these, and some
handsome, well-kept mansions to the most handsome of all, the
ample Craigie House that George Washington chose for a headquarters in 1775, and that Longfellow later occupied when he was
a Harvard professor.

Toiling through the sticky heat of the midsummer tourist
season, the visitor will no doubt inspect the other obligatory
sights, such as the bare and beautiful churches of the Colonial
period which lie near the Cambridge Common, at peace among
the abominable traffic. He can inspect the famous glass flowers
in Harvard's Botanical Museum, or wander in weary awe through
the five floors of anthropological displays at the Peabody, or
"do" the paintings and sculpture in the Busch-Reisinger and

Fogg Museums. Amazed at Harvard's accumulated loot, he may seek relief among the shops along Massachusetts Avenue, just outside the Harvard Yard. They offer him books, skin-diving equipment (or skis, if he comes at the end of summer), books again, conservative suits and thin neat ties, books once more, cameras, tobacco pipes, prints: very much a university row. He may look for the heart of Harvard, its Yard, perhaps entering through the gate inscribed

BY THE GENERAL COURT OF MASSACHUSETTS BAY
28 OCTOBER 1636 AGREED TO GIVE 400£
TOWARDS A SCHOALE OR COLLEDGE . . .

Inside is a surprisingly quiet precinct—a medley of buildings of various dates, designs, and sizes, scattered among lawns and trees that are the home of a breed of sophisticated grey squirrels. The tallest building is the Memorial Church, with an ambitious white spire. The most thickset is the Widener Library, which confronts the Church.

The yard is a congenial area. Though there are university police at the main gate, you can get into it by a dozen different routes. Young wives wheel their babies along its paths. Pigeons wheel and alight, unalarmed. Yet the tourist, especially in mid-summer, out of term, cannot get much sense of Harvard. He ought to see the Yard at ten or eleven or twelve in term-time, when the paths are thick with Harvard boys and Radcliffe girls in transit from one class to another. Even then he would miss much, for universities do not reveal very much of themselves to the out-sider. If he happened to be in Cambridge in early June, though —more precisely in June, 1960, when I too was there, at the end of a year as visiting lecturer—he might, like me, catch glimpses of half a dozen aspects of Harvard.

In mid-June the last written examinations, the last orals were over. The grades were settled, beyond protest. The prizes were being awarded and announced: $50 for an essay on Dante; the James Gordon Bennett award, which went to a thesis on *Bertrand Russell—The Plea for "Sane" Nuclear Politics;* prizes for essays on the collapse of the Weimar Republic, and on the political thought of André Malraux; a $250 award, carried off by a Radcliffe girl, for a thesis on *The Fall of Hyperion: The Moral Function of the Poet;* and so on. Radcliffe students, living a few blocks away in their own Yard, had disposed of their hired bicycles. The secondhand bookshops were up to their necks in discarded texts. Each day the back page of the *Harvard Crimson,* the student newspaper, advertised things for sale—1950 Chevrolets, 1958 M.G.'s, studio couches, microscopes, guitars. There were rooms to let, appeals for passengers to drive to San Francisco and share expenses.

The annual exodus was under way. It sounded, to judge from the conversations in the Yard or on "Mass Ave," as if nearly everyone was off to Europe for at least a month. Many were going by chartered flight, at bargain rates. Some of the oarsmen on the Charles were bound for Henley. Rhodes Scholars discussed longer destinies. The faculty, too, were in motion. Their families might be vacationing already, mulatto-hued from sunburn, at Martha's Vineyard, or in New Hampshire, or on Cape Cod. The husbands talked of sabbatical leave in Paris, research at the British Museum, a conference in Stockholm, meetings with friends in Madrid or Amsterdam. Edmund Wilson, a visiting professor in 1959-60, was leaving for Wellfleet on the Cape. Leon Edel, another visitor, who had been transcribing the huge collection of Henry James letters in the Houghton Library, was devising a Jamesian tour in Europe. Arthur Schlesinger Jr. and John Kenneth Galbraith were flying to Berlin to attend the Congress for Cultural Freedom. Later they and others would fly to Los Angeles or Chicago for the party conventions. Robert Lee Wolff, a Byzantinist with a subsidiary passion for Victorian literature, was going to Aberdeenshire—to the back of the north wind—to consult material for his book on the Scottish fantasist George Macdonald. Paul Tillich, the theologian, was away for two months in Japan. Merle Fainsod, of the Russian Research Centre, was travelling somewhere between Pakistan and Indonesia.

There were arrivals as well as departures: parents and relatives on hand for Commencement, and the Class Reunions, stratified in a living geology.

The strata lay as deep in time as the Class of 1905 and as near modernity as 1957. The two most conspicuous layers were formed by the Class of 1935 and the Class of 1910, celebrating their twenty-fifth and fiftieth reunions and displaying their respective dates on the bands of special (though conservative) straw hats. Proprietary-wistful, the alumni of 1935 and their families were to be seen by the hundred around Cambridge: Marquandish men who had made their way in the world and always found that Harvard was part of that world, well-groomed and fairly athletic men, with faces younger than their bodies; appropriate Marquandish wives, with bodies younger than their faces; and their children, half-awed, half-mutinous, both older and younger than their years, carrying Harvard emblems and being forcibly photographed against the bronze statue of John Harvard in the Yard. Student guides ushered them among the buildings to indicate changes in their lost landscape—the northward spread of the natural sciences, the Lamont Library with its Poetry Room, the manuscript acquisitions of the Houghton Library, the thuggish new towers of Leverett House, the brand-new Quincy House (an undergraduate college with sand-murals by Nivola, so hotel-chic in plan and décor that it has been nicknamed the Quincy-Hilton). Cocktail parties were arranged for the Class of 1935, a concert of the Boston *Pops,* a lobster dinner, sundry lectures and symposia, and a memorial service for classmates and wives. At the end of the reunion the group quietly disclosed that it had scraped together for the *alma mater* a class gift of half a million dollars.

The Class of 1910 had a less strenuous schedule. But, well-treated Rip Van Winkles, they too had their special occasions— an "Ivy League March" written expressly for them, a gathering at the Brookline Country Club. The grandson of Ralph Waldo Emerson, normally resident in Concord, put in an appearance. So did Walter Lippmann, whose own seventieth anniversary had some months earlier been celebrated with a *Festschrift* volume of essays. A third member, T. S. Eliot, was not present, though he had briefly visited Harvard the previous autumn and though he had loyally completed his questionnaire for the 560-page Class Report. ("Tom," according to the Class Secretary, "was very shy and introspective in college.")

Commencement day, the grand finale, came on June 16th. Radcliffe College, officially separate, undoubtedly equal, and unofficially merged with Harvard, held its Commencement the day before. Harvard's affair was staged in the Yard, in the great quadrangle between the Widener Library and the Memorial Church. Fourteen thousand ticket-holders assembled under the trees. The day was, if anything, excessively sunny. Ladies in silk fanned their programmes and, with the mild displeasure of people who are accustomed to seats in the stalls, pointed out to their husbands that *some* people were in the shade or were nearer to the distant platform and would enjoy a superior view. But though it was uncomfortable on the wooden chairs, the atmosphere was extraordinarily affable. How good to be *inside* the Yard! (And so might the casual, excluded tourist think.) Harvard had taken over the town for the day: the police outside had even placarded the parking-meters to concede the triumph. Governor Furcolo came in pilgrimage from the Boston State House with his jogging, portly escort of National Lancers, sweating in the costumes of Polish cavalry of Napoleonic vintage as they had ritually sweated on the same annual errand for over a century.

A black wedge, the Academic Procession, began to move through a lane in the multitude, headed by President Pusey. Mortarboards and top hats bobbed above the heads of the spectators. Somewhere among the top hats was Senator Kennedy in his capacity as Harvard Overseer. The procession reached the platform and subsided into place. A bell rang from the church tower. The Sheriff of Middlesex County, uniformed in black and red, thumped his sword three times to call the meeting to order. In the ensuing silence, his voice divinely clear through the loudspeakers, the Preacher to the University offered a prayer. An anthem from the University Choir. Then three brief orations: one by a West Indian student in Latin ("Who can understand *that?*" whispered a wife close to me, her husband frowning back at her); one on "Education and Social Concern," full of exemplary sentiments; and a mellifluous tribute to Harvard's international spirit by an Englishman from the Business School. Another anthem.

Then, phalanx by phalanx, announced by their deans and greeted with polite applause, the candidates for degrees from the graduate schools, fearsome in their collectivity, their sheer manhourage of application, their square-yardage of diploma. Four hundred and ninety-three from the School of Arts and Sciences, including 189 Ph.D.s; 136 from the School of Education, primed to teach the teachers how to teach; 39 architects, landscapers, and others from the School of Design; a regiment of 573 from the right-bank Business School (of these, 554 Masters in Business Administration); 45 savants in Public Administration; 142 survivors of the Medical School; 11 Doctors of Dental Medicines; 71 qualified experts in Public Health; 524 nimble in case-studies (case-hardened, in the hoary joke) from the Law School; and a final 42—not very many, perhaps, in view of President Pusey's summons to a religious rebirth—from the Divinity School. In all, 2,076 postgraduate degrees.

Swiftly dispatched, they made way for the undergraduates of Harvard College, the 991 members of the senior class, who had already undergone several days of feasting and exhortation. One hundred and nineteen of them had just been commissioned into the armed services through the ROTC programme. All had received their diplomas from the masters of their "houses" (Leverett, Adams, Eliot, Winthrop, Lowell, Kirkland, Dunster, Quincy), and had had the chance to attend dances and parties and the customary moonlight cruise in Boston Harbour. Just over half the class, President Pusey declared, had graduated with honours, twenty-two of them *summa cum laude*.

After the seniors of Harvard College, the guests. The audience squinted at the tiny figures on the dais in an effort to see which celebrities were about to be presented with honorary degrees. The secret had been efficiently kept. As each of the fifteen recipients rose for his one-sentence citation and his allowance of applause, there was a gratified sense that in honouring others Harvard had reasserted its own prestige as an arbiter of reputation. Nothing for publicists or charlatans. A few just rewards for the faithful: a degree, for instance, to Mr. Pratt of New York, an alumnus who had formerly directed the $82½ million fund-drive. Some recognition for scholarship and research: to René Wellek the literary critic and to Sir Macfarlane Burnet the Australian authority on virus diseases. Above all, accolades for the great world, the world of which the Yard wished to be a microcosm— for Robert Menzies, Prime Minister of Australia; for Paul-Henri

Spaak of Belgium and NATO; for Eugene Black, president of the
International Bank (who also got degrees in 1960, as it chanced,
from Yale and Princeton); for Lucio Costa, designer of Brazil's
new capital; for Llewellyn Thompson, America's current ambassador to Moscow.

A few more items to end the ceremony. The rotund music of
the Commencement Hymn (words by an alumnus of 1856):

> Deus omnium creator,
> Rerum mundi moderator,
> Crescit cuius es fundator,
> Nostra Universitas,
> Integri sint curatores,
> Eruditi professores,
> Largiantur donatores,
> Bene partas copias. . . .

A benediction. The last flourish from the Sheriff of Middlesex
County. Then the gathering disintegrated, surfeited and content.
There would be more speeches later that day, from Mr. Menzies
and M. Spaak. But the University's year, and mine with it, was
virtually done with.

Such affairs are as a rule better handled in England. This
must be admitted even if one dislikes them. In America they are
often half-hearted or pompous or a little vulgar or—in the big
universities—borne down by weight of numbers. Harvard's Commencement impressed and even stirred me. It was managed with
dignity and precision. It seemed both solemn and debonair.

The impression lingered in the next few days, as I went back
to my room in the Widener Library and began to clear the desk
for the permanent occupant, a professor who had been away on
leave. I remembered my initial surprise on hearing that several
of the hundred private studies in Widener are allotted to retired
professors. The historians Samuel Eliot Morison and Frederick
Merk are among them. I admired the piety that underlay this
courtesy and the tact required to administer it. I found further
instances of benevolence and privilege among the papers in my
desk. There were the well-printed faculty agenda (or "dockets"),
each of which had some such note as this:

The Committee appointed to prepare a Minute on the Life and Services of the late Wilhelm Reinhold Walter Koehler, *William Dorr Boardman Professor of Fine Arts, Emeritus,* will present the Minute to the Faculty.

The same spirit seemed to reside in other documents: invitations, for example, to dinners and meetings of the Colonial Society of Massachusetts, the Massachusetts Historical Society, the American Academy of Arts and Sciences—each of these an institution with a substantial headquarters in or near Boston. The Academy sponsors the excellent periodical *Daedalus,* edited by the Harvard physicist Gerald Holton. There were further reminders of Boston-Cambridge life in the notices of a Courbet show at the Boston Museum of Fine Arts, and of Rembrandt drawings exhibited at the Fogg; and in the programme of concerts given by the Boston Symphony in the Sanders Memorial Theatre (which revived memories for me of packed benches; of the giant Latin Inscription about the stage; of the marble statue of James Otis forever protesting at the Writs of Assistance; of the names of Civil War dead in the sombre foyer; of two of the musicians who uncannily resembled Adenauer and Selwyn Lloyd).

I came upon notices of a lecture-series by George Kennan (who drew immense crowds) and a talk by the playwright Lillian Hellman (whose play *Toys in the Attic* opened in Boston); and upon invitations to dinners of the *Crimson,* the Signet Society, the Nieman Fellows (journalists selected for a year of meditation at Harvard), the Junior Fellows (a group of graduates who work undisturbed by Ph.D. requirements). There were announcements of receptions held by the *Advocate* (a literary magazine) for W. H. Auden and other authors. I turned over posters about plays, an appeal for the Poets' Theatre, leaflets on nuclear disarmament (a movement in which David Riesman and the historian Stuart Hughes were involved), a programme of the festival organised by Quincy House, which included a reading by Arthur Kopit (Harvard '59), author of a play entitled *Oh Dad, Poor Dad, Mamma's Hung You In The Closet And I'm Feelin' So Sad.*

All these mementos added to the effect made by the Commencement. In sum they compose the conventional picture, the one that has been so often drawn, of Harvard the powerful, the brilliant, benign, and cosmopolitan: *Fair Harvard,* or "Imperial Harvard" as it was labelled not long ago in a magazine article. This is Harvard as the tourist, the successful student, the heart-warmed alumnus, or the flattered foreigner may see it.

There were other papers in my desk—the kind of stuff swept under the carpet when "Fair Harvard" is being posed for another portrait.

There were memoranda about unsatisfactory students, the hopelessly inept few who had somehow hung on thus far. More disquieting were the general run of undergraduate essays, of the middle range between the excellent and the execrable. In bulk such essays conveyed an impression of a Harvard that is in examiner's parlance Fair Only. They were full of jargon and approximation. They seemed unable to penetrate imaginatively beyond the immediate past—beyond, say, 1950. The freshmen used the 1776-And-All-That clichés of high school. The juniors and seniors had acquired another set of clichés, the vogue-words of college life: *dichotomy, empathy, ambiguity, concept, symbol, paradox.* A high proportion of undergraduates would go on to graduate school. Were they travelling a route from naïveté by way of modishness to dullness? In their natural history, did the freshmen evolve into the stalemen of the graduate treadmill, those apprentices of Academe bound to an indefinite but usually protracted term of servitude?

I knew some first-rate graduate students. I met others who seemed prematurely old and cautious, as if they were absorbing the vices of academic life before they had a chance to grasp its virtues. I felt sorry for such students to see them emerge from the library stacks, myopic in the sunlight, hugging the dark green book-bags that are part of the Harvard costume, weighed down by inner burdens of information, treading along with the same resigned rhythm as their pregnant wives: youngsters winded in their twenties.

Now and then I was oppressed by the clutter and inhumanity of the educational process in America. In such moments I wondered whether it is much more than a series of expensive sausage machines: whether despite the semblance of energy and efficiency it has not almost broken down, so that it is alternately too cruel and too lenient to the product, mangling and skimping in careless sequence. Or whether its problems, like those of traffic on the American highways, are not multiplied by the very measures (more highways, more college buildings and classes) that are meant to solve them. American reformers bewail the small sums that are spent on education. To the visitor the remarkable fact is that so *much* is spent; the system suffers more from intellectual than material poverty. Harvard is only one among the hundreds of colleges affected by the pervasive mediocrity, the permissive slackness of American secondary education. But is Harvard entitled to congratulate itself on the undoubted brilliance of its best students? These are the ones that bring glory to Harvard and solace to those who teach there. Does Harvard make them; or do they make Harvard? Does Harvard draw them merely because of its long-acquired prestige? Would they educate themselves, no matter how bad their school or college?

Two suspicions haunt the teacher, or should from time to time:

(a) that he is powerless: his bad students remain bad, while the good ones are good in and of themselves;

(b) that he is not powerless, but that he has been derelict: standards are low and he is in part responsible.

In what ways could Harvard be held responsible for the mediocrity of its average students?

One piece of evidence, though obviously unreliable, is the *Confidential Guide to Freshman Courses*. This booklet, an annual production compiled and marketed by students (similar tip-sheets exist, I think, at Yale and other colleges), is not entirely destructive. It pays high compliments to certain professors. But a number are scolded: *A* is heavy, *B* irrelevant, *C* facetious, *D* inaudible. The comments on "section men" are even harsher. Harvard's large lecture-courses are broken into discussion sections conducted by graduate students and instructors, who also do most of the work in marking papers. Harvard relies even more than other colleges on this expedient. The teaching staff, like an army commanded by generals and sergeants, has a generous establishment of senior figures, and a big shifting population of lowly, part-time Nicholas Nicklebys, with a void between these extremes.

The assistants who worked with me were admirable. I heard less enthusiastic verdicts on some of their colleagues.

Occasional undergraduates grumbled to me that Harvard was "too big" and "mechanical." They attended vast lectures given by celebrated professors whom they never met, and section meetings conducted by nervous assistants whose grading of papers and examinations they did not trust.

"Harvard," I was told, "hires big names for the sake of the name. Then these *prima donnas* begin to resent interruptions to their own careers. They let substitutes lecture for them. They're too busy to revise their lectures, so they give the same stuff year after year. They find students a nuisance. Go and see them in office-hours and you feel you are intruding if you stay more than five minutes."

The complaint was not universal. But it seems to have some foundation. The undergraduates probably have less cause for grievance than the graduate students (in Arts & Sciences: I cannot speak for the other graduate schools; those in the Law School seemed more than content with their lot). In the College, students after their first year live in Houses, each with a well-intentioned if not very comprehensive tutorial system. Freshman seminars are being organised. But for the graduate students it may be a long and lonely haul, with not much chance to meet the faculty informally. There are plenty of social functions at Harvard but they have a tinge of caste-structure about them. The cordiality between unequals has an element of calculation on both sides.

Plodding towards his Ph.D., teaching several hours a week, the Nicholas Nickleby often becomes bemused by Harvard's reputation. Unwilling to take a job in the academic backwoods he hangs around Cambridge, yearning to be kept on though his chances are negligible. The same anguish in more acute form afflicts the faculty member who has been teaching for several years but who has not achieved tenure. The emotion is of course not confined to Harvard yet it is more poignant there than in other American universities. It represents a reversal of the national psychological drama of the Rejected Father: this is the drama of the Rejected Son. Will the assistant professor be banished, or can he by luck and magic and worthiness reach the snug harbour of an associate professorship? Here is *The Quest for Permanence* (to borrow the title of a book on another subject recently published by the Harvard Press). Even those who triumph in the ordeal are said to reveal its after-effects for years.

One after-effect is complacence. What the promoted teacher may have previously described to his friends as a game of chance, or even a rigged game, he now naturally regards as a game of skill, a test of altogether exceptional merit. Indeed "complacence" is the commonest charge levelled against Harvard. Among the entertainments provided for the alumni of 1935 was a lecture on "Harvard's Place in Outer Space." Whoever chose the title certainly meant it as a joke. Was it though a slightly smug private joke, an instance of the bland we-happy-fewness detectable in the whole Commencement ceremony?

I talked about these matters with a friend from the Middle West who insisted that the special odour of Harvard was "sickly with decay:" it was the sweet unbearable smell of success.

He was an intellectual, far angrier with his country than any Englishmen I know are angry with theirs. He was disgusted with what he called the "Effluent Society." He was disgusted with himself for having been drawn at all to Harvard, where he held a sort of peripheral post. We stood together one day on the slim bridge over the Charles that links the Business School with Harvard proper. It was a sunny day and I remarked on the benignity of the scene. Unlike most Harvard people, he reacted violently. The whole place, he said, was a fake. He had nothing against the Business School, except a fundamental objection to all business schools. He thought this one was a pretty good specimen, though Harvard sneered at it privately. But he hated its colonial architecture, and that of most of the 20th-century buildings of the university. It was "morticians' architecture."

"They fake an American past that was never so glossy and prosperous. Like Colonial Williamsburg, only bigger, and they have people actually living in *this* place part of the year to make it more lifelike. You know those funeral parlours in the Colonial style, with a lamp lit in each window and a guarantee that every room is air-conditioned? No indelicacy—that's Harvard. Worse still, they put everyone into Houses, just because Oxford and

Cambridge have colleges. Here in Lowell House there's even a High Table where they wear dinner jackets now and then. You can't *do* that to Americans, at least not to real ones. Either we're Americans or we're nothing."

I was amused by his estimate of Harvard's Anglophilia and suggested that the situation was more complicated than he recognised. I reminded him that though there are pictures of Dear Old England hanging in the Harvard Club in New York, they are confined to the Men's Room. A view of D. W. Brogan's college, Peterhouse, is placed above the urinals. Ought Englishmen, ought Denis Brogan in particular, to feel complimented or insulted?

My friend was not interested in this problem. He wondered, though, why there was an occasional English boy with a title among the Harvard undergraduates.

"From what I know of England, he must have tried first to get into Oxford or Cambridge and they must have turned him down. No offence to you"—my friend knew that I teach at Manchester University—"but he wouldn't be seen dead in Birmingham or Manchester. So he comes here. The Redbricks would be too grubby: he can pass Harvard off as 'amusing.' Harvard the next-best-thing."

I pointed out that many American colleges have built in the colonial idiom. The reply, perhaps illogical, was that Harvard should have known better. I mentioned the newer buildings. Again they did not pass muster. My Middle Western companion thought them inferior—and I agree with him—to the best of the recent construction nearby at M.I.T. It was all a question, I told him, of one's attitude to piety. There were evidences of a kind of piety all over the Boston-Cambridge area: for example, in the frequent use of the word *memorial*—Storrow *Memorial* Drive, Sanders *Memorial* Theatre, and so on. My friend's response?

"Exactly. The whole area is a mausoleum. There's a saying that although today Berkeley is known as the Harvard of the West Coast, in a couple of years Harvard may get called the Berkeley of the East Coast. *I* think it may get called the Forest Lawn of the East Coast. Take the little *Lampoon* building at Harvard.

The *Lampoon* used to be a funny magazine. Now it's like the
Embalmers' Monthly. You know why if you go inside their place.
It's full of old stuffed animals and old framed jokes. Or take
the Signet. They have lunches and their own clubhouse. But
they're extinct too. Once you could find F. O. Matthiessen there
every day, and men like Perry Miller, and really talk. It was
marvellous for undergraduates. Now, Matty's dead and the spirit
has gone out of things. And you know what they have for deco-
rations? Old menus and a few pressed roses! They have a rose
that T. S. Eliot used to own. Think of that—that's Signet for you,
and all of Harvard."

Another day I lunched with a professor from a college a few
miles away. Bitterly and conspiratorially he analysed the badness
of some of Harvard's departments. Too many men, he claimed,
were appointed because they had the right names, private incomes,
Boston connections. Harvard wanted to keep the tone up, to have
the big houses on Craigie and Brattle occupied by Harvard people.
I asked him—he was Jewish—whether there were any traces of
anti-Semitism in Harvard appointments.

"Traces? Until the war Harvard never gave permanent appointments to Jews—at any rate, not in the College. Things have
changed since then. But they like to appoint their own Jews—
people with Harvard Ph.D.s." With an air of open-mindedness
he admitted that this might be an unfair criticism: "After all,
Harvard prefers to appoint *everyone,* not just Jews, from inside."

I had a third conversation with a friend from California, a
man with strongly liberal opinions. Harvard's, he said, was a
"painless liberalism," a matter of fighting small battles that they
could not possibly lose. "They think they lead the country—
that's just a delusion. Setting an example means showing real
courage, not merely passing resolutions. Rich private institutions
like Harvard have nothing to worry about. Let them face the
legislature as they'd have to do in a state university—in fact let
them have to deal with the Massachusetts legislature. You
wouldn't get a squeak out of most of this faculty."

Finally, a friend who is a Harvard professor mentioned the
Society of Junior Fellows as one of Harvard's failures. When the
Society was organised, it was, he said, a brave attempt to get

away from the Ph.D. nonsense. The first Fellows were bright and argumentative. Now they were diligent and polite. "There's too much S.C.R. mystique—silver candlesticks, sherry, nice gentlemanly conversation. It's a come-down from the days of Henderson and Whitehead."

Such comments found a response in me, not only because they were a relief after hearing so much of the other, "Fair Harvard," but also because of my own post in an English Redbrick.

I was mildly chagrined to discover that for many Americans, as for many of my own countrymen, there are only two real universities in Britain (*L.S.E.* might be a third, though some Americans speak as if it passed out of existence with the death of Harold Laski). In Britain I was tired of those Oxford-and-Cambridge anecdotes, of the conversational boat-race with only two conceivable entries. At some Harvard cocktail parties it was almost like being back in England: the initial enquiry as to which of the two one taught at, the faint bewilderment on hearing that it was neither, the subsequent introduction (a few drinks later) as being "Mr. Cunliffe from Birmingham," or Liverpool, or Leeds. So I could not help being sympathetic to the criticism that Harvard was living too comfortably, off unearned income. I was half-ready to envisage Berkeley as an American Redbrick, and to hope that it would vanquish Harvard in the contest for top place on the academic prestige-scale.

I was a little bothered, too, by the Harvard thinness that exasperated my Middle Western acquaintance: its loss of nerve when its complacence could not cover the situation. A generation ago Malcolm Cowley observed of American expatriates that they were always shouting for Harvard and Yale to carry the ball, but that they could not repress the belief that the game was in the bag for Oxford and the Sorbonne. Before Cowley, Henry Adams and others dissected the vulnerabilities of Boston-Cambridge. The symptoms are still discernible. Boston, as Elizabeth Hardwick recently asserted,[1] has become more dowdy and provincial and less able to sustain the pretence, except in a pathetically solipsist way, that it is the Hub of the Universe. Harvard

---

1. Elizabeth Hardwick, "Boston," *Encounter*, Nov., 1959.

has become much less provincial since Henry Adams' time. But its inherited pieties are not always very robust. Otherwise how could there be so much veneration for a "character" such as "Copey" (Charles T. Copeland), a bygone professor of English who was pitiably proud of his few aphorisms ("To eat is human, to digest divine" is one of them)? Some of the Harvard mannerisms—an arch weariness in the voice, a way of carrying head and hands—seem perculiarly derivative, and bring to mind again the contention of our Middle Westerner: namely, that whatever Harvard stands for, it cannot be achieved without a surrender of some essential Americanness.

In sorting out reactions so varied and somewhat contradictory it is useful to consider what Harvard has in common with other universities. Like every university in the world it is a disappointment. I am not thinking of minor deficiencies—personal feuds, curricular rigidities, and the like—but of a larger failure, the failure inherent in all institutions whose aim is in part professedly moral.

In universities as among religious bodies—the closest parallel— we are aware of and cannot forgive the difference between *ought* and *is*. What they might be is so tremendous. What they are is so inevitably humdrum, so tantalisingly a substitute for the Good Life. Universities generate myths, therefore, of intellectual ferment in other eras or in other places, of the one-time great and their rapt audiences, of glorious eccentrics who made life continuously surprising and rich. Perhaps it is healthier to believe such myths than to believe that the greatness has been attained in one's own time and place. Certainly it is more usual. This is why the undergraduate becomes frantic in pursuit of the Good Life, as he hears the laughter from another room, the applause from a lecture he did not attend; or why the teacher becomes cynical, and convinced that his students worsen each year; or why on splendid institutional occasions one has the uneasy feeling that the setting and the ritual are superior to the people involved in them. The measure of Harvard, as of any university, is calibrated in failure: by the size of the gap between aspiration and actuality.

Harvard has more particular features that it shares with all or some American Colleges. Like the rest it is affected by the prior weaknesses of American schooling, by the frighteningly high cost of education, by the growing number of students around the nation and the growing competition for places, and by the cautious, deceptively cool tone of current American life. Harvard's atmosphere might well seem a little flat to a visitor from another continent, though probably not if he is from Western Europe. Party politics caused less excitement in 1960 than the issue of Negro segregation. Woolworth's, one of the chain-stores that had experienced sit-in demonstrations at the lunch-counters of its Southern branches, was methodically picketed in Cambridge by Harvard and Radcliffe students. There were similar activities in various college communities.

Harvard can be grouped in a number of ways. It is one of the private educational institutions, like Chicago and Columbia, which have one thing above all in common: the need to raise money, a need they feel far more acutely than the state tax-supported institutions. Harvard is also in the "Ivy League" of Eastern colleges and universities. They are a miscellaneous group but as a whole they are socially and intellectually fashionable. The "Ivy League" overlaps with what can be called the "Big League," of universities which are listed at the top of the academic prestige-polls. Harvard, Yale, and Princeton are in both. They share pride of place in the "Big League" with California (Berkeley), Chicago, Columbia, Michigan, Pennsylvania, M.I.T. (in a special category), and a few others. In other words Harvard is not *sui generis*. It does not occupy in the United States the place occupied by Oxford in Britain, or by the Sorbonne in France. To write of it as though it were *the* American university, in the sense of being without serious rivals, would be quite misleading.

On the other hand, to speak of Harvard as *the* American university, in the sense of typifying them all, would be equally misleading. It does hold a unique position, if only because it is regarded as and regards itself as unique. Other Ivy League institutions may be Anglophile: Harvard is deemed the most Anglophile. Other universities may have a good conceit of themselves: Harvard is considered the most conceited. Even the men who told me of Harvard's weaknesses assumed without question that it is still the most conspicuous academic target in America. They might

predict that it would slip from first place. They might insist that
some of Harvard's boasted programmes—for instance, the plan
of "general education" for freshmen—were actually pioneered
elsewhere. They still conceded that Harvard leads the rest in a
total assessment of social prestige, intellectual celebrity, and
popular renown. Not all its departments were in the first rank.
There were plenty of young Americans in high school who not
only did not aspire to go to Harvard, but who knew next to
nothing about it. Even so, cumulatively Harvard came first. Before long Berkeley might surpass it: their relative standings fas-
cinate American professors. Yet Berkeley itself has no doubt that
Harvard is *the* rival. It can cull professors from practically anywhere else in the United States: Harvard faculty tend to stay put,
in the conviction that they have already reached the promised
land.

This being so, the criticisms that are made of Harvard can be
seen as unavoidable consequences of American life, and of Harvard's very strengths.

If the average students leave something to be desired, so do
average students all over the United States—and indeed not
merely in the United States. The Harvard average is far above
the national average. As for the Nicholas Nicklebys, I dislike the
habit of entrusting so much instruction to graduate students. But
it is a national habit and there are arguments in its favour. Nor
can I think of any practicable reform that would abolish it: the
cost of higher education would rise inordinately. I regret the
sickly attachment to Harvard of so many of the graduate students; but what else is to be expected while Harvard's prestige
remains so high? Such circumstances—and I include here the
situation of faculty who do not have tenure—are reminiscent of
the tight, despairing atmosphere of British universities where
promotion is concerned. In Britain there are more able men
than senior posts to put them in, and there is a roughly comparable gulf between senior and junior academicians. But the
parallel is accidental. The problem arises in Harvard only because so many of its products wish to stay there. Loss of will,
self-hatred, and hatred of Harvard are engendered; but one cannot say that Harvard is to blame.

Possibly the eminent professors *are* spoiled. Some of them have outside commitments. The Schlesingers and Galbraiths are, however, untypical in this respect; and in any case Schlesinger and Galbraith are widely known and much admired by Harvard students. They and their colleagues are more distracted by outside events than would be the case in such smaller colleges as Amherst or Dartmouth. Constant, informal contact between teacher and student is impossible on the Harvard scale. Something is lost in intimacy, but I think more is gained in general vitality. It is not only Harvard that has this difficulty to reckon with. All over the United States the college professor is in demand as consultant, editor, researcher, TV performer, policy-maker, speech-writer. Business and government both want him. Professors in the Big League are especially sought after. They are bid for, where they are thought to be open to bidding, by rival universities. To secure one of these men is a great prize. Harvard's prestige depends on having a generous share of scholars who enjoy national reputations. One Harvard professor told me that he had lately taught at a small though respectable liberal arts college. He published a book which was deservedly praised. Soon after the first enthusiastic reviews he received a telephone call from McGeorge Bundy, Dean of Arts and Sciences, to ask him whether he would like to come to Harvard. He came.

According to gossip, Harvard has not invariably succeeded. One hears rumours that X and Y could not be lured from Columbia. But usually A, B, and C can be lured; and it is no wonder that now and then Harvard's satisfaction at the process communicates itself unpleasantly to the outsider. At least it is an active, not an inert complacence.

Anglophilia is more difficult to write about. Even a disgruntled Englishman is pleased to find his country and his culture held in such esteem. The main difficulty, though, is that the word does not adequately define the phenomenon. Proper Bostonians and good Harvard men may admire some features of English life. But it is a culture rather than a country that they revere; and an ideal version of a culture—the England that might have been. And they admire it as an ally, or more precisely as a factor in their *own* equation, rather than as a mother-country. Nineteenth-century Boston-Cambridge has been dismissed as "genteel." Many Americans reject its spirit. The combination of intellect and gentility has not been favoured in the United States. It has often taken on a querulous, defensive, snobbish, inbred, nostalgic quality. But Boston-Cambridge at its best was far from being a conscious, weak imitation of England. It was capable of remarkable integrity and vigour.

Harvard's contribution varied in weight. A century ago it was a prim parochial college. Fifty years ago, transformed into a University by the long, energetic, and unpopular leadership of President Charles W. Eliot, it was still unlikeably staid. Nearly all its students were white, Protestant, Anglo-Saxon, and from the north-eastern states.[2] President Abbott Lawrence Lowell, following Eliot, brought Harvard nearer to greatness, and so did *his* successor, President James Bryant Conant.

To-day it exhibits an interesting mixture of conservatism and radicalism. A third of the undergraduates are from New England, and two out of five from private schools. But those figures should be turned round, so as to stress that Harvard now draws its students from all over the country and that the majority are from public high schools. The trend will increase with the stiffening competition for places. The sons of alumni are by no means certain of being admitted. While there are still only a handful of Negro students, Harvard has ceased to be overwhelmingly Protestant and Anglo-Saxon. About a quarter of the undergraduates are Jewish and the proportion is higher in some of the graduate schools. The transition has been remarkable, and relatively swift. Hence the apparent confusion in popular American conceptions of Harvard: that it is "stuffy" and yet "long-haired," snobbish and yet left-wing, exclusive and yet a "Jew college."

---

2. W. E. B. DuBois, a Negro who graduated from Harvard in 1890, says that by this period students from elsewhere were beginning to resent "the way New England students were dominating . . . college affairs. The class marshall on commencement day was always a Saltonstall, a Cabot, a Lowell, or from some such New England family." In 1890 the outsiders managed to elect their own candidate, a Negro, as class orator. ("A Negro Student at Harvard," *Massachusetts Review*, Spring 1960, p. 446.)

The transition was also deliberate. Other Ivy League colleges have changed likewise, but not quite so wholeheartedly. Historic New England gave priority to intellect. The idea survived, somewhat debased and debilitated but still not without worth, in the image of the gentleman-scholar. To it, perhaps just in time to save Harvard from sterility, was added the newer zeal for pure intellect: intellect, that is, judged without regard for doctrinal soundness or social pedigree. The two styles combine a little oddly in the Harvard manner, but they do combine in Harvard intellectual life, and they do represent a concern for excellence.

"Excellence" has lately become a catchword of American educators. How to reconcile it with the American passion for democratic uniformity is an urgent conundrum. Those who approach the problem fairly discover that Harvard has been making honourable and reasonably successful attempts to solve the insoluble.

My Middle Westerner poured scorn upon the Colonial "houses" built in Lowell's day. But the house system was a reform, not a pale imitation of Oxbridge. Other American colleges, including many said to be more "democratic," accommodate their students in fraternity buildings; the unloved minority who fail to secure election live elsewhere, as social outcasts. Harvard used to have its "Gold Coast" of expensive private rooms for wealthy students, and felt little or no obligation to look after the less wealthy. The house system, also introduced at Yale, was an experiment in the hope of avoiding both sorts of evil. True, the Harvard clubs (AD, Porcellian, etc.) remain, but they are non-residential and peripheral to the life of the place, archaic survivals rather than an inner élite. There is no Harvard spectacle of triumph and despair equivalent to Yale's annual *Tap Day,* when the Yale societies (*Skull & Bones* and the rest) publicly select their new members. The Colonial style in architecture is a safe bore, but any alternative at the time—such as Yale's ventures in Gothic—might have been worse. The Harvard houses bunch together pleasantly; the warm brick is of an agreeable hue; and the river-setting helps a great deal. In recent years Harvard's architectural record has been far more enterprising than that of most British universities, though that may not be very high praise. It has even had the nerve to commmission a building from Le Corbusier, his first in North America.

Rebuttals, justifications. But is Harvard a great university?

I believe so, in part for reasons already suggested. It is old— the oldest college in the United States. Age alone does not guarantee eminence. William & Mary College in Virginia, the second oldest, would to-day not be listed among the first hundred, let alone the best dozen American colleges. But age is a benefit. Of the more venerable American establishments, Yale, Princeton, and Columbia have, like Harvard, maintained a high rank over a long period. Age confers a certain momentum, a self-assurance, a style of doing things, a resistance (especially important in America) to cheapjack innovation and to *Hurrapatriotismus* among the trustees. It ought to entail the survival of some old buildings, to give the eye delight, and to confront the two-dimensional young with the extra dimension of time past. With luck and good management there ought to be a gradual accretion of buildings, covering all stages of the university's history and grouped in a coherent community. Harvard does not have quite as much room as it requires. But the very concentration is an advantage. One ought to be able to walk around a university, or at worst resort to a bicycle. Vast campuses have a boring melancholy quality; in so much space one feels like a fatigued dwarf. All of Harvard's main buildings, apart from the medical and dental schools, lie within walking distance of one another. Life swarms around the Yard, and around Harvard Square with its newsstand where you may buy the papers and periodicals of half-a-dozen countries. Many of the faculty live close in. They pay dearly for the privilege. Rents are high and quarters sometimes cramped. But the community has held together.

And yet one learns to distrust places that are always talking about themselves as a "community." They are invariably claustrophobic, when D knows beyond conjecture whom E has invited to dinner and begins to brood over the question of why D was not also invited. University communities should not have to live upon their own resources. Their inhabitants should not consider themselves exiles from the great world. In Harvard's case, "Greater Boston" may not be a genuine metropolis but it is good enough. It provides congenial areas to live in—notably Boston's Beacon Hill, where a number of Harvard professors are elegantly situated. It is an attractive enough region for professors to remain in when they retire: contrast the humane yet sad settlement of emeritus homes, nicknamed "the Graveyard," at Princeton. Boston is run-down and laxly governed. But it has museums, libraries, orchestras, galleries, a harbour, publishing houses—a large-scale variety and activity. If it is provincial, as New Yorkers contemptuously believe, Bostonians do not know this. Their city has been in a mess for a much longer time than is generally realised, and they are used to it. Moreover, though Boston is only a few minutes away from Harvard on the subway, it does not smother Harvard as London tends to obliterate the scattered colleges of its university. On the other hand, Harvard people are not the sole guardians of academic culture. Nearness to a metropolis ought to involve, as in the Boston area, a proliferation of other colleges—and so more people to talk to and talk about. With M.I.T., Brandeis, Wellesley, Boston University and others near at hand, Harvard is in no danger of becoming a hermetic congregation. Nor need it strive to turn itself into a universal emporium. For instance, it does not need to create overnight an Institute of African Studies when there is already one in existence a couple of miles away at Boston University.

All the same, the university itself must be big in order to be great. There are obvious limits to desirable size. Above five or six thousand, the undergraduate population tends to become faceless to its teachers. But if the number is much smaller the college dwindles into an academy in which some branches of scholarship have only a token existence. And to the undergraduate college should be added graduate schools. For some of these, such as medicine and law, nearness to a large city is almost essential. Given this nearness, and a large and various university, other benefits follow—as they have for Harvard. It lies on one of the main academic trade-routes. Visitors pass through in quantity, not in an artificially stimulated trickle ("I know Professor Blank would like to continue this stimulating discussion, but I am afraid I must tear him away so that he can catch his plane back to. . . ."). There is a bigger selection of faces

to look at on the street. There are genuine bookshops, not places
that peddle greeting-cards and best-sellers. There are, as there
should be, more lectures, concerts, plays, and club-meetings than
the student can possibly attend. If they are so scanty that he can
go to all of them, there is a risk that he will be expected to go to
all of them and so be frog-marched into cultivation.

There should be women as well as men students. But colleges
should not become matrimonial agencies or country clubs. Radcliffe has been a boon to Harvard, for it too now stands at the
head of its league, as the most prestigious of women's colleges.
Radcliffe girls are often pretty, and often married to Harvard
boys. But they are not "co-eds" despite the fact of co-education.
They do not act as cheerleaders for the Harvard football team.
The Radcliffe Yard is not subject to the nasty imbecility of
"panty raids."

Harvard is a rich institution, in part through its own tireless
fund-raising efforts. Private colleges in America cannot survive
without such efforts. It is a question whether all will survive,
when state universities can come by funds so much more readily.
Here antiquity counts. Prestige begets prestige; money follows
money. Rich, loyal alumni (*largiantur donatores* . . .) have
long sustained Harvard. Time and money have endowed it with
a library of 6½ million volumes, fine art museums and scientific
collections. Faculty salaries are among the highest in the country.
Because it is big and prosperous already, Harvard can count on
liberal slices of money from the Federal government and from
foundations.

Attitude and vocabulary coarsen ("slices of money") in discussing this topic. Many American academics deplore the emergence of the "affluent professor" with his research budget and his
consultant fees, and the general intensifying of the hunt for
money. But historically, wealth and culture have been con-
comitant. Bad libraries breed bad books, though great libraries
will not infallibly breed good books. On the whole scholarships
lead to scholarship. Amenities are conducive to amenity. As
surely as Oxford or other ancient institutions, Harvard rests
upon money. Its capacity to attract money to-day and its good
sense in spending it are crucial.

What is going to happen to Harvard? Will Berkeley have supplanted it half a century from now? In Berkeley's favour are the westward drift of the Berkeleian prophecy, the California sunshine, the glitter of San Francisco, the resources of a rich state, the almost ferocious energy with which Berkeley applies itself to acquiring the best scholars, the best graduate students. Harvard's advantages are cancelled by some of these. But her lead in prestige means something. So does what has been more solidly accumulated—in business terms, the inventory as well as the good-will. Can even Berkeley match Harvard's library or its scientific collections?

The rivalry is dramatic. But it is not really relevant for Britain. Berkeley is hardly comparable with our Redbricks, or Harvard with Oxbridge. There are many other entrants in the competition and there is no chance that the leaders will outdistance pursuit. For this reason, among others, Harvard's eminence pleased me. It seemed a great university because of a whole sum of virtues. Faculty and students were confident and earnest and quick—though admittedly the bulk of students do not write as engagingly as they talk. The place buzzed. My main complaint is a surly, ungrateful one: that I drank and dined too well too often in a succession of good-looking houses among good-looking and extremely intelligent people, and became insomniac from the combination of physical and mental indulgence.

True, the Harvard faculty has its dull men and its frumpish wives. There were repetitious smugnesses in the conversation and repetitious topics—*Zhivago,* Durrell, C. P. Snow, presidential politics, the satisfaction of being at Harvard. But in the main talk was wide-ranging and excellent.

Brendan Behan once said it was his ambition to be a "rich Red." I liked the rich Crimson tone of Harvard and felt that the blend of prosperous piety and exuberant vitality did not fall hopelessly short, in a world of imperfect universities, of the ideal of a great university. Any day, crossing the Yard, you might encounter along with a score of other exceptional men, Harry Levin, hurrying to lecture on Shakespeare; Van Quine, the philosopher; Werner Jaeger, the classicist; Talcott Parsons, the sociologist; Crane Brinton, the historian; I. A. Richards, stepping as if along a mountain path, with a knapsack on his back; ancient Roscoe Pound, emeritus of the Law School, smiling reminiscently to himself.

I believe Harvard will continue to be a rare centre, that is good to be in despite the stultifying traffic and the surrounding frowsiness and the unkind climate. I was always happy to return there from visits elsewhere. After the gigantic state universities, after the demureness of the smaller New England colleges, my spirit lifted again to catch the view of the Harvard skyline, to be greeted with snatches of music or the rattle of typewriters from open windows on the Cambridge streets, to hear the applause from lectures I had not attended and to join in the applause at other lectures I *did* attend. Harvard's snobberies seem to me harmless and even essential, its weaknesses minor, its virtues firm and undeniable. If I were an American I would want my son to go there, and I would suspect that only his own ability could get him in.

Princeton

JOHN PEALE BISHOP
(1892–1944)

Act of Darkness, 1935
Collected Essays, 1948
Collected Poems, 1948

JOHN PEALE BISHOP graduated from Princeton with F. Scott Fitzgerald and Edmund Wilson. He was in Paris, along with Malcolm Cowley, at the time of the Great Expatriation. His fine novel, *Act of Darkness,* was not much noticed when it appeared; and his poems and essays were not gathered together until after his early death. His reputation has, however, grown steadily since.

PRINCETON UNIVERSITY WAS FOUNDED IN 1746 AS A PRESBYTERIAN college and is now one of the most desired and desirable places in America in which to loiter through four years of one's youth. This establishment of a place whence good Calvinists should go forth—laymen if need be, divines if possible—was, from the first, doomed to failure. Calvinism requires a clear and mountainous air; Princeton is set near slow streams, and the air is always either softly damp or suave with sunlight. Although the trustees desperately made Jonathan Edwards president of the college, he could do nothing against the indulgent climate. It is evident that the cause was early lost, for the younger Aaron Burr, the first graduate to rise to distinction, destroyed a village virgin at sixteen and shot Alexander Hamilton when a little more mature. I drag in these somewhat doubtful details because it is my conviction that the University of Princeton is what it is largely on account of its site. Had it been left to Elizabeth (town), New Jersey, and named, as was originally intended, for Governor Belcher, its history and character might be quite otherwise.

This quiet leafy New Jersey town, continuously troubled by the sound of bells, still keeps a sense of its past. In Nassau Hall the Continental Congress sat in threatened assembly, and behind the second hand furniture shops of Witherspoon Street are the graves of a half dozen Signers. All but the most indifferent students are aware that a barren acre of cornland to the east of the town is the battlefield of Princeton. It is the privilege of certain towns to mumble over their past. Edinburgh, for example, wears its age proudly and obviously; little of London, except to the bearers of Baedekers, seems older than the Crystal Palace or the Albert Memorial.

Princeton is older than the rocks upon which it sits, perhaps because it needs but four years to establish a precedent in antiquity, so that, since the middle of the eighteenth century, forty generations of youth, each with its stiff customs and cries of revolt, have passed through the town on their way to middle age and mediocrity.

Tom D'Invilliers, the poetic feeder to the epigrammatic hero of *This Side of Paradise,* was aware of this when, with Amory Blaine, he crossed the campus on their last night before leaving for the war: "What we leave is more than this one class; it's the whole heritage of youth. We're just one generation—we are breaking all the links that seemed to bind us to top-booted and high-socked generations. We've walked arm and arm with Burr and Light Horse Harry Lee through half these deep blue nights."

The campus accepts this tradition and attempts an air of even greater age by borrowing an architecture of Oxonian medievalism. It is the fashion just now among intellectuals to decry this imitation of the English collegiate Gothic. But the only endurable form of American architecture is the ferro-concrete-skyscraper, which in such a village would be ridiculous. Colonial Georgian is American only by virtue of its early importation. Besides, it has already been used in its two adaptable forms at Harvard and the University of Virginia. No, I am unfortunately fond of the grave beauty of these towers and spires trembling upward, intricately labored and grey; of these grey quadrangles and deep slate roofs, at night hooding under dormer windows' solitary lights, the slate only less luminous and blue than the sky uplifted above it; of Seventy-Nine stately, in red brick, and Holder, enclosing with cloisters and arches a square of sunlight and sod. . . .

Here it is possible that the student should believe himself in a rich current of life. Here no dreamer in his ivory tower, no drunkard, driveling and about to pass out under the table, is farther removed fom actuality than the sophomore sunning his white-flanneled legs in front of the soda shops on Nassau Street. The trains that pass three miles away, plying between New York and Philadelphia, loaded with bankers, clergymen, fertilizer agents, Italian immigrants and cigar drummers, are only so many swift blurs trailing a long foam of smoky cloud across a wash of summer green. Life outside exists—for weekends and eventually for more troublesome purposes—but there is no immediate reason to bother about it. After four years, the undergraduate becomes so studiously lackadaisical, so imperturbably serene, that a young Princeton alumnus looks little better to him than a bank president or a United States senator.

For during these four years he will have heard an affirmation of the older aristocratic tradition—such as it was—of the Middle States, that barbarous gentility, that insistence on honor and physical courage, which America as a whole scarcely preserved after the eighteenth century. He will have found life more nicely adjusted than he is likely to find it again in his youth, and he will have had leisure in which to adjust himself after the turbulence of adolescence. During these years he will, according to his measure, acquire a more gracious conduct: the puritan will be forced toward tolerance; the philistine will become less raucous. And some will find the pathetic beauty of the wisdom of dead men and come with the fervor of contemporary discovery upon the books of those who have written beautifully of themselves.

Cut off from the present, it is possible to stare with a wild surmise at the past. In New York and Chicago, Dr. Johnson must remain a rather shadowy corpulence, ghostily closeted in bookstores. In Princeton, his too solid flesh becomes as substantial as Mr. Chesterton's. Even Tiberius descends from the monstrous and tragic cloud in which Tacitus has enveloped him and dwindles to a studious and able administrator quite as credible as, say, the Honorable Josephus Daniels. Dante may be found at the end of a dreary term in Italian. And the young Swinburne, flamboyant and incarnate, with tossing red hair and wobbly knees, emerges from the Chancellor Green Library with the 1866 volume in his tiny hands.

The campus, already aloof, becomes the more circumscribed because of a lack of girls in Princeton. There are some few, but they are hedged about or wear flat-heeled shoes or serve epigrams with cucumber sandwiches or—but enough. Of course, every once in a while some unwary student returns from vacation sad-eyed and engaged, and, in my generation, there was likewise a society known as the Grousing Club, from whose adventures Fitzgerald drew heavily in his thesis on petting. But in ordinary times the ordinary student contents himself as best he can with masculine society and regards proms and houseparties as something of a nuisance.

Trenton is near by, but bad form. Except for a few undiscriminating freshmen, who ride by trolley on Saturday nights to dance with rouged but chaste shopgirls, the place does not exist. New York and Philadelphia are possible, both socially and by reason of the Pennsylvania Railroad. One mournful professor recently told me that everyone spent the weekend in Princeton except the students. Certainly these absences are more frequent than before Prohibition, when the Saturday night drinking parties at the Nass afforded passable amusement. Then, at least, weekends were not talked about, whether one went to Philadelphia for the Assembly or to New York for more ribald amusement.

II

What shall be said of the Princeton social system and the upperclass clubs, of which so many bitter and uninteresting things have been said already? The clubs have been called undemocratic, as if a goosestep method should be applied to choosing one's friends. They have been assailed as snobbish, when many a poor but honest student has found that neither poverty nor honesty could keep visitations of upperclassmen and election committees from his door. It has been said that they accustom the undergraduate to a too luxurious manner of living. Even this is, I am afraid, a fiction, for, if the architecture is at times pretentious, the food is unfortunately simple and wholesome— and it is to be remembered that the clubs are, first and last, eating clubs.

No, the trouble with the clubs is that, once in them, they matter so little after having seemed to matter so much. During the first two years even quite sane students look upon these formidable buildings on Prospect Street as having the awesomeness of the College of Cardinals and as bearing the hereditary privileges of the stalls of the Knights of the Garter. The President of Ivy—the most ancient of the clubs—is regarded more enviously than the President of the University, the Captain of the football team, the Governor of the State or the Prince of Wales. But once the elections are over, it is difficult for even the election committees to maintain their fervor.

These elections are held in the spring term of sophomore year, usually the first week in March. Invitations are sent out to a limited number of sophomores, who move among their own class, sounding out their friends and desirable acquaintances. A day or so later the bicker begins, and committees of upperclassmen from each club are free to approach the sophomores. The campus takes on an air of Old Home Week in a faintly alcoholic Bedlam. Juniors and seniors harass and harangue the amorphous sections; names are brought up to be blackballed or passed. Eventually—no one ever knows quite how—the sections are formed and signed up. The delirium ends, and the sophomore starts self-consciously to cultivate these bosom friends of a week's standing or, in loneliness and it may be with heart-burnings, broods over his failure to realize himself.

Many an arrival at this season has based his success on brilliantine and a gift for silence. For at times it seems as if nothing matters much but that a man bear an agreeable person and maintain with slightly mature modifications the standards of prep school. Any extreme in habiliment, pleasures or opinions is apt to be characterized as "running it out," and to "run it out" is to lose all chance of social distinction. Talking too loudly at Commons, an undue concern over the souls of unconverted Chinese, drinking more liquor than can be held quietly and steadily, dressing too dowdily or too flamboyantly, the display of more money than necessary for maintenance on a plane with one's peers—all these are "running it out" and wooing damnation. I knew one able youth who barely got into a club on the ninth ballot because his legs were bowed so that he walked like a sailor in a heavy gale. Another sank far below his hopes after boasting too loudly and complacently of his goings-on in New York. Still another failed altogether because he wore pale yellow shorts and was near-sighted.

These somewhat naïve standards may be violated on occasion by the politician or the big man, but to the mere individualist they will be applied with contempt and intolerance. There are certain activities—all of them extra-curriculum—which have a recognized social value, though what a man does counts rather less at Princeton than elsewhere, certainly less than at Yale. Most influential are those sports which play to large crowds—football, baseball, track and crew. Closet athletics, such as wrestling and the parallel bars, are almost a disadvantage.

Outside of athletics, the most powerful organization is the Triangle Club, an unwieldy and smart assemblage, which each year tours a dozen cities, presenting a musical comedy written, book and music, by the undergraduates on a lively but slightly antiquated model. The English Dramatic Association, with a record of Elizabethan comedies, Molière and Shaw, is looked on askance, and the more recent Theatre Intime regarded as a little queer.

Of the publications, the *Daily Princetonian* is received, journalism being, as readers of the *New York Times* know, a highly reputable pursuit. The *Nassau Literary Magazine* suffers from its pretentious title, although literature is admitted in the curriculum. The Philadelphia Society, which is only the Y.M.C.A. in a Brooks suit, is socially and politically powerful. There is more to be said on this subject, but this should be enough to give a hint of the undergraduate's mind at the mid-point of his career.

Yet I do not wish to cry down the clubs. They are pleasant enough places in which to loll over a second cigarette at break-fast, with the sun striping the cloth and the bell for your nine-ten class, which you are quite conscious you are cutting, ringing outside. And dinner is crowded but intimate, with amiable kid-ding from the professional jesters and all the amenities of youth save wine. After dinner, the idlers saunter toward the movies, and a few will, for an hour, lean across the fire or, in warmer weather, stare wistfully into the blue emptiness of evening, as if youth were immutable and time had stopped. If the judg-ments on which the elections are based are immature, it is that the sophomores are themselves immature, the average age being but nineteen. The periodical revolts are raised not, as the leaders suppose, against the clubs, but against the intolerance of the young and youth's contempt for all that do not walk after their own way, whether because of some austerity of soul or weak ankles.

Once the division into clubs is made, it is largely ignored. Many of the idols of sophomore year are discovered to have not only clay feet but clay heads as well. The Secretary of the Tri-angle Club fails to be elected president; the promising athlete becomes ineligible. And a new valuation begins, based more on the individual and less on powerful friends. In the meanwhile, the junior has probably discovered that Princeton is a uni-versity and gives himself somewhat belatedly to such education as may be had in the two years that remain.

For it is unfortunately true that the first two years are spent on studies so general and elementary that they might well have been completed in preparatory school. Despite the fact that the entrance requirements of Princeton are as high as those of any university in the country, the average boy at entrance is little better than literate.

This is not the place to go into the defects of our educational system, but it is idle to rail at the universities for their lack of accomplishment while the average American boy of eighteen re-mains so hopelessly untrained and uninformed. The sole pre-

tense of the preparatory schools seems to be (1) that they prepare
their charges for college entrance exams, which is true and the
beginning of their inadequacy; and (2) that they build character,
which means that they uphold a sweet and serious ideal deriving
somewhat from Tennyson's death-mask of the Victorian Prince
Consort and somewhat from the most unselfish of the Boy Scouts.
But I don't know that anything can be done about it, so long as we
keep up a pretense of universal education.

At the beginning of the junior year, the student is free to
choose a department in which henceforth he concentrates his
energies. History and Economics gather the fairest crowds, with
English and the Romance languages holding those who hope
for an easy two years or who believe that Princeton can best be
appreciated by following beautiful letters. Science, mathematics,
and the ancient languages keep only small and serious groups.

During these last two years the ends of education are directed
toward upholding the humanities and establishing a more intimate relation between student and instructor. This last is done
chiefly through the preceptorials, small and conversational
groups, which supplement the more formal lectures. The aim
of the faculty now becomes, in theory at least, the inculcation of
that form of education so abhorred by H. G. Wells, for Princeton
does not attempt to make good citizens, but to create a respect
for ideas and to make the student aware how intolerably men
have suffered that beauty and wisdom might have form. Education is conceived as being quite as useless as a drawing by da
Vinci, and as having nothing to do with training a man to vote
intelligently for Democratic congressmen or to become a more
earnest member of the Christian Endeavor Society. There is a
certain amount of social service hocus-pocus extant on the campus, and occasionally revivalists appear with theatrical gestures
and voices like Dunsany gods, but they do little harm and represent a compromise rather than an aim.

These things are goodly and well enough for the average
undergraduate, but the exceptional boy will not come off so
happily. If he does not flunk out—which he is more than likely
to do through indifference or boredom—he will waste most of his
time, unless he discovers a more intimate relation with the

faculty than the classroom allows or contemptuously devotes himself to reading outside his courses.

III

My first view of the Princeton faculty was in the autumn of 1913. I had been herded along with some four hundred other freshmen into the seats of Marquand Chapel—a hideous brownstone building, recently burned, to the rich delight of all those who care more for Christian architecture than for Christian instruction. My legs were lost in bulky corduroy trousers; my somewhat skimpy shoulders were evident under a tight black jersey. A black skullcap (the sole remaining vestige of this once compulsory uniform) fidgeted between my knees.

An old man, rosy as a stained-glass prophet and only a little less severe, flapped by in a gown of black. "That's St. Peter, the sexton," whispered an informed freshman.

The organ began—an orgulous roll—and the academic procession passed slowly down the aisle beside me: gowns of voluminous black, hooded with orange, sapphire and crimson; the pale robes of the Doctors of Oxford and Cambridge, the rich proud reds of the Académie Française: mortar boards and beef-eater caps of crushed velvet, brilliant or black.

Presently they were seated in semi-lunar tiers in the chancel, and a speech began, tactful with platitudes. But I did not hear it. I was intent on the aspect of these grave, serene and reverend scholars; philosophers grown old in the pursuit of Truth, mathematicians entranced by the dizzying splendor of numbers, humanists who dined nightly with Lucretius, Erasmus, Pico della Mirandola and Sir Thomas More. I came out of the chapel still dazed by the sight of these noble creatures and was told to run home by bawdy sophomores eager for horsing.

Have I given you, gentle and credulous reader, a true impression of the Princeton faculty? The question is obviously rhetorical. I have not. I have looked on many academic processions since that day and have never been able to see more than a number of bored elderly gents, tricked out in cotton wrappers, black with an occasional gaudy streamer or color, worn over their everyday Kuppenheimers.

But if the faculty is not, as I supposed in my credulous eagerness, a noble body of rapt scholars, neither is it exclusively composed of the kind of professors made famous by their own published platitudes and the satires of intelligent critics. Most of them are old boys with a weakness for pedantry. They play golf in knickerbockers and are not more than ordinarily absent-minded. If they are in their craft disinclined to face facts, their conversation is more full of good sense than is the average businessman's of their years. They lead, indeed, a cloistered life, and many of them are as chaste as the very gargoyles on their scholastic cells. They are jealous of their privileges and regard a doctor's thesis as the only substitute for an initiatory vow in their cult. But they are not moralists using the arrows of Apollo to point a Sunday text. If they deplore the text of Petronius Arbiter, it is not because of the horrible decay of Roman morals, but because of the decadence of Neronian Latin and the mutilations of the manuscript.

There are, of course, this being America, moral enthusiasts and pallid respectabilities who deplore the vagabondage, the thyrsus-twirling and harlot-hunting of the poets they pore over, and who would be mightily disturbed "should their Catullus walk that way." I have not forgotten that lecture where an hour was spent trying to bring the late Percy Bysshe Shelley safely into the Anglican Church. But neither have I forgotten that the wisest of the English faculty are as anxious that the student escape the dominance of the Victorian tradition as Mr. Ezra Pound might be in their place.

For beyond the pedants and the prudes there are still a few wise and gracious individuals, who are more than pedagogues and—on occasion—less than scholars. They do not write moral essays for the *Atlantic Monthly* nor contribute to the Sunday edition of the *New York Times,* having little in common with the box-office hokum professor, that crabbed and senile androgyne who rushes weekly into print to uphold his little store of dogma and to deplore with recent sorrow the death of Elizabeth Browning and Thomas Carlyle. Neither are they erudite non-intelligences, chattering over marginalia, useless phantoms in a noisy and passionate world. They are, rather, quiet-mannered gentlemen, urbane and skeptical, content to uphold the dignity of the scholar in an age without dignity and crassly uneducated. Sometimes I feel that they are all that is permanent in Princeton, when I return and find that all the men who were young with me are gone. Much of the grave charm of the place is due them, and I had rather the elms of McCosh Walk were cut down and burned away than that a single one of them should move from his chair.

After four years at Princeton, what remains beyond a piece of black-printed parchment, waxed and tabbed with a colored string? What beyond the recollection of Sage Tower, misty and strange, standing like a gray alchemist over October's gold; of the days of the big games, with broad orange banners over the towers and the gay, opulent, easy-going crowds come down in motors or by train; of my own small room in Witherspoon with books, dingily red and brown, or with golden blazonries, and the portrait of Georg Gyze, wistfully serene; of rolling marbles down the declining floor to bump against a lecturer who had droned overlong; of examination rooms, intense, hot and cigaretteless? What beyond the recollection of torchlight processions, the "Whoop 'er up" song and the gargoyles creeping out into the crimson glare; of drunken students drilling imaginary squads under midnight windows; of the mid-year prom and the gymnasium diaphanous in streamers of apple-green and pink; of arriving drunk at the Phi Beta Kappa dinner and passing out before the roast; of students leaving a little sorrowfully and without illusion for the war, after farewell parties which began on Perrier Jouet '93 and ended on Great Western; of Holder Court under a decrescent moon, softened by snow as by age, startled by the sudden sound of reveling footsteps under the arches?

What remains beyond these and other such recollections? Well, not much, to be frank: a few friends whom time has proved, men with whom I have shared many things and who are after my own kind; a few books I should not otherwise have read; a smattering of Italian and the ability to pronounce Middle English passably well. But it is enough. If I had a son who was an ordinarily healthy, not too intelligent youth I should certainly send him to Princeton. But if ever I find myself the father of an extraordinary youth I shall not send him to college at all. I shall lock him up in a library until he is old enough to go to Paris.

On Wisconsin!

DAVID BOROFF
(1917-   )

Campus U.S.A., 1961

DAVID BOROFF, a teacher, attained nationwide notice as a journalist, first, in the *New York Post*, then in various magazines, chiefly *Harper's*. His best work has dealt with universities and colleges and has been gathered together in *Campus U.S.A.* He is currently conducting a survey of journalism schools throughout the United States.

THE CASUAL VISITOR TO MADISON, WISCONSIN, IS OFTEN BEMUSED BY the sight of rival state capitols, a mile apart on the main thoroughfare. The loftier of these buildings bulks large behind a huge statue of Abe Lincoln, seated, brooding, and timeless. No state capitol, this is Bascom Hall, the antique nerve center of the University of Wisconsin, in many ways the prototype of the Big Ten and certainly one of the most vigorous examples of public higher education. The way the two capitols confront each other across a mile of department stores and dress shops is by no means fortuitous, for at Wisconsin the relationship between legislature and university is intimate, contentious, and fruitful. The university occupies the higher ground, and this, too, has symbolic overtones. "Madison is the only place where the academician looks down on the politician," an alumnus observed. And it is clear that no politician can propel his career by attacking the university. Even Senator McCarthy, at his snarling worst, refrained from taking on Bascom Hall, despite its history of liberalism at least equal to that of Harvard.

The University of Wisconsin, encompassing hill and wood and plain and fronting the waters of Lake Mendota, is a merging of dizzying polarities. It is a state institution with relaxed admission standards. ("Any high school graduate in the state who really wants to can shoulder his way in," an official admitted.) Nevertheless, it is one of America's great universities, with a Ph.D. production rate—the Dow-Jones average of the academic world— up among the leaders. Amiably schizophrenic, it is at once an intellectual center and a playground for adolescents with an indomitable appetite for fun. It is where rural Wisconsin meets urban sophistication. Beer cascades endlessly, as one might expect in Wisconsin. Yet at the Student Union, where 3.2 beer is dispensed, five times as much milk is consumed. At 10 A.M. huge farm boys sip containers of milk while waiting for their next class. UW is the seat of liberalism, and its academic freedom statement of 1894 still reverberates, but the supervision of student life is repressively mid-Victorian. (Here rural values triumph, and the gaunt presence of mythical Aunt Minnie of Kaukauna is heeded.)

The collision of opposites engenders little comment. Last spring no one saw anything surprising in two adjacent art exhibitions at the Student Union. One was a cornball collection of Norman Rockwell's Americana; the other, a group of impenetrable and tortured canvases by German expressionists. At the Union, the Hoofers, stolid partisans of ski trail and mountain, are next door to as arty a theater crowd as can be found west of Chicago. The silos and pigpens of the School of Agriculture border the tennis courts alive with shapely girls in short-shorts. It is a school where fusty professors are football-happy, and the annual Military Ball must share the limelight with the annual *anti*-Military Ball. Its lake is legendary, but for much of the year it is locked in a Siberian winter. A final paradox: UW is in the heartland of America, but its personality is ineradicably European as well. The university has sturdy departments of Germanic and Scandinavian studies, and its new president, Conrad Elvehjem, is a proud member of the Ygdrasil Norwegian Literary Society.

In short, UW is an academic cosmos, where the enterprising student can find almost anything he wants. The statistics are awesome. To its 18,000 students on its Madison campus (13,000 undergraduates, 5,000 graduate students), UW offers a staggering

1,350 courses in 88 departments, ranging from the most crassly vocational (Office Procedures) to the most magnificently esoteric (Advanced Sanskrit). It has a physical plant worth more than $88 million, and its annual operating budget exceeds $62 million. One thousand scholars, out of a faculty of 3,000, hover over 1,500 research projects. Students from every state and 84 foreign countries jam its frat houses, dorms, and rooming homes. The main campus is so far-flung that there is a bus from the faculty parking lot to Bascom Hall. Its marching song, "On Wisconsin," is known to more millions than any other and has been endlessly pirated. Its Memorial Union has served as a model throughout the country. It used to have the best boxing team in the college world, although its male students are slow to anger.

The unique flavor of the school—the way citizen-student and administrator stand nose to nose—was reflected in a recent meeting of the Contemporary Trends class at which President Elvehjem was a speaker. A sport-shirted student got up and asked bluntly if friction between the president and Dr. Joshua Lederberg was responsible for the departure of the Nobel Prize winner to the promised land of Stanford University. This struck Dr. Elvehjem as an entirely reasonable question, and he explained Lederberg's departure in terms of shifting research interests.

The populist tradition at UW is strong. The chauffeur of former President Edwin Broun Fred used to work in the paintshop. When a call would come from the president, he would jump out of his overalls and into a business suit in order to drive the president to meet a sultan or another visiting dignitary. Nor is rank much heeded. Unlike many parvenu schools which are acutely rank-conscious, UW prefers the egalitarian "Mister."

Populism is also deeply imbedded in the "Wisconsin Idea," the conviction that the university belongs to the people and should render service to it—"a wedding of soil and seminar." This is expressed in extension centers (in places with vaudeville gag names like Sheboygen), in agricultural research stations, and in the university's resident artist, Aaron Bohrod, going on tours of the state talking art to farmers and their wives. As part of its extension service, the university will answer almost any question asked by a responsible citizen. The late Selig Pearlman, professor of labor economics, said reverently, "Wisconsin civilized the United States." He meant such things as workmen's compensation and social security in which the state, under the leadership of university personnel, pioneered.

The Wisconsin Idea is housed institutionally in the Wisconsin Alumni Research Fund, a huge enterprise which subsidizes research in such disparate areas as antibiotics, mink reproduction, heart-valve repair, development of new cheeses, etc. Some revolutionary advances were achieved at UW—for example, dicumarol, an anti-coagulant which allegedly saved former President Eisenhower's life. The Alumni Fund helps make Wisconsin one of the great research centers in the country.

The Wisconsin Idea is epitomized in Jim Wimmer, a twenty-four-year-old student who managed Gaylord Nelson's successful campaign for the governorship and was appointed the governor's executive secretary. A sociologist on campus was unable to see me because he was busy testifying at the state legislature in behalf of the Menominee Indians, who are in traumatic transition from federal to state control. The Wisconsin Idea is represented, too, by the history professor who does a radio broadcast throughout the state and on one occasion received a letter which stated succinctly: "Dear Professor . . . Please drop dead."

Wisconsin used to boast that it has more cows than people. UW, however, is no cow college. In fact, its "Ag" students are the new Organization Men of farming, headed for careers in food processing, farm machinery, or government service. Authentic bumpkins can be found among the short-course students in farming (noncredit), for whom only grade school education is required.

Social cartographers abound at UW, and some are quick to divide the students into Langdon Street (fraternity row), the dorm crowd, and the Independents. Langdon Street is identified with fun, anti-intellectual vigilantism, and a consumption of beer little less than heroic. The dorm students—most of them at the far end of the campus—are reputed to be small-town or rural, ingenuous, and intellectually unformed. Their typical majors are home economics, agriculture, and education. (Engineering students occupy an undefined limbo; it is not a chic major, but no one would suggest that it is easy.) The Independents (called

GDI by Langdon Street—Goddamned Independents) spill out of rooming houses and apartments to oppose Langdon Street Philistia. They provide the soldiery of dissent on campus and man the few frail barricades of radical causes.

There is a sharp urban-rural dichotomy at UW. A sociologist summed up the rural ambiance: "The rural kids tend to be absolutist in matters of religion and family. They see divorce as an evil; they lean towards 'familism,' with relatives as part of the inner family. They are not really independent because of the extended family pattern. The university is expected to stand *in loco parentis*. We're really euchred into a semi-parent position."

Emeritus President Edwin B. Fred, who spent his boyhood on a Virginia farm and forty-seven years of his adult life as a member of the Wisconsin faculty, claims that after they have been on campus a year, it is impossible to tell a farm boy from a city sophisticate. But other observers demur.

A graduate assistant in English from New York City observed: "The urban students are more acute; they catch on faster. But they sometimes have a superficial brightness. Rural kids are ingenuous, friendly, and less artificial." They are also almost totally lacking in irony, and he described with amusement the Chicago girl who sits and smiles with an assured sense of superiority whenever he indulges in irony. Her smile says, "You and I get it, but the others surely don't."

Martha Peterson, the amiable and perceptive Dean of Women, observed that big-city girls with problems "have a big thing about going to the psychiatrist." On the other hand, to refer a small-town girl for therapy, "you have to sneak up on her."

The small-town girl sets modest goals. She is unlikely to think of a glamorous career in the State Department, and some with a four-point index (as close as you can get to scholastic charisma) are content to settle for elementary school teaching.

Miss Peterson tells of the occasion when she invited ten small-town dorm girls to a Sunday night supper at a friend's lake house. "We fed them well, and they ate beautifully," she recalled. "But we couldn't really get a conversation going except for some mild complaints about the food in the dorms. For the most part they sat around and read back copies of magazines." The next week Miss

Peterson received ecstatic notes from the girls affirming what a marvelous time they had and telling how they had written home about the memorable evening.

There are striking differences in social life too. A rural boy came to a house-fellow and asked him for "some topics of conversation for a date." Another bucolic gallant is in the habit of carrying three-by-five cards with deft little conversational gambits neatly typed on them. Formals, in particular, scare them to death.

Sex morality has its rural and urban variations. Generally speaking, rural girls become involved in intimate relationships because of deep and solemn love. They are often appalled at the cavalier way some of the more sophisticated girls have affairs with only a mild affection or a hazily defined intellectual compatibility as sanction.

Carnal anarchy prevails no more at UW than at other universities. Certainly, the administration exercises a steely-eyed vigilance. (A recent satiric skit has the president saying: "I spend 90 per cent of my time regulating the sex life of students, football for the alumni, and parking for the faculty.") Nevertheless, in warm weather there are beaches and cars. In the winter, according to a dorm supervisor, "sex is more challenging." Satyrs don't gambol in Midwestern groves, but it would be naive to assume too much sexual quiescence. However, students feel little need to dramatize their sexual liberation. In fact, this generation of students is much given to trappings of virtue. A member of a big "social" frat said: "Oh, the boys talk about sexy girls. They like to take them out once or twice but don't want to go steady with them." And the women students, for the most part, are girdled in propriety. However, one girl, a free-wheeling Independent, observed tartly, "The vividness with which so many nice girls describe what happens to *other* girls would suggest that they're not as pure as they say."

Recently, a mass-circulation magazine featured a provocative article entitled "Are We Making a Playground out of College?" In it, UW was severely castigated as a high capital of frivolity. *The Daily Cardinal*, UW's student newspaper, said ruefully: "We can see the looks on the faces of Grandma Jones and her neighbors in Superior, Sinsinawa, Silver Lake, and Spread Eagle when they read this week's *Post*." Then in a more vigorous spirit, the newspaper affirmed: "We've made Wisconsin a playground; it's up to us to reconvert it into an institution of higher learning." A student leader, however, declared: "I'm proud that we're a college playground. They refer to us as the dead generation, but the fact that we pull some of our humorous events is a distinguishing feature."

Other students, peering wistfully behind barricades of books, asked, "Boy, what have we been missing!" A young man in the student senate explained, "When visitors from Iowa come on a weekend, they tend to overdo things, because this is supposed to be a big play school. Students, however, don't go out on a nine-month bender." Then he pondered a moment and added judiciously, "Not unless they can adjust to it." "Adjust or drown," another boy said mirthfully as he hoisted his can of beer.

How much fun is enough? Has the university attained a balance between the life of ideas and extracurricular activity, or is the very notion of a great university sponsoring the elaborate apparatus of fun an absurdity? Some faculty members think so. "Our prestige goals are wrong; they're largely social," a professor said firmly. ("College professors everywhere think their students are stupid," an administrator countered.) This much is clear: the pursuit of fun is ubiquitous. There is little surcease from the relentless sequence of Homecoming (floats and parades), Humorology (skits), Campus Carnival, Haresfoot ("All our girls are men, and everyone's a lady"), weekends on lakes for which fraternities charter busses, dances, and parties, parties, parties. One of these was a "Pink and Blue Party" in which, in an unwitting parody of themselves, the boys came in blue, the girls in pink, "and they were all supposed to look like children."

There may be something amiss when only seven students turn up for academic freedom forum, while thousands mill around at Campus Carnival. (It is only fair to point out, however, that Dr. J. Robert Oppenheimer and Mrs. Eleanor Roosevelt drew capacity crowds when they gave talks.) Or it may simply be as one corn-fed girl remarked, "When we work, we work hard; when we play, we play hard."

This playfulness sometimes has an unexpected element of

social criticism. The word "Mickey Mouse," UW argot for trivial, is constantly in use, as if the students are looking uneasily over their own shoulders. A few years ago, a naval ROTC unit was proudly doing close-order drill in a crowded stadium between halves of a big football game. Suddenly, out of Badger Block, the chauvinist cheering section, came a derisive song: "M-I-C-K-E-Y-M-O-U-S-E. That's the way you spell Mickey Mouse." Throughout the enormous stadium, students picked up the chant gleefully.

Fraternity and sorority row incurs a good deal of animus about UW's over-developed play habits, since the Greeks are the chief artisans of organized fun. And beer consumption is the hallmark of the fraternity man. (State Street leading away from Bascom Hall is lined with beer joints.) A girl from Sweden described beer parties as "just a huge noise." She explained, "You don't even get to know the boys because they're drunk before you even get settled." A sorority girl frowned at the mention of beer. "It gets to be an obsession with some boys," she said. "At a party I asked for a coke. My date was so embarrassed, he asked me to pour the coke into an empty beer can."

A frat boy, with a scrupulous sense of the fitness of things, said, "We want lots of milk on the table during the week and lots of beer on Friday and Saturday nights."

I attended a fraternity party—liquid and raucous—in which the empty beer cans were placed neatly on top of one another in the shape of a pyramid. It mounted to the ceiling as the evening went on. Another party had a rock 'n' roll combo (Blackjack Corfines and his Hound-dogs), and couples twitched spasmodically to the music. At still another party, girls in drastically cut-down dungarees, and boys in overalls sang folk songs while the housemother sat in the next room reading a magazine.

UW students take a wry pride in having fathered the panty raid. There was also a small flurry of phone-booth jamming, some of it engineered by a local department store which offered prize money for a contest in front of the store. But UW's particular genius for horseplay expresses itself in the water fight. After Wisconsin comes the deluge. Students pelting each other with buckets of water may conceivably be some kind of Jungian fertility ceremony. It is certainly part of the rites of spring.

I arrived in Madison on a soft spring night, the first warm evening of the year. More than a thousand students milled around Langdon Street under the benevolent surveillance of the police. (In the old days they used to fire their pistols over the heads of the students.) Aside from some small skirmishes, a major dousing did not develop.

The students offered a persuasive rationale. They had endured a bitter winter. "You didn't know which was more confining," a student explained, "the four walls of your room or the snowbanks outside." Girls would get up in the morning, reach into their closets, and wear *everything*. (As a gesture of defiance at the weather, they continued to wear sneakers.) Springtime is the great liberation. People are friendlier; they can even say "Hello." (In the winter, their heads are bent against the wind.) Couples can hold hands without fear of frostbite. And the cracking of Lake Mendota, which had just taken place a few weeks before, was apparently sheer drama. There were hourly reports from ebullient students on the thunderous breaking of the ice. The water fights—"the annual virus" an official called it—are simply a response to the urge to do something that students feel on the first warm days.

To this the administration says a peremptory "No." And, curiously, in a school with a great libertarian tradition, the machinery of suppression is grim and ponderous. A few years ago, the fraternities "got the big knock" as a result of a riotous water fight, and were required to police themselves. On Langdon Street, during the abortive water fight, there were fraternity officers—a crew-cut Gestapo in Bermudas—taking names of frat men who were present.

Nevertheless, the drive against the aquatic Freedom Fighters is only partly successful. *Cardinal* gleefully reported that a dorm water fight in which wastebaskets, water cups, shoe boxes, and plastic bags were pressed into service, produced "the closest cooperation" attained by any function in that house. In a women's dorm—the girls are generally avid handmaidens in water warfare—trash cans were removed by the administration and holes punched in them to forestall their use as weapons. The hapless girls had to wait months for the trash cans to come back.

Water occasioned another controversy last spring. There was a furor last spring about the delay in setting up the piers along the shores of Lake Mendota. The administration wanted the fraternities to pledge that bodies wouldn't go hurtling into the deep. "Residents do not realize the dangers inherent in mass dunking," an official stated primly. The students vociferously demanded their piers. When delay persisted, they prepared an effigy of one of the dorm supervisors with the legend, "Thanks for the piers." At the last minute, the effigy burning was averted. The pathos of the episode is that the object of their wrath was no martinet but one of the new breed of personnel technicians, desperately bent on "understanding" the students. The administration is now considering a kind of voluntary mass deportation. They hope to have old-fashioned launches carrying students on the lake at a nickel a ride from Langdon Street to the playing fields and Picnic Point. Their objective is to kill off Langdon Street's hegemony over organized horseplay.

There are some indications of a trend away from overblown fun. The Junior Prom, a venerable tradition at UW, was recently abolished. And an imposing symposium, organized around the theme "The Challenge of the Sixties," was a striking success and was well attended by students.

Social life at UW has characteristic *élan*. The girls, of course, are coolly marriage-conscious. The ratio of men to women—two to one—is helpful. ("I just wish they would admit it," a boy said testily.) The royal road to matrimony was outlined to me: lavaliered in the soph year; pinned in the junior year; engaged in the senior year. To be sure, there are anxieties. A sorority girl confessed that if she is dateless on Saturday night she hesitates to be seen on Langdon Street. A frat boy remarked that he is taunted by his brothers if he chooses to study on Friday evening. "I think it's a freshman's school," a sophomore girl said. "Freshman year is a big blast. You're a new face and it's all snow and beer and fraternities. Then when you're a sophomore you see the boys on the street, and it's just 'Hi.' In the meantime, they're looking over the new crop."

The Greeks and Independents glare at each other balefully. (The dorm crowd, though populous, is reputed to be out of things, insulated by a bucolic torpor.) The Independents watch the pageantry of play with awed disapproval. The fraternity houses strike them as indecently sybaritic—some are remarkably luxurious—or childish. (One frat house is ornamented with a toilet bowl and a Model T Ford at its entrance.) Sorority girls are stereotyped as trench-coated, short-haired, and rah-rah. "The sorority stuff," a Student Union activist observed, "is even more Mickey Mouse than the Union. Here are seventy-five girls who are automatically my friends because we all paid our dues." A literature student said dispassionately: "I see them all looking and talking alike. They're just interested in trivia. I suppose I am too, but their trivia are not mine." A graduate assistant in art made the telling point that the Langdon Street crowd are afraid to draw well in art class for fear of being outstanding. "It's the same in criticism," he added. "They hesitate to criticize each other."

The fraternity boys do their share of glowering. "The Independents are just people who don't fit into groups," one of them said. And an angry polemicist summed up the bohemian fringe: "They scorn conformity, yet they all look alike. Each gray face and each black-stockinged leg, and each uncombed head looks like every other. They scorn the tennis-shoed and beige trench-coated Bascom Hall cult without realizing that they are just as conformist."

The sexes occasionally snap at each other too. A girl wrote a letter to *Cardinal* lamenting the "lost, strayed, and/or probably extinct mature male." She appealed for someone "individual enough to wade barefoot in a puddle or walk down the street eating a double-dipped ice-cream cone . . . a conversationalist who doesn't have to rely on the latest adventures of *Maverick* or *Gunsmoke*."

A young man shrilled against the campus Messalinas who flaunt their charms in tight sweaters and skirts. "I'm in favor of clean, decent sex appeal," he expostulated, "but it's not one bit funny when a man can't even walk down a street without having his emotions unreasonably stimulated by females. Don't girls realize what their sexiness does to a man? Girls are not flowers which men merely desire to look at."

Sooner or later, everybody meets at the Memorial Union, the self-styled "living room" of UW. Occupied daily by about fourteen thousand people, it is at once cultural heart of the university, lounge, dining room, art gallery, workshop, forum, dance hall, meeting room, theater, and more. (It also has an ineffably lovely lake-side dining terrace on the lake.) No student need stray from campus, for the Union is both Parnassus and juke joint. On a Saturday night last spring, the Dolphins (water ballet) were splashing synchronously at one end of the campus; in the Union actors were posturing elegantly in scenes from *The Importance of Being Earnest;* and a costume dance was in progress in a ballroom, where a Burmese student did an interminable fire dance. Meanwhile, the Rathskeller (invariably called "the Rat") churned with talk, boy met girl in cavernous corners of the gloomy cellar, the jukebox jumped, and all activity, solemn or gay, was well lubricated by a steady flow of 3.2 beer—and milk.

The Rat is the hangout for bearded rebels, sandaled folk singers, and foreign students, as well as for small-town types enthralled by the colorful outlanders. But despite a lot of official rhetoric about the more than nine hundred foreign students, all is not well. A campus survey revealed that though students are willing to live in the same house with members of minority groups, they are reluctant to date them. Over half would not date a Negro or Oriental; a third side-steps social contact with Latin-Americans. Not unexpectedly, fraternity and sorority people are less tolerant than others.

"If that boy from India calls, I'm not in," a girl left word with her roommate. Others date foreign students as an adventure in exoticism. "Did you see who I was with last night?" they then ask their friends.

The bulletin boards proclaim the teeming diversity of campus life. Under the sign for the Annual Military Ball (ROTC formal) is the announcement of the third annual anti-Military Ball (informal with recorded music) whose theme is "The Street Where You Lived, or Dig You Later, Atom Crater." The anti-Military Ball's attendance doubled not long ago (from 200 to 400) and was enlivened by an attempted kidnapping of their leaders as a reprisal for the kidnapping, by parties unknown, of a guard at the Military Ball. Even grave political issues begin to sound like something out of an old-fashioned college musical at UW.

A friend of mine who leafed through *The Badger,* UW's yearbook, gasped incredulously, "My God, it's a Sears, Roebuck catalogue!" Indeed, students respond in much the same way to the profusion of activity. One said, "The nice thing is that you can walk out on a group, and it will still be there when you want it." Another observed, "Wisconsin offers a real-life situation. It has everything—even an Oberlin if you want it." (In the Midwest, Oberlin is considered a prairie Harvard.) The *everything* includes a quaint UW game or dance called "limbo," in which a boy or girl, by bending his knees and arching his back, inches under a rope while everyone chants, "Limbo, limbo, limbo." A shapely girl remarked matter-of-factly, "A more seductive routine for a girl has yet to be choreographed."

UW, of course, is the home of Big Football. Even serious students respond to the zip and sparkle of a football weekend. One professor described football as the only real communal activity at the university, and he spoke with genuine affection of the march to the stadium ("Nobody would think of driving.") To the highly sophisticated, football is a kind of secret vice publicly enjoyed. No intellectual will openly espouse it though he may attend all the games.

A professor who grew up in the Midwest defined his attitude: "I like football. I like the pageantry. But colleges ought to hire good football teams and stop pretending the game has anything to do with education." One faculty member suggested that the Chicago Bears be hired as artists-in-residence.

President Elvehjem pointed out that the athletic budget is a modest million dollars against $15 million for research. "When you have 18,000 students on campus and no football to let off steam, you'll have more panty raids." As for the drive to win (1960 record: 4—5), the football coach wants the team in the top ten to keep it even with the university's academic standing.

The coaching staff, by the way, shrewdly resists the impulse towards punditry so characteristic of coaches at other schools.

(The attraction of the life of the mind for muscle-merchants has long been underestimated.)

Football players have become seriously devalued in recent years. They are Saturday's children, neglected the rest of the week. No longer heroes, they are just hulking mercenaries to many students. "Animal farm" was the scornful epithet of one student. A huge 6'5" linesman ("They're not all as big as me") studied his bruised hands and spoke of the plight of the gladiators: "I think students look down on football players as animalistic. And maybe we are. Other people can sit at their desks, but we have to keep moving. You know, we'll be walking up the hill, and suddenly we'll start shoving each other."

Some years ago, before the wider world beckoned, it was a ritual for many Brooklyn College students to attend UW's summer session to savor the delights of an out-of-town school. The idea of a lake on campus—swimming between classes—seemed deliciously frivolous after the gray austerities of a subway school.

A Brooklyn College girl, darkly pretty and intense, wrote of her experience last summer: "Such things are not for you, I said to myself. You'll prance off to Brooklyn College (with its fine faculty), major in education, marry, have a boy and a girl, and become President of Hadassah. You'll never room with a girl from Kalamazoo and fight off a Lutheran from Texas. You'll never have coffee with an Ethiopian whose father is in the UN, discuss Israel with an Arab, and segregation with a Negro from the South." Her own impact on UW was almost as dramatic as its own on her. She described a moment of sheer Gauguinesque splendor when, after a swim, she shook out her lustrous black hair. "The boys just went wild," she wrote. "They looked at me as if an electric shock passed through their bodies."

What about the intellectual life at UW? Estimates vary. A recent study reveals that the university, despite its open-house philosophy, is getting higher-ranking students from high schools than do the country's colleges as a whole. (In 1959, 60.7 per cent of the freshmen were from the top quarter of their class, while only 2.7 per cent were from the bottom quarter.) Fred Harvey Harrington, the able vice-president in charge of academic affairs, said flatly, "Students are better academically then they were."

The range of ability is wide. According to an informal estimate by an English professor, one-third of the students have difficulties in expressing themselves. The faculty chants dolorously about the intellectual insufficiencies of their students. "I gave an exam and used the word 'expendable,' " one man reported. "A number of students asked what it meant."

But it is the flaccidity of intellectual life that grieves the faculty. "It's difficult to get them to talk," a distinguished teacher of literature observed. "They're so accustomed to a passive role. You have to pull it out of them. They submit to authority; they hesitate to risk their intelligence. It's almost as if they were painted on the wall." Then he added compassionately: "I often think there are too many of them and too few of us."

A girl made a bold assertion about mass education in one of her courses. Her instructor challenged her thesis. "I take it back," she said meekly.

A social scientist complained about intellectual quietism on campus: "They don't inquire about religion. There is an organized religious structure, and they accommodate themselves to it. They take for granted that they're going to be married—and married soon. This represents a decline in individuality, for when you marry you limit your individuality. You take on a conservative component.

"They simply don't feel enough. The job of the social scientist is to get people to think objectively about subjects for which they feel some passion. But these kids are not impassioned about anything."

There is, to be sure, a free commerce of ideas on campus. Recently a Marxist ideologist spoke to students about racial segregation, and shortly thereafter a priest advanced "Christian arguments for capitalism" to the members of the Conservative Club. It is UW's proud boast that it was the last college campus to maintain a chapter of the Labor Youth League, an allegedly Communist-front group. (Former President Fred fought the American Legion on this issue.) The small group finally died of inanition, and the shriveling-up process was no doubt accelerated by the student handbook which let students know that LYL was on the Attorney-General's list. Both the students and the administration opposed loyalty oath in connection with the National Defense Education Act.

Student intellectuals fall into at least four elites: the New Idea group (editors of the literary magazine, who, according to one critic, "have not budged an inch from the avant-garde"); foreign intellectuals; scientists; and fraternity boys with a taste for ideas, who have tired of frat-house fatuities. (One professor asserts that there are many intellectuals immured in a kind of cozy concentration camp on Langdon Street. "Our job should be to help them break out," he said.)

The Green Lantern, an eating co-op, is one of the more spirited intellectual enclaves. Reputed to be vaguely leftist and aggressively bohemian, its members are full of a strident but cheerful insurgency—not without a sly consciousness of the absurdity of some of their postures. Raffish, Saroyanesque, they hunch over cigarette-scarred tables in their cooperative cave (the co-op is in a cellar) and intone slogans for new crises. The hard core is from New York, shaggy-headed and fiercely intellectual, wise-guy heirs of the dead wars of the thirties. Around them are a few pretty girls, surfeited with the inanities of Langdon Street, and some small-town boys awed by the sheer articulateness of these avatars of protest. ("They come as Taft conservatives and leave as socialists," one of the ideologists said.) Nevertheless, one boy called me stealthily by phone to protest his innocence of the heresies I heard expressed. He was opposed, he said, to creeping socialism, which would suggest that the contagion of ideas has limits. "I go there only because the food is cheap," he explained.

The Green Lantern denizens express themselves with aphoristic pungency. Football: "We sit on the steps and watch the parade of citizens go by. Then we listen to the roar." ROTC: "You march up and down in the Quonset Hut, and guys with little stripes yell at you." Fraternities: "They metabolize a lot, but their ends are trivial." Wisconsin boys: "Naive but very decent; free from the oppressive neurosis of New Yorkers." Themselves: "We're not rebels; we all had happy childhoods." They even have a social chairman to betoken their normalcy.

Particularly exhilarating are visits by candidates for office in student government. These poor innocents are badly roughed-up by the cerebral hoods of the Green Lantern.

The final word, however, belongs to a Wisconsin girl who fled the joys and terrors of the co-op. "I could stand the talk," she explained, "but I couldn't endure the dirt."

No doubt, the most talked-about student at UW was Richard S. Wheeler, *The Cardinal's* acidulous commentator on manners and morals. An unabashed student of Mencken, Wheeler assailed the liberal pieties in a prose of unusual trenchancy. The students seemed to take a curious pleasure in the pummeling they receive. "The notorious Wheeler," a student called him, and another gravely explained that Wheeler is bitter "because the Midwest isn't like the East where he once lived."

"The trouble with fraternities," Wheeler wrote at a time when the university passed the 1960 clause outlawing discrimination, "is not that they are undemocratic but rather not aristocratic enough." He dismissed idealism as "a malignant tumor of adolescence . . . a kissing cousin of superstition and fantasy." He raised hackles with a column on necking: "Every time a young lady necks, she's taking a lesson in frigidity. . . . A half-hour's sabbatical in the bathroom with a good book is infinitely more pleasurable." After the piece appeared, he received calls from irate young men whose erotic maneuvers had been repulsed by young ladies brandishing Wheeler's column.

Wheeler also did deadpan interviews with Badger beauties to "make them look like the dumb blondes they usually are." One guileless doll prattled on in this fashion: "I think psychology is so interesting. One professor has a wonderful theory, and at the end of the semester you really believe him, and then next semester another professor refutes everything. I would say that psychology is a science . . . it's good, but it has its bad aspects too." Another beauty confessed: "I was thinking of attending Radcliffe, but it's unnatural. All those girls living just for their weekends. That's not moral."

The faculty at UW is considered strong and no more factious than most. Salaries are good but not good enough. The average for a full professor is $11,069; associate professor, $8,288; assistant professor, $6,827; instructor, $5,614. The campus, described as "sublime" by a visiting Englishman, is supposed to be worth easily $1,000 a year, but assent to this quaint notion by faculty is not easily obtained. Nevertheless, many faculty people, modest salaries notwithstanding, live in handsome suburban developments. There are even some futuristic homes which make East Coast suburbia look timid and unadventurous.

The strongest departments are biochemistry and history. There is some uneasiness among the arts people about the research boons that scientists have for the asking. There was the hope that after President Fred, a man in the humanities or social sciences would be elevated to the presidency in a kind of rotation. (Elvehjem is a biochemist who has done distinguished work in vitamin B-1 complex.) Nevertheless, there has not been too much grumbling about research money. A normal teaching load is three courses a week (nine teaching hours), and the university expects scholarly output from its faculty.

"Formally, we are slaves; factually, we are free men," the late Selig Perlman explained. The price of freedom in a university is the evermultiplying body of faculty committees. "Spending all your time milling around is a consequence of faculty democracy," Vice-President Harrington explained. (Psychologist Carl Rogers, father of nondirective counseling, had to be approved by ten committees when he was appointed recently.) A solution to all this backing and filling is to cut down on the size of committees and their functions. This is currently being considered.

Faculty members range from strenuously informal types in sport shirts and tennis shoes to a Harvard Ph.D. in pencil-thin tie, scrupulously narrow suit, and a faintly supercilious manner, who seems determined to maintain an outpost of gentility among the corn cribs. Careerism rockets along at UW, and relief is in sight only when one is a full professor with tenure. There is also fierce inter-collegiate rivalry for academic talent, and former President Fred used to keep a scoreboard of faculty people who went to the University of Michigan—the big rival—and vice versa.

UW has a Midwestern bonhomie. A man who taught at the University of Chicago asserts that there is far more communication among departments at UW. Nor is there any of the usual churlishness directed against the School of Education, since let-

ters and science faculty members vote on all matters pertaining
to that school, and there are joint appointments to both schools;
for instance, a history professor will also teach the history of
education. There is even a measure of good will towards deans.
"At least they're scholars and researchers," a faculty member
said grudgingly.

I talked with a sociologist, full of that ponderous jargon without which the social scientist feels undressed. After discussing
"well-structured family inter-actional patterns," he turned to life
in Madison and plunged into a racy and uncluttered idiom. "Boy,
this town's a drag," he said. "Occasionally, my wife and I want to
get something to eat late at night, but Madison folds up at 1
A.M. On New Year's Eve there are the same people counting
noses to see who is at whose party."

There are hundreds of graduate assistants at UW who lead
a strangely amphibian existence. They often teach sections for
professors with whom they, in turn, take courses. Moreover,
though they have faculty status, they take upper-division courses
with undergraduates.

Being a graduate student means the big change from directed
to autonomous study. ("You grow up overnight.") It also involves a search for an academic father—a professor in the student's
area of scholarship. Relationships are close, and there are very
few students languishing for years while sweating out their Ph.D.

Teaching can be vexatious for graduate assistants. Some status-
minded undergraduates test them arduously before final acceptance. Then there is often a lack of coordination between quiz
sections and the big lecture section. "But Mr. Whitley said at
the lecture . . ." Often, Mr. Whitley said nothing of the kind.

It is characteristic of UW as an open society that the phone
numbers of faculty members, and their addresses, are published
in a directory available to all students. Students phone at all
hours of the day and night—sometimes for the flimsiest of reasons.

How effective are graduate assistants? An argument in their
behalf is that they make small classes possible. Nor are they all
neophytes. Many have taught elsewhere, and the great concentration is between the ages of twenty-six and twenty-eight. President Elvehjem asserted baldly: "Some are very good. I think I

did some of my best teaching when I was a graduate assistant."

It was former President Fred who observed that it is UW's unique habit "to haul all our dirty linen in front of Abe Lincoln's statue and wash it in public." In recent years, the proposal to erect a new building in Bascom Woods, near the famed carillon tower, provoked a spirited controversy. Everyone had his say— the woods are sacred—and the building plan finally squeaked through by a narrow margin. The university's grandiose buildings program has generated some student resentment. The new Chadbourne Dormitory, eleven stories of Miami Beach decor with a huge "W" on top, was quickly tagged the Chadbourne-Hilton. "How much is the university going to waste?" a sullen student asked.

A long-term student campaign to end compulsory ROTC was successful in 1960, and with voluntary military training came a new curriculum that became a pattern for ROTC throughout the country. Under it a good share of the instruction is in academic subjects, such as geography, military history, and speech, given by the university's own faculty, not by armed forces officers.

But the most acrimonious dialogue had to do with apartment regulations and the supervision of student life. "Apartment living is new and will increase," an official pointed out, "but the rules are old and outmoded." In truth, they smacked unpleasantly of a police state. A student living in a building into which an unmarried woman moved was required to move out. A forty-five-year-old New Zealander lived in the same building as a seventy-one-year-old woman. Hailed before the Student Conduct Committee, he protested, "Really, I had no designs on her." A student living in an apartment was required to report a roommate who entertained a female. ("But I was asleep," a boy protested.) This rule, to be sure, was contemptuously ignored.

After considerable debate, the faculty finally relaxed its vigilance and allowed entertaining in apartments without chaperones. But with its decision, it issued a warning that students must accept full responsibility for apartment life.

There was a fuss a few years ago over whether or not the university has the right to discipline a student for misbehavior in his home town during the summer vacation. A faculty member suggested the commonsense policy of "When they're off the hill, the hell with them." He added: "We're not in the business of building character. I doubt if some of us are qualified. Instead we should be concerned with building minds." Perhaps the ultimate in official doubletalk was attained by an administrator who declared piously: "I believe that when the average student comes to the University of Wisconsin, he is old enough to accept responsibility but young enough to need guidance."

The university views itself—its progress and grandeur—with uneasy pride. UW is so ambitiously extended that the new shibboleth on campus is balance: between teaching and research, between undergraduate work and graduate study, between the liberal arts and professional education, between service to the state and service to the nation. How to establish a sound alignment of parts is an administrator's nightmare.

Maintaining quality in a school determined to give everyone a chance is also a headache. The fact that eight state schools have changed over from normal schools to four-year colleges may, in the future, drain off weaker students who would otherwise come to UW. The university now gives advanced standing to particularly able high school graduates, and it is instituting an honors program—but with a peculiarly egalitarian twist. "Our hope is to help gifted students without tagging them," the president stated. "Our bright people will learn by rubbing shoulders with average ones."

A great tradition is a burden as well as a joy. Has Wisconsin already had its great day? "There is little doubt that it lost some of its fire between the wars," Vice-President Harrington said. "There was a deflation of idealism, and other states began to originate things." At present there is a resurgence, but to attain distinction in a highly competitive period is another matter. UW people cast a troubled look at the West where the University of California—the General Motors of higher education—has been raiding faculty remorselessly. "Our problem," Harrington said, "is to see if we can keep the two dozen or so innovators on campus."

The University of Wisconsin grew out of a noble vision. "There is something extraordinary about Wisconsin," an administrator said. "After all, it's just an ordinary little state, its population no larger than that of Brooklyn. Yet this small state has created a great university."

At the conclusion of his inaugural address, President Elvehjem declared, "Give us, then, the hills to climb and the strength to climb them." Students wheezing up Bascom Hill would no doubt find this funny, but they too have been touched by the vision.

Christian Gauss as a Teacher of Literature

EDMUND WILSON
(1895–   )

Axel's Castle, 1931
The Triple Thinkers, 1938
To the Finland Station, 1940
Memoirs of Hecate County, 1952
The Shores of Light, 1952

EDMUND WILSON is widely regarded as our best American critic; his *Axel's Castle* was the first successful attempt on this side of the Atlantic to come to terms with French *Symbolisme* and with the works it influenced, including Proust's *A Remembrance of Things Past* and James Joyce's *Ulysses.* Mr. Wilson never, however, confined his interest to literature. He has observed politics and society and history; radical politics in the thirties, for instance, and more recently, the American Civil War and the plight of the American Indian. Mr. Wilson is also a writer of short fiction and of one full-scale novel, *Memoirs of Hecate County.* He has never taught regularly, but has maintained an abiding interest in education ever since his encounter in Princeton with Christian Gauss, an encounter whose meanings are explored below.

WHEN CHRISTIAN GAUSS OF PRINCETON DIED ON NOVEMBER 3, 1951, I was asked by the Princeton *Alumni Weekly* to write something for a set of tributes that were to appear in the issue of December 7. I sent the editor, who wanted a column, only part of what I had written in response to this request, and even this was much cut before it was printed. I have now further elaborated my original memoir, and I am including it here to serve as a sort

From *The Shores of Light* by Edmund Wilson (New York: Farrar, Strauss & Company, 1952). Reprinted with the permission of Edmund Wilson.

of prologue, for it indicates to some extent the point of view from which I started off in my criticism of the twenties.

I have been asked to write about Christian Gauss as an influence on my generation at Princeton. Since we knew him as a teacher of literature only—I was in the class of 1916, and he did not become dean of the college till 1925—I shall speak mainly of this side of his activity.

As a professor of French and Italian, then, one of the qualities that distinguished Gauss was the unusual fluidity of mind that he preserved through his whole career. A teacher like Irving Babbitt was a dogmatist who either imposed his dogma or provoked a strong opposition. Christian Gauss was a teacher of a different kind—the kind who starts trains of thought that he does not himself guide to conclusions but leaves in the hands of his students to be carried on by themselves. The student might develop, extend them, transpose them into different terms, build out of them constructions of his own. Gauss never imposed, he suggested; and his own ideas on any subject were always taking new turns: the light in which he saw it would be shifted, it would range itself in some new context. It bored him, in his course on French Romanticism, to teach the same texts year after year; and with the writers that he could not get away from, he would vary the works read. With the less indispensable ones, he would change the repertory altogether. If Alfred de Vigny, for example, had been featured in the course when you took it, you might come back a few years later and find that he had been pushed into the background by Stendhal. Christian would have been reading up Stendhal, and his interest in him would seem almost as fresh as if he had never read him before. He would have some new insights about him, and he would pass these on to you when you came to see him, as he was doing to his students in class. I know from my own experience how the lightly dropped seeds from his lectures could take root and unfold in another's mind; and, while occupied in writing this memoir, I have happened to find striking evidence of the persistence of this vital gift in the testimony of a student of Romance languages who sat under Gauss twenty years later, and who has told me that, in preparing his doctor's thesis, he had at first been exhilarated by an illusion of developing original ideas, only to find the whole thing in germ in his notes on Gauss's lectures. But though his influence on his students was so penetrating, Gauss founded no school of teaching—not even, I suppose, an academic tradition —because, as one of his colleagues pointed out to me, he had no communicable body of doctrine and no pedagogical method that other teachers could learn to apply. If one went back to Princeton to see him, as I more or less regularly did, after one had got out of college, one's memory of his old preceptorials (relatively informal discussions with groups of five or six students) would seem prolonged, without interruptions, into one's more recent conversations, as if it had all been a long conversation that had extended, off and on, through the years: a commentary that, on Christian's part, never seemed to be trying to prove anything in any overwhelming way, a voyage of speculation that aimed rather to survey the world than to fix a convincing vision. In his role of the least didactic of sages, the most accessible of talkers, he seemed a part of that good eighteenth-century Princeton which has always managed to flourish between the pressures of a narrow Presbyterianism and a rich man's suburbanism. It is probable that Christian was at home in Princeton as he would not have been anywhere else. He was delightful in the days of his deanship, in the solid and compact and ample yellow-and-white Joseph Henry house, built in 1837, where there was always, during the weekends, a constant going and coming of visitors, who could pick up with him any topic, literary, historical or collegiate, and pursue it till someone else came and the thread was left suspended. Though by this time so important a local figure, he seemed always, also, international. He had been born of German parents in Michigan, and German had been his first language. In his youth he had spent a good deal of time in France. He had no foreign accent in English, and, so far as I was able to judge, spoke all his languages correctly and fluently; but French, Italian and English, at any rate, with a deliberate articulation, never running the words together, as if they were not native to him. One did not learn a bad accent from him, but one did not learn to speak the Romance languages as they are spoken in their own countries. On the other hand, the very uniformity of his candid tone, his unhurried pace and his scrupulous precision, with his slightly drawling intonations, made a kind of neutral medium in which everything in the world seemed soluble. I have never known anyone like him in any academic community. He gave the impression of keeping in touch, without the slightest effort—he must have examined all the printed matter that came into the university library—with everything that was going on everywhere, as well as everything that had ever gone on. It used to amuse me sometimes to try him out on unlikely subjects. If one asked him a question about the Middle Ages, one absolutely got the impression that he had lived in Europe then and knew it a first hand.

This extreme flexibility and enormous range were, of course, a feature of his lectures. He was able to explain and appreciate almost any kind of work of literature from almost any period. He would show you what the author was aiming at and the methods he had adopted to achieve his ends. He was wonderful at comparative literature, for his reading had covered the whole of the West, ancient, medieval and modern, and his memory was truly Macaulayan (an adjective sometimes assigned too cheaply). He seemed to be able to summon almost anything he wanted in prose or verse, as if he were taking down the book from the shelf. (He told me once that, in his younger days, he had set out to write something about Rabelais and had presently begun to grow suspicious of what he saw coming out. On looking up Taine's essay on Rabelais, he found that he had been transcribing whole paragraphs from it, his unconscious doing the work of translation.) He was brilliant at revealing the assumptions, social, aesthetic and moral, implicit in, say, a scene from a romantic play as contrasted with a scene from a Greek tragedy, or in the significance of a character in Dante as distinguished from the significance of a character in Shakespeare. I remember his later quoting with approval A. N. Whitehead's statement, in *Science and the Modern World,* that, "when you are criticizing the philosophy of an epoch," you should "not chiefly direct your attention to those intellectual positions which its exponents feel it necessary explicitly to defend. There will be some fundamental assumptions which adherents of all the variant systems within the epoch unconsciously presuppose. Such assumptions appear so obvious that people do not know what they are assuming because no other way of putting things has ever occurred to them." Gauss had always had a special sense of this. But he was interested also in individuals and liked to bring out the traits of a literary personality. His commentary on a poem of Victor Hugo's— *Le Mendiant* from *Les Contemplations*—would run along something like this: "A poor man is passing in the frost and rain, and Victor Hugo asks him in. He opens the door *'d'une façon civile'* —he is always democratic, of course. *'Entrez, brave homme,'* he says, and he tells the man to warm himself and has a bowl of milk brought him—as anybody, of course, would do. He makes him take off his cloak— *'tout mangé des vers, et jadis bleu'*—and he hangs it on a nail, where the fire shines through its holes, so that it looks like a night illumined by stars.

> Et, pendant qu'il séchait ce haillon désolé
> D'où ruisselaient le pluie et l'eau des fondrières,
> Je songeais que cet homme était plein de prières.
> Et je regardais, sourd à ce que nous disions,
> Sa bure où je voyais des constellations.

"This sounds impressive, but what does it mean? Not a thing. We have not been told anything that would indicate that the old man is full of prayers. It is a gratuitous assumption on the part of Hugo. That the cloak with its holes reminded him of a heaven with constellations has no moral significance whatever. Yet with his mastery of verse and his rhetoric, Victor Hugo manages to carry it off.—I don't mean," he would add, "that he was insincere. Rather than live under Louis Napoleon, he went into voluntary exile—at considerable personal inconvenience— for almost twenty years. He lived up to his democratic principles, but he was always a bit theatrical, and he was not very profound."

I include such reminiscences of the classroom in the hope that they may be of interest in putting on record Gauss's methods as a teacher, for the work of a great teacher who is not, as Gauss was not, a great writer is almost as likely to be irrecoverable as the work of a great actor. Not that Christian was ever in the

least histrionic, as some of the popular professors of the time
were. On the contrary, for all the friendliness of one's relations
with him outside class when one eventually got to know him,
his tone was sober and quiet, his attitude detached and impersonal. This was partly due to shyness, no doubt; but the impression he made was formidable. He would come into the classroom without looking at us, and immediately begin to lecture,
with his eyes dropped to his notes, presenting a mask that was
almost Dantesque and levelling on us only occasionally the clear
gaze that came through his eyeglasses. When he made us recite
in Dante, he would sometimes pace to and fro between the desk
and the window, with his hands behind his back, rarely consult-
ing the text, which he apparently knew by heart. In the case of
some appalling error, he would turn with a stare of ironic amazement and remonstrate in a tone of mock grief: "You thought
that barretry was the same as banditry? O-O-oh, Mr. X, that's
too-oo ba-a-ad!" This last exclamation, drawled out, was his only
way of indicating disapproval. His voice was always low and even,
except at those moments when he became aware that the class
was falling asleep, when he would turn on another voice, loud,
nasal, declamatory and pitilessly distinct, which would be likely
to begin in the middle of a sentence for the sake of the shock-
value, I think, and in order to dissociate this special effect from
whatever he happened to be saying—which might be something
no more blood-curdling that a statement that André Chénier
had brought to the classical forms a nuance of romantic feeling.
When this voice would be heard in the class next door—for
it penetrated the partition like a fire-siren—it always made people
laugh; but for the students in Gauss's own room, it seemed to
saw right through the base of the spine and made them sit forward intently. When it had had this effect, it would cease. He
was never sarcastic and never bullied; but the discipline he maintained was perfect. Any signs of disorder were silenced by one
straight and stern look.

Nevertheless, though Christian's methods were non-dramatic,
he had a knack of fixing in one's mind key passages and key
facts. His handling of Rousseau, for example, was most effective
in building up the importance of a writer whom we might other-

wise find boring. (In this case, he *has* left something that can
be used by his successors in his volume of *Selections* from Rousseau, published by the Princeton University Press—though, as
usual with Gauss's writing, the introduction and notes have little
of the peculiar effectiveness of his lecture-room presentation.) He
would start off by planting, as it were, in our vision of the panorama of history that critical moment of Rousseau's life which,
since he did not include it in the *Confessions*, having already
described it in the first of his letters to M. de Malesherbes, is
likely to be overlooked or insufficiently emphasized (compare
Saintsbury's slurring-over of this incident and its consequences
for Western thought, in his *Encyclopaedia Britannica* article):
the moment, almost as momentous as that of Paul's conversion on
the road to Damascus, when Jean-Jacques, then thirty-seven,
was walking from Paris to Vincennes, where he was going to see
Diderot in prison, and happened to read the announcement that
the Academy of Dijon was offering a prize for the best essay
on the question, "Has the progress of the arts and sciences contributed to corrupt or to purify society?" Such an incident Gauss
made memorable, invested with reverberating significance, by a
series of incisive strokes that involved no embroidery or dramatics.
It was, in fact, as if the glamor of legend, the grandeur of history,
had evaporated and left him exposed to our passing gaze, the
dusty and sunstruck Jean-Jacques—the clockmaker's son of
Geneva, the ill-used apprentice, the thieving lackey, the vagabond
of the roads—sinking down under a tree and dazzled by the
revelation that all the shames and misfortunes of his life had
been the fault of the society that had bred him—that "man is
naturally good and that it is only through institutions that men
have become wicked." In the same way, he made us feel the pathos
and the psychological importance of the moment when the six-
teen-year-old apprentice, returning from a walk in the country,
found for the third time the gates of Geneva locked against him,
and decided that he would never go back.

Christian admired the romantics and expounded them with
the liveliest appreciation; but the romantic ideal in literature
was not his own ideal. In spite of his imaginative gift for entering into other people's points of view, he was devoted to a certain

conception of art that inevitably asserted itself and that had a tremendous influence on the students with literary interests who were exposed to Gauss's teaching. Let me try to define this ideal. Christian had first known Europe at firsthand as a foreign correspondent in the Paris of the late nineties, and he had always kept a certain loyalty to the "aestheticism" of the end of the century. There was a legend that seemed almost incredible of a young Christian Gauss with long yellow hair—in our time he was almost completely bald—who had worn a green velvet jacket;[1] and he would surprise you from time to time by telling you of some conversation he had had with Oscar Wilde or describing some such bohemian character as Bibi-La Purée. It was rumored —though I never dared ask him about this—that he had once set out to experiment one by one with all the drugs mentioned in Baudelaire's *Les Paradis Artificiels*. He rather admired Wilde, with whom he had talked in cafés, where the latter was sitting alone and running up high piles of saucers. He had given Christian copies of his books, inscribed; and Christian used to tell me, with evident respect, that Wilde in his last days had kept only three volumes: a copy of Walter Pater's *The Renaissance* that had been given him by Pater, Flaubert's *La Tentation de Saint Antione* and Swinburne's *Atalanta in Calydon*. And it was always Gauss's great advantage over the school of Babbitt and More that he understood the artist's morality as something that expressed itself in different terms than the churchgoer's or the citizen's morality; the fidelity to a kind of truth that is rendered by the discipline of aesthetic form, as distinct from that of the professional moralist: the explicit communication of a "message." But there was nothing in his attitude of the truculent pose, the defiance of the bourgeoisie, that had been characteristic of the fin de siècle and that that other professor of the Romance languages, Gauss's near-contemporary, Ezra Pound, was to sustain through his whole career. How fundamental to his point of view, how much a thing to be taken for granted, this attitude had become, was shown clearly in a conversation I had with him, on

---

1. I learn from Mrs. Gauss, who has shown me a photograph, that the realities behind this legend were a head of a blond bushy hair and a jacket which, though green, was not velvet.

some occasion when I had come back after college, when, in
reply to some antinomian attitude of mine, or one that he imputed to me, he said, "But you were saying just now that you
would have to rewrite something before it could be published.
That implies a moral obligation." And his sense of the world
and the scope of art was, of course, something very much bigger
than was common among the aesthetes and the symbolists.

Partly perhaps as a heritage from the age of Wilde but, more
deeply, as a logical consequence of his continental origin and
culture, he showed a pronounced though discreet parti pris against
the literature of the Anglo-Saxon countries. In our time, he carried on a continual feud—partly humorous, yet basically serious
—with the canons of the English department. I remember his
telling me, with sly satisfaction, about a visiting French professor,
who had asked, when it was explained to him that someone was
an authority on Chaucer, "Il est intelligent tout de même?" Certain classical English writers he patronized—in some cases, rightly,
I think. Robert Browning, in particular, he abominated. The
author of *Pippa Passes* was one of the very few writers about
whom I thought his opinions intemperate. "That Philistine beef-
eating Englishman," he would bait his colleagues in English,
"—what did he know about art? He writes lines like 'Irks care
the crop-full bird? Frets doubt the maw-crammed beast?'" When
I tried to find out once why Browning moved Christian to such
special indignation, he told me, a little darkly, that he had greatly
admired him in boyhood and had learned from him "a lot of
bad doctrine." He said that the irregular love affairs in Browning
were made to seem too jolly and simple, and insisted that the
situation of the self-frustrated lovers of *The Statue and the Bust*
had never been faced by Browning: If "the end in sight was a
vice," the poet should not have wanted to have them get together; if he wanted them to get together, he ought not to have
described it as a vice, but, on the other hand, he ought to have
foreseen a mess. "He is one of the most immoral poets because
he makes moral problems seem easy. He tells you that the good
is sure to triumph." He would suggest to you an embarrassing
picture of a Browning offensively hearty—"not robust," he would

say slily, "but robustious"—bouncing and booming in Italy, while the shades of Leopardi and Dante looked on, as Boccaccio said of the latter, *"con isdegnoso occhio."* The kind of thing he especially hated was such a poem as the one, in *James Lee's Wife*, that begins "O good gigantic smile o' the brown old earth." . . . Of Byron—though Byron's writing was certainly more careless than Browning's—he had a much better opinion, because, no doubt, of Byron's fondness for the Continent as well as his freer intelligence and his experience of the ills of the world. He accepted Byron's love affairs—he had nothing of the prig or the Puritan —because Byron knew what he was doing and was not misleading about it. As for Shakespeare, though Christian was, of course, very far from the point of view of Voltaire, there was always just a suggestion of something of the kind in the background. He knew Shakespeare well and quoted him often, but Shakespeare was not one of the authors whom Christian had lived in or on; and he always made us feel that that sort of thing could never come up to literature that was polished and carefully planned and that knew how to make its points and the meaning of the points it was making. He was certainly unfair to Shakespeare in insisting that the Shakespearean characters all talk the same language, whereas Dante's all express themselves differently. For Christian, the great poet was Dante, and he gradually convinced you of this in his remarkable Dante course. He made us see the objectivity of Dante and the significance of his every stroke, so that even the geographical references have a moral and emotional force (the Po that finds peace with its tributaries in the Paolo and Francesca episode, the mountain in the Ugolino canto that prevents the Pisans from seeing their neighbors of Lucca); the vividness of the scenes and the characters (he liked to point out how Farinata's arrogant poise was thrown into dramatic relief by the passionate interruption of Cavalcanti); and the tremendous intellectual power by which all sorts of men and women exhibiting all sorts of passions have been organized in an orderly vision that implies, also, a reasoned morality. No Englishman, he made us feel, could ever have achieved this; it would never have occurred to Shakespeare. Nor could any English novelist have even attempted what Gustave Flaubert had achieved

—a personal conception of the world, put together, without a visible seam, from apparently impersonal descriptions, in which, as in Dante, not a stroke was wasted. He admired the Russians, also, for their sober art of implication. I remember his calling our attention to one of the church scenes in Tolstoy's *Resurrection*, in which, as he pointed out, Tolstoy made no overt comment, yet caused you to loathe the whole thing by describing the ceremony step by step. This non-English, this classical and Latin ideal, became indissolubly associated in our minds with the summits of literature. We got from Gauss a good many things, but the most important things we got were probably Flaubert and Dante. John Peale Bishop, who came to Princeton intoxicated with Swinburne and Shelley, was concentrating, by the time he graduated, on hard images and pregnant phrases. Ezra Pound and the imagists, to be sure, had a good deal to do with this, but Gauss's courses were important, too, and such an early poem of Bishop's as *Losses*, which contrasts Verlaine with Dante, was directly inspired by them. Less directly, perhaps, but no less certainly, the development of F. Scott Fitzgerald from *This Side of Paradise* to *The Great Gatsby*, from a loose and subjective conception of the novel to an organized impersonal one, was also due to Christian's influence. He made us all want to write something in which every word, every cadence, every detail, should perform a definite function in producing an intense effect.

Gauss's special understanding of the techniques of art was combined, as is not always the case, with a highly developed sense of history, as well as a sense of morality (he admirably prepared us for Joyce and Proust). If he played down—as I shall show in a moment—the Thomist side of Dante to make us see him as a great artist, he brought out in Flaubert the moralist and the bitter critic of history. And so much, at that period, was all his thought pervaded by the *Divine Comedy* that even his own version of history had at moments a Dantesque touch. It would not have been difficult, for example, to transpose such a presentation as the one of Rousseau that I have mentioned above into the sharp concise self-description of a character in the *Divina Commedia*: "I am the clockmaker's son of Geneva who said that man has made man perverse. When for the third time the cruel captain closed the gates, I made the sky my roof, and found in Annecy the love Geneva had denied". . . .

With this sense of history of Christian's was involved another strain in his nature that had nothing to do with the aestheticism of the nineties and yet that lived in his mind with it quite comfortably. His father, who came from Baden—he was a relative of the physicist Karl Friedrich Gauss—had taken part in the unsuccessful German revolution of 1848 and come to the United States with the emigration that followed it. The spirit of '48 was still alive in Christian, and at the time of the first World War an hereditary hatred of the Prussians roused him to a passionate championship of the anti-German cause even before the United States declared war. Later on, when Prohibition was imposed on the nation, the elder Gauss, as Christian told me, was so much infuriated by what he regarded as an interference nothing short of Prussian with the rights of a free people that he could not talk calmly about it, and, even when dean of the college and obliged to uphold the law, the American-born Christian continued in public to advocate its repeal, which required a certain courage in Presbyterian Princeton. It was this old-fashioned devotion to liberty that led him to admire Hugo for his refusal to live under the Second Empire, and Byron for his willingness to fight for Italian and Greek liberation. "Everywhere he goes in Europe," Christian would say of Byron, "it is the places, such as the prison of Chillon, where men had been oppressed, that arouse him." When he lectured on Anatole France, he would point out the stimulating contrast between the early France of *Sylvestre Bonnard*, who always wrote, as he said, like a kindly and bookish old man, and the France who defended Dreyfus, made a tour of the provinces to speak for him and remained for the rest of his life a social satirist and a radical publicist. In the years when I was first at Princeton, Gauss called himself, I believe, a socialist; and during the years of depression in the thirties, he gravitated again toward the Left and, in *A Primer for Tomorrow* (1934), he made some serious attempt to criticize the financial-industrial system. In an inscription in the copy he sent me, he said that my stimulation had counted for something in his writing the book. But I was never able to persuade him to read Marx and Engles at firsthand: he read Werner Sombart instead; and I noted this, like the similar reluctance of Maynard Keynes to look into Marx, as a curious confirmation of the theory of the Marxists that the "bourgeois intellectuals" instinctively shy away from Marxist thought to the extent of even refusing to find out what it really is. Yet Christian had read Spengler with excitement—it was from him that I first heard of *The Decline of the West*—immediately after the war; and he never, in these later years, hesitated in conversation, to indulge the boldest speculations as to the destiny of contemporary society.

He was a member of the National Committee of the American Civil Liberties Union, and he made a point, after the second war, of speaking to Negro audiences in the South. On my last visit to Princeton when I saw him, in the spring of 1951, he talked to me at length about his adventures in the color-discrimination states—how the representatives of some Negro organization under whose auspices he had been speaking had been unable to come to see him in his white hotel, and how, as he told me with pride, he had succeeded, for the first time in the history of Richmond, in assembling—in a white church, to which, however, he found the Negroes were only admitted on condition of their sitting in the back pews—a mixed black and white audience. As he grew older, he became more internationalist. He foresaw, and he often insisted, at the end of the first World War, that nothing but trouble could come of creating more small European states, and, at the end of the second war, he was bitterly opposed to what he regarded as the development of American nationalism. He complained much, in this connection, of the intensive cultivation, in the colleges, of American literature, which had been carried on since sometime in the middle thirties with a zeal that he thought more and more menacing to sound international values. I did not, on the whole, agree with him in disapproving of the growth of American studies; but I could see that, with his relative indifference to English literature, he must have conceived, at the end of the century, an extremely low opinion of American. He took no interest in Henry James and not very much in Walt Whitman. He told me once that Henry Ford had said, "Cut your own wood and it will warm you twice," not knowing that Ford

had been quoting Thoreau. For Christian, the level of American
writing was more or less represented by William Dean Howells,
the presiding spirit of the years of his youth, for whom he felt
hardly the barest respect. It was absolutely incredible to him—
and in this I did agree with him—that *The Rise of Silas Lapham*
should ever have been thought an important novel. "It wasn't
much of a rise," he would say. Yet the "renaissance" of the
twenties—unlike Paul Elmer More—he followed with sympathetic, if critical, interest.

Christian Gauss was a complex personality as well as a subtle
mind, and one finds it in some ways difficult to sort out one's impressions of him. I want to try to deal now with the moral qualities
which, combined with his unusual intellectual powers, gave him
something of the stature of greatness. In some sense, he was a
moral teacher as well as a literary one; but his teaching, in the
same way as his criticism, was conveyed by throwing out suggestions and dropping incidental comments. In this connection, I
want to quote here the tribute of Mr. Harold R. Medina, the
disinguished federal judge, from the symposium in the *Alumni
Weekly*. It expresses a good deal better than anything I was able
to write myself, when I drafted this memoir for the first time, the
penetrating quality of Gauss's power, and it is interesting to me
in describing an experience that closely parallels my own on the
part of an alumnus of an earlier class—1909—who was to work
in a different field yet who had known Christian Gauss, as I had,
not as dean of the college, but as teacher of literature.

"Of all the men whom I have met," Mr. Medina writes, "only
four have significantly influenced my life. Dean Gauss was the
second of these; the first, my father. From freshman year on I
had many courses and precepts with Dean Gauss and during my
senior year I was with him almost daily. He attracted me as he
did everyone else; and I sensed that he had something to impart
which was of infinitely greater importance than the mere content of the courses in French Literature. It was many years after
I left Princeton before I realized that it was he who first taught
me how to think. How strange it is that so many people have the
notion that they are thinking when they are merely repeating the

thoughts of others. He dealt in ideas without seeming to do so; he led and guided with so gentle a touch that one began to think almost despite oneself. The process once started, he continued in such fashion as to instil into my very soul the determination to be a seeker after truth, the elusive, perhaps never to be attained, complete and utter truth, no matter where it led or whom it hurt. How he did it I shall never know; but that it was he I have not the slightest doubt. His own intellectual integrity was a constant example for me to follow. And to this precious element he added another. He gave me the vision of language and literature as something representing the continuous and never-ending flow of man's struggle to think the thoughts which, when put into action, constitute in the aggregate the advance of civilization. Whatever I may be today or may ever hope to be is largely the result of the germination of the seeds he planted. The phenomena of cause and effect are not to be denied. With Dean Gauss there were so many hundreds of persons, like myself, whom he influenced and whose innate talents he developed that the ripples he started in motion were multiplied again and again. In critical times I always wondered whether he approved or would approve of things I said and did. And this went on for over forty years."

"To instil into my very soul the determination to be a seeker after truth . . . no matter where it led or whom it hurt." I remember my own thrilled response when, in taking us through the seventeenth canto of the *Paradiso*, Christian read without special emphasis yet in a way that brought out their conviction a tercet that remained from that moment engraved, as they say, on my mind:

> e s'io al vero son timido amico,
> temo di perder viver tra coloro
> che questo tempo chiameranno antico.

—"If to the truth I prove a timid friend, I fear to lose my life [to fail of survival] among those who will call this time ancient." The truth about which Dante is speaking is his opinion of certain powerful persons, who will, as he has just been forewarned in

Heaven, retaliate by sending him into exile—a truth which, as Heaven approves, he will not be deterred from uttering. Another moment in the classroom comes back to me from one of Christian's preceptorials. He had put up to us the issue created by the self-assertive type of romantic, who followed his own impulse in defiance of conventional morality and with indifference to social consequences; and he called upon me to supply him with an instance of moral conflict between social or personal duty and the duty of self-realization. I gave him the case of a problem with which I had had lately to deal as editor of the *Nassau Lit*, when I had not been able to bring myself to tell a friend who had set his heart upon contributing that the manuscripts he brought me were hopeless. "That's not an impulse," said Christian, "to do a humane thing: it's a temptation to do a weak thing." I was struck also by what seemed to me the unusual line that he took one day in class when one of his students complained that he hadn't been able to find out the meaning of a word. "What did you call it?" asked Christian. "Didn't you call it something?" The boy confessed that he hadn't. "That's bad intellectual form," said Christian. "Like going out in the morning with your face unwashed. In reading a foreign language, you must never leave a gap or a blur. If you can't find out what something means, make the best supposition you can. If it's wrong, the chances are that the context will show it in a moment or that you'll see, when the word occurs again, that it couldn't have meant that." This made such an impression on me that—just as Mr. Medina says he has been asking himself all his life whether Christian would approve of his actions—I still make an effort to live up to it.

I love to remember, too, how Christian began one of his lectures as follows: "There are several fundamental philosophies that one can bring to one's life in the world—or rather, there are several ways of taking life. One of these ways of taking the world is not to have any philosophy at all—that is the way that most people take it. Another is to regard the world as unreal and God as the only reality; Buddhism is an example of this. Another may be summed up in the words *Sic transit gloria mundi*—that is the point of view you find in Shakespeare." He then went on to an explanation of the eighteenth-century philosophy which assumed that the world was real and that we ourselves may find some sense in it and make ourselves happy in it. On another occasion, in preceptorial, Christian asked me, "Where do you think our ideals come from—justice, righteousness, beauty and so on?" I replied, "Out of the imaginations of men"; and he surprised me by saying, "That is correct." This made an impression on me, because he usually confined himself to a purely Socratic questioning, in which he did not often allow himself to express his own opinions. I felt that I had caught him off guard: what he had evidently been expecting to elicit was either Platonic idealism or Christian revelation.

It was only outside class and at secondhand that I learned that he said of himself at this time that his only religion was Dante; yet it could not escape us in the long run that the Dante we were studying was a secular Dante—or rather, perhaps, a Dante of the Reformation—the validity of whose art and morality did not in the least depend on one's acceptance or non-acceptance of the faith of the Catholic Church. Christian would remind us from time to time of Dante's statement, in his letter to Can Grande, that his poem, though it purported to describe a journey to the other world, really dealt with men's life in this, and we were shown that the conditions of the souls in Hell, Purgatory and Heaven were metaphors for our moral situation here. The principle of salvation that we learned from Dante was not the Catholic surrender to Jesus—who plays in the *Divine Comedy* so significantly small a role—but the vigilant cultivation of "il ben del intelletto."

Some of those who had known Christian Gauss in his great days as a teacher of literature were sorry, after the war, to see him becoming involved in the administrative side of the University. I remember his saying to me one day, in the early stages of this, "I've just sent off a lot of letters, and I said to myself as I mailed them, 'There are seventeen letters to people who don't interest me in the least.'" But the job of the Dean's office did interest him —though it seemed to us that it did not take a Gauss to rule on remiss or refractory students. He had never liked repeating routine, and I suppose that his department was coming to bore him. He made, by all accounts, a remarkable dean—for his card-catalogue memory kept all names and faces on file even for decades after the students had left, and the sensitive feeling for character that had been hidden behind his classroom mask must have equipped him with a special tact in dealing with the difficult cases. His genius for moral values had also a new field now in which it could exercise itself in an immediate and practical way, and the responsibilities of his office—especially in the years just after the war, when students were committing suicide and getting into all sorts of messes—sometimes put upon him an obvious strain. Looking back since his death, it has seemed to me that the Gauss who was dean of Princeton must have differed almost as much from the Gauss with whom I read French and Italian as this austere teacher had done from the young correspondent in Paris, who had paid for Oscar Wilde's drinks. The Gauss I had known in my student days, with his pale cheeks and shuttered gaze, his old raincoat and soft flat hat, and a shabby mongrel dog named Baudelaire which had been left with him by the Jesse Lynch Williamses and which sometimes accompanied him into class—the Gauss who would pass one on the campus without speaking, unless you attracted his attention, in an abstraction like that of Dante in Hell and who seemed to meet the academic world with a slightly constrained self-consciousness at not having much in common with it—this figure warmed up and filled out, became recognizably Princetonian in his neckties and shirts and a touch of that tone that combines a country-club self-assurance with a boyish country-town homeliness. He now met the college world, unscreened, with his humorous and lucid green eyes. He wore golf stockings and even played golf. He interested himself in the football team and made speeches at alumni banquets. Though I know that his influence as dean was exerted in favor of scholarships, higher admission requirements and the salvaging of the Humanities—I cannot do justice here to this whole important phase of his career—the only moments of our long friendship when I was ever at all out of sympathy with him occurred during these years of officialdom; for I felt that he had picked up a little the conventional local prejudices when I would find him protesting against the advent in Princeton of the Institute for Advanced

Study or, on one occasion, censoring the *Lit* for publishing a "blasphemous" story. One was always impressed, however, by the way in which he seemed to have absorbed the whole business of the University.

We used to hope that he would eventually be president; but, with the domination of business in the boards of trustees of the larger American colleges, it was almost as improbable that Christian would be asked to be president of Princeton as it would have been that Santayana should be asked to be president of Harvard. Not, of course, that it would ever have occurred to anyone to propose such a post for Santayana, but it was somehow characteristic of Christian's career that the idea should have entered the minds of his friends and that nothing should ever have come of it. There appeared in the whole line of Christian's life a certain diversion of purpose, an unpredictable ambiguity of aim, that corresponded to the fluid indeterminate element in his teaching and conversation. He had originally been a newspaper correspondent and a writer of reviews for the literary journals, who hoped to become a poet. He was later a college professor who had developed into a brilliant critic—by far the best, so far as I know, in our academic world of that period—and who still looked forward to writing books; I once found him, in one of his rare moments of leisure, beginning an historical novel. Then, as dean, in the late twenties and thirties, he came to occupy a position of intercollegiate distinction rather incongruous with that usually prosaic office. Was he a "power" in American education? I do not believe he was. That kind of role is possible only for a theorist like John Dewey or an administrator like Charles W. Eliot. Though he was offered the presidency of another college, he continued at Princeton as dean and simply awaited the age of retirement. When that came, he seemed at first depressed, but later readjusted himself. I enjoyed him in these post-official years. He was no longer overworked and he no longer had to worry about the alumni. He returned to literature and started an autobiography, with which, however, he said he was unsatisfied. In October of 1951, he had been writing an introduction for a new edition of Machiavelli's *Prince*, and he was pleased with it when he had finished. He took Mrs. Gauss for a drive in the car, and they talked about a trip to

Florida. He had seemed in good spirits and health, though he had complained the Saturday before, after going to the Cornell game, where he had climbed to one of the top tiers of seats, that he was feeling the effects of age—he was now seventy-three. The day after finishing his introduction, he took the manuscript to his publisher in New York and attended there a memorial service for the Austrian novelist Hermann Broch, whom he had known when the latter lived in Princeton. While waiting outside the gates for the train to take him back to Princeton, with the evening paper in his pocket, his heart failed and he suddenly fell dead.

One had always still expected something further from Christian, had hoped that his character and talents would arrive at some final fruition. But—what seems to one still incredible—one's long conversation with him was simply forever suspended. And one sees now that the career was complete, the achievement is all there. He has left no solid body of writing; he did not remake Princeton (as Woodrow Wilson in some sense was able to do); he was not really a public man. He was a spiritual and intellectual force—one does not know how else to put it—of a kind that it may be possible for a man to do any of those other things without in the least becoming. His great work in his generation was unorganized and unobtrusive; and *Who's Who* will tell you nothing about it; but his influence was vital for those who felt it.

Chè in la mente m'è fitta, ed or m'accora,
la cara e buona imagine paterna
di voi, quando nel mondo ad ora ad ora
m'insegnavate come l'uom s'eterna. . . .

How Badly Can You Teach?

GEORGE WILLIAMS
(1902–   )

Some of my Best Friends are Professors, 1958

GEORGE WILLIAMS has had two life-long interests, students and birds. He has taught English to students for a number of years at Rice Institute and he was also on the staff of the Houston Museum of Natural History. The essay which follows is a kind of bird watcher's guide to the American professor.

PROFESSORIAL BUCK-PASSING

IT IS AN OLD ARMY GAME FOR COLLEGE PROFESSORS TO HOLD GRAVE conferences and make dire public announcements on the inferior quality of the modern high school graduate; for the high school teachers to be scandalized by the poor quality of the junior high school graduates; for the junior high school teachers to speculate about what is going to happen to the world if the elementary school teachers continue training children so poorly; for the elementary school teachers to blame all their classroom troubles on uncooperative parents; and for parents to write letters to the papers, and besiege school boards, and hold councils of war, all intended to turn the responsibility back to the teachers and the school system and the curriculum and the methods of instruction.

As a commentary on the constant professorial lament that the poor training of the modern high school student is responsible for the poor scholastic showing of the modern college student, I should like to make five short observations:

First, no freshman ever knows as much as he should—neither

does any sophomore, any junior, any senior, any graduate student, or any professor. If the freshman already knew all he ought to know, there would be no need for him to come to college. It is precisely for the reason that he does not know as much as he ought to know that his parents send him to college, and society is glad to have him there.

Second, it is my impression that the high schools are doing at least as good a job now as they ever did, and in most cases they are doing a better job. In thirty years of university teaching I have noticed a steady improvement in the basic cultural attainment of most students. This improvement may be due to the fact that more and more high schools are dividing their courses of instruction into two groups, one for students intending to go to college, and the other for students not intending to go to college. Thus the colleges have to deal with only a pre-selected group, which has been specifically prepared for college work.

Third, whether or not the high schools are doing a good job, it is the business of the college professor to take whatever material the gods send him, and teach it. If the material happens to be bad, then the business of the professor may be a little more difficult. But that is all the more reason why he should look to his competence as a teacher. He is certainly not benefiting the nation by throwing out 40 per cent of the students who come to him, and refusing to give them any kind of "higher" education.

Fourth, so-called poor high school preparation does not necessarily make a poor college student. When I was a very young man I taught in colleges in one of the most backward of the Southern states. The colleges were compelled by law to admit any student who could show a diploma from any high school in the state—at a time when this state contained some of the most underprivileged schools in the nation. I found that about 10 to 15 per cent of these students were completely out of place in college. But the others were as responsible and responsive, as eager to learn, and as capable of learning as any students I have had since. It just happens that the alumnus of my own university who has become the science professor of whom the university is most proud, a man of worldwide reputation, came from a little non-accredited high school in which several of the teachers did not even have the B.A. degree.

Finally, if a student has learned to write reasonably "correct" English, and to read English with a fair measure of understanding, he needs no further preparation for the university—unless he happens to be planning a career in science, in which case he will need mathematics through algebra and plane geometry. Practically all college courses except English and some of the science courses are taught at the beginner's level; and even some of the science courses (biology, geology, and psychology, for example) require no previous preparation in high school. If a student can read English and write English well, he is prepared for college. Too often those professors who complain that their freshmen are "unprepared" are merely trying to rationalize their own failure.

STUDENT READING VERSUS PROFESSORIAL WRITING

At this point I wish to digress for a moment to speak of a very special complaint that professors are forever making about their freshmen. Not being able to prove that high school graduates are unprepared in specific ways for college work, the professors have settled on *poor reading ability* as one major defect that seems ubiquitous. They have made "reading ability" the mainstay of their complaints, as well as of their entrance examinations.

The professors are on safe ground here. For one thing, it is quite possible that young people today, accustomed to visual and auditory education through television, cinema, and radio, cannot absorb the printed page as well as their grandfathers did. But I have never seen any actual evidence to prove that this is so. And even if it is so, "Other gifts have followed, for these, I would believe, abundant recompense." The modern high school graduate knows more about music, drama, geography, politics, recent history, science, mechanics, and adjustment to society for the sake of a happy and socially useful life than his grandfather ever did. Moreover, even if it should be true that the modern youth is more responsive to visual and auditory education than to literary education, we need not be too alarmed. When, several centuries ago, youth in the Western world ceased memorizing lessons and reciting them by rote, and began to depend more and more on the printed word, I am sure that the professors of the day felt that education was being debased. Some modern educators undoubtedly feel the same way when they suspect that the old reading instrument is being replaced by the new visual and auditory instruments. But that groping, inquisitive, prying, discontented temperament that has brought the human species this far is not likely to fail man now; whatever instrument best helps him satisfy his insatiable curiosity, he will use. The professors need not worry; if the human animal becomes extinct, it will not be through intellectual lethargy, but its opposite.

Another reason why it is possible for professors to demonstrate the inability of modern students to read properly is that it is virtually impossible for any writer to say any but the simplest things in English, and hope to be understood. If any ten professors can read any fairly abstract or complex passage, in English, and derive exactly the same meaning out of it, they have performed a miracle. Yet each one of these same professors expects his students to derive exactly the same meaning from their reading that he would derive. If they fail to derive his meaning, he announces far and wide that the modern student cannot read.

Absolutely at random I open the number of the *Journal of Higher Education* (a strictly professorial project) that happens to be lying on my desk, and find this sentence at the beginning of an article by Dean Herbert Stroup of Brooklyn College:

> The two most commonly advocated aims of student activities are overly familiar: the development of the personal maturity of the individual student, and the growth of democratic citizenship responsibility on the part of the students.

Almost every word of it is ambiguous, and capable of misinterpretation. One has only to ask just who it is that has *aimed* and *advocated*; and what "commonly" means; and what "student activities" the author is talking about (love-making, studying, eating, playing tennis, or what?); and who is "overly familiar" with these "aims" (I, for one, never heard of them till this moment); and exactly what the phrases "personal maturity" and "democratic citizenship responsibility" mean; and who is to determine what is "growth" and what is degeneration—in order to see how easy it would be for a dozen different students to get a dozen different meanings out of this sentence . . . and then be accused of not knowing how to read. This is not hair-splitting; it is an intensely serious matter. Three students asked to paraphrase the first phrases of this sentence might say:

> The two most commonly advocated aims of the college program of studies . . .
> The two most commonly advocated aims of student social affairs on the campus . . .
> The two most commonly advocated aims of the intramural athletic program . . .

Three other students asked to paraphrase "personal maturity" might substitute the phrase "the ability to assume the financial responsibility of a family," or "the ability to get along with other people without being selfishly demanding," or "the stable relationship of a person toward God." Who could say that any of these students did not know how to read? Yet how many of these six different interpretations (together with their many permutations and combinations, and other interpretations of still other phrases in the sentence) would be counted right in the scoring if this sentence appeared on a college entrance examination? And who can say that just such a sentence would not appear on an examination? After all, did not a college professor and a dean write it?

If it should seem that this sentence is accidentally ambiguous, here are the last sentences of the same article:

> It is clear that there are strengths and weaknesses in all the intentions as theoretical means of understanding student activities; some combination would enhance the final truth of the matter. Further study, bolstered by empirical investigation, is required to establish the validity of such constructs and to determine their mode in concrete situations.

I myself would be at a complete loss if I were asked to tell what these sentences mean; and doubtless most young high school graduates would be little better off.

If it still seems that the article is accidentally ambiguous, here are the first few and the last few sentences of the very next article (also written by a professor who might be grading students on their ability to read) in the same number of the *Journal of Higher Education*. All the sentences are studded thick with words, phrases, and ideas so vague that the meanings they bear must vary enormously with every individual reader who carefully considers them:

> The college of liberal arts utilizes many educational agencies to achieve its aims. The emphasis placed upon extra-classroom activities depends upon the philosophy of education which predominates in a particular college. The use of the term "extra-classroom" involves a point of view in respect to the breadth and inclusiveness of the curriculum.

> Curtailment of liberal education to the point of neutralization will be deplorable and shortsighted educational statesmanship. Any intelligent reorganization of the resources of the college of liberal arts demands a proper evaluation and adequate utilization of extra-classroom activities.

Even when English is used at the kindergarten stage of simplicity, it can seldom be pinned down to exact and unambiguous meanings which anybody can "read" to the complete satisfaction of everybody else. If I say to a small child, "Drink your milk," I am expecting him to interpret the command in a far more precise way than I may be justified in doing. The child may set his cup on the floor, and lap up the milk as he has seen his puppy doing; or he may dip it up with his cupped hand; or he may soak his napkin in it, and then suck the napkin. He is, in all these cases, following my command, he is drinking his milk. Not being a mind reader, how could he tell that when I said, "Drink your milk," I actually meant to say, "Raise the edge of your cup to your mouth, open your mouth slightly, insert the edge of your cup into the slightly opened mouth, tilt the cup just a little, pour a small quantity of milk into your mouth, swallow that milk, then tilt the cup a little more, and repeat the process till the cup is empty." Sometimes those professors who grade students on their "ability to read" expect the students to be, not readers, but mind readers.

But it is not only the language itself that prevents accurate reading; it is the language as used in the textbooks, essays, articles, study-sheets, and instructions that the professors write, and expect their students to "read." Not one third of the professors who complain so bitterly about the inability of their students to read well can write precisely and intelligibly, or express themselves precisely and intelligibly in lectures, or ask precise and intelligible examination questions. In printed books by acquaintances of mine, I have seen expressions like "The substance divides into two unequal halves"; I have seen laboratory directions instructing students to "Draw a square about twice as long as broad"; I have seen examination questions asking students to "Discuss the use of various technical devices in *Huckleberry Finn*"; I have heard lectures crammed with sentences like "The idea of history, philosophically reinterpreted, may well serve to express the value aspect of unfolding significance of reality as we know it especially in human activities"; I have seen psychological tests which asked the subject to fill the blank in the sentence, "4 is to 8 as 8 is to _____," where any answer but "12" was counted wrong; I have graded papers (my own and other professors') in which every student in the class had the identical wrong answer, making it perfectly apparent that the instructor had failed to make himself clear on the matter involved. Yet professors are gravely concerned because "Our students just can't read."

Reading is always a relative matter—relative to what certain words mean and imply to the writer and what they mean and imply to the reader; relative to the personal backgrounds of the writer and the sometimes very different personal backgrounds of the reader; to the educational backgrounds of the writer and the sometimes very different educational backgrounds of the reader; to the philosophical outlook (theological, political, economic, etc.) of the writer and the sometimes very different philosophical outlook of the reader. A good many professors of English would have difficulty reading a textbook on nuclear physics to the satisfaction of any physicist; and a good many physicists would have difficulty reading a textbook of prosody to the satisfaction of any English professor. But these technical difficulties are among the least: it is the personal experiences and differences in background that make accurate reading so rare. Thus "liberal" and "conservative" carry very different meanings, emotions, and implications to different Americans; "democratic" is a word of praise in both America and Russia, but it bears contradictory meanings to Americans and to Russians; "God" is one thing to a Roman Catholic priest, and a very different thing to a well-educated Hindu; some Americans would interpret "segregation" as an unmitigated evil, some as an unmitigated blessing, and a sentence like "Ending racial segregation in America will have profound effects on the nation as a whole" might be paraphrased by one student, "Ending racial segregation in America will create grave dangers for the country as a whole," and by another student, "Ending racial segregation in America will benefit the entire nation."

Much of the time the professorial complaint that "Our students just can't read" amounts actually to one of two things: first, that "Many professors and other academicians just can't write"; or second, that "The experiences and thought patterns of the students are just not uniform with those of the professors." Most professors in most universities find it quite disturbing to encounter a student whose mind is not attired in the same uniform as the professors'.

All this does not mean that every student who graduates from high school "knows how to read." Far from it! Undoubtedly the high schools are giving their students less and less practice in reading. Nevertheless, the professorial excuse that "Our students just can't read" is too often assigned as a cover-up for professorial lack of empathy, imagination, power of clear self-expression, judgment in choosing well-written material for the student to read, and (above all) ability to awaken the student's interest in the reading material.

How to Teach Freshmen Badly

Once the prospective freshman has convinced the authorities that he "knows how to read," and has been admitted to the university, and has got his courses arranged to the satisfaction of the curriculum people, he starts attending classes.

It is not the least of the sins of the universities that many of the basic courses in the all-important freshman year (just when the student is establishing fundamental values and attitudes about learning) are taught by young graduate students. These young teachers lack experience, and have usually had little counsel on the methods or the ideals that a university teacher should have, no real indication from older faculty members that good teaching is an important goal, and no great incentive (and very little time) to do anything well except try to make A's in their own courses and write acceptable dissertations. In English, foreign languages and mathematics, this condition prevails almost universally; it is not so common in the sciences, in history, and in economics, but in even these courses a large amount of instruction is done by young undergraduate and graduate assistants who have had little experience and no training in the art of teaching. Just last week the Dean of Sciences of a university with almost 20,000 students told me: "When we hire young fellows and assistants, we ask ourselves only one question: Is the young man capable of going ahead and doing good research as a graduate student? We don't give a damn about his teaching ability. We let the students sink or swim; it's their affair, not ours."

Though few deans and departmental heads are quite that blunt about the matter, I know of no dean or departmental head in any university who, when the chips are down, actually feels or behaves any differently. As a result, the freshman, right when the pattern of his entire experience of higher education is being set, is guided and dominated in much of his basic college work by untrained young instructors whom nobody expects to be good teachers. What is more, these young instructors are otherwise occupied in matters that the entire university considers far more important than teaching; they are often abominably conceited; they have no concept about what higher education is for in relation to the individual and to society, and no understanding of human nature; they are only half-informed in the subject that they pretend to be teaching; and they usually hide their ignorance and inexperience with a callow cynicism and a hard-boiled cruelty that is appalling.

This is no exaggeration. It is the usual world of the freshman, the one that gives him his first impressions of university life, and that establishes most of his fundamental attitudes toward higher education for the rest of his university career. That university faculties should treat their freshmen like this, and still lament that it is only the very rare and occasional freshman who develops a love of his subject, an interest in learning, an enthusiasm for intellectual experience, is one of the best illustrations of inconsistency and of the almost criminal negligence of most universities.

How to Teach Upper-Classmen Badly

In the postfreshman years the student has more experienced, but not necessarily better, teachers. Reasons for the lack of improvement are, principally, five.

First, it is rare to find any teacher who has not succumbed, mentally and temperamentally, to the pressures of the system in the matter of examination, grades, and credits. The ideal he holds up to himself is to teach "a good stiff course"; and the ideal he holds up to his students is to make good grades on the examinations, and get credit for the course. He does not try to make his students understand how there can be pleasure in learning; he does not try to lead them to want to learn more and more all their lives; he does not try to show them how questions and problems lie lurking dangerously at the very fountainhead of the knowledge he is trying to impart. Among the academic courses, only a few (10 to 20 per cent) make any attempt to link the student's learning with the pressing intellectual, artistic, political, social, moral and religious problems that he must face daily; among the science courses the percentage is still smaller. The professor makes the grade the thing. The student learns his facts and his scientific processes, gets his grade, wins his credit, graduates, and thereafter applies his education to no problem except that of making money. And the professor doesn't care.

A second reason why teachers of the upper classes are seldom good teachers, no matter how experienced they may be, is that they have somehow got the notion that "upholding the standards of the university" means essentially giving many low grades. This is a fallacy deeply ingrained in every university that I know anything about, and in almost every professor. Again and again I have heard professors mention the high percentage of bad grades among students majoring in their departments, and the low percentage of students who finally manage to get degrees from their departments. When questioned, they say with obvious pride, "I am doing what I can to uphold the standards of the university." Again and again I have seen lifted eyebrows and significant glances when some professor confessed that nobody failed in one of his courses. I have heard chairmen of committees sit down to go over grades of students at term's end, and say, "Let's see how many of the bastards we can get rid of." I can remember that, even when I was a 'student, I heard a number of the administration sneering about the greatest professor and the most inspiring man I ever knew: "The old fool never fails anybody in his courses!" There is no doubt that a large number of professors think that their success as teachers depends directly on the number of bad grades their students make. If any professor gives enough bad grades, he will soon get a reputation with the university administration, with his colleagues, and throughout the graduate school as being one of the ablest and sharpest members of the faculty. It is no joke that if a young professor just arrived on the campus wishes to establish himself solidly, he has only to start giving many bad grades, and talking earnestly and in public about "upholding the standards of the university."

A third reason why professors are likely to be bad teachers I have already mentioned in another connection. It is the idea (maintained in spite of their own personal experience to the contrary) that learning is unpleasant *work*. "The world feels," says Jacques Barzun, "that drudgery, discipline, and conformity are the social virtues par excellence"—and the educational virtues, too. It is plain to most professors that, unless a student expends blood, sweat, and tears, he is not getting an education. This is a relic of the Hebraism (Puritanism and Victorianism) that Matthew Arnold criticized. In some ways, Whitehead's book on education is a vessel of this old tradition: "The essence of education is that it be religious . . . A religious education inculcates duty and reverence." In strong contrast is Plato: "Do not train boys to learning by force and harshness, but lead them by what amuses them." It is a fearful comment on the university

classroom that 80 to 90 per cent of the students undoubtedly regard it as a boring necessity, a dull adjunct to those really exciting
portions of university life, the dances, the athletic contests, the
sororities and fraternities and clubs, the social functions. If one
questions the percentages hazarded here, one has only to listen
to the cheers that go up when a professor announces that the class
will not meet next time, and the boos when it is announced that
some scheduled dance or athletic meet has been arbitrarily cancelled.

The typical professor accepts this situation with resigned stoic-
ism, just as he accepts age and sickness, and takes refuge from it in
his own researches. It does not occur to him to try to make his
classes as fascinating as a basketball game, or as pleasant as playing bridge in the student lounge. Indeed, the bitter truth is that,
if he does try to make his students like his classes, his colleagues
look askance at him as a "popularizer." He must be dull and hard
if, in professorial eyes, he is to be great. Not one professor in fifty
can understand that the process of learning can be, and should
be, in Milton's words, "so sweet, so green, so full of goodly prospects, and melodious sounds on every side, that the harp of
Orpheus were not more charming." Instead, professors (and university administrations) believe that the student seeking an education must expect none of those "refined and delicate pleasures
that spring from research and education," but only toil, trouble,
pain, and tedium. If the student is not able to pay this price, then
he is a shallowpate; and if the professor does not demand it, he
is a "popularizer."

A fourth reason for bad teaching is mere negligence or indifference on the part of the professor. He may simply not try to be a
good teacher. This attitude may arise from any one or more of
several causes. The professor may be lazy; he may not want to stir
himself sufficiently to teach well. Or he may be so interested in
his own researches in library and laboratory that he considers
teaching a distraction to which he gives as little time and thought
as possible. Or he may be extremely ambitious for advancement,
and, knowing that advancement in all major universities depends
upon frequent publication rather than good teaching, he may deliberately (and selfishly) pare down to a minimum the time he

gives to his classes. Or he may have outside interests that keep him too busy to be a good teacher—part-time jobs in business or industry, his own investments, do-it-yourself projects, hobbies, off-campus lecturing, political activity, his own family, and so on. Or, paradoxically, he may be so engrossed in administrative activities on the campus, so absorbed in the work of faculty committees, so occupied with matters of public relations, so busy being what the students like to call a "wheel," that he has little time or energy left over for the mere human beings who compose his classes.

Negligence or indifference (from whatever cause) in teaching is widespread, well recognized, and generally tolerated or even encouraged in the universities. Only in the most flagrant cases of absenteeism or neglect does anybody (from the president and the dean on down) venture to suggest that the professor ought to pay more attention to his teaching duties. Indeed, the professor who pays too much attention to his teaching duties is definitely suspect on the campuses of most major universities. People wonder whether he is a good researcher who may get the university's name in the learned journals, or an aggressive personality who may win good publicity for the university in the public prints. Of course, something may be said for the negligent or indifferent professor. Often he cares so little about teaching that he does not bother to give "a good stiff course" in which he distributes many bad grades; instead he allows his classes to run themselves, more or less, and leaves the students to their own devices, some to learn and some to fritter away time. On the other hand, these negligent and indifferent professors are often just the ones who insist most emphatically (for rather obvious psychological reasons) that their students "get down to business."

A final reason for poor teaching among the professors is lack of a personality that can put itself in rapport with many types of student personality, understand how to interest and stimulate young minds, and perceive the many facets that many minds may discover in most types of human knowledge. Too many professors are cynics who can do nothing but ridicule the ignorance of students; too many are determined factualists who beat down imagination and creativeness; too many are "disciplinarians" who think that classrooms and the process of learning should never be any fun to students; too many are academicians whose thinking moves always in formal grooves and who are quite unable to comprehend differences of interpretation; too many have such high regard for "truth" that they discourage all independent thought for fear that the young person may be "wrong"; too many, insensitive to the feelings of other people, or unsympathetic toward universal human weaknesses, antagonize students permanently by unjustly accusing them of cheating, refusing to believe or to accept honest excuses for absences or late work, making no allowances for normal human lapses of attention or deviations from the straight-and-narrow path of industry; too many of them have developed (as a result of early maladjustments and insecurities) an inferiority complex that results in certain typical personality traits, including compensatory arrogance, morbid suspicion, fear that students will discover professorial weaknesses, timidity that masks itself as unfriendliness, intolerance of disagreement, sometimes downright sadism. To be sure, professors are not the only people in our society likely to have the personality weaknesses mentioned here. But the professors are likely (for reasons outlined in a previous chapter) to have more of them than other people; and besides, they are so situated that their personality weaknesses, by operating on students at a very impressionable period of life, can do immeasurably more harm than those of most other people.

Upholding the Standards

Since the Russians scared the wits out of us with their *sputniks,* we have been hearing a continuous uproar in the public press, in educational circles, and in legislative halls, about the need for raising the standards of American education. I have already said that a very large number of professors are honestly convinced that the only way to "uphold the standards of the university" is to give many bad grades.

There is a story that Professor E. G. Lorenzen, of Yale University's law school, while acting as a visiting professor at another college, inquired about this college's grading policies. The Dean answered, "Flunk as many as you want." To which Professor Lorenzen replied, "I don't flunk my students. I teach them."

But I myself, in thirty-five years as a faculty member of universities, have yet to hear one faculty member say in open faculty meeting that the best way to "uphold the standards of the university" is to be a skillful and inspiring teacher. Instead, there is continual talk about "tightening the curriculum," "more efficient procedures for the selection of applicants for admission," "increasing the course load," "greater concentration on major subjects," and similar matters, together with complaints about the "inefficiency of the high schools," the "hopelessness of competing with TV," or even "the incurable stupidity of the human race." I have never heard any professor suggest that the failure of a student is also the failure of his professor. The two or three professors I still remember from my own student days as outstanding persons, scholars, and teachers, almost never found it necessary to give a failing grade to any student. And now that I myself am a professor, I never set down a failing grade for a student without a feeling of contrition and humiliation. I feel that, through ignorance or lack of skill or indifference or selfishness, I have betrayed some young person who was depending on me. I am ashamed that I have not "upheld the standards of the university."

If a teacher is a good teacher he ought to be able to make his students understand what he is trying to tell them. The students are all about the same age, have similar educational backgrounds, and (if they have graduated honestly from high school) are essentially intelligent. If he fails to make them understand, so that a considerable portion of them fail, or almost fail, he is almost certainly a poor teacher. But try to get anybody around a university to admit to such a heresy! In all my years of teaching, I have known of only one professor whose savage failing-rate (over 50 per cent of his class) was questioned by the authorities of the university; but even they did not question him because they lacked faith in his teaching ability, but because he was bringing some very unfavorable publicity to his department.

It is true that a professor may be an excellent teacher and able to make his students understand the course, yet assign them such a heavy load of work that only a few of them can complete it. For example, he may teach them how to solve a certain type of long problem, but then assign them fifty such problems to complete overnight; or he may give them an excellent understanding of a historical period, but then assign them 5000 pages of source material to be read in one week. By making such assignments, and giving poor or failing grades to the students who do not complete them, he fancies that he is "upholding the standards of the university." But here we encounter once more that schizophrenic trait that is so common among professors. Presumably the university exists for the purpose of educating students; but if the "standards" of the university (in this case, the load of work required) eliminate a large number of students from the university, the whole purpose of the university is defeated. Yet universities seem proud of this inconsistency.

The professorial mind seldom seems to realize (or perhaps it just doesn't care) that dropping a student on account of failure may solve a troublesome problem for the professor here and now. But a student who has failed, and is dropped from the course or from the university, is *not* a solved problem. In relation to his own future career, and in relation to society at large (which is supplying the money for the university) the student who has failed is a more serious problem than ever. A student who can do only 25 problems out of the assigned 50, or who can read only 2500 pages out of the assigned 5000, is by no means a total loss to himself or to society; yet (having completed only 50 per cent of his assigned work) he is dropped from the rolls. His life, and his possible future contribution to society, have been considered less important than the necessity of "upholding the standards of the university." He has become a sacrifice to a vague and abstract "high standard" arbitrarily set by his professors. I do not perceive how such a sacrifice can be justified either from a democratic, humane, individualistic point of view, or from a nationalistic, socialistic, utilitarian point of view. In these days of increasingly intense competition with the Communist world, our nation can not afford to let even a little of its brain-power go to waste.

If all of us who are in any way concerned with higher education would remember that "high standards" which large numbers of students cannot live up to mean only one of two things—either that the professor involved is a poor teacher, or that he is making unrealistically heavy assignments—we might be a little more successful than we have been in improving the quality of higher education in America. Practically everybody seems to think that a university has demonstrated its "high standards" when a large number of its students make poor grades, or fail completely. It is an almost hopeless task to try to make everybody (especially the professors) see that a university in which large numbers of students make poor grades, or fail, actually has very low standards of teaching, or a very unrealistic (and even dangerous) comprehension of its function as an educational institution in a democracy—a democracy threatened, as never before in its history, by the growing power of a hostile nation.

IMMORALITY AMONG THE PROFESSORS

What the universities, and the professors themselves, can do about all these weaknesses will be suggested in a later chapter of this book. The nub of the whole matter, however, for both the university administration and the professor is to have the desire for better teaching, or at any rate to establish better teaching as an ideal more significant than it now is in the university world. Much could be accomplished by a mere arbitrary, deliberate, officially announced and publicly supported change in administrative policy.

The majority of professors are not actually bad men; they do not *want* to do evil. But the whole university community fails, as a rule, to see that the obligation of good teaching is essentially a moral obligation. When any man sees another human being in need of help, and can help him, and does not help him, but passes by on the other side, that man is immoral. This is even more acutely true if the passer-by is an adult, and the human being in need of help is a young person. Even elephants, wild cattle, and baboons band together to protect their collective young. It does seem as if college professors (and university administrations) could demonstrate as much morality as elephants, cattle, and baboons. But a very large percentage of college professors (and university administrations) do not practice that much morality. A very large percentage of them make no special effort to help their fellow man in ways that are almost more important than matters of life and death, for though to save a man's life is important, to give him a life worth saving is almost equally important. When generations of young people come to university professors asking to be shown how to have a life worth saving, and are turned away because the professors are willing accessories to the formalism of examinations-grades-credits systems, or because the professors think that "upholding the standards of the university" by giving bad grades is more virtuous than good teaching, or insist that learning be unpleasant, or are selfishly busy or negligent or indifferent, or are dominated by certain character traits that are harmful to young people but that can be altered, these professors are being immoral. The only way they could be more immoral would be to commit murder.

This immorality of the professors and of the universities is widespread, and it is growing. The universities are leading no moral revivals these days. Instead, the moral revivals are being led by ecclesiastical showmen, religious quacks, leaders of cults, well-meaning but abysmally ignorant missionaries, and all the other ragtag and bobtail of sensationalism and superstition. This is not as it should be. The professors and the universities should be showing the way to a higher and more universal morality. But they lack the will and the spirit for it. They should have got the habit of morality in their own classrooms; but it is there that the majority of them daily commit almost the worst of immoralities. This is a basic tragedy of modern America.

The Teacher and Sex

ALEXANDER SUTHERLAND NEILL
(1883–   )

The Problem Teacher, 1944
Summerhill, 1960

A. S. NEILL'S books are propaganda for an extraordinary school for difficult children which he runs at Summerhill in England—and for his radical notions about how to educate them. His experimental approach has been a center of interest and controversy from which new insights have come into the difficult problem of freedom and constraint in the schools, and, especially, into the role of sex in the educational process.

IT IS A HUMAN RIGHT OF EVERYONE WHO HAS REACHED SEXUAL maturity to have a sex life. Today this can only be had in marriage, and all extra-marital relationships are condemned by law and morality. Owing to the marriage stipulation many teachers have no sex life at all. There are thousands of women who, for one reason or another, have never found or taken a husband, and many of these women teach in our schools, indeed the more respectable a girls' boarding school is, the more spinsters there are on the staff. Men teachers have sometimes to work for years before they can afford to marry and set up house. Owing to the respectability of their profession they cannot easily have a sex life that is taboo in the eyes of morality. The teacher in the big city may have comparatively safe opportunities, but the teacher in a small town or village has too many eyes to evade.

Let us consider the consequences, the price society pays for its sexual morality. Repressed sex always becomes converted into something else, often anxiety, sometimes nervous breakdown, probably sometimes physical breakdown, often just pure irrita-

The Problem Teacher, New York: International Universities Press, 1944.

tion and hate of life. Anxiety is the commonest direction that repressed sex takes, and linked with it is an incapacity to work well,

The man or woman who is sex-starved may try to find a substitute for love in masturbation, but owing to the fear-giving precepts of early childhood, the masturbation is associated with feelings of guilt, and these feelings produce anxiety and more anxiety. Masturbation is no cure for sex-starvation in the adult.

In our moral society we have not only, as I have pointed out, the daydreaming of the children during a lesson: we have also the phantasying of the sex-starved teacher. This is often attached to fear of authority, and such teachers live in dread that the head will come into the room and catch them bending. A sex life does not abolish fear: it abolishes the neurotic fear, the phobia. Fear of bombs is not neurotic but fear of mice or spiders is. Fear of school inspectors in the days when they had power over the teacher's salary was a real fear: fear of an inspector today is an unreal fear. It is an emotion attached to the wrong thing. This is another evil result of sex repression: the sex emotion is transferred from its original, unattained or unattainable object, and it can attach itself in a negative form to other objects, children perhaps. Only a teacher who is not having a sex life will flare up if a child writes a sexual word on the wall.

It is one of the tragedies of education that a married woman is not allowed to teach. Not that marriage itself is an exact criterion: many married women never get a full sexual satisfaction owing to their inhibitions or to the inhibitions of their husbands. A married woman, however, has at least the chance of a sex life whereas her unmarried sister has none.

This brings up the vexed question of women teaching boys. The usual argument is that they cannot keep control. I say control be damned. Children should be taught by both sexes. Boys require a mother substitute: girls a father substitute. The difficulty is that today these substitutes are so often without a sex life. One result is that the teacher of either sex has an unconscious sexual attitude to the children. This is seen in favouritism. Sometimes an unmarried man will attach his emotions to an attractive little girl in his class; sometimes the unmarried woman teacher has a like attitude to a boy. Sometimes the emotion is so strong that when the favourite is absent the day's work is dull and tiresome. I hasten to say that this emotion is never conscious, at least the underlying sex emotion is never conscious. It is a fact that emotions can be quite dissociated from age, and a man of forty can have a "pash" on a girl of ten, because the man of forty whose adult sex life is not in order, regresses to emotions long past. This follows easily because in childhood sex and love are frowned on so much that early fixations are formed, fixations that live on till death. Many people have dream love figures that haunt them: they seek some golden girl that long ago thrilled their emotions. I thought that this could occur only in a civilisation like the white one which suppresses sex so strongly, but recently, on reading *Black Hamlet*, the life story of a Rhodesian native by Wulf Sachs, psychoanalyst, I found that the native met a beautiful girl for half an hour when he was young, and her image clung to him all through his life.

Often the dream girl has her origin in the love for a sister, the dream boy in love for a brother. The growth of a human should be such that early fixations are gradually dropped or in other words, freedom lies in the breaking away from the family. In the case of the sex-repressed teacher the temptation to break away may be weakened by the constant association with the family in the form of many little brothers and sisters.

One of the great dangers connected with the sex-inhibited teacher is that of conversion of sex energy into jealousy. I found in myself that my anxiety lest two young people should sleep together had, as its main root, my own infantile jealousy. I know of a large girls' school where the staff shows its dislike of visible breasts, and the girls come to be ashamed if they do not look like flat-chested boys. This is not only caused by jealousy on the part of the sex-starved women: it has another root also —it springs from the scorn of sex that the unsexed person develops. "Anyway sex is an overrated thing. We must do all we can to ignore its existence."

It may be masculine arrogance on my part when I say that women teachers who have no sex life are more dangerous to children than men teachers in the same predicament. It is a sad fact that a woman ages more rapidly than a man, and a man can look forward to a sex life even if he is sixty. A woman who has let her youth slip by without having a sex life, has little opportunity of beginning one when her peach-like charm has gone. Hence the oldish woman renounces sex as unattainable, while the oldish bachelor hopefully glances at the ankles of the young girls. Lack of a sex life seems to lead to more irritation in a woman than in a man. That may be because sex life means more to a woman in this way—that when she is deprived of sex she is also deprived of motherhood. Fatherhood does not mean so much to a man as motherhood to a woman. The male animal usually has no interest in his offspring, and with men the interest often does not come until the child has lost its early ties to the mother.

What is then the solution? That only married teachers should be allowed to deal with children? Do we not all know married teachers who are as bad as unmarried ones? Haven't you and I known scores of married headmasters who were cruel brutes, married women who were shrews?

That brings me back to the theories of Dr. Wilhelm Reich. I have already mentioned his belief that repressions show themselves in the muscles, appearing as stiffness and cramping. These repressions are primarily sexual, so that all the muscles of the body are, as it were, fortifications guarding the sexual apparatus from danger. When the child is corrected morally he stiffens his stomach. I took that with a large grain of salt when I first heard of it from Reich, but on examining the small children of Summerhill I was astonished to find that the ones who had been brought up without morality had soft stomachs, while the children of the religious and moral had stiff stomachs.

Reich contends that because of sex prohibitions few men and women in a civilized country ever get the fullest enjoyment from the sex act. He holds that muscle tension prevents a true orgasm reflex. The result is that many women have sexual intercourse without a real orgasm (a fact that every doctor and psychologist has known for years). Many men perform the act without getting the enjoyment they desire, and not infrequently one hears a man or woman say: "It's an overrated pastime."

Reich's theory is the only one that explains the reason why married life is so often unsatisfactory. It explains the raging virago of a wife who nags all day long: it explains the husband who seeks pleasure out of his home most of the time, and I don't mean only sex pleasure: I mean his darts and clubs and hobbies. Married life is now synonymous with love life, indeed, marriage is the greatest obstacle that love can meet, for marriage involves permanency, and love cannot be made permanent by law: love should be free.

The question arises: What is love? What is the difference between love and lust?

It is a question that must be faced without the evasion we call modesty. The desire for physical contact between the sexes is based on the physical genital organs. Without them there would be no falling in love nor sexual desire. Desire can spring up without love, and this is especially true when people are young. This desire would be described as lust. It is the sex element that is condemned by morality while its equivalent in the animal world is taken for granted. No one has any moral feelings about the attraction of a bitch in season for any dog.

The moral attitude is that animalism is something low, an attitude that conveniently enough applies only to the sex element, for the fact that only the "higher" animal man wages war, and bombs women and children, and hates, is completely forgotten. Thus we have the hypocritical belief that the loss of virginity is "worse than death."

It is not easy for an honest man to understand why the marriage ceremony raises animalism to a higher level. There are marriages that are founded on a love that lasts, but there are countless marriages in which the love element dies sooner or later. To anyone of comparative honesty such marriages are more degrading than the worst prostitution. So long as love is unfree marriage will be accepted as the only respectable means of having a love life. That marriage is the greatest danger to love is certain: its possession, its bondage, the economic dependence of the wife on the husband, these are all fatal to love, because marriage is static and love dynamic. Emotion can be repressed but it cannot be destroyed. If Mrs. X falls in love with Mr. Y her social surround-

ings may prohibit her from ever consummating that love, and the
price is a heavy one: her married life must become a lie, her
sex life with her husband must be an unhappy prostitutionary
one, her children, infected by her unhappiness, must suffer and
be unhappy. Worst of all she is haunted by a sense of guilt, even
though she has never kissed the man she loves. It is the story of a
million women, of a million men. It is the story that explains
why countless women find the sexual act unpleasant, why countless men find it unsatisfactory. Marriage is the surest way of converting love into lust.

Love is lust with tenderness added. In love both parties have
the same tenderness to each other after sexual intercourse as before. If love is absent the man generally wants to get away from
the woman after the act. Under a sane sex morality love would
be the only criterion of sex behavior: men and women would
sleep together solely because they wanted each other, and no
third party would have any right to interfere or to forbid.

However, since we do not live in Utopia, we must look at things
as they are today. In our schools stand thousands of teachers who
either accept morality or feel themselves coffined and confined by
it. How does their attitude affect the childen?

It is not easy to say. What a child acquires unconsciously is still
a hidden secret, only partly guessed at. One thing is certain, however, that the unconscious of the teacher does in a mysterious way
affect the unconscious of the child. A sex-repressed head-mistress
will quite unconsciously give her girls a guilty feeling about sex.
The mere fact that sex as a topic is taboo in schools denotes that
the new generation, having no education on the subject, is forced
to accept the current morality of sex. True there are teachers who
try as well as they can to obviate this by giving sex instruction
about the bees and the pollen. One young man of my acquaintance tells me he feels like blushing when the word pollen crops
up in conversation: it is obscene to him. Sex instruction can get
nowhere until we tell children truthfully that the chief element
in sex is pleasure, for it is the pleasure of sex that makes it taboo.

Reich's view of sex repression has wide social significance. According to him the repression of sex has a grim purpose behind
it. The state (capitalism) sees in sex repression a powerful means

of keeping the working class in its place. Sex repression, so to speak, castrates the workers, makes them oxen without fire and energy, so that they have never the guts to fight for their rights. He shows that in life there are two great instincts—hunger and sex. Marxism takes up the hunger, that is, the economic instinct, and by giving the workers power over the means of production, hopes to make the new world. Reich says that hunger is only part of the story, that until the world is free from sex repression it will fail. Here he instances Russia which began with a surge of sex freedom, but is now as moral as any bourgeoise State with its laws against homosexuality and abortion, and its disapproval of early sex life. Reich contends that the sex revolution must accompany the economic revolution if there is to be a new civilization that will endure. Therefore, in his long work with the revolutionary movement in Germany he concentrated on youth and sex, trying to give youth a sex education at the same time as being given a political one.

Here his work should be of vital interest to teachers, especially teachers of working class children. His book *Der sexuelle Kampf der Jugend* (The sex battle of youth) will, I hope, soon be available in English. In this book he emphasizes the misery of sex among the younger workers, how that they have no place for love, how that as a substitute for love they seek furtive, unsatisfactory sex congress in corners and lanes: how that they are mostly ignorant of preventatives and in any case are too poor to supply them. It is the book of a brave fighter for freedom, and, so well have the powers above drilled the poor into morality, it is a book that has raised more hate and passion among Socialists and Communists than any book I know. To fight to abolish Capitalism is respectable, but to fight to destroy the sex morality that, with the Church, is the mighty supporter of all that Capitalism stands for, is to put yourself beyond the pale of civilization. Reich wants to see a new morality, founded on love and not on vested interests.

If Reich's analysis of society is right, and personally I believe it is, what harm is being done by the teachers' acceptance of conventional sex morality? The schools are producing not only wage slaves but sex slaves. I have a great admiration for men like Harry Pollitt and Willie Gallacher, but in their trenchant and well-informed speeches and articles they never touch the subject of sex. What is the use of smashing Capitalism if we are to retain capitalist morality? Sex is the creative force in life and our revolutionaries hope to remake the world by ignoring it, hope to remake it by their heads alone. Rebels with a sense of guilt are handicapped from the word go. This is why so many rebels are haters: they hate the rich rather than love the poor: they hate not as free men but as bound men. They think that their chains are from Capitalism and they are quite unaware that the strongest chains are those of their own repression, not only sex repressions but spiritual repressions.

Spirituality naturally brings us to religion. I may not be qualified to write about religion because I have no conscious religion. I live without it, as do the children in my school. We live as honestly and as humanely as any gospel band of Christians. We simply have no need for it, and my experience of children has proved to me that there is no innate desire in a child to seek formal religion, no innate desire to pray or to fear a God.

But I was brought up under religion in Scotland, and to some degree I can look back and see it with some objectivity. I see a religion that is topsy-turvy, a religion that has called God the Devil and the Devil God. The God of my youth had nothing to inspire anyone with love: he was a God of fear, of prohibition, of hate, of vengeance. He forced us to say nay to life.

The Devil was different: he had all the best tunes: he was on the side of the best pleasure: he never condemned. In truth he gave out love instead of fear. He was always on the side of life, while God was preoccupied with death. He loved the flesh, while God extolled the spirit. He in effect said: There is nothing sinful in sex, while God cried: Flee from the sins of the flesh if you will avoid the wrath to come. Looking back I now understand why as a small boy I pictured Heaven as a small place and Hell as one of enormous population. "Heaven for holiness: Hell for company."

Thus to me religion is inimical to human nature. Not the religion that Christ preached, the religion of love and loving your enemies, but that religion never got beyond words, so that last week very few Christians were shocked when the Primate in the House of Lords advocated using war against the Dictators.

Thus when sexuality is condemned on religious grounds, I ask: on what religious grounds? The religion of the Archbishop of Canterbury or that of Jesus? The religion of love or the religion that props up the capitalist system? It is a question that should be answered. Organised religion, like everything else that is organised, is dead spiritually, yet this corpse, paradoxically enough, has the power to negative human lives. It has the evil power of making generations say nay to life, because it fears life. Hence it is easy for religion to steal the sex emotions and convert them for its own use. How many sex-starved women seek their emotion in religion? Many. The sex emotion is converted into an anti-sex emotion, really a death emotion. Religious people unconsciously seek death, but oddly enough, they do everything they can to keep on living.

Sex repression and economic suppression allow much emotion to go to seed, so that when a Hitler comes along the emotion can be showered on him. Emotion for a Hitler is fundamentally the same emotion that goes to religion. In some of his followers it is an emotion of worship. It is not without significance that the South Germany greeting has changed from: Gruess Gott to Heil Hitler. The coming war will be to many a holy crusade, and as long as we have an unattached emotion springing from a repressed sex emotion, we shall have our Hitlers and wars and poverty and exploitation.

I have wandered far away from the school and the teacher. That is as it should be, for the teacher's job is only partly in the school. He is part of society and if society is what I have described it as being, he is part of the whole suppressive complex that is a conspiracy against human nature and human pleasure. And by sticking only to his school subjects he is helping to perpetuate that society: he is helping to bolster up a civilisation that denies economic and sexual freedom to human beings. I am not suggesting that he should suddenly announce to the Board of Education that he intends to keep a harem openly: all I hope to do is to make him a little more conscious of what his job really means, a little more aware of the forces behind the society which pays him to instruct the young, to keep their feet in the straight and narrow path that leads to a capitalist heaven.

If the teacher's attitude to sex is a limited one he is not in the position to understand or to help children with sex difficulties. The teacher with a guilty conscience about masturbation cannot help the child who is tortured with a like conscience. The so called dull child who daydreams his class life away is so often the child who cannot solve the awful problem: Is sex sinful or not? All the discipline or talking in the world cannot help such a child, but the sympathetic understanding of the teacher can. Worries about sex take up more of a child's libido than all the school subjects in the world. The teacher who fears to face the sex question sees only the ability or inability to do arithmetic or to behave well in class. He sees only the outer shell of the child.

Many people indignantly assert that too much importance is attached to the sex question. They declare that children are not obsessed by sex. I once taught in a coeducational school in London, where the pupils were all of good middle class. In two years I never heard a sexual word, indeed, I discovered that boys of fifteen did not know the vulgar words for excrement or even the sex organs. I was greatly puzzled but light dawned upon me when the head master held a long lecture on the enormity of a boy of nine's offence in kissing a girl of eight. But I did not realise how much the apparent sexlessness of the middle class was a myth until I had a school of my own. I find that children of five from middle class homes react to freedom by showing an intense interest in sexual and excremental affairs, so much so that their language is sometimes awkward when the wrong type of visitor is being shown round the school.

Children seem to know the character of visitors by instinct. When modern young people come along prepared to hear·choice language, the children glance at them and remain silent, but if disapproving Aunt Mary shows her face in the garden there is a lurid stream of obscenity. Here it is of interest to say that my wife, who had no religious training as a child, can smile when Aunt Mary is shocked at the language, while I, with deep-rooted memories of Scots Calvinism, conduct Aunt Mary around with some trepidation. This statement is of greater value than the whole of this chapter: it shows that repressions formed in early childhood remain in some form or another . . . in my case after long psychoanalysis. I am aware that there is in myself something of Aunt Mary, and that is why I am so passionately eager to give children an environment which will give them inner freedom from Aunt Maryism all their lives. For Aunt Maryism is against life.

This subject leads naturally to a question that teachers often ask me: "Is it necessary for a teacher to be psychoanalysed?" Hitherto I have answered: "Yes. You can't deal with others if you are unaware of your own unconscious." I have lost my certainty now, although I still believe that analysis goes a long way. I have been saying for years that psychology could not advance far until it joined up with physiology, until body and soul were seen as a unity. That is why Reich interested me: he was the first psychologist I had met who considered the body at the same time as he considered the psyche.

It is a known fact that in any psycho-therapeutic treatment the cure can only come from an emotional abreaction. It is useless to interpret a dream if the interpretation arouses no emotion in the patient. I can say to a patient: "Your dream is simple. It shows that you are in love with your brother's wife, and you have a repressed wish to kill your brother and marry his wife." The chances are that the patient will accept this interpetation objectively without releasing any emotion in the process. But that is not the worst of it: he will automatically form another repression which will strengthen the resistance against analysis. He will get the whole bag of analytical tricks in his head but his heart will harden, and his emotional release will be impossible.

The Freudian analysis does not crudely blurt out explanations of hidden complexes: it attempts to wait till the patient more or less tumbles to the emotional truth himself. But analysis costs time and money and few of us can spend four years and a thousand pounds on an analysis.

The teacher is never well enough paid to afford a long analysis, and in any case analysis is only an attempt to counteract past influences. *The teacher's ideal should be an education that will produce children who do not need analysis.* Even if he never had an hour's analysis, he should be aware of the factors in early life that produce later damage, and to some extent he can acquire that by reading: I say to some extent because when we are blind to our own complexes we cannot see the complexes of children. That would not matter so much if every school had a psychologist on the staff, a dynamic psychologist, not one trained in Intelligence Tests and Stimulus Reactions.

Every teacher should know the dangers of suppressing sex interest, of introducing fear, of making children insincere. He should be aware of the ordinary mind mechanisms—projection, identification, transference, etc. Possibly the most vital for him is that of projection, so that when he feels angry with a child he has some power to say to himself: "My anger is in me, it is against myself. I am projecting it on to the child."

One difficulty is that there are so few books that can really help the teacher to an understanding of child psychology. Books on psychoanalysis usually deal with more or less pathological cases. One will give the impression that the child's interest in its excrement is the central point of child nature: another that the child's interest in "mother's penis" is the be all and end all: a third that the little girl's desire to urinate like a boy is the chief factor. It isn't that the writers are wrong, for there is truth in most of them: it is that their books appear to make psychology so one-sided and so limited. In a popular health magazine a woman of the Adlerian school answers parents' queries, and often she writes good sense, but she seems to attach no importance at all to sex, and she gives explanations in terms of power when they obviously should bring in sex as a very important cause.

The teacher should study all schools, taking from each what he feels he can accept, realising all the time, that no psychologist has the Gospel, that the subject is still primitive, at the stone age but probably now getting into the bronze age. He should be warned that his own repressed attitude to sex may make him overvalue the psychology of Dr. Alfred Adler, a doctrine that is apt to attract the timid ones whom Freud scared away with his sex theory. But now that Freudianism is so respectable Adlerianism may begin to lose ground, for Freudianism only shows up causes: it does not translate its theories into action. Reich says: "If we free sex repressions, what then? What is the patient going to do about sex actively? How can our proletarian youth have a sex life even if they get rid of their repressions? They have no facilities. Therefore the sex question is a political question: we should aim at changing society so that sex can be free." The Freudian would say: "That is not our affair. I deal with the individual, and it is not my job to help him to a sex life: all I do is to show him what is behind his sexual lack of satisfaction, and then he can do what he likes. It isn't for me to advise him in any way. Nor is it my province to reform society so that sex repression will be abolished."

The Freudian says to his patient in effect: "You can say what you like, you can live out your complexes in words, but I shall never help you to do what you like." That may be the reason why Freudian analysis seldom or ever recommends a parent to send a child to Summerhill, for it is a school where a child can do what it likes all day long, so long as the others do not complain that its doing interferes with the peace of mind. I have an uneasy feeling that the Freudian fears freedom as much as the Calvinist did. Freud was welcomed in England as a distinguished refugee: Reich has been driven from country to country. It is always a dangerous thing to advocate real freedom.

Instruction Without Authority

JACQUES BARZUN
(1907–   )

Darwin, Marx, Wagner, 1941
Romanticism and the Modern Ego, 1943
Teacher in America, 1945
The House of Intellect, 1959

JACQUES BARZUN is Provost of Columbia University and head of its Graduate Division. His approach to education is not that of a literary amateur but of a professional administrator. Yet Mr. Barzun has influenced the American intellectual community not only as an academic, but also as an author and the founder (along with Lionel Trilling and W. H. Auden) of the widely respected and influential *Mid-Century Book Club.* His concern with art is, like his interest in education, moral rather than merely formalistic; and his many books are both provocative and informative.

AT THE SAME TIME AS THEY FOSTER THE BLURRED MIND, THEN, THE elementary and secondary schools postpone and finally make unpalatable the ancient discipline of work. But it would be a mistake to suppose that college brings about a radical change. How could it? There are mountainous arrears of ignorance, and little habit of study to bring to bear upon them. And there are, besides, the collegiate forms of philanthropy, make-believe, and the desire to play. The best thing that has been found so far to remedy a part of the incompetence carried forward from high school is "general education"—the attempt to show the young how abstract "subjects" hang together to form the traditions by which the world lives. In good hands general education courses at least teach a youth how to read.

But no way has yet been found to teach him how to write. The sole magic that could make freshman composition succeed would be the belief on the part of both student and teacher that writing mattered, that the instructor was bored by dullness, offended by barbarisms, and outraged by nonsense. Then the student might begin to feel, through his written work, a moral responsibility for his intellectual acts. As things are, he writes in order to gain three credits, work off a degree requirement, and "satisfy" the English department, which has been delegated by the rest of the faculty to demand payment of this debt of honor. Members of the other departments can apparently do without clear prose, though, some ask for it, grumbling at its permanent scarcity. More often, they rely on powers of divination to glimpse historical or literary or scientific truth through the mists of adolescent incoherence which they themselves would find it grievous and perplexing to correct.

This is not to say that the best liberal arts colleges do not achieve remarkable results as remedial institutions. In four years they often manage to reawaken the high school graduate narcotized by the special dullness of the eleventh and twelfth grades. The college, moreover, sometimes gives the able student a command of one of the elements—language, logic, or number—which have hitherto eluded him: the cripple is first given a crutch and then taught to walk without it.

But these cases must be rare in proportion to the total college population, or we should not hear the continual complaints of those who admit to the professional schools. Dean William C. Warren, of the Columbia University School of Law, tells us in his Report for 1955: "We have found that few of our entering students, however, carefully selected, possess these skills (reading and writing) to the extent needed for law study."[1] In England, a recent outcry of the Medical Council after a reading of examination papers led Mr. Alex Atkinson to write for *Punch* a lively parody entitled "How I Done My Research."[2] Taken together

1. Report of the Dean of the School of Law, Columbia University, 1955, 5.
2. Alex Atkinson, "How I Done My Research, "*Punch*, October 12, 1955, 416.

with similar indications from France and Germany, this suggests a democratic phenomenon, the signs of which began to be noticed soon after the turn of the century.

But in the United States the condition is aggravated by that indifference to central subjects which colleges continue from the lower schools. Dean Erwin N. Griswold of Harvard complained some time ago of capable applicants to his Law School who offered college records showing no literature, mathematics, philosophy, physical science, or foreign languages, but consisting wholly of courses in Principles of Advertising Media, Office Management, Principles of Retailing, Stage and Costume Design, and Methods in Minor Sports.[3]

"Real life," it would seem, has crept in and ousted academic subjects, that is to say, not only those which are best for furnishing the mind and giving order to thought, but those which are alone capable of being taught theoretically. This fundamental distinction, elementary to the trained intellect, is virtually forgotten in the zeal of educators to "offer" as a course whatever is a namable activity of man. This willingness matches the student's penchant for avoiding hard conceptual work in genuine subjects and for playing at others, which depend on practice for their meaning and whose so-called principles are but platitudes or tautologies. For the intellectually lazy, Methods in Minor Sports is as far as thought can reach. The student's desire to prolong his earlier "activity" is understandable, but its indulgence is in fact a fraud practiced upon him, for his courses will neither increase his literacy nor impress his prospective employers. Meantime the law school that accepts him because of his "general intelligence" has the task of starting him on his ABC's.

Colleges whose main curriculum is academic are not thereby saved from another kind of make-believe, which frequently leads a student to drop philosophy or English for journalism or business admistration. In a university college, these "enlivening" subjects are taught by men from the marketplace, whereas the academic ones are taught by young graduate assistants (section men), who are subject to the professional's fallacy. They look upon college

---

3. Dean's Report, Harvard Law School, 1954-1955, 12-13.

students as future specialists of their own kind and speak to them of nothing but the methods and minutiae of scholarship. For example, if the college offers an introductory course in the civilization of India, scholarly standards require that it be taught by a student of Sanskrit. This is reasonable, but experience shows that one would have to supply a keeper or a policeman before one could stop a young Sanskritist from spending class time on doubtful etymologies and disputed points in the literature. That his students cannot follow, and are bored and discouraged, does not deter him for many years. Meanwhile one understands why Milton said, "I hate a pupil teacher."

No doubt some graduate assistants and young instructors are capable of good teaching, but something is radically false in a "philosophy" which says that the college student should receive a general and liberal education, and which makes its teachers the living refutation of that ideal.

There is worse. The majority of assistants teaching in our universities are neither born scholars nor aspiring to be educated men. They are caught in a maze—preoccupied with their own studies and examinations, with their young families and the cost of living. For all but the best, the main responsibility in research and teaching consists in amassing facts and avoiding factual error. What they do in the "third hour" of the course is try to correct the wrong impressions gathered from the textbook or the lecture of the senior professor—in short, coach the group to pass with a gentlemanly C the monthly quizzes and final examinations. The whole tendency of the arrangement is to enthrone the thought cliché, to give it value as a passport, to convince the student that this facsimile is what learning and intellect consist of.

Occasionally—for we must not forget the large number of intelligent people studying and teaching in any college—an embryo of intellectual discussion comes into being; fledgling ideas begin to fly about. But the young instructor, and sometimes the senior man, are not able to keep the collective thought alive. Where would any of them have acquired the art or the manners for it? The students have no skill in making their ideas clear or in meeting a point. One or two speak too much and too fast; a few others struggle with a weak vocabulary and faulty grammar to give body to phantom thoughts; while the dumb majority are confirmed in their suspicion of Intellect as directionless quibble. At best, the instructor straightens out the group on matters of fact and the accepted generalities of the subject. He almost never imparts principles for the conduct of the understanding, and he certainly does nothing that would spontaneously kindle in his students a bias in favor of Intellect.[4]

It is these underprivileged minds which in the last two years of college are expected to "specialize," do research, write an honors thesis. This is an attractive change from sitting, taking notes, and giving back in writing a faint approximation of memories associated with boredom and pain. At this point, surely, some men begin to receive intellectual training. But just as often, perhaps, the misdirection only grows worse. The instructor is an able specialist himself, and he puts his pride in treating his charges as fellow scholars. This means that he never dreams of telling them how to use a library or write a sentence. "Maturity" and high scholarship alike require that all such trivia be glossed over, and the time reserved for issues arising out of the assigned topic. The good student has long been accustomed to having opinions on issues, but he flounders among the technicalities of research and devices of expression which alone would make those opinions tenable. Details become more and more unmentionable as the tutorial hours grow loftier in contents. The students expect nothing but "suggestions"—and praise. I remember a very able young lady, a graduate *magna cum laude* from one of our leading university colleges, and who burst into tears when she received from me her third failing grade in a row for her weekly papers in historiography. Conversation brought out the fact that she had worked in college with two distinguished scholars and had never received less than A- on her written work.

---

4. When the lack of this bias in public opinion is deplored, it should be remembered that the remedy cannot be given by preaching. Respect for Intellect, if not born in the home, must be aroused in school and college by a sight of the teacher's ordinary attitudes toward ideas, minds, books, words, and their fit use. When one reads in the press of Paris and New York of the willful damage caused by college students to public library books during information contests, one concludes that college everywhere leaves the barbarian as it found him.

She added very candidly: "Of course, they made comments like yours in the margins, but they never marked me down for it." The moral of this liberality is not hard to draw, and a clever student draws it almost unconsciously: grades and critical comments are part of the ritual she has been familiar with since infancy. It does not mean anything. What really matters, more than ever, is "independent thought," and "original" point of view, creativity. Has she not reached the stage of higher education? Outwardly, yes, but who could say higher than what?—the phrase has the indefinite suggestion of "the better hotels."

Although college teachers are out of touch with high school teachers—inexcusably so—and university people are at war with educationists, the culture sees to it that the organic looseness of the lower schools infects the higher. Students are after all but pupils grown taller, and their bad habits become unspoken demands to which, owing to the sensitivity of our manners, teachers and institutions respond.[5]

This lack of strain begins with the "flexibility" which colleges irrationally make their principal boast. All their rules, they announce, are made to be broken, and their curriculum adapts itself to the meanest understanding. Each institution offers hundreds of courses in case someone should want them. They are made attractive—and flexible in substance—by "imaginative" titles, e.g., "Drama and Dreams," "Evil and the State Since 1900." The response to this offering is also flexible; it fluctuates, there is a perpetual boom-and-bust in subject matter. Now Russian is the rage and thousands are taking it who will never progress beyond bungling; at times economics is up and government is down; at other times, it is the reverse. English and psychology maintain their lead, based, regrettably, on their relative ease. Behind this show, and influencing the participants, is a series of unexamined beliefs: Psychology helps you get along, English prepares for delightful jobs in publishing: economics

5. The great Shakespeare scholar and keen observer of educational systems, Wolfgang Clemen, of the University of Munich, has noted the phenomenon in an article, "The Avalanche of the Masses Falls on the University," the subtitle of which is: "The Level of the Teachers Sinks with That of the Students." *Die Zeit,* March 20, 1958.

leads to executive posts, and government to being employed by international agencies—the vocational urge is strong, but seldom enlightened. For these courses are quite properly not training courses, and they rarely mesh together to form a reasonably complete theory of the subject. They are just departmental electives, some of which the department hopes will be popular. Any four or six or eight will make a "major"; and once the semester examination is passed, the knowledge acquired is sealed off from whence it came. No one other than the student has any right to ask for it again.

While this absence of a curriculum properly so called costs the college increasing amounts of money in staffing, record-keeping, and counseling, educators spend their no less expensive time asking what a liberal education is. Thus a former United States Commissioner of Education, who now heads a five-million-dollar institute for educational research, sends out a circular in which he says apropos of liberal education that "a more descriptive definition in terms of human behavior is needed for our times," and he asks his correspondents to "draw up a list of such intellectual, attitudinal, and spiritual qualities which you believe represent the results of a liberating education—if I may use a term which is not as ambiguous and emotionally colored as Liberal Education."

Meanwhile the student, whom one would suppose fully liberated, virtually licensed, chooses his "work" as best he can. If not guided by the thought of a job, he is likely to be moved by some interest in the present; the lower schools have given him the taste for the contemporary. Being thought more marketable, "more real," the smell of the present almost takes the curse off learning. Woe to the teacher or textbook that refuses to be up to date, either by holding lessons for today or by leading up authoritatively to the events of last week. The truth is that dealing with the contemporary prepares the mind poorly for a thoughtful life, shortening judgment and distorting perspective. The contemporary, moreover, is extremely difficult to assess and teach, though dealing with it makes the teacher popular. His references to the living satisfy in students the illusion of being at last in the know. Colleges feed that craving by engaging resident artists, poets, musicians, and statesmen, and combining their courses with "informal conferences." For once again, the best way lies through comfort, and comfort is happy confusion, mental promiscuity, or as is said in the Hebrides, "all through ither."

In addition to this costly liberating, the college follows the schools in their posture of wooing. When under democracy education ceases to be a privilege and becomes a right, the student's motive and attitude change. The class turns into a clientele to be satisfied, and a skeptical one: teach me if you can.[6] The mood follows naturally upon the child-rearing experts' demonstration that "lock-step teaching" is hurtful to the very young, because their development is uneven. They must be ready or feel a need. By extension, there is now no point outside the professional schools at which the student is told: *this* you must know, now and forever. The enlightening belief that some kinds of ignorance are culpable is gone.

In the sciences the notion of cumulative, indispensable knowledge has survived, and with it, in many places, an instructive severity. Yet there are ways of "taking" and "passing" mathematics or physics which "satisfy" high school and college instructors without visible gain in knowledge. When this is true, in science or other subjects, it is not always due to the teacher's incompetence in the abstract. More often it comes from his relation to the student, which is no longer one of a legitimate authority met by willing submission, but one of popularity-seeking met by patronizing tolerance. Where formerly the student who did not like or admire his teacher might feel hatred, he now feels a friendly sort of contempt. And though the modern student may like without contempt, he is not apt to admire: the feeling is not in our manners and therefore not in his emotional vocabulary. A teacher is liked because he is a "good guy"; and he and his colleagues are "just people" as books on the subject keep re-

6. The cliché is current in colleges that students who came or returned under Veterans' benefits after the recent wars were uniformly eager and enterprising in their studies. My experience suggests that this impression was vivid but not uniform. I found many excellent students, and as many who sat on their federal haunches, resisting what they had come to get.

minding us.[7] A faculty of good guys would make the ideal college, one of friendly and informal equals, warm as a family.

Free fraternizing between teacher and taught is in fact recognized as one of the great advantages of the small college.[8] Students can visit their instructors at home, "size up" their wives and children, and ascertain that they are all "human." The more human, the less likely that the demands in course will be heavy or strictly adhered to. For under our manners it is not conceivable that a man should break bread with you, call you by your first name, and without anger or unpleasantness, exact the fulfillment of your obligation. There would be in it no love of human error, no mercy: it would be rank justice.

The drive for popularity is, on the teacher's part at least, quite unconscious; and so is the inequity that results from being human at every turn. The special permissions, arrangements, and extensions of time that stretch academic rules into meaninglessness are not seen as doing an injustice to those who observe these rules, because students are not seen as competing with one another, nor indeed as engaged in work which belongs to the life of grown men.[9] These three notions—competition, work, and the life of men—are obscured by the pervasive democratic ideas of individual goals, self-development, and liberating education. In college, though life is near and the present beckons, the appropriate life-likeness of performance and failure is largely absent. The institutional aim is rather to push through as many as possible. If a grade is required for an honor or privilege, a student who misses that grade stands a fair chance of getting it nevertheless by appealing to his instructor in the name of all that hangs on his success.

So alien are justice and competitive effort to the academic world that recently a leading university abolished the require-

7. "Teachers Are Persons—And So Are Pupils, says Educator in Witty New Book." Circular from Henry Holt and Company about Charles H. Wilson's *A Teacher Is a Person*, New York, 1956.

8. The first fraternizer, however, is said to have been an instructor in chemistry at Harvard, in the late seventies, Charles E. Munroe (1849-1938).

9. It is noteworthy that, like their elders, who are to one another "the boys" and "the girls," the modern college man is a boy.

ment of high standing for scholarship students, on the ground that it made these students nervous and put them in a different academic category from the rest, who can pass with a low C. It is amusing to reflect that in Russia, where capitalism is cursed for its competitiveness, competition in schools is the norm, whereas in the capitalistic West it has all but disappeared.[10] When an American teacher awakens to his duty and fails the incompetent, there is an outcry. Students, parents, and often other teachers, object—no doubt correctly—that it is "out of line."

What is *in* line is the abdication of the teaching power. The claim itself is given up in an ambiguous cliché, regrettably echoed by Mr. William Faulkner when he was about to serve at Princeton: "Nobody can really teach anybody else anything."[11] If this means that there must be an active learner, it is true; but if it means that all teaching is self-teaching, then schools are wasting even more of the country's money than I suspect.

The question resolves itself again into that of work, and except for self-support, work is not inevitably associated with college studies. Periodically, the faculty utters the wish that students would "read more on their own" and were "capable of independent work" but they do not enforce their will. Taking notes on lectures that duplicate the text, or reading the text, or last-minute cramming from so-called review books suffices for most courses. But is not this work? No, it is at best industry, a virtue not to be despised, but lacking the essential element of work, which is passion. It is passion in work and for work that gives it its dramatic quality, that makes the outcome a possession of the worker, that becomes habit-forming and indeed obsessional. Of all the deprivations that modern life imposes on intellectual man, the abandonment of work is the cruelest, for all other occupations kill time and drain the spirit, whereas work fills both, and

---

10. A conversation with an educational official from behind the Iron Curtain informs me, since the sentence above was written, that Soviet mass education has not been so competitive as the West believes, but has been plagued by many of the same defects as American education. For the earlier view, see Jules Moch, *Les U.R.S.S. les yeux ouverts*, Paris, 1955.

11. *New York Times*, March 8, 1958.

in the doing satisfies at once love and aggression. That is the sense in which work is "fun," with an irresistible appeal to man's love of difficulty conquered—a pleasure altogether different from that for which educators have turned school subjects into activities and play. Under the habit of play, drudgery, when it comes, remains drudgery, instead of an accepted purgatory close to the heaven of work. No man who works in the sense I mean can despise himself, even if the work is below his deserts, or its perfection short of his ideal.

An inkling of these truths is doubtless behind the talk of creativity which I may seem to be inconsistent in decrying. I do so because (as I said earlier) the word has become another excuse for caprice, for nonwork; and because I still attach importance to the word "creation." Industry is not work, and work is not creation. If by what is already a metaphor we call Michelangelo a creator, if we say that Poe created the short story, if we may even say that a new dress from Paris is a creation, then we must not say that Sally's finger-painting and the college boy's short story, and the homemade costumes of amateur theatricals are creations. I am not worried about the effect of the misnomer on Michelangelo; I am worried about its effect on students and their parents, who will have been deprived by philanthropy of yet another intellectual awareness. Pitted only against their own capacities in school, denied the stimulus of failure by a world seemingly hungry for their crumbs of creativity, the talented young remain innocently conceited and hurtfully ignorant of both the range of common achievement and the quality of genius. I have talked with many brilliant students who could scarcely believe that their work was not readily publishable, at any length and without the alteration of a comma. Had they not always been known as gifted? Had they not won prizes? All they needed was a word from me to an editor: influence must aid achievement. They also considered it unjust that it should take ten or a dozen years of not especially agreeable work to prove oneself in a profession. A nurtured subjectivism about their own creativity made the thought of unrecognized effort as revolting as the statement that their work did not as yet equal the best. For the verbiage of "self-evaluation" in school had encouraged their critical discontent only about others; their own aims, measured by sheltered ambitions, had never failed except from extraneous causes.[12] And that is how, when a whole society concurs in mistaking and mis- calling the varieties of work, the notion of excellence departs.[13]

To judge by words, the academic world is very much alive to the desirability of maintaining standards. Not a minute passes without some reference to this sacred duty. Carrying it out is another thing. Here again few are incompetent or dishonest in the abstract; but the lack of clear notions and express demands produces the same effect as incompetence and dishonesty. The very customs of the academic grove militate against standards. The system of credits turns attention away from substance. The student amasses points in order to advance, as in the game of parchesi, but strange to say in the land of practicality, to ask what he can do is an invasion of privacy. As one student re- marked when rebuked for an illegible scrawl, "Well, it's *my* handwriting, isn't it?" At other times, on other subjects, the atti- tude is: "It's no good, I know, but whose is any better?" Exami- nations are in bad repute, and some teachers boast that they do not take them seriously. Whenever possible they substitute exer- cises believed to be more "genuine"—a report on the reading of

12. A group of young writers not long ago circularized sympathetic friends, asking help to overcome a situation they described as follows: ". . . the average first novelist thinks he has made the big move once he is published, only to find that the day after the reviews are printed, he is once more an anonymous figure. . . . We believe that one of the (reasons) is pure economics. . . ."

13. This is surely the result of spurring the critical spirit while leav- ing it undirected, of "thinking for oneself" without encountering the objections of a better thinker. I once had occasion to tell a group of graduate students that any of them would be lucky to achieve the fifth or sixth rank among historians. The remark was prompted by their dissatisfaction with all they knew: Gibbon was a bore, Macaulay a stuffed shirt, Hegel and Michelet were fools, Carlyle and Buckle frauds —this from students who could not write ten pages of readable and properly documented narrative. Pointing out that even second and third-rate men, such as Milman, Bancroft, or Grote, were the superiors of these students' own instructors, who were by definition superior to the students themselves, was a sobering thought quite foreign to their ex- perience.

three books, a long term paper, a set of questions worked on at home. Sometimes these do disclose ability, a general brightness coupled with responsible behavior. But we knew that our young in college were intelligent and nice; the question is, why are they there?

It is an unchallenged commonplace that what you learn in college does not matter. What does matter is not agreed upon: some say "contacts," others "atmosphere." College is "broadening," "liberating," "stimulating." How? Lectures, it appears, are no longer in favor; hence lecturers do not take the trouble they once did to organize, dramatize, and deliver, though they still address hundreds, sometimes in scattered colonies viewing closed-circuit television. Small classes *are* in favor, but I suspect more for "human" than for intellectual reasons. In small classes more reading is done, perhaps, and more "participating," but somehow not much more instruction. There is often about the small class something of the illusion of work one finds in the committee meeting. It can be an agreeable chat. In general, the net worth of the time and energy spent in college would seem to be a residue of miscellaneous experience. The contents and coherence of the work the degree stands for are secondary; otherwise it would not be possible to do what so many are praised for doing—combine a fatiguing part-time job with athletic or other activities while giving a token performance in class. These sturdy campus heroes by common consent receive for their moral and physical endurance the kind of honoring that properly belongs to scholastic achievement.

The observer is driven to conclude that under democratic conditions of equality mixed with envy, the college degree is the last remaining mark of class. Any doubt that this generality applies in other than the American democracy is dispelled by the tone of such arguments as the following taken from the usually sagacious English journal, *The Economist*: "Are the universities—Redbrick obediently following Oxford and Cambridge—going to continue to regard themselves as existing only to turn out an elite of highly trained, urbanely specialized race of men and women, and to gear their whole approach and teaching methods to endlessly reproducing dons and higher civil servants? Or are they going to accept the logic of expanding higher education—which is . . . also to make the mass of people now just below 'university standard' more educated than they are? . . . The universities and technical colleges together should be engaged in training the talents and broadening the lives of the top tenth of the nation's intelligence . . . and thereafter the whole first quartile should be regarded as collegeworthy. When that happens it cannot possibly be maintained that the methods evolved for dealing with the top five per cent should be applied to everyone. Everything must change—the varieties of degree, the methods of selection, and above all, the idea that ordinary . . . graduates are merely a menial by-product of the universities' main task of producing firsts in arts and science for top jobs."[14]

In the United States it is certainly social desire that presses the demand for more colleges to accommodate the new generations. Except among academics themselves the vivid awareness of a need to train the nation's talents comes only as an afterthought-cliché. Indeed, even the best-informed part of the public has no accurate idea of the merits of various colleges. Its opinions are fifteen years behind the times—except as to social ranking. But snobbery apart, the dividing line of the college degree is now part of the economic system as well as of accepted manners.[15] Someone has computed that seventy-one occupations require a B.A. When what is euphemistically called a noncollege graduate succeeds as a business executive making twenty-thou-

---

14. *The Economist*, March 1, 1958, 734.

15. One need not take seriously the demand for "Girls with Doctorates," which a hotel in Las Vegas advertised in January, 1957, presumably for a floor show. But an unpublished series of interviews with adult students taking evening classes at a large university supports the generality about degrees and snobbery. One woman, married to a doctor, answered the question, "Did you ever feel handicapped without a college degree" by saying, "No, not at that time." She went on to explain that at the army camp where her husband was stationed, "there wasn't any way one couple could be said to be better off than another," but by discovering that she had no college degree, "they had me placed and down I went in the esteem of everybody . . . It made me want to go to college." She also found that her husband, who has told her she was "so bright she didn't need to go to college," represented her to others as a graduate of the institution she was only beginning to attend.

sand dollars a year it is news.[16] I have known three or four persons of ability and education who, for lack of a diploma, had great difficulty obtaining employment corresponding to their unquestioned talents. No wonder that once a young person has a foot in college, he (or his parents if he is unconcerned) will do anything to reach the goal. For the great majority the name of the college matters no more than its curriculum, faculty, or standards.

Mass education, in short, has rediscovered the convenient badge of the English "pass degree." Does the present unrest mean that we are about to install a true "honors degree"?[17] Some think that this is unnecessary because our many kinds of graduate schools choose the best minds and give them, at long last, the genuine higher learning. This is inexact. A few leading law and medical schools are able to guess at who may be the ablest and subject them to a discipline. But the rest, including the non-professional graduate schools, lack the opportunity and often the desire. As at every earlier step in schooling, graduate admissions have regard to promise rather than achievement; they are the gambles of a futurist on students whose ability and knowledge are incommensurable. Hence the student body is mixed and the training uncertain. Outside the professional schools, graduate instruction follows the routines of an apprentice system designed eighty years ago, when numbers were small and scholars were dedicated beings.

In some ways, indeed, it is in the modern graduate school that the falsity which permeates our schooling is most flagrant and seemingly least remediable. We have seen one aspect of the fraud in describing the teaching of undergraduates by harassed and unprepared graduate students. The same disparity between ends and means is reproduced in such accepted practices as giving promotion for research to men appointed and salaried for teaching. Research worth having can only be hoped for, not com-

16. "Boy Who Couldn't Graduate Becomes $20,000-a-Year Sales Executive at 18," *New York Times,* June 8, 1958.

17. Mr. Conant has suggested that high school diplomas should indicate rank and quality by carrying on their backs the student's full record. He thinks it unjust that there should be a dual standard, high and low, for obtaining the same certificate. *New York Times*, July 17, 1958.

manded; yet in the best schools teaching is deemed inferior to it and a nuisance. This judgment is expressed in the coveted research professorships, and even more vividly in the inducements recently held out by the wealthier state universities to the members of poor ancient ones: the distinguished man is offered a high salary, frequent leaves of absence, funds for research, and no duties. The highest prize of the teaching profession is: no teaching. For the first time in history, apparently, scholars want no disciples. And perhaps, seeing those that come forward, they are right. In any case, they accept sterilization at a high fee, while the funds voted by legislatures and foundations to "increase facilities" serve in fact to remove the best minds from the classroom.

By the lore of graduate schools, to publish what is "new" is the only accepted way to contribute to knowledge. It follows that originality is sought also in the work of graduates, whose general information is lacking or recently acquired, whose technical training, if they are fortunate, dates from a senior thesis, and whose ability to write a page—let alone a book—has never been developed by suitable exercises. As in college, the pretense is that "mature persons" having free choice can educate themselves by following lecture courses which are assumed to be "advanced" and which may be taken in any order and combination. After a suitable number of lectures and one or two seminars, in which students read papers haltingly in front of their uninterested peers, the comprehensive oral examination suddenly looms demanding of the candidate a breadth and depth of knowledge equal to the sum of the same in the heads of his half-dozen examiners. In most subjects, few attempts are made to educe principles from ever larger masses of facts and to relegate detail to handbooks. The sum total of many specialties is required of the student, no matter how many years of his adult life are swallowed up in the preparation. Many give up. The rest go in for cramming, which after the strain of the vomition leaves a man reflecting that there was one week in his life when he knew a great deal.

The institution built on these assumptions crowns them all with the affectation of having nothing to do with the preparation of teachers. It would consider itself disgraced if it gave courses

in pedagogy or in the history of education. It knows and wants
to know nothing of the verified facts about learning, memory,
and habit; about temperamental differences in verbal and visual
powers; about anything that might prepare its graduates for the
age-old difficulties in imparting knowledge. It sends out "masters" and "doctors" in the humanities—the academic study of
literature, music, and the plastic arts—who have not an inkling
of the psychology of perception—just as if Helmholtz and William James had never lived. And these cripples, many of whom
have taught undergraduates while earning a license to teach,
are seldom enabled to correct their own patent deficiencies as
speakers, writers, and judges of work. Though it is upon them
as inspirers of the next generation in college that the continuity
of scholarship depends, no opportunity exists to tell them of such
elementary faults as mumbling, disjointed utterance, and unorganized thought. In short, the graduate school reproduces on a
lofty plane the errors of omission chargeable at every stage since
the fifth grade.

No exertions by isolated teachers in college or graduate school
can make up for the prevailing lack of the rudiments. The very
mixing of those who can with those who fumble or grope destroys morale and turns every advance into a perpetual rebegin-
ning. The net result is a general spoilage of the native ability
which should be exploited from its earliest appearance. But to
find and exploit talent as we exploit our other natural resources
presupposes a body of schoolteachers who are at least intel-
lectualized. This we almost certainly lack. We cannot be sure
until we release our present teachers from professional superstitions, irrelevant duties, economic cares, and social oppression.

This seems a large order, yet much of it could be carried out
by the simple expedient of letting teachers alone in winter and
making them read books in summer. Their minds are today the
least of their assets, in everyone's estimation including their own.
Teachers have been the victims—often the willing victims—of
that longing for a happy world, which not only has made the
school an anti-intellectual hothouse, but designed the Parent-
Teachers' Association as a vestibule to utopia. There the teachers have given the last of their energies to justifying themselves

by projecting impossible goals and pretending to enjoy with their audience's offspring a most unnatural bliss. In these public relations with the parents any respectable notion of teaching sank under the hypocrisies of the well-intentioned.

This subduing of intellect to pedagoguery and the cash nexus is so consequential for the discussion of money in a later chapter that it must be noticed here with the aid of an example. Since teachers in the public schools are presumably in no position to resist their masters, the taxpayers, I shall cite recent events at an old-established private preparatory school. The headmaster, not an educationist, invited a number of influential parents for a discussion of the school and its needs, chiefly financial. The first error imposed by our manners was that the headmaster must be mealy-mouthed and pretend that what the school needed was not money so much as parental criticism and advice. The second error was that the parents naïvely believed this transparent lie and acted on it. After the week-end in question, typical remarks were transcribed and circulated. Amid ordinary good sense, one read the following:

"The parents have a feeling of not being wanted. They need a tip as to how to act. . . ." Another complained: "We've seen a good bit of the housemaster, but we haven't seen the teachers because we've felt they've been too busy . . ." Another: "Your communications from the school tend to be formal and cold . . . it would be better if you went on to say that of course housemasters and teachers are interested and available for discussion, etc."

"Available for discussion, etc."—togetherness![18] That is the summit we have reached after three thousand years of arduous *paideia*. "A key point to the role of the parents," the school report goes on, "is to develop their understanding of the *why* behind the policies, programs, desires, and needs of the school." To parents who want such a role it would be useless to explain that

18. As one can see daily in the press, schemes are numerous for bringing parents and children together in the same classroom, e.g., "Parents Joining Children in Art." *New York Times,* July 8, 1957. This is another manifestation of the self-centered family, the sanctuary of innocence and incest combined.

teaching is not an agglutinative principle but a separating, a detaching principle. Teaching is to get rid of the pupils, not to inherit their parents.

When parents begin to meddle in the direction of schools, the teachers' defense of "the educational process" calls forth a jargon which is in good part responsible for the general decline in literacy—for how can we expect children to think and speak clearly when their elders in talking of school do neither? In order to suggest a perpetually gay adventure, everyone refers not to difficulties but to "challenges"—the challenge of or to our schools; each new class is a challenge to the school; when the P.T.A. convenes, the division of home economics "prepares to meet the parents' challenge" by furnishing coffee and cake and explaining how a new scheme was tried out (indeed, a "research experiment") with results that were "exciting."

Contrary to the common experience, a teacher's excitement seems never to stop. Yet, on sober reflection, a teacher who is free of false zeal should feel no more challenged by a new class (and no less) than any good craftsman by a familiar task; and should feel no more excitement in the classroom (and no less) than a surgeon at the operating table. Nor have parents any business challenging schools and teachers in another sense, as if here were policies to mistrust and candidates to elect. Notwithstanding, the political mixture of inquest and boasting continues, in the superlative mood of the advertiser and the mass media. A childish idea of wonder and surprise, of rescue and giant-killing, informs this agitation and colors it with megalomania.

What makes the pretense of dramatic thrills all the more absurd is that the practitioners lay claim, through another set of jargon words, to the results of a science called "educational research." There is, as a matter of fact, no such science. The results are vitiated in advance by the nonexistence of the entities they refer to. No doubt the children observed, the events counted, the test papers scored, are genuine objects in the world of experience; but the generalities inferred from them are either tendentious or tautological. They tell us over again in polysyllables what does not need saying, or they command us to foster in children certain motives or attitudes arbitrarily chosen, rather than others that are equally "natural" and therefore equally "found" by psychology. To the extent that psychology is a science, it prescribes nothing but merely describes. If our social bias did not lead us to prefer, say, co-operation and creativity, psychology could find excellent natural motives driving the young to hostility and imitation, on which an admirable system of repression could be built. Human capacity is more varied than educational researchers know, though their methods insure that they shall never find this out.

This simple intellectual point would be better appreciated than it is if that other creature of educational research, the hircocervus buzzing in a void, did not distract us with its capacity for dispelling sense. Try for example to think of any practical judgments that could be based on the answers to the questions I shall quote from a so-called "evaluation study" of a small liberal arts college. The few I have chosen were among those called "major" by the expert, who produced upward of a thousand. The remainder required the students, faculty members, and trustees to "measure" degrees of importance, intensity, and the like by writing 1, 2 or 3 as part of their answers; that is how "science" came into the inquiry. But the "major questions" required no "measurement":

"What is the major assumption underlying the program? What are the educational objectives of the students and the faculty? What is the relation of these objectives to the major assumptions? What evidence now exists to show the extent to which the objectives are now being attained?"

Let me interrupt here to make sure that the familiar sound of the words does not produce the illusion of meaning. The major assumption of any program is that it is good. The educational objective of any sane student is to be taught and receive a certificate of work done. The relation of the objective to the assumption is that if the assumption is true—i.e. the program (including its execution) is good—the objective will be reached more often than not, i.e., more students will learn and profit than fail. As for evidence that the whole thing works, it exists in the common sense to have things continue as they are. All I have said is of course truism; none of it differs from one school to the next; none of it is worth saying or asking—unless you

want an answer like this: "The major assumption of our distinctive program is that a balanced and enriched curriculum,
broad in concept but carefully adjusted to the growing needs
and motivations of the individual student, will help in the development of the whole person through the liberating influence
of the arts and sciences considered as a contribution not only to
personal well-being but to future service as a member of a democratic community."

The "self-evaluation" I have used does not dwell in abstrac-
tions throughout. But its concreteness is typically "educational"
in presupposing a godlike knowledge of human character. Thus:
"What is the nature of the faculty-student relationship? What
is the value of these relations? Can an instructor who is a poor
counselor at first become a good one? Do creative writing majors
get an increased appreciation of the work of others? Do science
students know as many facts as they should?" And—very apt for
a girls' college: "Do students who apply and are accepted have
irregular profiles?"[19]

It would be difficult to demonstrate the absurdity of these
questions to anyone who lives in the atmosphere in which they
sound genuine. But that would only be because of the gap between words and experience in the dream world of professional
educators. He who can read and understand other writers—
philosophers, poets, political theorists, scientists—is, after comparison, entitled to say that the language of educational research does not point to the common experience of teaching and
ignores the rules of common discourse.

This last conclusion is confirmed when one receives from a professor of higher education at a great university a printed inquiry
such as this, which I reproduce entire:

> Would you like to have a comparable overview of an important
> book in higher education on your desk periodically? A card is
> enclosed for your response.

Or again, when one reads in the paper that "Paul V. Gump and
Jacob S. Kounin, of Wayne State University, noted that a 'high

---

19. A technical reference to the graph representing test results in
several subjects.

firmness correction' such as a proper reprimand accompanied by leading the child by the hand or looking at him pointedly had a salutary effect on other misbehavior-bent children in the group. They observed that 'high clarity' statements such as 'Don't take the blocks away when Johnny's using them' were more effective than 'low-clarity' statements such as 'Stop it!' "[20]

This "experiment" seems to have rediscovered that infants respond to the intellectual virtue of explicitness. But when year after year schoolteachers are told that to be an educator means remembering the Gump-Kounin principle of high firmness correction, their minds acquire, so to say, permanent dampness factor which extinguishes any spark of intellect in them or those committed to their care.

To be sure, the country still numbers a great many excellent teachers who know their own minds and speak them clearly. They are the ones who, when the book salesman comes around with blurbs and study aids for what he calls the language arts, rebuke him by saying: "I am a teacher of English." Without such teachers, spreading their light from the first grade to the last, there would be no hope for the host of intelligent youth, and we who teach in the upper years would never encounter the able and intellectual student, as we periodically do. But the self-aware and defiant minority of teachers who teach is overborne by the weight of school administrators, of a diffident or defeatist public opinion, and of an atmosphere heavy-laden with the science of nonthought.

Its opposite, the power of articulate thought, is obviously the only force than can penetrate and dissolve this pall that hangs over and darkens our schools. In another system than ours we might have hoped that textbooks would counteract the weakness of teachers, for textbook writers are usually university men with some energy of mind and a special talent for exposition. But this is not always so, and in a country where leading scholars will not condescend to review textbooks, where in fact, most text-

---

20. *New York Times*, September 2, 1957.

books are not reviewed at all, the miasma of the teachers' college and the P.T.A. often beclouds the printed page.

Besides, the writing of a text is no longer in the sole hands of the author, who in any case is often tempted to give up his principles by the great pecuniary rewards held out to him. In the "processing" (the publisher's term), a textbook is submitted to a dozen or more teachers "in the field." The field refers not merely to the subject matter but to the field of action, the classroom, where local prejudices and sacred illiteracies obtain. Against these, the textbook writer must defend his words and views, squaring his mind with those of anonymous critics who are often his inferiors in learning and sense. His vocabulary at any rate cannot go beyond what "science" says is right for the "age group." Frequency lists rule the mind of America and see that it remains average. For high schools, no text can describe New England's colonial trade as lucrative; it must read "profitable." The word hegemony is unknown, and there is apparently only one adjective in common use to qualify strife, resentment, controversy, quarrel, and enmity—the adjective "bitter."

To offset this aridity, the modern textbook is magnificently illustrated and printed. At no time in the history of schools, I imagine, have children been given such beautiful maps, such interesting pictures of contemporary objects and persons, such clear scientific diagrams and fine typography, in short so perfect a page to study from. To those who have brought about this revolution, all thanks and honor are due. But their pride in show is a hindrance to other efforts. Textbook publishers do not sell to their readers but to the middlemen, the school administrators who order by the hundred thousand for groups of states. This lucrative, nay profitable, outlet justifies the expense of producing richly illustrated books, for it is patent that the buyers believe to a man in the supreme merit of visible attractions. What buyers and sellers cannot see is the great gap in quality between the visual and the conceptual matter they thrust on the pupil. They know from nineteenth-century psychology that imagination and memory do not work alike in everyone, some being visual, some auditory, some muscular. But they forget the two limitations of visual aid—let alone the interests of the "muscular" memorizers.

Pictures by themselves say little, or are ambiguous. To teach "social problems" with photographs of domestic situations and then ask, "What problems of human relations does the picture suggest?" and "What seems to be happening in the picture?"[21] is to confirm the pupil in thought-clichés rather than add to his knowledge and give it complexity.

Moreover, it is evident that visual memory and the power to summon up ideas are not the same. Unless the student learns to turn a verbal account into the right vividness in his mind's eye and conversely to frame his imaginings in words, he always remains something of an infant, a barbarian dependent on a diagram.

The power to summon up image-with-word and word-with-image is in truth the most completely undeveloped in our schooling. We keep it weak by the very means we think most advanced. Perhaps the abandonment of grammar which has come about in the wake of the new "scientific" linguistics, is too negative to be called a means, but it fitly represents the flight from articulateness. Meanwhile, the lavish use of things to see has turned pointing from bad manners to the lazy teacher's secret of success. Finally, in the universal use of the so-called objective test, both influences are wedded. Taking an objective test is simply pointing. It calls for the least effort of mind above that of keeping awake: recognition. And it is recognition without a shock, for to a veteran of twelve years old, the traditional four choices for each question fall into a soothing rhythm. No tumult of surprise followed by a rallying generalship and concentration, as in facing an essay question; no fresh unfolding of the subject under unexpected demand, but the routine sorting out of the absurd from the trivial, or the completing of dull sentences by word- or thought-clichés.[22] No other single practice explains

---

21. A new method for teacher' colleges, according to the *New York Times*, September 20, 1956.

22. The first discussion, so far as I know, of objective tests regarded from the intellectual point of view (as against that of convenience or handling large numbers) is an article in *The American Scholar* (Spring, 1959) by Mr. Banesh Hoffman, Professor of Mathematics in Queens College. It begins with an illustration of the penchant of objective-test makers for the thought-cliché: "*Emperor* is the name of (a) a string

more fully the intellectual defects of our students up to and through graduate school than their ingrained association of knowledge and thought with the scratching down of check marks on dotted lines.

With mass education this so-called "technique of educational measurement" is spreading. The Educational Testing Service announces a "Project in Malaya to Train Specialists,"[23] while the American public is fobbed off with reassuring references to "test reliability studies," the "translation of educational goals into behavioral terms," and similar apings of the genuine tests and conversion formulas of physical science. The making of a single objective test costs about twenty thousand dollars and takes two years' work by a squad of experts. When it is made and used it is then necessary to warn college admissions officers not to compare the various test scores of applicants: "The phenomenon of statistical regression. . . . would tend to penalize students with high SCAT scores and give an advantage to those with low SCAT scores. If the SCAT is being used as the selection test, it should be administered to *all* applicants."[24] Whether such tests and their comparisons are deemed scientific or not, the inexactitude of science as regards the individual is a subject that deserves the attention of all who understand what is meant by the rights of the person and the obligations of intellectual rigor. These are doubtless what Sir Alfred Zimmern had in mind when he called "the two unmentionable letters," I.Q., "those deadly enemies of self respect."[25]

---

quartet (b) a piano concerto (c) a violin sonata." The answer (b) is correct, but so is (a), one of Haydn's quartets being also the "Emperor," though not as widely known. Mr. Hoffman goes on to point out the imprecisions of wording, errors of fact and inconsistencies of expectation that characterize current aptitude and subject matter tests, notably in the sciences.

23. *E.T.S. Developments*, September, 1957, I.

24. *Examiner's Manual*, Cooperative School and College Ability Tests, Second Supplement, 1956, 3.

25. Sir Alfred Zimmern, Fourth Honors Day Address, Brooklyn College, October 15, 1947.

In theory and practice alike, then, and from top to bottom, American education serves other ends than Intellect. This state of fact, which has just begun to draw critical fire from various quarters is, as I said at the outset, the logical result of what we think and feel as a massive egalitarian democracy. The schools are made of our flesh and bone, our thought and emotions, which means that if we want to cut away any part and reshape others, we must be willing to bleed and feel pain. No amount of re-shuffling within the present curriculum and rebaptizing of "objectives" in the catalogues will accomplish anything. More will than we have ever used about "education" is needed to make the least of our hopes into a deed.

And the first step to willing is the intellectual one of saying what we mean and meaning what we say. The philanthropy I have assigned as one cause of futility in our schooling connotes much more than kindness to the child. The debate is not on that point. Nobody wants to return to the school run like a bad prison, by terror and flogging. The question is not about kindness but about instruction: Is the school a place of teaching or of psychologizing? Is it to prolong vicariously the parents' love of innocence and act out their dream of a good society, or is it to impart literacy? And are we to wait till *after* the Ph.D. to get it?[26] When, finally, is the school to sort out types of mind and, assuming that all can read, write, and count, enable each kind to acquire the facts and principles relevant to their calling and their tastes?

To encompass such ends the school must know what it wants, not in the form of vague private or public virtues, but in the form of intellectual powers. It must stop blathering about sensitivity to the needs of others, and increasing responsibility for bringing about one world, and say instead: "I want a pupil who can read Burke's 'Speech on Conciliation' and solve problems in trigonometry. I want young men and women who can read French prose and write English. I want academic high school graduates who can remember what the Missouri Compromise

---

26. Many a man now teaching has learned to write by seeing his thesis rewritten under his eyes, one word at a time, by his sponsor.

had to do with the Civil War, and who will carry over into college their familiarity with logarithms and the techniques of the chemistry laboratory." And having said these or similar things after due consideration, the school must enforce what it has said. It must pass judgment on performance and let accomplishment be known, quite as if it had the importance of a record in a track meet.[27]

Education with us has too long been a device for equalizing merit. Thinking of education as the open door to economic and social advancement, we have made schooling, or the token of it, available to all. Let us, we have said, favor the young who work their way through college, and make allowances for a poor showing; let the city spend half a million on retarded children but not a cent on the intelligent, for that would again widen the gap; and let us not make the bachelor's degree stand for anything exaggerated in the way of brains. The equal opportunity it affords *after* college cannot be widespread if we are strict about getting into college and staying there.

Once this reasoning is perceived, the puzzles about mass education disappear. The system of credits and electives permits an education to be made out of interchangeable parts; everybody fashions the same B.A. out of subjects variously difficult: Spanish as well as Greek, elementary geology as well as quantitative chemistry, will "satisfy" the ostensibly stern requirement of a science and a foreign language. And for other "prescribed" subjects the "blind-spot" excuse will bring a waiver and a substitution.

The bookkeeping system has another democratic advantage: it conceals the fact that there may be a relation between Intellect and ancestry. This is a delicate question to raise, but sooner or later someone will have to bell the cat. The connection I speak

27. It is hardly more than a year ago that the College Entrance Examination Board consented to "bare" the test takers' scores—at the insistence, be it noted, of the pupils themselves. But when one reads that the director of science in the New York City schools was appointed to his post after failing the qualifying examination a first and then a second time, passing it on his third try, though others achieved the feat the first time, one can hardly wonder that people think "exams are the bunk." *New York Times*, August 14, 1958.

of may or may not be found in heredity; its farthest cause does not matter so long as the obvious influence of domestic habit is known and seen to be cumulative after two or more generations. There is no mystery about it: the child who is familiar with books, ideas, conversation—the ways and means of the intellectual life—before he begins school, indeed, before he begins consciously to think, has a marked advantage. He is at home in the House of Intellect just as the stableboy is at home among horses or the child of actors on the stage. Medical schools recognize this truth when they give preference to applicants who are children of physicians. Sometimes, it is true, the specialty of the house causes rebellion and revulsion. But when it does not, it produces what we want in able minds—concentrated power. This does not preclude the genius or great scholar from being born on the farm or in the blacksmith shop; there is nothing fated about the harvest of talents. But it is historically true that two of the prime elements of intellect, continuity and concentration, go together. One has only to think of the long list of distinguished men that have sprung, in England and in Germany, from the Protestant clergy.

The generation born just after the wars of nationalism, between 1860 and 1880, retained traditions of intellect and presumably could have transmitted them, not intact, perhaps, which no tradition can ever be, but unimpaired. That generation fathered one of intellectual cripples by being itself emotionally lamed. Circumstances blighted its hopes—in the disillusion of the First World War, the failure of Parliamentary liberalism east of the Rhine, the Great Depression and the Second World War, each seeming a disproof of the power of reason. But the intellectuals of that era also took a hand in their own maiming. Their manners betrayed them, as we know, and they yielded the point of reason while pursuing their liberal, democratic aims. In creating public schools they refused to sort out of the crowd those most capable of learning. In turning individual militant liberalism into socially protective liberalism, they idealized all downtrodden minorities including children, and instead of "liquidating ignorance" hunted down Intellect as an ogre to destroy. Complacency did the rest by making them forget the economics of kindness: give-and-take was replaced by give-and-give, known in child-rearing as the permissive system, though better described as "All for Love." So defined, the formula of liberal philanthropy and science has to come to mean: "Nothing for Mind."

Yet no secret formula or special device is needed to make the most of our inherited wealth of intellect; simply do not penalize it as is now done in deference to theory, whether political, social, or psychological. Do not assume, for instance, that the child of professional parents who shows this natural advantage has been pushed or forced and must be saved from neuroticism by "contact" and group activities that bore him. His boredom is, I agree, a dangerous sign in a future committee member, but if we want his other talents, as scientist, scholar, linguist, poet, or mathematician, we must not let him lose his advantage; we must maintain his impetus. If he does not "develop evenly" let the sociable side of him delay its flowering, instead of adjusting it at the expense of his possibly unique powers: that too would be kindness, democracy, and opportunity. Let him throughout his schooling share classes with all the rest and get used, without priggishness, to the prevalence of slow wits. But do not wait till college or middle life to let him be the intellectual that nature and domestic circumstance prepared; that is, do not hold back the hare till near the end of the race to spare the feelings of the tortoise: the notion that she won is a fable.

The Good Teacher

SIDNEY HOOK
(1902–   )

The Hero in History, 1943
Education for Modern Man, 1946
From Hegel to Marx, 1950
The Quest for Being, 1961

SIDNEY HOOK has played a key role in the transmission of the ideas first formulated by John Dewey into the mainstream of American thought. He is not only a brilliant teacher, but also the author of cogent books on current philosophy and politics. Not content with mere detached scholarship, Professor Hook has been a committed fighter for academic freedom, and has helped inspire the effort to establish for America a body of liberal ideas, independent of conventional radicalism and conventional patriotism alike.

If the modern teacher will think of himself not so much as a schoolmaster but as a lifemaster doing from another angle what the social worker does in his sphere, then he will be striving for all the knowledge available which could help him in his task. He will try to educate a generation of youth which combines emotional stability with a flexible mind; yet he will only succeed if he is capable of seeing each of the problems of the new generation against the background of a changing world.

—KARL MANNHEIM

ALL PLANS FOR EDUCATIONAL REFORMS DEPEND ON THE TEACHER for their proper realization. Unless carried out by a personnel sincerely imbued with the philosophy animating the reforms and trained in the arts of effective teaching, they are doomed to failure. Everyone who remembers his own educational experience remembers teachers, not methods and techniques. The teacher is the kingpin of the educational situation. He makes and breaks programs. The initial difficulties and growing pains of progressive education were primarily caused by a scarcity of competent teachers. It still remains a source of great difficulty.

The major role of the teacher in the educational process has led some writers to the conclusion that, once students have been assembled for purposes of instruction, the good teacher is all sufficient. Given a good teacher, they assume, further concern with educational content and method is unnecessary. He has an unfailing natural sense of what it is right to teach and how to teach it. He does not even need a well appointed classroom. One end of a log will do. Invariably someone will recall an individual of whom he will say: "He did not know anything about pedagogy but he was a great teacher."

Such a position is understandable as a reaction to the view that anybody can be educated to be an educator. It manifests a healthy skepticism towards the overdeveloped curriculums of professional schools of education in which courses are needlessly proliferated. But there is little to be said for it as a serious response to the problems of instruction. If *what* a student learns depends altogether on *who* his teacher is, the result is sure to be a disorderly cross-patch pattern. The traditions and knowledge and skills which our age requires as a common soil in which to cultivate individual variety could hardly be developed. The diversity in temperament of these uniquely endowed persons, and in the direction of their interests as well as ideas, is much greater than among those who cannot spin an entire educational curriculum out of their innards. Such diversity within limits is desirable, provided students are exposed to the varied stimuli of several outstanding personalities. But this is not likely to be the case. For the number of these extraordinary teachers is not large enough to go around. And what the educational system of America needs is at least a million good teachers.

Teaching is an art and like all arts it can be learned with varying degrees of proficiency. Some are so gifted by nature that they can perform as good teachers without learning the arts of teaching, just as some singers can have brilliant musical careers without studying voice culture. On the other hand, there are some individuals who are naturally so handicapped for a teaching career that instruction in the teaching arts can do as little for them as musical study for the tone deaf. Most teachers fall between these two extremes. It is a crime against students to permit individuals of the second kind to enter the ordinary classroom as teachers, no matter how great their gifts may be in other respects or in other fields. Whatever teaching is, it should at least not be an obstruction to learning. But it is certainly no crime, it is not even a hardship, to require of naturally gifted teachers —those who are to the teaching manner born—that they learn the formal rudiments of the art of teaching. They can always improve their skills. An enormous amount of time can be saved by familiarizing oneself with teaching devices and techniques even if one already possesses the educator's insight and an adequate educational philosophy. No one who has not actually attempted to teach the details of a curriculum can properly appreciate the great difference that mastery of specific ways and means can make in motivating interest, facilitating communication and starting a train of thought in students which runs its course to the click of understanding. There are some things that are best learned *not* on the job. And although we can rely on any teacher to learn by trial and error experience, why should the students pay the price for that experience?

The most satisfactory teaching in American education is being done on the most elementary levels wherever plant facilities are adequate. The least satisfactory teaching is being done on the highest levels. By the "highest" level I mean, not the university, which is or should be primarily a research institution, but the liberal arts college. If we must tolerate a disparity in effective teaching, it is, of course, preferable that the best teaching be done on the lowest level, at the most susceptible age, rather than on the highest, when habits have already hardened. But there is no justification for the disparity, and were the public aware of the actual volume of bad teaching on the college level something would be done to remedy a scandalous situation. Practices are countenanced in colleges which would not be suffered for one moment in any good elementary or secondary high school, and I am not referring here to lecturing and unsupervised study which are sometimes assumed to be the distinctive procedures of college instruction. That some college instruction is excellent does not gainsay the fact that the quality of most of it is bad. Exceptions do *not* prove the rule; neither do they disprove it when the rule is true for the most part.

There are many causes for the comparative deficiencies of college teaching. First is the failure to clarify the function of liberal education, and the dual role the faculty is expected to fill as teachers and research workers. The second is the absence of any training in college teaching, indeed in any kind of teaching, despite the fact that there are certain common psychological and philosophical principles which hold for all varieties of instruction. The third is the indifference, almost hallowed now by tradition, to pedagogical questions. Officially many college teachers, especially if they feel secure because of length of service or publication, profess not to care whether they are good teachers or not. Little serious effort is made to evaluate how well the aims of college instruction are being carried out.

Before discussing the qualities which make for good college teaching and which should serve as criteria in the selection of teachers, I wish to say a brief word about each of the causes of the present state of college teaching.

The historical association between the college and the university has led to administrative confusion about the prerequisites of teaching in both institutions. Insofar as a university is an institution of research, it can use anybody—the blind, the deaf and the halt—provided only he has a brain. Capacity or incapacity to teach is strictly irrelevant. The only relevant question is whether this man or that can make a contribution to truth. University students are, or should be, mature men and women who are in a sense cooperating with their professors in the quest for truth. They should be expected to discount the personal and superficial mannerisms in those who are guiding their research, and fend for themselves.

The primary function, on the other hand, of the liberal arts teacher is to help young men and women to achieve intellectual and emotional maturity by learning to handle certain ideas and intellectual tools. This requires scholarship, and *familiarity* with current research but not necessarily the capacity to engage productively in it. It is alleged that the good liberal arts teacher will also be interested in doing creative work in his field. This is true for many but cannot be held true for all save by peculiar definition. It is certainly not true—and no one will be bold enough to make it true even by definition—that the good research worker will be an effective undergraduate teacher. Consequently, in selecting college teachers, once scholarly competence in the subject matter has been established, the primary consideration should be whether they give promise of being good teachers—and not, as is the case now, of whether they give promise of being good research workers. There is no necessary connection between a gift for discovery and a gift for lucid explanation, not even between a gift for discovery and a gift for teaching which evokes the desire for discovery in others. Until the liberal arts college is emancipated from its tutelage to the university, it will not find the teachers it needs.

It is notorious that most college teachers have never taken a course in methods of teaching, even in their own subject matter—and are proud of it. In most institutions, after an instructor survives a preliminary three-year teaching period he can stay put for life. Whether he survives depends basically on his contributions to the world of research—and this world, particularly in the humanities and social sciences, may be served in many curious ways—and only incidentally on his skills as a teacher. Only incidentally—because in few colleges does there exist an established method of evaluating teaching. Hearsay, student popularity, enrollment figures build up a picture, as often false as reliable, of what transpires in the classroom. Teaching is rarely supervised and, when it is, the credentials of the supervisor do not always pass critical muster. In most institutions, visits to the classrooms of one's colleagues are not considered good form. This hypersensitiveness to observation increases when departmental lines are crossed. There are exceptions, of course, but they must not blind us to the general rule.

The indifference and professed contempt of the liberal arts teachers as a group to problems of teaching is partly a reaction to the activities of schools of education. Standards of scholarship are lower in these schools. Not infrequently subject matter courses in the liberal arts are offered in schools of education by individuals who would not qualify on academic grounds for teaching in liberal arts colleges. And yet, when no subject matter courses are offered and instruction is given in methods of teaching, these courses are characterized as vapid and empty. In other words, there is a tendency for liberal arts faculties to damn schools of education not only for what they do poorly but for what they do well. There is a legitimate place for schools of education as teacher training institutes, not as rivals to the liberal arts colleges. In addition to stress on methods and techniques, strong curricular emphasis should be placed on the philosophy and psychology of education—themes, however, that are much too important to be left only to schools of education. A more genuine cooperation between liberal arts colleges and schools of education might begin at a point which enables the latter to serve the former by taking over the pedagogic training of its candidates for teacher's posts, leaving certification, on the basis of mastery of subject matter, strictly alone.

The function of the teacher is among the most important in our culture. He not only transmits essential knowledge and skills but, when he takes his calling seriously, strongly influences the formation of habits and the development of a philosophy of life. Yet this high calling is not valued by the community at its true worth nor, ironically enough, by teachers themselves. "Schoolmaster," "professor" are epithets of derision, and the odor of genteel poverty is repellent even to those who regard it as a sign of election. In boom periods the profession is deserted by a scramble for better paying jobs; in times of depression it is swamped by those who hanker for security. Social disesteem has operated as a principle of selection and bred a type noted for timidity. On paper, college faculties are responsible for all matters pertaining to educational policy and organization; in fact, they have, or rather exercise, less authority than do their glorified clerks. Faculty participation in democratic control of colleges is a favorite theme—for discussion.

The first step towards much-needed reforms in the selection of teachers is the stabilization of the economic conditions of the profession. This should take place on a plane high enough to liberate teachers from gnawing worry about making ends meet. Once this is achieved, the democratization of the college would be much easier to carry out. For the timidity of teachers grows largely from the knowledge that they face a restricted market for their services in which competitive bidding is only for a few, that administrators fight shy of "trouble-makers" even in a good cause, and that the price teachers pay for independence may be loss of a vocation—the only one for which they are trained.

This first step, however, must be accompanied by a rigorous revision of the process by which teachers educate and select their successors. The revision cannot be accomplished overnight, for we must begin where we are and educators themselves must undergo some reeducation. What is needed is the will to begin, since the knowledge of what constitutes a good teacher is widely distributed. The formulations of the traits which identify the good teacher vary, but it is possible to list those that are observable wherever there is agreement that a good teacher is in action.

A good teacher is not good for all purposes and in all circumstances. In the army, in the church, in the political party, in the penitentiary, as they are presently constituted, a good teacher as we shall define him cannot be used. What makes a good teacher, like what makes a good education, must be considered in relation to certain values. What we are seeking are the criteria of a good teacher in a democratic society whose educational system has embraced the fundamental aims we have previously outlined.

(a) The first criterion is intellectual competence. By this I mean not only the truism that the teacher should have a mastery of the subject matter he is teaching and that he should keep abreast of important developments in his field, but that he should have some capacity for analysis. Without this capacity, he cannot develop it in his students. There are different levels and types of analysis but what they have in common is an understanding of how to approach problems, of how to take ideas apart, of how to relate our language habits to our intellectual practices. Capacity for analysis is something different from mere possession of the dry-bones and heaps of knowledge. Insofar as the distinction can be made, it is bound up more with method than content. Whatever information a teacher imparts, he must know (and wherever relevant be able to explain) how it is reached, what its validity depends on, and the role of empirical and conventional elements in the answer.

Another element in intellectual competence is a sense of relevant connection. The good teacher should be well oriented in some other fields besides the one in which he may claim to be a specialist. He should be able to follow the thread of an argument or the ramifications of a problem without concern for what a subject is called or for departmental non-trespass signs. I have heard a professor of political science bitterly complain that the economics department was teaching government, too! If the teaching was good, he should have applauded it. On the other hand, not everything in the world is interrelated and, if it were, not all of it would be equally relevant to a specific problem. The most obvious evidence of bad teaching is classroom "thinking by association," in which by a series of grasshopper jumps topics are dwelt on that have no logical connection with each other. The usual result is that the original problem, where there is one, is lost sight of.

Related to intellectual competence is the willingness to countenance, if not to encourage, rational opposition and spirited critical dissent by students. The inquiring mind even among youth sometimes probes deeply. Only a teacher unsure of himself will resent embarrassing questions to which the only honest reply must be a confession of ignorance. Intellectual independence is such a rare virtue that the good teacher positively welcomes it despite the occasional excesses of youthful dogmatism and exuberance. For many years I refused to believe that any liberal arts teacher would actually penalize a student for intellectual disagreement. But the evidence is overwhelming that in many colleges this is far from exceptional, and that students are often fearful of venturing a defence of ideas and attitudes incompatible with those held by their teachers. In one institution, a teacher of philosophy did not conceal from his students his conviction that to embrace the metaphysics of materialism was to reveal a moral deficiency in character. Anyone who expected a recommendation from him was warned to look to his philosophy. In another institution, a bright member of the Young Communist League bitterly complained to his English teacher who had given him the lowest possible passing grade. In answer, he was told that anyone who believed in dialectical materialism deserved nothing better. A few years later, a young woman who had a perfect record in all her subjects took the same course with the same teacher and received the only C in her college career. On inquiring the reason she was told that no student who disbelieved in dialectical materialism deserved anything better. The teacher had become converted and had changed his mind about dialectical materialism—a speculative doctrine really irrelevant to the subject matter of his course. But he had not changed his intellectual ways. He was sincerely convinced that he had the truth on both occasions, but lacked the wit to realize that the students' reasons for embracing truth or error were far more important, in their educational experience, than the question of the validity of dialectical materialism. In the last decade, more than one class of students has been punished for the tortuous intellectual pilgrimages of their teachers—particularly at the hands of a certain school of militantly doctrinaire teachers who, despite the fact that their opinions veer as if by order from year to year, regard themselves as qualified to settle the most delicate problems of economics, politics, history, philosophy and religion with a zeal and confidence that specialists, handicapped by genuine knowledge, shrink from assuming.

(b) Intellectual competence is necessary but not sufficient for good teaching. It must be accompanied by a quality of patience towards beginners which accepts as natural the first groping steps towards understanding by the uninitiated. The "simple" and the "obvious" are relative to antecedent skills and knowledge. Failure to see and act on this is responsible for intellectual browbeating by otherwise competent teachers and for the air, deliberately only half-concealed, of suffering the hopeless stupidity of those who are stumbling their way forward. The intellectually quick, and all teachers should be quick, have a tendency towards intellectual impatience. The impatience but not the quickness must be curbed. Patience is something that can be learned, except by certain temperaments who should never be entrusted with a class. Good teaching is not found where a star teacher holds forth for the benefit only of his star pupils, but where some participating response is evoked from every normal member of the class. Nothing is easier than to yield to the pleasures of colloquy with the exceptional students of a class—and nothing more unfair to the rest, in whom this builds up intense resentments, oddly enough not against the teacher, but against their exceptional classmates. Special provision should be made for the instruction of superior students but a good teacher does not let their special needs dominate the class.

(c) The third characteristic of good teaching is ability to plan a lesson, without mechanically imposing it on the class, in those subjects where basic materials have to be acquired, and to guide the development of discussion to a cumulative result in subjects in which the seminar method is used. The bane of much college teaching is improvisation. Improvisation is not only legitimate but unavoidable in motivating interest and finding points of departure or illustration for principles. But it cannot replace the planful survey of subject matter and problems, nor provide direction to discussion. It is delightful to follow the argument wherever it leads. But it must be an argument.

Where improvisation is chronic and draws its materials from autobiography, teaching sinks to its lowest level. In my own experience I recall teachers who rarely knew what they were going to talk about before they came to class. Usually they would talk about themselves or their families. Over the years, when members of their successive classes came together, they were able to construct a fairly accurate composite family portrait. The personalities of such teachers rarely possessed a richness or power that might justify taking themselves as subject matter. The contempt in which intelligent students held them was checked only by the teachers' power to distribute grades—a power which they wielded with a whimsical irresponsibility.

Naturally, the responsibility of the teacher for the progressive organization of subject matter varies with elementary and advanced classes, and he will proceed differently in presenting a lecture and in conducting a tutorial. Nothing I have said suggests the necessity of a detailed lesson plan which is as often a drawback as an aid even in the secondary schools. What the teacher must aim at is to make each class hour an integrated experience with an aesthetic, if possible a dramatic, unity of its own. Without a spontaneity that can point up the give and take of discussion, and a skill in weaving together what the students themselves contribute, preparation will not save the hour from dullness. The pall of dullness which hangs over the memories of school days in the minds of many unfortunately envelops the whole question of education.

(d) Another important quality the good teacher possesses is knowledge of human beings. He is in a sense a practical psychologist. He knows something more about people than the laws of their learning curves, and what he knows he has not found in textbooks on psychology. The more one studies students, the more differences they reveal. These differences need not be relevant to what they are trying to learn; but sometimes they are. A teacher devoid of this knowledge cannot solve the problem of motivation or evoke full participation from his class. Nor can he tell when to temper the wind, when to let it blow, when to build up self-assurance in the pathologically shy, when to deflate the bumptious. Unable to diversify his challenges, he cannot teach with proper justice and discipline in a class of miscellaneous talents. He may have a standard for the group; he should have a standard for each individual in terms of his special needs—whether they be disabilities or advantages. Except on the frontiers of knowledge, subject matter cannot be continuously fresh. The great bulk of what is taught to students in every institution except graduate schools of universities is "old stuff" to their teachers. To stay intellectually alive as one traverses familiar ground year in and year out is not easy. It can be done, of course, by rotating assignments, by taking sabbaticals and, most important of all, by strong theoretical interests in one's own field and related fields. But to stay intellectually alive in the classroom is something else again. Yet for the sake of students one must be alive there if nowhere else. The new developments in one's field seldom bear upon the fundamentals of college instruction and the minutiae of scholarship have meaning only to those who are already well instructed.

The secret of intellectual vitality in the classroom, when a theorem is being derived for the twentieth time or when an elementary point in the grammar of a foreign language is being explained, or when the nerve of an old philosophic argument is being laid bare, lies in experiencing the situation as a fresh problem in communication rather than one in personal discovery. Or, putting it a little differently, it consists in getting the students to reach the familiar conclusion with a sense of having made their own discovery. The task is to make as many as possible see as much as possible of what they have not seen before. It is this perennial challenge, which cannot be adequately met without a knowledge of people, that keeps the good teacher alive. If he does not recognize it, he is a pedagogical automaton, and almost always a bore.

Where knowledge has not yet been won and the authority of method does not point to inescapable and well-tested conclusions, the love of truth can be relied on to generate its own enthusiasm. But where knowledge is already warranted by methods that are themselves warranted, and where originality is likely to be little more than a craving for attention or an expression of conceit, the love of truth by itself cannot be relied upon to make a lesson exciting. There is something suspicious about any mind that can be thrown into raptures of enthusiasm at stated intervals, and in pretty much the same language, too, by the statement of truths he has been purveying to students term in, term out. Such enthusiasm is synthetic and the students know it.[1]

---

1. There is a story told on the campus of an eastern college of an art teacher, now happily no longer teaching, who used to lecture by what might be called the method of sustained respiration. In treating of a certain figure in the history of art, at a fixed point in his course, he would draw a deep breath and, in a mounting crescendo, declaim the artist's wonders. One day he began as usual. "He had no sense of form, he had

There is a crackle of interest always present in the classroom of a good teacher no matter how trite or time-worn the theme. It is supplied not merely by the teacher's love of truth but by the students' desire to discover the truth, and by the teacher's interest in that desire and in the arts of gratifying it. In the end, the good teacher makes himself superfluous and the good student learns the art of self-education. But it is literally in the end.

(e) He knows man best who loves him best. A teacher cannot love all his students, nor is it wise to love any of them. The knowledge appropriate for good teaching requires an emotion not so strong as love but also not so irrational. This emotion is sympathy. The good teacher must like people and be interested in them as people, and yet he need not like or be interested in everyone. I am speaking of a general personality trait. It need not find universal expression in every action. But without it an intellectually competent teacher may do more harm than good. There is such a thing as sadism in educational life. Teachers have enormous powers to make students miserable; and, where they are chosen haphazardly, there will always be some who will visit their frustrations and disappointments upon those before them, usually under the guise of being strict disciplinarians. The incidence of insanity is higher among teachers than among any other profession, and the academic community is no freer from phobias like antisemitism than the rest of the community. It requires only one teacher to ruin a student's career.

Sympathy is a positive attitude of imaginative concern with the personal needs of others. Benevolent neutrality and mechanical application of rules, no matter how scrupulous, are no substitutes for it. If justice is based on understanding, then without sympathy there cannot be true justice. For understanding is never complete without the sympathy that awakens our organs of perception. Those who teach large numbers and never get to know their students have a tendency to regard all but a brilliant few as a dull, cloddish mass. Reduce the number in each class,

---

no sense of color, he had no sense for religion or morals, he broke all the rules of good drawing . . ." and before he could finish, back chorused the class with his punch-line, "But my God! could that man paint!"

foreshorten the perspective, and no one worthy of being a teacher will fail to see the interesting variety of potentiality in every group. Even outside the classroom it takes two people to make one bore. And, next to ideas, persons are the most interesting things in the world. In each person there is some unique quality of charm, intelligence or character, some promise and mystery that invites attention and nurture. The teacher who seeks it will find it.

Students respond to sympathy for their special intellectual needs like plants to sunshine and rain. They undertake more and achieve more. A certain danger exists that they may at the beginning undertake tasks in order to please their teacher or not to disappoint him but, if proper guidance is furnished, their own sense of growing mastery of a task and its increasing significance, provides intellectual momentum. The function of the teacher at this point is unobtrusively to raise the stick of achievement higher and to offer criticism without killing self-confidence. Students rarely disappoint teachers who assure them in advance that they are doomed to failure. They do not, of course, always live up to the more optimistic expectations of their teachers but they invariably do the better for it.

It is easy to caricature what I am saying by pretending that this is a demand that the teacher be a nurse or a psychiatrist to his students or that he serve literally in *loco parentis*. It would be helpful, naturally, if a teacher were to know the chief relevant facts about those students who need psychiatrists or nurses, if only to put them in proper professional hands and thus prevent them from serving as a drag on other students. But the teacher should not essay the role of amateur psychiatrist or nurse. His sympathy must be primarily directed to his students as growing intellectual organisms in a growing intellectual community, in the faith that they will become integrated persons capable of responsible choice. He cannot cope with all their emotional needs or assume the responsibilities of family and society, priest or judge. He must be friendly without becoming a friend, although he may pave the way for later friendship, for friendship is a mark of preference and expresses itself in indulgence, favors and distinctions that unconsciously find an invidious form. There is a certain distance between teacher and student, compatible with sympathy, which should not be broken down—for the sake of the student. A teacher who becomes "just one of the boys," who courts popularity, who builds up personal loyalties in exchange for indulgent treatment, has missed his vocation. He should leave the classroom for professional politics.

What I have said flows from the faith that imaginative sympathy towards the needs of the individual student, based on an intelligent appraisal of his equipment and achievements, will enhance his powers of growth. This faith may appear utopian or romantic. Those who are so impressed usually confuse two things: whom we shall teach and how we shall teach. If, at any level or for a specific purpose, a student is uneducable, a large assumption but sometimes obviously true, he should either be directed to a field in which he is educable, or committed to an institution for the feeble-minded, for that is where people who are absolutely uneducable belong. But so long as a teacher finds himself before a class in which there are varied talents, varied capacities for educability, he is under an obligation to help each one develop the best within him. That is what he is there for. If he accepts his obligation gladly and not as a chore, he will find that the results are worth the effort.

What to teach and how to teach must be distinguished from the problem of certification of student competence. Competence is a relation not only to subject matter but to comparative performance and to a set of conditions, far from fixed, defined by the nature of the task for which competence is required. There is also something that may be called a "conventional" element in the determination of competence. This is clearest when, because only a certain number can be certified, all whose achievements fall below this number are failed even though their achievements surpass those of individuals who have been previously certified. Competence established by position on a comparative scale can be ascertained even by those who are not teachers. What the teacher alone can supply is testimony of intellectual and personal qualities which he is uniquely qualified to observe. This testimony together with other data of measurable competence should determine the educational decision to advance, to hold, or to transfer the individual student. The basic consideration should be: what action will educationally most profit the individual without too great a cost to others? Detailed rules cannot wisely be drawn *in abstracto*. For all sorts of factors, sometimes even the state of the nation, may affect their formulation.

To develop the best in each student, therefore, emphatically does not mean that the teacher believes that all students are equally good, or that when he must rate them he should rate them all in the same way, or that he must sacrifice "standards"— a blessed word which is the hardest-worked substitute for thinking on educational matters among college teachers. Those who mouth the word most loudly as soon as any proposal is made to liberalize liberal education do not know what "standards" actually are, their source, their history, and that "standards," too, must face a test which requires other standards. They usually maintain that their own standards are absolute and objective, but no two of them agree with each other. It is notorious that one college's *Pass* student is another's *cum laude,* and that even in the same college one professor's A is another's C. Time and again it has been experimentally proved that the same teacher, irrespective of subject matter, rates the same paper differently, when he has not identified it as such, depending on matters that have nothing to do with education. Those who talk in absolutes here are only absolutizing their own subjectivity. Those who are militantly self-righteous about the number of students they regularly fail rarely stop to ask whether the fault lies in their own teaching or in the kind of standards they are using. I have heard teachers urge the imposition of standards which would obviously have barred them from any possibility of a college education if the proposed standards had been applied in all fields when they were students.

The teacher's working standards in the classroom should be distinct from the rules that determine the next step in the educational career of the student, i.e., whether he is to pass or fail. These working standards cannot be adjudged "high" or "low," for they should be nothing else but the realization of the fundamental ends of the educational process itself through the use of the most appropriate means that will insure the maximum intellectual growth of every student entrusted to him. If these are his working standards, the teacher will never be satisfied that this maximum has been finally reached. For with every intellectual achievement new vistas of knowledge open before us.

(f) The good teacher, to close our inventory of his traits, possesses vision. It is the source both of his intellectual enthusiasm and his detachment in the face of inevitable failures and disappointments. Without vision he may become a kindly technician, useful in a limited way. But he cannot inspire a passion for excellence. The vision may take many forms. It may be a doctrine—but he must not preach it. It may be a dream—but he must not keep talking about it. It may be a hope, an ambition, a work in progress, so long as it is not merely personal and has a scope or sweep of some imaginative appeal. But it must not obtrude itself into the details of instruction. Its presence should be inferrable from the spirit with which the instruction is carried on. It should operate in such a way as to lift up the students' hearts and minds beyond matters of immediate concern and enable them to see the importance of a point of view. Wherever an intellectually stimulating teacher is found, there will also be found some large perspective of interest that lights up the corners of his subject matter. If students catch fire from it, it should not be in order to believe some dogma but to strengthen them in the search for truth and to become more sensitive to visions that express other centers of experience.

The best teacher possesses all of the qualities we have mentioned to a pre-eminent degree. But the best teacher is to be found only in a Platonic heaven. Good teachers, however, who exhibit some or all of these qualities are to be found on earth. They can become, can be helped to become, and can help others to become, better teachers. If a resolute beginning is made by those who educate and select teachers, in time the community will discover that a new spirit and morale is abroad in the teaching profession. It will discover that a good teacher is a dedicated person, strong in his faith in what he is doing, worthy not only of honor in a democracy but of a place in its councils.

Pupils into Students

JACQUES BARZUN

(For a note on Jacques Barzun, see page 380.)

Madam, we guarantee results—or we return the boy!
—PRESIDENT PATTON, LATE OF PRINCETON.

TO PASS FROM THE OVERHEATED UTOPIA OF EDUCATION TO THE REALM of teaching is to leave behind false heroics and take a seat in the front row of the human comedy. What is teaching and why is it comic? The answer includes many things depending on whether you think of the teacher, the pupil, the means used, or the thing taught. But the type situation is simple and familiar. Think of a human pair teaching their child how to walk. There is, on the child's side, strong desire and latent powers: he has legs and means to use them. He walks and smiles; he totters and looks alarmed; he falls and cries. The parents smile throughout, showering advice, warning, encouragement, and praise. The whole story, not only of teaching, but of man and civilization, is wrapped up in this first academic performance. It is funny because clumsiness makes us laugh, and touching because undaunted effort strikes a chord of gallantry, and finally comic because it has all been done before and is forever to do again.

All the knowledge, skill, art, and science that we use and revere, up to Einstein's formulas about the stars, is a mere repetition and extension of the initial feat of learning to walk. But this extension does not take place by itself. Most of it has to be taught, slowly and painfully. There was a time when Mr. Einstein was not quite sure what eight times nine came to. He had to learn, and to learn he had to be taught. The reason teaching has to go on is that children are not born human; they are made so. The wretched foundlings that were occasionally discovered in rural parts of Europe a hundred years ago walked on all fours and grunted like beasts.

And we not only want human offspring but more particularly Western, American-speaking, literate, twentieth-century men and women, endowed furthermore with all sorts of special religious, moral, and intellectual characteristics. In short we want a very definite product, and it is our ability to make the plastic young animal develop certain desirable traits which makes men fall into the educational fallacy I denounced earlier. We speak of "molding the mind of a child" and G. B. Shaw denounces us as abortionists. But both he and we are wrong. Though the young mind is plastic and skillful handling can accomplish miracles, instruction *and* distortion are alike limited by forces of which we know nothing, except that they exist. We bottle up our ignorance and label it Heredity and Environment and there we stop. We should add something about will and temperament and then forget about the limitations, in order to concentrate on what *can* be done. Then we may ask, How is it done? And finally, What should we teach, and to whom? When we have answered these questions as reasonably and practically as possible, we shall, I think, find that the sulphur-and-brimstone nebula of Education has disappeared like a pricked bubble.

II

Since I am going to tackle these concrete questions in a somewhat autobiographical manner, I had better indicate here and now the sources of my experience. One never knows what accidents turn out to be advantages, and I am not yet sure my early apprenticeship was not a disadvantage, but the facts must be stated, for they contributed to the result and may be freely used against me.

I taught my first class at the age of nine. All I remember about it is that it had to do with arithmetic and that the room seemed filled with thousands of very small children in black aprons. The explanation is that with the shortage of teachers in France towards the middle of the last war, there were sporadic attempts at establishing the so-called Lancaster system of using older pupils to teach the younger. Lancaster himself, who lived a hundred

years before, was only trying to meet the teacher shortage of the
Napoleonic Wars, but he became an educational fanatic who
believed that "any boy who can read can teach, although he knows
nothing about it." I don't know what the "it" refers to, whether
the art of teaching or the subject matter, but in any case this
maxim, like so many others in education, is only half true.

It served, however, to apprentice me to my trade. Not that
I stayed very long in it that first time. Indeed, my maiden effort
possibly drove me into the retirement of a protracted illness. I
recovered, only to relapse, not once but many times—into the
habit of teaching. Having learned English and come to this
country to rejoin my father, previously sent on a good-will
mission, I found myself exchanging French lessons for further
work in reading and speaking American. I had the good fortune
to come in contact with a fine group of high school teachers, and
since advanced mathematics and beginning philosophy are taught
earlier abroad, I was able to tutor boys of my own age in those
subjects also.

All this while I vaguely felt the force of Milton's angry words:
"I hate a pupil teacher." But whenever I made mental casts in
the direction of more easy-going professions, like diplomacy or
finance, I was brought back to my destiny. In my second year in
college, I had my first academic offer. I happened to be coaching
two graduate students in the French educational theorists on
whom they were to be examined—Rabelais, Montaigne, and
Rousseau. My students, middle-aged men, apparently spoke of
me to their sponsor and I received a note asking me to call on
him. He was head of a department in a large university and I
thought at the time that he scarcely lived up to the dignity of his
position. For when I was announced by his secretary and he saw
me, he laughed in my face. He had not been told that I was
about seventeen and he was on the point of offering me an
instructorship.

This experience should have soured me against all academic
entanglements but circumstances prevailed. The period just before 1929 in this country, and particularly in the metropolis,
offered the active-minded college man innumerable opportunities
to achieve financial independence even before the bachelor's
degree. So I found myself writing and tutoring in very profitable

fashion before I thoroughly knew that I had chosen the two most back-breaking jobs in the whole world. Combined with study, this was an adventure of distinctly sociable character. A group of us—all classmates—maintained a perfectly legal and honest tutoring mill, whose grist renewed itself as we managed to put the backward rich through the entrance examinations of famous colleges not our own. School authorities smiled on our work and we ended by taking on all kinds of academic cases. No subjects were barred. If a retired minister came who wanted to read *Hamlet* in Esperanto (one did) we supplied an instructor who spoke the language like a native. At times our facilities were strained and some of us found ourselves tackling subjects with a bare head start over the pupil. But it was excellent practice and most broadening to the tutors. As a natural subsidiary enterprise we undertook high-class literary hackwork. We compiled statistics, contributed to the lesser encyclopedias, and worked up the raw material for public addresses by public men. We referred to ourselves as Ghosts, Incorporated.

When the time of my graduation came, in 1927, the die was cast. I knew I wanted to keep right on with both occupations, though no longer as piece work. Meanwhile I had formed an attachment to the Muse of History and was encouraged in it, chiefly by two men—Harry James Carman, now Dean of Columbia College, and Rexford Guy Tugwell, then Professor of Economics in that institution and now Chancellor of the University of Puerto Rico. Commencement emotions were hardly past when the director of the Summer Session asked me whether I was willing to teach an introductory course. I said I should like nothing better. He wanted to know with whom I had taken that same course. I told him. "You can teach it anyway." That was my *Hoc age.* I have been at it ever since, with breaks for study and travel and excursions into neighboring institutions.

It is over a quarter of a century since I first obeyed the summons to teach and I can only hope the habit has not become a compulsion. "Oh to sit next a man who has spent his life in trying to educate others!" groaned Oscar Wilde. My belief is that the last thing a good teacher wants to do is to teach outside the classroom; certainly my own vision of bliss halfway through a term is solitary confinement in a sound-proof cell. But feeling this way, I often wonder what originally made the impulse to teach take root. In the lives of so many good men one reads that they "drifted into teaching." They drift out again. It is clear that teachers are born, not made, and circumstances usually permit rather than compel. It is impossible to think of William James *not* teaching or of his brother Henry consenting to give a simple explanation. For many people, doing is far easier than talking about it.

From which I conclude that the teaching impulse goes something like this: a fellow human being is puzzled or stymied. He wants to open a door or spell "accommodate." The would-be helper has two choices. He can open the door, spell the word; or he can show his pupil how to do it for himself. The second way is harder and takes more time, but a strong instinct in the born teacher makes him prefer it. It seems somehow to turn an accident into an opportunity for permanent creation. The raw material is what the learner can do, and upon this the teacher-artist builds by the familiar process of taking apart and putting together. He must break down the new and puzzling situation into simpler bits and lead the beginner in the right order from one bit to the next. What the simpler bits and the right order are no one can know ahead of time. They vary for each individual and the teacher must grope around until he finds a "first step" that the particular pupil can manage. In any school subject, of course, this technique does not stop with the opening of a door. The need for it goes on and on—as it seems, forever—and it takes the stubbornness of a saint coupled with the imagination of a demon for a teacher to pursue his art of improvisation gracefully, unwearyingly, endlessly.

Nor is this a purely mental task. All the while, the teacher must keep his charge's feelings in good order. A rattled student can do nothing and a muddled teacher will rattle or dishearten almost any student. The teacher must not talk too much or too fast, must not trip over his own tongue, must not think out loud, must not forget, in short, that he is handling a pair of runaway horses—the pupil and a dramatic situation.

Patience is a quality proverbially required for good teaching, but it is not surprising that many good teachers turn out to be impatient people—though not with their students. Their stock of forbearance gives out before they get home. What sustains them in class is that the situation is always changing. Three successive failures to do one thing may all seem identical to the bystander, but the good teacher will notice a change, a progression, or else the clear sign that the attempt must be postponed until some other preliminary progress has been made.

It is obvious that the relation of teacher to pupil is an emotional one and most complex and unstable besides. To begin with the motives, the forces that make teaching "go," are different on both sides of the desk. The pupil has some curiosity and he wants to know what grownups know. The master has curiosity also, but it is chiefly about the way the pupil's mind—or hand —works. Remembering his own efforts and the pleasure of discovery, the master finds a satisfaction which I have called artistic in seeing how a new human being will meet and make his own some part of our culture—our ways, our thoughts, even our errors and superstitions. This interest, however, does not last forever. As the master grows away from his own learning period, he also finds that mankind repeats itself. Fewer and fewer students appear new and original. They make the same mistakes at the same places and never seem to go very far into a subject which, for him, is still an expanding universe. Hence young teachers are best; they are the most energetic, most intuitive, and the least resented.

For side by side with his eagerness, the pupil feels resentment arising from the fact that the grownup who teaches him appears to know it all. There is, incidentally, no worse professional disease for the teacher than the habit of putting questions with a half-smile that says "I know that one, and I will tell it you: come along, my pretty." Telling and questioning must not be put-up jobs designed to make the teacher feel good about himself. It is as bad as the Jehovah complex among doctors. Even under the best conditions of fair play and deliberate spontaneity, the pupil, while needing and wanting knowledge, will hate and resist it. This resistance often makes one feel that the human mind is made of some wonderfully tough rubber, which you can stretch a little by pulling hard, but which snaps back into shape the moment you let go.

It is exasperating, but consider how the student feels, subjected to daily and hourly stretching. "Here am I," he thinks, "with my brains nicely organized—with everything, if not in its place, at least in a place where I can find it—and you come along with a new and strange item that you want to force into my previous arrangement. Naturally I resist. You persist. I begin to dislike you. But at the same time, you show me aspects of this new fact or idea which in spite of myself mesh in with my existing desires. You seem to know the contents of my mind. You show me the proper place for your contribution to my stock of knowledge. Finally, there is brooding over us a vague threat of disgrace for me if I do not accept your offering and keep it and show you that I still have it when you—dreadful thought!—*examine* me. So I give in, I shut my eyes and swallow. I write little notes about it to myself, and with luck the burr sticks: I have learned something. Thanks to you? Well, not exactly. Thanks to you and thanks to me. I shall always be grateful for your efforts, but do not expect me to love you, at least not for a long, long time. When I am fully formed and somewhat battered by the world and yet not too displeased with myself, I shall generously believe that I owe it all to you. It will be an exaggeration on the other side, just as my present dislike is an injustice. Strike an average between the two and that will be a fair measure of my debt."

At any stage in learning, this inner dialogue between opposite feelings goes on. It should go on. Teaching is possible only because there is a dialogue and one part of the mind can be used to rearrange the other. The whole secret of teaching—and it is no secret—consists in splitting the opposition, downing the conservatives by making an alliance with the radicals. It goes without saying that I am not using these words here in their workaday sense. My meaning applies to the multiplication table as well as to anything else. The conservative part of the pupil's mind is passive, stubborn, mute; but his radical minority, that is, his curiosity and his desire to grow up, may be aroused to action. The move forward is generally short; then the conservatives return to power; they preserve, they feel pride of ownership in the new acquisition and begin to think they had it as a birthright. This rhythmical action is one reason why teaching and learning must not go on all the time, nor at an accelerated pace: time and rest are needed for absorption. Psychologists confirm the fact when they tell us that it is really in summer that our muscles learn how to skate, and in winter how to swim.

If I have dwelt on the emotions of teaching and being taught, it is because many people believe that schooling only engages the mind—and only temporarily at that. "I've forgotten," says the average man, "all I ever learned at school." And he mentally contrasts this happy oblivion with the fact that he still knows how to open oysters and ride a bicycle. But my description of teaching applies equally to physical things and to metaphysical. We may forget the substance of American History but we are probably scarred for life by the form and feeling of it as imparted by book and teacher. Why is it that the businessman's economics and the well-bred woman's taste in art are normally twenty-five years behind the times? It is that one's lifelong opinions are those picked up before maturity—at school and college.

This is why a "teacher's influence," if he does exert one, is not so big a joke as it seems. Notice in the lives of distinguished men how invariably there is a Mr. Bowles or a Dr. Tompkins or a Professor Clunk—whom no one ever heard of, but who is "remembered" for inspiring, guiding, and teaching decisively at the critical time. We can all see the mark left by a teacher in physical arts like tennis or music. The pupils of Leopold Auer or Tobias Matthay can be recognized at forty paces by their posture and even in a dark room by the sound they make. For in these disciplines the teacher usually falls back on direct imitation: "Hold your hand like this," or more simply, "Watch me." Well, much good teaching is of the "watch me" order, but the more abstract the knowledge, the less easy it is to imitate the teacher, and the genuine student wants to do the real thing in a real way *by himself*.

Consequently, the whole aim of good teaching is to turn the young learner, by nature a little copycat, into an independent, self-propelling creature, who cannot merely learn but study— that is, work as his own boss to the limit of his powers. This is to turn pupils into students, and it can be done on any rung of the ladder of learning. When I was a child, the multiplication table was taught from a printed sheet which had to be mem-

orized one "square" at a time—the one's and the two's and so
on up to nine. It never occurred to the teacher to show us how
the answers could be arrived at also by addition, which we already
knew. No one said, "Look: if four times four is sixteen, you
ought to be able to figure out, without aid from memory, what
five times four is, because that amounts to four more one's added
to the sixteen." This would at first have been puzzling, *more*
complicated and difficult than memory work, but once explained
and grasped, it would have been an instrument for learning
and checking the whole business of multiplication. We could
temporarily have dispensed with the teacher and cut loose from
the printed table.[1]

This is another way of saying that the only thing worth teaching anybody is a principle. Naturally principles involve facts and
some facts must be learned "bare" because they do not rest on
any principle. The capital of Alaska is Juneau and, so far as
I know, that is all there is to it; but a European child ought not
to learn that Washington is the capital of the United States
without fixing firmly in his mind the relation between the city
and the man who led his countrymen to freedom. That would
be missing an association, which is the germ of a principle. And
just as a complex athletic feat is made possible by rapid and
accurate co-ordination, so all valuable learning hangs together
and *works* by associations which make sense.

Since associations are rooted in habit and habits in feelings,
we can see that anything which makes school seem a nightmare
or a joke, which brands the teacher as a fool or a fraud, is the
archenemy of all learning. It so happens that there is one professional disease, or rather vice, which generates precisely this
feeling and whose consequences are therefore fatal. I refer to
Hokum and I hasten to explain what I mean. Hokum is the
counterfeit of true intellectual currency. It is words without
meaning, verbal filler, artificial apples of knowledge. From the

---

1. I find that General Grant complained of the same thing: "Both
winters were spent in going over the same old arithmetic which I knew
every word of before and repeating 'A noun is the name of a thing',
which I had also heard my Georgetown teachers repeat until I had
come to believe it." (*Memoirs*, New York, 1894, p. 20.)

necessities of the case, nine tenths of all teaching is done with words, whence the ever-present temptation of hokum.

Words should point to things, seen or unseen. But they can also be used to wrap up emptiness of heart and lack of thought. The student accepts some pompous, false, meaningless formula, and passes it back on demand, to be rewarded with—appropriately enough—a passing grade. All the dull second-rate opinions, all the definitions that don't define, all the moral platitudes that "sound good," all the conventional adjectives ("gentle Shakespeare"), all the pretenses that a teacher makes about the feelings of his students towards him and vice versa, all the intimations that something must be learned because it has somehow got lodged among learnable things (like the Binomial Theorem or the date of Magna Carta)—all this in all its forms gives off the atmosphere of hokum, which healthy people everywhere find absolutely unbreathable.

In a modern play, I think by A. A. Milne, this schoolmarm vice has been caught and set down in a brief dialogue which goes something like this:—

GOVERNESS. Recite.
PUPIL. "The Battle of Blenheim." (*Long pause*)
GOVERNESS. By?
PUPIL (*silence*).
GOVERNESS. By Robert Southey.
PUPIL. By Robert Southey.
GOVERNESS. Who was Robert Southey?
PUPIL (*pause*). I don't know.
GOVERNESS. One of our greatest poets. Begin again.
PUPIL. The Battle of Blenheim by Robert Southey one of our greatest poets.

As this example shows, hokum is subtle and I will forbear to analyze it. It hides in the porous part of solid learning and vitiates it by making it stupid and ridiculous. I remember once giving a short quiz to a class of young women who had been reading about the Renaissance. I asked for some "identification" of names and put Petrarch in the list. One girl, who had evidently read a textbook, wrote down: "Petrarch—the vanguard of the new emphasis." I spent a good hour trying to explain why this parroting of opinion was not only not "correct" but blind hokum, hokum absolute. It was not an easy job because so many teachers and books deal exclusively in that cheap commodity. The child's instinct is first to believe the Word, spoken or printed; then with growing good sense to disbelieve it, but to trust to its hokum value for getting through by "satisfying" the teacher. Great heavens, what satisfactions!

To carry my anecdote one step further, I believe I made a life-long friend and a convert to decent learning by persuading my student that almost any honest mistake would have been truer than the absurdity she was palming off. Some might better have been trivial: "Petrarch was an Italian"; or flippant: "Wrote poems to a girl named Laura"; or downright mistaken: "Also spelled Plutarch," rather than do what she did. My difficulty—and this is the important point—was in convincing her that I meant what I said, in breaking down the strongest superstition of the young, which is that everybody but themselves prefer make-believe and live by it.

III

So far as it concerns teachers, this superstition is not limited to the young. The reason why the "big world" scorns the "academic world" is precisely this, that remembering its school days, the big world is sure that all learning is hokum, and all teachers Old Pretenders. No doubt a good many teachers are. For some minds in any profession it is the path of least resistance to deal in shoddy phrases and use what brief authority is available to cram them down others' throats. But in teaching, this tradition —if it may be called one—has been rapidly dying out. It has been scotched like the custom of formal lecturing from cold-storage notes. Progressive education in this country, if it has done nothing else, should forever be honored and given thanks for insisting on genuine, hand-to-hand teaching, as against the giving out of predigested hokum. The older way was a hangover from the one-time union of the teaching and the preaching professions. Not that preaching is synonymous with hokum, but that when the ministry was the gateway to teaching, the Tartuffian attitude was compulsory. The teacher had to be more moral—which usually meant more conventional; he had to talk pious; to be gravely noncommittal and to support the established order in detail; he had to look and act—though the word is blasphemy —like a divine.

Since the advent of lay education—roughly the last seventy-five years—much has changed. No longer does the academic man resemble the description that Sherlock Holmes gives of his great antagonist, Professor Moriarty: ". . . clean shaven, pale and ascetic looking, retaining something of the professor in his features. His shoulders are rounded from much study, and his face protrudes forward and is forever slowly oscillating from side to side in a curiously reptilian fashion." Try as I may, I cannot think of any of my colleagues who has "retained something of the professor in his features," reptiles though they may be. They look like any other Americans; they are no more roundshouldered than bank presidents, they play golf and tennis and watch football, they marry and beget children, laugh and swear and have appendicitis in a thoroughly normal way. They are far less absent-minded than waiters in restaurants and they do not look a bit more like one another than a comparable number of doctors or mechanics.

Moreover their lives are as full of routine and excitement as that of any other group, and the excitement is not purely mental either. My own introduction to collegiate teaching, for instance, was marked by a seriocomic sequence reminiscent of Hollywood. A big bruiser of a student whom I had failed came to my office threatening bodily harm, then hounded me by phone, wire, and letter, pleading that I should pass him "in the name of Christian brotherhood," for he had "powerful friends in Brooklyn." Nothing happened, but two years later, the tide as it were turned in my favor. I mean that another student, an impressive-looking, middle-aged man in an Extension course, made a point of showing his gratitude, first by inviting me to his Turkish restaurant and then by intimating that if I had any enemies he would only be too glad to get rid of them for me gratis. Unfortunately by then I had mislaid the address of my disgruntled Brooklynite.

Even if the academic man is popularly thought of as a Hamlet sicklied o'er with the pale cast of thought, do not underrate thought. Remember how many corpses Hamlet managed to pile up by the end of the play and what relief it was. Given the chance, men of thought readily turn men of action because their minds do not shrink from the unfamiliar; think of all the professors now in government service, dealing on the whole as well as any regular bureaucrats with thoroughly live situations. Or returning to the hurly-burly of human passion, think of the academic tradition of private murder, begun (fittingly at Harvard) in 1849 with Professor Webster's dispatching of his colleague Parkman. Oliver Wendell Holmes—the elder and the greater one, that is, the doctor—has some wonderful testimony on that case and he is himself a witness to the variety, power, and unpredictability of the teaching faculty. They have furnished every kind of talent, crankiness, and devotion, and they have also, I trust, contributed their share to the nation's suicides, lunatics, and embezzlers. I even read last week in the news that a professor in the Army had been a hero. It is true that the young man was called an *ex*-professor, but we may put that down to the understandable jealousy of journalists.

A student of mine, to whom I once pointed out some of these facts to rebut the customary charge of being out of the world, answered with what seems at first a plausible distinction between the teacher and the man of action. "Anyone," he wrote me, "who does not spend most of his life working at something to which he is either indifferent or antagonistic cannot claim to share the common experience of mankind. Do I sound bitter? I am." The final comment gives the game away, and the argument is moreover based on a misconception. First, there are millions of people who work at things they like. Most professional men are in that class, and they pay for the privilege by working harder and cheaper than other people. Second, it is utterly untrue that teachers lead a life of elegant leisure, doing only what they like.

In recounting my apprenticeship I called teaching backbreaking work and later I hinted that steady teaching is a task that would fray the nerves of an ox. These are both sober statements. An hour of teaching is certainly the equivalent of a whole morning of office work. The pace, the concentration, the output of energy in office work are child's play compared with handling a class, and the smaller the class, the harder the work. Tutoring a single person—as someone has said—makes you understand what a dynamo feels like when it is discharging into a nonconductor.

Most teachers in colleges teach three hours daily five days a week, and their friends gape and stare: "You're through for the day at twelve!" The fact is that at twelve o'clock a teacher who has done his stint is as limp as a rag. In the next chapter I shall show in more detail what he has done to get into this state. In speaking now of the bare effect, I am not thinking of feeble constitutions or neurotic personalities, but of the average man or woman who might readily find other employment. Nor shall I go on to harrow the reader with accounts of primary and high school teaching, characterized by huge, unruly classes, longer hours, and usually—for the women at least—housework on getting home; and private schools impose other chores to fill the teacher's day. I stick to college teaching, which is supposed to be a sinecure. At noon, the best effort of the day has been put in. Then comes lunch, usually spoiled for relaxation by being combined with a committee meeting. The afternoon goes to conferences with students, a mass of clerical work, professional correspondence, and snags of all sorts involving plant and personnel—all this very akin to hospital work because in both places time and considerateness for persons are the dominant concerns.

By five or five-thirty, this do-nothing king of a professor goes home—to his family if he has one, to his books and papers, which he cannot help having. If he is a young instructor, he has many new preparations—perhaps four hours' work to every three class hours. If he is an old hand, he not only reprepares for surety but he is exploring some field of his own; he is reading and reviewing books, keeping up with periodical literature, carrying on debate with his colleagues all over the world, and supervising the written work of his advanced students. He has worked seven hours abroad and probably will work four more at home, while his businessman neighbor is quietly enjoying bridge with friends or worry by himself. No teacher gets through his day's work that day and hence no teacher has ever lived who did not regularly sigh, "Thank God it's Friday!"

"Yes, yes, of course, but he has four months in the summer

with nothing to do." On any campus around the first of June, this is a dangerous remark to make. Most teachers are then gasping for their three weeks' rest before the Summer Session opens. And those who are taking what is ironically called "the summer off" are planning only a modest vacation. Getting acquainted with one's family, swimming and loafing or fishing, are an absolute necessity, if the teacher's battery is going to be recharged for the next bout. But the four months cannot de devoted wholly to this body culture. The wretched slave has dragged with him to his summer camp: one Ph.D. candidate's manuscript stuck in mid-passage and so bad he will himself rewrite it; six current nonprofessional books which he must read if he is not to become an illiterate; three folders full of notes to be organized for his own next work; and two new volumes in his field, one in German and one in French, which he gullibly accepted for review last December. Teaching in America is a twenty-four-hour job, twelve months in the year: sabbatical leaves are provided so you can have your coronary thrombosis off the campus.

In England, they arrange things somewhat better. Terms are shorter and vacations longer. More people loaf, and teaching is on the whole as active and probably a good deal more effectual. For in our American university, with a few exceptions justified by age or eminence or incurable laziness, the faculty reaches the end of term frazzled and the students dizzy with work. Not that all students work, but that those who do, overwork. As for the instructor, he hurtles from term to term, wishing he could echo in his own behalf the tremulous cry that William James uttered near the end of his career: "For thirty-five years I have been suffering the exigencies of being . . . [a teacher], the pretension and the duty namely, of meeting the mental needs and difficulties of other persons, needs that I couldn't possibly imagine and difficulties that I couldn't possibly understand; and now that I have shuffled off the professional coil, the sense of freedom that comes to me is as surprising as it is exquisite. . . . What! not to have to accommode myself to this mass of alien and recalcitrant humanity, not to think under resistance, not to have to square myself with others at every step I make—hurrah! it is too good to be true."

The College Student in an
Age of Organization

DAVID RIESMAN

(1909–   )

The Lonely Crowd (with Nathan Glazer), 1950
Faces in the Crowd (with Nathan Glazer), 1952
Thorstein Veblen, A Critical Interpretation, 1953
Individualism Reconsidered, 1954
Constraint and Variety in American Education, 1956

DAVID RIESMAN majored in biochemical sciences at Harvard and went
on to the Law School. He then served as clerk to Supreme Court Justice Louis Brandeis, practiced law independently, taught law, and
worked as an executive and legal adviser for a large corporation. In
1946 he was appointed professor of social sciences at the University of
Chicago and began the book that made him famous, *The Lonely
Crowd.* Now at Harvard, he is active in SANE and other organizations
dedicated to social protest. Though not always finished in style, Mr.
Riesman's work is redeemed by the moral passion which has given
force and direction to his varied career.

THIS PAPER WAS ORIGINALLY PRESENTED AS A LECTURE TO AN
audience which included students, faculty, and alumni.[1] In addressing myself primarily to the students, already a highly
self-conscious group, I was reluctant simply to list once more the
labels the older generation has already pinned on them: apathy,

Reprinted by permission from *The Chicago Review,* Vol. 12, No. 3.
(Autumn 1958).
    1. I am indebted to a grant from the Carnegie Corporation for an
opportunity to investigate problems of higher education discussed in
this article. An earlier version was published in *Sequoia* (Stanford Literary Magazine), Vol. III (Winter, 1958).

conformity, security-mindedness, coolness, beatness, and so on. Such labels do have a certain truth, and I shall try to delineate what it is; but they also conceal about as much as they reveal. They conceal the fact that the college generations of the 1920's and 1930's, now nostalgically admired, were on the whole far less responsive, serious, and decent than students in comparable institutions today. They conceal the fact that the apparently negative qualities of apathy and conformity must be seen as an aspect of the high intelligence and sensitivity of this generation of students, who know more than their elders did and who have, justly, more to be afraid of.

In my lecture, I was able to count on a discussion period in which i might partially clarify the misunderstandings so loaded a theme was bound to generate and in which the students could (and did) talk back. Furthermore, I could respond to some alumni who attacked the "softness" and lack of political and civic responsibility of the students, first by reminding them of how ancient and inevitable was the theme of parents' complaints against the softening of the children whom they had themselves indulged, and second by emphasizing the difficulties sensitive and concerned young people face today precisely because the manifest hardships with which earlier Americans coped have been, for millions, eliminated, while new challenges, appropriate to an age of abundance, still remain to be discovered.

My principal theme, however, was not to defend students against the common ethnocentrism of their elders but to help explain them to themselves, and to show how some of the students' attitudes toward the world, as shaped in school and college, are not so much a reaction to that world as it is as a reaction-formation in the psychoanalytic sense, that is, a defense which has become unrealistically overgeneralized. College students today often act as if they believed that work in large organizations, and, beyond that, work in general, could not be basically or humanly satisfying (or at times even honest), but was primarily a way to earn a living, to find a place in the social order, and to meet nice or not-so-nice people. This is a conclusion which, I shall suggest, is partly projected upon the occupational scene as the result of experience with the curriculum in college and university

—and as the result of experience also with college and university as organizations which are viewed as bureaucratic, monolithic, and unchangeable, at least by many students.

I do not think it the primary task of education to prepare students for their later occupational roles, or indeed any narrowly specialized roles, nor to teach them to enjoy work regardless of its quality and meaning. Rather, the relation of education to later life should be a dialectical and critical one. If, however, one result of going to college is to become alienated from work per se and defeatist about the possibility of altering one's relation to it, then it seems to me one ought to re-examine academic institutions themselves and to see, as students, whether anything in them or in one's own attitudes or both might be changed.

I.

In the spring of 1955 several hundred interviews were done (at the behest of *Time*) with seniors at twenty colleges throughout the country, most of them colleges of some or of great distinction.[2] The seniors were supposed to be reasonably representative, but what this was taken to mean and how it was applied at various colleges and universities varied greatly. A good many student leaders were chosen, a good many bright people, but hardly any women got in (a questionnaire circulated by *Mademoiselle* gave me somewhat comparable data concerning college women). When I first examined the interviews, and now again when I have once more gone over them, I have been struck by what appears to be a not quite conscious ambivalence toward work in large organizations. On the one hand, the majority are planning to enter large organizations in pursuit of their careers: big corporations, big government, big law offices, and so on. Only a few seek independence in their work, either in terms of old-fashioned ideals of entrepreneurship or in terms of desire to become a foreign correspondent, to enter politics, or to follow some other individualistic

---

2. For fuller discussion of these interviews see "The Found Generation," *American Scholar*, XXV (1956), 421-36. I am indebted to Miss Robin Jackson of the Center for the Study of Leisure at the University of Chicago for assistance in analyzing these materials.

or exotic calling. (Moreover, hardly anyone expresses resentment against his prospective Army service on the ground that the Army is a large organization; there is no eagerness for service, but rather resignation to it as one of the givens of life.)

And yet, when these young people are asked about their lives outside of work, a very different picture emerges. There bigness and scale are definitely not valued. Only a tiny fraction want to head for the metropolis, even if their career aims might make such a location convenient. They want the suburbs—not later, after some bachelor start has been made in the big city, but now, on graduation. The great majority either are already married or plan to get married soon (even if there is no special one in mind at the moment); they plan to start having children at once and to begin building a community-centered life in the suburbs. They envisage a two-car but usually not a two-career family, in which the prospective wife will be active in the P.T.A., with subsidiary assistance from the husband, and in which both spouses will concern themselves with a manageable bit of real estate—a suburban neighborhood in which they can at once be active and hope to make a difference. It does not occur to them that they might be gifted and energetic enough to make a difference even in a big city. Rather, they want to be able to work through a face-to-face group —the postcollegiate fraternity of the small suburbs. Correspondingly, the very emphasis on family life which is one of the striking and in so many ways attractive qualities of young people today is an implicit rejection of large organization. The suburban family with its garden, its barbecue, its lack of privacy in the open-plan house, is itself a manifesto of decentralization—even though it makes use of centralized services such as TV, clinics, chain stores, and *House Beautiful.* The wish to build a nest, even if a somewhat transient one, is a striking feature of the interviews, in contrast with the wish to build a fortune or a career which might have dominated some comparable interviews a generation earlier.

This pattern—the acceptance of large organizations combined with tacit and uncrystallized resistance to them—appears not only in the respondents' emphasis on the family but also in what they say about their plans for and attitudes toward their future work. I get a sense from the material, and from other comparable data, of a certain withdrawal of emotional adherence from work. To be sure, it has become fashionable to speak of one's work or other activities in deprecatory terms and to adopt a pose of relative indifference to the larger goals of an organization. In an era of political, economic, and cultural salesmanship, such deprecation is a way to guard against being taken in, against being exploited for ends outside one's self. It is as if one had constantly to conduct psychological warfare against an outside enemy. But, as in any such process, students become to some extent the victims of their own defenses. They come to believe that work cannot really be worth doing for its own sake, whether or not it is done on behalf of a large impersonal organization—a fear of overcommitment to one's work even while one is at the workplace. In the course of getting rid of earlier collegiate or rah-rah enthusiasm, these young people have come to feel the work is not worth even their part-time devotion, and perhaps that nothing, except the family, deserves their wholehearted allegiance.

We see the same attitudes, of course, among the junior echelons now engaged in work. One hears them talk of their benevolent company as a mink-lined rat-trap, or speak of the rat-race, or refer to fights over principle as ruckuses or blowups—if somebody cares, he is said to blow his top. In a number of business novels, of which *The Man in the Gray Flannel Suit* is representative, it is taken for granted that a sensible fellow, and indeed an honest one, will prefer suburban domesticity and a quiet niche to ulcerous competition for large business stakes, despite the view from the top and the interesting climb.

Attitudes such as this are, of course, an aspect of the general cultural shift, not confined to students and not confined to those who seek employment in large organizations; similar attitudes turn up in some measure even among those who, studiously avoiding such organizations, look for a professional career in which they hope to be their own masters. Scholars, for example, are not immune to distaste for their work, nor are architects or physicians. But while I don't intend to imply that a life without any boredom is conceivable, except for a very stupid person, still I think we are witnessing a silent revolution against work on the part even of those relatively privileged groups who have been free to choose their work and to exercise some freedom in the doing of it. This reflects, in part, the fact that much work is meaningless per se, save as a source of income, prestige, and sociability; but it also indicates, as I have already implied, that people too readily accept their work as it comes, without hope of making it more meaningful.

William H. Whyte, Jr., summarizes some of these tendencies in his writings (notably in *The Organization Man*) and points out that some large organizations, worried about the decline in work-mindedness and devotion, are seeking to substitute an ideology of corporate loyalty, a "social ethic," for the inexorable attachment to work which was requisite in the building-up of an industrial society. Indeed, he shows how the corporation, in order to compete with the family, takes over much of the aura of domesticity, as if to say: "We may be a large organization to outsiders, but within we are, if not a happy family, at least a happy suburb, neighborly, protective, close, and clean." Such spokesmanship underplays the potential excitement of the work itself—and I believe that much work in large organizations can be intensely exciting—and overplays the fringe benefits.

What I want to stress is the fact that not all large organizations are alike, despite the sorts of institutional similarities investigated by sociologists; and of course that not all positions in them are alike. Many, although their top executives clamor for creativity and independence of mind, largely manage to process these qualities out of "their" people in the lower ranks. Others stockpile talent and expect it to keep as gold keeps at Fort Knox. Still others make products or provide services which are either antisocial or useless. But here and there one finds companies which face real and not contrived problems and apply to them an intelligence which is often remarkably disinterested and, in the best sense of the term, "academic." Young people in search of challenge and development would do well to seek out such relatively productive climates rather than to assume offhand (as is true of so many brand-name products) that they are all alike except for the advertising and the label. And this search is necessary precisely because many of the motives which impelled work in the older generation have fortunately become attenuated—motives such as money for its own sake, power, and fame—goals, that is, whose emptiness became evident with their attainment. Our industrial and commercial plant no longer "needs" such compulsive attachments to work which are based not on any genuine creative impulse but on the drying-up of other alternatives.

There is a further issue concerning work in large organizations where again differentiation is required. I refer to the conception that work in organizations requires surrender of independence of judgment, if not of integrity. When I was in college, there was a prevalent feeling among the more sensitive that this was true only of business and commercial organizations, not of governmental or philanthropic ones, and young men debated whether they would enter Wall Street and make money or enter government or teaching and be saved. This dichotomy has in large measure vanished, although traces of it do survive among the less cynical. For instance, I have known many graduate students in social psychology who believe that if they teach they can be honest, but that if they work in market research they will serve manipulation and corruption, and will have no power over their own work. Such judgments oversimplify the ethical dilemmas of any calling, and are in addition snobbish: one can find hucksterism (often hypocritically veiled) among academic people in search of reputations, grants, and promotions, as well as among market researchers and other businessmen. Indeed, I am inclined to think that at present many observant young people don't need to be persuaded of this; many are actually overpersuaded to the point of believing that every occupation is a racket and that at best some of the racketeers are less pious about it than others. And this, I suspect, is one of the reasons they tend to withdraw emotional allegiance from their work: with the impression that they have no control over it anyway, that all is in the hands of the mysterious men upstairs who run the show. If there is greater widsom in the belief that all occupations, like all forms of power, are corrupting in some degree, there is also greater resignation, greater passivity and fatalism.

II.

Where are such attitudes learned and confirmed? Even at some of the leading colleges, the more intellectual colleges—the col-

leges which produce literary magazines—the relation of students
to the curriculum has a certain alienated quality, in the sense
that the students do not believe they have any control over their
own education.

Let me give a few examples. In the last few years I have visited
a number of colleges of high quality—colleges which turn out
eminent professional men, scholars, and scientists; and I have
made it my business to talk with students informally, to read
their student newspapers and, where possible, student council
reports. At a number of these institutions, the livelier students
complain of the educational fare they are getting, of the very little
contact the curriculum makes with the problems that are meaningful to them. Sometimes they feel that opportunities for a civilized
and intellectual life on campus are wanting—for example, that
there are few inviting places to study or to talk, that social pressures in dormitories force any intellectual life out of the group
setting, that student publications are either dominated by the
school administration or devoted to "campus news" and trivia,[3]
that the bookstore is inadequate, or that the library is geared to
research needs, rather than to attract undergraduate browsers.
They often feel they have no access to the faculty for other than
merely routine matters. Sometimes students complain about the
prerequisites of a department which serve its monopolistic aims
or protect its mediocre teachers from boycott rather than serve
any defensible pedagogic aims. Yet when I ask such students what
they have done about these things, they are surprised at the very

3. Faculty members are by nature print-oriented people, and the
student newspaper can often have an impact on them even when they
pretend not to take it seriously. A student paper, devoted as many are to
sports, social activities and chit-chat about personalities, and complaints
about parking privileges, can often serve to confirm the faculty's own
image of the students as more or less nice and well-off barbarians who
are there to help pay the freight for research and an occasional promising graduate student. Such an image turns then to justify itself in a
vicious circle, concealing from the faculty and often from themselves
minorities in the student body who could become more responsive to
intellectual and cultural stimulation. (For a note on the local press in
influencing the climate for or against academic freedom, see "The Role
of the Press in Academic Freedom: A Proposal for Research," PROD,
I [January, 1958], 3-8.)

thought that they could do anything. They think I am joking when I suggest that, if things came to the worst, they could picket! They think I am wholly unrealistic when I say that many on the faculty might welcome student initiative in revising the curriculum, or that it might be possible to raise modest sums of money among alumni or others to bring visiting lecturers, poets, and such to the campus, or to furnish commodious rooms for interest-group meetings. When I tell them that the Harvard House Plan came about in considerable measure because of the report of a student council committee in 1926 which caught the attention of the philanthropist Edward Harkness, they shrug—that must have been a golden era, they say; nothing like that could happen now. Of course, as long as they think that, they will conduct themselves accordingly.

What is perplexing in this outlook is that the students appear to be so very realistic about the organization they are living in. They harbor no illusions about the faculty, the administration, the trustees. Yet they act as if the structure these men have created or inherited were part of the universe. It seems hardly ever to occur to students that a faculty is not a unit but a set of factions, often in precarious balance, and that student activity might conceivably help tip the balance.[4] And in spite of all that they know intellectually (and as children of vulnerable parents) about their power over their teachers, they don't put this power to use to improve the quality of their education.

---

4. Since these lines were written, I have come across several instances of energetic student activity. In the spring of 1958, students at the University of Wisconsin submitted a petition to the administration requesting more challenge and stimulation in their courses and in their educational program generally; President Fred has circulated this to the faculty. During the same period, students in the College at the University of Chicago have organized to defend the undergraduate General Education Program against attempts to subordinate it to the requirements and prerequisites of the graduate departments. One problem in all such cases is that students may not realize the ways in which their actions may strengthen the hands of faculty members sympathetic to their interests; they may interpret a rejection by authorities as an indication that what they did was futile—and, of course, since college generations change rapidly, they may not be around long enough to see the effect of what they did.

At a low-level college it may be that the students have too much power. My colleague Everett C. Hughes has investigated institutions supposedly devoted to higher education where students make it impossible for the professor to demand anything of them beyond routine and comfortable performance; for instance, if they are asked to read a book they consider too difficult, they will turn in blank pages on an examination concerning it. Professors even at good and serious colleges have to preserve their own autonomy like any other professional group, and I am not recommending that they conduct customer research and guide themselves by a popularity poll. But I don't think it follows from this that they must remain innocent of educational sociology and psychology, unaware of the harm they do, or indifferent to the indifference they help breed.

In fact, it is the very quality of some of these professors and of the institutions at which they teach that helps to create in a paradoxical way feelings of passivity and helplessness among their students. Not only have students become better in the better colleges in recent decades, but professors have become ever so much more erudite and competent. One seldom finds any longer at a first-rate university the platform ham actors or dreary pedants who were all too common even when I was an undergraduate. The most difficult and avant-garde books—often those considered not long ago subversive or ribald—are on the freshman reading list at many institutions, and while the market for textbooks is better than ever because education is everywhere such a boom industry, there are also many textbooks which take account of new knowledge and are reasonably sophisticated. "Sophisticated" is in fact the word for much current higher education: the professor is one-up on the student and the student knows it.[5] This is one of the

---

5. When I presented this lecture at a leading college, I was asked whether at colleges like this or like Columbia there isn't a conformity to non-conformity which appears sophisticated and takes form, for example, in sexual promiscuity. I responded, "I would agree with you [the questioner] that in many of our colleges today a person who doesn't engage in the now hardly shocking activities of drinking and sex may be looked on as square and may feel that he is a hick. I would also think that the need to be sophisticated is on the one hand a kind of mantle in which a young person has to wrap himself to feel that he

cases where general social advance brings unanticipated negative consequences in its wake. Vis-à-vis such professors students feel even less qualified than heretofore to influence their fate as students; and so they tend to leave matters in the hands of the constituted authorities, preserving (like GI's in the Army) only their privilege of griping.

III.

Why is it that students, often so precocious about many things —about each other, about sex, about their families, and occasionally even about national and world affairs—are so comparatively inattentive to what concerns them as closely as does their curriculum? For one thing, it seems to me that students don't want to believe that their activities might make a difference, because, in a way, they profit from their lack of commitment to what they are doing. I don't mean that they are not industrious students— they often are, much more so today, as I have said, than prior to World War II. They go through the required motions of working, but they seldom get really involved with the content of their courses. It is here that the better, more conscientious students sabotage their own education and restrict production: true enough, they turn out the credits and the grades, but they do not believe that it really matters in any fundamental sense what they think and feel.

When I have discussed this with students, they have often told

is anybody at all, and on the other a tremendous danger, and that the fear to be naïve is one of the ways in which young people prohibit themselves from being educated. Not only young people. The need to have a sophisticated reaction to anything prevents one from knowing what one's reaction to it actually is. I see people often going to the theater or reading a book which is not fashionable but is nevertheless good, a book or play from which they might learn something, and already beginning while they are in it to have the necessary negative reactions they can share with their friends, so that they won't be thought enthusiastic or naïve or simple-minded. This happens in class, too. I sometimes regret that good books are read in school; I sometimes think only really bad books which nobody could possibly like ought to be read so that good books can't be destroyed!"

me that it doesn't pay to be too interested in anything, because
then one is tempted to spend too much time on it, at the expense
of that optimal distribution of effort which will produce the best
grades—and after all they do have to get into medical school,
keep their scholarship, and please their old man. Now I am convinced that grades contaminate education—they are a kind of
currency which, like money, gets in the way of discovering their
intellectual interests—but here, too, the students in their realism
are often being somewhat unrealistic. They assume, for one thing,
that it is hopeless to try to alter the curriculum so that it might
penalize them less for serious interest in one topic at the expense
of others, or so that there might be more emphasis on reading
and discussion, and more opportunity for independent thinking.
And here, also, the students have a distorted image of what will
actually make an impression on their teachers either now or later.
On this point I have some evidence to back me up. After I had
tried in vain for some time to persuade graduate students at
Chicago that they could be more independent in their course and
thesis work without any heroism, any martyrdom, any loss of
life-chances, there was a thesis done by a student which documented my arguments.[6] The student went around to the departments and asked them which students in recent years they had
recommended for jobs or advanced training or fellowships, and
which they had not. Then he interviewed some of these students
in various categories of faculty blessing or disapproval, looked at
their grades, and so on. He concluded that those students frequently fared best who were not too obedient, who did not get
an undiluted, uncomplicated straight-A record. (The straight-A
students, in fact, sometimes slipped by without anyone's noticing.)
Rather, the students who were often most successful were a bit
rebellious, a bit off-beat, though not entirely goof-offs; these were
the students apt to appeal to a faculty member who had not entirely repressed a rebelliousness of his own that had led him to be
a teacher in the first place—a faculty member who was looking
for signs of life, even if they gave him a bit of trouble at times.

---

6. Julius Roth, "Paths to Success and Failure in Social Science Graduate Study," Ph.D. dissertation done for Committee on Human Development, University of Chicago, 1954.

To be sure, such a student had to do well in something to earn this response, but he was often better off to have written a brilliant paper or two than to have divided his time, like an investment banker his money, among a variety of subjects. Those students who were the most self-consciously opportunistic and realistic in allocating their time and emotional accent were in fact sacrificing themselves unprofitably, suffering not only now during the studies which they regarded as an anteroom to life but later on as well.

Now, not all departments at Chicago were alike in this matter; some gave more play to defiance and deviation than others. Moreover, this study encompassed only the social science departments. I am sure that institutions differ very much in this respect. But that is just the point I want to emphasize: by concluding prematurely that all organizations are alike, that all demand the same kinds of conformity, students not only surrender the chance to experience an atmosphere that is freer and more conducive to their own development but perpetuate a myth that then controls their passage through jobs in later life.[7] If the University of

7. In the discussion period I was asked if I would comment on retaliation, that is, the realistic dangers that a student would incur by, let us say, offending a professor whose recommendation to medical school is important. I replied: "I am not recommending martyrdom; I am recommending a greater realism. Not long ago I visited a southern state university where I was told by a student that, if a student protested anything that the administration did, he would be fired. And this was not in the touchy area of race relations (a particular case had come up with respect to some sorority girls who had gotten in trouble with the dean of women). It seemed to me that this was an atrocity story which was not likely to be so, which I investigated as best I could; and I came to the conclusion that the students had created a legend, making the administration even more vindictive than in fact it was. They could therefore say to themselves that they couldn't take risks because they magnified the risks. I am suggesting that many students who are afraid of retaliation are unrealistic about the complex motives of the faculty member in question who might or might not retaliate; there are people who, if one attacks them, like one better for it, and there are many others who will retaliate; and so one has to watch rather than to dogmatize.

"What I am saying is that students or members of an organization are likely to create a kind of myth of the damage that would be done by departure from routine, because this is apparently protective for them,

Chicago or even one's department itself can't be changed from below, how can one expect to change General Motors, or *Look* magazine, or the big hospitals of San Francisco? And if that is so, then why not settle for the fringe benefits, for a position of moderate respectability and adequate if not dazzling salary?

At work here is a characteristic social pattern in which individuals, hesitant to reveal feelings they have scarcely voiced to themselves, are misled about what in effect could be done if they expressed themselves, thereby discovering others who might share their views. (Sociologists refer to this process as "pluralisitc ignorance.") Leadership, of course, whether in poliitcs or in other affairs, often serves to help a group change its apparent mood to conform to its actual or potential but repressed views— but leadership also may, and frequently does, serve to continue enforcing the repression. Even in a large organization, radical and what were previously regarded as "impossible" changes come about almost instantaneously, once people discover that views they had previously regarded as unacceptable or idiosyncratic are in fact widely shared.

What happened in Hungary during the rebellion was apparently this on a large scale. People suddenly discovered that they were surrounded not by potential informers but by allies who had all along shared their hidden misgivings about the imposed Communist regime. Often no more than a look was necessary to communicate this; often a leader with the courage of his convictions unlocked the secret reservations that even party members

---

although in the long run it is harmful to them: it makes it unnecessary for them to look at specific cases and to decide what they really are and what they can accomplish. It may be said that the fear of admitting to being a coward is too great among many of these students; a student can't admit that he is a coward even in small matters, and he may therefore exaggerate the risks. I'm not saying that it couldn't happen, that a student wouldn't be penalized and might not get into medical school; I'm not saying even that he should not try for medical school if he has these convictions; rather, I'm saying that he ought to see exactly what risks he would realistically run with a minimum of harm to himself and with a maximum advantage. In a society of relatively full employment for the well-educated, people have more traditional fears than are justified."

had harbored—and here the students and intellectuals were of the greatest importance. Once this discovery was made, and a union formed of those who had been gulled about what "public opinion" was, it was very difficult to erase the lesson and to re-impose conformity, not of outward behavior, but of inward misconception and feelings of isolation and even guilt.

I confess that at times during the Hungarian and Polish insurrections, when I read the declarations of the Polish newspaper *Po Prostu* or of the Budapest Petofi Club, I felt a certain envy, realizing that the fight for freedom and for realism was in some paradoxical way easier where people were grossly and outrageously oppressed, in comparison with our situation where oppression is benevolent at best and usually bearable at worst. Our large organizations endanger and deceive their members, not by indecency and terror, but precisely by amiability and good will. (Of course, there are exceptions, but I am speaking in very general terms.) Students at the good colleges can't feel that it is worth making a fuss—let alone, of course, starting a revolution—to reduce the number of courses in which the lecturer merely repeats the outside reading, or otherwise to have themselves treated as no longer in high school. Their rebellion takes the very muted and even unconscious forms I have been describing, in which dissatisfaction shows up in withdrawal of allegiance to one's outfit, one's task, and eventually one's self.

IV.

Now there are, as the example of Hungary shows, situations in life which are beyond our control. There is nothing to be said for the posture of those pious but naïve Americans who believe that by virtue of noble declarations the tides of evil will be rolled back and righteousness triumph. Nothing is so simple-minded as the businessman who feels that if only he were let loose in Washington, everything would be straightened out. Such a man doesn't even recognize the extent to which his own business is supported by investment decisions made by large organizations, whether so-called private or public—the extent to which our prosperity rests on capital budgets controlled by a very few individuals.

The students know better, of course; they know that there are many decisions out of their conceivable control, decisions upon which their lives and fortunes truly depend. But what I am contending is that this truth, this insight, is over-generalized, and that, being believed, it becomes more and more "true." Not only do we fail to spot those instances in which intervention might change things quite substantially, but we fail to develop the competence and the confidence in ourselves that are necessary to any large endeavor. In that sense, despite our precociousness, we fail to grow up; we remain the children of organization, not the masters of it.

For Americans, there is something paradoxical about this development. Americans in the past have not been overimpressed by mechanical achievements. Workers in a steel mill are not awed by the giant rollers, and we take for granted that we are not awed by any large physical construction by our hands and brains. Contrary to the prevalent impression abroad that we are slaves to our machines, we are actually relatively uninvolved with them, and we surely do not feel dominated by them. But it seems to be different with the organizational machines. These are as much the product of our thinking and our imagination as any technological feat; yet, as Erich Fromm has said, we worship like idolators the product we have created—an image not of stone but of other images.

V.

It is a commonplace observation that in organizational life we use arguments to convince others which we think will appeal to them, even though they don't convince us. We try to persuade people to behave justly to Negroes because discrimination makes the United States look bad in the Cold War—as if that were why we ourselves behaved decently. Or we persuade businessmen to give money to colleges for all sorts of public-relations reasons, playing on their fear of radicalism or federal control or whatnot, whereas we ourselves devote our lives to education for quite different reasons. You will see that all arguments of this nature have two qualities: they patronize the other person and they perpetuate pluralistic ignorance. It can be contended that there may be occasions when we must appeal to others as they are, not as we would like them to be—when there isn't time for idealism. But, in our realism, we often make mistakes about what others will actually respond to, and we sacrifice the integrity and clarity of our argument to our false image of what will go over. The result: we conclude that one can't be honest while working for an organization, that one can be honest only when one is at home with one's family in the suburbs.

There is another result as well, namely, that we often end up in doubt as to what we ourselves think. We come to believe what we say to others and thus become "more sincere" in the subjective sense, but at the price of becoming still more confused as to what is actually so: we are the first victims of our own propaganda. No wonder we end up without emotional ties to what we do, for it is no longer we who do it, but some limited part of ourselves, playing a role. Not recognizing that we have done this to ourselves, we attribute to organizations the power and the primacy we have lost. And then, as I have said, we strike back, not directly, but by a kind of emotional attrition in which we lend to our work willingness without enthusiasm, conscientiousness without creativity.

I am sure that many college students who are not only serious but dedicated know this as well as I do. Such students have managed to make college serve their purposes and have in this way gained some rational confidence that they will be able to do the same in the organizations they will enter later—whether these are universities, business concerns, or the many voluntary organizations through which we Americans carry out much of our communal work. What I have principally sought to do in these remarks is to encourage greater and more differentiated realism than many young people already possess—a realism which does not take for granted the social structures which seem so impressive but which looks for the points of leverage where one's own effort, joined to that of others similarly freed from mythology, might make a difference. In many situations, there is more leeway than students think, and college is a good place to find this out.

Let me again make it quite clear that I understand the positive functions of what sometimes appears as mere apathy or passivity among students; for passivity toward revivalist manias and crusades is a sensible reaction, a sign of maturity.[8] Moreover, as I noted at the outset, students are not at all apathetic about many fundamental things, among them personal relations, family life, and in many cases the arts. But even these attachments may be in danger. If one is apathetic about one's work, with all that such an attitude implies for one's relation to social and personal creation, it is hard to prevent this apathy from spreading to other areas. Freud thought that children's curiosity, repressed in the realm of sex, became as a result crippled quite generally—that is, the malignancy of repression tended to spread. This danger we have all but overcome. But the comparable spread of apathy and disenchantment from work to family life—indeed, even to sex—seems to me an analogous development. My concern is that

8. In the discussion period I was asked whether the professional study of the emotions in the social sciences had not contributed to affectlessness, to the vogue of the cool student. I responded: "Yes, the externalization of what was previously internal may affect not only the discourse and rhetoric of the emotions but their felt quality. I had had misgivings of just this sort when I began teaching psychoanalytic theory to undergraduates, but I came to the conclusion that the general intellectual culture was moving so rapidly in this same direction that the educational system couldn't stop and put up a wall of ignorance: all it could do, at best, was to go beyond the general culture, and with full awareness of these matters. But I do believe that the loss of a sense of mystery in personal relations—even the current emphasis on honesty and sincerity—is not an unmixed blessing; people are often pushed to a point at which their emotions have no chance to build up within them before being dissipated by talk.

"The social scientist who works in this area, like many psychoanalysts, suffers markedly from this problem. He has to wonder whether he has any private life when his energies and gifts are turned, among other things, to the study of private life. This seems to be less of a problem for novelists; at any rate, they are heartier about it. But, as I have said, I see no remedy in silence, in hoping that the problem will go away; we can only seek in college to transcend or deepen the level of discourse about the emotions in movies, television, popular literature, and popular social science."

young people today, by playing it cool and fearing to be thought squares, may create a style of life, not only in work but in every dimension of existence, which is less full, less committed, less complex, and less meaningful than midcentury opportunities allow.

The Educational Elevator

C. WRIGHT MILLS

(1916–1962)

White Collar, 1951
The Power Elite, 1956

C. WRIGHT MILLS was notable during his short but active life for his effort to persuade his fellow sociologists that commitment rather than objectivity is the proper goal of scholarship. Sometimes more an impassioned prophet than a restrained analyst, he wrote books which no one could ignore. His studies of bureaucratic structures which stifle personality included, naturally enough, one of the structure of schools, and especially universities. Just before his death, he became deeply involved in the polemics over Castro and the meaning of the recent revolution in Cuba.

"SUCCESS" IN AMERICA HAS BEEN A WIDESPREAD FACT, AN ENGAGING image, a driving motive and a way of life. In the middle of the twentieth century, it has become less widespread as fact, more confused as image, often dubious as motive, and soured as a way of life.

No other domestic change is so pivotal for the tang and feel of society in America, or more ambiguous for the inner life of the individual, and none has been so intricately involved in the transformation of the old into the new middle classes. Other strata have certainly been affected, but the middle classes have been most grievously modified by the newer meanings of success and the increased chances of failure.

To understand the meaning of this shift we must understand the major patterns of American success and the ideologies characteristic of each of them; the changing role of the educational system as an occupational elevator; and the long-run forces, as well as the effects of the slump-war-boom cycle, which lift or lower the rate of upward movement.

1. Patterns and Ideologies

During booms, success for the American individual has seemed as sure as social progress, and just as surely to rest on and to exemplify personal virtue. The American gospel of success has been a kind of individual specification of the middle-class gospel of progress: in the big, self-made men, rising after the Civil War, progress seemed to pervade the whole society. The ambitious springs of success were unambiguous, its money target clear and visible, and its paths, if rugged, well marked out; there was a surefootedness about the way middle-class men went about their lives.

The idea of the successful individual was linked with the liberal ideology of expanding capitalism. Liberal sociology, assuming a gradation of ranks in which everyone is rewarded according to his ability and effort, has paid less attention to the fate of groups or classes than to the solitary individual, naked of all save personal merit. The entrepreneur, making his way across the open market, most clearly displayed success in these terms.

The way up, according to the classic style of liberalism, was to establish a small enterprise and to expand it by competition with other enterprises. The worker became a foreman and then an industrialist; the clerk became a bookkeeper or a drummer and then a merchant on his own. The farmer's son took up land in his own right and, long before his old age, came into profits and independence. The competition and effort involved in these ways up formed the cradle of a self-reliant personality and the guarantee of economic and political democracy itself.

Success was bound up with the expansible possession rather than the forward-looking job. It was with reference to property that young men were spoken of as having great or small "expectations." Yet in this image success rested less on inheritances than on new beginnings from the bottom; for, it was thought, "business long ago ceased to be a matter of inheritance, and became the property of brains and persistence."

According to the old entrepreneur's ideology, success is always linked with the sober personal virtues of will power and thrift, habits of order, neatness and the constitutional inability to say Yes to the easy road.[1] These virtues are at once a condition and a sign of success. Without them, success is not possible; with them, all is possible; and, as is clear from the legends of their lives, all successful men have practiced these virtues with great, driving will, for "the temple of Fortune is accessible only by a steep, rugged and difficult path, up which you must drag yourself."

The man bent on success will be upright, exactly punctual, and high-minded; he will soberly refrain from liquor, tobacco, gambling, and loose women. "Laughter, when it is too hearty, weakens the power of mind; avoid it." He will never be in a hurry, will always carefully finish up "each separate undertaking," and so "keep everything under control." He will know "that Method makes Time," and will "promptly improve small opportunities" by diligent attention to detail. He will gain an ease and confidence of endeavor, for self-reliance in all things will insure a moral presence of mind. Also, "a man's self-respect, and the respect of his wife and children for him and themselves, will increase continually as his savings augment."

To honesty, he will add "a great degree of caution and prudence"; then honesty, besides being rewarded in the hereafter, will here and now, be "the surest way to worldly thrift and prosperity." He will come to understand that "religion and business . . . are both right and may essentially serve each other"; that "religion is a mighty ally of economy . . . Vices cost more than Virtues . . . Many a young smoker burns up in advance a fifty-

---

1. The statement of success ideologies in this section is based on thematic analyses of some twenty books, selected at random from files of the New York Public Library, ranging from 1856—Freeman Hunt's *Worth and Wealth* (New York, Stringer & Howard)—to 1947—Loire Brophy's *There's Plenty of Room at the Top* (New York, Simon & Schuster).

thousand-dollar business"; and more broadly, that religion forti-
fies the "integrity which is a man's best 'reserve stock.' "

This inspirational ideology does not often concern itself with
the impersonal structure of opportunity, the limits the economy
sets to the practice of personal virtues; and when it does, personal virtues still win through: "The men who are made by
circumstances are unmade by trifling misfortunes; while they
who conquer circumstances snap their fingers at luck." Yet in
relating the detailed means of success, this literature also reveals
a good deal about its social conditions. It seems to have been
directed to rural and small-town boys. If city boys have better
education, country boys have greater "physical and moral pre-
eminence." In providing instruction in "polish," it indicates in
detail how the rural "bumpkin" must conduct himself in country town and larger city to avoid being laughed at by city slickers.
The aspiring boy is cautioned never to be "boisterous" nor have
"free and easy manners . . . The manners of a gentleman are a
sure passport to success." The city, in this literature, is imagined
as a goal, but more importantly, there is a Jeffersonian warning
about the evils of the city and the practical admonition that
"Businessmen . . . are not accidental outcroppings from the great
army of smooth-haired nice young clerks who would rather
starve in the city than be independent in the country."

Occupationally, the legendary road runs from clerk and then
bookkeeper in the country retail store, then to drummer or
traveling salesman, and finally, to business for oneself, usually
as a merchant. "He who seeks for the merchant of the future
will find him in the clerk of today," but the intermediate step is
very important and much desired. To the clerk, the drummer is a
source of advice about promising locations and opportunities for
new stores; the drummer can inspect opportunities for himself
and learn about a wide variety of commodity "lines." He also
learns to judge others quickly and shrewdly "so that in making a
statement he could follow in his hearer's mind its effects, and be
prepared to stop or to go on at the right moment." In fact: "All
that goes towards making a man a good merchant is needed on
the road by a traveling salesman."

The legendary fork in the road is often "a business career

versus farm life or life in a factory." But whatever its occupational content, it is identified with a moral choice: "Keeping on the right side" versus "being lost." He who fails, who remains a clerk, is "lost," "destroyed," "ruined." That end can be met by going either too slow or too fast, and the "easy success" of a few prominent men should not "dazzle other men to destruction."

The entrepreneurial pattern of success and its inspirational ideology rested upon an economy of many small proprietorships. Under a centralized enterprise system, the pattern of success becomes a pattern of the climb within and between prearranged hierarchies. Whatever the level of opportunity may be, the way up does not now typically include the acquisition of independent property. Only those who already have property can now achieve success based upon it.

The shift from a liberal capitalism of small properties to a corporate system of monopoly capitalism is the basis for the shift in the path and in the content of success. In the older pattern, the white-collar job was merely one step on the grand road to independent entrepreneurship; in the new pattern, the white-collar way involves promotions within a bureaucratic hierarchy. When only one-fifth of the population are free enterprisers (and not that many securely so), independent entrepreneurship cannot very well be the major end of individual economic life. The inspirational literature of entrepreneurial success has been an assurance for the individual and an apology for the system. Now it is more apologetic, less assuring.

For some three-fourths of the urban middle class, the salaried employees, the occupational climb replaces heroic tactics in the open competitive market. Although salaried employees may compete with one another, their field of competition is so hedged in by bureaucratic regulation that their competition is likely to be seen as grubbing and backbiting. The main chance now becomes a series of small calculations, stretched over the working lifetime of the individual: a bureaucracy is no testing field for heroes.

The success literature has shifted with the success pattern. It is still focused upon personal virtues, but they are not the sober virtues once imputed to successful entrepreneurs. Now the stress is on agility rather than ability, on "getting along" in a context of associates, superiors, and rules, rather than "getting ahead" across an open market; on who you know rather than what you know; on techniques of self-display and the generalized knack of handling people, rather than on moral integrity, substantive accomplishments, and solidity of person; on loyalty to, or even identity with, one's own firm, rather than entrepreneurial virtuosity. The best bet is the style of the efficient executive, rather than the drive of the entrepreneur.

"Circumstances, personality, temperament, accident," as well as hard work and patience, now appear as key factors governing success or failure. One should strive for "experience and responsibility with one's chosen field," with "little or no thought of money." Special skills and "executive ability," preferably native, are the ways up from routine work. But the most important single factor is "personality," which ". . . commands attention . . . by charm . . . force of character, or . . . demeanor . . . Accomplishment without . . . personality is unfortunate . . . Personality . . . without industry is . . . undesirable."

To be courteous "will help you to get ahead . . . you will have much more fun . . . will be much less fatigued at night . . . will be more popular, have more friends." So, "Train yourself to smile . . . Express physical and mental alertness . . . Radiate self-confidence . . . Smile often and sincerely." Everything you say, everything you do, creates impressions upon other people . . . from the cradle to the grave, you've got to get along with other people. Use sound sales principles and you'll do better in 'selling' your merchandise, your ideas, and yourself."

The prime meaning of opportunity in a society of employees is to serve the big firm beyond the line of a job's duty and hence to bring oneself to the attention of the higher-ups who control upward movement. This entails dependability and enthusiasm in handling the little job in a big way. "Character . . . includes . . . innate loyalty in little things and enthusiastic interest in the job at hand . . . In a word, thoroughly dependable and generally with an optimistic, helpful attitude."

"Getting ahead" becomes "a continual selling job . . . Whether

you are seeking a new position or are aiming at the job just
ahead. In either case you must sell yourself and keep on selling
. . . You have a product and that product is yourself." The
skillful personal maneuver and the politic approach in inter-
organizational contacts, the planful impressing of the business
superior become a kind of Machiavellism for the little man, a
turning of oneself into an instrument by which to use others for
the end of success. "Become genuinely interested in other people
. . . Smile . . . Be a good listener . . . Talk in terms of the other
man's interest . . . Make the other person feel important—and
do it sincerely . . . I am talking," says Dale Carnegie, "about a
new way of life."

The heraldry of American success has been the greenback;
even when inspirational writers are most inspirational, the big
money is always there. Both entrepreneurial and white-collar
patterns involve the remaking of personality for pecuniary ends,
but in the entrepreneurial pattern money-success involves the
acquisition of virtues good in themselves: the money is always
to be used for good works, for virtue and good works justify
riches. In the white-collar pattern, there is no such moral sancti-
fying of the means of success; one is merely prodded to become
an instrument of success, to acquire tactics not virtues; money
success is assumed to be an obviously good thing for which no
sacrifice is too great.

The entrepreneurial and white-collar ways of success, although
emerging in historical sequence, are not clear-cut phases through
which American aspiration and endeavor have passed. They now
co-exist, and each has varying relevance in different economic
areas and phases of the economic cycle. Each has also come up
against its own kinds of difficulty, which limit its use as a prod
to striving. In a society of employees in large-scale enterprises,
only a limited number can attempt to follow the entrepreneurial
pattern; in a society that has turned itself into a great salesroom,
the salesman's ways of success are likely to be severely competitive, and, at the same time, rationalized out of existence; in a
society in which the educational level of the lower ranks is constantly rising and jobs are continually rationalized, the white-

collar route to the top is likely to come up against competition it never knew in more educationally restricted situations.

2. The Educational Elevator

The American belief in the value of universal education has been a salient feature of democratic ideology; in fact, since the Jacksonian era, education for all has often been virtually identified with the operation of a truly democratic society. Moreover, the hope for more education has slowly been realized. Eighty years ago a little over half, but today over four-fifths of the children of appropriate age are enrolled in public elementary and secondary schools.

This massive rise in enrollment has strengthened the feeling of status equality, especially in those smaller cities where all the children, regardless of social or occupational rank, are likely to attend the same high school. It has aided immensely in Americanizing the immigrant. And it has spread and generally strengthened old middle-class ideologies, for teachers represent and reinforce middle-class attitudes and values, manners and skills. Yet, in spite of this reinforcing of old middle-class mores, mass education has also been one of the major social mechanisms of the rise of the new middle-class occupations, for these occupations require those skills that have been provided by the educational system.

In performing these functions, especially the last, American education has shifted toward a more explicit vocational emphasis, functioning as a link in occupational mobility between generations. High schools, as well as colleges and universities, have been reshaped for the personnel needs of business and government. In their desire for serviceable practicality, the schools have adapted themselves to changing demands, and the public has seemed glad to have its children trained for the available jobs.

The most fundamental question to ask of any educational system is what kind of a product do its administrators expect to turn out? And for what kind of society? In the nineteenth century, the answer was "the good citizen" in a "democratic republic." In the middle of the twentieth century, it is "the successful man" in a "society of specialists with secure jobs."

In the world of small entrepreneurs, little or no educational preparation was needed for success, much less to get along: one was stubborn, or courageous, had common sense and worked hard. Education may have been viewed as a main road to social equality and political freedom, and as a help in meeting opportunity so that ability and talent might be appropriately rewarded. But education was not the big avenue of economic advancement for the masses of the populace.

In the new society, the meaning of education has shifted from status and political spheres to economic and occupational areas. In the white-collar life and its patterns of success, the educational segment of the individual's career becomes a key to his entire occupational fate.

Formal requirements for entry into different jobs and expectations of ascent tend to become fixed by educational levels. On the higher levels, college is the cradle of the professions and semi-professions, as well as a necessary status-mark for higher positions. As the virtues and talents of the entrepreneur are replaced by the skills and prestige of the educated expert, formal education becomes central to social and economic success. Sons who are better educated than their fathers are more likely to occupy higher occupational positions: in one sample of urban males, studied by Richard Centers, some 46 per cent of the sons who were better educated than their fathers reached higher positions, whereas only 16 per cent of those whose education was poorer did. The educational link was specifically important in the U. S. Army during World War II: 64 per cent of the officers, but only 11 per cent of the enlisted men, had been to college.

The aim of college men today, especially in elite colleges, is a forward-looking job in a large corporation. Such a job involves training not only in vocational skills, but also in social mannerisms. Harold Taylor, president of Sarah Lawrence, writes: "The ideal graduate in the present employment market of industrial executives is a fraternity man with a declared disinterest in political or social affairs, gentile, white, a member of the football team, a student with a record of A in each course, a man popular with everyone and well known on the campus, with many memberships in social clubs—a man who can be imagined in twenty years as a subject for a Calvert advertisement. The large successful universities have confirmed this stereotype by the plans they make for the campus social life of the students and by the value system implicit in its organization . . . Even the liberal arts colleges seem bent upon becoming training schools for conservative industrial executives."

Although the middle-class monopoly on high-school education has been broken, equality of educational opportunity has not been reached; many young people are unable to complete their secondary school education because of economic restrictions. "Generally speaking," Walter Kotschnig concludes, "the children of large families in the lowest income brackets have little chance of graduating from high school. They have to leave school early to help their families. Most of them will never be anything but poorly paid unskilled workers for the simple reason that . . . education has become the main avenue to economic and social success. The situation on the college level is even worse . . ." The most careful study available reveals that in many cases the father's income rather than the boy's brains determines who shall be college trained.

The parent's class position is also reflected in the type of curriculum taken. Students of law, medicine, or liberal arts generally come from families having twice the yearly income of students in nursing, teaching, or commercial work. "Of the 580 boys and girls in a thousand who reach the third year of high school," Lloyd Warner and his associates write, "about half are taking a course which leads to college. One hundred and fifty enter college, and 70 graduate. These are average figures for the country as a whole . . . an average of some two hundred out of every thousand young people fail to achieve the goal toward which they started in high school."

The major occupational shift in college education has been from old middle-class parents to new middle-class children; the major shift via high-school education has been from skilled-worker parents to new middle-class children. Colleges and universities have been social elevators carrying the children of small business-men and farmers to the lower order of the professions. At the University of Chicago, for example, between 1893 and 1931, about 4 out of 10 of the fathers of graduates (bachelor degrees) were in business, commercial, or proprietary occupations. Only about one-fourth of these fathers were in professional service, but 62 per cent of the sons and 73 per cent of the daughters entered such service.

Mobility between generations probably increases from old to new middle classes during depressions, as, especially in the upper-middle brackets, parents seek to secure their children from the effects of the market. Rather than carry on his father's business, many a boy has been trained, at his parents' sacrifice, to help man some unit of the big-business system that has destroyed his father's business.

As the old middle classes have come to be distressed and insecure about their small-propertied existence, they have become uneasy about their ability to get their children into positions equal to or better than their own. At the same time, wage-workers have aspired to have their children attain higher levels. Both classes have emphatically demanded "educational opportunity" and both have sacrificed in order to give children better (more) education.

Thirty-five years ago John Corbin cried in the name of the educated white-collar people that education was as much a contribution to the nation's wealth as property, that education *was* the white-collar employee's "capital," the major basis of his claim to prestige, and the means by which he should close up his ranks. Yet, as a type of "capital," education carries a limitation that farms and businesses do not: its exercise is dependent upon those who control and manage jobs. Today, according to a *Fortune* survey, the idea of going into business for oneself "is so seldom expressed among college graduates as to seem an anachronism."

On the one hand, there is a demand for "equal educational opportunities" for all, which once unambiguously meant better and more secure positions for all. On the other hand, there are now strong tendencies, which in all probability will continue, for the educational requirements of many white-collar positions to decline, and, moreover, for the competition for even these positions to increase. As a result, the belief in universal education as a sacrosanct fetish has come to be questioned. This questioning, which began about the time of World War I, became more widespread during the 'thirties and came to sharp focus after World War II, represents, in Perry Miller's phrase, the "dislocation in a basic tradition."

Democratic ideologists now point out that almost 80 per cent of fifth-grade students, who are mentally capable of college education, never reach college, so millions of citizens, according to E. J. McGrath, U. S. Commissioner of Education, "go through life functioning below the level of their potential." This is undoubtedly true, but statisticians, occupational forecasters, and an increasing number of educational officials raise the question whether or not the occupational structure can possibly provide the jobs that are expected by college graduates.

During the last half century, college graduates, increasing four times as much as the general population, were involved in the expansion of higher white-collar occupations. So education paid off: ten years ago, college graduates earned one-third more than the U. S. average. Today, however, college graduates earn only one-tenth more than the U. S. average, and, according to an informed prediction by Seymour E. Harris, in twenty years "it won't pay to be educated." By then, instead of 3 million living college graduates as in 1930, there will be between 10 and 14 million. In order to meet their expectations, the professions would have to absorb between 8 and 11 million of them, yet between 1910 and 1940 professions expanded less than 2 million. There are warning cries among educational ideologists, recalling the contributions made by "disappointed intellectuals to the rise of fascism in Europe," and there are maneuvers and proclamations among school officials which reflect shifts in the role of education in the American success story.

Chancellor William J. Wallin of the New York State Board of Regents has decried higher education for all, declaring "that the country might produce 'surplus graduates' who, embittered with their frustration, would 'turn upon society and the government, more effective and better armed in their destructive wrath by the education we have given them.' " "Equality of opportunity," Harvard President Conant has recently said, "is one of the cardinal principles of this country. . . . Yet at the same time, no young man or woman should be encouraged or enticed into taking the kinds of advanced educational training which are going to lead to a frustrated economic life." "For a large majority of young Americans, a four-year college education was not only 'needlessly expensive,' but 'socially undesirable.' "

One of the most popular solutions now being proposed is the establishment of several educational ladders, each reaching to different levels of the occupational hierarchy. Such ideas are now rather widely, although informally, being put into practice in U. S. high schools. The principal of one high school says: "This educational system is a terrific waste of money and time to the city, since so few people can by any chance become members of the white-collar class and so many must follow some vocational line. . . . It is surprising how many people in 8C want the prestige of a white-collar job. So I point out how poor the pay is and endeavor to point out how hard it is to fit oneself for such a job and to make a success of it; the majority of them are unfitted for any such work. . . . I am giving all the groups A, B, and C a talking to, explaining the disadvantages of the white-collar job to all of them." "There is clear evidence," comments sociologist Lloyd Warner, who gathered these quotations, "that our educational system is now permitting too many to use high school and college for the purpose of attaining unavailable professional and managerial positions, with resultant failure and frustration and loss of social solidarity."

Education will work as a means of success only so long as the occupational needs of a society continue to demand education. The recognition that they might not has led to the idea, in Kotchnig's words, of giving "the masses of young people a general and special education in keeping with their abilities, while preparing leaders for the 'several *élites*,' thus breaking down the one-sided emphasis on the intellectual careers." Confronted with such ideas, "Progressive" educational theorists add to them the assumption that tests, measurements, placement services, and vocational guidance can at early ages select those who should go on, via education, to higher positions and those who should terminate their education, and hence their occupational chances, at lower levels.

We have thus come a long way from the simple faith in "equal educational opportunity" as part of the American pattern of success. First, with education a highly specialized channel for elites with high class chances, the major avenues of advancement do not involve education: independent men, who are "making themselves," compete on the open market and find their own levels.

Second, with the democratization of education as political demand and economic need, the occupational structures require literacy and some skills, and bring about a period of success via education. The single ladder is not questioned, the ideology of equal opportunity means that all top positions are competed for by all those with the ability to climb the educational ladder.

Third, almost all occupational mobility requires education, but as supply exceeds demand, education is stratified bureaucratically, by sorting out the young through tests and measurements. There are increased tendencies to manage the education-occupation structure and steer it; and magical notions of the environment are given up. As demand for educated people falls behind supply, as educated occupations are divided and rationalized, as enrollments continue to rise, the income and prestige differences between the more-educated and the less-educated masses decrease. Among those who are not allowed to use the educated skills they have acquired, boredom increases, hope for success collapses into disappointment, and the sacrifices that don't pay off lead to disillusionment.

A Dog in Brooklyn, A Girl in Detroit: A Life Among the Humanities

HERBERT GOLD
(1924–   )

The Prospect Before Us, 1954
Love and Like, 1960
The Age of Happy Problems, 1962

HERBERT GOLD has written six novels as well as many short stories and essays. His talent is essentially a fictional one, and in a piece such as the one below, his technique is narrative rather than expository. Two concerns central to Mr. Gold are our youth and our schools. He seeks to be a spokesman for the first as well as its critic, and has from time to time tried to earn his living in the second. What he has learned is, in part, embodied in what follows.

WHAT BETTER CAREER FOR A BOY WHO SEEKS TO UNRAVEL THE meaning of our brief span on earth than that of philosopher? We all wonder darkly, in the forbidden hours of the night, punishing our parents and building a better world, with undefined terms. Soon, however, most of us learn to sleep soundly; or we take to pills or love-making; or we call ourselves insomniacs, not philosophers. A few attempt to define the terms.

There is no code number for the career of philosophy in school, the Army, or out beyond in real life. The man with a peculiar combination of melancholic, nostalgic, and reforming instincts stands at three possibilities early in his youth. He can choose to be a hero, an artist, or a philosopher. In olden times, war, say, or the need to clean out the old West, might make up his mind for him. The old West had been pretty well cleaned up by the time I reached a man's estate, and Gary Cooper could finish the job. Heroism was an untimely option. With much bureaucratic confusion I tried a bit of heroic war, got stuck in the machine, and returned to the hectic, Quonset campus of the GI Bill, burning to Know, Understand, and Convert. After a season of ferocious burrowing in books, I was ready to be a Teacher, which seemed a stern neighbor thing to Artist and Philosopher. I took on degrees, a Fulbright fellowship, a wife, a child, a head crammed with foolish questions and dogmatic answers despite the English school of linguistic analysis. I learned to smile, pardner, when I asked questions of philosophers trained at Oxford or Cambridge, but I asked them nonetheless. I signed petitions against McCarthy, wrote a novel, went on a treasure hunt, returned to my roots in the Middle West and stood rooted there, discussed the menace of the mass media, and had another child.

By stages not important here, I found myself teaching the Humanities at Wayne University in Detroit. I am now going to report a succession of classroom events which, retrospectively, seems to have determined my abandonment of formal dealing with this subject. The evidence does not, however, render any conclusion about education in the "Humanities" logically impregnable. It stands for a state of mind and is no substitute for formal argument. However, states of mind are important in this area of experience and metaexperience. However and however: it happens that most of the misty exaltation of the blessed vocation of the teacher issues from the offices of deans, editors, and college presidents. The encounter with classroom reality has caused many teachers, like Abelard meeting the relatives of Eloise, to lose their bearings. Nevertheless this is a memoir, not a campaign, about a specific life in and out of the Humanities. Though I am not a great loss to the History of Everything in Culture, my own eagerness to teach is a loss to me.

2

News item of a few years ago. A young girl and her date are walking along a street in Brooklyn, New York. The girl notices

that they are being followed by an enormous Great Dane. The
dog is behaving peculiarly, showing its teeth and making restless
movements. A moment later, sure enough, the dog, apparently
maddened, leaps slavering upon the girl, who is borne to earth
beneath its weight. With only an instant's hesitation, the boy
jumps on the dog. Its fangs sunk first in one, then in the other,
the dog causes the three of them to roll like beasts across the
sidewalk.

A crowd gathers at a safe distance to watch. No one interferes.
The becalmed curiosity of teevee viewers.

A few moments later a truckdriver, attracted by the crowd,
pulls his vehicle over to the curb. This brave man is the only
human being stirred personally enough to leave the role of
passive spectator. Instantaneously analyzing the situation, he
leaps into the struggle—*attacking and beating the boy*. He has
naturally assumed that the dog must be protecting an innocent
young lady from the unseemly actions of a juvenile delinquent.

I recounted this anecdote in the classroom in order to introduce a course which attempted a summary experience of Humanities 610 for a monumental nine credits. There were a number of
points to be made about the passivity of the crowd ("don't get
involved," "not my business") and the stereotypical reaction of
the truck driver who had been raised to think of man's best friend
as not another human being but a dog. In both cases, addicted to
entertainment and clichés, the crowd and the trucker could not
recognize what was actually happening before their eyes; they
responded irrelevantly to the suffering of strangers; they were not
a part of the maine. This led us to discussion of the notion of
"community." In a closely knit society, the people on the street
would have known the couple involved and felt a responsibility
toward them. In a large city, everyone is a stranger. (Great art
can give a sense of the brotherhood of men. Religion used to do
this, too.) "Any questions?" I asked, expecting the authority of
religion to be defended.

An eager hand shot up. Another. Another. Meditative bodies
sprawled in their chairs. "Are all New Yorkers like that?" "Well,
what can you do if there's a mad dog and you're not expecting it?"

"Where does it say in what great book how you got to act in Brooklyn?"

I took note of humor in order to project humorousness. I found myself composing my face in the look of thought which teevee panelists use in order to project thinking. I discovered a serious point to elaborate—several. I mentioned consciousness and relevance and the undefined moral suggestion implied by the labor which produces any work of art or mind. A girl named Clotilda Adams asked me: "Why don't people try to get along better in this world?"

Somewhat digressively, we then discussed the nature of heroism, comparing the behavior of the boy and the truck driver. Both took extraordinary risks; why? We broke for cigarettes in the autumn air outside. Then, for fifty minutes more, we raised these interesting questions, referring forward to Plato, Aristotle, St. Thomas, Dostoevski, Tolstoi, William James, and De Gaulle; and then boy, dog, girl, truck driver, and crowd were left with me and the crowned ghosts of history in the deserted room while my students went on to Phys Ed, Music Appreciation, Sosh, and their other concerns. Having been the chief speaker, both dramatist and analyst, I was exalted by the lofty ideas floated up into the air around me. I was a little let down to return to our real life in which dog-eat-dog is man's closest pal. Fact. Neither glory nor pleasure nor power, and certainly not wisdom, provided the goal of my students. Not even wealth was the aim of most of them. They sought to make out, to do all right, more prideful than amorous in love, more security-hungry than covetous in status. I saw my duty as a teacher: Through the Humanities, to awaken them to the dream of mastery over the facts of our lives; I saw my duty plain: Through the Humanities, to lead them toward the exaltation of knowledge and the calm of control. I had a whole year in which to fulfill this obligation. It was a two-semester course.

Before she left the room, Clotilda Adams said, "You didn't answer my question." Fact.

Outside the university enclave of glass and grass, brick and trees, Detroit was agonizing in its last big year with the big cars. Automation, dispersion of factories, and imported automobiles were eroding a precarious confidence. Fear was spreading; soon the landlords would offer to decorate apartments and suffer the pain. Detroit remembered the war years with nostalgia. Brave days, endless hours, a three-shift clock, insufficient housing, men sleeping in the all-night, triple-feature movies on Woodward and Grand River. Though the area around the Greyhound and Trailways stations was still clotted with the hopeful out of the hill country of the midsouth and the driven from the deep South— they strolled diagonally across the boulevards, entire families holding hands—some people suspected what was already on its way down the road: twenty per cent unemployment in Detroit.

The semester continued. We churned through the great books. One could classify my students in three general groups, intelligent, mediocre, and stupid, allowing for the confusions of three general factors—background, capacity, and interest. This was how we classified the Humanities, too: ancient, medieval, and modern. It made a lot of sense, and it made me itch, scratch, and tickle. Series of three-form nice distinctions. According to Jung and other authorities, they have certain mythic significances. The course was for nine credits. All the arts were touched upon. We obeyed Protagoras; man, just man, was our study. When I cited him—"Man is the measure of all things"—Clotilda Adams stirred uneasily in her seat: "By which Protagoras no doubt meant Woman, too," I assured her. She rested.

Now imagine the winter coming and enduring, with explosions of storm and exfoliations of gray slush, an engorged industrial sky overhead and sinus trouble all around. The air was full of acid and a purplish, spleeny winter mist. Most of Detroit, in Indian times before the first French trappers arrived, had been a swamp and below sea level. The swamp was still present, but invisible; city stretched out in all directions, crawling along the highways. Though Detroit was choked by a dense undergrowth of streets and buildings, irrigated only by super-highways, its work was done with frantic speed. The Rouge plant roared, deafened. The assembly lines clanked to the limit allowed by the UAW. The old Hudson factory lay empty, denuded, waiting to become a parking lot. Then the new models were being introduced! Buick! Pontiac! Dodge! Ford and Chevrolet! Ford impudently purchased a huge billboard faced toward the General Motors Building on Grand Boulevard. General Motors retaliated by offering free ginger ale to all comers, and a whole bottle of Vernor's to take home if you would only consent to test-drive the new Oldsmobile, the car with the. . . . I've forgotten what it had that year. All over town the automobile companies were holding revival meetings; hieratic salesmen preached to the converted and the hangers-back alike; lines at the loan companies stretched through the revolving doors and out onto the winter pavements. But many in those lines were trying to get additional financing on their last year's cars. The new models were an indifferent success despite all the uproar of display and Detroit's patriotic attention to it. Searchlights sliced up the heavens while the city lay under flu.

Teachers at Wayne University soon learn not to tease the American Automobile. *Lèse* Chrysler was a moral offense, an attack on the livelihood and the sanctity of the American garage. Detroit was a town in which men looked at hubcaps as men elsewhere have sometimes looked at ankles. The small foreign car found itself treated with a violent Halloween kidding-on-the-square, scratched, battered, and smeared (another Jungian series of three!). A passionate and sullen town, Detroit had no doubts about its proper business. All it doubted was everything else.

I often failed at inspiring my students to do the assigned reading. Many of them had part-time jobs in the automobile industry or its annexes. Even a Philosopher found it difficult to top the argument, "I couldn't read the book this week, I have to *work,*" with its implied reproach for a scholar's leisure. But alas, many of these stricken proletarians drove freshly minted automobiles. They worked in order to keep up the payments, racing like laboratory mice around the cage of depreciation. Certain faculty deep thinkers, addicted to broad understanding of the problems of others, argued that these students were so poor they *had* to buy new cars in order to restore their confidence. The finance companies seemed to hear their most creative expressions, not me. Deep in that long Detroit winter, I had the task of going from the pre-Socratic mystics all the way to Sartre, for nine credits. Like an audio-visual monkey, I leaped from movie projector to records to slides, with concurrent deep labor in book and tablet.

We read *The Brothers Karamazov,* but knowing the movie did
not give credit. We studied "The Waste Land," and reading the
footnotes did not suffice. We listened to Wanda Landowska play
the harpsichord on records. We sat in the dark before a slide of
Seurat's "La Grande Jatte" while I explained the importance of
the measles of pointillisme to students who only wanted to see life
clear and true, see it comfortably. Clotilda Adams said that this
kind of painting hurt her eyes. She said that there was too much
reading for one course—"piling it on. This isn't the only course
we take." She said that she liked music, though. All Moses had to
do was to bring the Law down the mountain to the children of
Israel; I had to bring it pleasingly.

We made exegeses. I flatly turned down the request of a dean
that I take attendance. As a statesmanlike compromise, I tested
regularly for content and understanding.

Then, on a certain morning, I handed back some quiz papers
at the beginning of class. Out on the street, a main thoroughfare
through town, it was snowing; this was one of those magical days
of late winter snowfall—pale, cold, clean, and the entire city
momentarily muffled by the silence of snow. The room hissed with
steam heat; a smell of galoshes and mackinaws arose from the
class. "Let us not discuss the test—let us rise above grades. Let us
try to consider nihilism as a byproduct of the Romantic revival—"
I had just begun my lecture when an odd clashing, lumping noise
occurred on Cass Avenue. "Eliot's later work, including 'The
Four Quartets,' which we will not discuss here. . . ."

But I was interrupted by a deep sigh from the class. A product
of nihilism and the romantic revival? No. It was that strange
tragic sigh of horror and satisfaction. Out in the street, beyond
the window against which I stood, a skidding truck had side-
swiped a taxi. The truckdriver had parked and gone into a drugstore. The cab was mashed like a cruller. From the door, the
driver had emerged, stumbling drunkenly on the icy road, holding his head. There was blood on his head. There was blood on
his hands. He clutched his temples. The lines of two-way traffic,
moving very slowly in the snow and ice, carefully avoided hitting
him. There were streaks of perforated and patterned snow,
frothed up by tires. He was like an island around which the sea

of traffic undulated in slow waves; but he was an island that moved in the sea and held hands to head. He slid and stumbled back and forth, around and about his cab in the middle of the wide street. He was in confusion, in shock. Even at this distance I could see blood on the new-fallen snow. Drivers turned their heads upon him like angry Halloween masks, but did not get involved. Snow spit at his feet.

No one in the class moved. The large window through which we gazed was like a screen, with the volume turned down by habit, by snow, by a faulty tube. As the teacher, my authority took precedence. I ran out to lead the cab driver into the building. An elderly couple sat huddled in the car, staring at the smashed door, afraid to come out the other. They said they were unhurt.

I laid the man down on the floor. He was bleeding from the head and his face was a peculiar purplish color, with a stubble of beard like that of a dead man. There was a neat prick in his fore-head where the union button in his cap had been driven into the skin. I sent a student to call for an ambulance. The cab driver's color was like that of the bruised industrial sky. "You be okay till the ambulance——?"

Foolish question. No alternative. No answer.

We waited. The class was restless. When they weren't listening to me, or talking themselves, or smudging blue books in an exam, they did not know what to do in this room devoted to the special-ized absorption of ideas. Silence. Scraping of feet, crisping of paper. We watched the slow-motion traffic on the street outside.

The cab driver moved once in a rush, turning over face down against the floor, with such force that I thought he might break his nose. Then slowly, painfully, as if in a dream, he turned back and lay staring at the ceiling. His woolen lumberjacket soaked up the blood trickling from one ear; the blood traveled up separated cilia of wool, which drew it in with a will of their own. There was a swaying, osmotic movement like love-making in the eager little wisps of wool. An astounded ring of Humanities 610 students watched, some still holding their returned quiz papers. One girl in particular, Clotilda Adams, watched him and me with her eyes brilliant, wet, and bulging, and her fist crumpling the paper. I tried by imagining it to force the ambulance through the chilled and snowfallen city. I saw it weaving around the injured who strutted with shock over ice and drift, its single red Cyclops' eye turning, the orderlies hunched over on benches, chewing gum and cursing the driver. The ambulance did not arrive. Clotilda Adams' eye had a thick, impenetrable sheen over it. She watched from the cab driver to me as if we were in some way linked. When would the authorities get there? When the medics? There must have been many accidents in town, and heart attacks, and fires with cases of smoke inhalation.

Before the ambulance arrived, the police were there. They came strolling into the classroom with their legs apart, as if they remembered ancestors who rode the plains. Their mouths were heavy in thought. They had noses like salamis, red and mottled with fat. They were angry at the weather, at the school, at the crowd, at me, and especially at the prostrate man at our feet. He gave them a means to the creative expression of pique. (Everyone needs an outlet.)

Now Clotilda Adams took a step backward, and I recall thinking this odd. She had been treading hard near the pool of blood about the cab driver, but when the cops strolled up, she drifted toward the outer edge of the group of students, with a sly look of caution in her downcast, sideways-cast eyes. Her hand still crisped at the returned exam paper. This sly, lid-fallen look did not do her justice. She was a hard little girl of the sort often thought to be passionate—skinny but well-breasted, a high hard rump with a narrow curve, a nervous mouth.

The two policemen stood over the body of the cab driver. They stared at him in the classic pose—one cop with a hand resting lightly on the butt of his gun and the other on his butt, the younger cop with lips so pouted that his breath made a snuffling sound in his nose. They both had head colds. Their Ford was pulled up on the snow-covered lawn outside, with raw muddled marks of tread in the soft dirt. When the snow melted, there would be wounded streaks in the grass. The cab driver closed his eyes under the finicking, distasteful examination. At last one spoke: "See your driver's license."

The cab driver made a clumsy gesture toward his pocket. The cop bent and went into the pocket. He flipped open the wallet, glanced briefly at the photographs and cash, glanced at me, and then began lipreading the license.

The cab driver was in a state of shock. There was a mixture of thin and thick blood on his clothes and messing the floor. "This man is badly hurt," I said. "Can't we get him to the hospital first?"

"This is only your *driver* license," the cop said slowly, having carefully read through Color of Hair: Brn, Color of Eyes: Brn, and checked each item with a stare at the man of the floor. "Let me see your chauffeur license."

"He's badly hurt," I said. "Get an Ambulance."

"Teach," said the older cop, "you know your business? We know ours."

"It's on the way," said the other. "Didn't you call it yourself?"

"No, one of the students . . ." I said.

He grinned with his great victory. "So—don't you trust your pupils neither?"

Shame. I felt shame at this ridicule of my authority in the classroom. A professor is not a judge, a priest, or a sea captain; he does not have the right to perform marriages on the high seas of audiovisual aids and close reasoning. But he is more than an intercom between student and fact; he can be a stranger to love for his students, but not to a passion for his subject; he is a student himself; his pride is lively. The role partakes of a certain heft and control. There is power to make decisions, power to abstain, power to bewilder, promote, hold back, adjust, and give mercy; power, an investment of pride, a risk of shame.

Clotilda Adams, still clutching her exam, stared at me with loathing. She watched me bested by the police. She barely glanced, and only contemptuously, at the man bleeding from the head on the floor. She moved slightly forward again in order to participate fully in an action which apparently had some important meaning for her. She had lost her fear of the police when she saw how we all stood with them. The limits were established.

The police were going through the cab driver's pockets. They took out a folding pocket knife and cast significant looks at it and at each other. It had a marbled plastic hilt, like a resort souvenir. It was attached to a key ring.

"Hey!" one said to the half-conscious man. "What's this knife for?"

"Where'd you get them keys?" the other demanded, prodding the cabbie with his toe.

"A *skeleton* key. These cab companies," one of the cops decided to explain to Clotilda Adams, who was standing nearby, "they get the dregs. Hillbillies, you know?"

I said nothing, found nothing to say. I now think of Lord Acton's famous law, which is accepted as true the way it was uttered. The opposite is also true—the commoner's way: Having no power corrupts; having absolutely no power corrupts absolutely.

The bleeding seemed to have stopped. The cab driver sat up, looking no better, with his bluish, greenish, drained head hanging between his knees. His legs were crumpled stiffly. He propped himself on his hands. The police shot questions at him. He mumbled, mumbled, explained, explained.

"How long you been in Detroit? How come you come out of the mountains?"

"Why you pick up this fare?"

"What makes you think Cass is a one-way street?"

Mumbling and mumbling, explaining and explaining, the cab driver tried to satisfy them. He also said: "Hurt. Maybe you get me to the hospital, huh? Hurt real bad."

"Maybe," said one of the cops, "Maybe we take you to the station house first. That boy you hit says reckless driving. I think personally you'd flunk the drunk test—what you think, Teach?"

I sent one of the students to call for an ambulance again. In the infinitesimal pause between my suggestion and his action, an attentive reluctant expectant caesura, I put a dime in his hand for the call. One of the cops gave me that long look described by silent movie critics as the slow burn. "They drive careful," he finally said. "It's snowing. They got all that expensive equipment."

The snow had started again outside the window. The skid marks on the lawn were covered. Though the sky was low and gray, the white sifting down gave a peaceful village glow to this industrial Detroit. Little gusts barely rattled the windows. With the class, the cops, and the driver, we were living deep within a snowy paper-weight. I felt myself moving very slowly, swimming within thick glass, like the loosened plastic figure in a paper-weight. The snow came down in large torn flakes, all over the buildings of Wayne University, grass, trees, and the pale radiance of a network of slow-motion superhighways beyond. Across the street, a modern building—glass and aluminum strips—lay unfinished in this weather. Six months ago there had been a student boarding house on that spot, filled with the artists and the beat, the guitar-wielders and the modern dancers, with a tradition going all the way back to the Korean War. Now there were wheelbarrows full of frozen cement; there were intentions to build a Japanese garden, with Japanese proportions and imported goldfish.

My student returned from the telephone. He had reached a hospital.

The cab driver was fading away. Rootlets of shock hooded his eyes: the lid was closing shut. A cop asked him another question —what the button on his cap stood for—it was a union button— and then the man just went reclining on his elbow, he slipped slowly down, he lay in the little swamp of crusted blood on the floor. You know what happens when milk is boiled? The crust broke like the crust of boiled milk when a spoon goes into coffee. The cop stood with a delicate, disgusted grimace on his face. What a business to be in, he seemed to be thinking. In approximately ten years, at age forty-two, he could retire and sit comfortable in an undershirt, with a nonreturnable can of beer, before the color teevee. He could relax. He could *start* to relax. But in the meantime—nag, nag, nag. Drunk cabbies, goddamn hillbillies. The reckless driver on the floor seemed to sleep. His lips moved. He was alive.

Then a puffing intern rushed into the room. I had not heard the ambulance. The policeman gave room and the intern kneeled. He undid his bag. The orderlies glanced at the floor and went back out for their stretcher.

I stood on one side of the body, the kneeling intern with his necklace of stethoscope, and the two meditative cops. On the other side was the group of students, and at their head, like a leader filled with wrath, risen in time of crisis, stood Clotilda Adams, still clutching her exam paper. There were tears in her eyes. She was in a fury. She had been thinking all this time, and now her thinking had issue: *rage*. Over the body she handed me a paper, crying out, "I don't think I deserved a D on that quiz. I answered all the questions. I can't get my credit for Philo of Ed without I get a B off you:"

I must have looked at her with pure stupidity on my face. There is a Haitian proverb: *Stupidity won't kill you, but it'll make you sweat a lot*. She took the opportunity to make me sweat, took my silence for guilt, took my open-mouthed gaze for weakness. She said: "If I was a white girl, you' grade me easier."

Guilt, a hundred years, a thousand years of it; pity for the disaster of ignorance and fear, pity for ambition rising out of ignorance; adoration of desire; trancelike response to passion— passion which justifies itself because passionate. . . . I looked at her with mixed feelings. I could not simply put her down. In order to *put down,* your own mind must be made up, put down. She had beauty and dignity, stretched tall and wrathful, with teeth for biting and eyes for striking dead.

"But I know my rights," she said, *"Mister.* My mother told me about your kind—lent my father money on his car and then hounded him out of town. He been gone since fifty-three. But you can't keep us down forever, no sir, you can't *always* keep us down—"

She was talking and I was yelling. She was talking and yelling about injustice and I, under clamps, under ice, was yelling in a whisper about the sick man. She was blaming me for all her troubles, all the troubles she had seen, and I was blaming her for not seeing what lay before her, and we were making an appointment to meet in my office and discuss this thing more calmly, Miss Adams. Okay. All right. Later.

The police, the doctor, the orderlies, and the injured cab driver were gone. The police car out front was gone and the snow was covering its traces. The janitor came in and swept up the bloodstains with green disinfectant powder. The frightened couple in the cab were released. They all disappeared silently into the

great city, into the routine of disaster and recovery of a great city.
I dismissed the class until tomorrow.

The next day I tried to explain to Miss Adams what I meant
about her failing to respond adequately to the facts of our life together. Her mouth quivered. Yesterday rage; today a threat of
tears. What did I mean she wasn't *adequate?* What did I know
about adequate anyhow? Nothing. Just a word. Agreed, Miss
Adams. I was trying to say that there were two questions at issue
between us—her exam grade and her choice of occasion to dispute
it. I would like to discuss each matter separately. I tried to explain
why putting the two events together had disturbed me. I tried to
explain the notions of empirical evidence and metaphor. I recalled, without successful communication, the story of the young
couple and the dog in Brooklyn.

She did not see why she shouldn't have at least a B on her
quiz. Her back was strong, her head was high, she didn't need to
be compared to no black dog in Brooklyn.

Finally I urged her to have her exam looked at by the head of
the department, but she refused because she knew in advance that
he would support me. "White is Right," she said.

"Do you want to drop out of the class?"

"No. I'll stay," she said with a sudden patient, weary acceptance of her fate. "I'll do what I can."

"I'll do what I can too," I said.

She smiled hopefully at me. She was tuckered out by the continual alert for combat everywhere. She was willing to forgive and
go easy. When she left my office, this smile, shy, pretty, and
conventional, tried to tell me that she could be generous—a
friend.

We had come to Thomas Hobbes and John Locke in our tour
through time and the river of humanities. I pointed out that the
English philosophers were noted for clarity and eloquence of
style. I answered this question: The French? Isn't French noted
for clarity? Yes, they too, but they are more abstract. On the
whole. In general.

The class took notes on the truths we unfolded together. Spring
came and the snow melted. There was that brief Detroit flowering
of the new season—jasmine and dogwood—which, something like

it, must have captivated the Frenchman, Antoine de la Mothe Cadillac, when he paused on the straits of Detroit in 1701. University gardeners planted grass seed where the patrol car had parked on the lawn. The new models, all except the Cadillac, were going at mean discounts.

"The 'Humanities,'" wrote Clotilda Adams in her final essay, "are a necessary additive to any teacher's development worth her 'salt' in the perilous times of today. The West and the 'Free World' must stand up to the war of ideas against the 'Iron' Curtain." This was in answer to a question about Beethoven, Goethe, and German romanticism. She did not pass the course, but she was nevertheless admitted on probation to the student-teacher program because of the teacher shortage and the great need to educate our children in these perilous times. Of today.

3

Humanities 610 provided ballast for the ship of culture as it pitched and reeled in the heavy seas of real life; I lashed myself to the mast, but after hearing the siren song of grand course outlines, I cut myself free and leaned over the rail with the inside of my lip showing.

It would be oversimplifying to say that I left off teaching Humanities merely because of an experience. Such an argument is fit to be published under the title "I Was a Teen-Age Humanities Professor." I also left for fitter jobs, more money, a different life. Still, what I remember of the formal study of Truth and Beauty, for advanced credit in education, is a great confusion of generalities, committees, conferences, audio-visual importunities, and poor contact. "Contact!" cried the desperate deans and chairmen, like radio operators in ancient war movies. And much, much discussion of how to get through to the students. How to get through? Miss Adams and Mr. Gold, cab driver and Thomas Hobbes, policemen and the faceless student who paused an instant for a dime for the telephone—we all have to discover how relevant we are to each other. Or do we *have* to? No, we can merely perish, shot down like mad dogs or diminished into time with no more than a glimpse of the light.

Words fade; our experience does not touch; we make do with babble and time-serving. We need to learn the meaning of words, the meaning of the reality those words refer to; we must clasp reality close. We cannot flirt forever, brown-nosing or brow-beating. We must act and build out of our own spirits. How? How? We continually need a new politics, new cities, new marriages and families, new ways of work and leisure. We also need the fine old ways. For me, the primitive appeal to pleasure and pain of writing stories is a possible action, is the way in and out again, as teaching was not. As a teacher, I caught my students too late and only at the top of their heads, at the raw point of pride and ambition, and I had not enough love and pressure as a teacher to open the way through their intentions to the common humanity which remains locked within. As a writer, I could hope to hit them in their bodies and needs, where lusts and ideals were murkily nurtured together, calling to the prime fears and joys directly, rising with them from the truths of innocence into the truths of experience.

The peculiar combination of ignorance and jadedness built into most institutions is a desperate parody of personal innocence, personal experience. Nevertheless, education, which means a drawing out—even formal education, a formal drawing out—is a variety of experience, and experience is the only evidence we have. After evidence comes our thinking upon it. Do the scientists, secreting their honey in distant hives, hear the barking of the black dog which follows them? Will the politicians accept the lead of life, or will they insist on a grade of B in Power and Dominion over a doomed race? We need to give proper answers to the proper questions. I would like for myself and everyone else to have more experience of the humanities.

Particular life is still the best map to truth. When we search our hearts and strip our pretenses, we all know this. Particular life—we know only what we *know*. Therefore the policemen stay with me: I have learned to despise most authority. The cab driver remains in his sick bleeding: pity for the fallen and helpless. And I think of Clotilda Adams in her power and weakness; like the cops, she has an authority of stupidity; like the victim of an accident, she is fallen and helpless. But someplace, since we persist in our cold joke against the ideal of democracy, the cops still have the right to push people around, Clotilda is leading children in the Pledge of Allegiance. We must find a way to teach better and to learn.

IV. CRISIS AND
NEW SPIRIT

The Future of the Humanities in General Education

I. A. RICHARDS
(1893–   )

The Meaning of Meaning (with C. K. Ogden), 1923
Principles of Literary Criticism, 1924
Practical Criticism, 1929

IVOR ARMSTRONG RICHARDS was born in England and educated at Cambridge, but has taught throughout the world, and has since 1944 been a Professor at Harvard, where he initiated the courses in General Education that have replaced more traditional work in Freshman Composition. He has pioneered in the development of new methods for teaching foreign languages, was one of the inventors of Basic English, and has helped revolutionize techniques for introducing students to the study of literature. He is a founding father of the school of close textual analysis of poetry known as "The New Criticism." He has, however, not been content to look back on past achievements, but is presently concerned with the possibility of bringing to education the techniques of modern mass communications.

> Even in that certain hour before the fall,
> Unless men please they are not heard at all.
> *The Fabulists*

AMONG THE GUESTS AT THE CONFERENCE ON THE HUMANISTIC Tradition in the Century Ahead, which formed part of the Bicentennial Celebration at Princeton last fall, were men and women with good claim to speak with authority—and still more with responsibility—for their subject. The occasion was felt to be

Reprinted from *Speculative Instruments,* by I. A. Richards by permission of the University of Chicago Press. Copyright, 1947, 1955 by the University of Chicago.

challenging. This conference had been preceded by one on nuclear physics and another on the social sciences; and the skilful planners of our programme arranged that we should be aware of this. It was hardly possible throughout the discussion not to wonder where—in the balance of forces that are shaping the future—the humanities did come in. Latish in our deliberations, somebody, perhaps unkindly, said that we had been talking a lot about our traditions. He questioned whether the physicists or the social scientists had said much about their tradition. He thought they were more likely to have discussed their *programmes*. The audience looked, it seemed to me, somewhat uncomfortable at that. But indeed all to whom the humanities matter may well feel uncomfortable—extremely uncomfortable, if not indeed distressed and alarmed—about what is happening and *not* happening in the humanities at present. And they matter—by definition as well as in fact—to every man, woman, or child who aspires to become or remain a human being.

The Conference on the Humanistic Tradition in the Century Ahead is one source of the following remarks. Another which should be mentioned is the course on Homer, the Old Testament and Plato as Sources of Our Common Thought which I am giving at the moment as part of the experiments under way at Harvard towards "General Education in a Free Society." The reflections thus prompted sum up to this. The antinomies focused in that title are very far from being resolved, anywhere or by anyone, either in theory or in practice. Certainly reverence and regard for famous books and a backward-looking trust that all will somehow yet be well are, as these very books might teach, an insufficient equipment with which to meet what does seem to be ahead. Conservatism, in a phrase, must continue to be revolutionary in its technique.

In the last hundred years the human race has multiplied threefold. In 1840 there were some 700 millions of us; now we are more than 2,200 millions. In the next fifty years there will be a further and still more critical increase—unless the worst happens meanwhile. Too much reflective attention cannot be given to this fact. It is far more relevant to the problems of our age—and especially to the future of the humanities—than has yet been generally realized. Quantitative factors, unless technique is developed in commensurate degree, can settle qualitative possibilities— disastrously.

Another new fact, even newer and more momentous, is equally relevant, though it is not so easy to state. *Minds have become more exposed than ever before.* (If any point deserves italics, this does.) And this exposure too is undergoing explosive increase. Mental and moral communications, within each culture and be- tween cultures, have suddenly expanded beyond anyone's power to foresee the consequences. The agencies at work—with one ex- ception—hardly need more than mention. They are mass educa- tion, with its stress on verbal or nominal literacy, motion pictures, radio, television, modern advertising, and—here is the exception —modern scholarship. These are the new forces which already expose every urbanized mind to a range and variety and prom- iscuity of contacts unparalleled in history. And this is but begin- ning. Already some of the effects are showing. It would not per- haps be a culpable exaggeration to suggest that this expansion of our spiritual communications—and the power of minds to in- fluence other minds which goes with it—has already made two wars of a world scale possible. There will at least be no doubt that this new mental exposure makes immense changes necessary in our conceptions of what the humanities have to do and how they can do it. Let us take a brief look at these agencies in action.

Mass education is of course our hope—our one hope, maybe. But in so far as it must use classrooms, how are we to get teachers able to give their pupils any power to select from among the in- fluences to which they become ever more open? Present economic and social conditions repel almost all who might be capable of doing so, and teaching conditions frustrate those whose imagina- tion and devotion still make them enter the profession. And through the decline of the family and for a thousand other well- known reasons there is now incomparably more for the teacher to do. The humanities, being the hardest things to teach, suffer most. They are the hardest to teach because wisdom, which they exist to cultivate, cannot be cut and dried. Much in other subjects can.

Correspondingly the preparation of a teacher in the humanities is the hardest of all—which brings me to the not, as yet, sufficiently vexed topic of modern specialized scholarship. I have to explain its appearance in my list of disruptive agencies threatening the wholeness of present and future minds.

Modern scholarship is a fearful and wonderful as well as an unprecedented thing. It is unprecedented, I believe, in character as well as in scale, though I would listen eagerly to a modern scholar who was interested in just this historical question. Like so much else which should give us pause, modern scholarship is the product of admirably ingenious innovations in technique, on which Thamus' words to Theuth (*Phaedrus,* 275) are to the point: "Most ingenious Theuth, one man has the ability to beget an art, another to estimate the good or harm it will do to those who are to use it." The words apply equally to the ingenious doings of the nuclear physicists and to all inventions which may threaten us with nuclear fission of our minds. In scholarly technique the innovations are the modern dictionary, the book index, bibliography, the specialized journal, and the museum. Most of them seem to be eighteenth-century inventions. At any rate, as they affect us today they are recent. And it is relevant to note that Chinese scholarship only admitted an index to a book within the memory of those still living: an index being considered a subversive thing which would lead to superficiality and to disrespect for the teacher's authority—grounded on long and deep familiarity with a corpus rather than on quick glances at references.

However this may be, modern scholarship certainly requires ever more intensive and prolonged training of a sort which is of hardly any value to a teacher in general education. It is training in the administration of a vast body, an illimitable proliferation rather, of facts, comments, opinions, and mere phrases, too extensive and diverse to form, in any mind not of a very rare order, any coherent, much less any directing or confirming, view of essential human purpose. Moreover, since this proliferation proceeds geometrically, training in its administration, as we well know, becomes departmentalized, then subdepartmentalized, and scholarship, in so far as it is *that,* becomes less and less useful to a teacher. It may fit him to continue as a specialized researcher —within "areas" or on "points" with no known relevance to any side of the world crisis. It quite certainly does not give him what he needs as a teacher of the humanities—reasonably rich and considered views of a person's human relations to other persons. Worse still, it is intensive distraction from the hard essential task of maturing such views. Worst of all, this training has now become professional qualification offered competitively by rival institutions.

I would not be misunderstood here. This recent achievement of a method by which scholarship becomes accumulative and responsible to a controlled record is one of the glories of our age. It ranks with the partly parallel achievements in mathematics and experimental inquiry. Together with them it holds our infinite promise to man, and must go on. But, for the time being, as with physics, biology, and psychology (on which last I touch later) its present dangers rather than its remote promises should concern us most. It is preventing us from supplying our greatest need— teachers able to help humanity to remain humane.

Literature—a deep enough *and leisurely enough* familiarity with what the best minds have thought and felt about people— used to produce such teachers. Modern scholarship positively gets in the way. The critical apparatus of approach to the great things keeps them from their would-be student. He is daunted incessantly by the thought that somewhere there is something which would, if he only knew it, help him to understand better. He comes to distrust the direct approach, and lives in an unhealthy terror of his ignorance—which will anyhow for all men and to time's end be infinite. He forgets that we do not help ourselves or others by collecting more facts and comments, but by understanding more clearly our problems and theirs. We learn best to do this by reflecting upon such problems and by seeing them through the eyes of the best minds. So we lose our best teachers.

To turn now to mass media. Radio, TV and the screen might provide some remedy for this loss. It is possible to believe, sometimes, that they could become the instruments of our salvation. But we will agree, without difficulty, that they are not that now —for well-known and chiefly technical reasons. Radio, TV and the screen propagate most successfully the most superficial, the most facile, and the least educating elements of a culture. This is partly because, as programmes, they have to *go on*. They have

to change, every fifteen minutes or twice weekly. There is no time
for what they present to be deeply pondered, thought over, returned to and considered afresh. Therefore, it rarely is worth
such reconsideration. But in every culture it has been the things
which received the most lasting and recurrent attention—the
books re-read again and again, the stories and sayings known and
familiar from infancy to old age, the rites repeated throughout
a lifetime, the perennial monuments, the enduring ideas, the
constant aesthetic institutions—which have done the most part
of the work of the humanities. Mass media, at present, replace
such continuous shaping forces by an incessantly shifting play of
light and confusing impacts. It is not surprising that they are of
little help in seeing life steadily and seeing it whole.

For these and other reasons, just when the humanities are more
than ever needed and at a decisive turn of human fate, they
are becoming through multifarious distraction—ranging from
the movie to the graduate school—inoperative and ineffective.
But what is this turn of fate? It is the juncture, at last, of the
sciences with the humanities. A juncture is a meeting together, a
convergence of different principles into one event; it is also a
crisis. What are meeting now head on are two unreconciled ways
of conceiving man and his good and how to pursue it. Both wish
him well, but they differ radically as to how he can be helped.
The physical and social sciences alike—being applications of
methods of observation and calculation—conceive men as units
subject to forces playing upon them *from without*. A man is a
complex unit, no doubt—the psychologist is the last man to
overlook this—but differences between men are, for science, to
be accounted for in terms of past influences (genes, prenatal supply, early nurture, education, etc.) and present conditions. Any
inquiry based upon experimentation and comparison develops
such a conception; it abstracts, in its own defence, from other
aspects. Thus a man's desires and opinions and beliefs, the
springs of his action and sources of his triumphs or sufferings,
are likewise, for science, to be studied from without. If they are
investigable at all by science, they must be public and they must
be manipulatable; that is the methodical crux. It is the modes of
such manipulation and the resultant behaviour which are really

being studied. To the psychologist education is control of *behaviour*. Not unnaturally, therefore, mass influence techniques, by which groups in Germany, Japan, and elsewhere have controlled the behaviour of vast masses of population (though the behaviour was unfortunate), have come to offer—to better hands, no doubt—alluring prospects of doing man good even against his will.

In contrast, the humanities pin a faith, which is experimentally still ungrounded, on the ideal autonomy of the individual man. He is happiest who is least able to be changed from without, as Socrates averred (*Republic*, 381). Man is not a thing to be pushed about, however kindly or beneficently. He is a spirit who learns —not as a slave learns (*Republic*, 536E), but by exercising the freedom which is his being.

I should illustrate this opposition. I may do so best by an extract from page 18 of *Who Shall Be Educated?*, by Lloyd Warner and R. J. Havighurst, though the authors would, I hope, be horrified by the implications I am about to find in their sentences.

We will look at our American social system, which largely controls our behaviour, much as we would at a complex maze in which animals learn to behave. In such a system we must be taught to learn our way around as we grow up if we are to live normal lives and to behave normally as adults. This is true for all the Tom Browns, Katherine Greens, and Joe Sienkowitzes of our society. Growing up consists in learning how to behave, and learning how to behave means acquiring the proper responses to the batteries of social stimuli which compose our social order.

It is the last sentence to which I would draw most attention. Should "learning how to behave" mean anything like that? To a humanist (or a Platonist) it should mean learning the *what's* and *why's* of human good—what man's duties and responsibilities and his right relations to his fellows are, and learning how to stick to them under the terrible pressures of pleasure and pain—stronger than any lye or potash (*Republic*, 430)—which for ever try to force us from them. We only learn through understanding the differences and connections between things. It is possible, no doubt, to load the phrase "acquiring the proper responses" with all this moral teaching. If we do so, of course, all is well! And I will only have been expounding for my authors their full intention. But is that what the sentence suggests? Does it not much rather suggest some smooth adjustment to and conformity with current fashions in morals, a facile acquiescence in socially acceptable mass-circulated doctrine?

Speaking of fashions, we need be no very deep students of social science to know that the heaviest massed "batteries of social stimuli" directed upon young and old today are the ads. I listed advertisements among the disruptive agencies to which minds are now more exposed than ever before. It seems agreed that Goebbels and his gang learnt much from American advertising techniques. Even though we believe in the virtues of immunization to such attacks, we will do well to consider more seriously than is customary what the ads may be doing today to the humanities. Consider Christmas for a moment.

> O never rudely will I blame his faith
> In the might of stars and angels

wrote Coleridge. But how about using the might of stars and angels in an attempt to sell one's wares? What's wrong about that? On a page of both stars and angels, under a caption: "*And the Angels bring . . .*" we look to see what they do bring, and read, "*Heavenly gift robes and lingerie along the moon-lit trail leading to our star-studded Christmas collection . . .* LUCKY STAR, *above left . . . is all dressed up to go lounging in a cherubic rayon crepe . . . Radelle Constellation . . . shining brightly on the angel's arm, dream gown of celestial rayon . . . matching figure-moulding slip for heavenly* array . . . ," not to mention "*panties that lovely women prefer to wear behind the* 'seens,' " and lastly, that no insult should be lacking, "MOONLIGHT MADONNA GOWN!" To attend for a second seriously to such exploits will make one wonder if he has lost his sense of humour. But it is more unwise never to reflect upon what an incessant exposure to this sort of thing may be doing to us, if only to the language which channels our inheritance. I have shown this ad to a meeting of teachers of English. My chairman, a superintendent of secondary schools in a great city, took a little umbrage. "Didn't it at least show," he asked, "that the writer had profited by a sound grounding in the classics?" He seemed to think this was a proper outcome of a literary education.

We fail, I think, to realize how omnipresent these degradations are, or how much they may blur and disable the spiritual organs they play with and for what mean purposes. Was so much so skilfully designed to enfeeble and betray human judgment over directed on a previous generation? We need men inspired by Irving Babbitt's noble and tireless scorn to go on pointing to them. I will add but two examples:

In my first our hero is sitting—drinking his beer—in his over-stuffed chair, his dog at his feet, the radio on, his floor strewn with papers whose headlines read, "Cities Bombed," "Famine," "Air Raids." The paper still in his hand says, "Invasion!" Under the picture comes:

IN A WORLD OF STRIFE

THERE'S PEACE IN BEER

In these bewildering times, where can a man turn to replenish the wells of his courage . . . to repair the walls of his faith?

Courage—if you please! Faith—I ask you! Is it surprising that such great words as these have become suspect: so that when people hear or see them they assume they are being got at? Where these words are no longer understood, men no longer understand themselves.

My second: Edison Company placarding the subways in war-time with a bright-windowed villa thus legended: *"In a World of Darkness be thankful for the Light Within"* or some such words. The light within—meaning their products! The strange and dismaying thing about all this is that to those responsible it will be the idea that there is anything objectionable here which will be strange. For this is not blasphemy. Would that it were! It is trivialization, which is truly dangerous. Blasphemy provokes. The trivialized mind is supine, at the mercy of slick manipulators. The outcome can be generations of dehumanized social animals in place of self-controlled, self-judging, self-ruling men and women.

Manipulation and exploitation—for the benefit of the operator, or of the subject—that is the chief danger man incurs through the decline of the humanities. The humanities are his defence against emotional bamboozlement and misdirection of the will. The student of science—without the support of that which has been traditionally carried by literature, the arts and philosophy—is unprotected; the main doctrines and positions which keep man humane are insusceptible, at present, to scientific proof. Present-day science, in fact, like dialectic in Plato's day (*Republic,* 539) or popular philosophizing in pre-Nazi Germany, tends to break them down. Without a vigorous and widespread upkeep of the humanities every country comes to be populated chiefly with "supposititious sons" (*Republic,* 538), And science in the absence of the traditional communal loyalties can only supply their lack by indoctrination in what will probably be (as the samples run so far) nationalistic myths. Dangers due to new weapons will heighten men's susceptibility to such doctrines and also the temptation to teach them. Thus a very gloomy prospect looms up—deriving radically both from the decay of the humanities and from the exuberant vitality of the applied sciences.

It is not, however, the probability of more, and far more destructive, wars which most alarms a humanist. Circumstances are today too easily imaginable in which planetary disintegration would be a welcome release. What is daunting is the possibility that man may be permanently warped through these tensions— that the ideals which made him human may be destroyed—*before* their work can be taken over by science. For that science—or something into which science, given time and education by the humanities, can develop—is the inheritor of their task seems to me a tenet that no true humanist, remembering Book VII of his *Republic,* can yield, any more than he can truly, as a humanist, despair of man.

The Crumbling Ivory Tower

LESLIE A. FIEDLER
(1917–   )

An End to Innocence, 1955
Love and Death in the American Novel, 1960
No! In Thunder, 1960
The Second Stone, 1963

LESLIE FIEDLER has in recent years come to be known as a writer of fiction, poetry, and especially of polemical essays dealing with literature, politics and religion. What he has had to say on these subjects has not always produced assent, but it has always sparked fruitful controversy. His views on the nature of American literature, in particular, have caused even those who most disagree with him to see that subject in a new light. Mr. Fiedler is, however, primarily a teacher, who, since his education at New York University, Wisconsin and Harvard, has been a Professor of English at Montana State University, and has lectured at colleges and schools all over America, Europe and the Middle East. He has occasionally paused long enough to ponder the meaning of his experience in teaching, as the essay below attests.

BEFORE BEGINNING WHAT MUST BE IN THE END A RATHER MELANCHOLY account of higher education in the United States, I should like to remind myself of the virtues implicit in a system which I find myself and my more congenial colleagues continuing to foster and deplore with almost equal vigor. The chief of these virtues is the essentially American notion, at once absurd and noble (absurd perhaps, noble certainly), that more and more young people—eventually the majority of our youth—can profitably be exposed to four years of education beyond the primary and high school level; indeed, that such a majority must, for the

Reprinted from *Heights Daily News,* New York University, and the *New Leader.*

health of the whole community, be so exposed. It would be easy
to comment cynically that the real intent of American society is
not so much to educate its young for a total of 16 or 17 or 18
years (the term is lengthened at both ends, kindergarten and pre-
kindergarten as well as post-secondary) as to keep them for an
ever-growing period off the labor market and the streets and out
of the homes in which they begin and those in which they are
destined to end: to provide an artificially prolonged adolescence
for all—a paradisal state between infantile dependency and full
maturity—whose extent depends not on biology but on the
economics of our affluent society.

There is nothing shameful about all this. Adolescence is a luxury item produced late in evolutionary time, and it is neither
surprising nor reprehensible that Americans are proud of being
able to provide it in larger amounts than any other people at any
other moment of history. We want more for our adolescents,
however, than mere escape from the restrictions of the family and
the demands of the market-place; we should like them, in that
leisure which the labor and luck of their ancestors has brought,
to acquire skills, talents, bodies of knowledge, practical and esoteric, even the capacity for certain refined pleasures—so that
finally they will not only be better producers and earners (able
to provide for their children still more leisure) but less anxious
and bored than their parents.

That American society does not quite know how to do this is
disheartening but not astonishing. What *is* astonishing is that
the society is willing to keep paying for attempts at accomplishing
what it never quite understands or knows it really wants, and
that in the course of doing so it has provided, for the few able
to profit, an asylum from its own worst pressures, a community
within the larger community dedicated, unlike its parent (though
how tenuously, how approximately only those within realize), to
a respect for fact and a hunger for freedom—both of which are
subversive in the truest and best sense, subversive of all systems
of political compromise and social accommodation. In a world
where "service" is universally demanded, the universities alone
are licensed to subvert; though naturally the language in which
this patent is expressed is far from frank or even lucid. To "free

the mind" or "liberate the spirit," these are the conventional names for the kind of education, the dangerous enterprise to which our colleges are pledged.

Understandably enough, the end of liberation by which the academic subcommunity lives is betrayed a hundred times each day, out of timidity, confusion or simple weariness; but nonetheless it survives the weakness of its proponents as well as the strength of its opponents. The bitterest self-criticism of professors arises out of their sense of having failed this end, and the attacks of their enemies are directed at their continuing resolve to pursue it. Certain men outside the academies, to whom freedom and intelligence seem equally threatening, can never remember, perhaps never knew, why certain others inside have been granted the legal right (outward symbol of a deeper inward privilege) of working only nine months a year, with class schedules of nine or 10 or 12 hours a week. To explain that men within the university, (ideally, at least) never cease to work during their waking hours, that for them no line can be drawn between pleasure and paid performance, between self-indulgence and social labor, would be to aggravate misunderstanding in a world where most adults endure a perpetual disjunction between what they want and what they do that ends by making their jobs tedious and their leisure unprofitable.

Yet our society not merely permits but continuously subsidizes its universities and colleges. Though, on the one hand it must whip itself on in the effort with scare-talk about Russia and the race for survival, and on the other, it demands payment for its minor economic sacrifices by insisting that higher education provide certain lower forms of entertainment: football and basketball games, parades with floats, public debates, choral performances of popular songs, dramatic representations of mediocre Broadway plays, inspirational talks at Rotary and Ladies Clubs, competitions to choose state representatives for the Miss America Contest, summer schools and writers conferences—not all worthless, to be sure, but all smacking somehow of the minstrel show and the gladiatorial combat. After all, entertainment is "service" more clearly than scholarship or criticism or art; and for their general exemption from "service," the universities must be will-

ing to make occasional forays into the world of the socially useful
or delightful, to please those who foot the bill. In the end, however, such incidental services as higher education provides tend
to be thought of first in the minds of administrators and then in
those of the faculties themselves, not merely as a price paid for
certain privileges, but as an end, even the end of the whole
higher educational system.

To win games begins to matter, to draw large audiences and
send them away pleased, to accumulate cups and trophies, to book
more and more celebrities and to produce them, to "cover" more
and more meetings of even more disparate organizations, to sing,
fiddle, recite, win friends, grant M.A.'s in education and diplomas
in creative writing—or, on a higher level of "service," to contribute to the campaign efforts of presidential candidates, to sit
on cabinets and boards, to help win the cold war. Beside such
public and publicized efforts, other academic objectives, more
central and more important, begin to seem pretty pale: the private pursuit of perhaps useless facts, the unspectacular triumph
over one's own limitations and prejudices, the lonely experience
of really reading a poem, looking at a picture, or following a
mathematical proof. Finally the difference between professor
and Rotarian, citizen of the Republic of Letters and booster for
Our Town, grows slighter and slighter; and the university threat-
ens to become merely one more Service Club, meeting five days
a week for classes instead of once for lunch. The same man finds
no difficulty in being at once a professor of physics, a Lion, an
Elk and a Kiwanian—beyond remembering his lunch dates.

The university can endure any indignity but the collapse of
the values that make it an independent and dissenting community
in the greater world; it can surmount even the non-intellectual-
ism (always on the verge of becoming outright anti-intellectualism) which causes one professor to sneer at another for being too
"brilliant" and one student to snub another for answering too
often and too intelligently in class. It can persist despite the failure of most schools in the United States to define their own
ends, their own reason for being, despite the contemptuous refusal almost everywhere to wrestle with the idea of the university
itself. It can continue somehow to function though administrators

exhaust themselves in politicking and the pursuit of funds, under-graduates falsify themselves in the wrongheaded effort to become "well-rounded," graduates collaborate in their own desiccation and teachers expend their spirit in producing the trivial, ill-written commentaries on commentaries by which they earn their promotions. The bill of particulars is not hard to compile. Every-where the same replacement of humanistically trained admin-istrators by the manipulators of statistics and IBM machines; everywhere professors confronted by the necessity of grading with a set of five or six symbols the worth of experiences unmeasurable except at the end of man's life and before the Bar of Heaven; everywhere the chaos of curricula determined by petty inter-departmental bickering and antiquated theories of culture no one troubles to remember; everywhere the shameless illiteracy of professional "specialists" oblivious to all but the "literature" of their narrow fields.

It is difficult to say which is more irksome, the petty harass-ments (the splitting of the day into 50-minute segments signaled by bells, and the Pavlovian cutting off of discussion at such sig-nals; the polite hostility of the average student to learning and his eagerness to dissipate his meager spirit in a host of activities; the hypocrisy implicit in student "social regulations" concerning drinking, hours and sex, and the more general hypocrisy standard between faculty and students who pretend to be engaged in a common enterprise which neither could define to the satisfaction of the other), or the major cultural catastrophes (the general decay of language, for instance, manifested on the one hand by the spread inside the university of bureaucratic jargon with the con-sequent breakdown of communication between administration and faculty, left with no living common tongue in which to medi-ate their conflict of interests; and represented on the other by the difficulty of convincing students, conditioned by editorials and advertisements, that the function of words is to illuminate rather than misrepresent).

And how finally can one tell the difference between what is petty and what is major in the tragi-comedy of academic life? What is one to make, for instance, of a world in which what are called "struggles for academic freedom" turn out to be ritualized quarrels between supporters of yesterday's liberalism and defenders of day-before-yesterday's whiggery or reaction; and where, meanwhile, smugness and timidity are hailed as sweet reason by a generation brought up to distrust generalization and unguarded enthusiasm? And how does one find in any event time and space for such distinctions when he is buffeted by the sheer pressure of numbers, numbers, numbers—as the whole system bloats and strains its seams? And yet the universities do not go down, their very anarchy providing unsuspected islands on which teacher and student can confront each other over the pages of a book which decades of earnest ineptitude have not managed to kill.

Even the continued immoderate growth of the student population will not prove fatal to higher education unless the faculty is led to believe not merely that it is (somehow) better to educate more but that to educate more is (in itself and without further qualification) better. Even the flooding of the teaching profession by cautious status-seekers ready to settle for a minimum sort of security will not undermine our colleges and universities unless such status-seekers are led to believe not merely that higher wages would be good to have but that such higher wages are a sole and sufficient prerequisite for good teaching.

There is, in fact, a widespread movement these days among trustees, boards of education, state legislators, college presidents and some faculty members to "solve" the problem of higher enrollments by granting ever greater salaries to relatively fewer teachers; so that, though classes become more and more unwieldly, less and less efficiently taught, the troubled conscience of the instructor, aware that his assignments grow shorter and his reading of them more perfunctory as the teacher-student ratio climbs toward 1:20, can console himself with the books and records he can buy, the trips abroad he can take as his pay goes up. And the students? Whatever nagging sense of guilt toward them survives a rapidly rising standard of living can be allayed by giving speeches on "service" to graduating high school seniors and returning alumni.

I sat recently through a series of interviews of prospective university teachers, many of whom were asked what had determined their choice of so odd a vocation. Most of them answered, alas, that they dreamed of "service to mankind" or "contributing to the march of humanity" or "making a maximum contribution to society." One such servant of mankind, I recall, spoke of having a hard time deciding whether he was called to dentistry or teaching, confessed that he remained still a little uncertain about whether cleaning teeth or giving instruction in freshman aglebra was in fact a greater "service." But finally a single candidate appeared who said in response to the question, "My God, they pay you for *reading*, for—for doing what you want to do anyway!" It is in him and in the surviving few like him that I invest my diminishing hopes for my own profession; for in the end I discover that my notion of the proper motto for a university is not the *Perstare et praestare* of my alma mater but the slogan which Rabelais tells us was inscribed over the gates of the Abbey of Thélème: *Fais ce que voudras,* do what you will. If there is a future for the American university, it lies in the pursuit not of "service" but of freedom: the identity—under the auspices of the intelligence—of action and will.

The College of Liberal Arts and Sciences

ARTHUR EUGENE BESTOR
(1908–   )

Education and Reform at New Harmony, 1948
Backwoods Utopias, 1950
Educational Wastelands, 1953
The Restoration of Learning, 1955

ARTHUR BESTOR, educated at Yale, first made his reputation as an American historian, winning recognition for his efforts in this field both at home and in England. In the late forties and in the fifties, however, the rapid rise in school enrollments led him to switch his attention to the educational situation in colleges and high schools. His displeasure at that situation he expressed in the vigorous polemic, *Educational Wastelands*. In 1956, he helped create the Council for Basic Education, an organization devoted to strengthening the study of basic subjects like English, mathematics, science, history and foreign languages.

THE FOUR-YEAR LIBERAL-ARTS COLLEGE IS A DISTINCTIVE FEATURE OF the English and the American educational systems, and it has made a distinctive contribution to the public life of Great Britain and the United States. The nature of the liberal-Arts college ought to be better understood than it is, for we are in danger of losing a uniquely precious part of our educational heritage through sheer inattention to its essential characteristics.

To compare the educational systems of different countries accurately is an exceedingly difficult task, and to offer generalizations concerning their theoretical (let alone their actual) structure is a rash proceeding. Nevertheless, such a generalization must be hazarded here. The actual standards and performance of the educational systems of other countries need not be examined at this time. Our present concern is with the theoretical relationship between secondary and higher education, or, more accurately, the way in which responsibility for secondary and higher education is theoretically apportioned among institutions of different levels. And, for purposes of this discussion, we are interested only in the student who proceeds through all the levels.

Secondary education, for such a student, is conceived of in all countries (if we except some of the American heresies that I have already discussed) as rigorous training in the fundamentals of the various fields of learning—languages, sciences, mathematics, history, and the rest. Secondary-school instruction differs from higher education (in the theory of most systems) in that it is carried out methodically, in a pattern of courses that are largely prescribed, with relatively little expectation that the student will engage in independent, wide-ranging investigations of his own. At the opposite pole is the educational scheme of the Continental university, and of those portions of English and American universities which are not embraced within the undergraduate college. University work, in this sense, is highly specialized. It is concerned with training for research or for one of the learned professions. Independent reading and original investigation are generally more important than course work. Students are largely on their own. The schoolmaster is gone, and in his place is the professor, interested not in what the student does day by day, but in the results he can demonstrate at the end of his academic career through examinations and a written thesis.

Here are two diametrically opposed educational procedures. On the Continent of Europe the student proceeds directly from the first to the second. Secondary education (in the *Gymnasium* or *lycée*) is more prolonged than with us; university work is from the beginning more independent and more specialized. The undergraduate college of England and America is interpolated, as it were, into this scheme. It is a transitional institution, in the sense that it partakes of the qualities of both the secondary school and the univerity, and it covers the years that on the Continent are divided between the two.

But the liberal-arts college is a great deal more than a mere transitional institution. It has a unique character of its own. And its distinctive features have had much to do, I am convinced, with producing among the educated classes of the United States (as also of England) the kind of mutual understanding that underlies our success in maintaining national unity and harmony in the midst of social and political changes as drastic as those that have rent the societies of Continental Europe apart.

What characteristics of the liberal-arts college can justify such a sweeping assertion? To put the matter simply, the liberal-arts college permits students to complete their fundamental intellectual training in an atmosphere of greater freedom than the secondary school can allow. And in the liberal-arts college, students move gradually toward specialization, mingling the while and exchanging ideas with comrades whose intellectual paths are beginning to diverge. A sense of sharing in a common intellectual life is produced by the liberal-arts college as it is not produced by any institution in the Continental educational system.

The secondary school, of course, provides a unity of background, but this is an enforced and even regimented unity. When freedom of choice is suddenly granted, in the Continental university, the sense of unity in intellectual life disappears in the pursuit of intensively specialized scholarly and professional training. Under this system, unity is associated with intellectual immaturity; mature intellectual life is compartmentalized, divided, self-consciously specialized. The English and American conception is different. As students approach intellectual maturity, the methodical preceptorial methods of the schoolroom are gradually relaxed, and a study of the fundamental intellectual disciplines is continued under conditions of freedom and individual responsibility that approximate those of the university. A free exchange of ideas among fellow students, at the level of intellectual maturity, increases and is encouraged. And as these students progress toward greater specialization, they explore among themselves the interrelations between their various fields, thus cultivating the habit of discussion and mutual understanding. They are preparing themselves for the kind of public life in which a fundamental unity of purpose and principle underlies even the most striking differences, thus permitting honest compromise. The liberal-arts college exemplifies, and prepares for the realization of, the motto inscribed upon our Great Seal: *E pluribus unum.*

Theory of course is very imperfectly carried out in practice. The contrasts I have made are admittedly too sharp, and the generalizations too sweeping. Nevertheless they help to make clear, I believe, the features of liberal education which we need to safeguard and strengthen in our colleges, if these are to serve, as they have served in the past, as the bulwarks of enlightened, harmonious, democratic public life.

The ideal of the college of liberal arts and sciences is to raise up a body of men and women who understand in common the fundamentals of intellectual life in its various branches, and who are able to apply to their own problems not one, but a choice of powerful intellectual techniques over which they have achieved some measure of disciplined control. The crucial problem is how to encourage young men and women to range freely over the various fields of knowledge and yet to maintain that unified comprehension which will enable them to understand and cooperate in one another's intellectual pursuits.

The kind of unity we require in intellectual life is the kind that comes when educated men are able to command several, not merely one, of the distinctive ways of thinking that are central in the modern world. There is no genuine unity of intellectual life if men have merely learned the same sets of facts from so-called "subject-matter" fields. There is merely a specious unity if men have been taught to think in their respective disciplines alone and have been offered merely a smattering of information *about* other ways of thinking. And there is only a narrow and shackled unity if one way of thinking has been exalted above all others and made the *sine qua non* of education.[1]

Men need to know a fair number of the crucial ways of thinking upon which modern intellectual life is based. This implies

---

1. Despite its many strong points, the so-called "great books" program seems to me at fault in this respect. It tends to emphasize dialectical argument at the expense of all those intellectual processes that call upon men to sift multifarious evidence and draw conclusions from it.

that the truly distinctive ways of thinking are reasonably limited in number, and that there is a recognizable hierarchy of importance among them. The implications of this must be squarely faced. Educational reform must begin with a courageous assertion that all the various subjects and disciplines in the curriculum are *not* of equal value. Some disciplines are fundamental, in the sense that they represent essential ways of thinking, which can be generalized and applied to a wide range of intellectual problems. Other disciplines, though equal in intellectual potency, are somewhat less central to the purposes of liberal education, either because they can be studied only after the fundamental disciplines are mastered, or because they represent highly specialized intellectual techniques, restricted in their range of applicability. Other courses in the modern curriculum do not represent disciplines at all, but offer professional preparation, or training in mechanical skills, or helpful hints on vocational and personal matters. Still other courses, alas, offer nothing at all, save collections of more or less interesting facts, opinions, or fallacies.

When we have the courage to specify which disciplines belong in the first category—that is, which ones are truly fundamental—then, and only then, can we begin to restore intellectual unity to the curricula of our schools and colleges. The decision may not be as difficult as it seems, for we are talking about disciplines, or ways of thinking, not about "subject-matter" fields. The basically different ways of thinking are few compared with the number of factual areas within which they can be applied. The method of controlled experimentation, for example, is one sort of disciplined thinking, and it underlies several different physical sciences. Mathematics is another distinctive way of thinking, historical investigation is a third, philosophical criticism a fourth. One can go on, but one cannot go on far without exhausting the ways of thinking that are genuinely fundamental, that are clearly distinctive, and that are susceptible of being introduced at the elementary- or high-school level and carried forward systematically in college. All choices have something of the arbitrary about them, but a decision that certain disciplines are fundamental and others not can be made on reasonable and judicious grounds.

Once these premises are accepted—and not merely accepted,

but believed with the kind of conviction that will lead to action
—then some plan for genuinely liberal education appropriate to
the mid-twentieth century becomes possible. Such a plan must
provide for specialization. It must also establish standards and
prerequisites that will permit an orderly progress from introductory to advanced work. It must consider the nature of the courses
that are best adapted to the instruction of the non-specialist. It
must develop a philosophy for guiding the student in his quest
for intellectual breadth. And it must set up a final test for
achievement in terms of knowledge and skill acquired, not of
credits accumulated. These various points will be taken up in
order in the remainder of this chapter.

Intellectual training is so laborious and time-consuming that
it tends to become specialized education in *a* discipline rather
than liberal education in *the* disciplines. Given the complexity of
modern knowledge, a high degree of specialization is an inescapable thing. In point of fact genuine specialization is not in
itself an evil. It is false specialization that we need to fear and
avoid.

One kind of false specialization is exemplified by the man who
imagines that he will be able to solve important problems by
using only one set of mental tools. No intellectual activity is ever
so specialized that it involves only a single way of thinking. If a
specialist is to solve new problems in his own field he must be
prepared to draw upon ways of thinking that have never yet
been applied to the problem. The greater his achievement as a
specialist, the broader must be his fund of general knowledge and
the wider his acquaintance with other ways of thinking. Specialization that is false because of its narrowness is also self-defeating.
Genuine specialization always involves the careful study of related fields.

A second type of false specialization in intellectual life is more
insidious. It arises from the failure to discriminate between an
intellectual discipline defined as a way of thinking and a field of
study defined in some other way—defined, say, as the body of
practical information connected with some specified vocation.
Now, vocational training, as an earlier chapter has shown, is perfectly compatible with liberal education, but it is not the same

thing. The *liberal* part of the training for any profession or trade is the part devoted to the scientific and scholarly disciplines that underlie the profession or trade. The *vocational* or *professional* aspect of the training is something added to liberal education. It should not be reckoned a *part* of liberal education at all.

A man's vocational or professional training is necessarily specialized. The liberal education upon which it is based need not be, but if it is, the specialization that is considered part of his liberal education can only be in one of the intellectual disciplines. There is no place in genuinely liberal education for a major in journalism, or home economics, or pedagogy, even though courses in these vocational subjects may be taken as supplements to a program in liberal education.

Because both specialization and the quest for intellectual breadth are recognized aims of the liberal-arts college, a problem arises over the proper grading of courses. In his special field an upperclassman or a graduate student will be pursuing advanced courses, but at the same time he may be receiving his first introduction to some other field. American colleges customarily assign different sets of numbers to courses of different levels. This is entirely reasonable. But they usually take another step, the logic of which is utterly specious. Thinking to uphold standards, they are apt to forbid a graduate student or even an upperclassman to enroll for full credit in a course the number of which indicates that it is on the introductory level. This is absurd. Where, may one ask, should a student be introduced to a new subject if not in an introductory course?

The consequence of this mechanical way of treating advanced credit is that the student enrolls in an advanced course without knowing anything of the fundamental processes of thought involved. An advanced student in history may need to commence the study of economics as a supporting discipline, but he is likely to find that to secure full credit he must enroll in an advanced course in the subject, though he has never mastered the introductory material. Not one student does so, but scores, and the instructor is forced to adjust his teaching to the situation. He cannot assume that his students possess a common fund of knowledge in the field or a command of certain clearly defined intellectual skills of a specialized nature. The supposedly advanced course becomes partly an introductory one. The compromise is unsatisfactory to all concerned. Thoroughly prepared students do not advance in disciplined thinking as far or as fast as they should, and new students are not initiated into disciplined thinking as systematically or as thoroughly as they ought to be.

If the introductory course is a really rigorous one, there is no reason why it should not be elected for full credit by upperclassmen and graduate students. Only in this way can advanced courses become and remain truly advanced ones, and a rational system of prerequisites be maintained. The difference between an introductory course and an advanced one has almost nothing to do with the chronological age of the student or his academic status. No one can vault lightly over the difficulties involved in learning the elements of an intellectual discipline merely because he happens to be a senior or a graduate student. He may learn a little faster, it is true, but he does not learn differently. In particular, he cannot skip essential steps in a process of thought. Knowledge, after all, *is* cumulative, and intellectual processes do advance through clearly defined stages of increasing complexity.

Once the difference between introductory and advanced courses is firmly established, we can deal more intelligently with the harder question of the kind of course that a student should be offered in a discipline outside the field of his special interest and effort. What, for example, does a student majoring in the discipline of history need to know of mathematical reasoning, of scientific investigation, of philosophical cricitism, of literary expression, of aesthetic comprehension? The answer is that he needs to know the things represented by the nouns or gerunds in the phrases above—that is to say, the nature of reasoning, investigation, criticism, expression, and comprehension, as these appear in their various special forms. He does not need to know all the different lines of inquiry pursued in a given field, but he needs to know its particular way of thinking well enough to grasp its special power and applicability.

Liberal education is training in thinking. It is not the mere communication of facts. What every student—specialist or non-specialist—should gain from a course is command, even if only limited command, of the processes of thought employed in the discipline he is studying. Far less than the specialist does the student from another field need to fix in his mind a multitude of facts already discovered and verified. These facts and formulas may be necessary parts of the equipment that a specialist requires for further work in the field; hence to him they are important in themselves. To a non-specialist, however, the facts and formulas are significant as examples, as the fruits of successful inquiry, as tests of the validity of some process of reasoning. Few are so important that they must be remembered for their own sakes.

To have solved a quadratic equation is the vital thing if one wishes to grasp the nature of algebraic reasoning. Whether to memorize the general formula of solution depends entirely on one's future use for it. Similarly, to have weighed historical evidence in order to reach a conclusion and to have explored the problems of historical causality are the crucial matters. The number of specific historical facts that the student remembers is of secondary importance. Actually a student will remember a great many facts without special effort if he has really entered into the process of investigation which produced them. His score on a factual test is thus an indirect, not a direct, measure of what he has learned. It can be a fairly reliable test (if not abused by the get-rich-quick technique of factual "cramming"), because the student who has thought a lot will remember a lot, and the student who remembers nothing has probably never thought at all. Memory and disciplined thinking do go hand in hand, but we must never forget that it is the latter that really counts.

So far as "general" education is concerned, these considerations lead to a conclusion the opposite of the one ordinarily accepted. The course for the non-specialist should emphasize theoretical reasoning to an even greater extent than the course for the specialist. The latter needs to know—and hence should be drilled to remember—facts, conclusions, and formulas for which the non-specialist has little use once he has grasped the reasoning involved. In practice, colleges and universities have acted upon a contrary premise. Courses originally planned for specialists have been adapted for general students by eliminating or reducing the discussion of methodology and theory, and crowding in as much purely factual information as possible. Such courses advance neither intellectual discipline nor mutual understanding among educated men.

If this reasoning is correct, the proper introduction to each of the great areas of knowledge is a rigorous course, emphasizing intellectual processes, in one of the fundamental disciplines lying within the area. In certain fields it may be desirable to create for the non-specialist a course somewhat different in structure and emphasis from that offered to the future specialist. In the sciences, for example, it is possible that a study of crucial principles in the historical order of their discovery (as President Conant has suggested) might be more effective for the non-specialist than the study of them in the systematic order in which they need to be known by the man who is to do research in the field. Two courses, equally rigorous and equally thorough in their use of laboratory techniques, are a possibility here. Needless to say, when alternative courses are offered, there ought never to be a qualitative difference between them. Every course must discipline the mind of every student who enrolls in it. In actual fact, however, separate courses in most fields are quite unnecessary. The typical introductory course in college would serve the needs of both specialists and non-specialists more effectively if it were reorganized in such a way as to pay *more* attention than at present to methodology, to rigorous thinking, and to abstract theory. If, however, classes for non-specialists seem necessary, the instructors in charge should eschew the encyclopedic approach, should select with care the topics that exemplify basic methodological and theoretical questions, and should concentrate upon making perfectly clear the kinds of thinking involved.[2]

Courses alone, even though properly organized for the non-specialist, will not guarantee breadth of intellectual understanding. A plan of study outside the field of specialization is needed.

---

2. The principles I have in mind are admirably exemplified by the series of *Select Problems in Historical Interpretation* prepared for use in undergraduate courses by various members of the Department of History at Yale, and by the proposals for scientific instruction embodied in James B. Conant's *On Understanding Science.*

And American colleges are only gradually emerging from an era
of complete planlessness. The free-elective system has long since
proved a faulty answer to the questions raised for education by
the increasing complexity of modern knowledge. It did not solve
the problem of integrating the new disciplines into an ordered
structure of learning; it simply dodged the problem. Under the
free-elective system, two programs of study might contain no element whatever in common. Worse than that, the very mechanics
of the free-elective system put all subjects on a par with one another, and tended even to treat advanced courses as if they were
quantitatively equivalent to elementary ones. It fostered the
belief that a man acquires a liberal education by adding so many
hours in one classroom to so many hours in another until he has
served his time in full.

American colleges have begun to put behind them the follies
of the free-elective system. But at best they have usually done no
more than apply palliatives to the evil. A college may force the
student to make his choices in such a way that each of the broad
areas of knowledge is represented somewhere and in some fashion
among the array of courses he offers for the degree. Or the college may institute omnibus courses designed to "survey" each of
these broad areas for the student, usually in his freshman or
sophomore year. Or it may seek in some other mechanical way
to produce unity by adding together disunities.

It must do a great deal more than this if it is really to restore
among liberally educated men a sense of participating in and
comprehending the varied ways of thinking that belong to modern intellectual life. To devise an adequate scheme for that part
of liberal education which aims to give a student breadth of
understanding is far more difficult than to devise a scheme for
that part which aims at intensive, specialized knowledge. The
difficulties are not insurmountable, however, provided we make
clear to ourselves exactly what we are after. We have failed, I
think, to do this, and we have masked our confusions under vague
and undefined terms like "general education."

The last-mentioned phrase has gained widespread currency in
the United States since the end of World War II, thanks largely,
I suppose, to the prestige of the Harvard report on *General Edu-*

cation in a Free Society (1945). In that document, as I read its arguments, general education" was simply a synonym for "liberal education." The report dealt with education in the basic intellectual disciplines, and it proposed various means for introducing students more effectively than before to a wider range of such disciplines. There was nothing anti-intellectual in its recommendations, but the term "general education," which was unfortunately chosen to describe them, was sufficiently ambiguous to be applied elsewhere to almost any kind of pseudo-educational program. On many campuses university administrators announced that they were following in the footsteps of Harvard, and proceeded to set up rambling, catch-all courses, geared to the meager abilities of the marginal student. In teacher-training institutions the professional educationists seized upon the term with glee and promptly introduced into the curriculum college versions of "life-adjustment" training. At one state teachers' college that I visited, a faculty member asked me in all seriousness whether a course in general education was not the proper place to teach good table manners to college students. Since "general education" has come to signify, in so many institutions, complete educational inanity, we ought to abandon the term forthwith and restore the traditional phrase "liberal education," which, despite frequent misuse, has never suffered such utter degradation as the new one.

To get back to first principles, liberal education involves three distinct kinds of intellectual training. It aims to give a student thorough, and hence creative, command of one discipline. It undertakes, in addition, to give him control over the basic and related intellectual skills that are necessary to successful work in his field of specialization. Finally, it seeks to give him breadth of intellectual understanding.

The last two of these objectives are not very clearly differentiated in most college programs. They need to be, if we are to deal effectively with the problems involved. For the sake of clarity, I should like to avail myself, in the paragraphs that follow, of a more or less arbitrary terminology. The term "major" will be given its usual meaning, the discipline in which a student specializes. The term "supporting fields" will be used to describe the work a student needs to do in the disciplines that are closely related to his "major." And the term "minor" will be used to describe the work outside the "major" and the "supporting fields"—the work, that is, which is designed to produce breadth of comprehension. This special usage needs to be borne in mind, for at present the term "minor" is used sometimes for the work in what I call the "supporting fields," and sometimes for that which I too call the "minor."

The fields that are necessary to "support" sound specialization include both the basic intellectual disciplines of general applicability, and the specialized disciplines that fall within the same general area as the "major." An adequately trained chemist, for example, requires knowledge of mathematics (one of the disciplines of general applicability) and also of physics (one of the related specialized disciplines). Similarly a well-trained historian requires knowledge of foreign languages and also of economics. For the most part the training in the disciplines of general applicability ought to be completed in the secondary school, and rigorous college entrance examinations should take care of the matter. Once minimum standards in English grammar and composition, in mathematics, and in foreign languages (at least one, and preferably two) are assured for college matriculation, the further requirements in these disciplines should be established in terms of the actual demands of each major field. Likewise, a rational plan of study in the related "supporting" disciplines needs to be worked out for each field of specialization. These requirements, it should be noted, are in the interests of sound specialization. They do not, by themselves, completely solve the problem of securing breadth of intellectual understanding.

The latter problem, indeed, is the most difficult of any that can arise in liberal education. Present-day attempts to solve it have proved, in my judgment, quite unsatisfactory. The existing "distribution" requirements of most colleges—that is, the requirements that specify work in a number of different areas—are at once too impatient, too mechanical, too ambitious, and yet too distrustful. They are too impatient because they do not take into account the time required to achieve a mature grasp of a subject. They are too mechanical because they do not go beyond scattering a student's effort. They are too ambitious because they expect an undergraduate to range over more fields than he is really capable of assimilating. And they are too distrustful because they assume no ability on the part of an individual to enlarge his range of intellectual powers through his own efforts.

It takes time to acquire a usable command of any intellectual discipline. This seems to me the most neglected fact in American educational thinking. Psychologists and physiologists make use of a concept that is relevant here. A stimulus must reach a certain intensity before it can produce a response. This critical point is called the *threshold*. Below the critical point the stimulus might as well not exist so far as any observable reaction is concerned. There is, it seems to me, such a critical point or threshold in intellectual training. The study of a foreign language, for example, if pursued for only a single school year, does not bring the knowledge of the language up to the threshold where it produces the desired response in the student—namely, a sense of being at home in the language. American colleges usually proceed on the theory that at least two college years of language study are necessary to reach this threshold. I believe, incidentally, that this figure is too low, but the important fact is that a threshold is tacitly recognized in the learning of a foreign language. My conviction is that such a critical point or threshold exists for every intellectual discipline, and that to disregard it is to doom any educational program to futility.

Unless we bring a student's command of a discipline beyond the threshold, we give him nothing that he can use for ordinary working purposes. We leave him bewildered and uncomprehending. Instead of opening a door for him, we may actually slam it shut. In the early stages of learning a new discipline, the student is mainly impressed with how much there is to be known and how unfamiliar and hence difficult the processes of reasoning are. Only when he reaches the threshold does he acquire pleasure and confidence as the reward of his labors. If we cut him off before he reaches the critical point, we frustrate the process of learning. The student carries his discouragement away with him, and usually convinces himself that he could never have mastered the discipline sufficiently well to make it a part of his own thinking. Thereafter he makes no real effort to understand it.

As a psychological compensation he is apt to convert what is actually self-distrust into active distaste for the discipline that he feels has betrayed him. If he becomes a teacher he communicates this feeling to his students, and they go through life with blindspots for certain disciplines, most of which are simply the consequence of bad teaching. The distaste of many students for mathematics, I firmly believe (and many mathematicians with me), is a measure of the number of elementary- and secondary-school teachers who are frightened of the subject because they have never been required to bring their command of it up to the threshold of genuine comprehension. And the neglect of foreign languages—one of the gravest weaknesses of our educational system—seems to me the result of a vicious circle, originating in the shame that most American teachers (including a great number of university scholars) feel, but suppress, concerning their own linguistic inadequacies.

This situation must be corrected in the elementary and secondary schools which are, with devastating success, killing off every budding intellectual interest by refusing to carry forward any disciplined study to the point where the student passes the threshold into confidence and enjoyment. In the college we must avoid the same mistake when we try to counter the evils of overspecialization. If we send a student into a multitude of courses without making sure that his knowledge of each discipline reaches the all-important critical point, we run the risk of producing not breadth but an almost neurotic narrowness of mind.

In my judgment, the college should approach the problem of producing intellectual breadth in a quite different way from the one it has customarily followed. I have already pointed out that the distinctively different ways of thinking are limited in number. There is another fact to be noted. For any given discipline there is another in which the processes of thought are of an almost opposite character. The discipline of chemistry, for example, is at an opposite pole from the discipline of literary criticism. The process of inductive generalization in history stands in the sharpest possible contrast with the process of deductive reasoning characteristic of mathematics. The college of liberal arts and sciences, I suggest, should recognize this fact and make it the principal basis of its efforts to encourage a wide-ranging comprehension on the part of students.

To be specific, I propose that the college should require each student to offer (besides his "major" and his work in its "supporting fields") a "minor" in some discipline that is as remote as possible, in its way of thinking, from the one to which his principal efforts are devoted. A physicist, for example, should choose his minor from one of the humanities; an economist from one of the biological sciences. Such a minor would not be a mere collection of courses, but a systematic program of study, which would bring the student well beyond the threshold of genuine understanding. Other plans, admittedly, disperse a student's efforts more widely, but dispersed effort is no virtue in an educational program. Dispersed effort is usually halfhearted effort. One virtue of such a minor as I have described would be that it would guarantee that all a student's work—outside his own field as well as in it—would be equally serious, equally rigorous, and equally productive of demonstrable intellectual power.

Would not such a program provide the essential basis for the intellectual breadth we are really seeking, and for the mutual understanding among educated men which we so desperately need? The danger in specialization is that a man will fail to recognize that there are cogent ways of thinking markedly different from those he customarily employs. This realization can be brought home to him by giving him a thorough grasp of one such divergent way of thinking. This experience should teach him, if he is a truly thoughtful man, that every disciplined field has its rationale and its reason for existence. It should teach him that no field is beyond his grasp, if only he will devote the requisite effort to understanding it. The arrogance that arises from narrow specialization will dissolve, and real unity of intellectual life will emerge. The liberally educated man will overcome the barriers that now keep specialists from fruitful conversation and collaboration. The liberally educated teacher (and all teachers should be such) will be able to explain to students of divergent temperament the processes of thinking in his own field because he will be able to relate them to processes of thinking in fields of remote and opposite character.

If the college aims to give a student true breadth of understanding, it should abandon the hopeless task of acquainting him with every one of the disciplines. Instead it should bring the student's efforts to a focus, first of all upon his own discipline with its related fields, then upon some discipline far beyond the normal horizon of his specialty. We cannot (to change the metaphor) enable him to conquer the whole world of learning in one undergraduate career. We can, however, assist him to win a foothold on two different continents. Thereafter we ought to be content to trust him, as an educated man, to plant his banner in whatever province he wishes and win control of it by his own efforts.

In the last analysis, moreover, the synthesis of knowledge must be the student's own achievement. Only the things that he can bring together in his own mind has he really learned. Only the intellectual skills that he can co-ordinate for his own purposes has he really mastered. It is the responsibility of the college not only to offer the courses that might produce such intellectual powers, but also to satisfy itself that the student has in fact acquired them. The degree should be awarded only when the college is so satisfied. Indispensable to a sound college program of liberal arts is a comprehensive examination at the end. This should test the student's command not only of his own discipline, but also, if possible, of the "supporting" fields that are a necessary part of fruitful specialization. Many colleges require such examinations; every college worthy of recognition should require them.

A way should also be found to examine the student's command of the field remote from his own that he has elected to study, lest the work there be considered by him a mere accumulation of credit hours. A comprehensive examination in this minor field of concentration, administered perhaps at the end of the sophomore or junior year, should form part of the pattern of the college which strives for genuine breadth and balance in its program. And if the work in the minor field is validated by an examination, then the field itself can safely be set up, if desired, on an interdisciplinary basis.

Liberal education—in both its specialized and its generalized aspects—can be placed on a sound basis only if we restore to the college curriculum as a whole the intellectual vitality that has so largely departed from it in recent years. We are not producing men and women with a general and liberal education by requiring students to elect specified fragments of a curriculum that has been pulverized into unrelated three-semester-hour courses, and in which the distinction between elementary and advanced work has been forgotten. We are not producing them by adding more "survey" courses. We shall not produce them until we go back to first principles and create a college curriculum which, as a whole and in its interrelated parts, provides ordered and progressive training in the various forms of disciplined thought. When we do this we shall at last train up specialists who are scholars and scientists in the highest sense, and citizens who are truly educated men. Liberal education will then become a reality, because it will introduce all men alike into that world of disciplined thought where scholars and reflective citizens meet on common ground.

On Science and Culture

J. ROBERT OPPENHEIMER
(1904–   )

The Constitution of Matter, 1956
Reflections on Science and Culture, 1961

DR. J. ROBERT OPPENHEIMER'S most renowned work has been in the field of quantum mechanics. After a brilliant career at Harvard, he received his doctorate at the University of Göttingen. He then undertook teaching and research at the University of California and California Tech. His research made significant contributions to atomic physics. He has concerned himself with the impact of atomic science in society and he has striven for understanding between natural scientists and humanists. He is currently director of the Institute for Advanced Studies at Princeton.

WE LIVE IN AN UNUSUAL WORLD, MARKED BY VERY GREAT AND irreversible changes that occur within the span of a man's life. We live in a time where our knowledge and understanding of the world of nature grows wider and deeper at an unparalleled rate; and where the problems of applying this knowledge to man's needs and hopes are new, and only a little illuminated by our past history.

Indeed it has always, in traditional societies, been the great function of culture to keep things rather stable, quiet, and unchanging. It has been the function of tradition to assimilate one epoch to another, one episode to another, even one year to another. It has been the function of culture to bring out meaning, by pointing to the constant or recurrent traits of human life, which in easier days one talked about as the eternal verities.

In the most primitive societies, if one believes the anthropol-

From *Encounter*, XIX (October, 1962).

ogists, the principal function of ritual, religion, of culture is, in fact, almost to stop change. It is to provide for the social organism what life provides in such a magic way for living organisms, a kind of homeostasis, an ability to remain intact, to respond only very little to the obvious convulsions and alterations in the world around.

To-day, culture and tradition have assumed a very different intellectual and social purpose. The principal function of the most vital and living traditions to-day is precisely to provide the instruments of rapid change. There are many things which go together to bring about this alteration in man's life; but probably the decisive one is science itself. I will use that word as broadly as I know, meaning the natural sciences, meaning the historical sciences, meaning all those matters on which men can converse objectively with each other. I shall not continually repeat the distinction between science as an effort to find out about the world and understand it, on the one hand, and science, in its applications in technology, as an effort to do something useful with the knowledge so acquired. But certain care is called for, because, if we call this the scientific age, we make more than one kind of oversimplification. When we talk about science to-day, we are likely to think of the biologist with his microscope or the physicist with his cyclotron; but almost certainly a great deal that is not now the subject of successful study will later come to be. I think we probably to-day have under cultivation only a small part of the terrain which will be natural for the sciences a century from now. I think of the enormously rapid growth in many parts of biology, and of the fact, ominous but not without hope, that man is a part of nature and very open to study.

The reason for this great change from a slowly moving, almost static world, to the world we live in, is the cumulative character, the firmness, the givenness of what has been learned about nature. It is true that it is transcended when one goes into other parts of experience. What is true on the scale of the inch and the centimeter may not be true on the scale of a billion light-years; it may not be true either of the scale of a one hundred billionth of a centimetre; but it stays true where it was proven. It is fixed. Thus everything that is found out is added to what was known before, enriches it, and does not have to be done over again. This essentially cumulative irreversible character of learning things is the hallmark of science.

This means that in man's history the sciences make changes which cannot be wished away and cannot be undone. Let me give two quite different examples. There is much talk about getting rid of atomic bombs. I like that talk; but we must not fool ourselves. The world will not be the same, no matter what we do with atomic bombs, because the knowledge of how to make them cannot be exorcised. It is there; and all our arrangements for living in a new age must bear in mind its omnipresent virtual presence, and the fact that one cannot change that. A different example: we can never have again the delusions about the centrality and importance of our physical habitat, now that we know something of where the earth is in the solar system, and know that there are hundreds of billions of suns in our galaxy, and hundreds of billions of galaxies within reach of the great telescopes of the world. We can never again base the dignity of man's life on the special character in space and time of the place where he happens to live.

These are irreversible changes; so it is that the cumulative character gives a paradigm of something which is, in other respects, very much more subject to question: the idea of human progress. One cannot doubt that in the sciences the direction of growth is progress. This is true both of the knowledge of fact, the understanding of nature, and the knowledge of skill, of technology, of learning how to do things. When one applies this to the human situation, and complains that we make great progress in automation and computing and space research but no comparable moral progress, this involves a total misunderstanding of the difference between the two kinds of progress. I do not mean that moral progress is impossible; but it is not, in any sense, automatic. Moral regress, as we have seen in our day, is just as possible. Scientific regress is not compatible with the continued practice of science.

It is, of course, true, and we pride ourselves on it that it is true, that science is quite international, and is the same (with minor differences of emphasis) in Japan, France, the United States,

Russia. But the culture is not international; indeed I am one of those who hope that, in a certain sense, it never quite will be, that the influence of our past, of our history, which is for different reasons and different peoples quite different, will make itself felt and not be lost in total homogeneity.

I cannot subscribe to the view that science and culture are co-extensive, that they are the same thing with different names; and I cannot subscribe to the view that science is something useful, but essentially unrelated to culture. I think that we live in a time which has few historical parallels, that there are practical problems of human institutions, their obsolescence and their inadequacy, problems of the mind and spirit which, if not more difficult than ever before, are different, and difficult. I shall be dealing with some traits of the sciences which contribute to the difficulty, and may here give a synopsis of what they are. They have to do with the question of why the scientific revolution happened when it did; with the characteristic growth of the sciences: with their characteristic internal structure: with the relation of discovery in the sciences to the general ideas of man in matters which are not precisely related to the sciences: with freedom and necessity in the sciences, and the question of the creative and the open character of science, its infinity: and with what direction we might try to follow in bringing coherence and order to our cultural life, in doing what it is proper for a group of intellectuals, of artists, of philosophers, teachers, scientists, statesmen to do to help refashion the sensibility and the institutions of this world, which need refashioning if we are at all to survive.

It is not a simple question to answer why the scientific revolution occurred when it did. It started, as all serious historians would agree, in the late Middle Ages and early Renaissance, and was very slow at first. No great culture has been free of curiosity and reflection, of contemplation and thought. "To know the causes of things" is something that serious men have always wanted, a quest that serious societies have sustained. No great culture has been free of inventive genius. If we think of the culture of Greece, and the following Hellenistic and Roman period, it is particularly puzzling that the scientific revolution did not occur then. The Greeks discovered something without which our contemporary world would not be what it is: standards of rigour, the idea of proof, the idea of logical necessity, the idea that one thing implies another. Without that, science is very nearly impossible, for unless there is a quasi-rigid structure of implication and necessity, then if something turns out not to be what one expected, one will have no way of finding out where the wrong point is: one has no way of correcting himself, of finding the error. But this is something that the Greeks had very early in their history. They were curious and inventive; they did not experiment in the scale of modern days, but they did many experiments; they had, as we have only recently learned to appreciate, a very high degree of technical and technological sophistication. They could make very subtle and complicated instruments; and they did, though they did not write much about it. Possibly the Greeks did not make the scientific revolution because of some flaw in communication. They were a small society, and it may be that there were not quite enough people involved.

In a matter of history, we cannot assign a unique cause, precisely because the event itself is unique; you cannot test, to see if you have it right. I think that the best guess is that it took something that was not present in Chinese civilisation, that was wholly absent in Indian civilisation, and absent also from Greco-Roman civilisation. It needed an idea of progress not limited to better understanding for this idea the Greeks had. It took an idea of progress which has more to do with the human condition, which is well expressed by the second half of the famous Christian dichotomy—faith and works; the notion that the betterment of man's condition, his civility, had meaning; that we all had a responsibility to it, a duty to it, and to man. I think that it was when this basic idea of man's condition, which supplements the other worldly aspects of religion, was fortified and fructified between the 13th and 15th centuries by the re-discovery of the ancient world's scientists, philosophers, and mathematicians, that there was the beginning of the scientific age. By the 17th century there were a handful of men involved in improving human knowledge, or "useful knowledge" as the phrases went, so that new societies like the Royal Society and the Academy were formed, where people could talk to each other and bring to the prosecution of science that indispensable element of working together, of communication, of correcting the other fellow's errors and admiring the other fellow's skills, thus creating the first truly scientific communities.

Just before Newton, Hobbes wrote:

> The Sciences are small power; because not eminent; and therefore, not acknowledged in any man, nor one at all, but in a few; and in them, but of a few things. For Science is of that nature, as none can understand it to be, but such as in good measure have attayned it.
>
> Arts of publique use, as Fortification, making of Engines, and other Instruments of War; because they conferre to Defence, and Victory, are Power.

It was the next century that put science in a context of fraternity, even of universal brotherhood. It encouraged a political view which was egalitarian, permissive, pluralistic, liberal— everything for which the word "democratic" is to-day justly and rightly used. The result is that the scientific world of to-day is also a very large one: an open world in which, of course, not everybody does everything, in which not everybody is a scientist or a prime minister, but in which we fight very hard against arbitrary exclusion of people from any works, any deliberation, any discourse, any responsibility for which their talents and their interests suit them. The result is that we face our new problems, created by the practical consequences of science itself, in the context of a world of two or three billion people, an enormous society for which human institutions were not really ever designed. We are facing a world in which growth is characteristic, not just of the sciences themselves, but of the economy, of technology, of all human institutions; no one can open a daily paper without seeing the consequences.

One can measure scientific growth in a number of ways, but it is important not to mistake things. The excellence of the individual scientist does not change much with time. His knowledge and his power does, but not the high quality that makes him great. We do not look to anyone to be better than Kepler or Newton, any more than we look to anyone to be better than Sophocles, or to any doctrine to be better than the gospel according to St. Matthew. Yet one can measure things, and it has been done. One can measure how many people work on scientific questions: one can count them. One can notice how much is published.

These two criteria show a doubling of scientific knowledge in every ten years. Casimir calculated that if the *Physical Review* continued to grow as rapidly as it has between 1945 and 1960, it would weigh more than the earth during the next century. In fifteen years, the volume of chemical abstracts has quadrupled; in biology the changes are faster still. To-day, if you talk about scientists and mean by that people who have devoted their lives to the acquisition and application of new knowledge, then 93 per cent of us are still alive. This enormously rapid growth, sustained over two centuries, means, of course, that no man learned as a boy more than a small fraction in his own field of what he ought to know as a grown man.

There are several points to keep in mind. One would naturally think that if we are publishing so much, it must be trivial. I think that this is not true: any scientific community with sane people would protect itself against that: because we have to read what is published. The argument not to permit the accumulation of trivial, unimportant things which are not really new, which do not add to what was known before, is overwhelming.

The second point is that one may say that every new thing renders what was known before uninteresting, that one can forget as rapidly as one learns. That is in part true: whenever there is a great new understanding, a great new element of order, a new theory, or a new law of nature, then much that before had to be remembered in isolation becomes connected and becomes, to some extent, implied and simplified. Yet one cannot forget what went before, because usually the meaning of what is discovered in 1962 is to be found in terms of things that were discovered in 1955 or 1950 or earlier. These are the things in terms of which the new discoveries are made, the origins of the instruments that give us the new discoveries, the origins of the concepts in terms of which they are discovered, the origins of the language and the tradition.

A third point: if one looks to the future of something that doubles every ten years, there must come a time when it stops, just as *The Physical Review* cannot weigh more than the earth. We know that this will saturate, and probably at a level very much higher than today; there will come a time when the rate of growth of science is not such that in every ten years the amount that is known is doubled; but the amount that is added to knowledge then will be far greater than it is to-day. For this rate of growth suggests that, just as the professional must, if he is to remain professional, live a life of continuous study, so we may find a clue here also to the more general behaviour of the intellectual with regard to his own affairs, and those of his colleagues in somewhat different fields. In the most practical way a man will have some choice: he may choose to continue to learn about his own field in an intimate, detailed, knowledgeable way, so that he knows what there is to know about it. But then the field will not be very wide. His knowledge will be highly partial of science as a whole, but very intimate and very complete of his own field. He may, on the other hand, choose to know generally, superficially a good deal about what goes on in science, but without competence, without mastery, without intimacy, without depth. The reason for emphasising this is that the cultural values of the life of science almost all lie in the intimate view: here are the new techniques, the hard lessons, the real choices, the great disappointments, the great discoveries.

All sciences grow out of common sense, out of curiosity, observation, reflection. One starts by refining one's observation and one's words, and by exploring and pushing things a little further than they occur in ordinary life. In this novelty there are surprises; one revises the way one thinks about things to accommodate the surprises; then the old way of thinking gets to be so cumbersome and inappropriate that one realises that there is a big change called for, and one recreates one's way of thinking about this part of nature.

Through all this one learns to say what one has done, what one

has found, and to be patient and wait for others to see if they find
the same things, and to reduce, to the point where it really makes
no further difference, the normally overpoweringly vital element
of ambiguity in human speech. We live by being ambiguous, by
not settling things because they do not have to be settled, by suggesting more than one thing because their co-presence in the
mind may be a source of beauty. But in talking about science
one may be as ambiguous as ever until we come to the heart of it.
Then we tell a fellow just what we did in terms that are intelligible to him, because he has been schooled to understand them, and
we tell him just what we found and just how we did it. If he does
not understand us, we go to visit him and help him; and if he still
does not understand us, we go back home and do it over again.
This is the way in which the firmness and solidity of science is
established.

How then does it go? In studying the different parts of nature,
one explores with different instruments, explores different objects,
and one gets a branching of what at one time had been common
talk, common sense. Each branch develops new instruments,
ideas, words suitable for describing that part of the world of
nature. This tree-like structure, all growing from the common
trunk of man's common primordial experience, has branches no
longer associated with the same question, nor the same words
and techniques. The unity of science, apart from the fact that it
all has a common origin in man's ordinary life, is not a unity of
deriving one part from another, nor of finding an identity between one part and another, between let us say, genetics and
topology, to take two impossible examples, where there is indeed
some connection.

The unity consists of two things: first and ever more strikingly,
an absence of inconsistency. Thus we may talk of life in terms
of purpose and adaptation and function, but we have found
in living things no tricks played upon the laws of physics and
chemistry. We have found and I expect will find a total consistency, and between the different subjects, even as remote as
genetics and topology, an occasional sharp mutual relevance.
They throw light on each other; they have something to do with
each other; often the greatest things in the sciences occur when

two different discoveries made in different worlds turn out to have so much in common that they are examples of a still greater discovery.

The image is not that of an ordered array of facts in which every one follows somehow from a more fundamental one. It is rather that of a living thing: a tree doing something that trees do not normally do, occasionally having the branches grow together and part again in a great network.

The knowledge that is being increased in this extraordinary way is inherently and inevitably very specialised. It is different for the physcist, the astronomer, the micro-biologist, the mathematician. There are connections: there is this often important mutual relevance. Even in physics, where we fight very hard to keep the different parts of our subject from flying apart (so that one fellow will know one thing and another fellow will know another, and they do not talk to each other), we do not entirely succeed, in spite of a passion for unity which is very strong. The traditions of science are specialized traditions; this is their strength. Their strength is that they use the words, the machinery, the concepts, the theories, that fit their subjects; they are not encumbered by having to try to fit other sorts of things. It is the specialised traditions which give the enormous thrust and power to the scientific experience. This also makes for the problem of teaching and explaining the sciences. When we get to some very powerful general result which illuminates a large part of the world of nature, it is by virtue of its being general in the logical sense, of encompassing an enormous amount of experience in its concepts; and in its terminology it is most highly specialized, almost unintelligible except to the men who have worked in the field. The great laws of physics today, which do not describe everything (or we would be out of business) but which underlie almost everything that is ever noticed in ordinary human experience about the physical world, cannot be formulated in terms that can reasonably be defined without a long period of careful schooling. This is comparably true in other subjects.

One has then in these specialisations the professional communities in the various sciences. They are very intimate, work closely together, know each other throughout the world. They are always excited—sometimes jealous but usually pleased—when one member of the community makes a discovery. I think, for instance, that what we now call psychology will one day perhaps be many sciences, that there will be many different specialised communities practising them, who will talk with one another, each in their own profession and in their own way.

These specialised communities, or guilds, are a very moving experience for those who participate. There have been many temptations to see analogues in them for other human activities. One that we hear much discussed is this: "If physicists can work together in countries with different cultures, in countries with different politics, in countries of different religions, even in countries which are politically obviously hostile, is not this a way to bring the world together?"

The specialising habits of the sciences have, to some extent, because of the tricks of universities, been carried over to other work, to philosophy and to the arts. There is technical philosophy which is philosophy as a craft, philosophy for other philosophers, and there is art for the artists and the critics. To my mind, whatever virtues the works have for sharpening professional tools, they are profound misreadings, even profound subversions of the true functions of philosophy and art, which are to address themselves to the general common human problem. Not to everybody, but to anybody: not to specialists.

It is clear that one is faced here with formidable problems of communication, of telling people about things. It is an immense job of teaching on all levels, in every sense of the word, never ending.

It has often been held that the great discoveries in science, coming into the lives of men, affect their attitudes toward their place in life, their views, their philosophy. There is surely some truth in this.[1]

---

1. Examples that are usually given include Newton and Darwin. Newton is not a very good example, for when we look at it closely we are struck by the fact that in the sense of the Enlightenment, the sense of a coupling of faith in scientific progress and man's reason with a belief in political progress and the secularisation of human life, Newton himself was in no way a Newtonian. His successors were.

If discoveries in science are to have an honest effect on human thought and on culture, they have to be understandable. That is likely to be true only in the early period of a science, when it is talking about things which are not too remote from ordinary experience. Some of the great discoveries of this century go under the name of Relativity and Uncertainty, and when we hear these words we may think, "This is the way I felt this morning: I was relatively confused and quite uncertain": this is not at all a notion of what technical points are involved in these great discoveries, or what lessons.

I think that the reason why Darwin's hypothesis had such an impact was, in part, because it was a very simple thing in terms of ordinary life. We cannot talk about the contemporary discovery in biology in such language, or by referring only to things that we have all experienced.

Thus I think that the great effects of the sciences in stimulating and in enriching philosophical life and cultural interests have been necessarily confined to the rather early times in the development of a science. There is another qualification. Discoveries will really only resonate and change the thinking of men when they feed some hope, some need that pre-exists in the society. I think that the real sources of the Enlightenment, fed a little by the scientific events of the time, came in the re-discovery of the classics, of classic political theory, perhaps most of all of the Stoics. The hunger of the Eighteenth Century to believe in the power of reason, to wish to throw off authority, to wish to secularize, to take an optimistic view of man's condition, seized on Newton and his discoveries as an illustration of something which was already deeply believed in quite apart from the law of gravity and the laws of motion. The hunger with which the Nineteenth Century seized on Darwin had very much to do with the increasing awareness of history and change, with the great desire to naturalise man, to put him into the world of nature, which pre-existed long before Darwin and which made him welcome. I have seen an example in this century where the great Danish physicist Niels Bohr found in the quantum theory when it was developed thirty years ago this remarkable trait: it is consistent with describing an atomic system, only much less completely than we can describe large-scale objects. We have a certain choice as to which traits of the atomic system we wish to study and measure and which to let go; but we have not the option of doing them all. This situation, which we all recognise, sustained in Bohr his long-held view of the human condition: that there are mutually exclusive ways of using our words, our minds, our souls, any one of which is open to us, but which cannot be combined: ways as different, for instance, as preparing to act and entering into an introspective search for the reasons for action. This discovery has not, I think, penetrated into general cultural life. I wish it had; it is a good example of something that would be relevant, if only it could be understood.

Einstein once said that a physical theory was not determined by the facts of nature, but was a free invention of the human mind. This raises the question of how necessary is the content of science—how much is it something that we are free not to find—how much is it something that could be otherwise? This is, of course, relevant to the question of how we may use the words "objectivity" and "truth." Do we, when we find something, "invent" it or "discover" it?

The fact is, of course, just what one would guess. We are, of course, free in our tradition and in our practice, and to a much more limited extent individually to decide where to look at nature, and how to look at nature, what questions to put, with what instruments and with what purpose. But we are not the least bit free to settle what we find. Man must certainly be free to invent the idea of mass, as Newton did and as it has been refined and re-defined; but having done so, we have not been free to find that the mass of the light quantum or the neutrino is anything but zero. We are free in the start of things. We are free as to how to go about it; but then the rock of what the world is, shapes this freedom with a necessary answer. That is why ontological interpretations of the word "objective" have seemed useless, and why we use the word to describe the clarity, the lack of ambiguity, the effectiveness of the way we can tell each other about what we have found.

Thus in the sciences, total statements like those that involve the word "all," with no qualifications, are hardly ever likely to occur. In every investigation and extension of knowledge we are involved in an action; in every action we are involved in a choice; and in every choice we are involved in a loss, the loss of that we did not do. We find this in the simplest situations. We find this in perception, where the possibility of perceiving is co-extensive with our ignoring many things that are going on. We find it in speech, where the possibility of understandable speech lies in paying no attention to a great deal that is in the air, among the sound waves, in the general scene. Meaning is always attained at the cost of leaving things out. We find it in the idea of complementarity here in a sharp form as a recognition that the attempt to make one sort of observation on an atomic system forecloses others. We have freedom of choice, but we have no escape from the fact that doing some things must leave out others.

In practical terms, this means, of course, that our knowledge is finite and never all-encompassing. There is always much that we miss, much that we cannot be aware of because the very act of learning, of ordering, of finding unity and meaning, the very power to talk about things means that we leave out a great deal.

Ask the question: *Would another civilisation based on life on another planet very similar to ours in its ability to sustain life have the same physics?* One has no idea whether they would have the same physics or not. We might be talking about quite different questions. This makes ours an open world without end. I had a Sanskritist friend in California who used to say mockingly that, if science were any good, it should be much easier to be an educated man now than it was a generation ago. That is because he thought the world was closed.

The things that make us choose one set of questions, one branch of enquiry rather than another are embodied in scientific traditions. In developed sciences each man has only a limited sense of freedom to shape or alter them; but they are not themselves wholly determined by the findings of science. They are largely of an aesthetic character. The words that we use: simplicity, elegance, beauty: indicate that what we grope for is not only more knowledge, but knowledge that has order and harmony in it, and continuity with the past. Like all poor fellows, we want to find something new, but not something too new. It is when we fail in that, that the great discoveries follow.

All these themes—the origin of science, its pattern of growth, its branching reticular structure, its increasing alienation from the common understanding of man, its freedom, the character of its objectivity and its openness—are relevant to the relations of science and culture. I believe that they can be and should be far more robust, intimate, and fruitful than they are to-day.

I am not here thinking of the popular subject of "mass culture." In broaching that, it seems to me one must be critical but one must, above all, be human; one must not be a snob; one must be rather tolerant and almost loving. It is a new problem; one must not expect it to be solved with the methods of Periclean Athens. In the problems of mass culture and, above all, of the mass media, it is not primarily a question of the absence of excellence. The modest worker, in Europe or in America, has within reach probably better music and more good music, more good art, more good writing than his predecessors have ever had. It seems rather that the good things are lost in such a stream of poor things, that the noise level is so high, that some of the conditions for appreciating excellence are not present. One does not eat well unless one is hungry; there is a certain frugality to the best cooking; and something of this sort is wrong with the mass media. But that is not now my problem.

Rather, I think loosely of what we may call the intellectual community: artists, philosophers, statesmen, teachers, men of most professions, prophets, scientists. This is an open group, with no sharp lines separating those that think themselves of it. It is a growing faction of all peoples. In it is vested the great duty for enlarging, preserving, and transmitting our knowledge and skills, and indeed our understanding of the interrelations, priorities, commitments, injunctions, that help men deal with their joys, temptations and sorrows, their finiteness, their beauty. Some of this has to do, as the sciences so largely do, with propositional truth, with propositions which say "If you do thus and so you will see this and that"; these are objective and can be checked and cross-checked; though it is always wise from time to time to doubt, there are ways to put an end to the doubt. This is how it is with the sciences.

In this community there are other statements which "emphasise a theme" rather than declare a fact. They may be statements of connectedness or relatedness or importance, or they may be in one way or another statements of commitment. For them the word "certitude," which is a natural norm to apply in the sciences, is not very sensible—depth, firmness, universality, perhaps more —but certitude, which applies really to verification, is not the great criterion in most of the work of a philosopher, a painter, a poet, or a playwright. For these are not, in the sense I have outlined, objective. Yet for any true community, for any society worthy of the name, they must have an element of community of being common, of being public, of being relevant and meaningful to man, not necessarily to everybody, but surely not just to specialists.

I have been much concerned that, in this world of change and scientific growth, we have so largely lost the ability to talk with one another, to increase and· enrich our common culture and understanding. And so it is that the public sector of our lives, what we hold and have in common, has suffered, as have the illumination of the arts, the deepening of justice and virtue, and the ennobling power of our common discourse. We are less men for this. Never in man's history have the specialised traditions more flourished than to-day. We have our private beauties. But in those high undertakings when man derives strength and insight from public excellence, we have been impoverished. We hunger for nobility, the rare words and acts that harmonise simplicity with truth. In this default I see some connection with the great unresolved public problems—survival, liberty, fraternity.

In this default I see the responsibility that the intellectual community has to history and to our fellows: a responsibility which is a necessary condition for re-making human institutions as they need to be re-made to-day that there may be peace, that they may embody more fully those ethical commitments without which we cannot properly live as men.

This may mean for the intellectual community a very much

greater effort than in the past. The community will grow; but I think that also the quality and the excellence of what we do must grow. I think, in fact, that with the growing wealth of the world, and the possibility that it will not all be used to make new committees, there may indeed be genuine leisure, and that a high commitment on this leisure is that we re-knit the discourse and the understanding between the members of our community.

In this I think we have, all of us, to preserve our competence in our own professions, to preserve what we know intimately, to preserve our mastery. This is, in fact, our only anchor in honesty. We need also to be open to other and complementary lives, not intimidated by them and not contemptuous of them (as so many are to-day of the natural and mathematical sciences). As a start, we must learn again, without contempt and with great patience, to talk to one another; and we must hear.

Education Automation

R. BUCKMINSTER FULLER
(1895–   )

Education Automation, 1962
No More Second Hand God, 1962

BUCKY FULLER, as he is known to everyone who knows him, was educated at Harvard and the United States Naval Academy, and has worked in industry all of his life—except for a term of service in the U.S. Navy. A practicing technologist and an inventor (he has invented the geoscope, the geodesic dome and a three-wheeled automobile among other things), he has scorned the narrow point of view typical of his profession, and has pondered the implications of technological change in a culture where the organization of industry seems to be replacing politics as a key factor in our lives. Given his choice of a topic on which to speak, he will always select "The World"—and on this broad subject he has lectured in colleges and universities all over the country. More prophet than teacher, more orator than writer, he has largely made disciples directly from the lecture platform, until recently when the Southern Illinois University Press published in book form some of his speeches and occasional essays.

I HAVE TALKED TO YOU ABOUT SOLVING PROBLEMS BY DESIGN competence instead of by political reform. It is possible to get one-to-one correspondence of action and reaction without political revolution, warfare, and reform. I find it possible today with very short electromagnetic waves to make small reflectors by which modulated signals can be beamed. After World War II, we began to beam our TV messages from city to city. One reason television didn't get going before World War II was because of the difficulty in distributing signals over long distances from

From *Education Automation: Freeing the Scholar to Return to His Studies* by R. Buckminster Fuller. Copyright © 1962 by Southern Illinois University Press. Reprinted by permission of Southern Illinois University Press.

central sources on long waves or mildly short waves. We were working on coaxial cables between cities, but during the war we found new short ranges of electromagnetic frequencies. We worked practically with very much higher frequencies, very much shorter wave lengths. We found that we could beam these short waves from city to city. Television programs are brought into the small city now by beam from a few big cities and then *re-broadcast* locally to the home sets. That is the existing TV distribution pattern. My invention finds it is now possible to utilize the local TV masts in any community in a new way. Going up to, say, two hundred, three hundred, or four hundred feet and looking down on a community you see the houses individually in the middle of their respective land plots. Therefore, with a few high masts having a number of tiny Retrometer light-beams, lasers, or other radiation reflectors, each beam aimed accurately at a specific house, the entire community could be directly "hooked up" by beams, instead of being broadcast to. This means a great energy saving, for less than 1 per cent of the omnidirectionally *broadcast* pattern ever hits a receiving antenna. The beaming makes for very sharp, clear, frequency-modulated signals.

In the beaming system, you also have a reflector at the house that picks up the signal. It corresponds directly to the one on the mast and is aimed right back to the specific beaming cup on the mast from which it is receiving. This means that with beam casting you are able to send individual messages to each of those houses. There is a direct, fixed, wireless connection, an actual direct linkage to individuals; and it works in both directions. Therefore, the receiving individual can beam back, "I don't like it." He may and can say "yes" or "no." This "yes" or "no" is the basis of a binary mathematical system, and immediately brings in the "language" of the modern electronic computers. With two-way TV, constant referendum of democracy will be manifest, and democracy will become the most practical form of industrial and space-age government by all people, for all people.

It will be possible not only for an individual to say, "I don't like it," on his two-way TV but he can also beam-dial (without having to know mathematics), "I want number so and so." It is

also possible with this kind of two-way TV linkage with individuals' homes to send out many different programs simultaneously; in fact, as many as there are two-way beamed-up receiving
sets and programs. It would be possible to have large central
storages of documentaries—great libraries. A child could call for
a special program information locally over the TV set.

With two-way TV we will develop selecting dials for the children which will not be primarily an alphabetical but a visual
species and *chronological category* selecting device with secondary
alphabetical subdivisions. The child will be able to call up any
kind of information he wants about any subject and get his latest
authoritative TV documentary, the production of which I have
already described to you. The answers to his questions and prob-
ings will be *the best information* that man has available up to
that minute in history.

All this will bring a profound change in education. We will
stop training individuals to be "teachers," when all that most
young girl "education" students really want to know is how they
are going to earn a living in case they don't get married. Much
of the educational system today is aimed at answering: "How
am I going to survive? How am I going to get a job? I must earn
a living." That is the priority item under which we are working
all the time—the idea of *having to earn a living*. That problem
of "how are we going to earn a living?" is going to go out the
historical window, forever, in the next decade, and education is
going to be disembarrassed of the unseen "practical" priority
bogeyman. Education will then be concerned primarily with exploring to discover not only more about the universe and its
history but about what the universe is trying to do, about why
man is part of it, and about how can, and may, man best function
in universal evolution.

Automation is with us. There is no question about it. Automation was inevitable to intellect. Intellect was found to differentiate out experience continually and to articulate and develop
new tools to do physically repeated tasks. Man is now no longer
essential as a worker in the fabulously complex industrial equation. Marx's *worker* is soon to become utterly obsolete. Automation is coming in Russia just as it is here. The word *worker*

describing man as a muscle-and-reflex machine will not have
its current 1961 meaning a decade hence. Therefore, if man is
no longer essential as a worker we ask: "How can he live? How
does he acquire the money or credits with which to purchase
what he needs or what he wants that is available beyond immediate needs?" At the present time we are making all kinds of
economic pretenses at covering up this overwhelming automation
problem because we don't realize adequately the larger significance of the truly fundamental change that is taking place in
respect to man-in-universe. As automation advanced man began
to create secondary or nonproductive jobs to make himself look
busy so that he could rationalize a necessity for himself by virtue
of which he could "earn" his living. Take all of our bankers, for
example. They are all fixtures; these men don't have anything
to do that a counting machine couldn't do; a punch button box
would suffice. They have no basic banking authority whatsoever
today. They do not loan you their own wealth. They loan you
your own wealth. But man has a sense of vanity and has to
invent these things that make him look important.

I am trying to keep at the realities with you. Approximately
total automation is coming. Men will be essential to the industrial equation but not as workers. People are going to be utterly
essential as consumers—what I call *regenerative consumers*, however, not just swill pails. . . .

Every time we educate a man, we as educators have a regenerative experience, and we ought to learn from that experience how
to do it much better the next time. The more educated our
population the more effective it becomes as an integral of regenerative consumer individuals. We are going to have to invest
in our whole population to accelerate its consumer regeneration.
We are going to be completely unemployed as muscle-working
machines. *We as economic society are going to have to pay our
whole population to go to school and pay it to stay at school.*
That is, we are going to have to put our whole population into
the educational process and get *everybody* realistically literate
in many directions. Quite clearly, *the new political word* is going
to be *investment*. It is not going to be *dole*, or socialism, or

the idea of people hanging around in bread lines. The new popular *regenerative investment* idea is actually that of making people more familiar with the patterns of the universe, that is, with what man has learned about the universe to date, and that of getting everybody inter-communicative at ever higher levels of literacy. People are then going to stay in the education process. They are going to populate ever increasing numbers of research laboratories and universities.

As we now disemploy men as muscle and reflex machines, the one area where employment is gaining abnormally fast is the research and development area. Research and development are a part of the educational process itself. We are going to have to invest in our people and make available to them participation in the great educational process of research and development in order to learn more. When we learn more, we are able to do more with our given opportunities. We can relate federally paid-for education as a high return, mutual benefit investment. When we plant a seed and give it the opportunity to grow, its fruits pay us back many fold. Man is going to "improve" rapidly in the same way by new federally underwritten educational "seeding" by new tools and processes.

Our educational processes are in fact the upcoming major world industry. This is *it*; this is the essence of today's educational facilities meeting. You are caught in that new educational upward draughting process. The cost of education will be funded regeneratively right out of earnings of the technology, the industrial equation, because we can only afford to reinvest continually in humanity's ability to go back and turn out a better job. As a result of the new educational processes our consuming costs will be progressively lower as we also gain ever higher performance per units of invested resources, which means that our wealth actually will be increasing at all times rather than "exhausted by spending." It is the "capability" wealth that really counts. It is very good that there is an international competitive system now operating, otherwise men would tend to stagnate, particularly in large group undertakings. They would otherwise be afraid to venture in this great intellectual integrity regeneration.

I would say, then, that you are faced with a future in which education is going to be number one amongst the great world industries, within which will flourish an educational machine technology that will provide tools such as the individually selected and articulated two-way TV and an intercontinentally networked, documentaries call-up system, operative over any home two-way TV set. . . .

I think that all the patterns I have been giving you are going to unfold rapidly and that primarily the individual is going to *study* at home. That is in elementary, high school, and college years. Not until his graduate work days begin will he take residence on campus. I am quite sure that the students of all ages will keep on going to "school houses" to get *social experiences* —or to be "baby-sat." We will probably keep the schools open in the evening because of the growing need for babysitters. Real education, however, will be something to which individuals will discipline themselves spontaneously under the stimulus of their own ticker-tapes—their individually unique chromosomes. Everyone has his own chromosomal pattern. No two persons have the same appetite at the same time. There is no reason why they should. There is no reason why everyone should be interested in the geography of Venezuela on the same day and hour unless there is some "news" event there, such as a revolution. However, most of us are going to be interested in the geography of Venezuela at some time—our own time—but not all on the same day. *Simultaneous curricula are obsolete*. We must make *all* the information immediately available over the two-way TV's ready for the different individual human chromosomal ticker-tapes to call for it.

There are two more things I would like to talk about if we have the time. I am a comprehensive designer—that is, I try to organize all the data and challenges and problems in such a manner that they may be solved by inanimate technology, as I mentioned to you earlier, rather than by organization reforms. Therefore, when I talk about educational problems, I am interested in how these can be satisfied by some kind of physical apparatus along the lines of the trend requirements I have been outlining to you. The kind of equipment that would be involved would be such as the two-way TV and the Geoscope and also what I call *automated education facilities.* We know about teaching machines, etc., today, and much of this is sound. In our consideration of equipment we must also include the environment-controlling structures which will house the computer-integrated equipment and activities.

I am going to give you one more "big" introductory concept that may shed considerable light on these problems and may lead to acquisition of logical apparatus of solution. C. P. Snow, the writer, has a great following today. He writes about "two worlds." His two worlds are the literary world and the scientific world. In the literary world, man writes the books that people can understand with least effort. They seem to be good romance books because they seem to fit many lives. Science writes in ways that require complete dedication of effort to comprehend. Snow says the dichotomy between the two worlds began approximately two centuries ago with the inception of the industrial revolution. In England it is as yet evident that the popular writers of a century ago and since were not helped by the scientist. The scientist tended to be preoccupied, obscure, and not interested in the literary man's needs. A pertinent fact that Snow does not mention is that the important scientific events were often withheld from the public because of their unique military advantages. The scientist's information began to be the grist of the industrial technology. The scientist was intimately tied up with industry, even though he didn't look upon his personal work in terms of economics. The scientist was aloof to the ultimate fact that industry was the user of the information that he was able to gather.

The literary man, not understanding either science or its technology, developed an animosity toward industrialization. Snow points out for us that in America this dichotomy was in evidence, for instance, in Emerson and Thoreau who were antipathetic to industrialization. As I grew up at the turn of the century I saw that society looked on industrialization as something noisy, smoky, and full of so-called "artificialities." (In my viewpoint, there is no meaning to the word "artificial." Man can only do what nature permits him to do. Man does not invent anything.

He makes discoveries of principles operative in nature and often finds ways of generalizing those principles and reapplying them in surprise directions. That is called invention. But he does not do anything artificial. Nature has to permit it, and if nature permits it, it is natural. There is naught which is unnatural.)

The literary and popular concept of industrialization grew out of erroneous definitions and terms. The static viewpoint was seemingly supported by the Newtonian statement that "a body persists in *a state of rest* (or in a line of motion) except as affected by other bodies." Primarily the norm was "at rest" and changes were therefore abnormal and undesirable. Changes were exploited from time to time only because of military advantage or because men could make large amounts of money out of the changes and not because of any social voting that the changes were constructively desirable. The literati just didn't try to understand change, and they stayed apart from science and abhorred the changes. Snow says the gulf between the scientist and the literati is now so great that the chasm is no longer spannable. He feels there has now developed an irreparable dichotomy between literary and scientific man. I do not agree with him as you shall learn.

Alfred North Whitehead came to Harvard University early in this twentieth century from the great universities of England. He said that one of the things that was very noticeable at Harvard was that this great private school was initiating a new kind of pattern. It was beginning to build and staff the great graduate schools. The graduate schools dealt in specializations. In England the special preoccupations could be taken up within the general university. There were no special schools. Whitehead said that the American populus applauded the high specialization, and Whitehead saw that this pattern was being followed by the other leading private schools, colleges, and universities. Of course, the public schools and public universities immediately followed suit, taking on the graduate school patterns, because the political representatives of the public saw that their constituents would want the state school to incorporate these educational advances of the rich man's private schools. So specialization in graduate schools also became the "thing."

Whitehead said this meant that we deliberately sorted out the students, sieved them, picked out the bright ones, and persuaded the brights to stay in the university and to go on to the graduate school. This meant that we began to make specialists out of our bright ones. The bright ones within their own special category of their special school went on to develop further special nuances within their special areas. This all worked toward expertism and hybridism in the educational pursuits. It meant that the bright ones would learn much about their special subject. The public thought this to be desirable, because people like the idea of an "all-star" team. They thought that if we took groups of all-stars and put them together our commonwealth would surely prosper.

Whitehead said, "So far so good, and everybody is applauding." But he then said that the educational hybridism would mean that these men who were of high intellectual capabilities would have very high intellectual integrity. As men of high intellectual integrity they would quickly discover that they were making great progress in highly specialized areas of inquiry and thus also they would know how little any other man outside of their own field could possibly understand of what was going on inside their own and inside any one field other than their respective specializations. Therefore, no specialist of integrity would think of going into some other expert's field and making quick assumptions as to the significance of that unfamiliar work. This would be considered preposterous. There would thus develop an increasing tendency to break down generalized communications and comprehensive prospecting between these experts. Certainly, they would not tend to join together and say: "I see I am developing this and you are developing that; if we associated them thus and so, such and such would be the economic consequences; therefore, let us do so by employing our credit as scientists with the banks in order to fund our undertakings." These men, Whitehead said, would do just the opposite and would become more and more subjective, growing into purer and purer scientists, to whom no banker would think of lending money on the basis of intellectual integrity alone. The scientists went in just the opposite direction of applied science. The more expert they were the less they would think of searching into the concept of how society might enjoy the fruits of their discoveries.

Whitehead pointed out that this system tended to break down the communication between the men of high intellectual capability in all special fields. Inasmuch as society wanted exploitation of the gains of their "all-star" teams, it meant that someone other than the prime intellects had to integrate and exploit their capabilities and their findings.

Then Whitehead said—which came as quite a surprise—inasmuch as we have deliberately sorted out the bright ones from the dull ones, we have inadvertently created a class of dull ones. Just as in mining, we have a big pile of tailings, and no one thinks much about tailings because they are interested only in the high-grade, quick-cash ore and the net metal that is taken out of the latter. He said that inasmuch as the "bright ones" are not going to be able to realize, integrate, and exploit their own potentials we will have to leave it to the not-so-brights to put things together. This is what I have termed "Whitehead's dilemma."

I have developed "Whitehead's dilemma" a little further than he could go at that time. I find that there is a second grade of men who get passing marks, but are not selected to be specialists, who, however, though not "gleaming bright" have a dull polish and are good healthy fellows who play good football and are liked by everybody. These second grade "clean ones" become the first choice for executives in business, which does integrate potentials of demand and supply. Then as corporation executives these not-quite-so-brights take on the pure scientist experts and cultivate them like special hybrid egg-laying hens in special houses. The corporations take on the task of putting appropriate specializations together to exploit the synergetic advantages thus accruing. The businessman becomes the integrator of the bright ones' capabilities. The business executive himself, however, tends to be a specialist of a less fine order. Pretty soon, he will say, for instance: "I am in the automobile business and don't know anything about stockings; so I am just going to stick to my automobiles." He might also say: "I find that an automobile won't run across an open field. Therefore it is only half of the invention—automotive transportation. The *highway* itself is a large part of the invention—high speed highway transportation." Automobiling is schematically like a monkey wrench—the ratchet half is the "highway," and the thumbscrew-adjustable traveling jaw is the "automobile." The automobile is literally geared by its tire-treads to the road. So the business executive might say: "An automobile company could not possibly afford to build the highways—it is a very difficult political matter; you have to have costly condemnation proceedings and so forth to get a highway through; it is all so expensive that our company would never make a profit if we took the responsibility of providing highways. All we can produce is automobiles. To get the show going, however, we will have a little auto race track over here, and we will have automobile shows in many big cities and at county and state fairs. We will get people very excited about the way our automobile can go and how fascinating it looks." Thus it went, and the people began to envision personal use and enjoyment of the automobile "if only they had a highway." What the auto executive did was to excite the people into demanding highways for the cars.

We next come down to a duller class of not-so-brights—much duller—who didn't even go to college. This much duller class is that of the politicians. The politicians saw that the people in general wanted automobiles and wanted to "joy ride"; so they immediately voted for highways to get the peoples' votes for themselves.

Thus, a much bigger geographical pattern of the automobile emerged than the domain of the factory and the auto executive's specialized territory. The bigger pattern was the total highway system—state, interstate, and federal. We also find that generally speaking *the geographically larger the physical task to be done, the duller the conceptual brain that is brought to bear* upon the integration of the scientific discoveries and their technically realized applications. Finally we get to international affairs, and you know what is happening today. The most highly polished of the dullest class, scientifically and intellectually speaking, may wear their striped pants very beautifully and be charming fellows, but they have not produced any mutually-acceptable, constructive, world peace generating ideas. They traffic successfully only in peoples' troubles and emergency compromises. One of the great mistakes that society has been demonstrating in our last century has been that of leaving the most important problems to the men who are bankrupt in creative thinking ability.

World War I marked the end of the old great masters of the water-ocean earth commerce. These were the world "bankers" who were the not-too-dull businessmen who had high courage and co-ordination and who developed successful world-pattern cartels and trusts quite transcendentally to any one nation's anti-trust laws or to any one nation's popular knowledge, advantaged by men's world-around preoccupations with their own respective domestic affairs. These old masters kept the world peoples in complete ignorance of their world planning and let it be thought that the latter was the consequence of their appointed local politicians' deliberations.

At Harvard just before World War I—and this was the time when I was having my little troubles there—the dilemma White-head was talking about was developing in a very interesting way. What Whitehead didn't ask was how Harvard could afford those graduate schools. The fact is that neither Harvard nor any other university has ever operated at a profit. Certainly, schools, colleges, and universities don't have surplus earnings accruing which they can reinvest. Establishing graduate schools wasn't something private colleges could do on their own. The explanation is that the graduate schools were *given* to Harvard and the other leading private universities.

The next interesting question is *who gave* them the graduate *specialty* schools? Well, the people who gave Harvard the schools were primarily the partners of J. P. Morgan and Company or they were men who were founders or presidents of companies whose boards were run by J. P. Morgan. J. P. Morgan or his partners were at that time on the boards of nearly every important, powerful company in America. Morgan or his associates were also partners in the great unseen syndicate of world commerce mastery up to World War I. . . .

Since World War I, the old masters have been extinct. Because they operated always in secret, they of course didn't announce their own demise. As they died secretly they inadvertently left many accepted patterns, such as, for instance, the "head men" on the world thrones and the university patterns which Whitehead described. As the new problems brought about by the old masters' demise arose, everybody began to turn to the local political head men and new head men who arose easily, pushing over the old who no longer had the support of the now defunct invisible masters. . . .

As a consequence, since 1918 world men speaking always under their conditioned reflex concepts of static geographical "nations" have been challenging the local political heads with the responsibility of getting them out of their troubles. Then suddenly, realistic "head men" haven't the slightest idea how to solve such problems. These were problems that only their old masters could solve. Nobody could have been duller in *world* strategems than the political leaders of the world's many separate nations. Ruthless, tough bluffing became the new winning technique, but it was implemented by the politicians' exploitation of their respective hybrid, economic slaves, the scientific specialists.

In respect to "Whitehead's dilemma" everybody today tends to believe that specialization is the best way to earn a living, by establishing one's own special monopoly at some strategic point in the specialization network. As a consequence of comprehensively undertaken specialization we have today a general lack of comprehensive thinking. The specialist is therefore, in effect, a slave to the economic system in which he happens to function. The concept of inevitable specialization by the brightest has become approximately *absolute* in today's social-economic reflexing. The fixation is false and is soon to be altered. . . .

At the World Affairs Conference in Colorado this last week, they brought Ludwig Von Bertalanffy together with me on five panels. Ludwig Von Bertalanffy is a great biologist. He is in the front ranks of the "academy." As a great scientist in biology, he discovered that there were comprehensive system behaviors in nature unpredicted by the behaviors of the systems' components, a phenomenon known to scientists as synergy. Von Bertalanffy, along with other mathematicians who had discovered synergy in

the theories of games and so forth, began to discover that there
were complex patterns which could never be apprehended, understood, operated on, or dealt with if we approached them only in
terms of their separate elements; that is, *literally* in an *elementary*
manner. Our whole educational process, all the way up from the
elementary school, is one of taking the child who has an innate
comprehensive coordinate capability (not only to teach itself to
walk but to be interested in the *heavens*) and give him differentiated parts—elements to work with. The prime patrons of the
planetariums and the like are the children, because they are spontaneously interested in the universe, that is, in the comprehensive
rather than in the specialty—the elements. We get them to school,
and we say forget the universe, and we give them A, B, and C. We
go toward the very opposite of comprehensiveness. We go to the
specialization right away. We render the children more and more
specialized from elementary school onwards. Ludwig Von Bertalanffy began to find that nature, as biology, did not tend toward
hybridism or more limited specialization by itself. Nature reverted
toward generalism. Nature tended to work toward broader adaptation, ergo, more comprehensive capabilities. As a consequence,
Dr. Von Bertalanffy was the scientist who developed an expression
you are quite familiar with today—General Systems Theory. Von
Bertalanffy employs his General Systems Theory subjectively. He
agreed with me that my *comprehensive anticipatory design science*
is an objective employment of systems theory and that I had discovered the same phenomenon that he had discovered through
completely different circumstances.

If we apply General Systems Theory to the analysis of our
total world problem, today we obtain an excellent view of the
techno-scientific, industrial theatre and the *socio-economic drama*
in which our swiftly evolving educational processes are going to
function and we can see far more clearly what the roles therein
may be of the kinds of new educational developments which I
have been describing to you. We will also be able to comprehend
better the problems that were insurmountable to the old "world
masters" and how the coming universities may now solve them
under the newer circumstances. . . .

What I now propose is that all the universities around the world be encouraged to invest the next ten years in a continuing problem of *how to make the total world's resources, which now serve only 43 per cent, serve 100 per cent of humanity through competent complex design science.*

The general theory of education at present starts students off with elementary components and gradually increases the size of the complex of components with which the student will be concerned. The scheme is to go from the particular toward the whole but never to reach the whole. . . .

I think that one of the most important events of the educational revolution is the present realization that we are going to discover that the child is born comprehensively competent and co-ordinate and that it is capable of treating with large quantities of data and families of variables right from the start.

When parents make babies they don't know what they are making. They don't know how to make what they make. All they do is "press a button." Ours and our babies' brains have a quadrillion times a quadrillion atoms already operative in coordinate patterning operation utterly transcendental to our conscious control. A quadrillion times a quadrillion atoms operative subconsciously in most extraordinary co-ordination make it possible, for example, for me to be communicating with you. We don't have anything consciously to do with the fundamentals of our communicating capability. Nor do we have anything to do consciously with pushing a million hairs out of our heads at preferred rates, colors, and shapes. We don't know how to consciously co-ordinate our heart beating and our breathing. We don't know at all how we charge energies back into the various glands of our systems. We really don't know what is going on at all, but we do co-ordinate it all subconsciously. What we do have in the brain is an extraordinary, orderly pattern manipulating capability to deal with that quadrillion times a quadrillion invisible atoms. This is all born into the child. The parent doesn't consciously put it there. Men may take no credit for the fundamentals of their relative success upon earth.

I will say that it is very clear to me that when a child stands up, breathing and co-ordinating all these complex patterns by himself and gets his own balance and starts drinking in the patterns of cosmos and earth he is apparently spontaneously interested in co-ordinating the total information—the total stimulation. He craves to understand—to comprehend. That is why he asks his myriad questions.

I am quite confident we are going to find ways of helping the child to co-ordinate his spontaneous comprehension of the *whole* instead of becoming a specialist without losing any of the advantages gained by yesterday's exclusive specialization. With general comprehension there will also come an entirely new way of looking at our mutual problems around the earth. We will not be easily influenced by ignorant persuasion and propaganda, such as pronouncements that "we are against this man and that man," and so forth. We are going to look at our problems quite differently than we do now. There will be a coordinated comprehensive continuation of development of the child in appreciation of the subconsciously co-ordinate design of humans not forcing them into prolonged special focus, yet accomplishing with automated tools and instruments far greater probing than was accomplished by the utter specialist while conserving the comprehensive comprehension of the significance to society of the increasing flow of discovered data.

Next, let us think carefully and daringly of the equipment we will need and that we won't need for the large, new research establishments for students staying longer and longer at the university, as the new major industry of mankind. At M.I.T., for instance, where I visited as lecturer for eight years, there are rooms full of special and expensive apparatus which everyone thought would put M.I.T. at the top of the heap. Room after room of this equipment is now obsolete—at best these collections of machinery make a dull museum. . . .

I would counsel you in your deliberation regarding getting campuses ready now to get general comprehensive environment controls that are suitable to all-purposes like a circus. A circus is a transformable environment. You get an enclosure against "weather" that you can put up in a hurry, within which you can put up all kinds of apparatus—high trapezes, platforms, rings, nets, etc. You can knock it down in a few minutes. That is the way the modern laboratory goes. In laboratories you can get the generalized pipette or whatever it is, the crucible and the furnace. You can put the right things together very fast, rig them up, get through the experiment, knock it down. It's one clean space again. You want clean spaces. The circus concept is very important for you. I would get buildings where it is possible for many to meet. On the Carbondale campus you have succeeded in getting some good auditoriums—but we need more auditoriums and more auditoriums time and time again. We want places where there is just a beautiful blank floor and beautiful blank walls upon which to cast our pictures or apply crayons. You don't have to put any "architecture" there at all. You don't have to build any sculptured architecture—use the ephemeral. Work from the visible to the invisible very rapidly.

I would not waste dollars on great, heavy, stone masonry and any kind of Georgian architecture, and I would forget all the old architecture and even the curricula patterns of any schools before this moment. You might better consider putting up one big one-half-mile-diameter geodesic dome over your whole campus and thereafter subdivide off local areas temporarily for various activities.

Anything that is static, forget it. Work entirely toward the dynamic. Get yourself the tools and ways of enclosing enormous amounts of space, and make it possible for large numbers of human beings to come together under more preferred conditions than have ever before come together. Then give them large clear spaces so that their privacy results from having sufficient distance between people or groups of people. Get over the ideas of partitions. Partitions are like socialism. They came out of living and working in fortresses where there wasn't enough room to go around, so they put up partitions—really making cells. Partitions simply say you shall not pass. That's all they do. They are improvised to make that which is fundamentally inadequate work "after a fashion."

There are four kinds of privacy: if I can't touch you, we're *tactilely* private; if I can't smell you, we are *olfactorily* private;

if I can't hear you, we're *aurally* private; and if I can't see you, we are *visually* private. Just a little space will take care of the first three. For the fourth—since we can see a great distance—all we need are delicate occulting membranes, possibly rose bushes or soap bubbles or smoke screens.

WORKS OF RELATED
FICTION AND DRAMA

Works of Related Fiction and Drama

The academic setting has been used for works of fiction ever since Nathaniel Hawthorne's unsuccessful first novel *Fanshawe* which appeared in 1828. Since then colleges and schools have been made the background of serious novels, stories and plays, as well as juveniles, popular shockers, detective stories and even works of science fiction. Seldom, however, have works of real literary merit been produced in this genre—and perhaps Hawthorne's failure can be taken as a sign, not just of his own technical inadequacy as a young man, but of the difficulty, the near-impossibility of producing an academic novel or play which is also a thoroughly successful work of art. Of all really considerable American writers, Thomas Wolfe is the only one who dealt centrally with university life in most of his major works; but even in his case, one feels that the descriptions of academic routines and teacher-student relationships are merely means to quite another end. More typical is the case of F. Scott Fitzgerald who made college life a chief subject only in a single book (and a group of stories) of minor importance in the context of his whole work. Nonetheless, the student interested in discovering the meaning of his own experience in school and of comparing it with the experience of other generations will find much of value in the following list, which provides a selected sample only of literature about life in college or, in some cases, of students out of college and in pursuit of pleasure. They are listed in chronological order.

Nathaniel Hawthorne, *Fanshawe*, 1828
F. Scott Fitzgerald, *This Side of Paradise*, 1920
Willa Cather, *The Professor's House*, 1925
Sinclair Lewis, *Arrowsmith*, 1925

Bravig Imbs, *The Professor's Wife,* 1928
Thomas Wolfe, *Look Homeward Angel,* 1929
William Faulkner, *Sanctuary,* 1931
George Weller, *Not to Eat, Not for Love,* 1933
Vardis Fisher, *Passions Spin the Plot,* 1934
 We Are Betrayed, 1935
Thomas Wolfe, *Of Time and the River,* 1935
 The Web and the Rock, 1939
George Stewart, *Doctor's Oral,* 1939
Wallace Stegner, *Fire and Ice,* 1941
Dorothy Baker, *Trio,* 1943
James T. Farrell, *My Days of Anger,* 1943
Albert Guerard, *The Hunted,* 1944
Robert Penn Warren, *At Heaven's Gate,* 1943
William Maxwell, *The Folded Leaf,* 1945
Helen Howe, *We Happy Few,* 1946
Donald MacRae, *Dwight Craig,* 1947
Calder Willingham, *End as a Man,* 1947
Shirley Jackson, *Hangsman,* 1951
Robie Macauley, *The Disguises of Love,* 1952
Mary McCarthy, *The Groves of Academe,* 1952
Theodore Morrison, *The Stones of the House,* 1953
Howard Fast, *Silas Timberman,* 1954
Randall Jarrell, *Pictures from an Institution,* 1954
Elizabeth Hardwick, *The Simple Truth,* 1955
May Sarton, *Faithful are the Wounds,* 1955
Myron Kaufman, *Remember Me to God,* 1957
Vladimir Nabokov, *Pnin,* 1957
Howard Nemerov, *The Homecoming Game,* 1957
Carlos Baker, *A Friend in Power,* 1958
Stringfellow Barr, *Purely Academic,* 1958
George P. Elliot, *Parktilden Village,* 1958
Monroe Engel, *The Vision of Nicholas Solon,* 1959
Mark Harris, *Wake Up, Stupid,* 1959
Eleazar Lipsky, *The Scientists,* 1959
John Aldridge *The Party at Cranton,* 1960
William Van O'Connor, *Campus on the River,* 1960
Vivienne Koch, *Change of Love,* 1960

Bernard Malamud, *A New Life*, 1961
Vladimir Nabokov, *Pale Fire*, 1962
Philip Roth, *Letting Go*, 1962
Louis Simpson, *Riverside Drive*, 1962
J. D. Salinger, *Franny and Zooey*, 1963
Herbert Kubly, *The Whistling Zone*, 1963
Jack Ludwig, *Confusions*, 1963

There are many fewer books of merit and truth enough to be considered among those which treat high school or prep life. Perhaps the following handful is a sufficient sample.

J. D. Salinger, *Catcher in the Rye*
Evan Hunter, *The Blackboard Jungle*
John Knowles, *A Separate Peace*
William Goldman, *Temple of Gold*

Good plays are even rarer, since college life on the stage almost inevitably turns into musical comedy highjinks or sentimental falsification. Four only seem really worth hunting up and reading.

James Thurber and Elliot Nugent, *The Male Animal*
Robert Hivnor, *Too Many Thumbs*
Edward Albee, *Who's Afraid of Virginia Woolf*
Robert Anderson, *Tea and Sympathy*

There are innumerable short stories of student life on various levels, most of them not much above the level of popular entertainment or ladies' magazine sentiment; and there are some short fictional studies of the problems of professors, though these seem to fit better the longer form of the novel. Scott Fitzgerald wrote several school stories of some interest, among them "The Freshest Boy," while Sinclair Lewis left one often anthologized attempt at least, "Young Man Axelbrod"; and William Saroyan, prolific in this area as elsewhere, tried his hand at many, including "First Day of School," and "Death of Children." John O'Hara's "Do you Like it Here?" has been frequently reprinted, as has James Thurber's "University Days"; and there was a time when a respectable freshman anthology scarcely dared appear without George Milburn's "Student in Economics." More recently such writers as Paul Goodman, Peter DeVries, Robie Macauley, Sylvan Karchmer and R. V. Cassill have turned to the genre. A notable attempt at dealing with the peculiar problems of university students at the present moment is found in Lionel Trilling's "Of This Time, of That Place." Trilling's story of a professor faced with the ambiguity of sanity and insanity in the mad world of the campus should be read by all. If one adds to this Salinger's brief tale "Franny," which serves as a sort of preface to the novella "Zooey," he will have a pair of stories which pretty well illuminates the plight of the bright college student in our time.

QUESTIONS AND TOPICS
FOR DISCUSSION

JEAN JACQUES ROUSSEAU *Emile*

1. What do you understand Rousseau to mean by "nature"?
Can you ever be quite sure in what sense he is using that slippery
term? Where in this essay does he come closest to defining it?
How close? Why is it of crucial importance to his thesis?
2. The goal of education, Rousseau tells us, is to enable man to
be "at peace with himself." What does he see as the forces which
may destroy that "peace"? What does he suggest we can do about
them? Do you find yourself in agreement with him on the possible sources of conflict? On his suggested remedies?
3. In what ways does the distinction which Rousseau makes
between "public and common" education, on the one hand, and
"private and domestic" education, on the other, resemble that
made in this book's Introduction between "conservative" and
"liberal" education? Do you take Rousseau's argument to mean
that any genuine "liberal" or "libertarian" education cannot
take place in a publicly supported school, or, indeed, in any kind
of school where large numbers of teachers confront masses of
students? What counter-arguments might be advanced against
this position?
4. "Life," says Rousseau, is the "trade" he would teach his
students. What subjects have you studied or are you now studying
in school which would seem to you appropriate in a curriculum
aimed at teaching life rather than some profession? Would the
same courses that help a man become a good citizen help him
also to lead a good "life," in Rousseau's sense of the word?
5. "It is ordinary people who have to be educated," Rousseau
remarks, "and their education alone can serve as the pattern for
the education of their fellows." What would be the response to
this of Cardinal Newman, Irving Babbitt, Arthur Bestor? How
would John Dewey have responded to such a theory? What is its
relation to the American educational system as presently consti-

tuted? What provision does it make (or does Rousseau make elsewhere) for the "gifted student"?

6. You have been reading a translation of Rousseau, but something of his manner and tone comes through. How would you describe these? Do you find any relationship between Rousseau's style and the point of view he uses it to expound? How logical is the structure of Rousseau's thought? How much of the impact of his essay depends on apt phrasing and strength of feeling rather than logic?

JOHN HENRY CARDINAL NEWMAN   *Liberal Knowledge Its Own End*

1. Read a paragraph of this essay and then a paragraph from Paul Goodman. What differences do you observe in the kind of writing? Which is the more effective? Why? Are the differences dictated only by concern with different subjects?

2. "Liberal Knowledge" "is at once its own end and at the same time carries the attribute of utility along with it." Do you agree with Newman's definition of "liberal knowledge"? With his definition of "utility"? Is what is called "liberal knowledge" on your campus as "useful" as technical training?

3. Newman defends liberal knowledge by citing Cicero, Cato and Aristotle. What relevance do they have to the scope and nature of university education in the twentieth century? Do other authorities in this text seem to you more relevant?

4. Do you think Newman's ideas apply to a secular public school in our time? What differences do you detect between Newman's vision of university education and the practice of education in your school?

5. "Liberal Education makes not the Christian, not the Catholic, but the gentleman." What does Newman mean by a "gentleman"? Does Newman's "gentleman" have a place in today's society? How would Newman deal with the educational and social problems raised by, say, Paul Goodman on "Jobs" and Martin Mayer in "The Senior-High-School Years"?

6. Do you find any differences between the way Newman

marshals his argument, and the method used by, say, Martin-
Mayer?

THOMAS HENRY HUXLEY   *Science and Culture*

1. Huxley utilizes literary allusion to make his case for scientific education. How many of these allusions can you recognize?
From what sources does he draw them? How does Huxley's use
of a literary tradition affect his argument?
2. Is Huxley's definition of "liberal education" adequate?
What, if anything, do you find lacking in it? Does it seem to you
in any sense "loaded"? How and where?
3. Compare Huxley's view of scientific education with Oppenheimer's. How do their views differ? How agree? Who makes the
better case for his point of view? Why?
4. Do any elements of Huxley's argument seem dated? Does
it seem to you that Huxley overstates the case for scientific education?
5. Compare Huxley's essay and Matthew Arnold's rejoinder.
Which seems the more convincing? Which the better organized?
Which the clearer? Which the more varied in tone?
6. Are the claims made by Huxley for "scientific education"
borne out by your experience with science courses in high school
or in college?

MATTHEW ARNOLD   *Literature and Science*

1. Compare the literary allusions of Huxley and Arnold. How
do they differ? How are they similar? Which uses allusion more
effectively?
2. Compare Arnold's definition of "liberal education" with
Huxley's. Which seems more adequate? Why? How would *you*
define a "liberal" education? A "scientific" education?
3. When Arnold illustrates the ignorance of a member of the
British Parliament who traveled in America, is his argument

convincing? Why or why not? In general, what sort of evidence does Arnold adduce to support his position?

4. Arnold has certain tricks of style. Identify some of these. Do they seem to you to enhance the effectiveness of his essay or to detract from it?

5. How does Arnold's notion of human nature differ from that of Huxley? Does Huxley make any overt or covert assumptions about human nature? What are these? Would Arnold or Huxley agree with Rousseau? Which would agree more with Newman? Which with Jerome Bruner and Paul Goodman?

6. Are the claims made by Arnold for "humane letters" borne out by your experience with literature courses in high school or in college?

PAUL GOODMAN   *Jobs*

1. Is the tone of this essay expository or polemical? How would you distinguish between the two? Would Mr. Goodman's essay be more effective were the tone different?

2. Careful reading of this essay will reveal lapses in sentence structure and paragraph development. Which sentences might be revised to advantage and which paragraphs might be given more coherent development?

3. "Man's work" is the production of "necessary food and shelter." Is this an adequate definition of the term in light of modern technology and the spread of automation?

4. Do you agree that work which is "hard, useful, and of public concern" tends to bring lower pay?" Cite some examples (other than teaching) which confirm or contradict Goodman's point of view.

5. Mr. Goodman insists that the public school system has "spurious" aims; does Martin Mayer agree? Do you? Which aims of your high school seem valid? Which spurious? How does one decide between legitimate and spurious aims for schools?

6. What principles underlie Goodman's criticism of society? What kind of society do you gather he would favor? What would be the nature of "work" in such a society?

ALFRED KAZIN   *The White Cool Record Book*

1. What view of education does "The White Cool Record Book" referred to in the title stand for?
2. What logical or psychological connections can you see among Theodore Roosevelt and Mr. King, the problem of character, Brownsville, and Mrs. B.?
3. This essay appears simply to describe the experiences of a young boy, though it reflects complex attitudes toward education. What are these attitudes? How are they communicated?
4. Kazin's school could hardly be called "progressive," at least as John Dewey defines the term. Arthur Bestor, on the other hand, implies that we should return to the "White Cool Record Book." What seem to you to be the virtues—and vices—of Kazin's school? What are the virtues and vices of schools more "progressive" in character?
5. Kazin begins and ends his essay with references to the "White Cool Record Book," yet the references are in vastly different contexts. What connection do you see between the first and the last references? How has the meaning attached to the Record Book changed?
6. Do Kazin's experiences confirm or deny the assertions of Neill?

MARTIN MAYER   *The Senior High School Years*

1. Without any overt comment, Mr. Mayer conveys his attitude towards three schools. How does he do this? Which school is most nearly like your own?
2. Do you agree that "teaching methods and the technology of education are astonishingly ill-developed." Which subjects seem to you to be the worst taught? How would you improve the teaching of them?
3. Mr. Mayer suggests that "extra-curricular" activities might play a larger part in education. Did you learn anything in your

own high school extra-curricular activities that is useful to you in college? What?

4. This essay presents vignettes of high schools along with sections of exposition. What is the governing principle of organization? How effectively does Mr. Mayer use it? Would an alternative organization have improved the essay? Compare Mayer's writing with Friedenberg's. Which is the more effective writer? Which seems to probe deeper?

5. Do you agree that "the task of the schools" is to "lead a child to be interested in almost anything within his range of comprehension?" Do you believe in secondary education for all? Which of Mayer's arguments on this score seem to you most persuasive?

EDGAR Z. FRIEDENBERG *The Impact of the School: The Clarification of Experience*

1. What does Friedenberg seem to be driving at when he says that in our society "tragedy is regarded as a problem"? How else might it be (or has it been) regarded? What connection does Friedenberg establish between this view and our attitude toward adolescents and the schools we provide for them?

2. Friedenberg says that he hopes to assume in his study "the detached interest of an observer from another planet." Is he successful? Explain. Do you think his is a desirable attitude? Justify your answer.

3. Which of the four functions Friendenberg attributes to the schools do you consider most important? Why?

4. There are a good many formal or technical terms in this essay: "ambience," "interaction," "methodology," "diastrophic," "security and status," "social heterogeneity," etc. Do you find these troublesome? Can their use be justified? How?

5. What is the distinction Friedenberg makes between "propaganda" and "the clarification of experience?" Between "clarification" and "mediation"? Does he seem to you to make a clear and convincing case?

JOHN DEWEY   *My Pedagogic Creed*

1. The key term in Dewey's creed seems to be "social." He speaks, for instance, of the "social consciousness of the race" into which presumably education inducts us. What do you take him to mean by this phrase?

2. How does Dewey define the "psychological" side of education? How does he understand its relationship to the social side?

3. How important to Dewey is the notion of "adjustment"? What reservations does he have about it as a social ideal?

4. What do you take him to mean when he speaks of education as being a "process" of living rather than a "preparation" for it? Do you feel this to be true of your own education up to now? Do you think it has been a real assumption of your teachers?

5. You probably find Dewey a little hard to read. What do you think is the source of the difficulty? How would you define his kind of language? How would you describe his way of making sentences?

JEROME BRUNER   *After John Dewey, What?*

1. Writing sixty-five years after John Dewey, Mr. Bruner has points of agreement and disagreement. Which writer speaks with more relevance to your own experience? In what respects?

2. Mr. Bruner speaks of our "reluctance to expose the child to the startling sweep of man and nature" because of our fear that "it might violate the comfortable domain of his direct experience." What do you think this statement means? Did your own school shelter you from the harsher aspects of human experience? How? In what ways did it prepare you for them?

3. What is the purpose of Bruner's summary of Dewey's position on "experience" in education? Is it a fair summary? How does Bruner make clear his judgment of Dewey?

4. Distinguish between "adjustment" and "competence" as used in this essay. Which was your high school chiefly interested

in? What means were used to achieve these goals? Is your college different in this respect?

5. Which courses you have taken so far most "reflect the changes through which we are living"? Do you think it possible or desirable for all school courses to do this? What other goals are equally important?

WILLIAM JAMES   *The Social Value of the College-Bred*

1. Cardinal Newman sees the aim of a University as the creation of a "gentleman"; William James believes that "it should help you to know a good man when you see him." Compare and contrast these statements.

2. When James speaks of the loss of influence of the university to the "ten cent magazines," he is dealing with the problem of mass media and their effect on the "tone" of the country. Compare the attitudes of this essay with those found in, for example, David Riesman's "The College Student in an Age of Organization."

3. "Tone," James writes, "is a terribly vague word to use." Why then does he use it? What does he mean by it? Could this essay make its point more effectively by the use of more concrete everyday language? Compare James' writing with that of Martin Mayer and Jacques Barzun. Which is more in the tradition of James?

4. "Real culture," according to James, "lives by sympathies and admirations, not by dislikes and disdains." What difference of meaning is there between the first pair of words and the second? How does James make this clear?

5. The charge made against democracy is that "its preferences are inevitably for the inferior." What connection is there between this and James' criticisms of the educational system?

IRVING BABBITT   *Literature and the College*

1. Babbitt attacks a specific attitude toward the study of literature. Can you gain from this essay a sense of what he is attacking?

On what grounds does he base his attack? Does he, in your opinion, make his case?

2. When Babbitt writes, "The humanities have ceased to be humane," what meaning is he giving to the adjective? Which courses you have taken were "humane" in his sense?

3. What does Babbitt think should be the place of literature in the college curriculum? Why? What is it he expects one to learn from the study of literature?

4. What are the chief antitheses set up by Babbitt in this essay? What is their purpose? Are they effective? How does Babbitt use irony to indicate on which side his own sympathies lie?

5. A democratic state needs an "aristocracy of character and intelligence." Are these the concern of schools? How does Babbitt define "aristocracy"? Does he agree with Cardinal Newman? With Jerome Bruner? Do you agree with Babbitt?

6. Babbitt's style is characterized by an extensive use of allusion. Do you find this baffling or helpful? In what respects?

ALFRED NORTH WHITEHEAD   *The Aims of Education*

1. Distinguish what Whitehead calls "culture" from what he calls "expert knowledge." Do you believe it is always possible to make this distinction? Is there a middle ground? In any event, what connects the two?

2. What are "inert ideas"? What is their effect on schools? What role have they played in fomenting revolutions?

3. Do you believe that "The only use of the knowledge of the past is to equip us for the present"? Why? What case can be made against that point of view?

4. What relationship is there in science between the "process of proof" and the "process of appreciation"? Exactly what does Whitehead mean by the latter?

5. Does what Whitehead says about the English system of examinations have relevance to our own? How?

6. This essay gives the sense of being spoken, not written—and of being an appeal, not just an explanation. Point out the

specific details in the text which give to it an oratorical and horta-
tory effect.

ROBERT MAYNARD HUTCHINS   *The Higher Learning*

1. Mr. Hutchins asserts that we have confused "science with
information, ideas with facts, and knowledge with . . . data."
How would you define each of these confusions?
2. He warns that a new brand of anti-intellectualism is now
arising. Have you detected it in your high school experience? In
college?
3. On what points would Mr. Hutchins and Irving Babbitt
agree? Disagree? Which seems to you to have a more solid grasp
of educational problems and their solution?
4. Babbitt says that "Our modern attitude might be . . . correctly defined as an attempt to study man by the methods of
physics and chemistry"; Mr. Hutchins asserts that "our program
has amounted to a denial of the nature of man." Do you find the
reasoning of each man valid? How so?
5. Many of the authors in this volume are concerned—even
dismayed—with the multiplicity of data available to the student
and the paucity of principles by which he may organize the data.
Hutchins hopes that we might "see again the connection of ideas,
and thus of subject matters," that "we might recapture . . . the
unity of thought." Does the multiplicity of data seem a problem
to you? Which author here offers the best solution to the problem?

HENRY ADAMS   *Harvard College*

1. At the end of the fourth paragraph, Adams describes the
Harvard class of 1858. What does he identify as the chief characteristics of that class? In light of the fact that he is looking back
at events long past, how much do you feel his account can be
trusted? How similar or different do you think college graduating
classes are now?

2. When Adams writes of Lee that he "had no mind; he had temperament," is he praising or defaming him? What does he mean by "mind"? By "temperament"? Which of these is more highly prized now?

3. Adams says Harvard was a "negative force" as far as he was concerned. Have you felt your own school experience to be "negative" in this sense? What might Adams have considered "positive"?

4. How would you describe the tone of this essay? How does Adams achieve it? Compare it with the tone of Malcolm Cowley's or John Peale Bishop's account of his schooling.

5. "The entire work of the four years could have been easily put in to the work of any four months in after life." Does this statement make Adams a cynic? Might the same be said of your work in high school? How so? How might education be more efficiently conducted?

MALCOLM COWLEY *American College, 1916*

1. Cowley opens with the melancholy assertion that his schooling "might be regarded as a long process of deracination." Does school inevitably destroy "roots . . . in the soil?" If so, to a good or bad effect?

2. Are students still taught to write "a standardized Amer-english as colorless as Esperanto"? Does Cowley write in this synthetic tongue? Do any of the essayists you have been reading?

3. What complaint does Cowley make against the Harvard of his day as far as a young writer is concerned? What suggestions does he make about what might have improved it? Is it the duty of a college to train writers?

4. What is the point of the anecdote about the "boy from my own city"? What connection has this small story with Cowley's argument against "culture" as a "badge of class distinction"?

5. Compare Cowley's arguments against Harvard with Adams', particularly with regard to Cowley's idea that Harvard gentility crushed "native" expression. Do Cowley and Newman mean the same thing by "gentility"?

MARCUS CUNLIFFE   *Harvard*

1. This essay is comprised of five sections. How are these sections combined to give the essay coherence?

2. Cunliffe criticizes "The prior weakness of American schooling;" The "frighteningly high cost" of it, the "Growing number of students;" and the "cautious, deceptively cool tone of current American life." Which of these features shapes academic life in your college? How do you protect yourself from these features?

3. Compare David Boroff's view of Wisconsin with Cunliffe's of Harvard. Which, would you say, seems more democratic? More stimulating? More advantageous to attend? Which seems more distinctly "American"? Is it possible to receive as good an education at one school as at the other?

4. In the essays of Adams, Cowley, and Cunliffe, what attributes of Harvard are consistent? What changes do you detect in Harvard in the three views? Does Harvard seem to you to be a better or a poorer university than it was in Adams' day? Why?

5. Compare Cunliffe's "Harvard" with Bishop's "Princeton." Do these schools have similar virtues? What are they? Vices? What are they?

JOHN PEALE BISHOP   *Princeton*

1. What role does irony play in this essay? Cite examples that demonstrate Bishop's ability to imply a meaning quite different from the one he seems to be stating.

2. Does the constant play of irony over the subject matter make it difficult to tell what the author's final attitude is toward the issues he raises? What in fact *is* it? How can you be sure?

3. Scott Fitzgerald once called a character in a novel whom he had based on Bishop "Tom D'Invilliers." What is the point of Bishop's calling himself by that fictional name?

4. Does one get out of this essay not only a sense of Princeton, but also a sense of the Princeton man, or simply a sense of a particular Princetonian called John Peale Bishop? Do any of the

essays on Harvard provide similar effects? Could a large, coeducational state university be written about in the same way?

5. Does the final sentence seem merely a wisecrack or a pleasant
note in which to bring things to a close?

DAVID BOROFF   *On Wisconsin!*

1. This essay is organized on the basis of oppositions and contradictions. Do you find this device merely mechanical or a way of
getting at truth? Does Boroff force his pattern, or does it flow
naturally? Refer to passages to justify your view.

2. Boroff comments on the contrast at Wisconsin between
"academic freedom" and "social restrictions." What is "academic
freedom" anyhow? Is it compatible with enforced moral taboos?
What is the situation in your college?

3. Among the oppositions described by Boroff, that between
"urban" and "rural" points of view gets the most attention. What
does he describe as the chief attitudes associated with each? Do
you find a similar clash of points of view in your own environment?

4. How does Boroff explain the contradiction between Wisconsin "liberalism" and the difficult situation of Orientals and
Negroes in respect to dates? Does his analysis seem to you clear
and adequate?

EDMUND WILSON   *Christian Gauss as a Teacher of Literature*

1. At the beginning, Wilson suggests that this essay is not only
a tribute to a man, but a definition of the critical principles from
which he himself started in the twenties. Summarize these principles.

2. Explain why and how Wilson uses Dante's *Divine Comedy*
as a motif for defining the essential characteristics of Christian
Gauss.

3. Wilson seems to believe that a teacher like Gauss could

have flowered only at Princeton. Would you agree with that assertion? Does the man he describes seem to you to fit into the Princeton described by Bishop, who was a classmate of Wilson's?

4. What are the "fundamental assumptions," which, Wilson tells us, Gauss learned from Whitehead were the chief clues to philosophy and literature? What might be some of the "fundamental assumptions" of the times in which you are living?

5. Wilson alludes with approval to Gauss' awareness that the "artist's morality" expresses itself quite differently from that of the churchgoer. Why is it important to teach this in connection with literature?

6. What finally does Wilson believe to be Gauss' importance? What was his contribution in and out of the classroom?

GEORGE WILLIAMS *How Badly Can You Teach?*

1. How valid are Williams' "five short observations" on the high school teacher as measured by your own experience? What light do Friedenberg's remarks about the high school cast on what Williams says? Does Williams or Friedenberg probe deeper and speak truer?

2. Against the charge that students cannot read, Williams asserts that professors cannot write. Can you find any of the faults he points out in the essays you have been reading? In Williams' own essay?

3. Williams argues against having graduate assistants and young instructors teach freshmen. What arguments might be advanced for so employing them? What justice (or injustice) would you say there is in Williams' complaints?

4. Do you believe that the ideal of a "stiff course" and the giving of too many low grades gets in the way of education? Do you agree with the notion of learning as "work" rather than "pleasure"?

5. What connection does Williams establish between "bad teaching" and "Hebraism," "Puritanism" and "Victorianism"? What do you take these terms to mean anyhow? Are they purely pejorative terms?

6. Many conventional academics find this essay to be a "piece of dishonesty" worth including in a student anthology only "for the purposes of student refutation." Do you agree? How would you go about refuting it? Defending it?

ALEXANDER SUTHERLAND NEILL   *The Teacher and Sex*

1. What attitudes in Neill remind you of Paul Goodman? Of George Williams? Do these three essays taken together define a "libertarian" view of education as opposed to an "authoritarian" one? What would some of its characteristics be? Which writers in this collection represent an authoritarian view?

2. What, according to Neill, is the relationship between sex and mental health? Mental health and good teaching? Whose psychological doctrines does Neill seem to have in mind? What special problems does Neill see when women teach boys? Do his views square with your experience?

3. What can be done about the problems Neill sees in our society? Is a reform of schools enough—or does he imply we need a change in our basic way of life?

4. What of Neill's style? How do you react to the use of profanity in an essay on education? Does Neill's essay have shock value only? Or does he make significant statements? Contrast the tone of Neill's essay with that of Cardinal Newman. Which appeals to you most? Why? Would you call Newman a prude? Neill an iconoclast?

5. Does Neill's belief that women without sex lives are more dangerous teachers than men without sex lives merely reflect his masculine arrogance?

6. Are you annoyed or embarrassed by anything in this essay? What? What in yourself or your education may explain this reaction?

7. One reader comments that Neill's essay "has no real connection with this section, for it deals with primary school teachers in England." Evaluate that comment.

JACQUES BARZUN   *Instruction Without Authority*

1. Barzun, like Bestor and Babbitt, seems to approve of an educational elite. How do his evidence and mode of argument differ from those of Bestor and Babbitt? Which of these three seems to make its point most effectively? Why?

2. Like Bestor, Barzun agrees that not all subjects in the curriculum are of equal value. How would the curriculum approved by Bestor differ from or agree with that approved by Barzun?

3. Barzun asserts that instruction is now without *authority*. What is the nature of the authority he seeks? What is its source? What is his major disagreement with the assumptions of Dewey?

4. Barzun argues that the weaknesses in our education reflect the weaknesses in our society. Why does he then argue for an "authoritarian" educational system in a democratic society?

5. Would you prefer to study with Barzun, or with Riesman, Mills, or Gold? Why?

SIDNEY HOOK   *The Good Teacher*

1. Which of John Dewey's principles are honored by Sidney Hook? Are they compatible with the view of the "school master" as a "life master," as expressed in the quotation from Karl Mannheim? Explain.

2. In what sense (according to Hook) can people be taught to teach? What does he mean when he says that "teaching is an art"?

3. Do you agree with Hook that the worst teaching in America occurs at the "highest levels," i.e., in the liberal arts college? Do you consider that Hook's solutions are the right ones for this problem?

4. What does Hook have to say about the difficult relations which ordinarily exist between liberal arts colleges and schools of education? Which side does he seem to feel is right?

5. Which of the criteria Hook lists for the "good teacher in a

democratic society" seem to you to apply to our society? Which might apply to a good teacher in any society?

JACQUES BARZUN   *Pupils Into Students*

1. Barzun speaks of teaching as "comic." One reason for his doing so is surely rhetorical, that is, he aims at attracting the reader's attention and convincing him. Do you think he succeeds? Have you ever thought of teaching as "comic" before? Do you believe it to be so now?

2. Why does Barzun write so much of himself in the first part of this essay? What is the relationship (in his case) between autobiography and general educational theory? Where have you acquired your own ideas about schools and learning?

3. If it is, as Barzun states, "obvious that the relation of teacher to pupil is an emotional one," of what use are studies of pedagogy and method in the classroom?

4. Barzun says, "Teaching is only possible because there is a dialogue." A dialogue between who and whom and about what? What about lecture classes? Is there any sense in which these are a dialogue?

5. Do young people, in fact, believe, as Barzun suggests, that "everybody but themselves prefers make-believe and lives by it"? What is "make-believe"? Is it possible for the teacher to undermine this belief? Do you share this "superstition"?

DAVID RIESMAN   *The College Student in an Age of Organization*

1. David Riesman begins and ends his essay with a reference to the cult of "playing it *cool*"; and Marcus Cunliffe has commented on the "cautious, deceptively *cool* tone of current American life." Do both these authors mean the same thing by *cool?* Is "playing it cool" as dangerous to yourself and to society as Mr. Riesman suggests? Explain.

2. "My principal theme," Mr. Riesman asserts, is "to help ex-

plain [students] to themselves." Edgar Friedenberg also takes this as his theme. What are the differences in technique in these two essays? Which is the more effective piece of writing? Why?

3. Riesman says that "We are witnessing a silent revolution against work" in part because we frequently "make products or provide services which are either antisocial or useless." Do you agree with Riesman? How so? How would you define "antisocial or useless" services? Would Riesman and Goodman define them in the same way?

4. At the beginning of Section III, Mr. Riesman asks why students are so "inattentive to what concerns them as closely as does their curriculum." How would you answer this question? Are students inattentive in this way?

5. Do you agree that "grades contaminate education"? How would you improve the grading system at your school? What alternative to that system do you propose?

C. WRIGHT MILLS   *The Educational Elevator*

1. Many of the essays in this volume concern themselves with the social and political milieu in which our educational system operates. How does Mills' view of the social function of education differ from that of Paul Goodman? David Riesman? Edgar Friedenberg?

2. This essay appears to be an objective description of certain changes in education. Does Mills have any emotional attitudes toward these changes? If so, how are these conveyed to the reader?

3. Is Mills criticizing his own education? Has he fallen into the trap of thinking the next generation is going to the dogs? What evidence from the essay can you cite in support of your opinion?

4. Compare Harold Taylor's description of the ideal graduate with that of Newman. Do these two seem to you adequate definitions of the college educated? Which seems more adequate? Why?

5. On what sort of data does Mills rely for his statements about "success and ideologies"? Do these seem to you valid? Does Dale Carnegie represent the values of contemporary college students?

Does the kind of evidence utilized by Mills throughout this essay seem to you both valid and adequate? Explain.

HERBERT GOLD *A Dog in Brooklyn, A Girl in Detroit: A Life Among the Humanities*

1. Is this a "short story" or an "essay"? What makes it different from the other esays in this collection? In what does it resemble Alfred Kazin's *A Walker in the City?*

2. What is Gold's major point? How can you tell, since he does not state it directly? Why, in short, doesn't Gold find himself convinced that he wants to teach humanities again?

3. What is the cause of the comedy of misunderstandings Gold relates: the attitudes of the students? the teacher? the nature of the books they were reading?

4. What is the importance of Clotilda Adams in this account? What notions about the relations of black and white does she bring to mind? What ideas about the irrelevance of that issue to certain larger ones of teaching and learning?

5. What do you make of the last sentence, "We must find a way to teach better and to learn." How much of what comes before really leads up to this? How much (from a thematic point of view) is irrelevant? Why is it included then?

I. A. RICHARDS *The Future of the Humanities in General Education*

1. Does Herbert Gold's essay cast light on what Richards has to say here? Does it undercut in any serious way Richards' position? Are there substantial areas of agreement?

2. What effect has the increase of population on the one hand, and the development of communications on the other, had on the teaching and learning of courses in the humanities?

3. How do Richards' assumptions about the place of humanities in the whole educational system, and in society itself, differ

from Babbitt's and Dewey's? To which of these does he seem closest?

4. In what way does Richards foresee Radio, TV and movies becoming "the instruments of our salvation"? What are the usual arguments against such a belief? Does he deal with those arguments?

5. What does Richards consider to be the basically different conceptions of man proper to scientists and humanists respectively? Does he foresee any possibility of mediation between the two?

LESLIE A. FIEDLER   *The Crumbling Ivory Tower*

1. In this essay you encounter one more specimen of a "libertarian" view of education. Is the "freedom" Fiedler speaks about the same as that advocated by, say Goodman and Neill? What do the authors to whom Fiedler refers (as compared with those cited by Neill) or his style (as compared to theirs) reveal about his point of view?

2. Define the word "service" as Fiedler uses it in this essay. What devices does he use to indicate his attitude toward the concept? What is his attitude?

3. Why does Fiedler think the faults of the academic system he lists are of no final account? What are for him the matters which really count? Does he make a convincing case?

4. How would you characterize the style of this essay? Does it seem to you more formal or loose? Closer to Babbitt or Neill? Or Newman? Is it possible to establish here once again a connection between the sentence style and diction of a writer and his overall point of view?

5. On what sort of note (cheerful? melancholy? cheerful-melancholy?) would you say this essay ends? The writer promises at the start that it will be "melancholy." Does he keep his word? What is the force of the "if" with which the final sentence begins?

ARTHUR EUGENE BESTOR *The College of Liberal Arts and Sciences*

1. "Educational reform must begin with a courageous assertion that all the various subjects and disciplines in the curriculum are *not* of equal value." Do you agree with the way Bestor ranks the disciplines? Why? Would you say Fiedler and Bestor have similar views on education, though one is libertarian and one is authoritarian?

2. Bestor in writing employs some fairly obvious devices (e.g., "These various points will be taken up in order in the remainder of this chapter."). Does he seem to you too mechanical a writer? Does his organization of material aid you in assimilating what he says?

3. Do you disapprove of the free-elective system? On what grounds would you defend or attack it?

4. Do Bestor's goals for the reorganization of college education seem to you to be valid? What factors has Mr. Bestor perhaps failed to consider? How would those factors bear on his proposals?

5. The elementary and secondary schools are "killing off every budding intellectual interest." Is this wholly true? Attack or defend this point of view from your own experience. What is the effect on you as a reader when an author is inaccurate or overstates his case? Do you see other points at which Mr. Bestor's arguments are open to question?

J. ROBERT OPPENHEIMER *On Science and Culture*

1. Mr. Oppenheimer employs scientific terms such as *homeostasis, cyclatron, static, quasi-rigid, analogues, resonants, light quantum;* do you find them baffling? Could you drop them in rewriting the sentences in which they appear without changing the sense?

2. This very carefully organized essay promises to treat six subjects, does treat them, and then draws conclusions. Describe

the principle of organization. Does it improve the comprehensibility of the essay? Compare the organization of this essay with that of Gold's essay. Which essay is more effective, moving, and to its point? Why?

3. "The principal function of ritual, religion, of culture is . . . almost to stop change." Explain this sentence. Do you agree with it? Explain. Would Friedenberg and Dewey agree with it?

4. What differences does Oppenheimer see between the study of science and the study of art? What similarities? What is his attitude toward art?

5. "Certitude" is the criterion of the sciences; define "certitude" as Oppenheimer uses the word. What does Mr. Oppenheimer mean by "depth, firmness, universality"? Are these valid criteria by which to judge art? Does "certitude" have a place in the criticism of art?

R. BUCKMINSTER FULLER   *Education Automation*

1. A key word in Fuller's discussion of automation and education is "regenerative." What meanings does this adjective have in the phrases "regenerative consumers" and "regenerative investment"? Does Fuller mean the same thing by it when he speaks of education as being "a regenerative experience" for educators? What is the importance of the concept of "regeneration" in his total argument?

2. At a crucial point in his discussion, Fuller refers to certain theories of C. P. Snow and Alfred North Whitehead. Why does he deal with them at this particular stage of his argument? What is the area of concern he and they have in common? In what respects does he agree with them? What are his major points of difference? Which is more vital to the development of Fuller's own thesis, the agreements or the differences?

3. Do you believe Fuller's contention that *"the geographically larger the physical task to be done, the duller the conceptual brain* that is brought to be upon [it]"? If the brains brought to bear on such large problems are "conceptually" dull, are they bright in any other sense? What sense? What defense could be

made for saving the first rate "conceptual brains" for other, narrower tasks?

4. What, according to Fuller, is the answer to the drive toward "specialization" sponsored by our graduate schools? What relationship does he see between "automation," which he has discussed earlier, and "General Systems Theory," which he comes to rather late in the essay? What is the connection of both to Fuller's hopes for beginning education at the comprehensive rather than the elementary level? Do you find any flaws in the logic by which he moves from the first of these concepts to the others?

5. Make a list of the terms in Fuller which you have not encountered in any of the other essays included here. Does the difference in vocabulary which separates Fuller from the other essayists seem to you to indicate any fundamental difference in approach? How would you define that difference? Which other essayists read come closest to Fuller's point of view?

6. The present selection is an abridgment of a long speech which Fuller gave before the student body of Southern Illinois University. What indications do you find in the style of its having been orally delivered rather than written? What influences do you find exerted by the kind of audience he was addressing? Generally speaking, do you consider it a virtue or a defect when an essay makes clear its occasion and its intended audience?

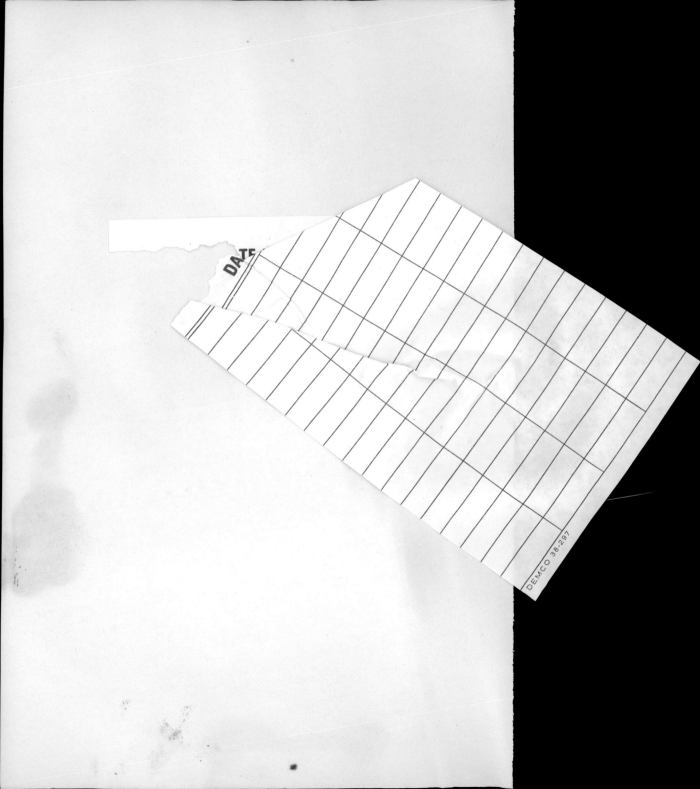

DATE

DEMCO 38-297